P9-DXM-564

GALLERY OF
Best
RESUMES

THIRD EDITION

DISCARD

DAVID F. NOBLE

jist Works®
America's Career Publisher

Gallery of Best Resumes, *Third Edition*
A Collection of Quality Resumes by Professional Resume Writers

© 1994, 2001, 2004 by David F. Noble

Published by JIST Works, an imprint of JIST Publishing, Inc.
8902 Otis Avenue
Indianapolis, IN 46216-1033
Phone: 800-648-JIST   Fax: 800-JIST-FAX   E-mail: info@jist.com

Visit our Web site at **www.jist.com** for information on JIST, free job search tips, book chapters, and ordering instructions for our many products! For free information on 14,000 job titles, visit **www.careeroink.com**.

Other books by David F. Noble:

Gallery of Best Cover Letters
Gallery of Best Resumes for People Without a Four-Year Degree
Professional Resumes for Executives, Managers, and Other Administrators
Professional Resumes for Accounting, Tax, Finance, and Law

Quantity discounts are available for JIST books. Please call our Sales Department at 1-800-648-5478 for a free catalog and more information.

Acquisitions and Development Editor: Lori Cates Hand
Proofreaders: Jeanne Clark, Michael Thomas
Interior Designer and Page Layout: Debbie Berman
Cover Designer: designLab, Seattle
Indexer: Virginia Noble

Printed in the United States of America.

07 06 05 04   9 8 7 6 5 4 3 2 1

   Library of Congress Cataloging-in-Publication Data

Noble, David F. (David Franklin), 1935-

 Gallery of best resumes : a collection of quality resumes by

professional resume writers / by David F. Noble.-- 3rd ed.

    p. cm.

 ISBN 1-56370-985-6

 1. Résumés (Employment) I. Title.

 HF5383.N62 2004

 650.14'2--dc22

                           2003026436

ISBN: 1-56370-985-6

Contents

Foreword vii

Acknowledgments viii

Introduction 1

How This Book Is Organized 2

This practical "idea book" of best resumes has three parts: best resume writing tips; a gallery of 178 resumes written by 71 professional writers; and an exhibit of 30 cover letters, together with tips for polishing cover letters. With this book, you have a treasury of quality resumes and cover letters that you can use as superior models for your own resumes and cover letters.

Who This Book Is For 3

This book is for *any job seeker* who wants to know how the professionals write resumes. It's for *active job seekers* who want top-notch ideas for creating a first-rate resume in today's competitive job market. It's for *all job seekers* who must have an ahead-of-the-pack resume—from *high school students* looking for their first jobs to *retirees* wanting to stay employed. This book is also for *career changers,* those *terminated* by downsizing, and the *overqualified,* who must look in new directions and tailor their resumes in special ways. Because of the wealth of quality resume models in this book, it is for *anyone* who wants examples of top-quality resumes to create an outstanding resume.

What This Book Can Do for You 4

This idea book can transform your thinking about resumes so that you have a better sense of what kind of resume is best for you and will help you schedule more interviews.

Part 1: Best Resume Tips 5

Best Resume Tips at a Glance 6

Best Resume Tips 7

Best Resume Writing Strategies 8

In this section, you learn experience-tested resume-writing strategies, such as how to put the most important information about you as a worker near the top of your resume, how to highlight key information so that it is seen, and how to showcase your experience and skills.

Best Resume Design and Layout Tips 9

This section shows you effective design techniques, such as how to use *white space* for an uncluttered look; how to use choice phrases from reference letters as *testimonials* in a resume; how to make decisions about *fonts* and *typefaces;* how to handle capital letters, underlining, italic, and bold-facing; and how to use *graphic elements* such as bullets, horizontal lines, vertical lines, and shaded boxes.

Best Resume Writing Style Tips 14

To help you make your resume error-free, you learn in this section practical writing tips, such as how to use *capital letters* in computer terms; how to use *hyphens* in words and phrases; and how to use *commas, semicolons, dashes,* and *colons* correctly.

Part 2: The Gallery 19

The Gallery at a Glance 20

How to Use the Gallery 21

Resumes on Special Paper 23

Special Paper Information 41

Resumes Grouped by Occupational Fields

Accounting..**43**
Advertising/Promotion **51**
Communications **59**
Customer Service **69**
Design/Architecture **75**
Education/Training **83**
Engineering **141**
Finance **155**
Healthcare **183**
Hospitality **233**
Human Resources **241**
Information Systems/Technology **259**
Law **283**
Law Enforcement **293**
Management **305**
Manufacturing **331**
Media..**339**
Sales and Marketing **347**

Part 3: Best Cover Letter Tips 363

Best Cover Letter Tips at a Glance 364

Best Cover Letter Writing Tips..365

Myths About Cover Letters..365

Tips for Polishing Cover Letters 366

A quality resume can make a great impression, but that impression can be ruined quickly by a poorly written cover letter. This section shows you how to eliminate common errors in cover letters. It amounts to a *crash writing course* that you won't find in any other resume book. After you read the following sections, you will be better able to write and polish any letters you create for your job search.

Using Good Strategies for Letters..366
Using Pronouns Correctly...367
Using Verb Forms Correctly..368
Using Punctuation Correctly 369
Using Words Correctly 373

Exhibit of Cover Letters 375

In this section, you learn how to evaluate 30 sample cover letters that accompanied resumes featured in the *Gallery*. After you study this exhibit, you will have a better feel for designing your own cover letters to make them distinctive and effective.

Appendix: List of Contributors 407

Occupation Index 417

Features Index 422

Foreword

You just have to ask whether the world needs yet another resume book. There are hundreds of them out there, and each year there is a new crop. So a legitimate question is, "Why is this resume book worthwhile?"

After looking at hundreds of resume books, I can tell you that most people who write them really don't know much about looking for work—and too few seem to know much about what makes a good resume. They often have backgrounds as personnel directors (who use resumes to screen people out, not in) or teachers (with little practical experience in actually looking for work). Nice people, I'm sure, but not all that well qualified.

Gallery of Best Resumes is different from most resume books for two reasons:

1. The resumes have all been created by people who write resumes for a living.

2. David Noble.

I think that these two reasons make this a more useful and important book. Let me explain.

While most books are based on one person's opinion of what makes a good resume, *Gallery of Best Resumes* includes resumes written by dozens of professional resume writers. These people make their living helping others produce good resumes, and they sent us their best work. This approach allows for a wide range of writing styles, formats, and designs that just is not possible through any other approach.

But behind this extraordinary collection of resumes is the author, David Noble. Educated in the classics and a graduate of prestigious universities, he brings to this collection a discipline of thought and an understanding of good writing that are simply lacking in most resume books. When I asked him to explain to me how this book was developed, he used this analogy:

> If Plato had been asked, "What is a resume?" he would have asked the questioner what it was for, how it was used, and what it did. Plato would then have tried to imagine the ideal form that a resume should take to fulfill those functions. That, David explained, is deductive reasoning (an advanced form of intuition).

> Aristotle, a pupil of Plato, responding to the same question, would have asked, "Who makes resumes?" and asked a number of those persons to show him examples. Aristotle would then have sorted through those examples and arranged them into types. From this, he would have determined what a resume is. That, David explained, is inductive reasoning (a scientific method).

Aristotle's method is the one that David used to examine the question, "What makes a resume a best resume?"

There are, it seems, some things that make one resume stand out above others. Instead of just making assumptions, David Noble examined hundreds of professionally written resumes. After careful analysis, he presents his conclusions in this book—along with lots of outstanding resumes.

One good thing about this book is that you don't have to read Plato or Aristotle to find out how to write a good resume. It's all here. You can examine carefully on your own the resumes presented in the *Gallery,* or spend some time learning from David the principles of resume writing and, more importantly, how to *use* a resume.

Michael Farr

Mike Farr is the author of many career planning and job search books, including his own books on resumes: *Same-Day Resume, The Quick Resume & Cover Letter Book,* and *America's Top Resumes for America's Top Jobs.* Collectively, his books have sold more than two million copies.

Acknowledgments

To all those who helped to make possible this third edition, I would like to acknowledge my appreciation. Again, I am most indebted to all of the professional resume writers who sent me many examples of their work for inclusion in this book and other books. These writers took the time—often on short notice—to supply multiple copies, files on disks, and any other requested information.

I want to express my gratitude to Mike Farr for his Foreword to this book and to Lori Cates Hand for overseeing this project.

Introduction

The *Gallery of Best Resumes,* Third Edition, is a new collection of quality resumes from professional resume writers, each with individual views about resumes and resume writing. All the resumes in the third edition are new. Some of the writers who contributed resumes to the first and second editions are represented in the third edition, but some are not for various reasons (the writer has retired, become inactive as a resume writer, changed careers, and so on). Other writers are new and contributing to my resume books for the first time.

Unlike many resume books whose selections "look the same," this book, like the first and second editions, contains resumes that look different because they are representations of *real* resumes prepared by different professionals for actual job searchers throughout the country. (Certain information in the resumes has been fictionalized by the writers to protect, where necessary, each client's right to privacy.) Even when several resumes from the same writer appear in the book, most of these resumes are different because the writer has customized each resume according to the background information and career goals of the client for whom the resume was prepared.

A decade has passed since the first edition, and the resumes in this third edition are "professional looking" for still other reasons. During the past ten years the resume writing industry has matured through the increase in the number of professional organizations for resume writers; the ready sharing of ideas at national conventions of these organizations; the easy access to e-mail and the World Wide Web; the greater availability of higher-resolution, lower-cost printers (black-and-white and color) for personal computers; and the increase in the number of books like this *Gallery* that display collections of quality resumes and cover letters by professional writers. Often these books serve as idea books that emerging writers use as they develop their own expertise. Then there was the rare appearance of Susan Whitcomb's *Résumé Magic,* which offers professional resume-writing advice that other professional writers have found useful.

Instead of assuming that "one resume style fits all," the writers featured in this *Gallery* believe that a client's past experiences and next job target should determine the resume's type, design, and content. The use of *Best* in the book's title reflects this approach to resume making. The resumes are not "best" because they are ideal types for you to copy, but because resume writers have interacted with clients to fashion resumes that seemed best for each client's situation at the time.

This book features resumes from writers who share several important qualities: good listening skills, a sense of what details are appropriate for a particular resume, and flexibility in selecting and arranging the resume's sections. By "hearing between" a client's statements, the perceptive resume writer can detect what kind of job the client really wants. The writer then chooses the information that will best represent the client for the job being sought. Finally, the writer decides on the best arrangement of the information, often from the most important to the least important, for that job. With the help of this book, you can create this kind of resume yourself.

Almost all of the writers of the resumes in this *Gallery* are members of Career Masters Institute (CMI), the National Résumé Writers' Association (NRWA), the Professional Association of Résumé Writers & Career Coaches (PARW/CC), or the Professional Résumé Writing and Research Association (PRWRA). Many of the writers belong to more than one of these organizations. Each organization has programs for earned certification. For example, writers who have CPRW certification, for Certified Professional Résumé Writer, received this designation from PARW/CC after they studied specific course materials and demonstrated proficiency in an examination. Those who have NCRW certification, for National Certified Résumé Writer, received this designation from NRWA after a different course of study and a different examination. For contact information about CMI, NRWA, PARW/CC, and PRWRA, see their listings at the end of the Appendix (List of Contributors).

How This Book Is Organized

Like the first and second editions, the *Gallery of Best Resumes,* Third Edition, consists of three parts. Part 1, "Best Resume Tips," presents resume writing strategies, design and layout tips, and resume writing style tips for making resumes visually impressive. Many of these strategies and tips were suggested by the resume writers who contributed resumes to the first and second editions. From time to time, a reference is given to one or more Gallery resumes that illustrate the strategy or tip.

Part 2 is the Gallery itself, containing 178 resumes from 71 professional resume writers throughout the United States, Australia, and Canada.

Resume writers commonly distinguish between chronological resumes and functional (or skills) resumes. A *chronological resume* is a photo—a snapshot history of what you did and when you did it. A *functional resume* is a painting—an interpretive sketch of what you can do for a future employer. A third kind of resume, known as a *combination resume,* is a mix of recalled history and self-assessment. Besides recollecting "the facts," a combination resume contains self-interpretation and is therefore more like dramatic history than news coverage. A combination resume and a functional resume are not always that different; often, all that is needed for a functional resume to qualify as a combination resume is the inclusion of some dates, such as those for positions held. Almost all of the resumes in the third edition of the *Gallery* are combination resumes.

The resumes in the Gallery are presented in the following occupational categories:

Accounting
Advertising/Promotion
Communications
Customer Service
Design/Architecture
Education/Training
Engineering
Finance
Healthcare
Hospitality
Human Resources
Information Systems/Technology
Law
Law Enforcement
Management
Manufacturing
Media
Sales and Marketing

Within each category, the resumes are generally arranged from the simple to the complex. Some of the resumes are one page, but most of them are two pages. A few are more than two pages.

The Gallery offers a wide range of resumes with features that you can use in creating and improving your own resumes. Notice the plural. An important premise of an active job search is that you will not have just one "perfect" resume for all potential employers, but different versions of your resume for different interviews. The Gallery is therefore not a showroom where you say, "I'll take that one," alter it with your information, and then duplicate your version 200 times. It is a valuable resource of design ideas, expressions, and organizational patterns that can help make your own resume a "best resume" for your next interview.

Creating multiple *versions* of a resume may seem difficult, but it is easy to do if you have (or have access to) a personal computer and a laser printer or some other kind of printer that can produce quality output. You will also need word processing, desktop publishing, or resume software. If you don't have a computer or don't know someone who does, most professional resume writers have the hardware and software, and they can make your resume look like those in the Gallery. See the List of Contributors in the Appendix for the names, addresses, phone numbers, e-mail addresses, and Web sites (if any) of the professional writers whose works are featured in this book. A local fast-print shop can make your resume look good, but you will probably not get there the kind of advice and service the professional resume writer provides.

In the *Gallery of Best Resumes,* you will notice a few resumes displayed in .pdf or .txt format. These formats are appropriate for the electronic submission of resumes or cover letters, which many employers now encourage because of timeliness and expediency in processing. Any of the resumes in this book can be prepared for electronic transfer. If you intend to apply online for positions, be sure you follow the submission guidelines posted by the employer. If they are not clearly explained, phone or e-mail the company to inquire. You don't want to be disqualified for a job that suits you well because you did not follow the steps for successful submission.

Part 3, "Best Cover Letter Tips," contains a discussion of some myths about cover letters, plus tips for polishing cover letters. Much of the advice offered here applies also to writing resumes. Included in this part is an exhibit of 30 cover letters.

The List of Contributors in the Appendix is arranged alphabetically by country, state or province, and city. Although most of these resume writers work with local clients, many of the writers work nationally or internationally with clients by phone or e-mail.

You can use the Occupation Index to look up resumes by the current or most recent job title. This index, however, should not replace careful examination of all of the resumes. Too many resumes for some other occupation may have features adaptable to your own occupation. Limiting your search to the Occupation Index may cause you to miss some valuable examples. You can use the Features Index to find resumes that contain representative resume sections that may be important to you and your resume needs.

Who This Book Is For

Anyone who wants ideas for creating or improving a resume can benefit from this book. It is especially useful for active job seekers—those who understand the difference between active and passive job searching. A *passive* job seeker waits until jobs are advertised and then mails copies of the same resume, along with a standard cover letter, in response to a number of help-wanted ads. An *active* job seeker believes that a resume should be modified for a specific job target *after* having talked in person or by phone to a prospective interviewer *before* a job is announced. To schedule such an interview is to penetrate the "hidden job market." Active job seekers can find in the Gallery's focused resumes a wealth of strategies for targeting a resume for a particular interview. The section "How to Use the Gallery" at the beginning of Part 2 shows you how to do this.

Besides the active job seeker, any unemployed person who wants to create a more competitive resume or update an old one should find this book helpful. It shows the kinds of resumes that professional resume writers are writing, and it showcases resumes for job seekers with particular needs.

What This Book Can Do for You

Besides providing you with a treasury of quality resumes whose features you can use in your own resumes, this book can help transform your thinking about resumes. There is no one "best" way to create a resume. This book will help you learn how to shape a resume that is *best for you* as you try to get an interview with a particular person for a specific job.

You might have been told that resumes should be only one page long; however, this is not necessarily true. The examples of multiple-page resumes in the Gallery will help you see how to distribute information effectively across two or more pages. If you believe that the way to update a resume is to add your latest work experiences to your last resume, this book will show you how to rearrange your resume so that you can highlight the most important information about your experience and skills.

After you have studied "Best Resume Tips" in Part 1, examined the professionally written resumes in the Gallery in Part 2, and reviewed "Tips for Polishing Cover Letters" and the cover letters in Part 3, you should be able to create your own resumes and cover letters worthy of inclusion in any gallery of best resumes.

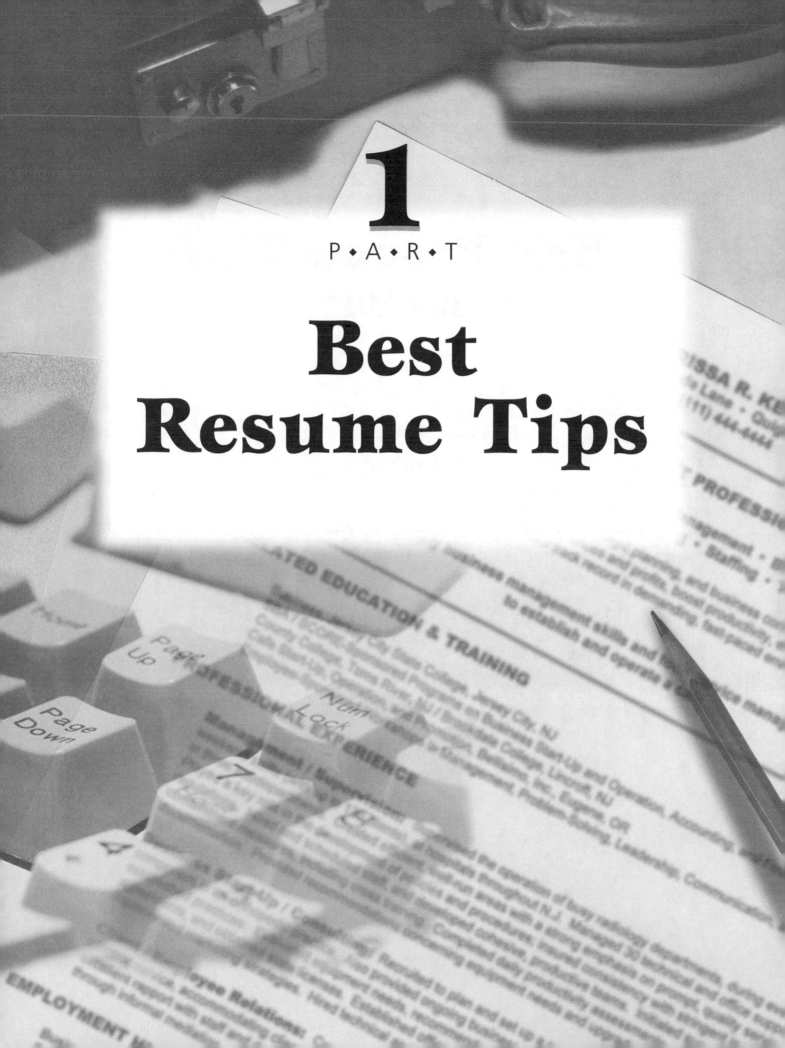

1
P·A·R·T

Best
Resume Tips

Best Resume Tips
at a Glance

Best Resume Tips 7

Best Resume Writing Strategies. 8

Best Resume Design and Layout Tips 9

Best Resume Writing Style Tips 14

Best Resume Tips

In a passive job search, you rely on your resume to do most of the work for you. An eye-catching resume that stands out above all the others may be your best shot at getting noticed by a prospective employer. If your resume is only average and looks like most of the others in the pile, the chances are great that you won't be noticed and called for an interview. If you want to be singled out because of your resume, it should be somewhere between spectacular and award-winning.

In an active job search, however, your resume complements your efforts at being known to a prospective employer *before* that person receives it. For this reason, you can rely less on your resume for getting someone's attention. Nevertheless, your resume has an important role in an active job search that may include the following activities:

- Talking to relatives, friends, and other acquaintances about helping you meet people who can hire you before a job is available

- Contacting employers directly, using the *Yellow Pages* to identify types of organizations that could use a person with your skills

- Creating phone scripts to speak with the person who is most likely to hire someone with your background and skills

- Walking into a business in person to talk directly to the one who is most likely to hire someone like you

- Using a schedule to keep track of your appointments and callbacks

- Working at least 25 hours a week to search for a job

When you are this active in searching for a job, the quality of your resume confirms the quality of your efforts to get to know the person who might hire you, as well as your worth to the company whose workforce you want to join. An eye-catching resume makes it easier for you to sell yourself directly to a prospective employer. If your resume is mediocre or conspicuously flawed, it will work against you and may undo all of your good efforts in searching for a job.

The following list offers ideas for making resumes visually impressive. Many of the ideas are for making resumes pleasing to the eye, but a number of the ideas are strategies to use in resumes for special cases. Other ideas are for eliminating common writing mistakes and stylistic weaknesses.

A number of the ideas have come from the professional resume writers who submitted resumes for the first edition of the book. The names of the writers appear in brackets after the relevant tips. Resumes that illustrate these ideas are referenced by resume number.

Some of these ideas can be used with any equipment, from a manual typewriter to a sophisticated computer with desktop publishing software. Other ideas make sense only if you have a computer system with word processing or desktop publishing. Even if you don't have a computer, take some time to read all of the ideas. Then, if you decide to use the services of a professional resume writer, you will be better informed about what the writer can do for you in producing your resume.

Best Resume Writing Strategies

1. **Although many resume books say that you should spell out the name of the state in your address at the top of the resume, consider using the postal abbreviation instead.** The reason is simple: it's an address. Anyone wanting to contact you by mail will probably refer to your name and address on the resume. If they appear there as they should on an envelope, the writer or typist can simply copy the information you supply. If you spell out the name of your state in full, the writer will have to "translate" the name of the state to its postal abbreviation.

   Not everyone knows all the postal abbreviations, and some abbreviations are easily confused. For example, those for Alabama (AL), Alaska (AK), American Samoa (AS), Arizona (AZ), and Arkansas (AR) are easy to mix up. You can prevent confusion and delay simply by using the correct postal abbreviation.

   If you decide to use postal abbreviations in addresses, make certain that you do not add a period after the abbreviations, even before ZIP codes. This applies also to postal abbreviations in the addresses of references, if you provide them.

   Do not, however, use the state postal abbreviation when you are indicating only the city and state (not the mailing address) of a school you attended or a business where you worked. In these cases, it makes sense to write out the name of the state in full.

2. **Adopt a sensible form for phone numbers and then use it consistently.** Do this in your resume and in all of the documents you use in your job search. Some forms for phone numbers make more sense than others. Compare the following forms:

123-4567	This form is best for a resume circulated locally, within a region where all the phone numbers have the same area code.
(222) 123-4567	This form is best for a resume circulated in areas with different area codes.
222-123-4567	This form suggests that the area code should be dialed in all cases. But that won't be necessary for prospective employers whose area code is 222. Avoid this form.
222/123-4567	This form is illogical and should be avoided also. The slash can mean an alternate option, as in ON/OFF. In a phone number, this meaning of a slash makes little sense.
1 (222) 123-4567	This form is long, and the digit *1* isn't necessary. Almost everyone will know that *1* should be used before the area code to dial a long-distance number.

222.123.4567 This form, resembling Internet addresses, is becoming more popular, particularly with people in computer and design fields.

Note: For resumes directed to prospective employers *outside* the United States, be sure to include the correct international prefixes in all phone numbers so that you and your references can be reached easily by phone.

3. **Near the top of the first page, include a Profile section that is focused, interesting, and unique.** If your Profile fails to grab attention, the reader may discard the resume without reading further. A Profile can be your first opportunity to sell yourself. For examples of effective Profiles, see Resumes 79, 92, 101, 109, 116, 121, 123, and many others.

4. **In the Experience section, state achievements or accomplishments, not just duties or responsibilities.** The reader often already knows the duties and responsibilities for a given position. Achievements, however, can be interesting. The reader probably considers life too short to be bored by lists of duties and responsibilities in a stack of resumes. See, for example, Resumes 68, 83, 105, 110, and 164.

5. **If you feel you must indicate duties, call attention to special or unusual duties you performed.** For example, if you are an accountant, don't say that you prepared accounting reports and analyzed income statements and balance sheets. What else is new? That's like being a dentist and saying, "I filled cavities and made crowns." What did you do that distinguished you from other accountants? To be noticed, you need to stand above the crowd in ways that display your individuality and work style.

6. **Instead of just listing your achievements, present them as challenges or problems solved, indicating what you did when something went wrong or needed fixing.** See, for example, Resumes 123, 172, and 173. [Young]

7. **When skills and abilities are varied, group them according to categories for easier comprehension.** See, for example, Resumes 34, 59, 80, 96, 154, and 162.

8. **Consider including a Highlights section to draw attention to special accomplishments or achievements.** See, for example, Resumes 6, 12, 29, 82, and 94.

9. **Summarize your qualifications and work experiences to avoid having to repeat yourself in the job descriptions.** See, for example, Resumes 12, 14, 27, and 121. [Lowry]

10. **Create a prominent Expertise section that draws together skills and abilities you have gained in previous work experience.** See, for example, Resumes 68, 78, 84, 111, 112, 113, 132, and 141.

Best Resume Design and Layout Tips

11. **Use quality paper correctly.** If you use quality watermarked paper for your resume, be sure to use the right side of the paper. To know which side is the right side, hold a blank sheet of paper up to a light source. If you can see a watermark and read it, the right side of the paper is facing you. This is the

surface for typing or printing. If the watermark is unreadable or if any characters look backward, you are looking at the "underside" of a sheet of paper—the side that should be left blank if you use only one side of the sheet.

12. **Use adequate "white space."** A sheet of white paper with no words on it is impossible to read. Likewise, a sheet of white paper with words all over it is impossible to read. The goal is to have a comfortable mix of white space and words. If your resume has too many words and not enough white space, the resume looks cluttered and unfriendly. If it has too much white space and too few words, the resume looks skimpy and unimportant. Make certain that adequate white space exists between the main sections. For examples that display good use of white space, see Resumes 26, 27, 29, 31, 37, 54, 57, 96, 97, 100, and 139, and many others.

13. **Make the margins uniform in width and preferably no less than an inch.** Margins are part of the white space of a resume page. If the margins shrink below an inch, the page begins to have a "too much to read" look. An enemy of margins is the one-page rule. If you try to fit more than one page of information on a page, the first temptation is to shrink the margins to make room for the extra material. It is better to shrink the material by paring it down than to reduce the size of the left, right, top, and bottom margins. If you do your resume on a computer, lowering the point size of the type is one way to save the margins. Try reducing the size of the text in your resume to 10 points. Then see how your information looks with the font(s) you are using. Different fonts produce different results. Be certain—in your effort to save the margins—that you don't make the type too small to be readable.

14. **Be consistent in your use of line spacing.** How you handle line spacing can tell the reader how good you are at details and how consistent you are in your use of them. If, near the beginning of your resume, you insert two line spaces (two hard returns in a word processing program) between two main sections, be sure to put two line spaces between main sections throughout the resume.

15. **Be consistent in your use of horizontal spacing.** If you usually put two character spaces after a period at the end of a sentence, make certain that you use two spaces consistently. The same is true for colons. If you put two spaces after colons, do so consistently.

   Note that an em dash—a dash the width of the letter *m*—does not require spaces before or after it. Similarly, an en dash—a dash the width of the letter *n*—should not have a space before and after it. An en dash is commonly used between a range of numbers, as in 2002–2004. If you use "to" instead of an en dash in a range of numbers, be sure to use "to" consistently in all ranges in your resume.

   No space should go between the *P* and *O* of P.O. Box. Only one space is needed between the postal abbreviation of a state and the ZIP code. You should insert a space between the first and second initials of a person's name, as in I. M. Jobseeker (not I.M. Jobseeker). These conventions have become widely adopted in English and business communications. If, however, you use other conventions, be sure to be consistent. In resumes, as in grammar, consistency is more important than conformity.

16. **Make certain that characters, lines, and images contrast well with the paper.** The quality of "ink" depends on the device used to type or print your resume. If you use an inkjet or laser printer, check that the characters are sharp and clean, without ink smudges or traces of extra toner.

17. **Use vertical alignment in tabbed or indented text.** Misalignment can ruin the appearance of a well-written resume. Try to set tabs or indents that control this text throughout a resume instead of having a mix of tab stops in different sections. Make certain that you understand the difference between tabbed text and indented text, as in the following examples:

    Tabbed text: This text was tabbed over one tab stop before the writer started to write the sentence.

    Indented text: This text was indented once before the writer started to write the sentence.

18. **For the vertical alignment of dates, try left- or right-aligning the dates.** This technique is especially useful in chronological resumes and combination resumes. For examples of left-aligned dates, see Resumes 35, 97, and 105. For right-aligned dates, look at Resumes 18, 21, 26, 98, 110, and 141.

19. **Use as many pages as you need for portraying your qualifications adequately to a specific interviewer for a particular job.** Try to limit your resume to one page, but set the upper limit at four pages. No rule about the number of pages makes sense in all cases. The determining factors are a person's qualifications and experiences, the requirements of the job, and the interests and pet peeves of the interviewer. If you know that an interviewer refuses to look at a resume longer than a page, that says it all. You need to deliver a one-page resume if you want to get past the first gate. For examples of two-page resumes, see Resumes 22, 67, 80, 115, and 134. For three-page resumes, look at Resumes 56, 84, 119, 127, and 133.

20. **Make each page a full page.** More important than the number of pages is whether each page you have is a full page. A partial page suggests deficiency, as if the reason for it is just that information on page 1 has spilled over onto page 2. There, it becomes evident that you don't have enough information to fill two pages. In that situation, try to compress all of your information onto the first page. If you have a resume that is almost two pages, make it two full pages.

21. **If your word processor can compress or expand text to fit one or more pages, use that feature.** For example, if you use WordPerfect and your resume is 1 1/4 pages long, use the Make It Fit feature to put all of your resume on one page. You can elect to alter margin width, line spacing, or font size (or any combination of these variables) to have WordPerfect compress your resume onto one page. Note that if your resume is 1 3/4 pages, you can use the Make It Fit feature to expand the document to two full pages. If you are a resume writer or write many letters, this feature is worth the cost of the program.

22. **When you have letters of recommendation, use quotations from them as testimonials in the first column of a two-column format or somewhere else in the resume.** Devoting a whole column to the positive opinions of "external authorities" helps to make a resume convincing as well as impressive. See, for example, Resumes 2, 12, 40, 56, 65, 80, and 102. [Culp-Coury]

23. **Unless you enlist the services of a professional printer or skilled desktop publisher, resist the temptation to use full justification for text.** The price that you pay for a straight right margin is uneven word spacing. Words may appear too close together on some lines and too spread out on others. Although the resume might look like typeset text, you lose readability. See also Tip 4 in "Tips for Polishing Cover Letters" in Part 3 of this book.

24. **If you can choose a typeface for your resume, use a serif font for greater readability.** Serif fonts have little lines extending from the tops, bottoms, and ends of the characters. These fonts tend to be easier to read than sans serif (without serif) fonts, especially in low-light conditions. Compare the following font examples:

Serif	Sans Serif
Century Schoolbook	Gill Sans
Courier	Futura
Times New Roman	Helvetica

Words such as *minimum* and *abilities,* which have several consecutive thin letters, are more readable in a serif font than in a sans serif font.

25. **If possible, avoid using monospaced fonts, such as Courier.** A font is monospaced if the space for each character is the same. For example, in a monospaced font the letter *i* is as wide as the letter *m*. Therefore, in Courier type *iiiii* is as wide as *mmmmm*. Courier was a standard of business communications during the 1960s and 1970s because it was the font supplied with IBM Selectric typewriters. Because of its widespread use, it is now considered "common." It also takes up a lot of space, so you can't pack as much information on a page with Courier type as you can with a proportionally spaced type such as Times New Roman.

26. **Think twice before using all uppercase letters in parts of your resume.** A common misconception is that uppercase letters are easier to read than lowercase letters. Actually, the ascenders and descenders of lowercase letters make them more distinguishable from each other and therefore more recognizable than uppercase letters. For a test, look at a string of uppercase letters and throw them gradually out of focus by squinting. The uppercase letters become a blur sooner than the lowercase letters do.

27. **Think twice about underlining some words in your resume.** Underlining defeats the purpose of serifs at the bottom of characters by blending with the serifs. In trying to emphasize words, you lose some visual clarity. This is especially true if you use underlining with uppercase letters in centered or side headings.

28. **If you have access to many fonts through word processing or desktop publishing, beware of becoming "font happy" and turning your resume into a font circus.** Frequent font changes *can* distract the **reader**, AND SO CAN GAUDY DISPLAY TYPE such as this.

29. **To make your resume stand out, consider using headings in unconventional type.** See, for example, Resumes 56 and 61.

30. **Be aware of the value differences of black type.** Some typefaces are light; others are dark. Notice the following lines:

A quick brown fox jumps over the lazy dog.

A quick brown fox jumps over the lazy dog.

Most typefaces fall somewhere between these two. With the variables of height, width, thickness, serifs, angles, curves, spacing, ink color, ink density, boldfacing, and typewriter double-striking, you can see that type offers an infinite range of values from light to dark. Try to make your resume more visually interesting by offering stronger contrasts between light type and dark type. See, for example, Resumes 10, 32, 43, 49, 67, and 93.

31. **Use italic characters carefully.** Whenever possible, use italic characters instead of underlining when you need to call attention to a word or phrase. You might consider using italic for duties, strengths, achievements, or company descriptions. For examples, see Resumes 55, 160, and 175. Think twice about using italic throughout your resume, however. The reason is that italic characters are less readable than normal characters.

32. **Use boldfacing to make different job experiences or achievements more evident.** See, for example, Resumes 7, 17, 19, 26, 28, 54, 83, 132, and many others.

33. **If you use word processing or desktop publishing and have a suitable printer, use special characters to enhance the look of your resume.** For example, use enhanced quotation marks (" and ") instead of their typewriter equivalents (" and "). Use an em dash (—) instead of two hyphens (--) for a dash. To separate dates, try using an en dash (a dash the width of the letter *n*) instead of a hyphen, as in 1993–1994.

34. **To call attention to an item in a list, use a bullet (•) or a box (▫) instead of a hyphen (-).** Browse through the Gallery and notice how bullets are used effectively as attention getters.

35. **For variety, try using bullets of a different style, such as diamond (♦) bullets, rather than the usual round or square bullets.** For diamond bullets, see Resumes 13, 67, 73, 84, 85, 95, 128, 140, 141, and 152. For other kinds of bullets, see Resumes 18, 20, 22, 39, 41, 43, 47, 53, 60, 63, 68, 77, 78, 87, 117, 151, 163, and 176. [Hosek]

36. **Make a bullet a little smaller than the lowercase letters that appear after it.** Disregard any ascenders or descenders on the letters. Compare the following bullet sizes:

    • Too small   ● Too large   • Better   • Just right

37. **When you use bullets, make certain that the bulleted items go beyond the superficial and contain information that employers really want to know.** Many short bulleted statements that say nothing special can affect the reader negatively. Brevity is not always the best strategy with bullets. For examples of substantial bulleted items, see Resumes 89, 130, and 177. [Noonan]

38. **When the amount of information justifies a longer resume, repeat a particular graphic, such as a filled square bullet or a right-pointing arrow bullet, to unify the entire resume.** See, for example, Resumes 79 and 112.

39. **Use a horizontal line to separate your name (or both your name and your address) from the rest of the resume.** If you browse through the Gallery, you can see many resumes that use horizontal lines this way. See, for example, Resumes 13, 27, 39, 65, 77, 104, and 162.

40. **Use horizontal lines to separate the different sections of the resume.** See, for example, Resumes 19, 20, 39, 58, 85, 94, 112, 126, 140, and 146. See also Resumes 66, 93, 129, and 131, whose lines are interrupted by the section headings.

41. **To call attention to a resume section or certain information, use horizontal lines to enclose it.** See, for example, Resumes 59, 76, 99, 132, 152, and 154. See also Resumes 30, 71, 117, and 144, in which one or more sections are enclosed in a box.

42. **Change the thickness of part of a horizontal line to call attention to a section heading above or below the line.** See, for example, Resumes 104 and 152.

43. **Use a vertical line (or lines) to spice up your resume.** See, for example, Resumes 6, 24, 50, 160, and 178.

44. **Use shaded boxes or headings to make a page visually more interesting.** See, for example, Resumes 18, 24, 30, 36, 44, 51, 62, 63, 143, 145, and 151. Compare these boxes with the *shadow* box in Resume 28.

45. **Try to make graphics match the theme of the resume.** See, for example, Resumes 6, 36, 43, 44, 57, and 63.

46. **If possible, visually coordinate the resume and the cover letter with the same font treatment or graphic to catch the reader's attention.** See, for example, Resumes 64, 44, and 24 and Cover Letters 9, 14, and 23, respectively. [Robertson]

Best Resume Writing Style Tips

47. **Avoid using the archaic word *upon* in the References section.** The common statement "References available upon request" needs to be simplified, updated, or even deleted in resume writing. The word *upon* is one of the finest words of the 13th century, but it's a stuffy word at the beginning of the 21st century. Usually, *on* will do in place of *upon*. Other possibilities are "References available by request" and "References available." Because most readers of resumes know that applicants can usually provide several reference letters, this statement is probably unnecessary. A reader who is seriously interested in you will ask about reference letters.

48. **Check that words or phrases in lists are parallel.** For example, notice the bulleted items in the Transitional Skills section of Resume 101. All the verbs are in the past tense. Notice also the bulleted list in the Executive Profile section of Resume 155. Here all the entries are nouns.

49. **Use capital letters correctly.** Resumes usually contain many of the following:

    - Names of people, companies, organizations, government agencies, awards, and prizes

    - Titles of job positions and publications

    - References to academic fields (such as chemistry, English, and mathematics)

    - Geographic regions (such as the Midwest, the East, the state of California, and Oregon State)

    Because of such words, resumes are minefields for the misuse of uppercase letters. When you don't know whether a word should have an initial capital letter, don't guess. Consult a dictionary, a handbook on style, or some other authoritative source, such as an official Web site. Often a reference librarian can provide the information you need. If so, you are only a phone call away from an accurate answer.

Follow headline style in headings with upper- and lowercase letters. That is, capitalize the first letter of the first word, the last word, and each main word in the heading, but not articles (*a, an,* and *the*), conjunctions (*and, but, or, nor, for, yet,* and *so*), and short prepositions (for example, *at, by, in,* and *on*) *within* the heading. Do initial cap long prepositions (of five or more letters; such as *about*).

To create a heading with "Small caps" (a Format, Font option in Word), first create a heading with upper- and lowercase letters. Then select the heading and assign Small caps to it through the Format, Font, Small caps command. Original uppercase letters will be taller than original lowercase letters now appearing as small capital letters.

50. **Check that you have used capital letters and hyphens correctly in computer terms.** If you want to show in a Computer Experience section that you have used certain hardware and software, you may give the opposite impression if you don't use uppercase letters and hyphens correctly. Note the correct use of capitals and hyphens in the following names of hardware, software, and computer companies:

LaserJet III	Hewlett-Packard	dBASE
PageMaker	MS-DOS	Microsoft
WordPerfect	PC DOS	Microsoft Word
NetWare	PostScript	AutoCAD
QuarkXPress	Photoshop	Windows

The reason that many computer product names have an internal uppercase letter is for the sake of a trademark. A word with unusual spelling or capitalization is trademarkable. When you use the correct forms of these words, you are honoring trademarks and registered trademarks and showing that you are in the know.

51. **Use all uppercase letters for most acronyms.** An *acronym* is a pronounceable word usually formed from the initial letters of the words in a compound term, or sometimes from multiple letters in those words. Note the following examples:

BASIC	Beginner's All-purpose Symbolic Instruction Code
COBOL	COmmon Business-Oriented Language
DOS	Disk Operating System
FORTRAN	FORmula TRANslator

An acronym such as *radar* (*ra*dio *d*etecting *a*nd *r*anging) has become so common that it is no longer all uppercase.

52. **Be aware of the difference between an acronym and an abbreviation.** Remember, an acronym is a combination of letters making a word that you can pronounce as a word. One kind of an abbreviation, however, is a set of uppercase letters (without periods) that you can pronounce only as letters and never as a word. Examples are CBS (C-B-S), NFL (N-F-L), YWCA (Y-W-C-A), and AFL-CIO (A-F-L, C-I-O).

53. **Be sure to spell every word correctly.** A resume with just one misspelling is not impressive and may undermine all the hours you spent putting it together. Worse than that, one misspelling may be what the reader is looking for to screen you out, particularly if you are applying for a position that requires accuracy with words. The cost of that error can be immense if you figure the salary, benefits, and bonuses you *don't* get because of the error but would have gotten without it.

    If you use word processing and have a spelling checker, you may be able to catch many misspellings. Be wary of spelling checkers, however. They can detect a misspelled word but cannot detect when you have inadvertently used a wrong word (*to* for *too,* for example). Be wary also of letting someone else check your resume. If the other person is not a good speller, you may not get any real help. The best authority is a good dictionary.

54. **For words that have more than one correct spelling, use the preferred form.** This form is the one that appears first in a dictionary. For example, if you see the entry **trav·el·ing** *or* **trav·el·ling,** the first form (with one *l*) is the preferred spelling. If you make it a practice to use the preferred spelling, you will build consistency in your resumes and cover letters.

55. **Avoid British spellings.** These slip into American usage through books and online articles published in Great Britain. Note the following words:

British Spelling	American Spelling
acknowledgement	acknowledgment
centre	center
judgement	judgment
towards	toward

56. **Avoid hyphenating words with such prefixes as** *co-, micro-, mid-, mini-, multi-, non-, pre-, re-,* **and** *sub-.* Many people think that words with these prefixes should have a hyphen after the prefix, but most of these words should not. The following words are spelled correctly:

coauthor	microcomputer	minicomputer
coworker	midpoint	multicultural
cowriter	midway	multilevel
nondisclosure	prearrange	reenter
nonfunctional	prequalify	subdirectory

    Note: If you look in a dictionary for a word with a prefix and can't find the word, look for the *prefix* itself in the dictionary. You might find there a small-print listing of a number of words that have the prefix.

57. **Be aware that compounds (combinations of words) present special problems for hyphenation.** Writers' handbooks and books on style do not always agree on how compounds should be hyphenated. Many compounds are evolving from *open* compounds (two different words) to *hyphenated* compounds (two words joined by a hyphen) to *closed* compounds (one word). In different dictionaries, you can therefore find the words *copy-editor, copy editor,* and *copyeditor.* No wonder the issue is confusing! Most style books do agree, however, that when some compounds appear as an adjective before a noun, the compound should be hyphenated. When the same compound appears after a noun, hyphenation is unnecessary. Compare the following two sentences:

I scheduled well-attended conferences.

The conferences I scheduled were well attended.

For detailed information about hyphenation, see a recent edition of *The Chicago Manual of Style* (the 15th edition is now current). You should be able to find a copy at a local library.

58. **Hyphenate so-called *permanent* hyphenated compounds.** Usually, you can find these by looking them up in a dictionary. You can spot them easily because they have a "long hyphen" (–) for visibility in the dictionary. Hyphenate these words (with a standard hyphen) wherever they appear, before or after a noun. Here are some examples:

all-important	self-employed
day-to-day	step-by-step
full-blown	time-consuming

Note that *The Chicago Manual of Style*, 15th Edition, now recommends that these hyphenated compounds should no longer be considered permanent, but should be written without a hyphen (or hyphens) when they appear after a noun (see again Tip 57).

59. **Use the correct form for certain verbs and nouns combined with prepositions.** You may need to consult a dictionary for correct spelling and hyphenation. Compare the following examples:

start up	(verb)
start-up	(noun)
start-up	(adj.)
startup	(noun, computer and Internet industry)
startup	(adj., computer and Internet industry)

60. **Avoid using shortcut words, such as abbreviations like *thru* or foreign words like *via*.** Spell out *through* and use *by* for *via*.

61. **Use the right words.** The issue here is correct usage, which often means the choice of the right word or phrase from a group of two or more possibilities. The following words and phrases are often used incorrectly:

alternate (adj.)	Refers to an option used every other time. OFF is the alternate option to ON in an ON/OFF switch.
alternative	Refers to an option that can be used at any time. If cake and pie are alternative desserts for dinner, you can have cake three days in a row if you like. The common mistake is to use *alternate* when the correct word is *alternative*.
center around	A common illogical expression. Draw a circle and then try to draw its center around it. You can't. Use *center in* or *center on* as logical alternatives to *center around*.

For information about the correct *usage* of words, consult a usage dictionary or the usage section of a writer's handbook, such as Strunk and White's *Elements of Style*.

62. **Use numbers consistently.** Numbers are often used inconsistently with text. Should you present a number as a numeral or spell out the number as a word? A useful approach is to spell out numbers *one* through *nine* but present numbers 10 and above as numerals. Different approaches are taught in different schools, colleges, and universities. Use the approach you have learned, but be consistent.

63. **Use (or don't use) the serial comma consistently.** How should you punctuate a series of three or more items? If, for example, you say in your resume that you increased sales by 100 percent, opened two new territories, and trained four new salespersons, the comma before *and* is called the *serial comma.* It is commonly omitted in newspapers, magazine articles, advertisements, and business documents; but it is often used for precision in technical documents or for stylistic reasons in academic text, particularly in the Humanities.

64. **Use semicolons correctly.** Semicolons are useful because they help to distinguish visually the items in a series when the items themselves contain commas. Suppose that you have the following entry in your resume:

    > Increased sales by 100 percent, opened two new territories, which were in the Midwest, trained four new salespersons, who were from Georgia, and increased sales by 250 percent.

    The extra commas (before *which* and *who*) throw the main items of the series out of focus. By separating the main items with semicolons, you can bring them back into focus:

    > Increased sales by 100 percent; opened two new territories, which were in the Midwest; trained four new salespersons, who were from Georgia; and increased sales by 250 percent.

    Use this kind of high-rise punctuation even if just one item in the series has an internal comma.

65. **Avoid using colons after headings.** A colon indicates that something is to follow. A heading indicates that something is to follow. A colon after a heading is therefore redundant.

66. **Use dashes correctly.** One of the purposes of a dash (an em dash or two hyphens) is to introduce a comment or afterthought about preceding information. A colon *anticipates* something to follow, but a dash *looks back* to something already said. Two dashes are sometimes used before and after a related but nonessential remark—such as this—within a sentence. In this case, the dashes are like parentheses, but more formal.

67. **Use apostrophes correctly.** They indicate possession (Tom's, Betty's), the omission of letters in contractions (can't, don't), and some plurals (x's and o's), but they can be tricky with words ending in *s,* possessive plurals, and plural forms of capital letters and numbers. For review or guidance, consult a style guide or a section on style in a dictionary.

68. **Know the difference between *its* and *it's*.** The form *its'* does not exist in English, so you need to know only how *it's* differs from *its.* The possessive form *its* is like *his* and *her* and has no apostrophe. The form *it's* is a contraction of *it is.* The trap is to think that *it's* is a possessive form.

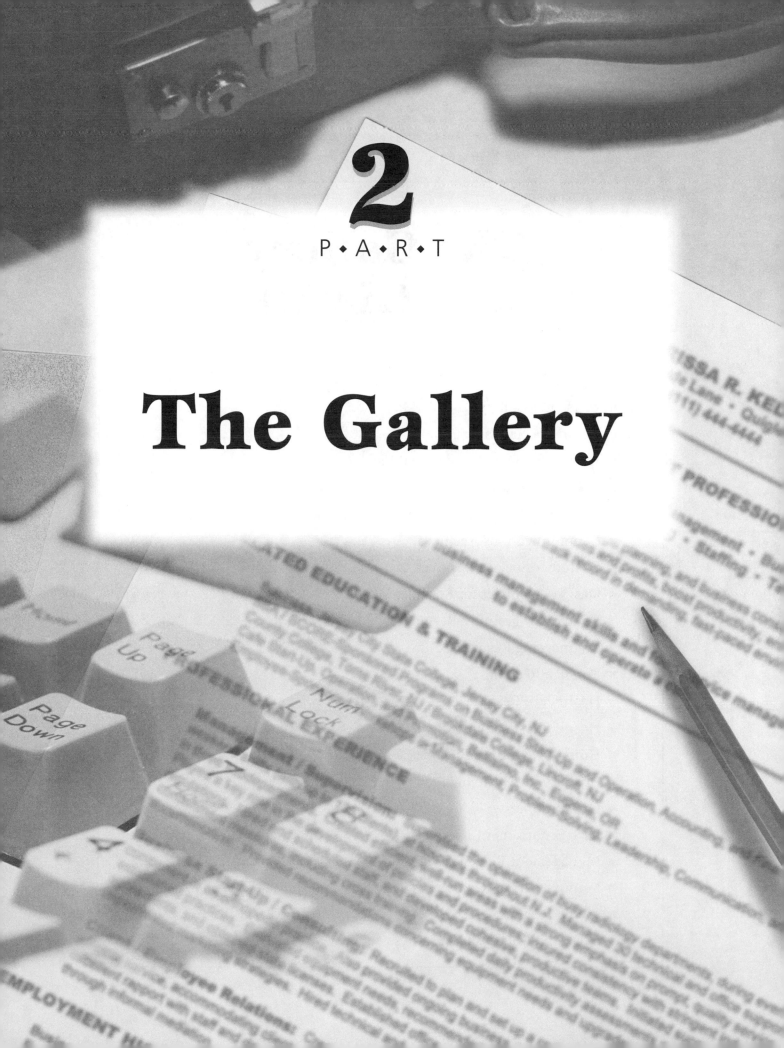

2
P·A·R·T

The Gallery

The Gallery at a Glance

How to Use the Gallery. 21

Resumes on Special Paper. 23

Resumes Grouped by Occupational Fields

   ■ Accounting Resumes 43

   ■ Advertising/Promotion Resumes 51

   ■ Communications Resumes. 59

   ■ Customer Service Resumes 69

   ■ Design/Architecture Resumes 75

   ■ Education/Training Resumes 83

   ■ Engineering Resumes. 141

   ■ Finance Resumes 155

   ■ Healthcare Resumes. 183

   ■ Hospitality Resumes 233

   ■ Human Resources Resumes. 241

   ■ Information Systems/Technology Resumes. 259

   ■ Law Resumes. 283

   ■ Law Enforcement Resumes 293

   ■ Management Resumes 305

   ■ Manufacturing Resumes 331

   ■ Media Resumes 339

   ■ Sales and Marketing Resumes 347

How to Use the Gallery

You can learn much from the Gallery just by browsing through it. To make the best use of this resource, however, read the following suggestions before you begin.

Examine the resumes on special paper at the beginning of the Gallery. These 16 examples show how quality paper can enhance the appearance of a resume. The papers range in color from off-whites to blues and include creams, tans, warm grays, and cool grays. Most of these papers are watermarked, and all are compatible with laser and InkJet printers, and photocopiers. All have a weight of 24 lb., which is widely used for resumes, and some contain recycled content. Some of the paper samples have subtle differences in texture that you can sense by rubbing your fingers over the surface and listening to the sound. Notice which colors are not included: orange, green, purple (the secondary colors), and darker values of any color.

Look at the resumes in the category containing your field, related fields, or your target occupation. Notice what kinds of resumes other people have used to find similar jobs. Always remember, though, that your resume should not be "canned." It should not look just like someone else's resume, but should reflect your own background, unique experiences, and goals.

Use the Gallery primarily as an "idea book." Even if you don't find a resume for your specific occupation or job, be sure to look at all of the resumes for ideas you can borrow or adapt. You may be able to modify some of the sections or statements with information that applies to your own situation or job target.

Study the ways professional resume writers have formatted the names, addresses, and phone numbers of the subjects. In most instances, this information appears at the top of the first page of the resume. Look at type styles, size of type, and use of boldface. See whether the personal information is centered on lines, spread across a line, or located near the margin on one side of a page. Look for the use of horizontal lines to separate this information from the rest of the resume, to separate the address and phone number from the person's name, or to enclose information for higher visibility.

Look at each resume to see what section appears first after the personal information. Then compare those same sections across the Gallery. For example, look just at the resumes that have a Goal or an Objective statement as the first section. Compare the length, clarity, and use of words. Do these statements contain complete sentences, or one or more partial lines of thought? Are some statements better than others from your point of view? Do you see one or more Objective statements that come close to matching your own objective? After you have compared these statements, try expressing *in your own words* your goal or objective.

Repeat this "horizontal comparison" for each of the sections across the Gallery. Compare all of the Education sections, all of the Qualifications sections, and so on. As you make these comparisons, continue to note differences in length, the kinds of words and phrases used, and the effectiveness of the content. Jot down any ideas that might be true for you. Then put together similar sections for your own resume.

As you compare sections across the Gallery, pay special attention to the Profile, Summary, Areas of Expertise, Career Highlights, Qualifications, and Experience sections. (Most resumes won't have all of these sections.) Notice how skills and accomplishments are worked into these sections. Skills and accomplishments are *variables* that you can select to put a certain "spin" on your resume as you pitch it toward a particular interviewer or job. Your observations here should be especially valuable for your own resume versions.

After you have examined the resumes "horizontally" (section by section), compare them "vertically" (design by design). To do this, you need to determine which resumes have the same sections in the same order, and then compare just those resumes. For example, look for resumes that have personal information at the top, an Objective statement, an Experience section, an Education section, and finally a line about references. (Notice that the section heads may differ slightly. Instead of the word *Experience,* you might find *Work Experience* or *Employment.*) When you examine the resumes in this way, you are looking at their *structural design,* which means the order in which the various sections appear. The same order can appear in resumes of different fields or jobs, so it is important to explore the whole Gallery and not limit your investigation to resumes in your field or related fields.

Developing a sense of resume structure is extremely important because it enables you to emphasize the most important information about yourself. A resume is a little like a newspaper article—read quickly and usually discarded before the reader finishes. That is why the information in newspaper articles often dwindles in significance toward the end. For the same reason, the most important, attention-getting information about you should be at or near the top of your resume. What follows should appear in order of descending significance.

If you know that the reader will be more interested in your education than your work experience, put your Education section before your Experience section. If you know that the reader will be interested in your skills regardless of your education and work experience, put your Skills section at or near the beginning of your resume. In this way, you can help to ensure that anyone who reads only *part* of your resume will read the "best about you." Your hope is that this information will encourage the reader to read on to the end of the resume and, above all, take an interest in you.

Compare the resumes according to visual design features, such as the use of horizontal and vertical lines, borders, boxes, bullets, white space, graphics, and inverse type (light characters on a dark background). Notice which resumes have more visual impact at first glance and which ones make no initial impression. Do some of the resumes seem more inviting to read than others? Which ones are less appealing because they have too much information, or too little? Which ones seem to have the right balance of information and white space?

After comparing the visual design features, choose the design ideas that might improve your own resume. You will want to be selective here and not try to work every design possibility into your resume. As in writing, "less is more" in resume making, especially when you integrate design features with content.

Resumes on Special Paper

Resumes at a Glance

RESUME NO.	OCCUPATION	GOAL	PAGE
1.	Corporate Facilities Manager	Facilities/Project Manager	25
2.	Operations Manager	Operations Manager	26
3.	Product Manager	Not specified	27
4.	Asst. Manager/Floor Supervisor	Not specified	28
5.	Security Director	Not specified	29
6.	Tennis Professional and Coach	Tennis Professional and Coach	30
7.	Event/Program Coordinator	Not specified	31
8.	Cardiology Account Manager	Meeting Planner	32
9.	Commercial Airline Pilot	First Officer, Airline	33
10.	Esthetician	Esthetician	34
11.	Dept. Chairperson/Teacher	Not specified	35
12.	Project Coordinator	Administrative Specialist	36
13.	Recording Engineer	Recording/Mixing Engineer	37
14.	Customer Service Specialist	Not specified	38
15.	Territory Sales Specialist	Pharmaceutical Salesperson	39
16.	Software Account Manager	Software Sales Manager	40

Cara Provalenko, CFM

5700 Main Street, Denver, CO 00000—caraprovalenko@email.com—303-000-0110

Facilities Manager—Project Manager—Strategic Planner with extensive experience in leading-edge facilities planning, design, and management.

- Exceptional results in fast-track, high-end capital construction, renovation, and relocation projects.
- Influential, team-building approach, conducting research, creating urgency, selling programs among cross-disciplinary teams, and driving results. Extensive professional network of industry leaders.

Experience

Corporate Facilities Manager, BOSTON MARKET CORPORATE OFFICE, Denver, CO, 1997–2004

- Developed and led a multidisciplinary project management team of 24.
- Provided strategic planning, site selection, lease negotiations, scheduling, construction budgets, and relocation of corporate headquarters to meet growth objectives.
- Designed and implemented an innovative office environment, achieving objectives for enhanced corporate image and improved communication, teamwork, and productivity.
- Negotiated contracts for utilities, telecommunications, and security services for 150 retail locations nationwide.

Project Manager/Space Manager, UNIVERSITY OF DENVER, Denver, CO, 1993–1997

- Managed facility utilization at a 3-million-sq.-ft. research campus. Directed, developed, and motivated professional staff and interns.
- Developed and administered a space management database for indirect cost recovery, asset tracking, and space utilization, increasing revenues by $1.5 million annually. Authored long-range facilities master plan.
- Spearheaded the conversion of paper-based facilities documentation to AutoCAD. Negotiated contract with architectural firm with built-in incentives for accuracy, collaboration, and timely completion.
- Created and implemented community outreach and public relations campaign to ensure support for 25 concurrent major capital projects valued at $200 million.

Facilities Designer/Project Manager, LOCKHEED MARTIN ASTRONAUTICS, Denver, CO, 1990–1993

- Functioned as architect, space planner, and project manager for a major aerospace contractor.
- Completed tenant-finish of research laboratories, high-security suites, and corporate offices. Developed scope of work, schedules, and budgets.
- Collaborated with purchasing departments in complex government-regulated bid development processes. Served as liaison to research scientists, corporate executives, and community members.

Education & Professional Activities

Bachelor of Science, Business Administration, University of Colorado at Boulder

Certified Facility Manager (CFM), Distinguished Member, International Facility Management Association

Combination. *Tracy Laswell Williams, Arvada, Colorado*

Horizontal lines appear as a separate line under the Experience heading and another under the Education & Professional Activities heading. Adequate white space makes the layout easy to grasp at a glance.

David Foreman

555 Center Street
Grove City, Pennsylvania 16127

724.555.3333
dforeman@aol.com

MANAGER
Operations • Process Improvement • Training

Your hard work, superb preparation, and "can-do" attitude were noted with pleasure by Fleet Training Group personnel. Your flexibility to adapt to rapidly changing situations and your ability to work as a team member have established you as an integral member of *Implicit's* elite crew. Your dedication, knowledge, enthusiasm, and drive for excellence are second to none.
—*R.T. Thompson*
Commanding Officer, USS Implicit

[Foreman] placed upon himself the task of improving the layout of forward berthing temporary racks. Using exceptional skill and resourcefulness, [he] modified the format ... enlarging the living space and privacy, turning the temporary racks from the worst to the best in forward berthing. This provided a big morale boost for the personnel. [Foreman's] personal initiative is an example of the "can-do" spirit of "Iron Men in Wooden Ships!"
—*A. G. Myers*
Commanding Officer, USS Enhance

[Foreman's] performance is excellent. He has, without question, gained respect and confidence from his superiors for his depth of knowledge, sound judgement, and initiative. An exceptional leader routinely selected to train new personnel on MCM techniques. ... [Foreman] is not only an excellent leader but also a dependable manager and administrator.
—*September 30, 1990*

[Foreman] is thorough, gifted, and meticulous in his leadership skills. ...[He] has distinguished himself as one who will "take the ball and run with it."
—*January 15, 1988*

➤ Strong leadership, strategic planning, project management, and team-building expertise. Create enthusiasm and build confidence in others.

➤ Design innovative workflow planning/prioritization strategies, resulting in improvement in productivity, efficiency, inventory issues, and cost savings.

➤ Able to multitask and make decisions. Flexible to changing priorities.

➤ Adept at recognizing/launching steps needed to attain objectives. Thrive on challenges to overcome obstacles with solutions that are technically sound and financially feasible. Learn new skills rapidly.

➤ Exceptional interpersonal and communication skills (network, collaborate, negotiate); build positive, effective business relationships with people from diverse cultures and at all professional levels.

➤ Motivate team by recognizing high standards of performance. Give feedback to encourage people to be open and to foster sense of trust.

PROFESSIONAL EXPERIENCE

Foreman Construction and Repair—Flower Mound, Texas   *1999–Present*
OPERATIONS MANAGER
- Manage daily operations of construction company, specializing in commercial and residential remodeling projects. Supervise team of 7–15 on job sites. Prepare estimates and negotiate contracts.
- Carry out all management functions, i.e., hire and terminate personnel, purchase material and equipment, and direct logistics and scheduling of construction projects.

Owens Corning Fiberglass—Flower Mound, Texas   *1994–1999*
TRAINING AND SAFETY INSTRUCTOR
- Revamped in-house OSHA course curriculum and instituted regular class schedule.
- Taught OSHA standards to employees; trained team members on effective presentation of material. Significantly improved employee compliance with established safety standards.

United States Navy—Seattle, Washington, and aboard ships worldwide   *1972–1994*
NATIONAL TEAM TRAINER (*1990–1994*)
- Traveled nationwide to evaluate team performance in the field. Delivered weeklong team-training workshops to optimize performance of teams under emergency and stressful situations.

OPERATIONS MANAGER (*1987–1990*)
- Wrote and implemented logistics for operations and training for 15 ships and their personnel. Directly managed 50 personnel, assigning duties, training, and work schedules, and directing the Preventative Maintenance System (PMS).
- Appointed to #3 management position on nuclear cruiser during Persian Gulf War.

Prior to Honorable Discharge in 1994, experience included 8 years as Navigator.
Held Secret Clearance.

EDUCATION / CONTINUING EDUCATION

B.S., Business, anticipated 2004, **current GPA 3.8,** American Intercontinental University

Commercial Plumber coursework, 1996–1998, Local 100

2

Combination. *Jane Roqueplot, Sharon, Pennsylvania*

Impressive testimonials, tip-bulleted skills, and a record of experience with major achievements display this worker as a recent graduate with an exceptional past.

BOB ANDERSON

banderson@dotresume.com

5 Graber Ferry Circle • Grand Valley, PA 00000 • Home: (555) 555-5555 • Cell: (999) 999-9999

QUALIFICATIONS SUMMARY

Medical marketing manager with eight-year history of utilizing strengths in strategic planning and communication to increase sales and improve market share.
- Track record of finding and converting new prospects.
- Special talent for building successful relationships with customers and prospects.
- Proven ability to lead cross-functional teams and direct-reports.
- Internet savvy; working knowledge of Microsoft Office with expertise in Word, Excel, and Outlook.
- M.B.A. in marketing plus e-commerce certification.

PROFESSIONAL EXPERIENCE

Product Manager   2/00–present
CLINITRAK, Blue Bell, PA

Report directly to vice president of marketing, overseeing marketing and development of all Web-based clinical documentation services. Define positioning and promotional strategies with focus on gaining recognition as high-end product line. Supervise four marketing and sales professionals. Interface with development staff to define product requirements and manage product life cycle. Establish relationships with luminary hospitals, clinics, and physicians. Own P & L for product line.

Accomplishments
- Grew market share 15% in spite of lagging economy.
- Recruited three highly regarded physicians to serve on advisory board.
- Established reputation for product line with requirements-rich, on-time releases.

Product Marketing Manager   11/96–2/00
TELEMED, Wayne, PA

Developed and implemented strategies for marketing medical transcription products to physicians and clinical practice groups. Managed cross-functional team in producing all marketing and promotional materials. Led initiative to move product line to Web and oversaw development of product Web site.

Accomplishments
- Helped increase sales of product line by 90% between 1996 and 2000.
- Doubled number of prospects following launch of Web site in 1999.

Assistant Product Marketing Manager   6/94–10/96
SUPERIOR MEDICAL SUPPLY COMPANY, Lawrenceville, NJ

Assisted manager in developing strategic plans to market examination room supplies to physicians and hospitals. Created all supporting promotional materials including brochures, newsletters, and press releases. Prepared presentations and delivered to prospects.

Accomplishments
- Attained 70% conversion rate for prospects attending presentations.

EDUCATION, CERTIFICATION

E-commerce Certificate, CBI Institute, Philadelphia, PA   5/02
M.B.A., Marketing, Keystone State University, Trenton, NJ   12/94
B.S., Journalism, Taylor State College, Lambertville, NJ   6/92

BUSINESS ORGANIZATIONS

Grand Valley Chamber of Commerce, Grand Valley, PA   7/02–present
- Initiated and led membership retention drive.
- Achieved 90% retention in 2003, compared with an average of 75% in the previous three years.

3

Combination. *Jan Holliday, Harleysville, Pennsylvania*

The writer fit this resume on one page by "paring the text and then decreasing the font size, leading [the space between lines], and margins." Horizontal lines help you spot the major sections.

Kendall Rose Coleman

76 Columbia Street   175 West 57th Street, Apt. E
Poughkeepsie, NY 00000   New York, NY 00000
555.555.5555   555.555.5555

Career Focus: Corporate Fashion / Fashion Merchandising

▸ *Profile*

Flexible and creative individual with organizational ability, a wide range of fashion industry knowledge and a good eye for trends in silhouette, color and fabric. Offering a high degree of motivation and maturity, plenty of energy, leadership aptitude, great communication skills and assertiveness. Proven ability to manage complex projects and collaborate with both creative and business teams. Combines an innate ability to forecast trends with solid academic preparation and extensive retail experience. Excellent interpersonal skills developed in fast-moving, customer-centric environments.

▸ *Highlights of Qualifications*

Retail Sales & Merchandising / Staff Management
Personalized Customer Service / Customer Relations
Computer Literate: Microsoft Word, Excel, PowerPoint

▸ *College Coursework*

Fashion History	Design Principles
Psychology of Fashion	Fashion Merchandising
Consumer Behavior	Color & Design

▸ *Specific Areas of Knowledge, Insight & Experience*

Research & Trend Analysis	Product Development	Working with personal shoppers & upscale clientele
Concept Board Creation	Business-to-Business Sales	Sourcing, Supplier Evaluation and Vendor Assessment
Buying & Marketing	Multi-Cultural Markets	Up-to-date knowledge of fibers, yarns, fabrics & finishes

Internship Experience and College Work Project Highlights

Soho Designs**, New York, NY   Assistant—Product Development, Design & Merchandising*   ***Fall 2001

Assisted the VP of Product Development of this novelty sweater manufacturer. Involved with developing and producing a product line from initial concept to reality with the challenge to forecast trends and translate them into profitable sweater designs. Evaluated sales patterns, researched fabrics and trims, and created complex business plans aimed at target customers. Also, created concept boards, met with suppliers and worked with technical designers, QA managers and internal teams.

Upscale Boutique**, New York, NY   Senior Sales Associate*   ***Fall 2000

Involved with selling and merchandising high-end hosiery in this upscale Soho boutique. Acquired experience in dealing with personal shoppers and a discerning clientele. Expedited deliveries and handled specialty and high-volume accounts.

Victoria's Secret**, Poughkeepsie, NY   Sales Associate*   ***Fall 1999

Dealt directly with customers and merchandised in-store displays. Made efficiency improvements and achieved high sales through a thorough knowledge of products and creative merchandising. Also managed cash and closed ending reports.

Education / Activities

B.B.A. in Marketing
Fashion Institute of Technology, New York, NY
Thesis: African-American Designers

Pre-Professional Activities
Fashion Club Member / Director, Annual Fashion Show
Dress for Success Volunteer / Earned 100% tuition & books

Employment History

Assistant Manager / Floor Supervisor Abercrombie & Fitch, Poughkeepsie, NY		**2003 to Present**
Hostess / Waitress City Street Café, Poughkeepsie, NY		**1997 to Present**
Store Manager Weathervane, Poughkeepsie, NY		**2002 to 2003**

4

Combination.   *Kristin M. Coleman, Poughkeepsie, New York*

Ornamental, wavy lines enclosing the centered headings are distinctive. A profile, qualifications highlights, relevant courses, and knowledge areas are all put before experience.

John Raymond

111 West Annie Lane ◆ Ferrytown, VA 00000 ◆ 000-000-0000 ◆ user@cox.rr.com

Achievement-oriented professional with exceptional administrative skills

Areas of Strength

Written/Oral Communication	*Biometric Technology*	*Background Investigation*
Airport and Airline Security	*Physical Assessment*	*Budget Administration*
Resource Management	*Cost Controls*	*Staff Development*
Sales and Marketing	*Forecasting*	*Team Leadership*

Professional Experience

Security Director, TransSecure Corporation   **2001–present**
- Coordinate the design and development of iris-recognition products and services from a security perspective.
- Act as liaison between company and airports/airlines to facilitate implementation of cutting-edge biometric security technology.
- Monitor all aspects of administration for budget of up to $250,000 per project, and teams of up to 18 members, ensuring successful completion of projects within timeframe and cost constraints.
- Register fingerprints and irises of frequent flyers in U.S. and U.K., achieving reduction in planing and deplaning security checks and reducing customer security expenditures.
- Ensure all Federal Aviation Administration rules and regulations that govern airport and airline security are complied with at all times.

Operations Manager, Detailing Services   **1987–present**
- Maintain P&L responsibility for auto and boat detail center with 4 full-time employees.
- Handle all aspects of operations administration, including budgeting, bookkeeping, payroll, and report generation.
- Prepare and submit financial documentation to professional accountant for tax reporting.
- Manage employee benefits programs, including recent implementation of group health benefits.
- Monitor facilities and staff members for adherence to all applicable health safety guidelines.
- Remain in compliance with regulations of the Equal Employment Opportunity Commission.

RELATED EXPERIENCE

Metropolitan Police Department
Served 20-year tenure, fulfilling responsibility of the following positions:

Recruiting Investigator—2 years:
- Performed in-depth background investigations of both civilian and police applicants.
- Interviewed prospective applicants for both police and civilian positions.
- Initiated and conducted recruitment drives at colleges and universities.

Employee Management Specialist—8 years:
- Provided expert testimony and served as liaison to the Washington D.C. Superior Court, in matters relating to violations of uniform standards of conduct, general orders, and criminal acts, as well as informing officials as to how the act was performed.
- Offered recommendations for pay status of uniformed officers charged with violations, including administrative and sick leave, and benefits.
- Issued leadership handbook to first-line supervisors.

EDUCATION

Bachelor of Science in Administration of Criminal Justice—Western University

Training: Police Academy, Background Investigation, Personnel Management, Employee Relations, Dignitary Protection, Race Relations
Honors: Reduction of Crime—Presented by Chief of Police
Memberships: American Society of Industrial Security, Fraternal Order of Police

Keywords: Aviation, Personnel Management, Security Technology, Workplace Diversity, Biometrics

5

Combination. *Lea J. Clark, Macon, Georgia*

Strength areas of diminishing length are placed in a four-row, three-column table without lines. From left to right, the columns are in turn left-aligned, centered, and right-aligned.

Henry James

13 Windmill Lane, Huntington, NY 11743 • matchpoint@mail.com • (555) 555-5555

Experienced Tennis Professional & Coach
Beginners through National Champions
Children, Teens & Adults / Special-Needs Populations

PLAYER PROFILE

- At 16 years old, ranked #1 in California.
- At 18, ranked 20th in U.S. national standings.
- Four years as a varsity tennis player, University of California at Los Angeles (UCLA).
- In 2001, in the 35+ Division, competed in two U.S. national tournaments, reaching the semifinals.

EMPLOYMENT HISTORY

Senior Pro, NORTHPORT TENNIS ACADEMY, Northport, NY	1997–Present
Senior Pro, OLD WESTBURY TENNIS CENTER, Old Westbury, NY	1996
Head Pro, SANTA MONICA TENNIS ACADEMY, Santa Monica, CA	1990–1995
Head Pro, LONG BEACH TENNIS CENTER, Long Beach, CA	1983–1990

HIGHLIGHTS

- Provide skills instruction and motivational coaching in individual and group lessons, including men's, women's, and doubles leagues.
- Instill confidence and provide encouragement to all students with special attentive support to children. Set goals for future performance and monitor progress. Answer questions, provide feedback, and otherwise communicate with parents, as appropriate.
- Coach nationally ranked players on advanced skill development. Currently serve as a traveling coach to a 15-year-old student ranked 12th in the U.S.
- Manage summer camp program, overseeing six instructors for children's groups, ages 6–12.
- As a clinic coach, run drills for 2-hour group practices, several times per week.
- Teach children and adults with physically limiting conditions.
- Participated in the Senior Professional Tennis Clinics Circuit (1997–2000).

EDUCATION

Bachelor of Arts, Psychology. UCLA, Los Angeles, CA

PROFESSIONAL TRAINING

Certified Professional, 1995–Present
UNITED STATES PROFESSIONAL TENNIS REGISTRY

USA Tennis High Performance Coaching Program, 2003
UNITED STATES PROFESSIONAL TENNIS ASSOCIATION, College Park, MD

USA Tennis Teachers' Conference, 2002, 2001 & 2000
UNITED STATES TENNIS ASSOCIATION

Tennis Workshop for Coaches, 2001
SMITH TENNIS ACADEMY, St. Petersburg, FL

National Clinician Workshop for Tennis Instructors, 2000
USTA / UNITED STATES PROFESSIONAL TENNIS REGISTRY

Tennis Clinician Program, 1998
ROSSMAN TENNIS UNIVERSITY, Marco Island, FL

6

Combination. *MJ Feld, Huntington, New York*

The candidate was concerned about his age—around 40. The writer left off the graduation date but showed the person's 35+ Division achievement, continual tennis playing, and training.

MARILYN NOLAN
22 Meadow Lane ▪ Chicago, IL 00000 ▪ (555) 555-5555 ▪ MNolan@media.net

■ PROFILE

Conferences ▪ Fund-raising ▪ Trade Shows ▪ Meeting Planning ▪ Cultural Programs

Creative professional with expertise in all aspects of successful event/program planning, development and management. Excel in managing multiple projects concurrently with strong detail, problem solving and follow-through. Demonstrated ability to recruit, motivate and build cohesive teams. Sourced vendors, negotiated contracts and managed project budgets. Superb written communications, interpersonal and presentation skills.

■ SELECTED ACCOMPLISHMENTS

Special Events Management:

Planned and coordinated conferences, meetings and events for companies, professional associations, arts/cultural, and other organizations. Developed program content and administered budgets. Arranged all on-site logistics, including transportation, accommodations, meals, guest speakers and entertainers, and audiovisual support. Coordinated participation and represented companies at industry trade shows. Recognized for creating and planning some of the most successful events ever held statewide.

- ◆ **Created cultural events for an arts organization that boosted membership enrollment.**
- ◆ **Organized 5 well-attended conferences for 2 national professional associations.**
- ◆ **Designed successful community educational campaigns promoting safety awareness.**

Fund-raising & Public Relations:

Created, planned and managed all aspects of several major fund-raising campaigns, resulting in a significant increase in contributions raised for each function over prior years. Recruited volunteers and developed corporate sponsorships. Generated extensive media coverage through effective promotional and public relations strategies. Created newsletters distributed to employees, customers and others.

- ◆ **Co-chaired capital fund campaign, raising $3.5 million for new facility.**
- ◆ **Coordinated 3 auctions, raising over $140,000 for an educational institution.**
- ◆ **Initiated successful publication, generating $25,000 to finance community programs.**

Sales & Marketing:

Selected by management to spearhead opening of regional office, including all logistics, staff relocation and business development efforts. Designed and implemented creative sales and marketing strategies to capitalize on consumer trends and penetrate new market. Coordinated and conducted sales training.

- ◆ **Developed and managed 17 key accounts generating $10 million annually.**
- ◆ **Recognized for managing top revenue-generating program company-wide.**
- ◆ **Consistently exceeded sales forecast and led region to rank #1 out of 6 in profitability nationwide.**

■ EXPERIENCE

Event/Program Coordinator, ARTS COUNCIL, BOTANICAL GARDENS & CULTURE EXCHANGE, Chicago, IL (1998–present).

Promoted from **Regional Manager, Account Executive** and **Financial Underwriter,** MARCON FINANCIAL SERVICES COMPANY, Chicago, IL (1988–2000).

■ EDUCATION

B.A. in Business Administration, Springfield College, Springfield, MA

Functional. *Louise Garver, Enfield, Connecticut*

The goal was coordinating museum events, originally an avocation, so the writer played up avocational activities. This resume generated a museum interview; the person was hired on the spot.

TATIANA STEVENS

77 East Neck Road   Lake Success, New York 22222   (555) 222-0000   TStevens@mtgplanning.net

◆

Meeting Planner

Highly motivated, energetic professional with more than 10 years of specialized experience in meeting planning services for major pharmaceutical clients across various disciplines of the medical industry. Articulate communicator with a proven ability to plan and synchronize the essential details of multiple meetings in an efficient and resourceful manner. Select qualifications encompass the following:

Key Account Management... Logistical Planning & Coordination... Vendor-Contract Negotiation...
Client Relations... Site Selection and Management... Budget Tracking and Reporting... Billing...
Print Materials... Participant Recruitment... Speaker Procurement... Staff Supervision...
Windows 2000; MS Word, Excel, Outlook, Meeting Trak; Internet Research, Database Management

◆ ◆ ◆

Master of Arts, Developmental Psychology, Stony Brook University, 1998
Bachelor of Arts, Psychology, State University of New York at Binghamton, 1995

Professional Experience

Medical Meetings, Inc., Farmingdale, New York   2000–present
2001–present   **CARDIOLOGY ACCOUNT MANAGER**
2000–2001   Project Manager

Exclusively manage the logistics and on-site management of more than 25 annual Advisory Board, Consultant, and Faculty Update meetings held nationwide for Jasper Pharmaceuticals.

- Orchestrate meeting planning services with a focus on needs assessment, vendor relations, cost analysis, set-up/audio-visual specifications, transportation, off-site entertainment, accommodations, and menu selection.
- Serve as direct point of contact for clients, vendors, and participants to ensure the smooth coordination of corporate events from early phases of planning to post-meeting support.
- Expertly consult on travel and entertainment options, employing information acquired during extensive business travels and advice from a cultivated network of DMC representatives across the country.
- Prepare, track, and summarize budgets for annual meetings and medical symposiums, and manage physician-participatory information utilizing an industry-specific database program.
- Diplomatically enforce negotiations with vendors to arrive at mutually agreeable, cost-saving solutions.
- Collaborate the efforts of creative teams and outsourced printers on the conceptualization and production of print material to facilitate the implementation of meetings.
- Effectively supervise meeting coordinators, exercising strong staff management and project leadership skills.

Homecare Medical Services, Inc., New York, New York   1993–2000
1997–2000   **MANAGER, MEETING SERVICES**
1996–1997   Program Coordinator, Visiting Faculty
1995–1996   Assistant Program Coordinator
1993–1995   Administrative Assistant

Promoted the planning, coordination, and management of 200 annual dinner meetings, as well as seminars, symposiums, and special events for a portfolio of leading pharmaceutical clients.

- Directed site evaluation and selection, vendor relations, budget management, participant recruitment, speaker procurement, creation and distribution of print materials, logistical planning, menu selection, audio-visual requirements, transfers, entertainment, and supervision of six meeting planners.

8

Combination. *Ann Baehr, Brentwood, New York*

Strong features are the shaded line above the name, the shaded Professional Experience heading, a profile (the paragraph under "Meeting Planner"), and expertise areas separated by ellipses.

JEFFREY JONES

<u>Current Residence</u>
5555 Kingman Blvd.
Las Vegas, NV 00000

SSN: 555-55-5555
Tel: (555) 555-5555

<u>Local Contact</u>
55-555 Poipounder Rd.
Honolulu, HI 00000

Seeking Entry-Level Position As...
FIRST OFFICER WITH PACIFIC AIRLINES

Profile: Experienced aviator with 9,000+ total flight hours, including 2,800+ hours of B737 time. Verifiable record of no FAA violations. Solid training record—have passed all commercial airline IOEs and check rides on first attempt. Continuous employment in aviation. Dependable employee—zero no-shows throughout career. Facilitate open communication and mutual respect among all workgroups.

Committed to Safety First • Firm Advocate of Crew Resource Management

RATINGS & CERTIFICATES

- Airline Transport Pilot: AMEL
- Commercial Privileges: ASEL
- Flight Engineer: TurboJet
- Flight Instructor: Instrument ASEL/MEL
- Medical Certificate: FAA Class I
- FCC Radio Operator Permit

FLIGHT HOURS

• **Total**	**9,650**	• TurboJet	2,952	• B737	2,846
• PIC	2,482	• TurboProp	4,122	• B727	103
• SIC	7,072	• MEL	7,288	• Instrument	734
• Stdnt. Hrs.	96	• SEL	2,361	• FE	379

OPERATIONAL EXPERIENCE

Commercial Airlines

Oct 97–Present	**Nationwide Airlines**—Atlanta, GA First Officer: B737-300/500
May 96–Oct 97	**West Coast Airways, Inc.**—Los Angeles, CA First Officer: B727 / Flight Engineer: B727
Jan 93–May 97	**Atlantic Airlines**—Raleigh, NC First Officer: EMB-120, BAE J41
May 92–Jan 93	**Scenic Air**—San Diego, CA First Officer: DHC-6-300

General Aviation

Jan 92–Apr 92	**Airtech, Inc.**—Las Vegas, NV *(FBO and Part 135 on-demand charters)* Assistant Chief Pilot
Apr 89–Dec 92	**Wallaby Aviation**—Portland, OR *(FBO)* Chief Flight Instructor/Fire Patrol

EDUCATION

B.A. in Business Administration, University of Oregon

9

Combination. *Peter Hill, Honolulu, Hawaii*

This experienced pilot was facing the possibility of a furlough by a major airline. The goal, profile, and multicolumn lists position the pilot for a transition to a smaller carrier.

Olivia Isabella

76 Columbia Street ✦ Frankfort, NY 00000 ✦ 555.555.5555

Esthetician

Offering comprehensive esthetic training, a degree in fashion and proven sales skills. Ready to utilize knowledge, creativity, excellent communications and integrity to help to understand the "whole" person and provide the perfect environment to stimulate mental, spiritual and physical well being. Possess a sound understanding of the most advanced facial techniques and exposed to the latest in skin care procedures.

Education & Credentials

The Metropolitan Institute of Esthetics, *New York, NY* **January 2003**
Completed 600-hour training program

AREAS OF SPECIFIC KNOWLEDGE	SPECIALIZED COURSEWORK
▸ Customized professional facial treatments	▸ Ionization / Pre- & Post-operative Care
▸ Marketing and promoting a skin care center	▸ Aromatherapy / European Facial Massage
▸ Balancing and controlling various skin conditions	▸ Skin Analysis / Masque Therapy
▸ Maintaining healthy skin from teen to maturity	▸ Bridal Makeup / Corrective Makeup

Oneida College, *Utica, NY* **May 2002**
Bachelor of Professional Studies in Fashion Merchandising GPA 3.2

SPECIAL PROJECTS, INFORMATION & VOLUNTEER ACTIVITIES
▸ Participated in the "Early Admission Program"—entering college as a high school senior.
▸ Assisted in creating visual displays for the Fashion Program (1999–2000).
▸ Volunteer Makeup Artist for Oneida's annual Silver Needles Award show (April, 2000).
▸ Completed a comprehensive and lengthy "capping" project that received high praise and an "A."

INTERNSHIP **Spring 2002**
SEVENTEEN MAGAZINE, NEW YORK, NY
Beauty Editor Assistant: Involved with "brainstorming" for article and cover ideas. Conducted research and assisted with actual article development/writing. Acquired considerable experience with facilitating focus groups that consisted of target readers. Gained insight into several aspects of the beauty industry. Also, attended team meetings, helped create promotional concepts and handled overall clerical duties.

Employment

AVON SALON & SPA, *NEW YORK, NY* **1/03 TO PRESENT**
Esthetician—Provide a variety of services in this upscale Aveda Concept salon. Experience includes waxing, customized facials and product sales. Receive extensive training at Aveda in Soho.

MARSHALL FIELDS DEPARTMENT STORE, *POUGHKEEPSIE, NY* **12/99 TO 2/00**
Worked as a Skincare and Makeup Artist for Clinique with responsibility for promotions and direct sales. Dealt extensively with customers, opened and closed counter and assisted with product marketing.

Additional Information

Trade shows attended include Ex-Tracts, 2002; and Aromatherapy, Fragrance & Personal Care, 2002

Attributes

Calm Demeanor
Well-Spoken
Perceptive Nature
Professional Appearance

Esthetic Skills

Skin Histology
Hydrotherapy
Massage Techniques
Customized Facials

Business Skills

Inventory Control
Merchandising
Customer Relations
Sales & Marketing

Qualities

Client Focused
Strong Sales Skills
Highly Organized
Keen Listener

Interests

Horseback Riding
Nutrition
Yoga (two years)

10

Combination. *Kristin M. Coleman, Poughkeepsie, New York*

A distinctive light font ties together information in the left column with the contact information and side headings in the wide right column. The page border binds together the two columns.

Jennifer Saks

7025 First Avenue
Pittsburgh, PA 99999
(555) 555-5555
jsaks@dotresume.com

Summary of Qualifications

Dedicated professional with master of science degree in administration and experience serving in progressively responsible leadership roles. Effective manager and coordinator. Proven ability to establish rapport and build relationships with people from diverse backgrounds. Team player. Talent for training and counseling. Creative with a flair for writing and orchestrating events. Fast learner. Adept at handling new challenges.

Highlights of Experience

Administration / Management—Proven ability to manage large groups, advise employees, administer programs, and coordinate major events.

- Recruited by supervisor to serve as department chairperson with responsibility for guiding programs and advising staff of 3.
- Received excellent evaluations for group-management and organization skills.
- Revived and administered incentive recognition program, resulting in improved performance among participants.
- Produced innovative historical musical; coordinated every detail with more than 20 administrators, staff members, and volunteers. Event hailed as "a huge success . . . the audience was amazed."

Communication / Interpersonal Relations—Frequently called upon by superiors and colleagues to act as group representative. Recognized as top-notch trainer. Superior writing ability.

- Chosen by peers to serve on advisory board—1 of only 5 selected from group of 50.
- Appointed by supervisor as 1 of 2 representatives to attend and report on district-level meetings.
- Selected from among 5 new employees to participate in roundtable discussion with superintendent.
- Designated by county chairperson to demonstrate teaching techniques to new instructors.
- Sought out by coworkers for assistance in creating lesson plans and delivering training.
- Developed professional research bulletins on a variety of topics, including cooperative groupings and group dynamics.

Education

M.S.A., Administration, Three Rivers College, Pittsburgh, PA, 3.8 GPA (2004)

B.A., English / Elementary Education, Mansfield University, Pittsburgh, PA, Scholarship (1997)

Employment History

Department Chairperson / Teacher—Reading, Writing, Math (1999–2004)
North Side Elementary School, Allegheny School District, Pittsburgh, PA

English Teacher (1997–1999)
Lakeside High School, Greene County Public Schools, Lakeside, PA

11

Combination. *Jan Holliday, Harleysville, Pennsylvania*

The applicant was seeking a career change. The Summary of Qualifications and Highlights of Experience play up her managerial, organizational, training, and social skills.

Emily Cho

(555) 555-5555
emcho@cho.com

113 Hickory Street
Cameron, CA 99999

PROFILE

*Conscientious, personable & energetic **Administrative Specialist** with 10 years of experience that encompasses Project & Document Management, Analysis, Marketing and Public Relations. Motivated self-starter who's earned a reputation for being proficient, hardworking and reliable.*

"You are a conscientious, dependable worker who is a definite asset to the company."

QUALIFICATIONS SUMMARY

Outstanding communications skills...Comfortable interacting with all organizational & cultural levels.

Highly Organized...Expert in multi-tasking & prioritizing. Skillfully manage large projects, start to finish.

Flexible & Adaptable...Assimilate quickly in transitions, switching roles as needed to maintain productivity. Embrace new concepts and methods.

Resourceful Problem Solver...Adept in anticipating & analyzing problems, then formulating solutions.

Detail-Oriented & Conscientious...Keen eye for errors and inconsistencies, striving for flawless output.

Computer Proficiency...MS Word, Excel, Access, PowerPoint; Visio.

"You have capably handled even the most challenging situations."

CAREER HIGHLIGHTS

- *Managed $500,000* annual department budget; helped process grant proposals. (State U.)
- Wrote and helped revise departmental policies and procedures. (Biz Ink)
- Edited and proofread manuscripts and worked closely with publisher on 7 books. (Coopers & Brent)
- Monitored, organized and evaluated information submitted by more than 20 managers; from that raw data, created accurate workflow reports. (Biz Ink; Coopers & Brent)
- As Interstate Liaison, helped promote *Cops in Shops*, a program to deter underage drinking. (Pathways)
- Helped launch new programs, collaborating with PR firms and ad agencies to obtain media coverage. (Pathways)
- Facilitated successful establishment of in-house library by researching logistics and overseeing setup process. (Pathways)
- Served as Project Manager of department's *Client Appreciation, Biz 2003*. Coordinated activities for 125 clients attending annual company event. (Biz Ink)

"You are appropriately decisive and have strong problem-solving skills..."

EMPLOYMENT HISTORY

Project Coordinator/Executive Administrative Assistant   2002–Present
Biz Ink—Cameron, CA—Payroll, Payroll-Tax & HRMS outsourcing company

Executive Assistant   2000–2002
Coopers & Brent LLP—Crescent Hills, CA—Publishing & Creative Services Group

Administrative Assistant   1999–2000
State University—Crescent Hills, CA

Executive Assistant/Marketing Coordinator   1994–1999
Pathways—San Marino, CA—Non-profit national organization promoting public awareness and programs to deter alcohol abuse

EDUCATION—Bachelor of Arts / Speech Communications / 1999—State University—Crescent Hills, CA

Comments above are excerpts from recent performance review.

12

Combination. *Gail Taylor, Torrance, California*

This candidate was relocating and looking for a challenging position with problem-solving responsibilities. Excerpts from performance evaluations support her quest.

202 Marley Avenue, Denver, CO 00000
(000) 000-0000
bandaide@waycool.com

Deirdre Janovic

CAREER INTERESTS   Recording/Mixing Engineer ◆ Staff Producer ◆ Studio Technician

PROFILE
- ◆ Knowledge of the music business developed through training in audio-video engineering, production assistance in a recording studio, and more than 6 years of experience in sales of musical equipment.
- ◆ Technical expertise with state-of-the art recording technology, as well as studio setup and basic maintenance.
- ◆ Good ear for music, with an understanding of the sound image desired by various performers.
- ◆ Ability to work comfortably under pressure and maintain a high energy level in an industry that emphasizes speed, flexibility, organizational skills, decisiveness, and effective interpersonal communications.

PROFESSIONAL EXPERIENCE

1999–Present
Niteglo Productions, Denver, CO
Engineer with a small recording studio specializing in hip-hop and R&B
- ◆ Started as an intern and was hired permanently after displaying initiative to take on various responsibilities in both the creative and business aspects of production.
- ◆ Operate a Mac-based console running Logic Audio Platinum program. Record and mix 32 tracks to produce master tapes.
- ◆ Set up and disassemble apparatuses such as instruments, mikes, and wiring for recording sessions in an efficient manner so that artists can make optimal use of scheduled studio time.
- ◆ From a library of more than a million samples, select sound effects that complement the music being recorded. Created the sound effects for more than 100 CDs.
- ◆ Participate in contract negotiations and meetings at major record labels to sell studio's productions.

1996–Present
Music Universe, Denver, CO
Sales Associate (part-time)
- ◆ Demonstrate features of various musical instruments and sound systems. Advise customers in selection of products best suited for their purposes.
- ◆ Prepare proposals that include all components necessary to equip a professional recording studio, with a breakdown of costs and alternative solutions.
- ◆ Generate approximately $250,000 in annual business, in part through networking at clubs where new bands perform. Consistently ranked as one of the company's top salespersons.

EDUCATION
University of Denver
B.A. Communications, May 2000
Concentration in TV and Video Production
Major Projects (available on request):
- ◆ Promotional video for current employer, Niteglo Productions
- ◆ Electronic press kit for a band called "Concrete"
- ◆ CDs of various artists

13

Combination. *Melanie Noonan, West Paterson, New Jersey*

Strong diamond bullets guide the eye down the page as an incentive to read all of the page and not just the top third of it. The full view is that of an engineer with sales experience.

Jennifer S. Peters
15 Bluebird Dr.
Milford, MA 01757
Home: (222) 555-7777
E-mail: jspeters@server.com

Key Qualifications

✓ Attentive, customer-centered attitude	✓ Detail-oriented with a talent for organization
✓ Outstanding oral and written communication skills	✓ Understanding of software design process
✓ Project leadership and supervisory experience	✓ Bachelor of Arts
	✓ Strong technological competence

Experience   Upton Tea Imports: Hopkinton, MA   1998–Present
Customer Service Specialist, Website Project Manager

Applied experience in company's customer service, order fulfillment, and warehouse departments to in-house software design and business process restructuring. Played a key role in daily customer service operations through order entry and management of e-commerce website.

- Integrated advanced shipping software that reduced time to label and dispatch packages by 50%. Trained shipping department employees and thoroughly documented new procedures.
- Collaborated with team programmer to test and deploy custom e-commerce website and back-end order processing software. Reinforced existing functionality with new features as website sales increased to 40% of annual revenue.
- Designed, promoted, and implemented new gift set product line that netted $20,000 during first year of availability.
- Authored more than 25 articles on history, culture, and consumption of tea for company's quarterly newsletter and website. Recognized among coworkers as a primary resource for information.

Education   University of Massachusetts Dartmouth: N. Dartmouth, MA   2000–2002
BA Anthropology, *Summa cum Laude*

- Achieved 3.985 GPA.
- Massachusetts Commonwealth Honors Scholar.
- Presented senior honors thesis at Sigma Xi Research Exhibition.
- Departmental Honors.
- Chancellor's List.

Nipmuc Regional High School: Upton, MA   1996–2000

- Achieved 3.9 GPA at Worcester State College.
- Attended college full-time during junior and senior years as participant in Massachusetts Dual-Enrollment Program.

Technology

• Microsoft Office	• Microsoft Visual Basic
• Internet and E-mail	• Adobe Photoshop
• HTML	• CorelDRAW
• Microsoft SQL Server	

References Available

14

Combination. *Jessica Robinson, Westborough, Massachusetts*

The resume lacks a stated objective because the individual was exploring multiple career possibilities. She was hired as part-time warehouse help, but her achievements reveal her worth.

FOSTER PORTER
44 Smith Street
Philadelphia, PA 11111
Home Phone 222.222.2222
Voicemail 333.333.3333
xxxxx@xxxxx.xxx

PHARMACEUTICAL SALES
Outstanding sales record, proven ability to close new product sales.
Strong public speaking ability, comfortable addressing large and small groups
on pharmacology and sales topics.
Excellent interpersonal skills.
Competent in Word, Excel, Access, PowerPoint.

Foster, your work at Wyeth has been outstanding. Staff trained by you become
some of our best employees, and your sales numbers stay at the top.
—Letter of commendation by supervisor, February 2002

PHARMACEUTICAL SALES EXPERIENCE
WYETH AYERST LABORATORIES, Radnor, PA   1998–2003
(A division of American Home Products, Madison, NJ)
Territory Specialist
- Achieved ranking in the **top 5% during 2002–2003** in eastern Pennsylvania.
- Increased sales **25%, 2000–2001.**
- Attended a self-improvement course through Career Development to improve sales skills and performance. **Promoted 4/00.**
- Chosen to develop training program for new hires.
- Developed long-term relationships with pharmacists, hospital personnel, and physicians in areas of Rheumatology, Neurology, Psychiatry, Orthopedics, Primary Care, and OB/GYN.
- Organized and presented continuing education seminars for medical personnel.
- Worked closely with SAMA—Spanish American Medical Association, 1998–2001.

ADDITIONAL EXPERIENCE
Quality Advertising, Inc., Philadelphia, PA   1995–1998
Media Planner
- Maintained a current and competent level of knowledge for Estée Lauder, Inc., including Prescriptives, Clinique, and Origins.
- Prepared and maintained advertising budget for fiscal year.
- Placed client advertising on network television, cable television, consumer magazines, and radio.

EDUCATION
University of Philadelphia, Philadelphia, PA
- Bachelor of Science, Communications/Business   1998

15

Combination. *Ellen Mulqueen, Hartford, Connecticut*

The resume displays the individual's outstanding sales record in a highly competitive field. The excerpt from the letter of recommendation is positioned and enhanced to stand out.

STEVEN FULLER
stevenfuller@email.com

5555 Silverlake Avenue	Residence 818.555.5555
Encino, CA 55555	Mobile 818.555.0000

SOFTWARE SALES MANAGEMENT
Special Expertise in Sales of Complex Software Solutions

Accomplished sales and marketing management professional who excels in strategic planning, marketing, sales and support of advanced technology solutions. Keen presentation, contract negotiation and communication abilities. Track record of training, motivating and coaching top-performing teams.

—Core Management Qualifications—

Strategic Business Planning • Consultative / Solution Sales • Competitive Product Positioning
Sales Training • Team Building & Leadership • Communications, Presentations & Public Speaking
Business Development • Strategic Alliances & Business Partnerships

PROFESSIONAL EXPERIENCE

ABC SOFTWARE GROUP, Los Angeles, CA • 1999–Present
Achieved fast-track promotion to positions of increasing challenge and responsibility.

Senior Software Account Manager (2002–Present)
Charged with driving software revenue growth and increasing market share in Consumer Products Cluster. Lead and coach team of 12 account representatives. Articulate ABC's software strategies to executive-level customers.

- Attained *President's Club* **status** by achieving **114% of quota** ($9.8 million).
- Closed **$3.8 million** deal with American Consumer Products Company by establishing reputation as trusted advisor to executive management.
- Achieved YTY overall software revenue attainment of **115%** (2002 over 2001).
- Surpassed revenue objectives for five (5) consecutive quarters.
- Grew YTY software revenue target by **200%,** achieving key wins across product family.
- Recipient of **2002** *Vice President's Award.*

Senior Software Specialist (2001–2002) / **Software Specialist** (1999–2001)
Sold software solutions to select Fortune 500 companies throughout Western Region. Completed extensive training in e-business application framework, Web-based applications, Web-to-host integration, Internet-based security, server-managed client environments and solution selling.

- Achieved *President's Club* **status** by selling **122% of quota** in 2000, **108% of quota** in 1999, and **128% of quota** in 1998.
- Established software sales training process; authored manual and trained new employees.
- Achieved **annual increases in revenue growth three consecutive years.**
- Forged strategic partnerships, capturing key wins at major companies.

EDUCATION

UNIVERSITY OF SOUTHERN CALIFORNIA, Los Angeles, CA
MBA—Concentration in Finance and Marketing; 1999
B.S. in Marketing; 1997

COMPUTER SKILLS

Proficient in popular applications, including Microsoft Windows, OS/2, Microsoft Office suite, Lotus SmartSuite. Strong knowledge of e-business software, including Business Integration, Foundation and Tools, Data Management and Analytics, Security and Systems Management and Collaboration SW.

16

Combination. *Vivian VanLier, Los Angeles, California*

A high-achieving software sales professional was seeking a new opportunity. Emphasis is on sales management skills, sales achievements, an MBA degree, and computer skills.

Special Paper Information

The papers are arranged from off-white to blue and from warm to cool colors, including warm grays and cool grays. Heavy textures are avoided because of their resistance to laser printing. Laser-printed characters on heavy textures tend to break up with frequent handling.

Besides comparing colors, compare subtle textures by rubbing your fingers rapidly over the surface and comparing sounds.

Not shown are 100% rag-content papers, which are ideal for resumes. Such papers feel more substantial and tend to be watermarked. Look for them in local stationery stores and office supply stores.

Resumes 1 and 2
Brand: Strathmore
Parent company: International Paper
Color: Soft White
Kind: Writing
Weight: 24#
Contains 25% cotton
Acid-free: Y
Watermarked: Y
InkJet compatible: Y
Laser compatible: Y
Copier compatible: Y

Resumes 3 and 4
Brand: Strathmore
Parent company: International Paper
Color: Ivory
Kind: Writing
Weight: 24#
Contains 25% cotton
Acid-free: Y
Watermarked: Y
InkJet compatible: Y
Laser compatible: Y
Copier compatible: Y

Resumes 5 and 6
Brand: Gilbert Neutech
Parent company: Gilbert
Color: Cream
Kind: Writing
Weight: 24#
Contains 25% cotton
Acid-free: Y
Watermarked: Y
InkJet compatible: Y
Laser compatible: Y
Copier compatible: Y

Resumes 7 and 8
Brand: Strathmore
Parent company: International Paper
Color: Soft Tan
Kind: Writing
Weight: 24#
Contains 25% cotton, 30% recycled content
Acid-free: Y
Watermarked: Y
InkJet compatible: Y
Laser compatible: Y
Copier compatible: Y

Resumes 9 and 10
Brand: Gilbert Neutech
Parent company: Gilbert
Color: Gray
Kind: Writing
Weight: 24#
Contains 25% cotton
Acid-free: Y
Watermarked: Y
InkJet compatible: Y
Laser compatible: Y
Copier compatible: Y

Resumes 11 and 12
Brand: Strathmore
Parent company: International Paper
Color: Soft Gray
Kind: Writing
Weight: 24#
Contains 25% cotton, 30% recycled content
Acid-free: Y
Watermarked: Y
InkJet compatible: Y
Laser compatible: Y
Copier compatible: Y

Resumes 13 and 14
Brand: Classic Crest
Parent company: Kimberly Clark Corporation
Color: Ember Blue
Kind: Writing
Weight: 24#
Contains 0% recycled content
Acid-free: N
Watermarked: Y
InkJet compatible: Y
Laser compatible: Y
Copier compatible: Y

Resumes 15 and 16
Brand: Fraser Synergy
Parent company: Fraser Papers
Color: Restful Blue
Kind: Writing
Weight: 24#
Contains 25% cotton, 50% recycled content
Acid-free: Y
Watermarked: N
InkJet compatible: Y
Laser compatible: Y
Copier compatible: Y

Accounting

Resumes at a Glance

RESUME NO.	OCCUPATION	GOAL	PAGE
17.	Accounting Clerk	Junior Accountant	45
18.	Adjunct Instructor	Not specified	46
19.	Assistant Controller	Not specified	48
20.	Accountant	Accountant	50

JAMES PARKER

222 Corner Lane Road • Bay Shore, New York 22222 • (555) 777-0000 • jraccountant@financialweb.net

---

Full-time accounting student with related experience seeking a part-time position in the capacity of

JUNIOR ACCOUNTANT

- Currently enrolled in a four-year accounting program; excel academically while working part time.
- Well-rounded experience working in retail sales environments across foodservice and clothing industries.
- Analytical problem solver with a strong figure aptitude and ability to quickly grasp complex concepts.
- Disciplined with a strong character developed from extensive athletics and community involvement.
- Personable with innate relationship-building qualities; communicate effectively in English and Spanish.

EDUCATION

Bachelor of Science, Accounting, expected May 2005
LONG ISLAND UNIVERSITY, C.W. POST, Brentwood, New York
Honors: Phi Eta Sigma, Freshman Honor Society   **Current GPA:** 3.9

Coursework: External Reporting, Tax and Business Strategies, Managerial Accounting, Corporate Finance, Principles of Accounting, Microeconomics, Macroeconomics, Calculus, Business Law, Marketing, and Statistics

WORK EXPERIENCE

➤ **Supermarket City, Riverhead, New York**   **11/01–present**

Accounting Clerk, Internal Audit Department, Corporate Headquarters
- Perform general accounting functions focused on high-risk audits of daily inventory for 47 stores, weekly disbursements of short-term payable accounts, and mandatory reporting activities for management review.
- Research, identify, and investigate over/under charges through review and analysis of vendors' aging reports for all store sites; and verify, reconcile, and approve payment for entry into network accounting system.
- Interface between major snack food and beverage vendors and Supermarket City's Accounts Payable/ Receivable departments concerning invoice discrepancy issues and account billing cycles that include vendor discounts.
- Assisted Personnel during tax season to trace high-risk fraudulent employee activities for all store locations.
- Interviewed all levels of personnel to investigate incidents of false Social Security identifications and W-2 forms to cases of embezzlement, with a focus on bookkeepers, cashiers, and field auditors.

Produce Clerk, Produce Department
- Assisted in broad areas of customer service, sales, marketing, staff training, quality assurance, inventory control, delivery verification, stocking, vendor relations, catering services, and product merchandising.
- Selected to train four part-time clerks at another store location on daily produce department procedures.

➤ **Sales Representative, Garment Department, Discount Suits Corp., Riverhead, New York**   **12/00–11/01**
- Assisted in storewide functions, including sales counter and cashiering activities, part-time employee training, inventory control, stocking, merchandise display, purchasing, loss prevention, and problem resolution.

COMMUNITY INVOLVEMENT & AFFILIATIONS

Active Member, Accounting Society, Long Island University, C.W. Post
Co-founder and Chairman, Bay Shore Alumni Student Association

COMPUTER SKILLS

Windows 2000/OSX; Microsoft Word, Excel, and Access; electronic tax research; Internet research; install, configure, and troubleshoot various hardware and software components

17

Combination. *Ann Baehr, Brentwood, New York*

A full-time accounting student wanted to become a part-time junior accountant. A strong summary of skills and good academic credentials appear before beginning work experience.

Mary W. Kingston—CPA, MBA

| 178 Stanton Drive | Cedar Park, Texas 78795 | 512-785-6857 | mkingston@aol.com |

Proffessional Summary

Degreed Accounting Professional with over 25 years of progressively responsible experience in a detail-oriented, multi-functional setting. Key accomplishments include

Led the audit of a multimillion-dollar construction project.
Developed and implemented multiple *accounting training programs.*
Implemented the concepts and procedures for multiple computerized systems.
Reduced processing time by 70% of raw material contracts, receipts and payments.

Accounts payable	Collections
Payroll	Financial reports
General ledger	System debugging
Financial statement preparation	Legal compliance examination

Professional Achievements

- Implemented payroll upgrades resulting in *increased payroll processing efficiency and accountability* by allowing department managers to input hours.
- *Corrected $3 million in errors* through identifying and debugging problems with the purchasing and accounts payable invoice matching system.
- *Improved accuracy, efficiency and overall effectiveness* of accounting month-end journals by implementing computerized systems combined with complex Excel workbooks.
- *Enhanced interdepartmental communications* through the development and implementation of training guides and programs in support of non-accounting personnel, including engineers, planning/schedulers, clerks and managers. Topics included sales tax issues, construction in progress, fixed-asset additions and disposals.
- *Strengthened the auditing division* by applying procedures and experience gained in national accounting firms and various small businesses.

Professional Experience

University of Texas, Austin, Texas   *2003–Present*
ADJUNCT INSTRUCTOR
- ❖ Teach college-level accounting classes: Intermediate II, Cost and Budget.
- ❖ Research, document and implement strategies for increased learning retention.
- ❖ Draft and present class content outline for College Dean approval.
- ❖ Lead students to master accounting concepts through formal and informal review/grading sessions.
- ❖ Incorporate "hands-on" industry application examples from professional experience.
- ❖ Mentor, counsel and guide students in career options that include the accounting profession.

18

Combination. *MeLisa Rogers, Victoria, Texas*

A resume makeover. The original lacked eye appeal, and a career objective added little to the document. This revision draws immediate attention to a summary of centered key

MARY W. KINGSTON—CPA, MBA
—Page Two—

Brackenridge Hospital, Austin, Texas   *2000–2002*
DIRECTOR OF ACCOUNTING
- ❖ Managed a staff of seven direct reports, including an accounting supervisor and six administrative personnel.
- ❖ Planned, organized and directed the functions of the accounting department, including accounts payable, payroll, general ledger and financial statement preparation; set goals and objectives for the department at all levels; partnered with the Assistant Administrator of Finance and Administration on special projects; managed outside vendors and auditors.
- ❖ Converted all accounting worksheets from Lotus to Excel and implemented improvements.

Hays County Community Hospital, San Marcos, Texas   *2000–2000*
ACCOUNTANT and CFO
- ❖ Developed procedures to track business office collections, posting and balancing.
- ❖ Trained and coached staff in procedures designed to improve accuracy and efficiency.
- ❖ Prepared financial statements by developing Excel spreadsheets to document work.

TP Chemicals, San Marcos, Texas   *1988–1999*
ACOUNTANT III
- ❖ Maintained financial books, prepared financial reports, mentored and coached accounting department personnel, provided support to Controller and enhanced the effectiveness and efficiency of the department.
- ❖ Supported, mentored, trained and delegated accounting activities to clerical help to expand their skills/abilities and to improve their self worth and value to the company.
- ❖ Developed concepts and procedures; analyzed, debugged and resolved general ledger interfaces with computerized work order/purchasing system and project accounting system.
- ❖ Prepared timely monthly accruals and reversals; posted interfaces, including inventories, work orders, construction in progress, fixed assets; closed timely the financial books, prepared and issued monthly financial reports for efficient and effective operation of the plant.

State of Colorado, Denver, Colorado   *1986–1988*
EXAMINER OF PUBLIC ACCOUNTS
- ❖ Performed financial audits and prepared financial statements for county school boards and county commissioners. Performed legal compliance examination for judges of probate, tax assessors and tax collectors.

EDUCATION and TRAINING

Masters of Business Administration, University of Texas, Austin, Texas, 1993
Bachelor of Science in Accounting, Cum Laude, University of Colorado, Denver, Colorado, 1974

Microsoft Word/Excel * WordPerfect * Lotus Quicken * Quick Books Pro * AS400 Query

AFFILIATES AND MEMBERSHIPS

Professional Association of Certified Public Accountants (PACPA)
CPA—Colorado and Texas
Texas Association of CPAs
Treasurer, Mission of Hope Recovery Outreach, Inc.

accomplishments and core abilities in a shaded box. Boldfacing makes additional professional achievements more visible. Unique compound diamond bullets unify the Professional Experience section. Centered section headings draw the eye downward through both pages.

PAUL KEENAN, CPA, CMA

Credentialed financial professional with expertise in GAAP and managerial accounting, excellent financial analysis skills, and a proven record in implementing effective cost-saving initiatives

PROFILE

Dynamic, results-oriented accountant with nearly ten years of experience that include five years as a controller in a manufacturing environment. Top-notch CMA with demonstrated expertise in cost accounting, financial analysis, and financial reporting. Hands-on leader with open management style who is effective at creating a team environment. Accomplished negotiator with excellent relationship-building skills. Strong track record in implementing initiatives that improve financial operations. Respected financial advisor schooled in the use of EVA™ metric system to guide corporate decision-making. Driven by challenge and the opportunity for development; thrive in diverse, fast-paced settings.

PROFESSIONAL EXPERIENCE

AFFILIATES OF AMERICA, New York, New York   Jan 1998 to present
Assistant Joint Venture Group Controller

Brought on to integrate financial operations of four affiliated companies with revenues totaling more than $800 million. Instrumental in building financial infrastructures and standardizing accounting procedures across all companies. Work closely with individual companies to prepare budgets and compile monthly and quarterly P&L forecasts. Coordinate monthly and yearly financial closing procedures.

- Served key role in the introduction, installation, and integration of new financial reporting system across four joint-venture companies. Successfully migrated existing data into new system while bringing books into compliance with general accounting standards.
- Introduced computerized production reporting, establishing a perpetual inventory system.
- Instituted procedures that standardized operational reporting, simplifying calculations such as ROI and allowing more accurate comparison between groups.
- Identified best practices among units and incorporated them throughout affiliated companies.
- Successfully lowered monthly closing time from 10 days to 3 days across all four companies through effective introduction and coordination of improved financial closing procedures.
- Instituted use of FAS Asset Accounting software to manage all property, plant, and equipment (PPE) with aggregate value in excess of $72 million.
- Created policies for the management and disposal of all capital assets to ensure assets are accounted for and charged to appropriate cost centers. Established new tracking system to simplify asset accounting.
- Effectively negotiated property and casualty insurance renewals with brokers, leveraging prior experience in the insurance industry to obtain the most favorable rates.
- Reported financial results based on the EVA™ metric system, calculating and presenting findings on a monthly and annual basis to provide financial data to enhance corporate decision-making.
- Working closely with Big 4 audit firm, prepared supporting documentation, flux analysis for sales and inventory, fixed assets, and accounts receivable and payable for both quarterly and year-end audits.
- Routinely develop clear, cohesive financial reports that identify opportunities for cost savings throughout joint-venture companies.

5 SIDNEY ROAD • BRIARCLIFF, NEW YORK 10001 • (333) 333-3333
pkeenan5@aol.com

19

Combination. *Carol A. Altomare, Three Bridges, New Jersey*

This resume displays two characteristics of executive resumes: smaller type and longer lines. These help to pack more information on two pages and still provide adequate white space.

JOHNSON GROUP OF NEW ENGLAND, Greenwich, Connecticut   Nov 1997 to Jan 1998
Assistant Vice President

Acting as broker, worked closely with underwriters to negotiate acceptable financial terms for casualty insurance programs targeted towards Fortune 100 client companies.

- Negotiated programs for major clients, providing expert financial analysis related to loss-sensitive programs.
- Won major contracts through persistence and determined negotiating.

ACE INSURANCE CORPORATION, New York, New York   Jan 1994 to Nov 1997
Account Executive—Actuarial Services

Serviced Commercial Property & Casualty accounts in the National Account Department. Assessed underwriting data, prepared insurance specifications, negotiated premium, and made presentations to clients.

- Served as key member of team that serviced insurance portfolio worth $1 million.
- Developed financial models for loss-sensitive/cash-flow insurance programs and introduced spreadsheets to simplify data analysis.
- Designed computer training program for employees.

EDUCATION

YORK UNIVERSITY, New York, New York
Bachelor of Science Degree in Accounting with concentration in Economics, May 1993

Post Graduation Education:
International Finance, Securities Analysis, Risk Management and Insurance, CPCU-7 Legal Environment, C/C++ Programming

CERTIFICATIONS & PROFESSIONAL AFFILIATIONS

Certified Management Accountant (CMA), 2004
Certified Public Accountant, New York, 1995

Member, The Institute of Management Accountants, 2001 to present

COMMUNITY ACTIVITIES

Member of the Board of Trustees & Volunteer Treasurer, Gentry Steering Committee, Yonkers, New York
- Manage books for this not-for-profit housing organization.
- Installed QuickBooks to automate accounting.

KEYWORDS

Accountant, controller, assistant controller, financial management, financial analysis, cost analysis, budgeting, general accounting, cost accounting, financial accounting, GAAP, accounts payable, accounts receivable, auditor, financial reporting, asset management, CPA, certified public accountant, CMA, certified management accountant, Economic Value Added (EVA™) metric system, manufacturing

Placing contact information in a footer on both pages makes room for important Profile information at the top of page one just below the person's name. Keywords near the end of the second page are useful in any online version. The individual got a call for an interview from every company he contacted.

James M. Olson

9803 Clinton Avenue ▪ Houston, TX 77068
(281) 000-0000 ▪ name@msn.com

ACCOUNTANT

Detail-focused, highly ethical accounting professional with a BBA in Accounting and work experience demonstrating consistent achievement of organizational and fiscal objectives and goals. Able to pinpoint discrepancies and errors to prevent continuing and potentially unnecessary cost expenditures. Willing to accept responsibilities beyond immediate job duties and take on special projects at management request. Proficient in Excel, Access, other MS programs, J.D. Edwards, and proprietary software. *Knowledge and skill areas include*

- Audits & Financial Statements
- Accounts Receivable/Payable
- Financial Reconciliations

- General Ledger Accounting
- Record/Systems Automation
- Financial Research Projects

- Strategic & Financial Analysis
- Audit Review Procedures
- Teamwork & Communication

Education

TEXAS UNIVERSITY, Houston, TX
Bachelor of Business Administration (BBA) in Accounting, 2000

Accounting G.P.A.: 3.5 / Member, Beta Alpha Psi—for Honors Accounting, Finance, and IT students

Relevant Experience

Accountant, CITY OF NAME, Anywhere, TX   2001–Present

Fully responsible for several core accounting functions within municipality of 200,000 residents, including preparing financial statements and monthly reports/reconciliations, analyzing expense reports, integrating technology to facilitate accounting tasks, and completing special research projects as needed. Assigned significant role in managing finances of WTMPA, organizing large bodies of financial data, and preparing all financial statements for 2001 and 2002 audits. *Selected Accomplishments:*

- **Records Analysis & Error Identification**—Researched, identified, and helped resolve several large discrepancies in receivables and payables, all favorable to City of Name:
    - *$100,000 in A/R account for City of Name's power purchases;*
    - *$20,000 underpayment for A/R in General Fund Account;*
    - *$10,000 excess in A/P for Internal Service funds.*
- **Policy Development**—Played key role in development of new travel policy, with projected elimination of problems previously stalling productivity of accounting and internal audit functions.
- **Financial Analysis**—Compiled analysis of franchise fees subsequently used by Assistant City Manager in evaluating potential effects of pending legislation.
- **Audit Review Compliance**—Prepared cash flow and financial statements for external auditors on 13 Internal Service and 10 Special Revenue funds, with zero notes from auditors on review documents.
- **Teamwork & Collaboration**—Coordinated project with legal division that revived dormant accounts and ensured proper disposition. Worked with Chief Accountant to construct new reporting model.
- **Technology Improvement**—Changed automatic accounting instruction table in J.D. Edwards system, leading to correction of multiple unnecessary entries and subsequent cost/time savings.

Collection Agent, CITYBANK, Irving, TX   1997–1998

Trained new employees on account software; prepared detailed financial/customer reports for management.

Manager, TANNING SALON, Irving, TX   1996–1997

Managed A/P, A/R, payroll, and other financial functions in addition to general management activities.

20

Combination. *Daniel J. Dorotik, Jr., Lubbock, Texas*

The area of interest is the Accountant information below the name and above the Education section. The pair of three-dimensional, horizontal lines works together as the top and bottom of a frame to direct attention to the Accountant information. In the Relevant Experience section, shadowed square bullets, boldfacing, and italic call attention to selected accomplishments.

Advertising/ Promotion

Resumes at a Glance

RESUME NO.	OCCUPATION	GOAL	PAGE
21.	Wait Staff	Not specified	53
22.	Account Supervisor	Marketing/Advertising Director	54
23.	Senior Advertising Manager	Advertising Director	56
24.	Cosmetic Technician	Events Planner	58

THOMAS DORAN   555 555-5555

EDUCATION

BA in Advertising; Minor in Marketing ACADEMIA UNIVERSITY, Camary, Texas   *Fall 2004*
17 hours Spanish

FOREIGN EXCHANGE PROGRAMS

THE CENTER FOR BILINGUAL MULTICULTURAL STUDIES, Citalynda, Zapata, Mexico   *Spring 2003*
Studied Spanish six hours a day, five days a week. Lived with Mexican family and other foreign students, and traveled throughout Mexico learning of foreign culture and economics.

- **Volunteered for Niños de la Calle.**

HUSTER HASS SCHOOL, Don Hogg, Holland   *Fall 2002*
Studied international marketing and management and organizational management for six months. Also studied Dutch law. Lived in dorm environment, and traveled throughout Europe learning of foreign culture. Helped organize school functions and give new-student orientations.

RELEVANT PROJECTS

ADVERTISING COALITION 2003 NATIONAL STUDENT COMPETITION
Selected out of 21 members to serve on creative team of three members. Created a four-year integrated marketing communications plan book for auto dealership, manufacturer of products for the transportation industry. Researching and analyzing industry; writing creative brief; designing Web page and magazine ads; and targeting portfolio to financial opinion leaders, stock and shareholders, employees, and customers.

- **Won second place at nationals.**

CAMPAIGN BOOK FOR STATE LOTTERY COMMISSION
One of a group of five compiling proposals for awareness campaign for state lottery. Six-member group creating 13 advertisements to be presented to lottery commissioner.

WORK EXPERIENCE

Wait Staff, HOME COOKIN' CORNER, Bullnose and Camary, Texas   *2002–Present*
Provided standard wait-staff services and balanced out cash and tips each day. Transferred from full-time summer job in Bullnose to part-time position in Camary.

- **Requested by regular customers.**

Director, WeeCare After-School Program, WEECARE, Camary, Texas   *2000–2002*
Oversaw five staff members who coordinated activities for 80 children ages 5–12. Handled discipline issues with both staff and participants and dealt with collection issues. Facilitated complete program organization and facility readiness.

- **Asked to return to director's position after study abroad.**

Full-time Daycare Counselor, WEECARE, Bullnose, Texas   *Summer 2000*
Organized arts and crafts and play activities for children and created projects. Interfaced with parents and handled issues. Acted as mentor to children.

ACTIVITIES

- Member, State Advertising Federation   *2003*
- Member and Social Chair, Kuptta Kai Fraternity   *2000–Present*
- Volunteer, Challenged Veterans Store   *1999*
- Volunteer, Heart Saving Association   *1998*

5555 55ᵗʰ Street ▪ Camary, Texas 55555 ▪ tdoran@yahoo.com

21

Combination. *Edith A. Rische, Lubbock, Texas*

This student had relevant experience both abroad and in academic competition. His goal was foreign advertising, so foreign language and exchange programs are highlighted. See Cover Letter 1 (page 377).

Christopher Rollins

138 Redwood Drive • Burlington Township, NJ 08016 • 609.555.5555 • CsRollins@earthlink.net

MARKETING DIRECTOR / ADVERTISING DIRECTOR
Expertise in Competitively Positioning Brands, Products and Services

Creative professional with a proven track record of successful projects from initial concept through completion. High-energy, results-oriented leader recognized for innovative tactics and strategies. Talent for building cohesive teams with strong problem-solving skills, able to manage time-sensitive projects with multimillion-dollar budgets.

Combine passion for marketing with commitment to contributing to an organization's bottom line. Consistently successful in conceptualizing, developing and orchestrating internal and external marketing initiatives to support national and international sales organizations. Excellent communications and interpersonal skills.

Areas of Expertise:

- Strategic Brand Planning
- Comprehensive Advertising Campaigns
- Direct Response Programs
- New Market & Customer Development
- Business Analysis
- Project Management

- E-Media
- Brand Building Goals
- Business Marketing and Promotions
- Cooperative Marketing
- Evaluate Market Trends
- Market Research Analysis

Professional Experience

HARRIS & SMITH COMMUNICATIONS, Cranbury, NJ (1999–Present)
A full-service, strategically driven agency, with $29 million in revenues and diverse capabilities in advertising, all forms of media promotions and public relations.

Account Supervisor

Lead the team responsible for Account Planning and day-to-day operations and management of key agency accounts. Responsible for setting budgets and forecasts, developing estimates and managing estimated vs. actual costs for all applicable clients. Hands-on involvement in each phase of client business, from campaign strategy through execution and program analysis.
- Conceptualized, designed and implemented programs ranging from brand salience to direct-response programs.
- Restructured underperforming accounts into profitable and successful client relationships.
- Created, planned and implemented programs ranging from strategic brand planning to direct-response campaigns for national and international brands including **Bank One/First USA, Nordica Skis, Fedders, Bank of America, Prince Sporting Goods, Yardville National Bank, SQN Banking Systems,** and **New Jersey Economic Development Authority.**
- Successfully planned, directed and launched the initial U.S. **ING DIRECT** campaign.

Continued

22

Combination. *Beverley and Mitchell I. Baskin, Marlboro, New Jersey*

A page border on both pages ties together the two pages visually. After a profile, a pair of lines enclosing Areas of Expertise directs attention to them. To recognize the value of boldfacing,

Page Two   CHRISTOPHER ROLLINS

Professional Experience *(Continued)*

PMG VENTURES, Narberth, PA (1994–1999)
A $25 million, 50-person international sports and entertainment marketing and management agency.

Director of Marketing (1997–1999)

Directed the design, creation and strategic planning for marketing campaigns for the Men's Worldwide Senior Tennis Circuit (WSTC), DiamondBack Racing, Limited Express Next Model Search and the Dave Schultz Wrestling Foundation. Developed integrated marketing programs with partners of the WSTC to maximize their sponsorship and achieve objectives. Some major accounts handled as sponsors were **Citi, Unilever, PricewaterhouseCoopers, Cadillac, U.S. News,** and **Circuit City.** Supervised and approved advertising media contracts for print, radio, TV and out of home. Successfully grew the company to 4 times its size in 5 years.
- Increased profits over a two-year period with budget reductions of 10%.
- Expanded WSTC sponsorships to record levels through innovative marketing concepts.
- Honored with the firm's "Man-of-the-Year" award for leading by example and for excellent performance.
- Trained and directed a staff of 10 regional marketing managers.
- Managed $1.1 million marketing budget for all U.S. events on the WSTC.

Creative Services Manager (1994–1997)
Initiated, planned and managed the implementation of the Creative Services department. Hired free-lance graphic designers and illustrators and developed them into a cohesive team during the firm's rapid growth period. Assumed full responsibility for all printed advertising and promotional materials, including magazine, newspaper, out-of-home advertising, pop displays, sales brochures, direct mail, posters, capability brochures, corporate identification and proposals.
- Led negotiations with service bureaus and other vendors on all contracts.
- Charged with full P&L responsibility for the department's budget.

BARNES MARKETING & COMMUNICATIONS, Media, PA (1993–1994)

Graphic Artist

Given creative control of the design and layout of numerous brochures, corporate newsletters, direct-marketing pieces and magazine and newspaper ads. Responsible for corporate identity on all media. Managed each project from concept through completion.

Education

ASHLAND UNIVERSITY, Ashland, OH
BS, Visual Communications, with honors, 1993
BS, Business Administration, with honors, 1992

Honors and Activities

Current participant with AmeriCare, helping to rebuild homes in the Northeast
Outstanding Achievement Award; Association of Graphic Communications, New York, NY
Honors Award for Outstanding Leadership, Ashland University

References available upon request

look just for it and let your eyes travel through the two pages. What you see first is what the applicant and writer want you to be certain to see: key information relevant to the target position and for convincing the reader that this particular applicant is someone to interview.

JOHN HARRISON

777 Winding Road
Alextown, New York 55555
(222) 555-0000
killersale@artofpersuasion.net

APPROACH • NEEDS • PRESENTATION • OVERCOME • CLOSE • SERVICE

ADVERTISING DIRECTOR

Accomplished advertising professional with a dynamic career leading a major media production company to success. Known for strengthening the organization to compete in competitive markets both directly and through leadership of others. Record for delivering innovative marketing concepts and strategies that work. Effectively manage the sales cycle process from client consultation to closing. Core strengths encompass

- **Key Account Development**
- **Solutions Selling & Marketing**
- **Team Building & Leadership**
- **Client / Public Relations**
- **Public Speaking**
- **Advanced Presentations**
- **Sales Analysis & Reporting**
- **Project Management**
- **Contract Negotiations**

PROFESSIONAL EXPERIENCE

Senior Advertising Manager   1985–2004
CABLE MEDIA PRODUCTIONS, INC., New York, New York
—*Animal World, Global Travel, Health Line*

- Spearheaded key account development programs that targeted, penetrated, and launched business growth throughout Northeast, Southeast, and Midwest regions.
- Overachieved projected sales volumes for 1999 by 74% with revenues in excess of $16 million.
- Established senior-level contact with 43 advertising agencies throughout New York City and Boston.
- Effectively negotiated and sold 30-second units of commercial advertising space to client agencies with major accounts that included Coors, AT&T, Lucent Technologies, Clorox, and Avon.
- Positioned Discovery Communications as a viable advertising avenue to target viewer audiences inclusive of preschool- to elementary-aged children, and adults in the 25–54 age category.
- Orchestrated the promotion of in-banner advertising and hotlinks.
- Secured Cable Media Productions' first million-dollar advertising sale with AT&T.
- Single-handedly negotiated and closed network's first online deal with Independent Films in 1998.
- Pioneered the organization's cross-channel promotion programs, heightening American Production's visibility with additional coverage in *U.S. News and World Report* magazine.
- Captured the interest of clients and professional audiences of up to 300 with powerful, invigorating presentations illustrating the benefits and value-added solutions of cable network advertising.
- Created innovative account-retention programs to protect key clients from competition.
- Pioneered the development of sales and marketing strategies and advertising plans.
- Chaired weekly competitive meeting to discuss season networks, market segments, and departmental issues with senior management, account executives, account planners, and sales assistants through open discussions and persuasive presentations.

— continued —

23

Combination. *Ann Baehr, Brentwood, New York*

This high-energy Advertising Manager's unique sales philosophy is prominently "advertised" within a pair of lines under the contact information to grab the reader's attention. A strong

JOHN HARRISON

Page 2

PROFESSIONAL EXPERIENCE
Cable Media Productions, continued

- Launched the business growth and development of this fledgling network cable start-up company.
- Developed convergence marketing proposals tailored to $500,000 budgets, mapping multifunctional advertising packages that incorporated the Discovery Channel's magazine, Website, and network.
- Spearheaded the development and execution of Internet-based hotlinks advertising.
- Collaborated with the International Education Society on the introduction of an online chat room to encourage post-viewing discussions among students.
- Technically astute and aware of our full product set, including software solutions.
- Allocated airtime programming that strategically assigned segmented advertising blocks on a regional level.

EDUCATION

Bachelor of Business Administration
PACE UNIVERSITY, Pleasantville, New York

SALES AWARDS

Recognized as one of the 25 Top National Sales Organizations, *Media and Marketing* magazine, 2002
Excellence in Salesmanship based on Meyer's Survey, 1997–2001

PARTICIPATORY MEMBERSHIPS

Vice President, American Management Association, 1995–present
Heart Walk Captain, American Heart Association, 1995–1998
Committee Member, Community Mainstreaming Program, 1995–1996
Committee Member and Fundraiser, National Committee for AIDS Research (NCFAR), 1994–1995

PROFESSIONAL DEVELOPMENT

Extensive presentations and skill-development workshops / Communispond / Speakeasy

profile ends with a three-column table of boldfaced core strengths. In effect, the two *bold* horizontal lines near the top of the first page enclose a hot zone that presents the information most likely to capture attention. A reader whose interest is sparked is more apt to read the rest of the resume.

AMY VESTAL

Target:

Events Planner

Profile:

Creative, detail-oriented person with planning, implementation, troubleshooting, and follow-up experience needed to orchestrate successful events. Proficient craftswoman with talent for providing finishing details that make nice presentations. Flower arranging, invitation and announcement designs, and color coordination make accessories festive, elegant, or just plain fun.

5555 55th Street
Flower, Texas 79000

avestal@aol.com

(555) 555-5555

Promotions and Value-added Projects . . . .

Increased sales by promoting Country Chic gift shop through teaching design and craft classes. Organized teas and brunches as well as acquired guest speakers on subjects such as quilting, gardening, and cooking. Planned showers from beginning to end for customers, to include invitations, decorations, food, etc.

Remodeled two-story residence to house gift shop.

Created sales brochures, advertising, crafty displays, and backdrops for unique photography studio that produced finished cut-out, stand-up photos mounted on wood.

Conceptualized and implemented plan to convert expensive laser cut-out process to a more cost-effective local operation with laser-like results.

Business Development and Revenue Growth . . . .

Restructured failing photo business, taking it from operating in the red to a profit-producing enterprise in only one year. Concentrated effort on marketing, networking, advertising, and recreating props and backdrops. Lowered overhead by researching less-expensive ways to cut out photos.

Utilized previous experience in retail sales and buying to conceive and launch gift-shop business. Used creative marketing ideas to attract customers.

Developed business savvy to keep expenses down while increasing profits. Areas of expertise include strategic planning, business proposals, budget projection and management, employee development, accounting, marketing, building a strong client base, and networking.

Additional Skills . . . .

- Able to relate at any level with people of varied beliefs and backgrounds
- Talent for building rapport and trust with clients
- Value organization and time management for efficiency and professionalism
- Use instructional communication style to relate information
- Friendly, personable, and approachable
- Focus on customer needs to ensure satisfaction
- Open to new ideas and enjoy brainstorming
- Solve problems effectively and make informed decisions

Employment History . . . .

Cosmetic Technician, Permanent Makeup, Flower, Texas	2002–2004
Substitute Teacher, Flower ISD, Flower, Texas	2000–2002
Sales Representative, ChemMate, Centerville, Texas	1999
Administrative Assistant, Northbrook Life Insurance, Ty, Texas	1998–1999
Owner, Stand-up Photography Studio, Centerville, Texas	1989–1998
Clothing Representative, Eastmart Wholesale, Ty, Texas	1989–1991
Jewelry Department Manager, Sammy's Dept. Store, Ty, Texas	1985–1986
Owner, Country Favorites, Poppy, Texas	1984–1987
Manager/Buyer/Designer, Elite Decorating, River Creek, Texas	1984
Manager, Golden Touch, River Creek, Texas	1980–1983

Education . . . .

Bachelor of Arts in Interior Design—Texas Vocational University   1989

24

Combination. *Edith A. Rische, Lubbock, Texas*

To de-emphasize many job changes, the writer presents a work history as just one-liners. Design elements of this nonconventional resume reflect the applicant's creativity. See Cover Letter 23 (page 399).

Communications

Resumes at a Glance

RESUME NO.	OCCUPATION	GOAL	PAGE
25.	Marketing Assistant	Marketing	61
26.	VP of Marketing	Creative Director	62
27.	Grant Writer	Not specified	64
28.	Public Relations Director	Public Relations	66
29.	Owner, Resume Service	Not specified	68

ARLENE STONE

AStone@email.com

500 West End Street #55
New York, NY 55555

Residence (212) 555-5555
Mobile (917) 555-5555

MARKETING POSITION—FASHION PUBLISHING INDUSTRY

Recent graduate with proven ability to produce results in a fast-paced environment with critical deadlines. Outgoing and articulate communicator who gets along well with public and coworkers at all levels. Works well independently as well as collaboratively in a team environment. Learns quickly and enjoys challenges. Computer skills include Microsoft Word, Excel, PowerPoint and Access. Experience includes

Writing • Research & Analysis • Media Kits • Presentations • Problem Solving & Troubleshooting.

EDUCATION

UNIVERSITY OF CALIFORNIA, Los Angeles, CA; May 2002
Bachelor of Arts in Communications; Minor in Marketing

PROFESSIONAL EXPERIENCE

STAR PUBLICATIONS—*MENS MONTHLY* MAGAZINE, New York, NY • 2002 to Present
Marketing Assistant
Relocated to New York after being accepted to position out of highly competitive applicant group from across U.S. Provide direct assistance to Advertising Director of prestigious men's magazine, gaining valuable hands-on experience. Day-to-day responsibilities vary and include the following:

- Prepare business proposals… Track competitive information... Run edit credits for various categories.
- Send out media kits to new clients, assemble presentations and manage contact card file. Collaborate with promotion department to organize databases for special events.
- Handle heavy phones, interacting directly with clients. Compose correspondence and memos, sort and distribute mail and manage complimentary subscription list.
- Track monthly expenses and coordinate travel arrangements.
- Organize weekly sales staff meetings and set up conference calls for outside offices.

MEDIA PRODUCTIONS, Hollywood, CA • Summer 2001
Production Assistant
Assisted in coordinating makeup and wardrobe for commercial and infomercial productions.

- Collaborated on identifying wardrobe theme; coordinated wardrobe selections with set decoration.

TOP SPORTS PUBLICATIONS / *FEELING GOOD* MAGAZINE, Woodland Hills, CA • Summers 1998 to 2001
Assistant / Intern
Worked closely with Editor-in-Chief, Fashion Editor, Beauty Editor, Senior Editor and Associate Editor of teen publication. Prioritized and coordinated multiple assignments, including transcriptions, research and follow-up. Contributed story ideas that resulted in publication, including the following:

- Assisted Fashion Editor at photo shoots. Contacted leading manufacturers to obtain sample merchandise; organized clothing for shoots; assisted with overall styling.
- Directly assisted in transforming and writing "Makeover" feature of magazine. Selected subjects; coordinated training with fitness instructors; arranged photo shoot; contributed to editorial staff meetings.
- Contributed ideas for retail accessories feature. Wrote captions, explaining new seasonal fashion trends.

25

Combination. *Vivian VanLier, Los Angeles, California*

Because the person's degree was only a year old and she graduated from a top-ranking university, education appears before professional experience. Bold italic emphasizes industry-related skills.

CARRIE M. FLAGER

507 SE 22nd Avenue
Portland, OR 55555

c_flager@yahoo.com

(000) 000-0000 Residence
(555) 555-5555 Mobile

Creative Director

Corporate Communications ▪ Corporate Image Development and Protection ▪ Special Events Coordination

PROFESSIONAL PROFILE

Dedicated Creative Director with 10 years of experience managing creative projects. Strong ability to think outside of the box. Recognized for discovering new and innovative ways of communicating sophisticated corporate image through top-notch presentation and development of traditions. Strong ability to set corporate image apart from average. Proven skill in developing high-impact marketing messages on meager budget. Flexible team player, fast learner, computer literate.

KEY STRENGTHS

Develop high-impact customer communications pieces

Design outstanding direct-mail campaigns

Organize well-attended special events, including conferences

Create and deliver unique presentations

Prepare sales presentations / materials for trade shows

Track and report marketing activities

Develop company literature, design brochures, prepare proposals

RECENT ACHIEVEMENTS

- **Solely responsible for corporate image** of company that grew rapidly from managing 200,000 covered lives in 1996 to well over 4 million in 2002. Current clients include **Sara Lee, Southern Baptist University, the State of Alabama, Intel, and National Car Rental.**

- Designed company image of much larger corporation than actual six-employee home-based business that it was. Through use of top-notch technology and **development of sophisticated company image, company grew rapidly from $200,000 in revenues in 1998 to projected $4.5 million today.**

- **Saved company $10,000 per year** by recommending that company drop dedicated fax lines for traveling regional employees and replace them with free online faxes so that any fax they received would go directly to their inboxes, no matter where they were.

- **Built a tradition that customers have grown to recognize and look forward to:** custom holiday cards that look like pharmacy benefit industry–related newsletters. Unique design stands out from rest of corporate holiday cards and **allows company to follow vision of doing things in a different way.**

- **Created company's most successful marketing piece:** puzzle holiday gifts. Clients must solve challenging puzzle for opportunity to win significant grand prize. **Result: Company is kept in clients' minds throughout the year.**

- **Organized conference that attracted twice as many attendees as hoped for,** broke even as desired, and was **rated extremely highly by attendees.** Designed all marketing materials, logos, communications, and conference materials. Sought sponsorship funding, managed all technical aspects of the speakers' presentations, and created opening presentation.

26

Combination. *Jennifer Rydell, Portland, Oregon*

The applicant remembered little about her two earliest jobs, but had too many accomplishments to fit after her most recent job on one page of the resume. The writer therefore

CARRIE M. FLAGER

PROFESSIONAL EXPERIENCE

NADIS, INC., Portland, OR   1997–2004
Vice President of Marketing (Creative Director)

Image / Process Development: Second employee hired for this former start-up pharmacy benefit consulting company with annual revenues of $4.4 million and 30 employees nationwide. Developed sophisticated company image despite humble beginnings working out of residential basement. Managed several departments over the years. Developed processes that streamlined company procedures. Trained new employees on proper procedures with regard to marketing materials. Created top-notch presentation that has consistently impressed much larger companies.

National Corporate Marketing: Controlled overall company image in all marketing materials in print and electronic formats, including online. Designed all marketing materials, including presentations, invitations, and brochures. Developed themes and traditions through promotional products. Managed national corporate marketing efforts at conferences and estimated ROI with such ventures. Created multimedia presentations for sales team and conferences.

Teamwork / Coordination: Coordinated with Accounting, Client Services, Sales, and Information Services departments to ensure streamlined creative / marketing image. Negotiated with multiple external vendors for printing services. Acted as mentor and leader for other office employees while maintaining position as only marketing person employed at corporate office.

SPRINT, Dallas, TX   1995–1997
Marketing Coordinator
Produced and organized requests for proposal (RFPs). Coordinated corporate sales meetings. Developed presentation materials for sales team and tradeshow kiosks. Acted as corporate liaison between clients and corporate management.

QWEST COMMUNICATIONS, Waco, TX   1993–1995
Art Director
Prepared and tracked news releases. Produced monthly newsletter, including editorial and layout. Designed corporate forms. Coordinated marketing and advertising campaigns.

EDUCATION

Bachelor of Arts in Graphic Art, Baylor University, Waco, TX, 1993

Additional Professional Development Coursework:

Adobe Illustrator 9 Levels 1 & 2, New Horizons, 2003
Adobe Photoshop 6 Levels 1 & 2, New Horizons, 2003

COMPUTER SKILLS

Hardware Platforms:	PC
Operating Systems:	MS Windows XP, 2000, and 98
Business Productivity Software:	MS Word; MS Excel
Presentation Software:	Astound Presentation 8.0; MS PowerPoint
Graphic Software:	Adobe Illustrator, Adobe Freehand; Adobe Photoshop; Adobe ImageReady
Web Design Software:	MS FrontPage

emphasized on page one the applicant's key strengths and accomplishments and then put her job descriptions on page two. Notice the quantification of recent achievements whenever possible. Boldfacing helps to make recent achievements stand out on page one; boldfacing helps to guide the reader's eyes on page two.

EILEEN ANDREWS

Accomplished teacher, trainer and administrator with extensive leadership experience and a flair for public relations and communications

SUMMARY OF QUALIFICATIONS

- Wealth of experience, including 13 years in highly visible and demanding leadership roles.
- Skilled grant writer with strong understanding of fund-raising strategies.
- Critical thinker. Able to develop compelling arguments.
- Outstanding interpersonal skills. Easily build productive, enduring relationships.
- Recognized as effective spokesperson for departmental programs and interests.
- Skilled in creatively promoting new products and programs.
- Energetic and organized. Able to effectively handle the demands of multiple projects.
- Committed to ideals of excellence.

PERTINENT SKILLS AND ACCOMPLISHMENTS

Grant Writing/Communications
- Working as a freelance grant writer, wrote effective grant proposals for organizations such as the Girl Scouts, Special Olympics, and the Los Alamos Chamber of Commerce.
- In leadership roles for local school board, wrote grant proposals to gain funding for key programs.
- Actively promoted all ancillary educational programs in the community. Represented township in the community-at-large.
- Developed the role of Director of Education, serving as liaison between the board of education and the local community.

Policy Development and Administration
- Established standards and goals and set up new policies and procedures to support them, bringing new credibility to the school system.
- Worked as liaison in helping individual groups set up consistent policies and procedures.
- As a member of the Board of Regents of financially troubled school, developed policy to ensure financial stability and initiated capital campaign.

Management
- Supervised activities of 350 employees and 500 volunteers in providing for the education of 1,600 children.
- Oversaw education budget in excess of $5 million. Hired and trained key employees.
- Stepped in as interim principal of troubled school and orchestrated its turnaround.
- Partnered with principal of struggling school and successfully facilitated the achievement of full-term accreditation.
- Effectively coached and mentored teachers and principals, helping them to hone their skills and motivating them to reach goals.
- Provided oversight function for district school.

52 YORK ROAD • READING, NJ 11111
HOME (222) 222-2222 • FAX (333) 333-3333 • E-MAIL andrews@aol.com

27

Combination. *Carol A. Altomare, Three Bridges, New Jersey*

The individual wanted to get out of education and was looking for anything that her background might qualify her for. The writer put together many versions of the person's resume.

Teaching and Mentoring
- Earned certificate in elementary education.
- Prepared training materials and delivered courses for students in all stages of life—children, college students, and adult learners.
- Initiated mentoring program for principals and entry-level teachers.
- Developed training and certification program for volunteer instructors.

Assessment
- Chaired 12 different visiting committees commissioned to evaluate schools and develop plans for improvement. Acted as resource to facilitate change.
- Assessed suitability of training materials for a given audience and program goal.
- Managed performance assessment of teachers and principals.

EMPLOYMENT HISTORY

Independent Contractor   2000 to present
Grant Writer

Los Alamos Board of Education, Los Alamos, NV   1981 to 2000
Director of Education, 1997 to 2000
Responsible for coordinating the activities and personnel of various groups and articulating the educational goals of the Board.
- Served as liaison between schools and state and federal government, and between the Board and the community.
- Developed policy handbooks.

Superintendent of Schools, 1996 to 2000
Responsible for hiring, supervising, and evaluating principals and maintaining school standards across schools in the local district.
- Chaired committees to assess schools and recommend plans for improvements.

Principal, Los Alamos School, 1990 to 1996
- Provided direction and leadership while handling day-to-day management issues.

Classroom Teacher, 1986 to 1990
- Taught 2nd and 7th grade, as well as 5th- to 8th-grade English.

EDUCATION

Master of Education in Educational Administration, University of California, 1990
Bachelor of Science in Elementary Education, University of California, 1986

KEYWORDS: Grant writer, development officer, critical thinking, leadership, administrator, development, liaison, public relations, mentor, program developer, policies, procedures, organizational skills, effective communicator, implementation, facilitator

This particular version was very successful in getting the applicant interviews as a grant writer/development officer. She even got an offer sight unseen from a local community college; on the basis of her resume, it was assumed that she could write. Note the use of keywords at the bottom of page two.

ELAINE KENNEDY

4736 Grande ▪ Dallas, TX 77777
Home: 555–555–5555 ▪ Cell: 555–555–5555 ▪ ekennedy@aol.com

SENIOR PUBLIC RELATIONS EXECUTIVE

Award-winning, forward-looking leader with more than two decades of senior management experience. Attested ability to assess and tackle critical situations and follow through to best outcome. Vision for high-return media opportunities and strategies that strengthen organizational market position and enhance revenue growth. Possess exceptional ability and knowledge to lead PR campaigns and issue management programs across multiple industries. Strong ability to influence thinking of others, forge strategic relationships, and build consensus. Agile in multitask environment with wide scope of activities. Skillfully lead cross-functional teams to achieve corporate, branding, and marketing goals.

AWARDS

Dallas Ad League Award: Regional Hospital Print Ad Campaign
Matrix Award: Venture Capital Conference for Ernst & Young
Matrix Award: Client Marketing Brochure
Regional Emmy: Best Newscast

CORE COMPETENCIES

- ❑ Strategic Planning & Positioning
- ❑ Corporate Identity & Reputation Management
- ❑ Promotions & Events Planning
- ❑ Media Relations & Scheduling

- ❑ Product & Brand Strategy
- ❑ Crisis Communications & Issues Management
- ❑ Multimedia Advertising & Placement
- ❑ P&L Management

EXECUTIVE EXPERIENCE

Ricklear Studios, Dallas, TX   **1994–Present**
Lead PR team to consistently maintain million-viewer-strong audience for Emmy-nominated television series for $500M television programming company of 250 employees.

PUBLIC RELATIONS DIRECTOR (1998–Present)
Direct in-house senior PR team and activities of selected partner PR firms in LA and NY in multiple product/brand marketing strategy support. Develop PR plans across full spectrum of marketing activities for $200M annual sales, including product launch, brand license, multimedia advertising, and customer communications. Exercise full P&L responsibility. Counsel president and CEO on critical issues management, media response inquiries, and corporate strategies. Corporate spokesperson, controlling all media relations.

- Doubled advertising equivalency results to $3M in 24 months, and reduced PR operating budget by $500,000 annually.
- Staged high-impact event that drew 20,000 consumers and demonstrated toy brand's sustained popularity to world press, retailers, and business partners for FAO Schwarz, New York 2001 International Toy Fair kickoff.
- Secured placements on *The Today Show, Rosie, Good Morning America,* and others by convincing national broadcast media producers on product national value.
- Produced more than 50 promotional videos, ranging from high-end film pieces to video news releases.
- Conceived, designed, and launched Electronic Press Room for company's corporate Website.

28

Combination. *Nick V. Marino, Bishop, Texas*

Involvement with a well-known children's show was judged to be "laughable" and therefore actually hampered this applicant in her job search. She was not taken seriously by firms for

ELAINE KENNEDY

Home: 555-555-555 ▪ Cell: 555-555 555 ▪ ekennedy@aol.com
Page Two

Ricklear Studios, Continued

MEDIA RELATIONS MANAGER (1994–1997)
Managed and coached PR staff in media placement of award-winning television programming brands and products. Responsible for $100,000 annual, multi-project budget.

- Developed publicity launch model that produced 30-minute ticket sellouts in most major cities for international live tour.
- Orchestrated 20-million viewership public service announcement for then-Governor George Bush.
- Secured coveted placement of stories, articles, and appearances In *USA Today, LA Times, NY Times, CBS This Morning, Today,* and *Donahue* through strong leadership of PR multimedia advertising team.
- Produced and directed more than 40 promotional videos.

Communication Counsel of America (CCA), Dallas, TX   1992–1994
Public relations firm providing crisis and issue management strategic response guidance to multibillion-dollar clients, such as U.S. Department of Energy, Westinghouse, Rocky Flats Nuclear Facility, British Petroleum—Alaska, and Syntex Pharmaceuticals.

CONSULTANT
Independent consultant brought in to manage high-stakes and sensitive PR projects. Advised on and developed client crisis strategies. Prepared executives on oral presentations for large government contracts. Developed technical witnesses for regulatory and legislative appearances. Trained companies in strategic negotiation techniques with communities and stakeholders for effective corporate goal attainment.

- Netted upwards of $1B in government contract awards, $750M in estimated CCA new-client presentations, and FDA hearings that achieved over-the-counter approval for Aleve, through careful preparation of Westinghouse, Coopers & Lybrand, and Procter & Gamble executives for high-stakes oral presentations.
- Created positive media and stakeholder relations for U.S. Department of Energy in release strategy of National Environmental Impact Statement for Nuclear Defense Facilities.

Kennedy Communications, Dallas, TX   1985–1992
Public relations, issues management, and marketing firm, serving multibillion-dollar clients, such as Hitachi Semiconductor, Campbell Travel, and Conoco Oil Company.

PRESIDENT
- Raised positive community response for Conoco Oil Company $25M community settlement.
- Developed TQM Quality Circles program for Hitachi.

Lewis & Partners, Dallas, TX   1980–1984
$20M ad agency serving multimillion-dollar clients, such as Ernst & Young, American Eagle Airlines, Donaldson, Lufkin & Jenrette, and Olivetti USA.

GROUP VICE PRESIDENT, PUBLIC RELATIONS
Founded and directed PR group, recruiting, training, and directing staff of 10. P&L responsibility. Oversaw consumer and B2B work. Billed $1M in annual fees.

- Established consistent emergency responses and elevated public confidence by authored Issues Management Plans for regional restaurant chain and American Eagle Airline Service.

EDUCATION
Bachelor of Journalism, University of Texas at Austin

which she was seeking an interview. The writer therefore avoided mentioning the "laughable" program but still showcased her related accomplishments. She immediately received interviews with this resume and in them could explain her involvement with the excellent, award-winning show.

CAROL A. YOUNG

3 TABBY DRIVE • FLEMINGTON, NJ 08822
OFFICE (908) 237-1883 • FAX (908) 237-2069 • CAA@WORLDCLASSRESUMES.COM

Credentialed résumé writer with a demonstrated commitment to providing superior products and top-notch service

SUMMARY OF QUALIFICATIONS

Independent, self-motivated, and conscientious professional with strong customer focus. Excellent writing skills with extensive experience developing marketing materials, customer communications, and job search documents. Able to draw on diverse experience to understand client needs and develop effective, targeted résumés.

PROFESSIONAL HIGHLIGHTS

- Opened résumé business, coordinating all aspects of start-up including creating and producing all business communications materials: brochures, business cards, flyers, and the company's Web site.
- Established proven record of accomplishment in writing winning résumés and other job search documents.
- With background that spans the fields of research, development, manufacturing, marketing, technical service, administrative customer service, career development, training and project management, successfully work with technical, administrative, and executive professionals at all levels.
- Competently draw out key information from clients to effectively market skills and abilities.
- Astute and analytical; always operate with the understanding that knowing and adapting to the audience is the key to effective communication.
- Recognized for leadership and commitment to quality improvement. Strong track record of providing outstanding customer satisfaction.

CERTIFICATION

Certified Professional Résumé Writer, Professional Association of Résumé Writers, 2001

EMPLOYMENT HISTORY

WORLD CLASS RÉSUMÉS, *Owner,* 2000 to Present
RESUME.COM, *Elite Writer,* 2000 to Present
LIBERTY LIFE, *Implementation Consultant,* Voluntary Benefits Group, 1999 to 2000
KAPLAN, *Prep Course Instructor and Tutor,* 1999 to 2001
YORK OIL CORPORATION, *Senior Research Engineer,* Fuels Marketing Support, 1995 to 1999
SPECIALTY CHEMICALS, INC., *Staff Engineer,* Petroleum Catalyst Group, 1990 to 1995

EDUCATION

STATE UNIVERSITY, Master of Education (Counseling Psychology), 1996
CITY COLLEGE, Bachelor of Science (Chemical Engineering), 1990

29

Combination. *Carol A. Altomare, Three Bridges, New Jersey*

Here is the resume writer's own resume. It is included in this Gallery to give an example of at least one professional resume writer's background. Note her degrees in science and psychology.

Customer Service

Resumes at a Glance

RESUME NO.	OCCUPATION	GOAL	PAGE
30.	Assistant Site Manager	Operations Manager	71
31.	Client Services Representative	Customer Service	72
32.	Operations Manager	Operations Manager	74

Ruben A. Rodriguez

2487 Coastal Bend Dr. Corpus Christi, TX 70376
(H) 361-878-3452 (C) 361-552-6523   e-mail: rod23@earthlink.net

RESULTS-ORIENTED
OPERATIONS MANAGER

Offers progressive inbound call-center operations experience defined by an aggressive promotional career path from agent to assistant site manager within four years, with current responsibility for customer-service call-center operations, staff development and budget forecasting. Extensive experience in the areas of customer service and quality assurance.

ACHIEVEMENTS

- Manage 150 Customer Service Representatives and 22 Manager/Support Staff with an average call volume of 10,000 customer-service calls per day.
- Managing direct customer-service programs for a variety of care products for Syrius Digicom.
- Creating financial models with forecasted revenue of $1 million per month and a year-to-date 5% budget variance.
- Achieved a gross profit of $4 million annually (2001).

PROFESSIONAL EXPERIENCE

SYRIUS DIGICOM—Corpus Christi, Texas   February 1999–Present

Assistant Site Manager—Operations   **May 2000–Present**
- Manage a supervisory team in regards to workflow allocation, performance appraisals, training, development and salary recommendations.
- Coordinate the daily operational objectives of performing departmental functions in an efficient, timely manner while meeting quality performance standards.
- Resolve customer and agent challenges through proactive investigation of issues in a liaison role, partnering with other departments, including the client.
- Implement and plan new projects and procedures as a result of a continuous review of current operating methods in relation to client/customer objectives.
- Budgeting and P&L responsibility.

Fraud Prevention Manager—Administrative Operations   **February 1999–May 2000**
- Developed and implemented fraud-prevention policy and procedures, which resulted in the lowest charge-back percentage among all Syrius Digicom call centers (half of one percent).
- Established customer-service guidelines in the Administrative Operations Department.
- Monitored the productivity of the Outbound Sales Department.
- Trained and managed 22 Fraud Prevention agents, 16 Administrative Operation agents and 3 Outbound Sales agents.
- Managed 2 Fraud Prevention Supervisors, 2 Administrative Operation Supervisors and 1 Outbound Sales Supervisor as well as functioned as an acting assistant site manager.

VTX TELESERVICES—Austin, Texas   1996–1998

Quality Assurance Supervisor
- Developed fraud-prevention guidelines.
- Responded to all charge-back issues.
- Managed customer complaint issues.
- Trained agents on quality assurance procedures.
- Supervised the call center on demand.

EDUCATION

Bachelor of Arts/Psychology   **1993–1996**
UNIVERSITY OF TEXAS—Austin, Texas

30

Combination. *MeLisa Rogers, Victoria, Texas*

The writer wanted to call attention to the applicant's achievements so that he could move to the next step of his career as a Call Center Site Manager. Note the lines, the box, and the shading.

DEBORAH GRAND

444 Beverly Road
Pittsburgh, PA 00000
333.333.3333
xxxxxxx@xxx.xxx

CUSTOMER SERVICE PROFESSIONAL

Problem Resolution ◊ *Marketing Research* ◊ *Results Oriented* ◊ *Strong Client Contact*

Extensive diversified business and marketing experience with focus on client service and account management. Self motivated, energetic. Efficient; organized; with strong analytical, logic skills and attention to detail. Excellent communication skills. Comfortable multitasking. Able to assess client needs and provide products/services to meet those needs. Interface effectively with diverse populations of clients and all levels of company personnel. Elected by peers as department representative for new-technology task force. Resolve client problems in timely manner to ensure satisfaction and loyalty. Extensive monthly documentation and data analysis.

COMPUTER SKILLS

Word, Windows, Excel, ACT, Outlook, PowerPoint, Mainframe and Network experience.

ACCOMPLISHMENTS

TROUBLESHOOTING
- Tackled and completed "difficult" projects abandoned by former incumbents.
- Installed hardware and software to interface with customers using different systems, coordinating needs with technical contacts.
- Identified products to meet clients' concerns and needs.

CUSTOMER SERVICE
- Linked customers with informational resources as value-added service.
- Nurtured relationships with key accounts, increasing frequency of call cycle from six to three weeks.
- Convinced customers to shift loyalties from competitors through unparalleled customer service and creative promotions.
- Leveraged position with new customers, offering impressive record for service and reliability.

PUBLIC SPEAKING
- Brought creative new vision to position by composing multimedia presentations for collateral marketing materials.
- Addressed groups of 20–30, on a volunteer basis, to promote company's commitment to the community.

31

Combination. *Ellen Mulqueen, Hartford, Connecticut*

Although this undergraduate is some way away from receiving her bachelor's degree, she has much to show for approximately 10 years of work experience. The writer first profiles the

Deborah Grand

ACCOMPLISHMENTS (continued)

MARKETING
- Outdistanced competitors by securing new business in the electronic commerce sector.
- Strengthened reputation of marketing department by providing timely, accurate responses and follow-up while simultaneously promoting new products.
- Nurtured long-term business relationships with clients, offering impressive record for service and reliability.
- Made inroads and headway with previously inaccessible clients.
- Ignited stagnant sales operation, showing 14% gain after four prior years of flat sales.
- Won service contract with long-time-sought institutional account.

TASK FORCES
- Participated in specialized training task force that planned and executed new technology upgrade.
- Selected for prestigious training team charged with updating skills of selected departments within the company.

PROFESSIONAL EXPERIENCE

Apex Company, Pittsburgh, PA
Client Services Representative   2002–2004

Credit Data Company, Pittsburgh, PA
Senior Account Executive   1997–2002

Quality Company, Pittsburgh, PA
Account Executive   1993–1997

EDUCATION

Pittsburgh College, Pittsburgh, PA
B.S., Management, degree expected in May 2005

Pittsburgh Community College
A.S., Business Administration

applicant's experience and diverse skills and then turns to her many accomplishments. These are effectively grouped under five side headings (Troubleshooting, Customer Service, and so on). Without these headings, the accomplishments would have been a long line of bulleted items without evident design.

DAVID DELGADO

752 Oakwood, Unit 6, Houston, Texas 77039   phone: 713-685-4527   e-mail: dda5563@attbi.net   pager: 887-524-8853

Bilingual Call Center Operations Manager offers extensive experience in a 24 / 7 inbound customer-service call-center operation with 100% management responsibilities of staff development / retention, budget forecasting, customer service, client management, quality assurance, product training, and performance management.

Professional Achievements

- Achieved a *$4 million* annual gross profit for 2001.
- Demonstrated keen ability to successfully manage and lead 150 Customer Service Representatives and 22 Manager / Support Staff to handle 10,000 calls per day while *exceeding client quality standards.*
- Orchestrated successful customer-service programs for *multiple TSS products.*
- Created financial models with forecasted revenues of $1 million per month and a year-to-date *5% budget variance.*
- Developed and implemented *fraud-prevention procedures* resulting in the lowest charge-back percentage among all TSS call centers of *.5%.*
- *Improved agent retention by 47%.*
- Spearheaded the development of interdepartmental communication avenues for the enhancement of *organizational performance.*
- Implemented client interfacing programs, resulting in increased *responsiveness to customer demands.*

Professional Profile

Business Results—financial forecasting, planning and budget adherence, strategy analysis for continuous improvement.

Operational Success—organizational policies / procedures, quality improvement programs, achieve performance management targets.

Resource Management—capacity management, telecom requirements, facilities management, staffing forecasting, workflow allocation.

Environmental Control—maintain a safe, productive environment for associates, consisting of fair and equitable relations.

Client communications—nurture client relationships while uncovering opportunities for additional client support.

Training and Development—improvement of product training and delivery through internal and external client / customer surveys.

Professional Call Center Experience

Triumph Satellite Systems, Inc.   Houston, Texas   1999–Present
Operations Manager, 2002–present
Assistant Site Manager / Operations, 2000–2002
Fraud Prevention Manager / Administrative Operations, 1999–2000

Amicom Teleservices   Phoenix, Arizona   1996–1999
Quality Assurance Supervisor

Education

Bachelor of Arts/Psychology, University of Arizona, 1996
National Honor Societies: Golden Key and Psi Chi.

32

Combination. *MeLisa Rogers, Victoria, Texas*

Compare this resume with Resume 30. The writer altered information to protect the candidate's privacy and took the data in two different directions. Resumes 30 and 32 present the same information two different ways.

Design/Architecture

Resumes at a Glance

RESUME NO.	OCCUPATION	GOAL	PAGE
33.	Senior Designer	Not specified	77
34.	Educational Coordinator	Design Artist/Production Asst.	78
35.	Architect	Architect/Project Manager	80

Aimeé Kufari

555 Henry Street • Apartment 5A • Brooklyn, New York • 55555 • 646.555.5555

Profile

A creative graphic design/illustration professional with more than seven years of proven talent; expert in designing graphics and illustrations for textbooks, catalogs, magazines and Web pages coupled with an amazing understanding of composition and color usage. Excellent project management skills. Ability to establish rapport with individuals at all levels, analyze needs and develop appropriate materials within project scope.

Areas of Expertise

Illustration • Graphic Design • Color Correcting • Logo Design • Brochure, Magazine and Newsletter Design

Computer Experience

Adobe Photoshop • Adobe Illustrator • InDesign • Dimensions • Streamline • QuarkXPress
Microsoft Word, Excel and PowerPoint • Mac and PC operating systems

Professional Experience

McGraw-Hill, School Division, 2001 to Present
Senior Designer: Produce artwork; design textbook covers and packaging for all educational CD-ROMs for grades K through 6; maintain total responsibility for color correcting, batching and scaling raw digital images. Primary liaison between department manager and junior designers; ensure that all assignments are completed within project scope.

Accessory Collaboration Network, 2000
Illustrator: Created illustrations of messenger bags, backpacks and tote bags for publication in nation-wide catalog.

Global Business Techniques, 1998 to 1999
Art Director: Designed corporate identity and branding image; developed business cards, letterhead and envelopes. Created all brochures; mini-magazines; newsletters; and trade-show, convention and corporate event banners and promotional giveaways: T-shirts, pins and postcards.

Hofstra University, 1994 to 1998
Art Designer: Designed and implemented all university publications, advertisements and brochures, including but not limited to student handbooks and course catalogs, *New York Times* magazine advertisements, posters for university club-sponsored events, invitations for faculty and staff university and alumni affairs and various departmental newsletters.

Freelance Design Experience

Two Side Advantage: Designed all marketing materials, including Website (www.twosidedvantage.isp), T-shirts, posters, bumper stickers, pins and print flyers promoting tours, documentaries and appearances.

U.S. Pastry Chefs: Solely responsible for design and implementation of the corporate identity and branding image, including brochures, newsletters, business cards and letterhead.

Jackie's Chocolate: Developed logo, business cards, letterhead, indoor displays and store-front signs; major contributor responsible for the design of all retail chocolate boxes.

Audio Vision: Created corporate identity, responsible for the design and implementation of a variety of magazine and trade publication advertisements.

Friendly Automotive: Designed logo and corporate image; created artwork for all marketing materials, including pamphlets and brochures; and designed direct-mail campaign postcards, T-shirts and coupon books.

Business Concepts of New York: Developed business cards, letterhead and envelopes for all corporate divisions.

Super 5678 Tattoo: Designed outside store-front sign, in-shop displays, business cards, T-shirts and print advertisements for various publications, including the *Village Voice*.

Education

New York Institute of Technology, Bachelor of Fine Arts, Graphic Design, 1994

33

Combination. *Deanna Verbouwens, Hicksville, New York*

The applicant wanted to correct color images for a magazine publishing house. The resume plays up her design experience and related artistic expertise and skills. Bullets capture attention.

Teri Boyd

32 Parons Court
Oakland, NJ 07445

(555) 123-5459 (C)
(201) 123-7689 (H)
Teri@boyd.com

DESIGN ARTIST/PRODUCTION ASSISTANT
"Producing creative design solutions for the future"

PROFILE: Talented, resourceful artistic visionary who is skilled in translating abstract concepts into practical solutions using computer graphics and artistic design. Strong background in graphic and presentation design. Portfolio at *www.teriboyd.com*. Adept at planning and organizing events and exhibitions. Superb communication skills.

Computer Expertise
- Adobe Photoshop 6 & 7, Adobe Illustrator 9 & 10, Microsoft PowerPoint and Word, FileMaker Pro 5.0, QuarkXPress 4.1 & 5, Macromedia Dreamweaver 4.0, Macromedia Flash 5.0, Painter 7.0

KEY QUALIFICATIONS

Design/Artistic Skills
- Detail-oriented graphic artist with exceptional creative and follow-through abilities.
- Able to effectively analyze and communicate creative ideas with clients.
- Landed major account by designing on-the-spot solution after 20-minute discussion with client.
- Innovative weave textile designer. Created unique technical solution for woven fabric project that resulted in significant production cost reduction.
- Experienced graphic designer and Web designer.
- Accomplished artist and draftsman with paintings exhibited in 7 New York metro-area art exhibitions.

Organization/Production Skills
- Co-organized and presented 7 painting exhibitions that featured personal paintings and other painters.
- Coordinated and administered training program for computer and software sales and training company. Supervised multiple classrooms and oversaw activities of 4 freelance trainers. Designed and developed curriculum.
- Created graphics for marketing department using Photoshop, Illustrator, Quark, and MS Office products.
- Developed and wrote a 50-page business plan for opening a small studio to display and sell paintings.
- Created and implemented an efficient filing system for organizing and storing software and educational material.
- Produced spatial and construction solutions for store product displays.

Communication/Teaching Skills
- Received Rotary Club Scholarship based on communication skills.
- Certified Technical Trainer (CTT), Adobe Certified Expert (ACE) Illustrator 9.0, Adobe Certified Expert (ACE) Photoshop 6.0.
- Adjunct Professor at 4 different colleges teaching Drawing 1, 2D Design, and Art Appreciation.

Education
- MFA in Fine Arts, SUNY, Buffalo, NY, 5/02
- BA in Fine Arts, Syracuse University, Syracuse, NY, 5/96

34

Combination. *Igor Shpudejko, Mahwah, New Jersey*

This applicant had done many things but not in the field she wanted to get into: production design. To de-emphasize her many short-term jobs, the writer focused instead on her skills and

Teri Boyd

EXPERIENCE SUMMARY

MAYWOOD COMPUTERS   Maywood, NJ
Educational Coordinator   2/01–3/03
Computer and software sales and training company. Taught desktop publishing classes consisting of 1–8 students for client companies. Supervised multiple classrooms and oversaw activities of 4 freelance trainers. Designed and developed curriculum.

WPF ASSOCIATES   Hackensack, NJ
Graphic Designer   8/00–1/01
Corporate presentation digital production studio. Developed MS PowerPoint and Adobe Photoshop and Illustrator designs for various types of presentations. Landed major account after designing graphic on the spot after short conversation with client.

JONES DESIGN STUDIO   Waldwick, NJ
Graphic Designer/Web Designer   1/00–8/00
Print and Web site production company. Prepared graphic designs for print and Web site using Dreamweaver, Photoshop, and Illustrator.

INGIS CORP.   Oakland, NJ
Weave Designer   2/98–1/00
Textile and design company. Analyzed textiles for redesigning to save manufacturing costs. Identified and corrected major technical flaw in one of the designs.

THE ARTWARE STORE   Mystic, CT
Store Manager   6/96–2/98
Ran art-supply store. Provided display solutions.

NORLELLEN STOKLEY INTERIORS   Ridgewood, NJ
Mural Artist   12/95–5/96
Produced murals, faux finishes, color compositions, and interior design surfaces.

Teaching Experience

Adjunct Professor, Drawing 1 and 2D Design Courses, Fall 99, Rockland Community College, Suffern, NY
Adjunct Professor, Art Appreciation and 2D Design, Fall 98, Bergen Community College, Paramus, NJ
Adjunct Professor, Art Appreciation, Fall 98, 99, Rockland Community College, Suffern, NY
Adjunct Professor, Drawing 1 and 2D Design, Spring 98, Purchase College, SUNY, Purchase, NY

Fine Art Exhibitions

Gallery of South Newark, Group Show, South Newark, NJ, Winter 01
Dactyl Foundation for the Arts & Humanities, Group Show, Soho, NY, Summer 00
Dactyl Foundation for the Arts & Humanities, Group Show, Soho, NY, Winter 98
SUNY Purchase Gallery, One-Woman Show, Purchase, NY, Spring 98
Paterson Museum, One-Woman Show, Paterson, NJ, Spring 97
Lena DiGangi Gallery, One-Woman Show, Totowa, NJ, Spring 96
Lena DiGangi Gallery, Group Show, Totowa, NJ, Winter 95
Bengert-Macrae Gallery, Group Show, Wyckoff, NJ, Spring 94
Catskill Art Society, One-Woman Show, Hurleyville, NY, Spring 92

put them on the first page. The applicant's key qualifications are grouped under three kinds of skills indicated in side headings. Boldfacing on the second page helps the reader see job positions and the art galleries where the applicant had exhibited fine art.

LINDA A. BUILDER
Licensed Architect

1227 Oak Avenue
Lantern, Texas 77391

331 271-9952
facsimile: 331 271-9953

ARCHITECT / PROJECT MANAGER with experience in the planning, design, and construction of diverse project renovations (major and minor) and architecture projects such as institutional, recreational, and health care facilities. Extensive background in **urbanism** and all infrastructure directing all project phases, from design through completion of construction, coordinating the efforts of contractors; architectural, engineering, and landscaping consultants; and government agencies. Excellent technical qualifications complement an **innate sense of creativity** in the design of aesthetically attractive, architecturally strong, and utilitarian space. Highly organized and proficient in AutoCAD. Meticulous, detail-oriented, perfectionist; work well under pressure.

AREAS OF PROFICIENCY

Experienced in all phases of design from program definition through working drawing; expertise in
- Construction estimating, cost analysis, feasibility studies, and project budgeting;
- Negotiation and contract administration;
- Inspection and supervision of construction.

▶ Solid design and construction experience in commercial projects, including landscaping, office buildings, schools, churches, hotels, and restaurants.

▶ Established a **regional reputation** for excellence and developed a loyal following. Highly successful for project profitability and investor ROI.

▶ Strong **management skills,** including personnel and project scheduling, employee and subcontractor supervision, budgeting and finance, problem solving, client relations, and quality control.

▶ Seasoned **sales and marketing skills.** Demonstrated ability to gain trust and confidence of prospects. Personable and highly ethical.

▶ Proven **communications ability** that is straightforward, honest, and articulate, yet tactful and diplomatic. Sincere sensitivity to unique needs and aspirations of all segments of a community. Active listening and consultation skills with talent for respecting and responding to divergent opinions and interests. Strength in blending idealism with political reality, and devising new methods to improve procedural and system efficiency.

▶ Computer literate: Microsoft PowerPoint, Adobe PageMaker, CorelDRAW, Harvard Graphics.

▶ Fully bilingual: Spanish and English.

CAREER HIGHLIGHTS

ARCHITECT
Planin Consultores, S.A., Caracas, Venezuela

1999	Designed, drafted, and supervised the building project for the new Emergency area for Adults and Pediatrics at the Hospital Clinico de Caracas.
1997	Remodeled living quarters on the second floor of the Caracas Hospital (4 models).

35

Combination. *Myriam-Rose Kohn, Valencia, California*

Contact information is presented in a balanced format and separated from the rest of the resume by a double line. The first paragraph is a profile of the applicant. Boldfacing enhances

LINDA A. BUILDER   Page 2

1996   Designed individual family units for private owner.
                Participated in all project phases from initial client contact and presentation through
                conceptual design; production of contract documents; interface with engineers and
                outside planning consultants; and development of interiors, finishes, and specifications.

1996   Key member of design team responsible for the renovation of the Adult Emergency area
                at the Public (County) Hospital in Caracas (Hospital Universitario de Caracas). While
                work was in progress, intervened and adjusted the specifications to improve production.

ARCHITECT
G.P. Arquitectura, S.A., Valencia, Venezuela

1998   Assigned as architect in charge for the Main Control Room project at the Energia
                Eléctrica (Electrical Energy) of Venezuela (ENELVEN / CAUJARITO), approximately
                1000 mt2.

1996   Designed and drafted the remodeling of the main offices at the Investment Bank of
                Welles Orvitz. Served as director of field operations. Reviewed project specifications,
                researched previous designs, and prepared designs for customer presentation and
                approval. Maintained in-house library of design materials and references.

ARCHITECT
Faculty of Architecture, University of Apure, Cabimas, Venezuela

1992–1995   Supervising Architect on several relocation projects, among which were the communities
                of *El Hornito* (252 acres, $300 million budget, 325 houses from 7 different models,
                church, elementary school, community center, clinic, and fishing processing center) and
                Villa Hermosa.

                Reviewed development proposals for adherence to county zoning and other ordinances,
                and aesthetically based design guidelines. Dealt with

                - zoning administration   - community development
                - site plan review and approval   - stormwater drainage
                - subdivision regulation   - surface hydrology
                - wastewater distribution   - parking lot design
                - design ordinance administration   - environmental impact
                - economic development   - public relations
                - historic preservation   - urban redevelopment
                - environmental impact and planning   - administrative management
                - policy analysis

                Directed and facilitated the design and construction of new development projects
                and improvements to transportation facilities, streets, sidewalks, and utility systems.
                Coordinated/supervised an interdisciplinary team of professional consultants and
                construction inspectors to meet individual project time and cost objectives. Analyzed
                impediments to project goals; quickly identified and implemented solutions.

                Prepared graphic files for inspection and critical path schedules; analyzed construction
                schedules from contractors. Monitored project construction daily and represented the
                interests of client at progress meetings. Prepared design revisions when required by
                unknown field conditions. Analyzed requirements of plans and specifications to deny or
                justify claims by contractors for extra work. Facilitated public involvement in planning
                decisions by communicating merits of project(s), which in turn promoted community good
                will and continued support. Explained or modified construction activity to respond to
                public concern. Assisted with final project designs and construction drawings.

information of interest to the prospective employer. Boldfacing also highlights certain skills in the Areas of
Proficiency section. The value of the applicant's bilingualism becomes evident in the Career Highlights section. Here and in the Education section, we may infer that Spanish is her native language and English her

LANDSCAPE ARCHITECT
Faculty of Architecture / Agronomy, University of Apure, Cabimas, Venezuela

1993   Collaborated with horticulturist Carmen Avila (partner in El Guacamayo Company) on the
              design and development of the exterior landscaping at *La Cabana Hotel* (Aruba, Antilles).
              Ensured *El Guacamayo Garden* was executed in accordance with client specifications.

PATENTS AND PUBLICATIONS

Faculty of Architecture
Research Institute I.F.A., University of Apure, Cabimas, Venezuela

In collaboration with Carlos Fidere, Dean, School of Architecture:
- Authored and published ***Informe Final,*** Relocation Project of the community of *El Hornito*. Presented
  material in Barcelona, Spain (1996).
- Authored, designed, and published ***Memoria Descriptiva,*** Relocation Project of the community of *El
  Hornito,* which became permanent reference in the library at the Faculty of Architecture.

EDUCATION

Diploma, **Architect,** University of Apure, Cabimas, Venezuela.

Completed highest level of English courses at Santa Fe University, Santa Fe, NM
Introductory computer and English courses, University of Apure, Cabimas, Venezuela
Courses in Excel for Windows, Beginning and Advanced AutoCAD.

second language. As you read the Career Highlights section, you learn quickly that an architect's activities
are essentially achievements because of the creative nature of those activities. The variety of projects and
the section on Patents and Publications are impressive.

Education/Training

Resumes at a Glance

RESUME NO.	OCCUPATION	GOAL	PAGE
36.	Pre-Kindergarten Teacher	Not specified	85
37.	Student Teacher	Not specified	86
38.	Substitute Teacher	Not specified	87
39.	Substitute Teacher	K–8 Elementary School Teacher	88
40.	Substitute Teacher	Not specified	89
41.	Substitute Teacher	Not specified	90
42.	Kindergarten Teacher	Elementary Education Teacher	91
43.	Kindergarten Instructor	Not specified	92
44.	Elementary Teacher	Elementary School Teacher	94
45.	Elementary Teacher	Not specified	96
46.	Elementary Teacher	Not specified	98
47.	Student Teacher	Special Education Teacher	100
48.	Special Education Teacher	Special Education Teacher	101
49.	Special Education Teacher	Special Education Teacher	102
50.	Student Teacher	Special Education Teacher	104
51.	Customer Service Associate	Secondary Ed. Instructor/Coach	105
52.	Middle School Teacher	History Teacher	106
53.	Student Teacher	History Teacher	108
54.	Japanese Teacher	Japanese Language Instructor	110
55.	Asst. English Language Teacher	Healthcare/Customer Relations	112
56.	Visual Arts Teacher	Visual Arts Teacher	114
57.	Student Teacher	High School Teacher/Coach	117
58.	Principal Intern/Math Specialist	Instructional Administrator	118
59.	Turnkey Trainer	Early Childhood Specialist	120
60.	Adjunct Instructor	Psychology Professional	122
61.	School Psychologist	School Psychologist	124

(continues)

(continued)

62.	Peer Education Teacher	Psychology Teacher	126
63.	Training and Doc. Specialist	Corporate Trainer	128
64.	Math Teacher/Cheerleading Sponsor	Corporate Trainer	130
65.	Teacher	Training and Development	132
66.	Co-Director of Education	Not specified	134
67.	Adjunct Instructor	Historical Researcher	136
68.	AT Program Manager	AT Program Manager	138
69.	Teacher/Dept. Chairperson	Not specified	140

AMANTHA McLAUGHLIN

Pre-kindergarten Teacher

454 Swordfish Drive • Brentwood, NY 55555 • (555) 555-0000 • no1teacher@planet.edu

"Did you hear the good news? Samantha McLaughlin wants to teach on Long Island!"

CERTIFICATION
New York State Permanent Certification in Elementary Education, K–6
New York City Permanent Certification in Early Childhood Education, Pre-K–6

EDUCATION

Master of Science, Elementary Education
LONG ISLAND UNIVERSITY AT C.W. POST, Brentwood, NY

Bachelor of Arts, Elementary Education
ENGLEWOOD COLLEGE, Englewood, NY

TEACHING EXPERIENCE

1997–present

Pre-kindergarten
9/99–present
First Grade
1998–1999
Kindergarten
1997–1998

PRE-KINDERGARTEN TEACHER
John Kennedy Elementary School, P.S. 18, Jamaica, NY

- Manage a structured, stimulating classroom with responsibility in all areas of teaching, assessment, behavior modification, and coordination of academic and social activities.
- Create a fun, warm, and exciting atmosphere where children play and learn while strengthening skills in areas of fine/gross motor development, math, reading, and writing readiness, and acclimate to daily routines and the school environment.
- Plan, develop, and institute educational activities that promote quality teaching in accordance with New York State teaching standards and Bloom's Taxonomy.

Thematic Units/Differentiated Lessons

Jungle Habitat, Farm Animals, Growth of a Seed, Shapes & Colors, Dental Hygiene, Martin Luther King, Self-expression, The Four Seasons, and Ocean Life

Employ an integrated approach towards teaching, utilizing the following methods:

Charts/Diagrams	*Learning Centers*	*Poetry/Reading*	*Compare/Contrast*
Writing/Big Books	*Cooperative Learning*	*Story Mapping*	*Five Senses*
Sentence Strips	*Group Discussions*	*Brainstorming*	*Bulletin Boards*
Sight Vocabulary	*Games/Puzzles*	*Role Playing*	*Cooking Projects*

- Proactively communicate with parents to acknowledge superior work and areas of concern through discussion, newsletters, progress reports, telephone calls, home visits; and encourage parent involvement/volunteer assistance throughout the school year.
- Collaborate weekly with musicians to provide children with basic music appreciation through exposure to a diverse range of musical instruments and lyrics.
- Successfully use enrichment activities and behavior-modification techniques as a motivator for completing projects, following rules, and maintaining classroom conduct.
- Encourage group participation, and develop students' character exercising a strong respect for self, others, the community, and diversity.
- Recognized as the only teacher to attend PTA meetings in three years, attend Parent-Teacher Conferences, and coordinate Meet the Teacher Night and monthly field trips.

1993–1997
PRE-KINDERGARTEN TEACHER
St. Agnes Head Start, Bay Shore, NY

1992–1993
PRE-KINDERGARTEN TEACHER
Lutheran Elementary School, Massapequa, NY

1979–1992
PRE-KINDERGARTEN TEACHER
Hauppauge Freedom Day Care Center, Hauppauge, NY

36

Combination. *Ann Baehr, Brentwood, New York*

The writer made the resume fun for a teacher who was changing districts. She displayed a catchy statement at the top and used a custom logo for the name. Note the strong teaching experience.

Sheilah J. Curtis

email@email.net

21 Grove Place
Ridge Township, MA 00000

Phone: (555) 555-5555
Alternative: (555) 555-5555

Lesson Planning / Student Evaluation / MCAS Preparation / Program Development & Implementation

EDUCATION / CERTIFICATION

Michigan State College, Township, MI
Bachelor of Science, Education, 2003
Majors: Elementary Education / Natural Science & Mathematics
Elementary Teaching Certification Grades 1–6

Alpha Phi Chapter of Alpha Upsilon Alpha, the honor society of the International Reading Association

Tri Beta Life Sciences Honor Society

Who's Who Among Students in American Colleges and Universities, 2003

QUALIFICATIONS

- Plan and develop daily lessons for up to 24 students in multicultural classrooms.
- Interact with mainstream special education students.
- Develop and implement learning units to integrate unique learning models.
- Championed innovative program-development project *"Words on Vacation,"* a communication skills-based strategy utilized to prepare students for MCAS testing.
- Expand learning styles, IEPs, and educational plans through design and development of hands-on, inquiry-based techniques.
- Establish and demonstrate interdisciplinary thematic units on subjects including biodiversity, biographies, and rocks and minerals.
- Actively participate in parent conferences, student evaluations, core meetings, and grade and departmental team meetings.

STUDENT TEACHING EXPERIENCE

Potter Road Elementary School, Framingham, MA   2/04–Present
Grade 4 Classroom

Longfellow School, Cambridge, MA   9/03–12/03
Grade 6 Classroom

Johnson Elementary School, Natick, MA   5/02–12/02
Grade 1 Classroom

Hemenway Elementary School, Framingham, MA   12/98–4/02
Grade 4 Classroom

PROFESSIONAL MEMBERSHIPS

International Reading Association
Massachusetts Marine Educators Association
Massachusetts Reading Association

Professional Portfolio Available

37

Combination. *Rosemarie Ginsberg, Framingham, Massachusetts*

This recent college graduate was entering the field of education. Education/Certification, honors, and Qualifications are put at the top. Only student teaching experience is put lower on the page.

Cheryl M. Stayton

732 Riverside Blvd., Beaumont, Texas 77403   703-584-5483 or 703-735-5425   cmstay1@aol.com

Enthusiastic new graduate with a
Bachelor of Science degree in Sociology / Psychology
brings a mature and solid background of organizational and analytical skills to
the job market.

Excellent Customer Service   Highly Efficient
Excellent Communications Skills   Dependable / Reliable / Flexible
Multi-task Oriented   Project Focused
Exceptional Organizational Ability   Results Oriented

EDUCATION

Bachelor of Science—Sociology/Psychology   Baylor University—2002

ACHIEVEMENTS

➢ *Awarded the highly recognized status of Order of Omega Honor Society* as a result of achieving a 3.0 GPA as a student at Baylor University.
➢ *Committee Coordinator of the Juvenile Autism Foundation* 5K-walk fund-raiser and serve the organization as an active contributor.
➢ *Managed a statistical research project* with a focus on the analysis of social effects of individual behavior as it relates to certain factors affecting their likelihood to be concerned with health-related issues in today's society.
➢ *Managed 100% of college career* through occupational research, course selection, and financial management through part-time employment.

EMPLOYMENT EXPERIENCE

Beaumont Independent School District—Beaumont, Texas   August 2002–present
Substitute Teacher—Grades K–5
- Manage classroom activities.
- Provide substitute teaching services with minimal disruption to daily curriculum.
- Implement creative activities to ensure assigned learning goals are met.

Comfort Day Spa—Waco, Texas   January 2002–July 2002
Administrative Assistant
- Managed and directed telecommunications and personally handled visitors to the spa.
- Managed and completed clerical tasks such as filing, reporting, data entry, and document processing.
- Administered customer service for both internal and external customers.

MAXCO, Inc.—Waco, Texas   May 2001–December 2001
Receptionist
- Managed and directed telecommunications, visitors, and vendors of the company.
- Administered customer service for both internal and external customers.

PROFESSIONAL ORGANIZATIONS AND TRAINING

Memberships in the following affiliations:
- Order of Omega Honor Society
- Pre-law Society
- Sociology Club

Proficient in MS Excel, MS Word, Keyboarding, Medical Terminology, and general office equipment.

38

Combination. *MeLisa Rogers, Victoria, Texas*

The applicant wanted to work in the city where she graduated so that she could work on her graduate degree. The writer pitched the resume to general as well as professional positions.

AMANDA L. O'BRIEN

3397 Ashland Road, Broomfield, CO 80044
(555) 555-5555 ◆ aobrien_azy334@maillink.net

K–8 Elementary-School Teacher
Classroom Experience ★ BA Degree

HIGHLIGHTS OF QUALIFICATIONS

★ Recent classroom-education experience (K–8) for the Denver Public School District.
★ Several strong letters of recommendation.
★ BA degree in Psychology.
★ Proven motivator. Favored by students, colleagues, and parents.
★ Trustworthy and reliable. Accustomed to the responsibility of 1000s of lives daily.
★ Fun and outgoing personality. Enjoys reaching out to children and making an impact.
★ Athletic. Coached a girls' basketball team for two years.
★ Computer skills include Windows, Microsoft Word, and Internet.

EDUCATION

Bachelor of Arts Degree—Psychology, 2001
Colorado State University, Fort Collins, CO

Key Courses:

Teaching the Special Child	Developmental Psychology
Educational Psychology	Adolescent Psychology

WORK EXPERIENCE

DENVER PUBLIC SCHOOL DISTRICT, Denver, CO   2002–2004
Substitute Teacher—Davidson Elementary

Full-time classroom teacher for students in grades 1–3, and Learning Disability (LD) students in grades 4–6. Enjoyed teaching a second-grade classroom for two weeks.

★ Reversed scores on Language Arts test from failing to 83% average.
★ Instructed LD students in math and reading.
★ Divided students into small, focused groups of six or fewer students.

UNITED AIRLINES, Denver, CO   1990–2001
Flight Attendant
Customer Service Agent

★ Obtained annual CPR certification and FAA-security clearance. Trained flight attendants.
★ Calmed in-flight crises and situations; remained the "go-to" problem solver for emergency issues, including heart attacks. Served as PR spokesperson on Frontier Airlines flights.

VOLUNTEER

Girls' Basketball Coach
Pike's Peak Academy, 1999–2000
Coached and mentored 7th- and 8th-grade girls.

39

Combination. *Matt Thompson, Seattle, Washington*

Evident energy and enthusiasm helped this candidate land a kindergarten teaching position. Phrases in the Highlights of Qualifications were chosen to avoid clichés such as "works well with people."

DAVID E. JOHNSON

2345 Mountainview Court
La Crosse, Wisconsin 55555
Home: (608) 652-9090 / Office (608) 383-5252

PROFILE

Dynamic and results-oriented teaching professional with superior interpersonal communication skills and 12+ years of experience in training, coaching, and motivating. Demonstrated capabilities in the following areas:

- Classroom Management
- Curriculum Development
- Parental Participation
- Instructional Materials
- Special Events Management
- Consultative & Group Instruction

TEACHING EXPERIENCE

LA CROSSE SCHOOL DISTRICT — WISCONSIN   1999 to Pres.
Substitute Teacher (Grades 1–8)
Taught a varied curriculum at 8 elementary schools within the district. Specifically requested by faculty to fill in and remembered by students for interesting and creative teaching methods. Experience in team teaching and adapting curriculum for special-needs students.

LA CROSSE EAST HIGH SCHOOL — WISCONSIN   1985 to 1986
Substitute Teacher & Asst. Coach (Grades 9–12)
Taught in all classrooms and served as Assistant Cross-Country and Track Coach for Varsity and JV teams.

LA CRESCENT SCHOOL DISTRICT — MINNESOTA   1983 to 1985
Substitute Teacher (Grades K–12)
Prepared lesson plans and developed units for physical education curriculum.

BUSINESS MANAGEMENT EXPERIENCE

GOLDMAN FOODS — LA CROSSE, WISCONSIN   1996 to Pres.
Store Director   1985 to 1995
Recruited to turn around unprofitable grocery store. Developed "back to basics" approach and built a team environment among 57 employees. Created an effective action plan, delegated responsibilities, and delivered sales growth of 8%, labor reductions of 1½%, and substantial increases in customer counts (+500/week).

EDUCATION

MARQUETTE UNIVERSITY — MILWAUKEE, WISCONSIN   1983
B.S. Education — Physical Education Major (4-year athletic scholarship)

CERTIFICATIONS

Wisconsin 43 Substitute (current)
Wisconsin 530 Physical Education (current)

INTERESTS

Distance running, softball, and soccer.

40

Combination. *Michele J. Haffner, Glendale, Wisconsin*

The applicant was transitioning to teaching after many years as a successful business manager. Strong testimonials offset a lack of teaching experience other than substitute teaching.

Stephanie Valentino

40 Trees Avenue ■ Huntington, New York 11801 ■ 631.555.5555

📖Qualifications: Talented and enthusiastic teacher with New York State Provisional Certification for grades K–6; excellent ability to motivate and excite students to learn; effective teaching techniques and communication skills.

📖Education:

Hofstra University, Hempstead, New York
Master's Degree, School of Education—Elementary, May 2003
G.P.A. 3.85

Binghamton University, Binghamton, New York
B.A., Liberal Art Studies, August 1995
G.P.A. 3.75
Activities: Member of Drama Club and Intramural Softball.

📖Teaching Experience:

Woodbury Park Elementary School, Woodbury, New York
Substitute Teacher, Grades K–6, September 2003 through Present
📖 Instruct each subject area based upon teacher's instructions and lesson plans.
📖 Implement strategies to engage students in active learning.
📖 Develop spontaneous lesson plans for all subject matters.
📖 Implement effective and efficient classroom management.

Central Elementary School, Manhasset, New York
Student Teacher, Grades 3 and 4, January 2003 through April 2003
📖 Prepared and instructed various language arts lesson plans, including grammar instructions on simple subjects, simple predicates, adjectives, and prefixes and suffixes.
📖 Created and taught reading lesson plans using confirm, predict, and revise; compare and contrast; note taking and listening skills.
📖 Conducted reading group sessions; created higher-order thinking questions for each session.
📖 Developed and instructed social studies units on the American Revolution, Declaration of Independence, and Martin Luther King.
📖 Prepared and taught math units on exploring division, mean, mode, median, range, and geometry.
📖 Created and administered classroom tests for math and science; graded tests and assigned homework.
📖 Developed and instructed hands-on science lesson plans in magnetism and electricity.
📖 Prepared weekly plan book and designed bulletin boards for the classroom and hallway.
📖 Implemented effective and efficient classroom management.
📖 Participated in teacher-parent conferences and faculty meetings.

📖Additional Professional Experience:

G.E.I.C.O., Woodbury, New York
Trainer and Claims Examiner, March 1997 through Present
📖 Create and present training seminars on negotiation skills, claims processing, and constructive and effective claim communication for new claim associates.
📖 Independently manage and analyze more than 175 active traumatic and catastrophic bodily-injury claims.
📖 Liaison between policyholder and attorney; communicate with all on a daily basis to settle claims or prepare cases for litigation or arbitration.
📖 Analyze cases and develop reports outlining specific case circumstances for distribution to judges, attorneys, and supervisors.
📖 Active member of Grassroots Committee.

R.H. Macy*s, Herald Square, New York, New York
Coordinator and Sales Specialist, Ralph Lauren Home Collection, May 1995 through March 1997
📖 Developed and implemented home collection floor displays.
📖 Responsible for soliciting and maintaining Tier 1 clientele.
📖 Analyzed year-to-date same-store sales; implemented new sale techniques to increase revenue.
📖 Assisted customers with all aspects of purchases.
📖 Recipient of Ralph Lauren Top Sales Specialist Club Award.

📖Skills: Proficient in Microsoft Office Suite 95/98; ability to efficiently perform Internet research. First Aid Certified, CPR.

📖Interests: Golf, creative writing, poetry, and softball; member of Multiple Sclerosis Society and Arena Playhouse.

41

Combination. *Deanna Verbouwens, Hicksville, New York*

This applicant had both corporate experience and recent teaching experience. The resume shows that all of her experience applies to successful teaching. Large type makes her name stand out.

Melody J. Courtney

87211 Jennywood Lane • Sherwood, Oregon 97140

555-555-5555 cell   *home 777-777-7777*

Elementary Education Teacher
Pre Kindergarten–5th Grade

Motivating students to explore the world around them, carefully guiding them through necessary and diverse situations to formulate questions and develop strategies with which to answer those questions, offering freedom in thought processes and learning.

Professional Profile

Success-driven recent graduate and ambitious **Elementary Education Teacher** with expertise in developing an intuitive connection with students, tuning in to their specific learning needs, and providing clear, concise, and complete hands-on exercises. Experienced in developing and implementing an appropriate curriculum and planning highly effective lesson plans. Able to immediately grab students' attention, provide a strong presence, and command mutual respect. Possess outstanding communication skills with students, staff, and parents. Highly adaptable, multi-disciplined, organized, competent, and loyal. Strong team player with effectiveness in promoting school policies and practices. Additional expertise includes **Health and Psychology** with emphasis in **Sports Coaching.**

Education

Bachelor of Science • Early Childhood / Elementary Education • *2003*
Western Oregon University • Monmouth, Oregon
• Honor Roll student with emphasis in **Health** and **Psychology**
Early Childhood Education • Oregon State University • *1998–2000*

History of Employment

Kindergarten Teacher • Columbus Elementary • McMinnville, Oregon • *2003*
Student Teacher • *Fourth Grade* • Columbus Elementary • McMinnville, Oregon • *2002–2003*

Caregiver • High Lookee Lodge Assisted-Living Facility • Warm Springs, Oregon • *2002*
Tenant care including administering medications. Provided cleaning, food service, and ground work for facility.

Membership Services Supervisor • Salem Boys and Girls Club, Swegle Branch • Salem, Oregon • *2001–2002*
Oversaw orientation of new members. Verified arrival and departure of 200 members daily. Supervised equipment check-outs and returns. Informed parents and members of upcoming events.

Concierge & Marketing / Sales • Eagle Crest Resorts • Eagle Crest, Oregon • *2000–2001*
Arranged hundreds of guest reservations daily. Advised businesses and traditional guests of local features to visit. Notified visitors of a variety of sales options being offered. Corresponded with guests, aiding in their vacation preparations.

Volunteer Activities

• Neighborhood Watch Co-Chairman • Preschool teacher's aide *(Fall 2001)* • Bible school teacher *(Summer 2000)*

42

Combination. *Rosie Bixel, Portland, Oregon*

A beginning mission statement in italic is followed by a Professional Profile with boldfacing to make Elementary Education Teacher, Health and Psychology, and Sports Coaching conspicuous.

Monique Agree

555 Taqueria Lane   Tampa, Florida 33629   (813) 555-7518

More than 6 years of experience teaching kindergarten. Outgoing, creative and ambitious professional who loves children and pushes for positive growth. Experienced with both gifted and emotionally handicapped students. ESOL certified. Functions well in a variety of settings. Volunteers for everything!

EDUCATION, CERTIFICATIONS, & TRAINING

University of Tampa	B.S. in Elementary Education	1998
University of Tampa	B.S. in Early Childhood	1999
Hillsborough County Schools	ESOL certified	2001

TEACHING & DEVELOPMENT EXPERIENCE

Kindergarten Instructor

DeCroes Elementary School   Tampa   2001–2004

Focus on determining each child's individual educational needs and developing a curriculum based on school's objectives.

- ☑ Developed improved curriculum to enhance the learning of the letters and sounds of the alphabet.
- ☑ Created a "center-based" atmosphere to encourage learning through play.
- ☑ Initiated multiple interactive activities to ensure that each child learned at their individual development level.
- ☑ Created stimulating and active learning environment with the addition of live animal pets in the classroom: an iguana, a rabbit, hamsters, birds and fish.
- ☑ Crafted a *Big Buddy* program and matched students with fifth-graders. Held parties and reading sessions, and did mutual projects.
- ☑ Communicated verbally and/or in writing with parents daily to update them on social and emotional development.
- ☑ Member of national award-winning team that created an exhibit titled *Under the Sea*. Project was an outgrowth of *Wading Through Florida,* a lesson and arts-and-crafts project created for kindergarten classes.
- ☑ Chosen as Teacher Liaison/board member for the PTA due to reliability, candor and sensitivity.

43

Combination. *Gail Frank, Tampa, Florida*

This kindergarten teacher was energetic, enthusiastic, assertive, creative, and fun loving. She wanted a resume that would make these characteristics evident so that she could find a

Monique Agree page 2

☑ Volunteered as Social Committee Chairman in order to improve social interaction and sharing among adult school staff.
☑ Solicited and secured local business support, donations and funding as a key member of Business Partnership Committee.

Intermediate Summer Instructor

Fins Elementary School   Tampa   Summer 1999

☑ Developed a hands-on program to prepare 4th-grade summer-school students for the 5th grade.

Gifted Summer Instructor, primary

Fins Elementary School   Tampa   Summer 1998

☑ Collaborated with a group of teachers to enhance the gifted curriculum, resulting in *Junior Detectives Go to the Zoo.*

Emotionally Handicapped Instructor, K–3

Reynolds Elementary School   Tampa   Spring 1997

☑ Worked with individual emotionally handicapped students. Goal was to enhance their problem-solving skills in order to control their emotional impulses.

Kindergarten Instructor

Gianni Elementary School   Tampa   1999–2000
Bayfront Christian School   Tampa   Fall 1998

PROFESSIONAL ORGANIZATIONS

☑ Hillsborough County Classroom Teacher Association (FTP/NEA)
☑ Hillsborough County Math Council
☑ Hillsborough County International Reading Association

ACTIVITIES

☑ Junior League of South Tampa	Monthly volunteer work	1999–present
☑ Social Committee member	School staff events	2001–present
☑ PTA member	Participate in events	2001–present
☑ Girl Scout/Brownie Troop leader	Lead troop in activities	2000–present

principal who was comfortable with them. The playful nature of the font and layout helps to communicate her enthusiasm. The apple graphic, plenty of white space, check-box bullets, and triple horizontal lines sustain interest across two full pages.

BETHANY MITCHELL

| 619 Winston Terrace | Longwood, CA 99999 | Teachkids@cc.com | (888) 000-0000 |

Elementary School Teacher—Grades K–5

PROFILE

- Energetic, insightful, resourceful teacher dedicated to helping children identify and enhance their unique potential for academic and personal achievement.
- Diligent educator who blends innovative and traditional methods to produce a solid foundation for lifelong learning.
- Combine challenge and fun to create a stimulating learning environment. Promote scholastic and social development by

  - Determining individual student interests, traits, and needs
  - Applying a variety of methods to fulfill the needs of diverse abilities and circumstances
  - Establishing trust by applying discipline with fairness and consistency
  - Developing problem-solving and critical-thinking skills by presenting challenges that boost self-esteem and performance
  - Promoting the concept of equality, regardless of racial, cultural, or economic differences
  - Reinforcing positive behavior by encouraging efforts and praising accomplishments

EDUCATION

Bachelor of Science, Elementary Education (K–8) Westfield University—Westfield, OK	1993
Certificate of Completion in Child Development & Elementary Education Longwood Community College—Longwood, CA	1986
Cross-Cultural Language in Academic Development (CLAD) Certification	2003

PROFESSIONAL TEACHING EXPERIENCE

Elementary Teacher—Combination Classes—Grades 1–2 & 2–3 Washington Elementary School—Longwood, CA	2001–2004
First-Grade Teacher Pearson Lane Elementary School—Perris, MI	1999–2001
First-Grade Teacher (Third Grade, Jan.–May 1995) Rosa Parks Elementary School—Sonoma, OK	1995–1999
Substitute Teacher, Grades K–5 Sonoma Public Schools, Education Service Center	1994
Preschool Teacher Great Beginnings Preschools—Crestview, CA	1993–1994

ACHIEVEMENTS

- <u>Met with every student's parent(s)</u> or guardian for Parent-Teacher Conferences (2000)
- Created a well-received First-Grade Orientation Night for Parents (2001)
- Site Chair Representative, K–3—Sonoma, OK (1996–1998)

44

Combination. *Gail Taylor, Torrance, California*

This teacher worked with young children, so the writer wanted to illustrate the teacher's character, understanding, dedication, caring, and creativity. The Profile and Rewards sections make

BETHANY MITCHELL

PAGE 2

SEMINARS/WORKSHOPS ATTENDED

- Creating a Balanced First-Grade Program: Teaching Skills & Literacy
- Practical Literacy Center: Strengthening Reading & Writing Instructions
- Maximize Your Students' Growth in Writing & Reading

PROFESSIONAL AFFILIATIONS

California Teachers Association ▪ National Education Association ▪ Michigan Education Association

REWARDS

[To Ms. Mitchell]

"I am going to miss you. You are my heart and my moon." ~ Ronnie, 1st-grader

"You are the best ever." ~ Bridget, 1st-grader

"Thank you for making Bridget's 1st-grade year wonderful and for everything you have given her." ~ Bridget's Mom

"Your continued support, assistance, and caring were big factors in getting us all through….A final thank you for all that you taught this year."

~ Mr. & Mrs. Banuelos, Parents

these characteristics evident from beginning to end. The crayons graphic at the end echoes the same graphic at the beginning. Shading for the headings helps to make evident the resume's sections. Testimonials in the last section make the resume's ending strong and convincing. See Cover Letter 14 (page 390).

Judy Cassidy
123 Main Street
Anytown, USA 19000-0000
(555) 555-5555

PROFILE

ELEMENTARY EDUCATOR with more than 20 years of experience fostering academic learning and enhancing critical-thinking abilities. Incorporate effective cooperative learning techniques and unique classroom management style to establish creative and stimulating classroom environment. Dedicated, resourceful teacher skilled in building rapport and respect with students and student teachers.

Honored with **New Teacher Mentor Award** for Outstanding Service (2004)

"Miss Cassidy is an exceptional teacher. She is respectful to and of her students, and that respect is reciprocated. Using a variety of materials and techniques, Miss Cassidy challenges her students to excel. Her classroom is a warm, nurturing atmosphere where children are called to be their best selves."   A.F., School Administrator

EDUCATION AND CERTIFICATIONS

Instructional II—Permanent Certification, State of Pennsylvania (2002)

Master of Arts—**ANY UNIVERSITY** (1994)

B.S., Elementary Education—**ANY STATE COLLEGE** (1988)

SELECTED CAREER HIGHLIGHTS

- Successful in developing and executing **Everyday Math Program** at John Smith Elementary School (1999). Implementation of program resulted in overall math grades improvement by 180 points in 2002 *(versus previous-year scores)* along with instituting greater math awareness and mathematical thinking among all students. Participated in ongoing staff development and district training sessions to ensure utilization of hands-on, cooperative learning approach along with reinforcement and assessment techniques.

- Selected to serve as **Middle States Team Evaluator** for Brooklyn Diocese School System (1998). Collaborated with four colleagues in accreditation process comprised of interviewing teachers, meeting with committee, writing evaluation report, and creating recommended action plan. Conducted comprehensive academic assessment in similar capacity as **Catholic Elementary School Evaluator** for Diocese of Camden (1995).

- Directed and facilitated **Multidisciplinary Learning Project** at John Smith Elementary School to meet promotional requirements for students graduating to fifth grade (1999–2002). Through intensive interaction, students developed research, writing, and computer skills to accomplish long-term school project *(with City Year members)* and effectively strengthen individual student knowledge, pride, and enthusiasm with 90% passing rate.

PROFESSIONAL TEACHING EXPERIENCE

Metropolitan Public School District   1999–Present

ELEMENTARY TEACHER—Fourth Grade

Four years of experience at John Smith Elementary School. Plan, implement, and evaluate various curriculum areas. Encourage cooperative learning and peer interaction, and increase achievement levels among disadvantaged and challenged students. Appointed by principal as Grade Chairman and Mentor (2000–2003).

45

Combination. *Darlene Dassy, Harleysville, Pennsylvania*

The applicant had been a nun serving the Catholic community more than 15 years. Nuns were moved around a lot, and she didn't want her resume to give the false impression that she was a

PROFESSIONAL TEACHING EXPERIENCE (continued)

Sacred Heart School   1995–1998

ELEMENTARY TEACHER—Third Grade

Three years of experience instructing students in subject areas of reading, integrated language arts, religion, and social studies. Coordinated and implemented language arts program for first- to fourth-grade students.

State Area Parochial School System   1989–1995

ELEMENTARY TEACHER—Third and Fourth Grade

- Saint Joseph Regional School
- Blessed Sacrament School
- Our Lady of Perpetual Help

Metropolitan Parochial School System   1978–1988

ELEMENTARY TEACHER—First and Second Grade

- Immaculate Heart of Mary School
- Our Lady of the Holy Souls School
- Saint Timothy School

TEACHING TESTIMONIALS

"Judith has, from the outset, displayed a level of professional competence and a striving for professional development which has benefited her students, our staff, and the entire school community in concrete ways. She introduced and implemented a variety of innovative classroom management strategies, such as Workshop Way and Integrated Language Arts, having been the first to pilot such a program in our school. She has challenged and motivated students to achievement and activities which have not only developed each child's personal gifts and talents, but also developed cooperative learning strategies to foster collaboration and interaction among her students."
                                                                                             G.S., Principal

"Judy's professionalism, enthusiasm, and talent as a teacher are evident on a daily basis. Judy employs a thematic approach, and the varied learning experiences the children have to showcase their talents are not just one-time activities but related to all curriculum areas. Judy is comfortable with and flexible in following many different styles of administration and has been recommended to assume leadership roles many times during her career."
                                                                                             F.B., School Administrator

PROFESSIONAL DEVELOPMENT COURSES

Attended and participated in various courses from 1998–2004, including

▪ The Middle Years Literacy Framework	▪ Professional Education for Central-East AAO
▪ Middle Years Balanced Literacy	▪ Rigby Guided Reading & Literature Circles
▪ Academy of Reading Program	▪ Improving Decision-Making/Values Clarification
▪ Bringing Curriculum to Life	▪ Improving Ability to Communicate Mathematically
▪ Accelerated Reading Program	▪ Everyday Math Program & PowerPoint for Educators

FORMAL REFERENCES AND CONTACT INFORMATION AVAILABLE UPON REQUEST

"job hopper." The writer therefore focused on the applicant's accomplishments, credentials, and teaching testimonials so as not to draw attention to dates of employment. The administrators' testimonials near both the beginning and the end are tributes to the candidate and the quality of her teaching.

KELLY MINOGUE

60 Maple Court • Princeville, New York 55555 • (222) 222-2222 Phone/Fax

Creative, high-energy teacher with excellent communication skills, a strong classroom presence, and a passion for helping children learn and grow

SUMMARY OF QUALIFICATIONS

- Candidate for State Teacher Certificate in June 2004 with nearly a year of teaching experience through the alternative licensing route program.
- Strong knowledge of effective teaching pedagogy and assessment methods.
- Extensive background in guiding children. Skilled in planning and coordinating appropriate learning experiences for children that are both fun and valuable.
- Demonstrated sensitivity to the needs of children from all backgrounds and ability levels.
- Team player with recognized leadership ability. Proven role model for children.
- Resourceful problem-solver with solid classroom management skills.
- Outstanding ability to build rapport and work cooperatively with others.
- Assertive and self-confident. Go-getter who thrives on new challenges and is motivated by the desire to instill strong values and love of learning in children.

CLASSROOM EXPERIENCE

CANTERBURY SCHOOL, Rosemont Park, New York   Sep 2003 to present
Elementary Teacher—Grade 5
Teach 5th-grade students, implementing all aspects of the academic curriculum in math, social studies, and language arts. Participate in parent-teacher conferences and HSA functions. Coach cheerleading squad.
- Successfully planned and taught thematic units on creative writing and world geography.
- Incorporated computer and art activities into the curriculum to expand learning opportunities.
- Effectively reinforced learning activities for classified students.
- Participated in technology training classes, introducing lessons to other teachers in unit.
- Led Varsity Cheerleading Team in competition, gaining first-place trophy and spirit award.

RELATED EXPERIENCE

COUNTRY DAY CAMP, Monroe, New York   Jun 1999 to Sep 1999
Senior Camp Counselor
Oversaw all group activities for 25 five- and six-year-old boys. Supervised junior counselor.
- Won Best Counselor Award as first-year counselor, effectively handling group generally acknowledged as one of the most difficult in camp.

SELF-EMPLOYMENT, Fog Harbor, Maine   Jun 1997 to Sep 1997
Live-in Nanny
Entrusted with the care of four children aged 5 through 12.
- Attended to all four children's needs around the clock, six days a week.
- Earned respect and cooperation of youngest boy, a difficult, undisciplined child, through empathetic consideration and effective interaction.

JILL'S KIDS, West Port, New York   Jun 1996 to Sep 1996
Swim Instructor
Planned and conducted swimming classes for 15 to 20 youngsters.
- Effectively planned lessons that provided appropriate instruction for children at all skill levels.
- Staged well-received swim show for the benefit of parents.

46

Combination. *Carol A. Altomare, Three Bridges, New Jersey*

The applicant got a good response from this updated version of an earlier resume done by the same writer. A two-line profile in italic fills a spot traditionally occupied by an Objective

PROFESSIONAL EXPERIENCE

LAKES PRIVATE LEDGER, Santa Rosita, California   Jan 2001 to Feb 2003
Advisory Operations Specialist
Served as liaison between account representatives and portfolio managers while handling range of portfolio support activities.

GLAVIN & ASSOCIATES, INC., Harper Point, New York   Sep 1999 to Jun 2000
Asset Manager
Assumed full range of asset-management responsibilities while participating in all phases of real estate advisory business. Monitored and evaluated 500 to 600 properties.

EDUCATION

Bachelor of Arts Degree, State University, Brunswick, New York, 1999

Activities:
Rho Zeta Tau Sorority, 1996 to 1999 (Held several leadership roles, including president.)
State University Varsity Cheerleading Squad, 1995 to 1997

CERTIFICATIONS

State Certification in Elementary Education (K–8), expected August 2004
Safety Clinic Coach Certification

COMPUTER SKILLS

Microsoft Word, Excel, PowerPoint, Explorer, Outlook. Netscape Navigator.

References Gladly Provided upon Request

statement. A well-developed Summary of Qualifications sells the applicant's merits. In the Experience sections, prose statements under the job title indicate responsibilities. Bulleted items indicate achievements. A number of professional writers use this effective duties-achievements format.

Allie L. Rees

alrees@yahoo.com
Home Address: 30 Summit Trail ▼ Sparta, New York 12345 ▼ 555.123.4567
School Address: 26 East State Street ▼ The Plains, Ohio 45780 ▼ 740.797.0000

"… Wow! Very attractive and engaging materials … love to see students 'beg' to learn using her created materials for the Learning Center … confident and positive; her students' self-esteem was enhanced by this … exhibited an excellent knowledge base and understanding of the nature and needs of students with special needs … she will be an asset in any educational environment."

~ Excerpts from Student Teaching Evaluations

OBJECTIVE

Special Education Teacher

Enthusiastic and creative educator offering a solid educational background, including B.S. in Education with a major in Special Education. Successful student-teaching experience and observations as evidenced by excellent evaluations from supervising teachers and university professors. Skilled in meeting the needs of special-education students—experienced in working with IAT, MFE, and IEP planning and implementation. Additional experience in testing and assessment.

EDUCATION & HONORS

OHIO UNIVERSITY, Athens, Ohio (June 2004)
Bachelor of Science in Education   Major in Special Education, Mild Moderate
Education GPA: 3.52/4.0 ▼ Overall GPA: 3.24/4.0 ▼ Successfully passed PRAXIS exam
Kappa Delta Pi Education Fraternity ▼ Dean's List ▼ POWER (Nationally Certified Peer Health Educator)

Computer Skills
Computer proficient—experienced in use of various forms of assistive technology, PowerPoint, Microsoft Office 98/2000/XP, Internet and e-mail functions

RELATED EXPERIENCE

Student Teacher—MORRISON ELEMENTARY SCHOOL, Athens, Ohio (January–March 2004)
  ▼ Developed and implemented lesson plans in K–4 Resource Room in conjunction with supervising teachers.
  ▼ Established attainable educational goals for students, which promoted personal and educational growth.
  ▼ Participated in IAT, MFE, and IEP planning sessions with parents, teachers, and administrators.
  ▼ Tailored educational curriculum to IEPs for children with a variety of disabilities.
  ▼ Gained experience utilizing the Stevenson program for presenting phonic patterns and testing.
  ▼ Created an entire learning center based on IEP goals—used Pokemon theme to significantly increase children's interest and participation.

Field Experience—MORRISON ELEMENTARY, Athens, Ohio (Spring 2003)
Field Experience—THE PLAINS ELEMENTARY, The Plains, Ohio (Fall 2002)
  ▼ Gained valuable experience observing a variety of teaching techniques and implementing daily lesson plans in diverse settings (K–6 classrooms).
  ▼ Served as a classroom aide and assisted with tutoring and assessing/teaching groups of 1–14 students with mild to moderate disabilities.
  ▼ Participated in data collection for the Positive Behavior Supports program implemented at Luke Middle School in Luke Valley, Ohio.

Child Care Counselor—WILLOWGLEN ACADEMY, Newton, New Jersey (Academic Breaks 2000–2002)
  ▼ Counseled children with severe behavior disorders.
  ▼ Gained experience working with autistic children while serving as a teacher's aide and working in group homes.

COMMUNITY INVOLVEMENT

  ▼ Tri-County Mental Health and Counseling—Volunteered with patients and planned recreational activities.
  ▼ Good Works—Volunteered at this temporary homeless shelter.

47

Combination. *Melissa L. Kasler, Athens, Ohio*

A challenge with education resumes for college graduates with the same credentials and experience is to separate an applicant from the competition. Quotations from evaluations can do just that.

Robert Valencia
404 Fortsolanga Lane
Bayshore, NY 11706
(631) 382-2425

Overview

Patient, understanding, and firm *Special Education Teacher* who enjoys enhancing the quality education of high-risk students. Combine a unique balance of humor, empathy, and stability into the classroom.

Summary of Qualifications

- Develop innovative classroom instruction consistent with educational plans and treatment goals. Integrate knowledge of New York State special education laws, rules, and regulations into lesson plans.

- Sensitive to students' backgrounds, interests, and handicaps. Fluent in Spanish and American Sign Language.

- Effectively manage behavior of students to create a safe physical and emotional classroom environment.

Education

Master of Science in Special Education, Dowling College, Oakdale, NY, 2000
Special Education Certification and New York State Certification, 2000

Bachelor of Science, Biology, State University of New York, Stony Brook, NY, 1998

Professional Employment

Special Education Teacher, Pine Street Middle School, West Islip, NY, 2000
Student Teacher, Pine Street Middle School, West Islip, NY, 1998

Teach various populations including students with ADD; mental retardation; visually impaired; deaf and hearing impaired; developmental and learning disabilities; and physically, emotionally, and behaviorally challenged.

Classroom Management and Presentation

- Provide a clear, consistent structure for the classroom that ensures that the academic, social, and emotional needs of each student are met within the guidelines of the IEP.

- Assess students' abilities and implement creative lesson plans to motivate student learning. Highly successful teaching techniques include Visualarticulation, photography for language use and awareness, personal picture diaries to aid students in recognizing basic concepts through symbols, and positive-reinforcement programs.

- Incorporate the latest technology in the teaching process, including computers with synthesized speech, interactive educational software programs, and audiotapes.

- Incorporate academic subjects with daily activities education; recommend integration/inclusion of students in mainstream education.

Interpersonal Skills

- Cooperate in a multidisciplinary team that includes parents, social workers, school psychologists, occupational and physical therapists, and school administrators.

- Review and present students' IEPs to parents, administrators, and classroom teachers.

Affiliation

New York State Special Education Teacher Association

48

Combination. *Linda Matias, Smithtown, New York*

A pair of horizontal half-lines directs attention to the Overview section. It has a brief profile and a Summary of Qualifications. Boldfacing helps to draw attention downward to degrees and positions.

Kalista Jabert

555 Adams Street, Lowell, MA 08152 (617) 453-9988

"...Kalista has been a godsend for my son...her attentiveness and commitment have resulted in him making progress we never dreamed of..." Parent of Student, 2003

Sensitive, creative and patient Special Education teacher with more than 12 years of experience in championing educational and developmental student needs. Masters-prepared professional who works collaboratively to develop innovative, age-appropriate solutions for behaviorally and emotionally challenged K–4 students.

Determined and tireless worker who forges strong relationships with other educators, administrators and parents. Additional experience in delivering presentations, writing grants and providing full-time care for special-needs children.

EDUCATION

Fitchburg State College, Fitchburg, MA
M.Ed. in Early Childhood Education,1997

Lesley College, Cambridge, MA
B.S. in Education
Dual Certification in Moderate Special Needs and Elementary Education with a Minor in Psychology

TEACHING EXPERIENCE

Special Education Teacher, Grades 1–4
Todd Alternative School—Lowell, MA
Fall 1998–Present

- Design and implement curricula to meet the individual needs of behaviorally/emotionally challenged special-needs students.
- Brainstorm and strategize comprehensive behavioral management plans with teachers, aides and parents.
- Chosen as Team Chairperson to lead development and implementation of individualized educational plans.

Fourth-Grade Teacher
Summer School Program—Lowell, MA
Summer 2003

- Implemented and supplemented age-appropriate curricula to meet the needs of fourth-grade students working below grade level.
- Received "Excellence in Teaching" award from school principal.

Inclusion Specialist
Concord Public Schools—Concord, MA
Summer 2001

- Designed interactive workshop to facilitate understanding of daily disability challenges faced by students.
- Trained staff of 25 to work with children of varying disabilities in a regular camp setting.
- Collaborated with staff and designed activities to include a seven-year-old girl with tuberosclerosis in the regular Concord Recreation Program.

49

Combination. *Gail Frank, Tampa, Florida*

The resume writer used a number of techniques to make prominent a special-education teacher's gifts and "tremendous dedication to her profession." A strong opening summary

Third-Grade Teacher
Donahue Elementary School—Lowell, MA
1995–1998

- Implemented and supplemented curricula in a regular third-grade classroom.
- Teamed with Chapter I, ESL and Special Education teachers and devised curricula to meet the individual needs of the student population.
- Developed and taught thematic units to enhance student involvement and participation, such as a class company owned and operated by students.

Behavior Management Program Teacher
Reilly Elementary School—Lowell, MA
1992–1995

- Developed a behavior-management program that provided a positive and nurturing environment for students in grades 1–4.
- Implemented strong comprehensive behavior modification programs to coincide with individualized academic programs.
- Conducted home visits that linked home and school as partners in development.

RELATED EXPERIENCE

Grant Recipient
Innovative Teacher Mini-Grant, The Reynolds Foundation

- Wrote extensive grant request that won funding for a teacher-developed unit to match the Massachusetts Curriculum Frameworks. Titled *Creating the Sky,* it was a program that allowed children to create a sky consistent with the Earth and Space Science Strand.

Camp Fatima Counselor, Exceptional Citizens' Week
Abraham, NH
Summers 1996–Present

- Selected as counselor at Camp Fatima: a charitable overnight summer camp for disabled children. Requested to return for 9 consecutive summers.
- Paired with one severely disabled camper and performed all living, health and personal-care needs for an entire week.
- Led local fund-raising events such as bake sales and donor drives throughout the year to benefit camp.

Behavioral Consultant
Lowell Public Schools—Lowell, MA
Spring 2002

- Developed and presented 5 interactive workshops for teachers and administrators on behavioral management at the Sullivan Elementary School.

highlights the applicant's master's degree, creativity, and "total package" for anyone seeking a special-ed professional. The quotation in the left column from a satisfied parent emphasizes the person's competence without seeming like bragging. The heading font adds a sense of playfulness.

CERTIFICATIONS:
Elementary N–6
Special Ed. K–12

𝔄lexandra 𝔖tack

931 Columbia Street ❧ Poughkeepsie, NY 00000   (555) 555-5555

Objective

Secondary Special Education Teaching Position
𝔅elieve that society benefits when all individuals are able to achieve their maximum learning potential.

Spirited, optimistic, and reflective individual with an outstanding attitude and a strong motivation to develop a caring learning community where students with exceptionalities can more fully participate. Offer positive interaction skills and the creativity necessary to accommodate unique needs. Respect a broad range of instructional methodologies and prepared to take collaborative approaches to teaching.

➜ Capable of making sound educational judgments (formed by theory, research, and best practices)

➜ Eager to promote understanding/respect for individual differences and unique learning needs

➜ Skilled at gaining the trust and respect of youth and conveying confidence in their abilities

➜ Possess a sound understanding of developmental issues and exposed to a wide range of disabilities

Education

Union College, Troy, NY	**May 2002**
B.A. in Psychology / Special Education / Elementary Education	GPA 3.49

Herkimer Community College, Herkimer, NY	**January 1998**
A.A. in Liberal Arts and Science—Humanities and Social Sciences	

Student Teaching

Connor Stevens High School (Westchester CSD)   1/02 to 3/02
Reading I & Reading II (Special Education)

Formulated intensive reading lessons, incorporating multiple modalities and engaging *all* students—inviting them to listen, share, explore, and reflect. Utilized Orton Gillingham methods and devised creative approaches to integrating literacy and technology. Established well-organized classroom routines, set appropriate academic expectations, and provided positive experiences to build self-esteem.

Titusville Elementary School (Mohawk CSD)   4/02 to 5/02
Sixth Grade (Inclusion Class)

Structured a positive and supportive environment that maximized student participation and success. Commended on effectiveness in teaching both small and large groups. Created integrated math and science lessons and made appropriate adaptations to address individual learning styles.

Freedom Plains Elementary School (Hyde Park)   9/01 to 12/01
Preschool (3 & 4 year olds)

Developed age-appropriate centers that incorporated proactive social-skill activities. Developed lessons that focused on reading and math readiness and incorporated enrichment activities. Utilized many hands-on activities, manipulatives, and discovery learning to develop large motor skills.

Additional Areas of Experience

- Devising developmentally appropriate lessons
- Cross-disciplinary coordinated service delivery
- Lexia Learning Systems/phonics-based programs
- Structuring a positive, encouraging environment
- Establishing clear expectations and class routines
- Adapting instruction based on ability levels

Volunteer Experience

Titusville School, *Cafeteria Aide / Playground Monitor*	**1999 to 2000**
Mohawk Elementary School, *Parent Helper, Kindergarten*	**1997 to 1998**
Pine Plains School, *Lunchroom Aide / Playground Monitor*	**1993 to 1994**

50

Combination. *Kristin M. Coleman, Poughkeepsie, New York*

This resume may look difficult to create, but it can be done as a three-column table in which the first column has the headings, the second is narrow for space, and the third is wide for the information.

TRAVIS KENSETH

9803 Clinton Avenue ▪ Lubbock, TX 00000 ▪ (000) 000-0000 ▪ name@ntws.net

FOCUS & OVERVIEW	**Career Target: Secondary Education Instructor & Coach** ▪ *Profile*—Enthusiastic, dependable teaching candidate with solid knowledge base/skills in instruction and coaching-related functions that include instructional strategies, scouting, student relations, special populations, and professional ethics. ▪ *Evaluations*—Earned recognition from university professors and supervisors in employment positions for consistently meeting and exceeding expectations. ▪ *General Traits*—Effective communicator and multi-tasker; adapt readily to changing circumstances. Value diversity within school groups; favor student-centered teaching. ▪ *Specific Skills*—Proficient in MS Office suite ▪ First-Aid Certification—Responding to Emergencies ▪ Strong knowledge in and advocate of functionalism theory in sports.
EDUCATION	**Teacher Certification Program** ▪ NORTHLAND COLLEGE, Northland, TX ❑ Expected completion in 5/04 for secondary education certification program. ❑ Engaged in combination of lectures, class assignments, and formal observations. **BS in Kinesiology, 2001** ▪ UNIVERSITY OF TEXAS, Austin, TX *Key Courses & Projects:* ❑ <u>**Administrative Theory/Practice in Athletic and Sport Regulatory Organizations**</u>—Analyzed process for securing professional position within sports industry; examined ethical, legal, philosophical, and professional development issues. ❑ <u>**Facilities, Equipment, and Budget for Athletics**</u>—Created and presented plan to class for construction of sports facility, including blueprints, materials, and cost analysis. Utilized software, Internet research, and phone calls to local businesses. ❑ <u>**Movement for Special Populations**</u>—Worked one-on-one with disabled student in locomotor and object control activities, followed by creation of adapted physical education lesson plan. Gained insight into mainstreaming of special ed. students. ❑ <u>**Coaching Football**</u>—Sent on assignment to scout TCU-UTEP football game. Applied extensive prior study of scouting techniques and proper formats to follow in charting plays, analyzing individual performances, and summarizing findings. *Additional Upper-Level Courses:* Sociology of Sports ▪ Coaching Football ▪ Motor Behavior ▪ Psychology of Sports Physiological Bases of Exercise & Sports ▪ Coaching Individual Sports **AA & AS Degrees, 1998/1997** ▪ WEATHERFORD COLLEGE, Weatherford, TX
WORK EXPERIENCE	**Customer Service Associate** ▪ HOME DEPOT, Austin, TX (1998–Present) ❑ Recognized frequently by customers for providing solutions to meet individual needs, leading to repeat/referral business and requests for personal service. **Courier** ▪ TEXAS BANK, Austin, TX (1996–1998) ❑ Managed multiple tasks effectively in deadline-driven environment. Delivered inter-office mail, transferred daily deposits, and prepared supplies for all branches. **Customer Service Representative** ▪ RENTER'S CHOICE, Austin, TX (1995–1996) ❑ Maintained excellent record of resolving problems and handling stressful situations that involved collection activities and challenging customers.

51

Combination. *Daniel J. Dorotik, Jr., Lubbock, Texas*

The applicant's work experience was unrelated to his career target, so the writer emphasized skills and school-related project work. Shading helps to distinguish headings from the information.

Meets Federal Highly Qualified Teaching Standards   *Available for relocation*

CARLTON MARNER

214 Central Street • Montgomery, Alabama 36100 • cm200@sss.com • ☎ 334.555.5555

WHAT I CAN OFFER YOUR SCHOOL AS A **HISTORY TEACHER** _____

- The **character** to establish and maintain classroom discipline.

- The **academic background** to make my subject come alive for your students.

- The **tact** to establish strong "partnerships" with peers, parents, administrators, and students.

EDUCATION AND RELEVANT INSERVICE DEVELOPMENT_____

- **Masters of Education in History Education,** Corona State University, Montgomery, Alabama, Aug 01

  Earned this degree while working 40 hours a week by day and carrying a full academic load at night. GPA: 3.75.

- **B.S., History,** Mark State University—Montgomery, Montgomery, Alabama, Aug 99. *GPA 3.95+, **Dean's List.** One of very few college students to be inducted into two national honor societies for* **academic achievement.**

- More than 32 hours of the following **inservice training** over the last two years alone:

DAT Inservice	Special Education Issues	Bullying Issues
Writing Assessment	Gifted Characteristics	Co-operative Discipline
School Safety	Yes, We Can Get Along	SAT 10
Special Education Team Development	SAT Testing and Interpreting Scores	Integrating Technology in the Classroom
7th Grade Writing Assessment	Effective Classroom Management	ESL
Teacher Mentorship Program		

- "Guidance Counseling," U.S. Army, five weeks, 85. *Selected by senior decision makers for this course. One of very few to have experience requirements waived.*

RECENT WORK HISTORY WITH EXAMPLES OF PROBLEMS SOLVED _____

- **School Teacher,** Tether Middle School, Montgomery, Alabama, Aug 01–Present

  Tether has an average total enrollment of 760, of which I teach five classes averaging 30 students per class, including mainstreamed special education students. AY is nine months.

  Turned around, gently but firmly, a disruptive special education student whose behavior had thwarted other teachers for months. Parents had become so frustrated that they sued— and won—to keep him enrolled. *Outcomes:* He **met every class's academic standards and passed**—a great confidence builder for him.

More indicators of performance your school can use ☞

52

Combination. *Don Orlando, Montgomery, Alabama*

This writer successfully presents fresh approaches in resumes. Information other than the candidate's name is at the top of the first page. A phone symbol signals the phone number. "What I

Carlton Marner	**History Teacher**	334.555.5555

Took on a challenge others shied away from: teaching a failing student whose parents had pulled him from school. Volunteered to work closely with school counselors to cover the entire curriculum at his home, after normal hours. *Outcomes:* **He's now learning at his grade level.**

Stepped in smoothly when an influx of Korean students, with nearly no proficiency in English, were mainlined throughout the school. With my wife's volunteer help, soon gave the newcomers confidence to learn to their potential. *Outcomes:* **Every Korean student getting straight "A's"** — after only one year with us.

Joined with one other faculty member to take on the additional duty of guiding the Student Council. Took the lead to reestablish close ties with community leaders. *Outcomes:* **Students raised nearly $5K for needy children over the last two years.**

- Full-time student. Completed **B.S., History** and **Masters in Education**, 97–01

- *More than 20 years of experience in positions of increasing responsibility as a non-commissioned officer in the U.S. Army, serving in these capacities from 76 to 97:*

Overhauled an education program I inherited that wasn't giving our team members the skills they needed to reach high school students. **Did the needs analysis** and then **built the right curriculum.** *Outcomes:* In three months, our group turned in its **best performance ever.** All done without spending an extra dime.

Reached out to faculty and administrators in local minority schools. Found a way to **equip their guidance counselors** with a **comprehensive assessment instrument** and the training they needed to use it well. Sponsored career days. *Outcomes:* **Demand** for our participation **grew steadily.**

LICENSURE _____

- Certified 6th- through 12th-grade history teacher, State of Alabama, expires 06.

COMPUTER LITERACY _____

- **Expert** in proprietary program that **matches people to jobs** and **assesses student values and aptitudes.**

- Fully proficient in PowerPoint, Excel, Word, Internet Search Methods, Harvard Graphics.

SKILLS USEFUL TO A DIVERSE STUDENT BODY _____

- Working knowledge of Korean language and culture.

Can Offer. . ." introduces the first main section. Comments in italic appear throughout the resume. Solutions to problems narrated in prose paragraphs are indicated as "Outcomes," with key information enhanced with boldfacing—a novel way to present achievements.

BRYSON CARSON
265 Charlotte Street
Cookville, NC 00000

(555) 000-7893 *home*
(555) 111-7893 *cell*
bcarson@hometown.net

HISTORY TEACHER
North Carolina License, Social Studies 9–12

PROFILE

Proactive, uncompromising focus on improving reading, writing, and critical-thinking skills. Use flexibility, resourcefulness, and organizational and interpersonal skills to assist that learning through a positive, encouraging environment.

Strengths

- Capable teacher thoroughly grounded in U.S., Middle East, World, and European history.
- Rapport-builder with parents (they think they're all alone out there), able to gain their involvement, trust, and respect in creating a participative environment.
- Adept, available, and adaptable classroom manager—combine discipline plan with effective procedures and varied lessons to attract the inattentive and enforce student accountability.
- Student motivator—can use cooperative learning, jigsaw, and other student-directed, process learning techniques to foster a team spirit and build teamwork and goal-setting skills.
- Develop useful daily lesson plans and instructional resources.
- Friendly, interactive, dependable.
- Some fluency in Spanish (can read Spanish newspaper).

"A page of history is worth a volume of logic."—Oliver Wendell Holmes

EDUCATION

B.A., History, Magna cum Laude, December 2003
North Carolina University, Polk, NC

Coursework

- U.S. History, Medieval Europe, Politics of the Middle East, Political Science, Chinese History (Revolutionary China), Afro-American History, Human Rights & International Politics, Humanities. Dean's List every eligible semester.

Student Teaching

- Hall High School, spring and fall 2003—11th-grade college-prep classes in U.S. history. Selected to teach AP U.S. history class due to knowledge of material.
  - Contributions included judging senior projects, proctoring end-of-course tests, and sponsoring the fledgling Debate Club.
  - Because my co-op was on the school improvement team, was able to observe planning and goal-setting functions in the effort to meet constantly changing requirements.
  - Participated positively in parent-teacher conferences.

"I teach skill in asking questions through my skill in asking the right questions...."

Honors & Affiliations

- Selected for Phi Alpha Theta History National Honor Society (high GPA and faculty recommendation).
- Selected by History Department faculty for the Mike Bolson History Scholarship as a promising student in the field of history, despite being on an education track.
- Participant, NCU History Association.
- Alpha Phi Omega National Service Fraternity—Chapter President; as Vice President of Service, initiated projects involving boys' and girls' clubs; fund-raising for pediatric brain tumors; highway beautification; food bank.

Cited by department faculty for original, critical thinking....

53

Combination. *Dayna Feist, Asheville, North Carolina*

The applicant was a man in his 50s whose previous careers were in the Navy, fishing, and manufacturing. When manufacturing moved to Mexico, he returned to college for a degree under a

bcarson@hometown.net · 111-7893 *cell* · 000-7893 *home*   **BRYSON CARSON**

Prior Education	**Diploma, Welding** (one-year program), 1980 WNC Technical Community College Coursework in Anthropology, Biology, Spanish, 1973 University of Massachusetts—Boston
PRIOR EXPERIENCE	BOILER OPERATOR: Culverton Textiles, Foster, NC—1981–1998 Operated steam and electric generating utility for largest textile mill of its kind in the world, on 10 acres, with its own waste-treatment and water-filtration system; a self-contained mini-city, it generated much of its own power. Member of 2-man team: managed electrical control room, maintenance, welding, machinery repair, pipefitting. ENGINEER: 100-foot Bluestocking fishing boat, Gloucester, MA—1971–1980 MACHINIST MATE: United States Navy—1967–1971 Served on the U.S.S. *Georgetown* (traveled to Mozambique Civil War, the Indian Ocean, and Havana, Cuba) and U.S.S. *Severn* (oil tanker refueling ships at sea in the Mediterranean). Trained Navy personnel (including firemen and 3rd class petty officers) to work with tools and operate equipment.
COMMUNITY REINVESTMENT	▪ Coached Roller Hockey for boys' and girls' clubs, ages 13–18, in league competition. ▪ Tutor, Afterschool Club, Salvation Army. ▪ Big Brothers/Big Sisters, 1981–1983. Mentored 7-year-old boy (gardening, movies, sports, homework). He moved to another state. ▪ Member of church Inquiry Committee—answer questions to assist one in deciding whether to join the church; prepare lesson plans and curriculum for those interested in doing so.

special teachers' program to teach history. His goal was a highly competitive position at the school where he student taught. The resume writer sought to show how this individual will bring "an interesting mixture of authority, geniality, and intelligence to the classroom."

Keiko Taniguchi

5555 Hula Lane, No. 5555 • Honolulu, Hawaii 00000
Tel: (808) 555-5555 • E-Mail: ktaniguchi@hawaii.rr.com

Seeking Position As...

Japanese Language Instructor

Profile: Recent M.A. degree graduate with 5 years of practical teaching experience. Demonstrated ability to design developmentally appropriate curriculum. Expertise in selecting effective methodologies to teach Japanese language and culture based on students' objectives and proficiencies. B.A. in International Business. **Core Skills:**

- Course Design
- Textbook Selection
- Supplemental Materials Design/Selection

- Classroom Management
- Testing Design/Administration
- Student Advising

Native Japanese Speaker
Advanced Oral and Written English Fluency
Resident of Hawaii

Education

M.A., Japanese Linguistics (Pedagogy emphasis), 5/2004
University of Hawaii—Honolulu, Hawaii
GPA 4.0/4.0

B.A., International Business, 8/1992
Women's College of Miami—Miami, Florida
Who's Who Among International Students
Graduated Cum Laude; GPA 3.56/4.0

Teaching Background

Japanese Teacher   Spring 2004
Japanese Practicum. Direct hands-on teaching in JPN 101 class.
University of Hawaii—Honolulu, Hawaii

- Collaborated with three other graduate students to teach listening, speaking, reading, and writing skills to class of up to 14 students.
- Designed, administered, and graded oral and written quizzes, and mid-term and final examinations. Provided appropriate feedback to students.

ESL Teacher   1/1996–4/1998
Nagoya City Junior College—Nagoya, Japan

- Taught English in language lab for classes of up to 50 students at a time. Designed listening skills curriculum. Developed mid-term and final examinations.
- Advised interested students on living/studying abroad and related test preparation.
- Substituted for professors and assistant professors in English department.

54

Combination. *Peter Hill, Honolulu, Hawaii*

The individual was a Japanese national who recently received an MA degree in Japanese Linguistics and was seeking a post as a Japanese Language Instructor at an advanced institute

Keiko Taniguchi
Page 2 of 2

ESL Teacher 2/1993–5/1996
NEON English Conversation School—Nagoya City, Japan

- Taught English conversation and grammar to Japanese students of English. Included TOEFL, TOEIC, and national English proficiency test courses.
- Planned and implemented developmentally appropriate curriculum focusing on oral communication skills.
- Managed class sizes of one to twelve students, from junior high school students to adults.

Business-Related Experience

Export Sales Coordinator 7/1992–2/1993
Tokyo Pens, Inc.—Tokyo, Japan

- Coordinated order fulfillment for China sales representative.
- Interpreted on behalf of company's English-speaking foreign visitors.

Assistant to Vice President (Internship) Spring 1992
U.S. East Bank, Asian Division—Miami, Florida

- Performed data organization using IBM PC.
- Translated annual reports from Japanese to English.

Assistant to Director (Internship) Summer 1990
Sister State Program, International Division—Miami, Florida

- Conducted data analysis and research on various tour programs in Maryland.
- Planned, developed, and arranged tour itineraries for Japanese tourists.

Additional Skills

Computer: Word, Excel, Internet Explorer, Outlook/Entourage, SPSS

Certified Interpreter of Japanese and English, Japan Interpreters Association

• • •

for management science. The writer highlighted skills the applicant acquired as an English teacher and included the business-related experience she had. Center-aligned main headings and certain key information make it easy for the reader to look down the middle of the pages and size up the resume's content.

Richard G. Murasaki

5555 Sandcrab Lane • Kailua, Hawaii 00000
Tel: (808) 555-5555 • Pager: (808) 555-5551
E-mail: rgmurasaki@islandnet.com

Executing a planned transition into...

Healthcare Administration Support / Customer Relations

Summary: Dedicated, resourceful professional with 14+ years of service-oriented experience in sales, education, business, and volunteerism. Readily develop rapport with superiors, colleagues, and customers. Proven ability to work effectively as part of a team and with people from other cultures. Confident, reliable, organized, and detail-oriented.

Core competencies include:

• Customer Service	• Communication Skills	• Teamwork Facilitation
• Interpersonal Skills	• Documentation	• Research
• Presentations	• Planning	• Organization

Fluent in Japanese • Basic Computer Literacy

Employment History

FUJIGAOKA HIGH SCHOOL—Fujigaoka, Japan   1999–2004
Largest enrollment in Western Japan; 150 faculty and staff members.

<u>Assistant English Language Teacher</u>: Partnered with native Japanese teacher to organize and lead English conversation classes of 8 to 50 students. Planned yearly course curriculum. Designed, administered, and corrected exams. Selected textbooks.

- Designed and implemented previously nonexistent pair work and group activities.
- Boosted student interest and involvement in class by designing unique lesson plans.
- Formed after-school English Conversation Club. Provided extracurricular English study activities and study-hall environment. Assisted students with college entrance exam preparation.
- Earned reputation as reliable source of information on studying abroad. Counseled students on options for future study.
- Reviewed incoming student entrance examination. Suggested revisions.

TOKYO LANGUAGE AND CULTURE CENTER—Fukuoka, Japan   1996–1999
Leading nationwide language school for business professionals.

<u>English Conversation Instructor</u>: Led English conversation classes for corporate managers and employees at companies such as Nippon Steel, Mitsubishi Chemical, and Asahi Glass. Prepared lesson plans, and taught and evaluated students.

- Persuaded school management to update and consolidate activity report/student evaluation preparation procedures. Saved time and resources for new and veteran teachers.
- Successfully guided students to an understanding of how to apply their English skills to real-world daily life and business situations.
- Regularly received positive evaluations from students regarding punctuality, consistent performance, and interesting/well-prepared lesson plans.

55

Combination. *Peter Hill, Honolulu, Hawaii*

This applicant had spent the past seven years teaching English in Japan. Drawing on the person's service-oriented experience, the writer positioned the individual for a customer service

Richard G. Murasaki

NATIONAL DIRECTORIES—Honolulu, Hawaii   1993–1995
Fortune 500 provider of Yellow Pages *advertising.*

> <u>Sales Representative</u>: Trained to be an effective and efficient salesperson. Promoted ad space in *Yellow Pages.* Canvassed assigned territory within given guidelines and deadlines.
>
> * Recognition: 3 regional awards for highest sales volume; 2 awards for paperwork accuracy; 1 award for highest sales volume for Maui campaign.
> * Demonstrated commitment to clients by emphasizing after-sales service.

SOUTH SHORE MARINE SERVICES—Honolulu, Hawaii   1987–1992
Commercial fishing vessel fueling company. Family business.

> <u>Manager/Accounting Clerk</u>: Handled all office administrative duties. Included customer service; company correspondence; advertising and promotions; purchasing and sales; payroll and accounting; recruiting, dismissing, and supervising personnel.
>
> * Fostered atmosphere of open communication and camaraderie among employees and with customers.
> * Ensured appropriate treatment of VIP clientele.

Community Activities

Volunteer: National English speech contest in Japan (8 years), local Cub Scout and Boy Scout troops (2 years each), and Rehabilitation Center of the Pacific (one summer).

Vice President: College student-church organization.

Education

Bachelor of Business Administration (Marketing)
University of Hawaii at Manoa—Honolulu, Hawaii

post in the healthcare field. A descriptive line in italic under each workplace in the Employment History section tells the reader something about each workplace. Underlining below each position held makes it possible to spot each position when the reader's eyes sweep across that section.

Barbara Joanne Blake *B.A., B.Ed.*

2222 Augusta View S.W.
Pinehurst, Alberta A1A 1A1
Phone: (444) 222-8888

Visual Arts Teacher
Intermediate & Senior

• • •

"Mrs. Blake is one of the most outstanding teachers I have met in my 22 years of teaching."

Creative and dedicated Visual Arts teacher committed to creating meaningful and stimulating art programmes to improve students' ability, creativity, appreciation, perception, awareness, concentration, confidence, and motivation. Exhaustive teaching experience in a wide range of visual media. Skilled in designing arts programs to complement core courses. Able to inspire children to stretch themselves and their work. Extensive leadership experience in school, volunteer, and community activities.

Teachable media include basic and advanced programs in

- Clay
- Free Form
- Group of Seven / Inuit Art
- Paint / Pencil
- Mixed Media
- Van Gogh
- Wire Sculpture
- Photography
- War / Militaria

EDUCATION & PROFESSIONAL DEVELOPMENT

Visual Arts—Part 3, Specialist	OISE, University of Augusta
Integrated Arts	Ontario Arts Education Institute
Meaningful Activities to Generate Interesting Classrooms	O.P.S.T.F.
English as a Second Language—Part 1	Pinehurst University
Canadian Art History	University of Ontario
B.Ed.—Visual Arts 2 / School Librarianship	University of Ontario
B.A.—Fine Arts	University of Manitoba

• • •

"She demonstrates an enthusiasm for the subject matter which is infectious."

TEACHING EXPERIENCE

Developed and implemented dynamic lessons designed to teach a rich variety of artistic techniques, appeal to multiple intelligences, and enrich student learning. Established dynamic learning environments that highlight student work and stimulate creative expression. Introduced and led Intermediate art clubs ("Creatots") that allowed students to create art projects for school and charitable initiatives (posters, play backdrops, etc.).

Placements include the following:

Bayridge Hill Elementary School, Berry Hill, Ontario **Visual Arts Teacher**—Grades 6, 7, & 8	1994–2002
Holy Trinity Catholic School, Berry Hill, Ontario **Visual Arts Teacher**—Grades 9 to O.A.C.	Oct.–Nov.1994
Bayridge Secondary School, Berry Hill, Ontario **Visual Arts Teacher**—Grades 9 to O.A.C.	1993–1994
Augusta Region Board of Education—Area Central **Occasional Teacher**	1990–1993
St. Avenue Secondary High School, Sarnia, Ontario **Visual Arts Teacher / Teacher-Librarian**—Grades 9, 10, & 11	1976–1980

• • •

"Barbara's creative mind, knowledge, and teaching ability combine to produce student work that is totally reflective of the keen interest, desire, knowledge, and skill level she has developed in her students."

56

Combination. *Ross Macpherson, Pickering, Ontario, Canada*

Quotations in the left column of each page acquaint the reader with the applicant's teaching abilities, enthusiasm, creativity, artistic skills, concern for students, effectiveness as a teacher,

• • •

"Barbara uses her incredible ability as an artist and art teacher to affect every aspect of school life."

CURRICULUM DEVELOPMENT

- **Art Action Team: Augusta Region District School Board (ARDSB)**—Selected to participate in the planning and facilitation of art workshops for teachers across the board.
- **Van Gogh: A Guidebook for Looking at Art, Grades 1–8**—Worked with ARDSB Art Consultant to develop an integrated curriculum kit on Vincent Van Gogh, including history, books, materials, prints, and activities.
- **Teach Art 3: A Visual Arts Curriculum Guide**—Invited by Heather Hearst to participate in focus group contributing to the development of a Grade 3 Art curriculum.
- **Outcome-Based Learning Study Team**—Served as Art Representative on school committee developing an outcome-based learning curriculum.

ARTS ADVOCACY

- Developed and directed *Arts Alive: Series 2003 Performing Arts Programme for Junior Kindergarten–Grade 8.*
- Coordinated *Careers in Art* After-School Speakers Series.
- Coordinated *Portraits of Our Past Art Show* in partnership with the Town of Berry Hill Heritage Centre.
- Coordinated Annual *Celebrate the Arts Night.*
- Presenter: Outdoor Education Weekend (Topic: Natural Dyes).

• • •

"[Barbara] has demonstrated extraordinary qualities of respect, dedication, and commitment to her students, to fellow human beings, and to her community."

SCHOOL & BOARD COMMITTEE INVOLVEMENT

- 10th Anniversary Committee (school mural)—Bayridge Hill Elementary School.
- Member of ARTSLINK Action Team Committee (ARDSB Millennium Project)—Secured Federal funding for program and coordinated school art shows board-wide.
- Committee Representative—ARDSB *Together We're Better* Conference.
- Intermediate Division Career Day Committee.
- School Fundraising Committee.
- Arts Representative—Bayridge Hill Elementary School.
- Staff Representative—Bayridge Hill Community School Advisory Council.
- Anti-Bullying Conference—Staff Support.

• • •

"The work displayed consistently by her students is to be marvelled at!"

EXTRACURRICULAR INVOLVEMENT

- Coordinated the Alternate Winter Sport Activity Program.
- Decorated display cases and bulletin boards to showcase student artwork and holiday themes.
- Annual Graduation Exercises Committee Coordinator (decorations).
- Coordinated art displays for Education Week .
- Volunteer Teacher (after hours)—Inuit presentations, watercolours, clay.

• • •

PUBLISHED ARTICLES

"CIA: 'Careers in Art' Program" – **Teachers Resource** (Curriculum & Instructional Services), ARDSB, Fall 1999.

helpfulness as a team player, global altruism, and positive influence on others. Such testimonials support all the factual data in the resume and help to win the reader over to the applicant as the one to consider seriously for a job opening. The easel graphic at the top of the first page prints in color. The applicant's

• • •

"[Barbara] is a fabulous team player and always looks for ways to help her colleagues. She has the biggest heart of anyone (save my immediate family) that I know."

• • •

"Under her leadership and direction staff, students, and parents have increased their knowledge of the plight of those less fortunate in other parts of the world."

• • •

"Barbara is a talented, dependable, knowledgeable, reliable, caring individual who continues to have a positive effect on those with whom she works and lives."

• • •

CHARITABLE / VOLUNTEER CONTRIBUTIONS (ACADEMIC)

- **Washington Hospital Burn Center Project**—Spearheaded a student relief project supporting victims of the September 11 Pentagon attack. Student contribution published in *Center Profiles*, the Washington Hospital magazine.

- **Canadian Feed the Children: Sierra Leone, Africa Project**—Coordinated school-wide initiative that provided 100+ knapsacks full of school supplies to children in Sierra Leone.

- **Project Love**—Created and led program that provided school supplies to schools in Ghana and Senegal.

- **Operation Shoebox: Covenant House**—Conceived and led a successful school-wide initiative that supplied 300+ shoeboxes of personal items to street children.

- **Help the Afghan Children**—Coordinated program to sell snacks during lunch period ("Loonie Tuesdays"). All proceeds quadrupled by CIDA and donated to World Vision.

- **Warm Hands Warm Hearts**—Initiated school program to collect winter clothing for Salvation Army.

CHARITABLE / VOLUNTEER CONTRIBUTIONS (NON-ACADEMIC)

- **Royal Canadian Air Cadets: 234 Banshee Squadron**—Clothing Coordinator, Parent Volunteer, and member of 30th Anniversary Committee.

- **Deer Creek Alliance Church, Deer Creek, Ontario**—Special Events Committee Member, Sunday School Teacher, and Coordinator of Grade 6 Sunday School Puppetry Program.

- **Augusta Region Skating Academy Winter Club**—Member of Board of Directors responsible for all publicity and communications.

- **Canadian Figure Skating Association, Central Augusta Section**—Developed and produced the programme booklet for the Sundial Sectional Championship (1994).

- **The Christian Alliance Church of Canada**—Created all conference stage decorations for the 10th Biannual National Assembly.

- **Bayridge Hill Elementary School**—Past President of parent-teacher liaison group (Partners in Education).

PERSONAL ACTIVITIES

Enjoy learning new crafts (calligraphy, stained glass, fabric arts, quilting), walking, and biking.

contributions "were so impressive that three pages were easily justified." If the writer were to keep the resume to two pages, the employer would not get to read about the person's charitable/voluntary work—information that is as diverse as it is impressive.

Jeremy Cloud

Current Address: 125 West Gibbs Street • Shade, Ohio 45701 • 740.696.0000
Permanent Address: 231 Louise Avenue • Racine, Ohio 45771 • 740.949.0000

High School Science Teacher

"Jeremy will make a great teacher ... builds great rapport with the students ... makes learning fun!"

– Sally Ball, Biology Teacher, Shade High School

PROFILE

Enthusiastic educator with an avid interest in all areas of science. Offering a solid educational background, including degree in Secondary Life Science as well as certifications in Project Wild and Project Learning Tree. Computer proficient. Seeking a high school teaching position with an interest in coaching track/cross country and/or advising extracurricular clubs.

EDUCATION & HONORS

OHIO UNIVERSITY, Athens, Ohio (June 2004)
Bachelor's Degree in Secondary Life Science
Major GPA: 3.24 • Dean's List

Relevant Courses
Microbiology ... Physics ... Chemistry ... Biology ... Plant Physiology ... Evolution

Certifications
Certified in Project Wild
  • Interdisciplinary conservation and environment education program exploring wildlife; supported by natural resource agencies

Certified in Project Learning Tree
  • Interdisciplinary environmental education program for educators working with students in Pre-K through Grade 12 focusing on the total environment: land, air, and water

RELEVANT EXPERIENCE

Student Teacher—NELSONVILLE-YORK HIGH SCHOOL, Buchtel, Ohio (April 2003–present)
  • Develop and implement lesson plans for anatomy, physiology, and biology classes

Tutor—PHILLIPS CENTER, Ohio University, Athens, Ohio (September–November 2002)
  • Effectively tutored student athletes in math, chemistry, and geology, resulting in improved test scores

ADDITIONAL WORK EXPERIENCE

Student Worker—BROMLEY DINING HALL, Ohio University, Athens, Ohio (June 2002–March 2003)
  • Utilized strong work ethic and excellent interpersonal communication skills while rotating through various areas of dining hall

Cashier/Baker—BRITISH PETROLEUM (BP), Bellevue, Ohio (Academic Breaks, October 2000–January 2002)
  • Performed a variety of duties with strong focus on providing superior customer service

Lifeguard—CEDAR POINT AMUSEMENT PARK, Sandusky, Ohio (June–September 2000)
  • Ensured safety of guests; responded successfully to a spinal-injury emergency

Combination. *Melissa L. Kasler, Athens, Ohio*

This person was a new graduate with a teaching degree. The cloud graphic was relevant to his last name and goal of science teaching. The graphic got many good comments, and the applicant got a quick job offer.

MARIA M. LEAL

(555) 555-5555 (H)   555 Quad Street, Prairie Stream, Texas 55555   **(555) 555-0000 (C)**
mariamleal@mindspring.net

INSTRUCTIONAL ADMINISTRATOR

HIGHLIGHTS OF QUALIFICATIONS

- *Master of Education in Educational Leadership from Greater Texas University, 2004*
- *Principal internship at Heartgood Elementary School, Spring 2004*
- *Thirteen years of teaching experience in a Title I School*
- *Expertise in elementary math curriculum, including cross-curricular integration, whole language, hands-on science, and math manipulatives*
- *Peer coaching/mentoring/team teaching experience*
- *Active participant in writing campus improvement plan, scheduling events, issuing waivers, writing grants, and projecting/preparing budgets*
- *Successful interaction with LEP, special needs, at-risk, and multicultural students*
- *Adept at building rapport with administrators, teachers, staff members, and students*
- *Proficient in both Mac and Windows-based computers*
- *Bilingual in English and Spanish*

CERTIFICATIONS

- *Mid-Management/Texas Principal Certification, 2003–Current*
- *Texas Teacher Certification (1st–8th Grades), Lifetime*

TEACHING EXPERIENCE

HEARTGOOD ELEMENTARY SCHOOL, Prairie Stream Independent School District, Prairie Stream, Texas   **1990–present**

Principal Internship (2003–2004)
Math Specialist, K–6 (2000–2003)
Self-Contained 3rd-Grade Teacher (all subjects) (1998–2000)
4th-Grade Math Teacher (1995–1998)
2nd- and 3rd- Grade Teacher (16 gifted students) (1994–1995)
Self-Contained 2nd-Grade Teacher (all subjects) (1990–1994)

Increased learning and TAAS/TAKS scores in self-contained and departmentalized classes using manipulatives, cooperative learning, hands-on activities, literature, thematic units, tutoring, and integrated subjects. Monitor math curriculum/instruction. Coach Creative Problem Solving Teams (previously Odyssey of the Mind) in grades 5–7. Taught and monitored gifted and talented students in grades K–6. Analyzed and disaggregated data from Benchmark Tests/Six Weeks Assessments, adjusting and modifying instruction to meet students' needs.

Key Contributions:

- *Frequently assume administrator's duties (discipline, ARD meetings, parent conferences, etc.), 1999–present*
- *Assist instructional specialists on district/school Benchmarks and TAAS/TAKS testing, 1999–present*
- *Organized and directed staff development training, 2000–2003*
- *Advanced Creative Problem Solving Teams to State Destination Imagination Competition, 2001, 2002, 2004; and to Global Finals, 2002*
- *Coordinate STARS (Student, Teachers Achieving Reading Success) Reading Mentor Program, 2000–2004; tutor participants*
- *Coordinated and scheduled school-wide TAAS/TAKS Tutoring Program, 1997–2003*
- *Assist Lego Team coach, 2001–present; and organized Summer Lego Academy, Summers 2002 and 2003*
- *Collaborated with two other teachers to restructure 1st-grade math curricula consistent with Sharon Wells 2nd–6th-grade spiral curriculum, 2001*
- *Mentored and tutored students in HOSTS Program, 1998–2000*
- *Scored into the 90th percentile on TAAS (a record for Heartgood), 1998c*

58

Combination. *Edith A. Rische, Lubbock, Texas*

The individual was a highly successful teacher applying for a principal position. A challenge for the writer was to condense a vast amount of information into two pages. There was room for

Maria Leal   **Page 2**

ACADEMIC BACKGROUND

Master of Education in Educational Leadership, 2003, Greater Texas University, Prairie Stream, Texas
   Mid-Management/Principal Certification

Master of Education in Elementary Education, 2001, Greater Texas University, Prairie Stream, Texas
   Area of Specialization: Elementary Math

Bachelor of Science in Elementary Education, 1995, Greater Texas University, Prairie Stream, Texas
   Area of Specialization: Elementary Reading

PROFESSIONAL DEVELOPMENT

- Sharon Wells Mathematics Curriculum Training (Grades 2–6), 1994–present
- Dual Language Training, 2002–present
- Gifted and Talented Update Training, 1999–present
- National Council of Teachers of Mathematics Conference, 2003, 2004
- Writing TAKS Training, January 2004
- Professional Development and Appraisal System (PDAS), June 2003
- Instructional Leadership Development, June 2004
- Math Academy for 5th and 6th Grades, August 2003
- Math TAKS Training, August 2003
- Reading TAKS Training, August 2003
- Conference for the Advancement of Mathematics Teaching, 1997–2003
- D-TEACH, Robo Lab Academy at University of Central Texas, Summer 2001
- Character Counts Training, 2002–2003
- Data Desegregation Training, Beth Manning, 1999–2004
- Gifted and Talented Students in the Regular Classroom, 2003
- PSISD Legal Issues Training, November 2000
- Captain Area Writing/Reading Summer Institute, June 2000
- Doing Math the Science Way, July 1999 and 2000

PROFESSIONAL ORGANIZATIONS

- Texas Council of Teachers of Mathematics, 2003–present
- National Council for Teachers of Mathematics, 2001–present
- Texas Classroom Teachers Association, 1995–present
- Prairie Springs Classroom Teachers Association, 1995–present

SELECTED EXTENDED PROFESSIONAL ACTIVITIES

- Lubbock Classroom Teachers Association, Faculty Representative, 2000–present
- Lubbock Classroom Teachers Association Conference Delegate, 2000, 2002, 2003, 2004
- Destination Imagination Intermediate Coach and Building Liaison, 2001–present
- Family Math Learning Night Committee/Chairperson, 2001–present
- Math Committee Chairperson, 1999–present
- Harwell Cheerleader Sponsor, 1999–present
- TAAS Building Co-liaison, 2000–2003

SELECTED CIVIC ACTIVITIES

- Member, Hispanic League of Prairie Springs, 2001–present
  - Super Seller, Holiday Fair, 2002
- Member, Hispanic Association of Women, 1999–present
  - President, 2003–2004
  - President-Elect, 2002–2003
- Board Member, Heartgood Neighborhood Association, 2003–present
- Co-coordinator, United Way Campaign, Heartgood Elementary, 2001–present
- Student Council Sponsor, 2000–2003

only selected community activities. An additional challenge was to combine 14 years of service at one school into a compact, reader-friendly format. As in many executive resumes, the feat is accomplished through smaller type, wider lines, and less line spacing. See Cover Letter 20 (page 396).

BERNADETTE JACKSON

77 Lincoln Avenue • Salt Lake City, UT 55555 • (555) 222-0000 • BJ12@educspecialist.edu

Position of Interest: **EARLY CHILDHOOD SPECIALIST**

Profile: Dedicated, resourceful, and passionate education professional with an accomplished career promoting quality education in the capacities of Elementary School Teacher and Early Childhood Resource Specialist.

Strengths: Administrative Acumen, Turnkey Training, Curriculum Development and Implementation, School- and District-wide Program Planning, School Improvement Initiatives, Student-Teacher Support, Classroom Teaching, Grant Writing, and Committee Involvement.

EDUCATION

City University of Utah—**Master of Arts in Elementary Education, 1994**
St. John's College for Women—**Bachelor of Arts, 1964**

LICENSES & CERTIFICATIONS

State of Utah Certified—**Certification for Administration and Supervision, 2002**
Utah State Licensed—**Early Childhood and Common Branches, 2002**

PROFESSIONAL EXPERIENCE

TURNKEY TRAINING

- Upon inception of Utah's Primary Standards in English Language Arts, served as a Turnkey Trainer for District 35 elementary schools.
- Attended grade-level conferences and presented new curriculums to district-wide faculty members.
- Provided teachers with practical strategies for differentiated lesson plans and multidisciplinary thematic units.
- Linked teachers with the Early Childhood Literacy Assessment System (ECLAS) as a vital assessment tool.
- Conducted one-to-one in-class demonstrations to familiarize teachers with lesson-specific materials, new teaching standards, and effective implementation techniques.
- Communicate with teachers to monitor developments in Language Arts and Social Studies while ensuring the effective application of teaching methods to accommodate classroom size and ethnic composition.

CURRICULUM & EDUCATIONAL PROGRAM DEVELOPMENT

- Formulated a Music- and Art-based program designed to teach Language Arts skills to a non-English-speaking student population from more than 40 countries (pre-Kindergarten through third grade).
- Developed a Whole Language Reading curriculum based on Scott Foresman's *Celebrate Reading* series.
- Guided the implementation of numerous parent-school communication programs.
- Developed and implemented a parent workshop, *Literacy Centers: What They Are and What They Teach*.
- PTA President's Council Evening Meetings: Conducted *Learning Math Through the Use of Manipulatives*.
- Designed monthly workshops for pre-Kindergarten teachers, educational assistants, and family assistants.

WORKSHOP DEVELOPMENT & COORDINATION

- Teaching Math through Music, Utah Early Childhood Conference, 2001
- Parent workshop: *When Will Your Child Read?* 2001
- Music workshop to facilitate reading, math, social studies, science, art, and music lessons, 2000
- Open-ended art workshop for pre-Kindergarten teachers at the school-wide level, 1999
- Early Childhood Literacy for Teachers, Kindergarten through Second Grade, 1997
- Good Literature Promotes a Love of Reading and Increases Skills for Teachers, 1996
- Training Kindergarten teachers to use new literature-based reading series, 1994
- ESL Trends, Methods, and Materials for Kindergarten Teachers, Kingsbridge Community College, 1990

— continued —

59

Combination. *Ann Baehr, Brentwood, New York*

The applicant had an extensive career in progressively responsible positions. The writer used functional sections to focus on select areas of interest right away. This resume helped the job

BERNADETTE JACKSON
Page 2

OVERSEAS TRAVEL & EXPERIENCE

England, France, Switzerland, Austria, Germany, Greece, Turkey, South Africa, India, and Nepal

Hazleton Scholarship, Summer Seminar Program, India, and Nepal, 2001
- Traveled across India, from New Delhi to Calcutta, and Nepal, receiving a hands-on education in broad aspects of various political systems, government structures, educational systems, sciences, art, music, customs, and traditions reflected in a social studies curriculum project developed upon return to the U.S.

Delegate Member, Citizen Ambassador Program, South Africa, 1996
- Attended workshops with South African teachers, administrators, and government officials.
- Conducted a workshop in Cape Town for teachers with more than 80 students.
- Successfully proposed the reassignment of classes to achieve a 1:20 student-teacher ratio; the Buddy System; cooperative learning; Family Literacy; and English as a Second Language for parents.
- Nominated as a member of the South African–American Early Childhood Congress.

COMMITTEE INVOLVEMENT

Chairperson, On-site Planning Committee, District 35, 1985–1998
- Spearheaded a one-year team effort to improve reading scores across all grade levels.
  - Led teams in the development and implementation of test sophistication materials designed to identify and evaluate the source of individual learning deficiencies with a focus on skill mastery.
  - **Successfully increased the school's reading scores by 14%.**
- Encouraged parents' participation on a daily basis and at meetings to share information and elicit valuable suggestions having an impact on the development of school-wide programs.

Member, Parents Advisory Committee, District 35, 1998–2002
Member, Early Childhood Community Coordination Committee, District 35, 1998–2002
Chairperson, Social Committee, District 35, 1987–1998

CAREER CHRONOLOGY

District 35, Salt Lake City, Utah
Early Childhood Resources Specialist, 1998–present

Public School 27, Salt Lake City, Utah
Teacher, Early Childhood Literacy through the Arts, 1997–1998
All-Day Kindergarten Teacher, 1990–1996
Second-Grade Teacher, 1986–1990
All-Day Kindergarten Teacher, 1984–1985

Public School 12, Salt Lake City, Utah
All-Day Kindergarten Teacher, 1983–1984
Second-Grade Teacher, 1982–1983
Vocal Music Teacher, Second through Sixth Grades, 1978–1982
First-Grade Teacher, 1974–1978

GRANT WRITING

President's Grant, Schoolyard Playground
Charlotte Hill Grant, School Band
$10,000 Implementation Grant for School Improvement Plans: Reading and Math Workbooks, K–6

seeker get a higher position in a tight market. Professional experience is clustered under three side headings, making it easier for the reader to comprehend the range of experience. The Overseas Travel & Experience, Committee Involvement, and Grant Writing sections are substantial additions.

TAYLOR RAINE

123 SUNNY KNOLL REST ■ POUGHKEEPSIE, NY 00000 ■ (555) 555-5555 ■ TAYLORRAINE@YAHOO.COM

PSYCHOLOGY PROFESSIONAL
Offering a well-integrated theoretical perspective, proven investigative skills and a strong interest in treatment research

PROFESSIONAL PROFILE

➢ Well-developed field research competence with adolescents, teens and other special populations

➢ Demonstrated ability to conduct a full range of in-depth assessments in an effort to establish baseline data

➢ Able to gather facts from a variety of sources and derive keen insights from seemingly disparate pieces of information

➢ Knowledgeable of developmental psychology and the specific levels of cognitive functioning for children of various ages

AREAS OF EXPERIENCE & STRENGTH

➢ Lesson Design & Development / Case Management Interdisciplinary Collaboration / Teaching

➢ Psycho-educational Evaluations / Developmentally Appropriate Interventions / Program Evaluation

➢ Empirical & Survey Research / Complex Data Analyses Policy Research / Evaluation Research Methods

➢ Group, Individual & Family Counseling / Program Development / Assessment & Treatment Planning

EDUCATION & CREDENTIALS

EDUCATION
James Madison University, Harrisonburg, VA
Doctor of Philosophy in Psychology (ABD)
Concentration: Health Psychology (2004)

Vassar College, Poughkeepsie, NY
Advanced Certificate in School Psychology (1998)
M.A. in Community & Counseling Psychology (1995)
Magna cum Laude

Mercy College, Dobbs Ferry, NY
B.A. in Psychology (1990), Summa cum Laude

DISSERTATION
Social Aspects of Childhood Obesity
Conducting research within a naturalistic setting

MULTICULTURAL INTERNSHIP / RESEARCH PROJECT
University of South Carolina, Columbia, SC (1998)
- Assigned to Bureau of Indian Affairs School, New Mexico
- Conducted holistic assessments of Native American youth

ADDITIONAL CERTIFICATIONS
Health & Fitness Instructor, American College of Sports Med.
Personal Trainer, National Strength & Conditioning Assoc.

PROFESSIONAL EXPERIENCE

Herkimer County Community College, *Herkimer, NY*   **2000 TO PRESENT**
Adjunct Instructor

Develop and instruct General Psychology courses. Secure guest speakers, participate in departmental and college activities, develop/integrate departmental curriculum and mentor/advise students. Devise weekly lessons that address current issues and perspectives in psychological science. Strive to maintain a thorough knowledge of instructional standards, practices and methodologies for adult learners.

Mohawk Central School District, *Mohawk, NY*   **1999 TO 2000**
School Psychologist

Served grades K–12 in a rural setting, working closely with parents, teachers, administrators and community agencies to identify needs through evaluation of skills, intellectual function, social adjustment and emotional development. Daily responsibilities also included crisis intervention. Served as a mentor to the special education staff and helped guide staff and families through complex system procedures. Also worked with learning specialists, testing experts and administrators to help ensure that the school operated within district guidelines and state mandates.

60

Combination. *Kristin M. Coleman, Poughkeepsie, New York*

Careful formatting makes this full, two-page resume easy to read. The writer achieves readability through smaller font sizes, narrower left and right margins, two-column arrangements, and

Taylor Raine   Page Two

PROFESSIONAL EXPERIENCE CONTINUED

Horry County School District, *Conway, SC*   **1995 TO 1996**

<u>**School Psychologist**</u>

Conducted psychological assessments of populations ranging from conduct disorders through developmentally disabled. Worked with students in kindergarten through junior high. Collaborated extensively with parents, teachers and community agencies to identify needs. Provided individual counseling to children and families on a full range of human issues from behavioral noncompliance to sexual abuse. Chaired the Committee on Special Education staffing initiatives.

Arlington Central School District, *Poughkeepsie, NY*   **1994 TO 1995**

<u>**School Psychologist**</u> **(Internship)**

Gained experience in a broad range of clinical case issues. Some cases required well-coordinated treatment programs that addressed the children's multiple and complex needs. Also gained experience with a variety of interventions, including functional behavior assessment, behavior intervention plans (classroom wide and individual), counseling and instructional modification.

New York State Regional Office of Mental Health, *New Paltz, NY*   **1988 TO 1994**

<u>**Residential Treatment Facility Case Manager**</u> **(Guidance Center)**

Facilitated referrals from schools, social services and psychiatric hospitals within a seven-county region. Coordinated and chaired regional preadmission and Certification Committee to determine eligibility for youth going into residential treatment facilities. Established therapeutic relationships with adolescent and young-adult inpatients. Maintained frequent contact with families in order to educate parents about the condition of their children and to reinforce the child's progress and strengthen connections between the child and family members. Scheduled, administered, formulated and reviewed assessment reports, ensuring that activities and specific goals were executed.

New York State Assembly / Speaker's Regional Office, *Utica, NY*   **1987 TO 1988**

<u>**Legislative Coordinator**</u> **(Internship)**

Conducted intensive and complex research on locally and nationally available services for children with serious mental illnesses. Research was used to support the Assembly Standing Committee on Mental Hygiene's efforts to pass Assembly Bill #7604. Provided a well-coordinated and comprehensive study, which examined the types of training, support and resources necessary for seriously mentally ill children. Praised for diligence and quality work. Received an outstanding letter of recommendation.

COMMUNITY WORK / PROFESSIONAL AFFILIATIONS

- ➤ American Psychological Association, *Student Member*
- ➤ Multiple Sclerosis Society, New York Chapter, *Volunteer*
- ➤ New York State Corp of Cadets Program, *Volunteer; 1 year*
- ➤ Office of Children and Family Services, *Volunteer; 1 year*

ADDITIONAL INFORMATION

- ➤ Computer Literate: MS Word / WordPerfect / SPSS
- ➤ Presently studying the Arabic language
- ➤ United States Army Reserve Officer, <u>Field Medical Assistant</u>
- ➤ New York State Air National Guard, <u>Avionics Apprentice</u>

adequate white space throughout. Boldfacing and underlining help important information to stand out. For example, once you realize that a job position in the Professional Experience section is bold and underlined, you can look for that kind of enhancement and see other job positions easily.

NANCY JOHNSON

SCHOOL PSYCHOLOGIST

555 Peachtree Road
Hauppauge, NY 55555
(555) 000-0000

EDUCATION / CERTIFICATIONS

Master of Arts, School Psychology, 2004—GPA 3.9/4.0
ST. JAMES COLLEGE, Buffalo, NY

Bachelor of Arts, Psychology, 2000—GPA 3.2/4.0
STATE UNIVERSITY OF NEW YORK AT BINGHAMTON, Binghamton, NY

New York State Provisional Certification, School Psychologist
New York State Initial Educator Certification, School Psychologist

PROFILE

Qualified school psychologist bringing a range of professional experience in the counseling and teaching of general and special education students throughout inner-city schools, group residency, and private day-care settings. Bring strong skills in areas of assessment, intervention, and prevention; program development and implementation; and a proactive approach towards promoting a home/school connection and awareness of supportive services and resources. Computer proficient: MS Office/Internet.

PROFESSIONAL EXPERIENCE

School Psychologist, Henry Hudson Public School District, Lakeview, NY   2000–present
   Blake Elementary School, Pre-Kindergarten–Sixth Grade, 2003–present
   Hillside Elementary School, Pre-Kindergarten–Third Grade, 2002–present
   Special Education Summer School Program, 2002
   James Elementary School, Pre-Kindergarten–Sixth Grade, 2000–2001
   Consultation Center, 2000–2001

- Perform evaluations and screenings to assess students' academic skills, learning aptitudes, emotional development, social skills, learning environments, and school climate, and determine eligibility for special education services to the Planning and Placement Team.

- Conduct counseling sessions to address issues affecting students' academic performance, social behavior, and mental health, and to develop tolerance, understanding, and appreciation for diversity.

- Administer/evaluate academic programs and behavioral management systems through Functional Behavioral Assessments, Behavioral Intervention Plans, and Individualized Education Plans.

- Provide teachers with student-tailored academic and behavioral management strategies designed to reduce students' risk of failure at a preventative level.

- Observe preschool-aged children in playgroup sessions, and consult with parents to obtain developmental and social histories.

- Keep students and parents current on important topics, community resources, and upcoming programs and events through Web page access, bulletin board postings, and pamphlets.

— continued —

61

Combination. *Ann Baehr, Brentwood, New York*

If it weren't for the page border, an interesting font (Castellar), a unique heading, and the Profile, this resume would have an otherwise standard chronological format. Horizontal lines

Nancy Johnson

School Psychologist, Henry Hudson Public School District, continued

- Co-facilitate a school-wide program providing third- through sixth-grade students with positive social and behavioral skills through role model students, motivational speakers, and community resources.
- Collaborate with the Family Support Team on the development of strategies designed to improve students' reading levels and to promote parental involvement in the Success For All program.
- Attend monthly staff meetings, professional development workshops, and school-wide activities.

School Psychologist Intern, Lexington Central School District, Landon, NY · · · 1999–2000
Shawnee Middle School, New Spring, NY
Lake Grove Middle School, Bloomington, NY

- Provided individual and group counseling and crisis-intervention services; consulted on academic, behavioral, and organizational issues; and developed behavioral strategies for the classroom.
- Conducted achievement and cognitive testing, and assessed emotional/social adjustment.
- Presented results of students with different handicapping conditions to the Committee on Special Education, and developed and implemented Individualized Education Plans.

Counseling Practicum, Pinkerton School District, Fishkill, NY · · · 1999

- Worked closely with students, parents, and professional teams to identify and resolve a broad range of issues directly impacting students' academic and social performance.
- Devised and presented counseling summaries on students' progress and future recommendations.

Residential Counselor, St. Mary's Youth Center, Fishkill, NY · · · 1998

- Supervised residential housing units provided to homeless youth, aged 16–21.
- Performed intake and exit evaluations, conducted on-site visitations to observe living conditions, and ensured full compliance with mandatory health and safety regulations.
- Collaborated with community representatives to provide clients with supportive services in areas of financial assistance, education, work and life skills, housing, childcare, and substance abuse.

Counselor, Kids Town, Fishkill, NY · · · 1998

- Coordinated and directed group activities for youth day camp and nursery programs.
- Integrated recreational activities to create an environment conducive to learning and social growth for a multicultural population of students of varying ages and learning disabilities.

Pre-School Teacher, Fishkill Developmental Center, Fishkill, NY · · · 1996–1998

- Implemented behavior reinforcement programs, performed formal evaluations, and collaborated with school psychologist and parents to identify and resolve problems.
- Co-taught individualized lessons and life skills within an integrated classroom environment.
- Adapted educational materials to facilitate the learning process at an appropriate pace.

PROFESSIONAL AFFILIATIONS

Member, New York Association of School Psychologists
Member, National Association of School Psychologists

help to call attention to the Education/Certifications section and the Profile. Boldfacing makes it easy to see the degrees and certifications. Boldfacing also helps the reader to spot in the Professional Experience section the various positions held. Right-aligned dates are easy to see down the right margin.

CHRIS CHAVEZ

55-555 Main Street • Honolulu, HI 00000
Home: (808) 555-5555 • Office: (808) 555-5551, Ext. 555
Cellular: (808) 555-5552 • E-mail: chavezc@coconut.org

AREAS OF EXPERTISE

Human Behavior

Adolescent Education

Peer Education/
Counseling

Peer Counselor
Training

Service Learning

Program
Development

Curriculum Planning

Classroom
Management

Procedures Planning

Parent/Student/
Teacher Liaison

Research

Workshops/
Seminars

*Relocating 6/2004
to San Francisco, CA*

PROFESSIONAL EDUCATOR
Making a Difference in the Lives of School Children

Dedicated educator seeking position as **Psychology Teacher.** 10+ years' related experience includes positions as high school counselor and teacher, substitute and volunteer teacher, and private tutor. Particularly adept at curriculum planning and program development. Task oriented. Solid organization and time-management skills.

M.S. in Educational Psychology • B.A. in Psychology

CAREER TRACK

Junior High Counselor/   4/2000–Present
Peer Education Teacher
Pacific Rim Institute—Honolulu, HI
Accredited K–12 private institution for girls. Total enrollment 2,500.

Assist 375 students with transition to high school. Provide personal and social counseling in areas of academic progress, career awareness, peer conflict, and other adolescent challenges. Train peer counselors.

• Developed peer education and counseling program from scratch within 1 year. Teach entire curriculum. Foster sense of community awareness by incorporating service-learning program with Young Students Club of Honolulu. Program currently has active student peer counselors.
• Revised faculty grade-check procedures, including comprehensive follow-up system. Resulted in improved communication among faculty, students, and parents.
• Rewrote counseling procedures to conform to national standards of ASCA, ACA, and APA.

Substitute Teacher   1999/2000 school year
Island Substitute Services—Honolulu, HI

Functioned as "on-call" substitute. Reported to various private schools on island of Oahu. Assignments varied from 1 day to 3 weeks. Class sizes of 20 to 30.

• Consistently followed teachers' curriculum requests. Accepted all assignments offered. Earned reputation for reliability.
• Acquired valuable teaching experience through assignments in various school settings.

Career Track Continued on Page 2 ⇨

62

Combination. *Peter Hill, Honolulu, Hawaii*

The applicant, a counselor, was relocating to another part of the country and was seeking a position as a psychology teacher. The writer directs immediate attention to the individual's

CHRIS CHAVEZ
Page 2 of 2

EDUCATION

**M.S. Degree,
Educational
Psychology**
3/2003

Accredited Distance
Learning Program of
Chicago University—
Chicago, IL
❋ *GPA 3.9/4.0*

**B.A. Degree,
Psychology**
1992

Chicago University—
Chicago, IL
❋ *GPA 4.0/4.0*

COMPUTER SKILLS

Internet, Outlook,
Outlook Express,
Eudora, Word,
Publisher, PowerPoint

Tutor   1997/98 school year
Tutors-R-Us—Honolulu, HI

Worked one-on-one with home-schooled or struggling students (1st through 9th grades). Kept student records. Wrote progress reports for in-house and parent use.

- Developed strong time-management skills. Required to cover large amounts of material in limited time.
- Obtained functional one-to-one communication skills through contact with children of various ages.

Volunteer Teacher   1992–1996
California Unified School District—Vista, CA

Taught basic Spanish to 2nd- and 5th-graders. Wrote weekly newsletter for 2nd-grade class and organized all activities. Also volunteered as ESL instructor until full-time teacher was hired. Class sizes of up to 27.

❋ *Previous experience as flight attendant with major airline.*

PROFESSIONAL DEVELOPMENT

Career Assistance Training	2002
State Counselor Association Conference	2001
Peaceful Intervention	2001
Psychobiology of Mental Control	2000
Statewide Conference on Conflict Management	2000
Counselor Education, Hawaii University	1997
National Student Assistance Program	1996

CERTIFICATIONS

Hawaiian Private School Professional Academic Certificate	2000
Hawaii Department of Health Substance Abuse Prevention Partner	2000
Student Assistance Training Certification	1999

AFFILIATIONS

American Psychological Association
American School Counselor Association
Hawaii School Counselor Association
American Counseling Association

---

formal education in psychology. The modified page border (not a full page) is attractive on both pages and unifies them visually. Shading in the left column on each page directs attention to Areas of Expertise on page one and to the Education and Computer Skills sections on page two.

Felicia Bowman

Corporate Trainer Available Immediately!

Summary of Qualifications

1 Master's degree in Adult Education/Training with hands-on delivery and development

2 Experience in training and program development for major corporation

3 Delivered dozens of workshops for team building, technical training and other workplace topics

4 Conducted analysis of work teams and job & task components and presented findings

5 Excellent computer skills, including development of online training and tools

6 Member: ASTD (national and local), SHRM, and ISPI

555 Wilshire Road
Tampa, Florida 33624
(813) 555-0248
fbowman@hotmail.com

Educational History and Degrees

For Felicia Bowman

University of South Florida
Adult Education–Training–Human Resource Development, M.A.
Tampa, Florida, 1998

University of South Florida
Psychology, B.A.
Tampa, Florida, 1995

Key Strengths

Creativity—Ability to create unique solutions, analogies and illustrations for complex problems

Patience—Ability to work with all departments with all levels of employees

Knowledge—Ability to use extensive insights in Adult Learners' understanding and information processing

Structured—Ability to plan and prepare programs and workshops in a long term, time-based critical path schedule in order to meet targeted launch dates

Communication—Ability to express complex ideas and important points in a way that is understandable and simple for the majority of Adult Learners

Professional Experience

Training and Documentation Specialist, Lockheed Martin
Lakeland, Florida, 1999–Current

Team member of highly creative Training Group for corporate offices and 3 major business sectors of this $27 billion company.

✓ Completed 12 major job and task analysis projects to document technical work processes.

✓ Designed 4 training programs, each in multiple forms of media, including the Internet, CD-ROM, PowerPoint and NetMeeting.

✓ Used interactive team development processes to assess the functionality of teams in the Shared Services division.

✓ Delivered 3 specialized training modules for highly technical computer systems.

✓ Facilitate team-building exercises, communication enhancement workshops and ongoing meeting facilitation.

✓ Offer constructive and strategic input on organizational structural changes.

✓ Participate in business development projects and strategic planning.

• Continued on Page 2

63

Combination. *Gail Frank, Tampa, Florida*

This corporate trainer was looking for a nontraditional format for a traditionally worded resume. She wanted to stand out from the pack when applying for jobs through the local ASTD chapter

Corporate Trainer—Felicia Bowman—page 2

Program Assistant, Counseling Center for Human Development, University of South Florida
Tampa, Florida, 1996–1999

Created policies, procedures and training for clients of USF's Counseling Center. Also provided administrative and computer troubleshooting support.

✓ Produced detailed publications and handbooks, including the Counseling Center's Handbook, internship materials and brochures.

✓ Designed and produced promotional materials and presentations for professional workshops to clients and university administration.

✓ Trained staff on Internet usage and software programs such as Microsoft Word, Excel, PowerPoint and Scheduler.

✓ Resolved client issues and provided customer service. Took incoming calls and provided referrals to other resources.

✓ Provided computer support for staff in the areas of software support and system troubleshooting.

✓ Conducted administrative support for the campus-wide Employee Assistance Program.

Program Assistant, University of South Florida, Veteran Services
Tampa, Florida, 1994–1995

Performed administrative and financial services in USF office that serviced veterans in their search for continuing education and employment.

✓ Reported directly to the Veteran Services Program Coordinator and ran the office when she was not present.

✓ Supervised 3 employees and ensured that reports and forms were properly filled out.

✓ Provided training in office procedures and policies.

✓ Handled all travel and budgeting administration.

✓ Solicited assistance from other campus offices in providing opportunities for work placement openings.

✓ Counseled veterans on their education and work options, and helped them define goals.

✓ Coordinated VA Work-Study Program for USF.

Courses Completed During Master's Program

Adult Education in the United States	Program Management
The Adult Learner	Foundations of Research
Methods of Teaching Adults	Consulting Skills
Instructional Design	Group Processes
Trainers in Business and Industry	Personnel Policy

Sample Presentations & Projects Completed During Master's Program

Experiential Learning in Adults

Presentation Skills Workshop

Future Trends in Adult Learning

Book Review: The Adult Learner, A Neglected Species

Andragogy Versus Pedagogy: Adults Are Different Than Kids

Professional Associations

Member of top local and national training organizations

National Chapter of American Society for Training and Development (ASTD)

Suncoast Chapter of American Society for Training and Development (ASTD)

Society for Human Resource Management (SHRM)

International Society for Performance Improvement (ISPI)

2 . . . .

(American Society for Training and Development). The writer chose a newsletter format and added the graphic of a trainer to convey the applicant's creativity and playfulness and to offset somewhat dry "trainer-speak." Master's degree coursework and presentations provide keywords.

555 ● 555 ● 5555

B. Rae French

1003 Ironton Avenue ● Skyview, Texas 79000
brfrench@nts-online.net

OBJECTIVE

Corporate trainer for large corporation that offers upward mobility.

SUMMARY OF QUALIFICATIONS

- BS in Interdisciplinary Studies with emphasis in Mathematics and Communications
- Eight years of teaching experience with measurable accomplishments
- Nine years of concurrent experience as sales representative for cosmetics line and portrait studio
- Director for live and video dramas; play actor
- Proven speaking, public relations, communication, and interpersonal skills

TEACHING EXPERIENCE

Math Teacher and **Cheerleading Sponsor,** MAC JUNIOR HIGH SCHOOL, Skyview, Texas   **1995–2000**
As teacher, trained individual students to increase their mathematical, logical, and reasoning skills. Ensured classroom safety, abiding by all safety requirements. As cheerleading sponsor (1997-2000), scheduled and organized special events such as pep rallies, fund-raisers, and tryouts. Motivated parents, staff, and cheerleaders to increase school allegiance. Authored directives.

Key Achievements:

- Advanced from teaching seventh-grade math to eighth-grade and freshman algebra.
- Instrumental in improving student assessment passing rate: 1998—86.2%; 1999—95.1%; 2000—97.6%; 2001—98%.
- Teaching techniques resulted in 100% of seventh-grade class passing TAAS Test (2000).
- Collaborated with other volunteer teachers to implement Saxon Math Program that produced amazing results.
- Invested large amounts of time working with cheerleaders; getting to know them, organizing tryouts, attending camp, and coordinating activities.
- Completely restructured cheerleading program: Organized paperwork, published schedules, involved other programs, established rules and guidelines, and utilized open communication with parents and administration.

Math Teacher, PROJECT INTERCEPT (ALTERNATIVE SCHOOL), Skyview, Texas   **1993–1995**
Organized and prepared curriculum to accommodate 7–12 grade levels. Taught as many as four subjects to students in class size of 8–10. Collaborated with other teachers in areas of discipline and student achievement. Utilized consistency and awareness to manage classroom.

Key Achievements:

- Gained recognizable progress with several difficult students through an accepting attitude and creative teaching techniques.
- Esteemed for motivating students, retaining their attention, and cultivating a zest for learning.

Continued ———————

64

Combination. *Edith A. Rische, Lubbock, Texas*

This teacher wanted to become a corporate trainer. The writer highlights transitional skills, such as writing directives, public speaking, and mentoring, which are relevant to a corporate

B. Rae French

Page 2

OTHER EMPLOYMENT

Portrait Consultant, PAUL'S PHOTOGRAPHY, Church Division, Skyview, Texas   **2001–2002**
Traveled multistate territory selling computer-generated portrait packages to church members. Created and presented attractive packages with best overall poses, motivating customers to make a purchase with warmth and sincerity.

<u>Key Achievements:</u>

- Ranked in top ten portrait consultants among 30 district representatives in first three weeks of employment.
- Trained for only four days rather than two weeks due to quick learning capacity.
- Outsold trainer in first two days as sales consultant.

Sales Consultant, PRECIOUS COSMETICS, Lubbock, Texas   *CONCURRENT*   **1993–Present**
Market product and conduct facials to sell cosmetic products. Recruit sales consultants. Attend regular training sessions and yearly conventions.

EDUCATION

Bachelor of Science in Interdisciplinary Studies, RELIGIOUS UNIVERSITY, Skyview, Texas   **1993**

- Major: Secondary Education in Mathematics and Communications
- Teacher certified by the Texas Education Association

AWARDS AND ACTIVITIES

- Active participant in improving TAAS scores instrumental in Mac Junior High's Texas Education Association rating as "Recognized" campus 1997, 1999, and 2001; and as "Exemplary" campus 2000
- Mentor in Leadership Training for Christ Program, 1996–2000
- Student Teacher of the Year, 1995
- Dean's List and National Dean's List, 1992–1993
- Participant in community and children's theater programs

SPECIAL SKILLS

- PC literate with working knowledge of MS Windows, Word, Excel, and PowerPoint; and Internet
- Electronics knowledgeable
- Piano, guitar, singing, and acting

environment. The writer also presents achievements such as successful teaching and program development to strengthen the candidate's hiring potential as a trainer. An unusual page border makes the resume distinctive. The use of bold and underlining helps achievements stand out. See Cover Letter 9 (page 385).

LORRAINE T. WILSON

919-223-8888
wilson @ email.com

2813 Twilight Avenue
Raleigh, NC 27613

TRAINING & DEVELOPMENT
Expert in delivering training programs that drive productivity and performance improvements

Dynamic training professional with an outstanding reputation for integrity and results. Effective interpersonal skills with an ability to meet and train people at their level. Skilled in facilitating groups through complex problem solving to action and improvement. Enthusiastic with a positive and motivating management style. Core competencies include the following:

- Strategic & Tactical Planning
- Performance Management
- Cross-Cultural Communications
- Train-the-Trainer Development
- Needs Assessment & Analysis
- Mentoring Programs

NOTABLE HIGHLIGHTS

Lorraine "is a highly skilled professional with a wealth of experience in working effectively with individuals and groups across the district to effect change."
Coordinator,
North Carolina Diagnostic & Learning Resources System

- Repeatedly selected by the county to serve as a consultant to *develop training materials for alternative assessments and lead training workshops.*

- Following the requirement of federal and state-mandated training procedures, *selected by the school district to develop the training modules and train 5,000 teachers to retain critical governmental funding.* Created the highly regarded and very effective PowerPoint presentation, "Solving the Puzzle," incorporating all learning modalities for ease of learning.

- *Created the highly successful community-based training program to prepare disabled students for the workforce.* Established long-term, mutually beneficial relationships with major employers, including the Sheraton, Marriott, St. Joseph's Hospital, Wal-Mart, Kash n' Karry, and Target. Served as the administration liaison monitoring student progress. *Enjoyed an unprecedented success rate in getting students hired into long-term employment.*

"She is an extremely well planned and structured individual. She models perseverance and encourages others to do the same…. Lorraine has an articulate ability to convey even complicated information in a very clear and concise manner."
Susan Smith,
Guidance Counselor

- *Chosen to author the curriculum and teach English to foreign-born nationals.*

- *Recruited to "train the trainer,"* authoring the program to successfully coach experienced teachers in the art of mentoring new teachers to reduce turnover.

- *Recruited by the University of North Carolina to develop the "Classroom Manager,"* standardized Web-based lesson plans.

- *Invited by North Carolina State University* to participate as a key member of the Special Education Consortium, conducting alternative assessment field testing for its Life Career Center *as a forerunner to becoming a state-certified trainer.*

65

Combination. *Cindy Kraft, Valrico, Florida*

This teacher also, with 20-plus years of teaching, wanted to transition to the world of corporate training. In the opening profile, the writer refers to skills and "core competencies" relevant to

LORRAINE T. WILSON   Page 2   919-223-8888

Evaluation Form Excerpts:

"Excellent presenter. Lively presentation of DRY topic!"

"Lorraine has an awesome personality."

"Wonderful job, Lorraine. Very informative, yet fun!"

"Fantastic job."

"Very informative and helpful."

"Good workshop. Brought everything together. Fun activities."

"Excellent! Excellent! Excellent!"

"Great instruction and activities."

"Good information. Well presented."

PROFESSIONAL EXPERIENCE

GREEN COUNTY SCHOOL DISTRICT, Raleigh, NC

Teacher—1999 to 2004
EMH Teacher, Central High School—1998 to 1999
VE/ESE Class Instructor, Springville Adult School—1992 to 1999
ESOL Instructor, Springville Adult School—1988 to 1992
ESE Department Head, Washington High School—1972 to 1998

Broad-based experience in training teachers and students within the 13th-largest school district in the nation. As Department Head, supervised and mentored paraprofessionals; served as liaison with outside agencies; and developed effective training materials.

- Developed the coaching programs that resulted in new teacher orientation and professional day training policies.

- Chosen numerous times to serve on committees aimed at improving teacher training.

- Proven record of success in teaching and graduating the most dysfunctional students.

- Repeatedly selected by the district as a model classroom for visiting foreign educators.

CERTIFICATIONS

North Carolina Certified Associate of Behavior Analysis (CABA)

EDUCATION

Master of Administration—University of Ohio, Athens, OH
Bachelor of Arts—Pennsylvania State University, York, PA

training. The testimonials in the left column on the first page and the evaluation form excerpts in the same location on the second page build reader esteem for the applicant. The boldfacing of notable highlights on the first page further enhances the applicant's image.

ALICE M. CAULFIELD

978 TURNER ROAD
SOUTHWICK, CONNECTICUT 66666
(888) 444-9999

QUALIFICATIONS

- ➢ Played a major role in developing the Audubon Society of Connecticut's new $4.5 million Environmental Education Center.
- ➢ Proven abilities in management, supervision, staffing, grant researching/writing, and budgeting.
- ➢ Established the education department at the Audubon Society of Connecticut's Environmental Education Center, and monitored significant growth of 20% in productivity and volume during the past year.
- ➢ Institute, direct, and coordinate all environmental education activities, including curriculum development, advertising, teacher training, summer camp, and personal appearances.

EMPLOYMENT

Audubon Society of Connecticut, Bristol, CT
Co-Director of Education, 2000–Present
Education Coordinator, 1998–2000
Education Specialist/Camp Director, 1996–1998
- o Hire and supervise staff of 26: 2 full-time, 5 part-time, 9 seasonal, and 10 interns/volunteers.
- o Reach 1,200 children per month and serve 28,000 total annual visitors to the Environmental Education Center.
- o Develop curriculum for children to adults, and conduct teacher workshops/training, conferences, and special events.
- o Supervise care of animals, act as liaison to other environmental organizations, and make public relations appearances.

Ella V. Sherman Zoo, Bristol, CT
Education Specialist, 1995–1996
- o Designed, implemented, and presented educational programs on zoo grounds for elementary schools, high schools, and colleges.
- o Presented a unique environmental curriculum for children at summer Zoocamp.
- o Trained and supervised counselors-in-training, ages 14–16.

Research Assistant, 1994–1995
- o Monitored activity of captive cheetahs to devise a behavioral ethogram and activity budget.
- o Developed an animal enrichment program.

Manchester Veterinary Ophthalmology Services, Inc., Manchester, CT
Veterinary Assistant, 1992–1994
- o Assisted veterinarian, Dr. Karen Bogart, during patient examinations and surgery.
- o Dispensed medications and assisted in office management.

Save the Seas Project, Mystic, CT
Education Intern, Summers 1990–1992
- o Presented marine life programs to small and large audiences throughout southern Connecticut.
- o Researched and prepared materials for children and teachers' science workshops.
- o Edited pollution manual to educate the public on current hazards in Mystic Bay.

66

Combination. *Edward Turilli, Newport, Rhode Island*

Distinctive design features help to capture the attention of the reader: the shaded box containing the contact information, the horizontal lines interrupted by centered headings to delineate

ALICE M. CAULFIELD   PAGE TWO

EDUCATION

University of Connecticut, Storrs, CT
Bachelor of Science in **Zoology.** *Concentration in* **Marine Biology,** 1992

University of Manchester, Manchester, England
Bachelor of Science, **Honors Biology**—*the Student Exchange Program,* 1990–1991
    Thesis: "Effects of Toxins on the Gill Cilia of the *Mytilus edulis*"

CONTINUING EDUCATION

Humane Society, Bristol, CT
Disaster Planning for Animals, 2002
Project Wild Environmental Training for Teachers, Bristol, CT
Project Wild Aquatic, Project Wet, Project Learning Tree, 2001–2002
Tri-State Bird Rescue and Research, Inc./New England Aquarium, Boston, MA
Wildlife and Oil Spills Seminar with OSHA Training, 1997
International Wildlife Rehabilitation Council, Storrs, CT
Basic Wildlife Rehabilitation Skills Seminar, 1996
Connecticut Emergency Management Agency/Humane Society, Hartford, CT
Dealing with Animal Issues in Disasters, 1996
University of Connecticut/Mystic Aquarium, Mystic, CT
Seminar in Marine Mammalogy, received graduate credit, 1995

VOLUNTEER

Mystic Aquarium, Mystic, CT
Animal Husbandry Volunteer, 1994–2000
- Cared for the pinniped, cetacean, and penguin collections, including diet preparations, exhibit maintenance, and behavioral conditioning.
- Assisted in rehabilitation and release of stranded pinnipeds.
- Provided support to staff during medical procedures and behavioral conditioning.
- Trained new volunteers, interns, and staff.

Save the Seas Project, Mystic, CT
Marine Mammal Monitoring Coordinator, 1994–1997
- Developed Mystic Bay Marine Mammal Monitoring Program and Guide.
- Organized and analyzed data obtained during monitoring program.
- Researched pinniped populations to assist in determining Bay population trends.
- Coordinated lectures and special events, while acting as liaison to field scientists.

PROFESSIONAL AFFILIATIONS

- Connecticut Environment Education Association Board
- American Zoo and Aquarium Association
- Mystic Aquarium, Honorary Member
- Southern Connecticut Disaster Animal Response Team
- Right Whale Consortium

CERTIFICATIONS

- Adult, child, and infant First Aid and CPR
- Pet CPR and First Aid: American Red Cross
- Basic Wildlife Rehabilitation

– REFERENCES PROVIDED UPON REQUEST –

the sections of the resume, and the shaded boxes at the top and foot of page two. Hollow circle bullets are not common, so these too help to make the resume distinctive. Second-page sections on continuing education, volunteer work, professional affiliations, and certifications add weight to the resume.

YVETTE SEITLIN

555 Andrews Road, Apt. 4   Pasadena, California 91030   323-555-6569   YvetteS@history.tulane.edu

HISTORICAL RESEARCHER

More than 9 years of experience in historical study and research. History Ph.D. candidate with understanding of war and its effects on civilians. Especially interested in study of Holocaust, its causes and its impact on survivors.

Dependable and intelligent professional who is extremely attentive to detail and produces quality work. Creative problem solver who manages ambiguity and deadlines well. Eager to make long-term commitment to Shoah Foundation and the Holocaust project.

EDUCATION

Ph.D. Candidate in History	Tulane University	New Orleans, LA	Expected Fall 2004
M.A. in History	Tulane University	New Orleans, LA	2000
B.A. in History & English	University of Massachusetts	Lowell, MA	Cum Laude, 1998

SUMMARY OF RESEARCH EXPERIENCE

- Currently preparing a dissertation on the reactions of Southern civilians on the Confederate homefront during the American Civil War.

- Wrote master's thesis on the responses of Southern women on the Civil War homefront.

- Hired as a Research Assistant for noted historian Edgar Byron-Smith. Researched, proofed, checked and approved footnotes and copy edited material to support research on 20th-century American culture. 2000–2002

- Hired as a Research Assistant for historian Gary Thompson. Conducted independent research, proofed, confirmed footnotes and copy edited to support his work on the history of public health in the state of Georgia. 1999–2001

- Researched, designed and set up "Made for the Trade: Seminole Tourist Art in the Twentieth Century," an exhibit at the Florida Museum of Natural History. 1998–1999

- Chosen to research, write and edit entry on "Women" for an upcoming Civil War encyclopedia.

- Published 4 book reviews in professional historical journals.

- Presented dissertation findings at 2 historical conferences, with 2 more proposed for 2005.

- Researched and prepared classroom teaching, class reading and assignments for instructor positions.

RELATED WORK EXPERIENCE

- Taught as an Adjunct Instructor at Lesley College, Boston, MA, for "Democracy, Dissent, and Disunion: The United States, 1815–1877." Summer 2003

- Assistant for "Cultural Diversity" at Tulane University. Fall 2000

67

Combination. *Gail Frank, Tampa, Florida*

Before completing her Ph.D., teaching full time, and doing research in history, this candidate wanted a position with Steven Spielberg's SHOAH Foundation to help document Holocaust

YVETTE SEITLIN
page 2

RESEARCH AWARDS

♦ Received a national grant: the Paul M. Frank Grant from the American Historical Association to do research in the archives of South Carolina. 2003–2004

♦ Received a national Women's Studies Research Grant from Duke University to support doctoral work. Spring 2003

♦ Received a College of Liberal Arts and Sciences Dissertation Fellowship from Tulane University to finish writing dissertation. 2002

♦ John Pozzetta Fellow, Department of History, Tulane University. 2002

♦ Grinter Fellow, College of Liberal Arts and Sciences, Tulane University. 1999–2000

♦ Richard J. Miaubach Fellow, Tulane University. 1997–1998

♦ Simon & Judic Klein Scholarship, University of Massachusetts. 1997

PUBLICATIONS

♦ "Women," in Howard S. Heidler and Marilyn T. Heidler, eds., <u>Encyclopedia of the American Civil War</u>. ABC-CLIO, forthcoming 2004.

CONFERENCE PRESENTATIONS

♦ "Untiring in Their Efforts: Female Outrage and Confederate Action," Southern Historical Association Meeting, Louisville, KY, November 8–11, 2005 (proposed).

♦ "An Army of Women: Defenders of the Confederate Homefront, 1864–1865," Fifth Southern Conference on Women's History, Southern Association for Women Historians, Richmond, VA, June 15–17, 2005 (proposed).

♦ "Full of Fire and Patriotism: South Carolina Women in the Path of Sherman," St. George Tucker Society Meeting, Washington and Lee University, Lexington, VA, June 4–6, 2002.

♦ "War Means Ruin and Misery: The Rape of the Confederate Homefront," Eleventh Annual History Forum at The University of North Carolina at Charlotte, April 16–17, 2001.

BOOK REVIEWS

♦ Julie A. Doyle, John David Smith, and Richard M. McMurry, eds., <u>This Wilderness of War: The Civil War Letters of George W. Squier, Hoosier Volunteer</u> (Knoxville: University of Tennessee Press, 2004) and J. Roderick Heller III and Carolynn Ayres Heller, eds., <u>The Confederacy Is on Her Way Up the Spout: Letters to South Carolina, 1861–1864</u> (Columbia: University of South Carolina Press, 2004) in <u>North Carolina Historical Review</u> (July 2004).

♦ John L. Heatwole, <u>The Burning: Sheridan in the Shenandoah Valley</u> (Charlottesville, VA: Howell Press, 2004) in <u>Civil War History</u> (forthcoming).

♦ Lucinda MacKethan, ed., <u>Recollections of a Southern Daughter: A Memoir by Cornelia Jones Pond of Liberty County</u> (Athens: University of Georgia Press, 2004) in <u>The Georgia Historical Quarterly</u> (forthcoming).

♦ Dorothy Denneen Volo and James M. Volo, <u>Daily Life in Civil War America</u> (Westport, CT: Greenwood Press, 2003) in <u>Civil War History</u> (forthcoming).

survivors. Originally, the applicant wanted a curriculum vitae, but it was not targeted to the position. The writer invented instead this combination CV-resume format to offer the best of both. It presents the applicant as a historical researcher but also has substantial detail for an academic environment.

Janet Elaine Ball

1000 Doner <> Ellis, OK 71000 <> jball@mail.net
Home: (903) 888-9999 <> Cellular: (903) 555-4444

Assistive Technology (AT) Program Management Professional
Certification and comprehensive experience in Special Education and Elementary Education

Areas of Expertise

Team Development, Leadership, & Empowerment	*Innovative Program Formulation & Enhancement*
Strategic Planning, Coordination, & Execution	*Operations Policy & Procedure Establishment*
AT Program Development & Management	*Organizational Pioneering & Systemization*
Fund-raising & Funding Acquisition	*Dynamic Presentations & Training*

Employment Chronicle

COPELAND COUNTY SHARED SERVICES ARRANGEMENT (CCSSA) — Ellis, OK (1998–Present)
Assistive Technology Program Manager

Direct assistive technology program in accordance with operational guidelines for approximately 1,200 students with wide range of disabilities within seven-school-district county. Coordinate/conduct assessments; formulate/revise AT reports, correspondence, and various district forms. Develop and direct core AT team consisting of occupational therapist, physical therapist, three speech-language pathologists, special education teacher, special education counselor, three diagnosticians, and vocational counselor. Train and provide technical service to CCSSA staff, district personnel, students, and parents.

Purchase, maintain, repair, program, and inventory equipment. Continually hone knowledge and proficiency of state-of-the-art assistive technology by attending conferences and trade shows. Train staff on new equipment/devices/software.

> *Significant Accomplishments*

> ➤ **Created operational guideline prototype** that was accessible by 97 districts in Region VII via intranet and adaptable for each district's requirements.
> ➤ **Established and launched AT program in Copeland County.**
> ➤ **Developed AT equipment library** and maintained inventory of 600+ items.
> ➤ **Completed 70+ assessments within four and a half years,** which provided more than 50 students with AT.
> ➤ **Spearheaded and presented numerous AT professional development inservices / workshops** to participants within Copeland County and Region VII.
> ➤ **Improved communications and synergy** among AT manager, district administrators, and interdisciplinary team.
> ➤ **Escalated awareness of AT program** and how it could benefit students with disabilities.
> ➤ **Convinced administrators to develop assessment protocols for Adaptive PE, Augmentative Communication, and Mechanics of Writing.**

REGION VII EDUCATION SERVICE CENTER — Tulsa, OK (1990–1998)
Assistive Technology Consultant

Provided assistive technology services to 99 Oklahoma school districts within a 17-county area. Orchestrated district-wide AT team development, AT assessment coordination/conveyance/reporting, device/product demonstrations and training, and policy/procedure establishment. Spearheaded AT program development in each special education program in Region VII and coordinated/facilitated continuing education to ensure cognizance and utilization of up-to-date devices and methodologies.

Managed loan library of 300+ AT devices and an AT Preview Center equipped with state-of-the-art devices and software. Represented Region VII in statewide AT consultant network and organized/participated in statewide conferences held four times per year. Planned, organized, and presented myriad six-hour workshops at regional and state level. Provided leadership, support, and federal/state policy dissemination to 32 AT program managers within region. Presented at two universities in Oklahoma each semester on topics related to assistive technology in public schools.

~ ~ **Continued on Page Two** ~ ~

68

Combination. *Ann Klint, Tyler, Texas*

This well-developed resume presents a wealth of information about a professional educator with more than 20 years of career experience. Like an executive resume, this document provides

Janet Elaine Ball

Home: (903) 888-9999 ◇ Cellular: (903) 555-4444 ◇ jball@mail.net
Page Two

REGION VII EDUCATION SERVICE CENTER (Continued)

Significant Accomplishments

➢ **Consistently received "excellent" evaluations from workshop attendees.** Regarded as creative presenter who delivers relevant information in enjoyable manner.
➢ **Pioneered Region VII Assistive Technology Program** that continues today.
➢ **Initiated Region VII AT Preview Center** and **Mobile Preview Center** (traveled to 32 special education program locations) to display various computer adaptations and relevant software for view/hands-on trial.
➢ **Planned, coordinated, and spearheaded every detail of three regional AT conferences.**
➢ **Established / implemented three-phase training framework** attended by 10 school districts/30 attendees during two-year period.
➢ **Accelerated number of AT items loaned from service center in excess of five times original amount.**
➢ **Created Region VII AT team,** which represented ideal paradigm; consisted of occupational therapist, educator for visually impaired, speech-language pathologist, PPCD teacher, and diagnostician.
➢ **Presented overview of assistive technology and technical solutions** to Tulsa Junior Club Physics Organization. Preceded hands-on seminar presentation designed to teach attendees fabrication/adaptation of toys for students.

TULSA INDEPENDENT SCHOOL DISTRICT — Tulsa, OK (1987–1989)
Preschool Program for Children with Disabilities Educator

CHILD DEVELOPMENT AND TREATMENT CENTER — Tulsa, OK (1987)
Summer School Teacher

RED OAK INDEPENDENT SCHOOL DISTRICT — Red Oak, OK (1983–1987)
Resource Teacher (1986–1987); **Homebound Teacher** (1983–1986)

FRIENDLY RESIDENTIAL CARE — Friendly, OK (1984–1985)
Evening Program Director
    Position held concurrently with Red Oak ISD. Spearheaded program for 12 mentally retarded adults.

LOS ANGELES SCHOOL DISTRICT — Los Angeles, CA (1982–1983)
Teaching Assistant — Resource Room

FRIENDS OF HANDICAPPED CHILDREN — Los Angeles, CA (1982–1983)
Qualified Professional for the Mentally Retarded (QPMR) / Program Director
    Orchestrated program in three group homes for cognitive-delayed adults. Held position concurrently with SDSD.

Education & Credentials

UNIVERSITY OF OKLAHOMA — Norman, OK
Numerous **Graduate** and **Undergraduate Courses**

TULSA COLLEGE — Tulsa, OK
B.A., Elementary Education and Mental Retardation (1982)

Oklahoma Teacher Certification — Elementary Education and Special Education

Honorary Distinction

Founder / Board Member / Fund-raising Chair, GENERATIONS TOGETHER — Tulsa, OK
(Extensively participated in constitution and operations manual development; director search; grant opportunity search; and fund-raising events to promote and acquire funding for start-up intergenerational daycare facility.)

much information through smaller font sizes and narrower margins (meaning wider lines). Careful provision of blank lines ensures enough white space so that the document does not seem cramped and so that sections, subsections, paragraphs, and bulleted lists can be seen and read easily.

e-résumé

Word Résumé

ASCII Résumé

Jennifer Saks

(555) 555-5555
jsaks@dotresume.com

Summary of Qualifications

Dedicated professional with master of science degree in administration and experience serving in progressively responsible leadership roles. Effective manager and coordinator. Proven ability to establish rapport and build relationships with people from diverse backgrounds. Team player. Talent for training and counseling. Creative with a flair for writing and orchestrating events. Fast learner. Adept at handling new challenges.

Highlights of Experience

Administration / Management — Proven ability to manage large groups, advise employees, administer programs, and coordinate major events.

- Recruited by supervisor to serve as department chairperson with responsibility for guiding programs and advising staff of 3.
- Received excellent evaluations for group-management and organizational skills.
- Revived and administered incentive recognition program, resulting in improved performance among participants.
- Produced innovative historical musical; coordinated every detail with more than 20 administrators, staff members, and volunteers. Event hailed as "outstanding . . . the songs and singing . . . [were] outstanding."

Communication / Interpersonal Relations — Frequently called upon by superiors and colleagues to act as group representative. Recognized as top-notch trainer. Superior writing ability.

- Chosen by peers to serve on advisory board — 1 of only 5 selected from group of 50.
- Appointed by supervisor as 1 of 2 representatives to attend and report on district-level meetings.
- Selected from among 5 new employees to participate in roundtable discussion with superintendent.
- Designated by county chairperson to demonstrate teaching techniques to new instructors.
- Sought out by coworkers for assistance in creating lesson plans and delivering training.
- Developed professional research bulletins on a variety of topics including cooperative groupings and group dynamics.

Education

M.S.A., Administration, Three Rivers College, Pittsburgh, PA, 3.8 GPA (2004)

B.A., English / Elementary Education, Mansfield University, Pittsburgh, PA, Scholarship (1997)

Employment History

Department Chairperson / Teacher — Reading, Writing, Math (1999 – 2004)
North Side Elementary School, Allegheny School District, Pittsburgh, PA

English Teacher (1997 – 1999)
Lakeside High School, Greene County Public Schools, Lakeside, PA

69

Combination. *Jan Holliday, Harleysville, Pennsylvania*

This Web resume is available in ASCII, or unadorned text, format and is kept simple with centered headings so that the viewer can easily size up and read the resume's information on the screen.

Engineering

Resumes at a Glance

RESUME NO.	OCCUPATION	GOAL	PAGE
70.	Research Associate	Environmental Engineer	143
71.	Project Manager	Environmental Engineer	144
72.	Manufacturing/Engineering Manager	Manufacturing Executive	146
73.	Construction Consultant	Engineer/Project Manager	148
74.	VP, Engineering and Land Surveying	Project Manager/Engineer	150
75.	Director, Operations and Training	Engineering Executive	152
76.	Industrial Engineer	Industrial Engineer	154

GEORGE CRANDALL, EIT

0000 Smith Avenue
Houston, TX 79000

Home: (000) 000-0000
name@lycos.com

Career Profile	**ENVIRONMENTAL ENGINEER-IN-TRAINING**

- Focused, analytical professional with strong engineering educational background complemented by work experience involving field research and evaluation projects.
- Able to balance creative thinking with logical design ideas; enjoy opportunities to develop solutions that address challenging environmental problems.
- Work effectively in both self-managed and team-based projects; maintain high ethical and quality standards, professional demeanor, and cooperative attitude.
- Use hands-on, detail-oriented approach in completing projects and assignments.

Knowledge & Skill Areas:

*Field Research • Report Writing • Experimental Design & Methods • Project Planning
Quality Assurance Standards • Research & Development • Environmental Hazards
Systems Analysis • Regulatory & Safety Compliance • Engineering Documentation
Environmental Sample Analysis • Risk Assessment • Client/Customer Communications*

Education

Masters of Environmental Engineering, 2002 / GPA: 3.75
Bachelors of Environmental Engineering, 2000 / GPA: 3.30
University, Houston, TX

Selected Upper-Level Coursework:

- Design of Air Pollution Systems
- Solid & Hazardous Waste Treatment
- Environmental Impact Analysis
- Environmental Systems Design

- Design of Wastewater Treatment Plants
- Groundwater Contaminant Transport
- Geoethnical Practices for Waste Disposal
- Environmental Law & Policies

Project Highlights:

- **"Best Bench Scale Demonstration Award"**—Worked with group of 6 students to plan, develop, and present winning bench scale model (addressing water quality issues) at 2 Design Competitions, 1999 & 2000, at the Waste Energy Research Consortium.
- **"Design of Wastewater Treatment Plants"**—Played key role in design project for treatment plant based on quality assurance and regulatory compliance factors. Delivered well-received presentation to Masters-level class upon completion.
- **"Environmental Impact Statement"**—Developed proposal-oriented report detailing most effective, environmentally sound strategies for controlling brushes within region.

Work Experience

Research Associate, 2002–Present
Research Assistant & Laboratory Technician, 1998–2001
Research Assistant, Summer 2001 (Texas National Environmental & Engineering Lab)
University, Houston, TX (1998–Present)

Conduct research, sample collection and analysis, experimental design, and explosives evaluations using high-performance liquid chromatography, and perform other related activities in positions involving field studies and frequent travel to various counties within East Texas region. Report directly to Laboratory Manager; additionally responsible for daily maintenance of weather stations.

- **Bioremediation of Explosives in Vadose Zone**—Conduct explosives contamination studies and evaluations for government agency Pantex to recommend strategies for remediation projects with highest potential for success.
- **Overall Work Performance**—Put forth consistent effort in meeting and exceeding job requirements; worked overtime hours and maintained full-time class schedule throughout employment. Recognized for intelligent, thorough work habits.

Activities

Society of Environmental Professionals—Member, 3 years; Secretary, 1 year
Civil Engineering Honor Society—Chi Epsilon

70

Combination. *Daniel J. Dorotik, Jr., Lubbock, Texas*

Including information about school-related projects is a way to offset a recent graduate's lack of much work experience. See, for example, the Project Highlights in the Education section.

CRAIG P. RICHTER, P.E.

163 Trinity Lane
Providence, North Carolina 28082
Home: (828) 442-9555   Cell: (828) 321-9422
crichter@blueridge.net

ENVIRONMENTAL ENGINEERING & PROJECT MANAGEMENT PROFESSIONAL
Expertise in Assessment, Design & Installation of Water/Wastewater Systems

---

Twenty years of experience in engineering planning, design, project financing (grantsmanship), advertisement/bidding, contract administration, construction management and startup services for numerous types of projects. Experience includes

- Wastewater Treatment Plants
- Wastewater Lift Stations
- Sanitary Sewer Lines & Force Mains
- Infiltration/Inflow Analysis
- Project Budgeting & Management
- NPDES Permitting
- Field Installation Management

- Sanitary Sewer Line Televised Inspection
- Wastewater Facilities Studies
  (201 Reports, Preliminary Engineering Reports)
- Toxicity Evaluation & Rate Studies
- Cross-Functional Team Leadership
- Intermunicipal Service Agreements
- Capital Improvements & Expansions

Strengths

> Skilled in establishing rapport and building long-term client relationships. Excellent problem-resolution skills; adept at assessing needs, communicating value and facilitating quality improvement through a win-win approach.
> Detail-oriented, organized, personable and enthusiastic leader with the ability to comprehend, coordinate and manage multiple projects while focusing on the overall scope.

Industry Experience

Extensive experience, including municipal, transportation, manufacturing and industrial clients.

Project Management

Directed diverse project teams, including engineers, CAD/CADD operators, technicians and construction observers. Managed external liaison affairs with elected municipal officials, city/town managers, council members, regulatory agency personnel, biologists/geologists, attorneys and directors of public works and utilities.

PROFESSIONAL EXPERIENCE:

Project Manager, **A. J. TAYLOR & CO., INC.**—Asheboro, N.C.   2001–2002

Directed more than 20 major projects in various phases (17+ water/wastewater; 1 storm water) in 11 months, representing aggregate engineering fees of $1.18 million. Worked on numerous other projects. Scope of responsibility included planning, design, permitting, grantsmanship, advertisement/bidding and construction supervision. Oversaw teams of project engineers and CAD operators. Managed projects using the Internet. Also traveled to project sites.

Operating & Management Achievements:

- Challenged to revitalize client relationships for several projects that were in various phases (including some behind schedule), improving communication, restoring credibility and delivering projects to achieve client satisfaction.

- Developed a marketing brochure (the first in company's 75-year history) on funding agencies, which was selected by the corporation's marketing director as a model and implemented companywide.

Representative Project Highlights:

- Directed preparation of Preliminary Engineering Report (PER) for the Tuscaloosa River Wastewater Treatment Plant Expansion for the Town of Mountain City, N.C. Personally presented PER to citizenry at public hearing, outlining company's plans to mitigate environmental impacts. Championed company's position, persuasively countering negative public comments and fostering goodwill.

- Managed the Basis of Design to establish project scope (i.e., type, size, dimensions and location of process equipment) and provide information on electrical issues. Proposed restructuring of project to separate the Basis of Design component from the design/preparation of plans and specifications.

71

Combination. *Doug Morrison, Charlotte, North Carolina*

This wastewater engineer with 20 years of experience had completed more than 100 projects. The writer selected several key projects to highlight the individual's diversified experience. The

Craig P. Richter   page 2

- As project manager, solidified tenuous client relationship with Tremont Water and Sewer Authority (TWASA) and secured new project, a PER and Environmental Assessment for upgrade and expansion of water and wastewater treatment plants, resulting in procurement of subsequent project contracts.

- Led successful turnaround of sanitary-sewer-line extension project for the Town of Carleton, N.C. Directed completion, returning project on track. Revised technical issues and obtained N.C. DOT approval.

- Won and managed Wastewater Treatment Plant Study project for Southern Mennonites, Public Works Division, Bryson City, N.C. Personally solicited, discovered and responded to existing RFP. Also served as project engineer; completed project within stringent timelines (30 days) and within budget.

Project Manager, **ALEXANDER FLEMING, INC.**—Philadelphia, Pa. & Charlotte, N.C.   1991–2001

Based in Philadelphia (1991–1999) and Charlotte (1999–2001). Managed 125+ wastewater, water and other environmental projects over 10 years. Worked on other projects in a supportive role. Project highlights include

- **Dilworth Elevated Water Storage Tank Improvement (Raleigh, N.C.):**
  Directed engineering services for improvements to control delivery of water during periods of high demand.

- **Muskrat Wastewater Treatment Plant (Melbourne Beach, Fla.):**
  Oversaw completion (final 20%) of an upgrade and expansion for facility. Provided contract administration, construction observation, operations and maintenance manual development, startup and plant performance troubleshooting.

- **Professional Tank Dismantling Services for the Duquesne Elevated Water Tank (Raleigh, N.C.):**
  Directed dismantling services for 500,000-gallon, riveted steel storage tank. Project included remediation of lead-contaminated soil, from identifying/profiling soil and obtaining bids for removal/disposal to overseeing removal/disposal procedures.

- **Final Design of Wastewater Treatment System Upgrades, Shakley Rail Yard (Shakley, Ind.):**
  Managed design of system upgrades for treating 170,000 gpd of oil wastewater. Project included relocation of roof rain leaders from diesel shop roof.

Previous Professional Experience: Project Manager, Smithfield Engineering & Surveying, Charlotte, N.C., 1987–1991; Project Manager, J. A. Jones Associates, Inc., Charlotte, N.C., 1978–1987.

EDUCATION:

B.S., Urban and Environmental (Civil) Engineering, 1980
Carnegie-Mellon University, Pittsburgh, Pa.
Professional Development:
- Confined Space Training, Alexander Fleming, Inc. (4 hours)
- Project Management Seminar, Penn State University & Alexander Fleming, Inc. (80 PDH), 2000–2001
- AutoCAD I & II, Central Piedmont Community College, Charlotte, N.C., 2000–2002

PROFESSIONAL REGISTRATIONS:

- P.E., N.C. (#16142), 1984–Present
- Inactive: S.C. (#19747), 1990; W.Va. (#21502), 1993; Ohio (#75966), 1993; Penn. (#039872), 1992

CERTIFICATIONS: Diplomate, American Academy of Environmental Engineers, 1991

PROFESSIONAL AFFILIATIONS:

Water Environment Federation; American Water Works Association; N.C. American Water Works Association & Water Environment Association

box pulls the reader's attention to his field and expertise. Bulleted, industry-specific keywords show the areas of expertise. Projects are referred to throughout the resume, especially on page one in the Project Management section and the Representative Project Highlights subsection, and in bulleted items on page two.

BARRY H. SCHMIDT

1817 Orleans Drive
Elk Grove Village, Illinois 60007

barrys@anyisp.com

Home: (555) 555-5555
Mobile: (000) 000-000

MANUFACTURING EXECUTIVE
Mechanical Engineering...Production...Plant Management

Seasoned professional with comprehensive experience and visible achievements in diverse manufacturing arenas, including machined parts, fabricated parts, plastic parts, die casting, mechanical power transmission, and powder metallurgy. Proven track record for implementing strategies that enhance productivity and profitability. Experienced in supervising engineers and technicians, as well as drafting and shop floor personnel. Recognized as an industry expert and published author on mechanical power transmission products. Academic credentials: MBA; BS in Physics.

Tradition of Performance Excellence in

- **Profit & Loss Responsibility**
- **Job Shop Operations**
- **Vendor Cost-Benefit Analysis**
- **Statistical Process Control**
- **Engineering Design Calculations**
- **Machining and Welding Operations**
- **Production Management**

- **Daily Plant Operations**
- **Staff Development**
- **Quality Assurance**
- **Creative Problem-Solving**
- **Job Costing and Routing**
- **Union Management Experience**
- **Continuous Process Improvement**

- **Computer literate** in MRP programs (MAPICS, Visual Manufacturing, ACCPAC, UA Corporate Accounting, PRO-MAN), AutoCAD 14, CADKEY, Windows 98, 2000, XP and MS Office applications.
- **Affiliations:** ASME, IEEE Magnetic Society, Charter Member—Chicago Chapter of Vibration Institute

PROFESSIONAL EXPERIENCE

REX-TEC CORPORATION   2001 to Present

Privately held, $2 million master distributor and manufacturer of mechanical power transmission products. 20+ years in business.

Manufacturing/Engineering Manager

Hired to develop new magnetic coupling product line, to offset 40% downturn in the machine tool industry (previous primary market for company); this included standardization of design, sourcing of components, and development of in-house manufacturing processes. Challenged with expanding sales of new product line from $100,000 to $1 million. Empowered with full accountability for manufacturing and assembly, design, application engineering, purchasing/vendor qualification, quality assurance, job costing, margin calculations, new materials evaluation and staff development. Advise President in all aspects of new business development, market expansion, capital expenditures and operating budgets. ***Key Accomplishments:***

- **Transformed company from warehouse distributor to a manufacturer, saving $10,000 per year in out-plant costs and offering 24-hour delivery and generating additional sales of $20,000 annually.**
- **Successfully developed new magnetic coupling product line, projected to generate a 56% profit margin.** This new product line is designed for small-quantity customers and large OEMs. Usually, this product is customized by individual OEMs for internal use or built by magnet manufacturers not offering a complete power transmission solution.
- **Increased profit margins by another 10%–15% after securing new vendors via E-sourcing.**
- **Achieved revenue increase in new product line from zero to $100,000 in the first year; projected to increase tenfold by FY04.**
- **Initiated and developed Quality Assurance procedures and manual and established a quality level for product manufacture, according to MIL-I-45208.**

72

Combination. *Joellyn Wittenstein, Elk Grove Village, Illinois*

This manufacturing executive had long-term experience in large organizations and drew on it to help his most recent employer, a considerably smaller company, expand its traditional product

BARRY H. SCHMIDT

CONTAINERS, INC.   1990 to 2001

Privately held $4 million manufacturer of steel industrial refuse containers and cart-dumpers; 25 years in business; customers included City of Chicago Department of Streets & Sanitation, BFI and Waste Management.

Plant Manager

Managed daily manufacturing operations and P&L of a 3-shift, heavy-gauge sheet metal and fabrication Union shop. Supervised 7 direct reports (3 foremen, buyer and engineering support staff) and 35 indirect employees (welders and assemblers). Responsibilities included purchasing materials and supplies, staffing, delivery, shop floor scheduling, vendor evaluation and selection, capital budgeting and implementation and reorganizing shop floor for maximum productivity. ***Key Accomplishments:***

- **Significantly reversed $100,000 operating loss to $750,000 profit in 9 months** by raising prices to reflect costs plus fixed margins, and preparing/adhering to monthly production schedules, which further decreased costs by eliminating production shutdowns for special product runs.

- **Reduced welding manufacturing costs by $500 per day through re-engineering of the labor force,** assigning lower-salaried material handlers to stock work cells and move semi-finished products to painting holding area, instead of highly paid welders, and adding a 3rd shift of painting operations to improve work flow.

- **Proactively negotiated payments with new vendors at a 15% cost savings on steel ($250,000) and established a new vendor for hydraulic cylinders at a savings of $50,000 per year at regular terms and no pre-payment,** after obtaining a large, multi-year contract and a pre-payment, preventing company from closing. Previously, the company had been paying bills on 120 days and many vendors had ceased business relationships or required advance payment on a year's worth of inventory.

POWER-TRANS, INC.   1976 to 1990

100-year-old privately held $30 million global manufacturer of mechanical power transmission products. Primary customers include Caterpillar, Gardner-Denver, GE, FMC, John Deere, WW Grainger and McMaster-Carr.

Director of Research & Development

Progressed from R & D Engineer to Senior Application Engineer, Quality Control Manager, and Engineering Manager, to Director of Research and Development. Contributed to company's growth from $6 million to $30 million during tenure. Managed design, application, manufacturing engineering and quality assurance departments, which included supervision of 13 direct reports. ***Key Accomplishments:***

- Created Quality Control Department and accompanying Quality Control manual, establishing the MIL-I-45208 Inspection System. Reduced scrap and return rate from $400,000 to $100,000 against $20 million in sales.

- Developed a super-strong, wear-resistant U-joint, using this design to secure multiyear, multimillion-dollar parts contracts for the M-1 tank, F-16 fighter, Harrier aircraft and Bradley fighting vehicle.

- Won the coveted "Bachner Award" after developing plastic universal joints and flexible couplings.

- Reduced costs of sintered products, saving 40,000 pounds of material (4% reduction) per year, lowering shipping costs by $30,000/annually, improving tooling life and increasing throughput.

- Developed new products including material development, tooling, vendors and manufacturing processes.

- Presented lecture series on power transmission couplings; also presented technical papers at industry conferences and authored magazine articles addressing flexible couplings, vibration and universal joints.

EDUCATION & TRAINING _____

- MBA, Olivet Nazarene University, Kankakee, Illinois (4.0 GPA)   2002
- MAPICS for the Engineer, GMD   1988
- Effective Engineering Management, NYU School of Continuing Education   1981
- Advanced Plastics Product Design Engineering   1979
- BS, Physics, Illinois Institute of Technology, Chicago, Illinois   1975

1817 Orleans Drive • Elk Grove Village, Illinois 60007 • 555-555-5555 • 000-000-0000 • barrys@anyisp.com

line. In the Professional Experience section, a brief company profile in italic under each company name helps the reader assess the applicant's career history. The heading Key Accomplishments in bold italic and the use of bullets make the individual's achievements in each workplace stand out.

Thomas P. Redmond, PE

256 Musket River Road • Washington, NJ 07882 • 908.555.5555 • TRedmond999@comcast.net

ENGINEERING / PROJECT MANAGEMENT
Maintenance Management ~ Project Engineering ~ Metals Industry

Results-driven and well-organized *Engineering Professional* able to combine a unique blend of formal technical education with a solid, hands-on background in the metals industry.

Extensive knowledge of manufacturing environments. Versatile team player with an ability to incorporate new concepts and interact with all levels of professionals. Expertise in industrial construction: foundations, structural steel, plumbing, and electrical. Work closely with management, consultants, vendors, and tradespeople.

Competencies Include

- ◆ Project Management
- ◆ Maintenance Management
- ◆ Equipment Selection & Installation
- ◆ Vendor Negotiations

- ◆ Troubleshooting
- ◆ Planning and Development
- ◆ Process Optimization
- ◆ Cost Reduction Strategies

Professional Achievements

As an Independent Consultant, and as a Maintenance Manager and Mechanical Engineer for Northeast Pipe Company, I developed expertise in the following areas:

<u>**Project Management**</u>—Provided design, project planning, and implementation for a variety of large projects that had a major impact on improving operations, efficiency, and profits.

- Specified, selected and managed the installation of a 150,000cfm pulse jet dust collector utilizing a 600hp blower, with more than 2,000 bags and 150-ft.-tall discharge stack. The project resulted in a drastic improvement in the air quality of the manufacturing area.
- Managed the design and implementation of a cooling tower for the cupola, for maintaining cool shell temperature. The 2,000-ton-capacity system included 150hp pumps running at 2,000gpm with extensive piping, all completed by in-house personnel.
- Renovated a 150-ft.-long annealing furnace with new burners, gas trains, blowers, ductwork, refractory, structural work, and new control room, to significantly increase production and efficiency.
- Directed the installation of seven air compressors, totaling more than 800 hp, in three climate-controlled rooms, to provide reliable shop air pressure.
- Consulted with a spray specialist on paint machine improvements in order to decrease paint use and improve the appearance of the product. Developed and managed the conversion process, which included a new spray system, all new controls, paint storage tanks, hydraulic unit, pipe conveying system, and overspray removal.

<u>**Industrial Maintenance**</u>—Managed a maintenance team of more than 50 employees covering three shifts of operation. Personnel included a superintendent, nine foremen, millwrights, electricians, machinists, carpenters, and mechanics.

- Maintained the entire foundry consisting of scrap-loading cranes, 60 tons/hr charging system, cupola system, pollution-control equipment, wastewater treatment plant, cooling towers, hot-metal cranes, core department, six casting machines, annealing furnace, quality control, pressure-testing equipment, cement-lining station, seal-coating station, pipe lifts, air compressors, machine shop, buildings and grounds, and mobile equipment.

Continued

73

Combination. *Beverley and Mitchell I. Baskin, Marlboro, New Jersey*

If it were not for the Employment history section on the second page, this resume would be altogether a functional resume. The applicant's name is large enough to be seen at a distance in

Page Two   THOMAS P. REDMOND, PE

Professional Achievements *(Continued)*

Environmental Compliance—Performed/supported storm-water testing and permitting, yearly stack testing, hazardous waste removal, solid waste storage, dust collector performance evaluations, monitoring well testing, wastewater treatment operations and testing, materials recycling program, and continuous emissions monitoring.

Operations—Supported operations in various capacities, including start-up, troubleshooting, environmental compliance, production upgrades, quality-control testing, maintenance, and new equipment commissioning.

Engineering Procurement—Procured items including pumps, bearings, gears, couplings, valves, pipe fittings, structural steel, fasteners, motors, cranes, gearboxes, hydraulic units, blowers, tooling, machined and fabricated parts, obsolete part substitutions, and pneumatic and hydraulic components.

Civil Engineering Design—Completed extensive design of reinforced concrete foundations, walls and slabs, structural steel building design and detailing, underground water supply and drain piping design, grading and paving throughout plant, and transit layout work.

Machine Design—Designed an assortment of machinery and machinery parts. Well-versed in fabrication and machining techniques and rebuilding of machinery (pumps, cylinders, gearboxes, cranes, lathes, etc.).

HVAC—Performed HVAC calculations, primarily blower and ductwork sizing. Designed, specified, and installed systems to provide furnace waste heat for pipe drying, fresh-air supply for control rooms, gas heaters for freeze protection, and infrared tube heaters for curing rooms.

Quality Control—Supported the plant's efforts in the ISO 9002 certification process. Experienced in product physical testing methods including Charpy impact, tensile, hardness, metallurgy, dimensional gauging, weighing, and pressure testing.

Piping—Designed and installed numerous piping systems for water, air, oxygen, nitrogen, natural gas, oil hydraulics, wastewater and sludge, powder conveying, fuel oil, and paint. Utilized several types of piping (carbon steel, stainless steel, cast iron, hydraulic tubing, copper, and plastic).

Materials Handling—Specified, operated, and maintained overhead cranes, forklifts, conveyor belts, pneumatic conveying systems, screw conveyors, bucket elevators, scissors lifts, conveyor chains, and pipe transfer cars.

Employment

- Independent Construction Consultant working on various construction projects   5/00–present
- Maintenance Manager, Northeast Cast Iron Pipe Co.   6/99–4/00
- Mechanical Engineer, Northeast Cast Iron Pipe Co.   4/90–6/99

Education/Professional

- New Jersey Professional Engineering License, 2002
- B.S., Mechanical Engineering—New Jersey Institute of Technology, 1989
- Computer skills include Internet proficiency, AutoCAD14, and Microsoft Word and Excel.
- Bilingual—English and Spanish

an average-size office. A profile, areas of competence, and achievements in a Professional Achievements section take up almost all of the resume. Boldfacing and underlining help the reader see the many areas of expertise indicated at length on pages one and two.

Martin G. Morrison, III, P.E., L.S.
234 Laurel Court • Freehold, NJ 07728 • 732.555.5555 (H & F)

PROJECT MANAGER / ENGINEERING
Professional Engineer ~ Professional Planner ~ Professional Land Surveyor

Competencies Include

- Engineering Management
- Inspection Bonding
- Municipal/Township Engineering
- Budget Management
- Storm Water Management

- Planning/Zoning Board Reviews
- Sanitary Sewer Design
- Site Development
- Staff Training/Motivation/Development
- Project Management

Profile

Results-oriented Professional Engineer and Manager...known for technical resourcefulness and creativity...interact with governmental agencies, privately owned businesses, and individuals.

Professional Experience

MARCO ENGINEERING AND LAND SURVEYING, New York, NY (2000–2003)
Vice President

Management and supervision of field survey crews and office personnel. Performed analysis of field work; prepared field schedules, topographical mapping, and right-of-way appropriation maps. Clients included the New York State Department of Transportation, the New York State Throughway Authority, the Metro-North Commuter Railroad, and the New York City Department of Design and Construction.

- Survey Project Manager for the LIRR East Side Access Project to Grand Central Station. This project employed a unique method of construction. Managed the scheduling, quality, and coordination of rail and topographic surveys with the Tunnel and Systems consultant.
- Managed the design survey for a noise barrier on the Grand Central Parkway, completing the project on time and within budget.
- Project Manager for the utility survey of the JFK Air Train Project for the Port Authority of NY/NJ. This project integrated light rail service between JFK Airport and New York City.
- Supervised the MTA-NYC Transit system project for a topographic, utility, and property survey of 12 subway stations in preparation for ADA improvements.
- Directed the site surveys for the New York State Department of Transportation on the following projects:
  - Completed the Hutchinson River Parkway safety improvements project on time and within budget. Prepared an Abstract Request Map for property acquisition for a pedestrian bridge, and a survey for ground photo controls using GPS, 3-D with GPS, and Einstein Loop.
  - The FDR Drive main roadways and service roads including a hydrographic survey of the East River for bulkhead treatment.
  - The rebuilding and rehabilitation of 3 bridges on I-95, requiring bridge structure surveys and roadway cross-sections.
  - The re-signing of the Henry Hudson Parkway from 72nd Street to Westchester County. Directed the topographic survey, the photogram metric survey, the ground survey, and the survey control report.
  - Supervised mapping of the Cross Bronx Expressway Right-of-Way, preparation of Abstract Request Maps for property acquisition, and a Right-of-Way report.
  - Successfully completed the survey of 3 bridges as part of the Van Wyck Expressway widening project.
- Project Manager for the New York City Department of Environmental Protection's Westchester Creek CSO Detention Site Preparation Survey, which was completed on time and within budget. Directed preparation of the site survey, the title search, and setting of the property corners.

74

Combination. *Beverley and Mitchell I. Baskin, Marlboro, New Jersey*

If it were not for the two-column list of competencies and the brief Profile, this resume would be essentially a chronological resume. Small, square bullets point to either responsibilities or

Page Two   MARTIN G. MORRISON, III, P.E., L.S.

Professional Experience (Continued)

CORMAN ENGINEERING, HIGHTSTOWN, NJ (1997–2000)
Project Manager

- As consultant to Marlboro Township, supervised inspections, bonded item compliance, bond reduction, billing, and recommendation for bond release.
- Managed the site-development surveys for a variety of projects in order to obtain final approvals from the Planning Board, Department of Environmental Protection, and other applicable agencies. Projects included an Assisted Living facility, a franchise restaurant, and a townhouse community.
- Responsible for the surveying and engineering of Sewer and Water Extensions, Stream Encroachment, Soil Conservation Service, Soil Erosion, and Sediment Control.

L & F ASSOCIATES, MIDDLETOWN, NJ (1995–1996)
Principal Engineer

Consulting Engineering assignment as Assistant Township Engineer for Holmdel Township.

- Supervised the administration and inspection of active bonded projects of 16 subdivisions and 21 site plans.
- Prepared estimates to determine quantities for bonded projects.
- Reviewed plans for Planning Board compliance.
- Provided day-to-day response to residential complaints and inquiries.

As the in-house Bonding Specialist, represented L & F at various Planning and Zoning Boards throughout New Jersey for plan review and meeting participation.

LOMAN, CARMICHAEL, GIFFORD & KASE, BRICK, NJ (1986–1994)
Associate, Project Manager

Managed the site-development engineering and surveys for several types of projects. Obtained approvals from local Planning and Zoning Boards, as well as other government agencies.

- Provided a unique roadway and log design for the Knob Hill Development, Howell Township, NJ, consisting of 24 homes. The road, lot grading, and detention area were constructed without affecting a wetland area in the middle of the site.
- Supervised engineering, surveying, and final approvals for the Shore Oaks Golf Course Development in Howell Township, NJ. The 450-acre site included 170 single-family homes and an 18-hole golf course. The project required a zoning change and offsite utility extensions for sewer, water, gas, and electric.
- Completed the site plan and survey for a 50,000-square-foot commercial warehouse, which involved wetlands delineation, stream encroachment applications, and sanitary sewer extensions to the site.

HAMMOND, FREEHOLD, NJ (1982–1986)
Corporate Engineer

- Responsible for the coordination and design of all corporate land-development projects.
- Managed the activities of in-house personnel, and supervised the coordination of outside contractors.
- Designed and directed the planning of water and sewer extensions, pumping stations, production wells, and water towers of the Adelphia Water & Sewer companies.

BOROUGH OF FREEHOLD, FREEHOLD, NJ (1975–1982)
Assistant Engineer

- Prepared plans and specifications for all contract work.
- Inspected and supervised all construction, maintenance, and repair work on streets, curbs, sidewalks, and drainage systems.
- In charge of maintaining the municipal tax maps and all surveying required for construction, reconstruction, and modifications to borough streets.

Education and Certifications

BS ~ Civil Engineering, NEW JERSEY INSTITUTE OF TECHNOLOGY, Newark, NJ
Licensed Professional Engineer—NJ, NY, PA, and CT
Licensed Professional Land Surveyor—NJ and NY
Licensed Professional Planner—NJ

achievements throughout the Professional Experience section. Diamond bullets point to a sublevel of projects completed at the most recent workplace. Page borders tie together the two pages. Larger-than-average "small caps" make the company names easy to see at a glance.

LOUIS G. AMES

457 Kimberly Drive • Wall, NJ 07719 • 732.567.2356 H • 732.569.8321 C • lames@monmouth.com

ENGINEERING EXECUTIVE

Metals Industry ~ Engineering ~ Manufacturing

Multi-dimensional hands-on business professional providing leadership, vision, creativity and business acumen in driving and managing business growth. Skilled in relationship building, metals, engineering and manufacturing line management. Accomplished in planning and executing projects from concept through production, with strong troubleshooting and problem-resolution skills. Highly organized and detail oriented. Demonstrating broad strengths and accomplishments in

Strategic Planning	**Project Management**	**Staff Management & Development**
New Business Development	**Quality Management**	**Crisis Management**
Business Management	**Product/Process Design**	**Troubleshooting/Problem Solving**
Lean Manufacturing	**Engineering Management**	**Contract Negotiations**
P & L Responsibility	**Training/Education**	**Customer/Vendor Liaison**
Production Management	**Financial Management**	**Marketing & Sales**
Plants & Facilities	**Manufacturing Techniques**	**Leadership/Motivation**

Twenty-seven years of experience in general management with progressively responsible management and technical positions. Adept at improving products and processes, and operational effectiveness with bottom-line results.
~ Operations Management/Lean Manufacturing/Engineering/Metals Industry ~

PROFESSIONAL EXPERIENCE—General Management/Operations/Sales

NEW JERSEY COMPUTER SCIENCE INSTITUTE, Newark, NJ
NJCSI in an accredited postsecondary vocational educational facility providing authorized instructor-led and hands-on IT training for the profit market. NJCSI is operated locally under the auspices of the NJ Department of Education and federally under the ASSCST. Organization employs 75–100 staff, maintains a 35% New Jersey market share selling services to the corporate and general population and ranks among the top 20 private for-profit training centers within the state.

Director of Operations & Training 1991–2002
Recruited to oversee daily operations of educational institute with full P&L responsibility for operations, maintenance, facilities, placement, corporate training and purchasing departments. Extensive knowledge of networks, Internet, database systems and programming processes.
- Recommended, acquired and implemented software, hardware and all IT equipment for the institution.
- Provided leadership and strategic direction for organization with emphasis on leading-edge technology.
- Reported directly to the President, implementing set agendas and achieving tactical/strategic goals.
- Authored and implemented overall budget, ensuring business objectives were achieved on a timely basis.
- Hired, evaluated and mentored staff, providing needed training and necessary staff changes.
- Instituted new consulting division with full P&L responsibility for sales, marketing and IT installations at all customer sites.
- Identified and assessed operational concerns, taking corrective actions when necessary.
- Introduced new technologies and innovations while increasing alliances and enrollment by 150%, resulting in doubling sales figures.

PROFESSIONAL EXPERIENCE—Engineering Management/Technical Operations

GAMMA METALS INC., Jersey City, NJ
Gamma Metals is the world leader in the development, manufacturing and sales of innovative materials used in the electronic assembly process with revenues of $130M annually. Clients include IBM, COMPAQ, Motorola, Seagate, Conner and the automotive industry.

Manufacturing/Key Manager 1990–1992
- Oversaw the production and distribution of solder paste and powder to domestic/international divisions.
- Managed myriad projects within budgetary restrictions, achieving corporate growth.
- Extensive knowledge and demonstrated experience of manufacturing, testing, and regulatory and quality operational issues associated with worldwide distribution.
- Authored and oversaw departmental budget.
- Liaison with domestic/international sales and marketing staff to improve overall product performance through modifications.
- Increased sales by 200% and reduced manufacturing downtime by 45% by introducing statistical process controls.
- Increased product shipments by 300%, reduced network by 75% and implemented JIT by testing to improve manufacturing techniques/production processes.

75

Combination. *Beverley and Mitchell I. Baskin, Marlboro, New Jersey*

Font sizes are smaller in this resume because there is more information to communicate to the reader. Strengths and accomplishments are placed in three columns after a profile. Boldfacing

LOUIS G. AMES   **PAGE TWO**

- Increased production output by 87% while gaining Union/Teamster acceptance and contract ratification by expanding weekly operation shifts.
- Graduate of *Corporate Quality Improvement Process* and instituted this process in preparation of ISO 9000 certification.

MEDICAL TECHNOLOGIES INC., Rahway, NJ
Medical Technologies, a start-up medical device (pulmonary and respiratory products) and consulting firm, with approximately 50 staff and $5M in annual sales.
Director of Manufacturing/Engineering 1985–1990
- Liaison with medical community and regulatory agencies.
- Senior staff member formulating key tactical and strategic programs impacting company operations.
- Led multidisciplinary teams responsible for product design, marketing and manufacturing.
- Hired, trained and motivated engineering staff, forming a cohesive approach to the product-development process.
- Improved current operational procedures to speed the documentation of medical device procedures to gain design, manufacturing and packaging approval within 90 days.
- Managed full project life-cycle, bringing a new product from design to manufacturing.
- Increased sales from $175K to $2.5M over four fiscal years by designing precision electronic/mechanical, durable medical equipment while creating manufacturing facility 2 months ahead of schedule and 15% under budget.

ELECTRO-CATHETER TECHNOLOGIES, Linden, NJ
Company designed, manufactured, marketed and sold adult and pediatric cardiovascular catheters employing 250 staff, with 2 production plants, and $25M in annual revenues. Ranked among the top 25 cardiovascular catheter firms in the country.
Vice President of Operations 1983–1985
Hired to institute ME department and facilitate the smooth transition of products from R&D to manufacturing.
- Key player closely working with suppliers to ensure that subassemblies and components meet engineering, quality and delivery standards.
- Investigated strategic alliances and partnerships, enhancing capabilities of engineering/manufacturing efforts and improving product line.
- Reduced transition time from R&D to manufacturing by 80%.
- Saved $200K in materials/assembly time within first two fiscal years by introducing 15-second ultrasonic welding cycle.
- Completed facilities by 10+% under budget for new products while increasing production.

BECTON DICKINSON & COMPANY, Rochelle Park, NJ
Division Senior Engineer 1980–1983

SECON METALS INC., White Plains, NY
Production/White Room Lead Engineer 1975–1980

EDUCATION
MONMOUTH UNIVERSITY, Long Branch, NJ
Master of Business Administration—Finance ~ Ongoing
MANHATTAN COLLEGE, Riverdale, NY
Bachelor of Science—Mechanical Engineering (BSME)

TRAINING
Total Quality Management (TQM)—Phillip Crosby Associates
Strategic Planning & Financial Analysis—American Management Association
Interactive Management & Stop Program—Dupont Corporation

CERTIFICATIONS
Adobe Certified Expert—Photoshop (ACE)
AutoDesk Certified Instructor
MCSE—NT 4.0 & MCT-NT 4.0

COMPUTER SKILLS
Microsoft Office (Word, Excel, PowerPoint, Access), WordPerfect, Lotus 1-2-3, AutoCAD 2002, Adobe Photoshop, Adobe Illustrator, Adobe inDesign, Web Design, E-mail and Internet, and accounting software packages.
Ability to identify computer components, and procure, build and troubleshoot computer systems.

makes the information in the columns stand out. In the Professional Experience section, boldfacing helps also to distinguish general management from engineering management and to direct attention to workplace names and job positions. Bold italic is used for the main section headings.

SEAN L. STEEPER

17 Woodcliff Road
Westboro, MA 01581

Home: 333-333-3333
slsteeper@hotmail.com

INDUSTRIAL ENGINEER
New Product Design • Manufacturing Process Redesign • Project Management

EDUCATION

University of Massachusetts ~ Amherst, MA
B.S. Industrial Engineering ~ Graduated with Honors ~ May 2003

RELEVANT COURSEWORK

Engineering Design • Systems Engineering • Computer Integrated Manufacturing • Production Systems
Production Engineering • Operations Research • Oral and Visual Communications
Industrial Psychology • Ergonomics • Quality Management

ACADEMIC PROJECTS

- Researched and recommended alternative methods for coating coronary stents for a leading manufacturer of cardiovascular products. Designed and manufactured prototype for spray-coating each stent, as opposed to the current practice of dipping them, which resulted in a 25% reduction in defects.
- Designed a facility and assembly-line layout to optimize production for an electronics products company.
- Generated a comprehensive Safety and Development Plan for a medical devices company.
- Created an ergonomically efficient material-handling trolley.

ENGINEERING EXPERIENCE

ABC Cardiovascular, Amherst, MA   5/02–10/02
Industrial Engineer, Co–Op

- Designed, developed, and implemented a unique device for facilitating the movement of coronary stent and catheter products from one workstation to another, resulting in a 20% decrease in scrapped product.
- Revised and simplified the Standard Operating Procedure for a label-printing machine that included detailed, easy-to-follow troubleshooting procedures and digital photographs.
- Analyzed production reports associated with a crimping machine and successfully identified one product that was consistently more prone to defects than others. Recommended machine adjustments to alleviate defects.
- Optimized floor space by rearranging and redesigning four production cells within a tightly constricted space.
- Member of a team to prepare for a critical FDA audit. Ensured machines were fully validated and safety guards were properly and securely in place.

ADDITIONAL EXPERIENCE

Albright Roofing and Painting, Framingham, MA   9/03–Present
Construction Laborer—Contribute to roofing and home painting projects.

Dunmore Plastering, Southboro, MA   Summers 01 and 03
Plasters Foreman—Organized and monitored building materials and inventory levels.

Independently Employed, Amherst, MA   1/99–5/01
Agricultural Contractor—Performed agricultural contract work for farmers.

76

Combination. *Jeanne Knight, Melrose, Massachusetts*

"The focus on Education, Relevant Coursework, Academic Projects, and Engineering Experience nicely positions this new graduate for a full-time position as an Industrial Engineer"—resume writer's note.

Finance

Resumes at a Glance

RESUME NO.	OCCUPATION	GOAL	PAGE
77.	Claims Dept. Manager/Supervisor	Not specified	157
78.	Customer Associate, Bank	Business Development Officer	158
79.	Dir., Online Dev. & Corporate Planning	Not specified	160
80.	Dir., Expense Mgmt. & Procurement	Senior Management Executive	162
81.	VP, Business Development Officer	Not specified	164
82.	Asst. VP/Trust Officer	Not specified	166
83.	Treasurer/Senior Controller	Finance Executive	168
84.	CFO, Treasurer, & Exec. VP	Chief Financial Officer	170
85.	Financial Services Representative	Internal Wholesaler	173
86.	Supervisor Trader/Account Executive	Financial Services	174
87.	Director, Investments	Not specified	176
88.	President/CEO/Director	Not specified	178
89.	General Partner, Real Estate	Real Estate Development Mgr.	180
90.	Customer Service	Financial Analyst	182

Helene Hirsch

46 Brook Hollow Road
Selden, New York 11700

(631) 382-2425
hirsch@online.com

Qualifications

➤ **Fifteen years** of progressive experience handling multiple lines of insurance claims.

➤ Experience in handling property claims, Commercial Auto Liability, Bodily Injury, and General Liability lines.

➤ Knowledge of applicable insurance contracts (commercial P&C), laws, and DOI regulations.

➤ Interfaced effectively with policy holders, claimants, physicians, medical providers, attorneys, and repair shops.

Work History & Summary of Key Skills

Claims Department Manager/Supervisor (15 years), ProCar Insurance, Garden City, New York

Initially hired as a Claims Representative Trainee and was quickly promoted to Senior Claims Representative and ultimately was selected as Claims Department Manager/Supervisor. **Prevented losses, contained costs,** and exercised initiative and independent judgment.

Effective Negotiation Abilities	Negotiated property-damage and personal-injury claims on both first- and third-party claims. Authority to **negotiate up to $500,000** per claim.
	Evaluated settlement strategies and alternatives. Determined settlement value and analyzed the potential costs, benefits, and risk of litigation.
	Attended mediation conferences and claim committee meetings to **achieve fair and equitable settlements.**
Keen Investigative Skills	Investigated commercial auto-property damage claims. Acquired information and maintained accurate records regarding accidents from policy holders and claimants.
	Conducted investigations of accidents, screened vehicles, researched missing information on claim forms, and processed claims from cradle to grave.
	Arranged independent medical exams, reviewed reports, and followed up on inconsistencies and/or coverage issues.
Strong Leadership Qualities	Managed a staff of 6 claims representatives, 2 claims processors, and 2 appraisers.
	Assigned incoming claims and **monitored process** to ensure accurate and timely handling of all claims. Held biweekly claim committee meetings to evaluate and delegate authority to settle third-party claims.
	Interviewed and trained staff in technical software, company procedures, and claims regulations/statutes.

Education

Bachelor of Arts, Finance, State University of New York at Stony Brook, Stony Brook, New York

Strong references available upon request

77

Functional. *Linda Matias, Smithtown, New York*

This insurance professional had been out of work for many years, so the writer did not include dates in the resume. She did mention the work duration of 15 years but embedded the information in the text.

Marta Jones

> *"Marta...I'll follow you anywhere with my money!"*
> **Laurence Tuck, Esquire**

Business Development Officer

Growing Client and Market Share in Retail Banking

Strengths

- Applying innovative marketing strategies to increase client acquisition, retention, and penetration.
- Building a solid client pipeline through referrals and focused efforts to create awareness and preference.
- Identifying client needs and desires and aligning them with product offerings.
- Identifying customer issues to achieve customer satisfaction levels that enable further sales.
- Leveraging personal entrepreneurial experience to build rapport with small-business clients.

Expertise

- Needs Assessment
- High-Impact Presentations
- Persuasive Communications
- Closing Skills

- Customer Acquisition
- Customer Retention
- Building Relationships
- Strategic Planning/Implementation

- Business Development
- Marketing Strategies
- Time Management
- Territory Management

Awards and Honors

Earned STAR Award (Top-Producer) 12 times.
Won bank-wide sales contest for acquiring 25 new customers in 1.5 days.
Top bonus earner in sales campaign for exceeding $200K/month funds managed for 6 consecutive months.

Career Achievements in Retail Banking

- ✓ Ranked #1 Sales Pavilion (branch) for 13 consecutive months. Ranked #1 Customer Associate within cluster for 13 consecutive months. Achieved #1 ranking with first month with funds managed over $100K.
- ✓ Attained 112% quota performance for 13 consecutive months.
- ✓ Transformed underperforming pavilion into #1 producing pavilion. Grew $200K of deposit products into $3M of deposit products in 12 months and $1M in loan products in 1 month.
- ✓ Established successful sales model adopted as standard. Mentored and trained 12 new hires.
- ✓ Operated pavilion single-handedly and outperformed combined sales of peers in typical pavilion setting.

Work History

Select Banking (Emica Bank, a subsidiary of Canadian Bank of Commerce)
Customer Associate   **February 2001–Present**

Establish new retail banking clients and deepen relationships with existing clients by devising creative business-development strategies and activities. Manage and maintain satellite site.

- ✓ Generated leads and interest outside of pavilion and immediate vicinity. Checked competitive rates daily.
- ✓ Maintained pipeline of 10 potential clients at any given time.
- ✓ Dedicated time for outbound calling to client base, resulting in further sales. Established and met goal of making 2 appointments with client base daily.
- ✓ Established deep relationships with key customers, fostering reliance and reducing competitive threats.
- ✓ Mentored/trained 12 new hires on sales strategies and tactics. (New hires receive 2 weeks of corporate training and 1 month with Marta.)
- ✓ Significantly improved sales results of faltering pavilion. Rebuilt relationship with store manager. Pavilion climbed from the lowest-performing to the top-performing pavilion.
- ✓ Selected to launch pavilion in the highly competitive Boulder market. Established key relationships with exclusive Realtors in the area to facilitate loan sales—resulted in $1M in loan sales in the first month.

12345 Francis St. • Longmont, CO 00000 • 555.555.5555

78

Combination. *Roberta F. Gamza, Louisville, Colorado*

The testimonial in the shaded box captures attention immediately, and a reader will want to read on. Because the box is placed at the top with the person's name, the contact information

Marta Jones

Family Services Counselor, Boulder Funeral Services, Boulder, CO   2000

Assisted families with final arrangements of loved ones, grief counseling, and resource follow-up.
As Community Services Counselor, sold pre-arranged cemetery and funeral plans and services.

- ✓ Achieved an above-average closing rate of 68% by aggressively prospecting (canvassing, cold-calling, and referrals).
- ✓ Acquired thorough product knowledge and effective presentation skills.

Principal, Design Consultant/Contractor
Design by Yvette, Denver, CO   1996–1999

Manage and market design and construction business, facilitating interior design projects for such firms as J. Peterson Associates, Inc., The Young Design Group, Architects Collaborative, and Burney and Associates, Inc.

- ✓ Served as contract/project manager for remodeling and new construction projects.
- ✓ Handled all phases of submitting/reviewing bids, obtaining required permits, estimating/billing materials and labor costs, and supervising contractors/laborers.
- ✓ Acquired extensive knowledge of building codes and scheduling.
- ✓ Tile and similar materials designs featured in prominent design publications.

Boulder Valley School District, Boulder, CO   1993–1996

Counselor, S.A.P.P. Program   1995–1996
Counselor/trainer for high-risk and minority youth. Applied outdoor cooperative activities to facilitate problem-solving skills, conflict resolution, and anger management.

Conflict Resolution/Mediation Supervisor, Elementary School Teacher, Grades 4 and 5,
Recreation Supervisor, University Hill Elementary School, Boulder   1993–1995
Designed/developed/implemented/facilitated district-wide Conflict Resolution/Mediation program instituted at Boulder Valley School District. Conducted seminars and training programs for faculty, parents, and students.

Education

Interior Design & Construction Management, Colorado State University, Fort Collins, CO, 1998–1999. Completed 90% of bachelor's degree before accepting full-time position.

Associates Program of Architectural Technologies, View Community College, Westminster, CO, 1995–1997.

B.A. Elementary Education, University of Colorado, Boulder, CO, 1994.

is pushed to the foot of the first page and repeated at the foot of the second page. Extra spacing between main resume sections makes the resume's design easy to grasp at a glance and invites the captured reader to continue reading. Boldfacing for workplaces and job positions is helpful as well.

EDWARD POTTER

752 Dexter Street #17
Santa Clara, CA 95050

edwardp@pacbell.net

408–666–2222 (home)
408–666–8000 (cell)

MANAGEMENT PROFILE

Business Intelligence management professional with a track record of significantly enhancing company operations. Define requirements aligned with strategic plans developed by senior management. Initiate partner relationships with IT staff to deliver critical decision-making information.

Key Strengths & Expertise

- Corporate strategic and tactical planning
- Project management to reduce risk
- Continuous process improvement
- Cross-functional team leadership
- Relational and OLAP database modeling

- Revenue-driven information management
- Focus on cost-effective problem solving
- Effective change agent and communicator
- Delivery of automated, accessible customer solutions
- Hands-on experience with Essbase, VBA, and Excel

PROFESSIONAL EXPERIENCE

Capsule Magic, Inc. / CapsuleMagic.com, Inc., Arcadia, CA / Santa Clara, CA   Jan. 2002–Feb. 2004

Director, Online Development & Corporate Planning (Capsule Magic, Inc.)

- Requested by senior management to remain with the newly combined company during the transition period to execute a comprehensive knowledge transfer, which included communicating the relationships among Web traffic, site transactions, direct and indirect revenues, and the expenses required to drive revenues.
- Designed and built multiple Essbase models, including a dealer-profitability model that provided margin visibility and analytical capability to Marketing, Sales, and Finance at the supplier and customer levels across several consumer and fulfillment brands.
- Interacted with IT and business managers to achieve data definitions suited to their needs and to create the necessary data sets.

Director, Online Development & Corporate Planning (CapsuleMagic.com)

- Managed the Finance and Business Intelligence team, which included a Financial Systems Manager, a Business Analyst, and a Web Site Analyst.
- Formed a cross-functional metrics team that worked with senior management to define operational reporting requirements and centralize tactical decision-making. Enabled transformation of a pro forma financial loss of approximately $1.0 million per month into a break-even situation by re-architecting the forecasting process for greater visibility and access to product-line managers.
- Delivered support to Marketing and Product Management for measuring and analyzing the success of new Web site features / products and online-marketing campaigns.
- Directed the development of tools to optimize partner / affiliate relationships from the standpoint of both cost and performance.
- Initiated a company-wide report inventory that identified over 500 existing reports. Communicated with business managers and IT staff to select critical reports for retention and thereby reduce the resource commitment needed to support the reporting function.
- Contributed significantly to preparing the company for sale to Capsule Magic. Key actions included
  - Modeled performance of major portal relationships to support the CFO and CEO in successful contract renegotiations.
  - Prepared due diligence materials, including driver-based models, to assist synergy modeling and analysis of historical expenses and revenues.
  - Designed and built an Essbase model to enable senior management to analyze and restructure the combined company prior to closing the sale.

79

Combination. *Georgia Adamson, Campbell, California*

This situation was complex: the applicant wanted to move to a higher management position, but the company he was leaving had been sold, and he had been asked to stay awhile to

EDWARD POTTER **PAGE 2**

Manager, Business Intelligence (CapsuleMagic.com)
➢ Interacted with the senior management team to clarify business objectives and develop corporate restructuring scenarios. Created and implemented strategies to transition the company from a dealer-referral model to one focused on the larger information-services market.
➢ Planned, directed, and implemented significant Essbase-related actions, including the following:
  ▪ With an outside consultant, developed a Hyperion Essbase model to provide actionable financial and transaction information, as well as accurate forecasting ability.
  ▪ Managed a consultant and a staff programmer, who developed front-end templates for entering data in and generating reports from Essbase.
➢ Developed the information architecture required for the IT staff to provide high-quality data for financial and Web site performance analysis.
➢ Teamed with the Director of Online Development to design a Web-traffic and transaction-analysis model that provided decision support for partner deal analysis and negotiation.
➢ Recruited by the company to investigate and resolve a number of problems. Key actions included partnering with the Controller to improve operating efficiency as well as board and SEC reporting.
➢ Promoted to a position as Director of Online Development and Corporate Planning.

Petroni Winery, Tracy, CA   Feb. 1999–Jan. 2002

Associate Financial Systems Analyst, Corporate
➢ Streamlined consolidation of domestic and corporate financials by re-engineering the International Finance reporting system. Prepared consolidated monthly reports and performed monthly closings.
➢ Contributed to successful migration of International to an Essbase system. Researched and identified opportunities to streamline and automate data flow in a mixed NT and UNIX environment.
➢ Created aids for management reporting and profitability analysis by developing Essbase front-ends using Excel and VBA. Trained key analysts in the front-end development process.

Associate Financial Analyst, International
➢ Analyzed and revamped the group's forecasting for Y2K and other potential problems, which involved dealing with information from subsidiary operations in 78 countries.
➢ Developed automation tools and leveraged corporate data systems (Data Warehouse / Data Marts) to eliminate manual data entry, reduce errors, and shorten the financial closing cycle.

Business Analyst
➢ Provided critical support to the cross-functional team that redesigned the company's domestic distribution network. Reduced the network design time of analysts and reduced annual costs more than $1.0 million by developing a database-driven, distribution-network-modeling application. Started with a pilot program in Louisiana, followed by nationwide rollout.
➢ Reduced tax overpayments and potential penalty exposure by designing and building a system to reconcile tax payments made by third-party warehouse operators. Trained Compliance staff in usage.

EDUCATION, PROFESSIONAL DEVELOPMENT, & AFFILIATIONS
➢ **M.B.A. in Finance**—one year completed, California State University—Hayward, Hayward, CA, 2000
➢ **B.A. in Political Science,** California State University—Hayward, Hayward, CA, 1997
➢ **A.A. in Political Science,** Mission College, Santa Clara, CA, 1995
➢ **Essbase Bootcamp,** FP&A Train, San Mateo, CA, June 1999: OLAP technology and Essbase application development
➢ **Visual Basic Programming,** Certificate of Merit, Tracy, CA, September 2000
➢ **Institute of Management Accountants (IMA),** member since 2000

facilitate the transition to the new entity. A number of his recommendations could not be shown as achievements because they had not yet been implemented. The writer decided to mention senior management's request that he stay on, and to refer to some of his suggestions that were implemented.

MICHAEL FISHER, MBA, CPA

717-222-8988
fisher@email.com
2283 Atlantic Avenue, York, PA 17404

SENIOR MANAGEMENT EXECUTIVE
Finance ... Change Management ... Procurement ... Purchasing

Visionary strategist with a demonstrated ability to deliver corporate objectives. Solid 13-year career creating market advantage; reducing and controlling expenses; and fostering a culture of teamwork, shared mission, and dedication to customer satisfaction. **Key strengths:**

"You quickly jumped in with both feet and made an immediate contribution to our team. Specifically, your analysis and projections of our financials and operational metrics within our group have been right on track."

John Jones
General Manager

Michael *"improved his revenue standing as the manager from the #6 position to the #2 position in about 60 days."*

Loren Hughes
Director
Consumer Ops

Leadership ... Pioneered a service program to improve customer service ratings that exceeded quarterly targets and captured the #1 position among 7 teams. The program was adopted by corporate and rolled out in 21 offices.

Cost Reductions ... Collaborated with intradepartmental managers and senior executives to implement a cost-reduction plan company-wide. Negotiated a telecommunications contract that generated $1.8 million in savings annually.

Change Management ... Drove the organization ranking from #6 out of seven to #2 in sales performance within 60 days by introducing an empowering, team-based management style.

Vendor Sourcing ... Consolidated temporary services sourcing from 50 providers to one national contract, generating $200,000 in annual expense savings.

Team Building ... Championed employee development, recognition, and open communication that positioned the call center as #1 in product retention within a 9-state region in 5 months.

New Product Launch ... Introduced incentives and measurement tools that positioned the territory as #1 in telephone sales within a 5-territory region.

Participative Management ... Partnered with the Communications Workers of America (CWA) union to create a performance-based work environment, establishing best-in-class benchmarks for management practices.

Training & Development ... Key member of a 6-person team tasked with developing sales effectiveness training and implementing a certification process. Drove 15% annual sales increases post-implementation, garnering the VP/GM "Shining Star" Award.

PROFESSIONAL EXPERIENCE

BANK OF AMERICA, York, Pennsylvania

Director of Expense Management & Procurement—2002 to 2004
Recruited to take over leadership of a department with a history of ineffective leadership, lack of performance, escalating expenses, and excessively high budgets. Manage a 15-person staff and $100 million expense budget; report directly to the Controller.

- Reduced expenses by $2.5 million through detailed reports and analysis of travel, telecom, express mail, copier leases, office supplies, document management, and cell phone policies.
- Partnered with the Human Resource Director to negotiate a 10% contract reduction on a national temporary services contract, yielding an annual expense savings of $200,000.
- Pioneered the department's first-ever incentive performance plans.

80

Combination. *Cindy Kraft, Valrico, Florida*

Most of the applicant's background was within the telecom industry. When that industry faltered with the economy, he was ready to transition to a new industry. "He submitted this

VERIZON, Tampa, Florida

Hired as a Senior Internal Auditor, launching a successful ten-year career holding increasingly responsible management positions with this Fortune 100 communications services company. Recruited for a special assignment as Finance Manager with P&L responsibility for a $200 million expense budget.

Manager of Sales/Service/Retention, Consumer Services — 2001 to 2002
Selected to drive sales and ensure customer service and retention. Managed 12 direct reports and 100 union-represented employees.

- Personally selected by senior management from among 1,000 candidates to participate in the Gateway Leadership Program.

- Completely turned around sales performance, taking the team from #7 to #2 in 60 days. Maintained the second-position slot for the balance of 2001.

- Initiated the customer service and satisfaction program that took ratings from #3 to #1 in 60 days.

- Built team unity and empowered employees to achieve corporate goals, establishing the team as #1 in product retention and beating the company's regional retention rate by 8%.

Manager of Sales Excellence, Consumer Services — 2000 to 2001
Personally chosen for leadership, product knowledge, vision, and financial expertise for this newly created position.

- Developed the Sales Effectiveness Training program that standardized training, strengthened the overall regional sales organization, and led to annual revenue increases of 15%.

Finance & Call Center Manager, Consumer Services — 1997 to 2000
Promoted to finance manager and within 12 months assumed additional responsibilities directing a 13-person team in the special-needs call center.

- Resolved a $20 million shortfall in sales goals to finish #1 in booked revenues by benchmarking internal performance, reallocating revenue goals between sales and service departments, and employing performance metrics for sales representatives.

Financial Analyst, Consumer Services Finance — 1996 to 1997
Conducted post-promotion marketing reviews for profitability; recommended marketing and operations funding prioritizations; reviewed income statement categories to evaluate financial trade-offs; and analyzed activity-based costing system results.

PRIOR RELEVANT EXPERIENCE

Financial & Compliance Auditor, FLORIDA AUDIT DEPT., Tallahassee, Florida — 1990–1992
Staff Accountant, Audit Staff, ERNST AND YOUNG, Nashville, TN — 1989–1990

EDUCATION

Master of Business Administration, University of Florida, Gainesville, Florida — 2001
Bachelor of Science in Accounting, Purdue University, West Lafayette, Indiana — 1989

CERTIFICATIONS

Certified Public Accountant (CPA) • Certified Internal Auditor (CIA)
Certified Information Systems Auditor (CISA)

resume and had three offers on the table simultaneously…two with banks and one with a restaurant." The shaded box with testimonials is an attention getter, buttressed by the list of key strengths of the same height and close to it. Bold italic makes these key strengths stand out.

BRADLEY SULLIVAN

669 Gillvrey Road   (555) 555–5555
Croton, New York 08890   bradsull@aol.com

PRIVATE BANKING ... COMMERCIAL LENDING ... MANAGEMENT

Consistent achievements as a top producer, increasing revenues, portfolios and profits through expertise in business development, relationship building, exceptional customer service and attentive followup. Recognized for managing the highest-quality portfolios.

Strategic planning and sales and marketing experience combine with qualifications in training, developing, coaching and managing staff to achieve performance objectives.

Licensure: NASD Series 7 and 63.

PROFESSIONAL EXPERIENCE & ACCOMPLISHMENTS

FIRSTBANK, New York, New York (1999–present)
Vice President, Business Development Officer, Private Clients Group (2000–present)
Private Banker (1999–2000)

Cultivate and manage new and existing client relationships of high-net-worth individuals and their related businesses. Develop sales plan for each relationship to provide an array of services: investment management, estate planning, credit and personal banking products. Continually expand referral network through contact with various internal business partners and external financial intermediaries. Coordinate events/seminars for new business development.

Results

◆ Successful track record of fee generation through sale of investment management accounts, surpassing industry benchmark for the market: $6 million in 2000 to $18 million in 2004.

◆ Selected based on product expertise and sales results to train business development officers of newly acquired organization in private equity investment products.

◆ Recognized for top sales performance in 1999, generating more than $4 million in fees.

BANK OF NEW YORK, New York, New York (1989–1999)
Fast-track advancement through progressively responsible positions in Private Banking. FirstBank acquired Bank of New York in 1995.

Vice President and Unit Manager, Private Banking Group (1993–1999)

Promoted to provide management direction to 2 business units with combined portfolios of $425 million in deposits, loans and assets under management. Designed and executed successful relationship-banking marketing plan for the sale of credit, trust (investment management and estate planning) and transaction products/services. Developed, coached and supervised team of 8 relationship managers and administrative assistants.

Results

◆ Evaluated and improved quality of the portfolios at both offices; credited for consistently maintaining the highest-quality portfolios, which included managing highly sensitive corporate relationships.

◆ Achieved revenue and customer-retention goals while increasing client profitability through relationship building, outstanding service delivery, cross selling and referral development.

◆ Contributed $1.5 million annually in fees through referral business to various banking divisions within the company.

continued...

81

Combination. *Louise Garver, Enfield, Connecticut*

This candidate was vying for an internal promotion in a highly competitive organization. The resume focused on his strong achievements and helped him land the next assignment. Note

Vice President, Private Banking Group (1990–1993)

Managed the Greenwood private banking office and staff. Managed $53 million portfolio (loans and deposits). Aggressively marketed and cross-sold all bank services. Reviewed and strengthened asset quality, including performing workouts, restructures and transfers of problem credits.

Results

♦ Consistently exceeded production goals for new loans, deposits and fee income. Recognized as an effective negotiator, generating highest level of fee income ($350,000 annually) division-wide.

♦ Turned around an adversarial relationship between consumer lending and private banking and forged a cohesive team.

Assistant Vice President, Private Banking Group (1989–1990)

Recruited to establish, build and manage the Westchester office's private banking operations. Designed marketing plan and originated new business by nurturing existing relationships and referral sources.

Results

♦ Built book of clients from zero base and managed top quality loan, investment and deposit portfolio ($7.1+ million) with no loan losses. Generated more than $50,000 in annual fees.

WEBBER BANK, New York, New York (1983–1989)
Banking Officer, Private Banking and Trust Division (1984–1989)
Banking Representative II, Community Banking (1983–1984)

Developed and executed an effective business development plan through intermediaries, colleagues and existing client base. Built and managed solid client relationships; communicated with other bank division personnel to effectively resolve any client issues.

Results

♦ Grew and managed $12 million deposit portfolio and $6 million loan portfolio.

EDUCATION

Columbia University, New York, New York
B.A. in Finance, 1983

PROFESSIONAL DEVELOPMENT / TRAINING

Credit Development Program
Fiduciary Banking
Management Information Systems
Asset Allocation Service and Estate Planning

how the achievements are presented as "Results" with diamond bullets. In most instances the bulleted information is quantified in dollar amounts. The pair of horizontal lines near the top of the first page encloses and draws attention to the first comments about the candidate's achievements.

Evelyn C. Murphy

1929 Hubbard Road
Midland, Michigan 48640

989-555-3333
murphy@internet.com

Accomplished administrator with excellent track record in positions of increasing responsibility. Recognized for delivering personalized client service. Respected by clients and colleagues. Experience in managing and performing administrative support functions. Comprehensive knowledge of legal issues relating to probate. **BBA** degree.

Functional Areas of Expertise
- ❖ In-depth client service & relationship building
- ❖ Probate, trusts, estates, and conservatorships
- ❖ Laws and procedures relating to municipal bonds
- ❖ Interaction with attorneys and court officials
- ❖ Assets and FET 706 worksheets
- ❖ Administrative & operations management

Personal Assets
- ❖ Analytical and highly detail-oriented
- ❖ Written and verbal communication skills
- ❖ Self-motivation and perseverance
- ❖ Vision
- ❖ Integrity
- ❖ Professional demeanor

Highlights of Accomplishments

- ❖ Instrumental in establishing policies and procedures for new charitable fund (Thomas Trust Foundation) with initial assets of $5 million. Served as Secretary to the Board. Spearheaded partnership with community service organization Zonta International. Organized and facilitated annual meeting.

- ❖ Served as Stock Transfer and Paying Agent for Fifth Third Bank. Solely responsible for facilitating stock transfers in adherence with stringent SEC policies and procedures.

- ❖ Selected to serve on focus group under auspices of North Central Bankers Association. Committee reviewed existing laws relating to conservatorships and evaluated appropriateness of future lobbying efforts on behalf of the association.

- ❖ Devised and implemented system to centralize word processing operations (prior to availability of personal computers). New system reduced support staff by half while increasing efficiency.

- ❖ Collaborated with computer programmer to develop software to handle specific financial transactions.

- ❖ Nominated for Midland Area Chamber of Commerce *Athena Award* (1995), established to recognize contributions by women in the business and professional community.

- ❖ Received *Zontian of the Year* award and *President's Award* from Zonta International of Midland.

- ❖ Honored with Fifth Third Bank *Community Service & Citizenship* award.

— continued —

82

Combination. *Janet L. Beckstrom, Flint, Michigan*

The applicant was a highly qualified individual, one of around 200 middle managers laid off from a regional bank. She had about 25 years of experience with the bank and considerable

Evelyn C. Murphy   989-555-3333

Career Path

Fifth Third Bank Estate Management, Inc. • Midland, Michigan   1978–2004
Assistant Vice President/Trust Officer—Personal Trust/Probate
- Administered 140 personal trust, estate, and investment accounts valued at $52 million. Acted as conservator, settled probate estates, administered revocable and irrevocable trusts and agency accounts.
- Ensured settlement of estates in accordance with deceased's wishes; negotiated with family members and others to achieve resolution.
- Interacted with clients on a one-to-one basis. Provided personal assistance and guidance in addition to delivering financial services, consistent with Client-First mission.

Assistant Vice President/Trust Officer/Corporate Trust Section Manager—Corporate Trust
- Managed high-profile (such as Jacobson Foundation and Bay Valley Estates) as well as routine bond accounts for municipal and governmental entities.
- Processed stock and bond transfers, bond trusteeships, and dividend and interest payments.
- Performed accurate recordkeeping (computerized and manual) resulting in consistently balanced accounts.
- Managed selected portfolios.
- Interacted with Securities & Exchange Commission and federal Bank Examiners during annual audits.

Manager—Corporate Transfer Agent section
Manager—Secretarial Services
Administrative Assistant—Employee Benefits

Education

Saginaw Valley State University • University Center, Michigan
Bachelor of Business Administration—Magna cum Laude   1998

Professional Development

- ❖ Personal Trust School—Midwest Trust Schools
- ❖ Certified Corporate Trust Specialist designation—Institute of Certified Bankers
- ❖ Corporate Trust III—Cannon Financial Institute
- ❖ Ongoing professional development and computer training

Community Involvement

- ❖ Zonta International District 321 [State of Michigan]—former Secretary/Treasurer (1998–2000)
- ❖ Zonta International of Midland—President (2002–2004), also former Recording Secretary, Treasurer, First Vice President, Director
- ❖ Community Children's Foundation—Treasurer, Board of Directors (current), and other leadership roles
- ❖ United Way, Bay & Midland Counties Chapter—Board of Directors
- ❖ Midland County Habitat for Humanity—former volunteer (managed 2,500-name mailing list)
- ❖ Safe House of Midland—former Board of Directors, Membership Committee

expertise in her area. The writer emphasized the applicant's banking and trust experience as well as her administrative background to make her more marketable. She was hired as an administrative assistant at an area medical center. Compound diamond bullets draw attention to key information.

RAYMOND MONROE
12 Main Street
New York, New York 00000
(555) 555-5555

FINANCE EXECUTIVE

**Finance & Accounting Management ... Banking & Cash Management ... Budgeting
Insurance & Risk Management ... Tax & Regulatory Compliance ... Information Systems**

Finance, public accounting and administration executive with diverse industry experience in retail/wholesale distribution, financial services and manufacturing. Proven ability to improve operations, impact business growth and maximize profits through achievements in finance management, cost reductions, internal controls and productivity/efficiency improvements. Strong qualifications in general management, business planning, systems technology design and implementation and staff development/leadership.

PROFESSIONAL EXPERIENCE

SOUTHINGTON COMPANY • New York, New York • 1991–2001
Treasurer/Senior Controller • 1993–2001
Corporate Controller • 1991–1993

Chief financial officer appointed to treasurer and Executive Committee member directing $500M international consumer products company. Accountable for strategic planning, development and leadership of entire finance function as well as day-to-day operations management of company's largest domestic division. Recruited, developed and managed team of finance professionals, managers and support staff.

Operations Achievements

- Instrumental in improving operating profits from less than $400K to over $4M, equity from $8.6M to $13.6M and assets from $29.7M to $44.4M.
- Boosted market penetration by 27%, which increased gross sales 32% through acquisition of 25 operating units as key member of due diligence team.
- Initiated strategies to redeploy company resources, resulting in 54% increase in gross margin by partial withdrawal from high-risk/low-margin product lines.
- Directed annual plan review process and strengthened accountability by partnering with senior-level department and district managers in all business units.

Financial Achievements

- Cut receivable write-offs $440K by developing credit policies, instituting aggressive collection strategies and establishing constructive dialogue with delinquent accounts.
- Negotiated and structured financing agreements, resulting in basis point reductions, easing/more favorable covenant restrictions and simplification of borrowing process.
- Saved over $2M through self-insurance strategy and an estimated $200K annually by positioning company to qualify to self-insure future workers' compensation claims.
- Designed executive and management reporting systems and tailored financial and operating reporting system to meet requirements of 100+ business units.

83

Combination. *Louise Garver, Enfield, Connecticut*

The candidate's first resume was his own bare-bones creation, and he was getting no interviews. He wanted to move to the next higher level as a finance executive. The writer created this

RAYMOND MONROE • (555) 555-5555 • Page 2

Southington Company continued...

Technology Achievements

♦ Turned around organization-wide resistance toward automation and streamlined procedures that significantly improved efficiency while reducing costs.

♦ Championed installation of leading-edge systems technology, resolving longstanding profit-measurement problems, and created infrastructure to support corporate growth.

♦ Implemented automated cash management system in over 100 business unit locations and reduced daily idle cash by 50% ($750K).

♦ Recognized critical need and upgraded automated systems to track long-term assets, which had increased from $28M to $48.8M in 5 years.

HAMDEN COMPANY • New York, New York • 1987–1991
Chief Financial Officer

Recruited for 3-year executive assignment to assume key role in building solid management infrastructure and positioning $15M company for its profitable sale in 1991. Directed general accounting, cash management, financial and tax reporting, banking relations, credit and collections, data processing, employee benefits and administration. Managed and developed staff.

♦ Converted company to small business corporation, saving $450K in taxes over 3-year period.

♦ Realized $195K in accumulated tax savings through strategies adopting LIFO inventory method, minimizing taxes on a continual basis.

♦ Secured 25% of company's major client base (50% of total sales volume) by leading design, installation and administration of computer-based EDI program.

♦ Reduced collection period from 3 weeks to 5 days by initiating new policies and procedures.

MADISON COMPANY • New York, New York • 1981–1987
Partner

Jointly acquired and managed public accounting firm serving privately held companies (up to $200M in revenues) in wholesale distribution, financial services and manufacturing industries. Concurrent responsibility for practice administration and providing accounting, business and MIS consulting services to corporate clients.

EDUCATION

B.S. in Accounting
New York University • New York, New York

Certified Public Accountant—New York

resume, which positioned the candidate well by emphasizing his achievements in multiple areas. The resume generated tremendous interest from recruiters and led to placement at the desired level. This resume won the Best Finance Resume category in a Professional Association of Resume Writers competition.

JEFFREY L. JACKSON

333 Lullaby Road—Cradlerock, MN 33333
999-555-6666—jljack@msn.com

CHIEF FINANCIAL OFFICER

Strategic Growth Management, Start-ups, Turnarounds

Equity and Debt Financing, IPO Process, M&A Experience and Restructure Operations

Senior executive with broad hands-on financial management and analysis background. P&L responsibility for national and international companies with multi-site divisions and gross revenues of more than $200 million. Skilled in integration of acquisitions. Identify and exploit opportunities to maximize ROI and create significant shareholder/VC value. Proven team builder who delivers effective CEO support and serves as a catalyst creating new business opportunities, establishing strategic partnerships and overcoming regulatory barriers. Broad administrative and operations management experience. Public company experience. CPA. Strengths:

- Turned around company, reversing $9,000,000 loss in one year by restructuring manufacturing and marketing operations. Completed international LBO with Merrill Lynch and Citicorp.

- Closed $2,000,000 source code sales contracts and negotiated software and system integration contracts of up to $5,000,000.

- Spearheaded decision to exit business venture to focus on core business. Acquired major competitor, solidifying market share.

AREAS OF EXPERTISE

- Financial Planning & Analysis
- General Accounting & Reporting
- Manufacturing Cost Systems
- Tax Planning

- Cash & Asset Management
- Human Resources
- Equity and Debt Financing
- Investor and Analyst Relations

- SEC Compliance & Reporting
- Sales & Marketing Strategies
- Credit and Risk Management
- Forecasting, Due Diligence

PROFESSIONAL EXPERIENCE

ABCD, INC., Cradlerock, MN, XXXX–XXXX
Publicly traded conglomerate providing Enterprise software and Internet technology, hosting and e-commerce solutions internationally with $800 million in revenues.

Chief Financial Officer, Treasurer and Executive Vice President, ABCD, INC., XXXX–XXXX
Publicly traded digital content management and e-commerce advertising software and services.

Recruited to lead reorganization, gain financial control and provide stability during CEO departure. Served as #2 in command with COO responsibilities. Led strategic decision to exit non-performing Internet advertising business to concentrate on core company Enterprise software. Took company from pre-reorganization revenues of $250,000,000 employing 1,200, globally, to post-reorganization revenues of $30,000,000 with 225 employees. Full P&L accountability. 8 direct and 42 indirect reports globally.

- Negotiated termination of $55,000,000 of pre-reorganization real estate and equipment leases, bandwidth and service contract commitments at a working capital cost 70% below investment banker's estimates. Preserved $20,000,000+ of working capital for company operations.

- Negotiated additional $25,000,000 inter-company working capital financing and positioned company for favorable inter-company ownership change.

- Created analytical models and reports to convey key issues. Developed strategies to quickly maximize cash flow and improve business processes. Provided product cost analysis, operational flow charting, short- and long-term cash flow forecasting, financial modeling and budget variance analyses. Managed IT/MIS, investor and analysts relations, SEC compliance and reporting; and directed capital expenditure process.

84

Combination. *Sally McIntosh, St. Louis, Missouri*

Normally two-page resumes become three or more pages when an individual has had a long career, held high positions within large companies, and accomplished much. Such is true for

JEFFREY L. JACKSON

Chief Financial Officer, XYZ, Inc., XXXX

Privately held $60 million joint-venture start-up of Internet operating network and infrastructure software development company with Sun, Novell, and Compaq.

Formulated and achieved projected business plan. Reported to Chairman of the Board. P&L responsibility.

♦ Positioned company for merger with corporate engineering infrastructure company.

Chief Financial Officer, EFGH, INC., XXXX–XXXX

Privately held start-up core company in roll-up and build-out plan providing technology and infrastructure solutions to the e-commerce industry with 450 employees.

Concurrently held COO responsibilities. Led financial dealings, potential public offering (pre-IPO and IPO roadshows) and investment analyses. Dropped IPO initiative prior to S-1 completion due to adverse market conditions. Participated in due diligence process of assessing potential investments. Focused on global customer base. P&L oversight. 2 direct and 8 indirect reports.

♦ Responsible for due diligence and supervised negotiations in acquiring premier systems integrator with 375 employees. Supervised integration of project management and technical proficiencies.

♦ Grew workforce from zero to 150 through acquisitions and organic growth.

RSTUV, INC., Chicago, IL XXXX–XXXX

VC core company in a roll-up plan within the high-end access control, CCTV, telecommunications and security software industry. Provides engineering design, installation and maintenance.

Chief Executive Officer, XXXX–XXXX
Chief Financial Officer, XXXX–XXXX

Brought in to turn around company and to evaluate the validity of the original roll-up plan. Built systems and procedures for operations and financial reporting required due to operating problems since XXXX acquisition. Worked directly with principals of the VC investment fund. Oversaw real estate and facilities management. Established best practices in cash management, contract cost accounting, financial analysis, forecasting, budgeting and reporting. Full P&L responsibility.

♦ Positioned company for sale to maximize return to investor group.

♦ Grew sales 10% by realigning marketing approach to target middle market.

♦ Won $5,000,000 installation contract for new terminal at Kennedy Airport.

MNOP, INC., Springfield, IL, XXXX–XXXX

Represented aftermarket products to automobile dealerships for resale to customers, including surface protection products and warranties, accessories, credit and insurance products. Company entered into joint ownership agreement with retail group operating in Canada.

Internal Business Consultant

Marketed products to larger automotive dealerships. Restructured marketing concept, product offerings and go-to-market strategy for potential franchise launch. Redesigned "point-of-sale" presentation system, materials and dealership sales training program.

♦ Improved gross margins 30% by renegotiating representation agreements and by acquiring highly competitive product line.

♦ Established contract sales employee program to place trained aftermarket personnel in dealerships.

this individual. Lines enclose profile information and help to separate visually the companies where the individual has held top executive positions. Diamond bullets point to stellar achievements quantified with high dollar amounts and significant percentages. Line spacing between bulleted items ensures adequate white

JEFFREY L. JACKSON

UVWX, INC., Springfield, IL, XXXX–XXXX
Privately held international manufacturer of children's clothing sold in 1,100+ specialty and department stores in the U.S., Canada and Japan. Company sold to international women's clothing company, XXXX.

Chief Operating Officer

Recruited to develop management systems in entrepreneurial company and to position company for IPO or sale/merger. Oversaw operations including sales, manufacturing, garment dye operations and administrative areas.

- ◆ Grew sales 10% and gross margins 8%, in first year, by developing retail concept and implementing multiple store operations.

- ◆ Saved 10% by bringing fabric management and cutting operation in-house.

MNOP, INC., Jacksonville, IL, XXXX–XXXX
Privately held manufacturer and importer of stainless steel and silverplated flatware and hollowware, and china and glassware. Also manufactured safety-critical precision forgings/assemblies for the foreign auto industry.

President and Chief Operating Officer, XXXX–XXXX
Executive Vice President, XXXX–XXXX
Member of Board of Directors, XXXX–XXXX

Completed $20 million leveraged buy-out of World Tableware International in XXXX from Insilco Corporation in association with Merrill Lynch Interfunding, Citicorp, U.S. and Citicorp, N.A., Taiwan, ROC. Obtained financial commitment prior to IPO roadshow offering process to obtain equity. Identified business drivers and key issues threatening survival of company turnaround. Increased product quality and manufacturing efficiency of Taiwan plant, improving competitive position, improving margins and increasing inventory turn. Acquired major competitor, solidifying market share.

- ◆ Defended and won United Trade Commission petition by Oneida to raise import duties.

- ◆ Secured $16,000,000 domestic and international refinancing to provide working capital for operations growth and strategic acquisitions.

- ◆ Grew sales 10% and improved gross margins 8% in first year by redefining product lines by market segment and simplifying pricing strategy.

Other positions held: 123 INC., **Chief Financial Officer/VC Sponsored Internal Consultant,** Springfield, IL, XXXX; 456, INC., packaged consumer goods, **Vice President Administration and CFO,** XXXX–XXXX; IJKL Corporation, diversified international Fortune 500 company in electronics, computers, communications, consumer goods, auto, publishing and housing industries, XXXX–XXXX; NOPQ Company, **VP Administration and Treasurer, Director of Internal Audit, Audit Manager,** XXXX–XXXX.

EDUCATION AND PROFESSIONAL AFFILIATIONS

BS in Business Administration and Accounting, American International College, Chicago, IL, XXXX

Certified Public Accountant, Minnesota

space, preventing the resume from looking cramped in spite of all of its information. Boldfacing makes the job positions stand out to the reader. The name, repeated in a header at the top of pages two and three, is kept in front of the reader.

THERESA RODRIGUEZ

215 54th Street ♦ New York, NY 00000 ♦ 212.555.1234 ♦ trodriguez@aol.com

OBJECTIVE: INTERNAL WHOLESALER
**Retirement Planning ♦ Life Insurance ♦ Mutual Funds ♦ Annuities
Pension Funds ♦ College Funds ♦ Disability Insurance**

SUMMARY OF QUALIFICATIONS
Award-winning bilingual financial services professional with diverse background in individual and corporate investment planning and management. **Earned Sales Production of the Year award (2003) for increasing sales by 10% during first six months of employment.** Skilled in identifying and maintaining new business opportunities and client relationships. Extensive experience facilitating presentations and workshops on financial planning and services. Outstanding communications and customer service skills with the ability to manage multiple clients and responsibilities.

PROFESSIONAL LICENSES
Series 7, Series 63, New York & New Jersey Life and Accident/Health

CAREER EXPERIENCE
Registered Financial Services Representative, MetLife Financial Services, New York, NY, 2001–present
  - ♦ Service 100+ existing and new clients on financial and insurance products and plans; facilitate monthly seminars on financial planning and debt management; develop marketing strategies to enhance customer base through mass mailings, cold-calling, referrals, walk-and-talks, expositions and educational seminars; analyze investment portfolios, review assets allocations, risk tolerance and objectives; administer life insurance, annuity and pension plan benefits to corporations, medical facilities and unions; provide medical benefits and employer-sponsored retirement plans to small-business owners.

Mutual Funds Sales Liaison, Salomon Smith Barney, Inc., New York, NY, 1999–2001
  - ♦ Provided 300+ financial consultants with mutual fund, portfolio content sales and marketing support; resolved 200+ client account discrepancies relating to dividend payments, performance analysis and 1099s; recommended fixed-income and equity products based on investors' objectives; developed and prepared weekly newsletter for 150+ employees detailing mutual fund updates and departmental issues; calculated and analyzed hypothetical illustrations on mutual fund performance and investment risks.

Registered Sales Assistant, Citigroup, New York, NY, 1998–1999
  - ♦ Worked directly with two financial consultants managing $350+ million in assets; researched performance of stocks, bonds and mutual funds; served as liaison between high-net-worth clientele, banking institutions and Citigroup; managed and maintained 200+ brokerage accounts; provided market data and research to top-tier investors; assisted financial consultants with presentations and trainings; transmitted daily client stock purchases through Post Order Entry System.

TECHNOLOGY SKILLS
Word, Excel, PowerPoint, Principia Pro, Morningstar, Investment View, Bloomberg, Internet

EDUCATION
BS, Business Administration—SUNY Stony Brook Harriman School for Management and Policy, 1998

85

Chronological. *La Dana R. Jenkins, Staten Island, New York*

The original resume was created with a resume wizard in MS Word and had a one-line summary. The writer altered the contact information, dates, and company information and mentioned the Sales Production of the Year award.

PATRICK M. JONES
615 Home Haven Pl. ◆ Brielle, NJ 08730
(732) 222-2222 ◆ E-mail: pjones@pjonesaddress.com

FINANCIAL SERVICES PROFESSIONAL

Talented and driven management professional with five years of experience in the trading and financial services arena. Possess effective combination of negotiation, closing, customer management and teambuilding skills that consistently contribute to operational objectives, even within volatile markets. **Hold Series 7, 24, 55 and 63 Licenses. Current CFA Candidate.**

QUALIFICATION HIGHLIGHTS

- Significant achievement in **analyzing current market conditions, monitoring volatile market activities and understanding industry comparisons.** Superior knowledge of NASDAQ Level II and NASDAQ Workstation.
- **Strong oral and written communication skills;** efficiently communicate with management, peers and customers.
- Excellent ability to **consistently maintain composure and remain productive in extremely high-pressure, time-sensitive environments;** experienced developing market-making operations.
- Demonstrated competencies in **customer service management with capacity to develop and maintain long-term, high-profit client relationships.**
- Recognized for strong work ethic and respected as contributing team player through consistent collaboration with co-workers, integrity and **commitment to success.**

RELEVANT EXPERIENCE

THE TRADING COMPANY — New York, NY   4.2002 to Present
SUPERVISOR TRADER / ACCOUNT EXECUTIVE

Charged with leading company's market-making operation project including development of all procedures, testing and implementation before transitioning to institutional trade desk as an Account Executive. Continually monitor all systems, manage customer inquires, cultivate new accounts and lead system usage training for clients. Established strategic sales plans, performed risk management and conducted extensive investment research to provide clients with optimum choice, service and product knowledge.

Key Achievements

- **Built both market-making and soft-routing operations** from scratch, based on knowledge of all NASD, SEC and compliance department rules/regulations.
- Realized market share improvement and increased sales within market-making operations by taking on more stocks.
- Delivered cost savings **($5K to $15K per day)** associated with market-making operations by devising "pecking order" of firms to access least expensive products first.
- Attained **personal sales increases of up to 75%** by reactivating older accounts and assuming management over client trades vs. client making their own grades.

86

Combination. *Kim Little, Victor, New York*

The "weight" of the globe graphic balances the contact information to the right.
A page border ties together the two pages visually. Boldfacing in the Qualifications Highlights section makes the most important information more evident. In the Relevant Experience section,

ABC ONLINE BROKERAGE SERVICES — Patterson, NJ   6.1998 to 4.2002
POSITION CONTROL MANAGER / EQUITIES TRADER

Initially hired as equities trader before promotion to Position Control Manager with accountability for 24 traders and expeditious order delivery. Produce risk/position surveillance reports and perform comprehensive end-of-day and monthly analysis. Provide system operations troubleshooting and frequently observe trader activity throughout the day. Trading responsibilities include management of proprietary account in high-volume, error-free environment.

Key Achievements

- Improved tracking of trader losses by creating automated monthly report.
- Researched and identified order-delay problems, **slashing free stock trades from 5% to 2.5%.**
- **Led "side by side" training** for new hires to determine their potential for working in pressure situations.
- Spearheaded introduction of **significantly improved customer order routing project.**
- Introduced employee evaluation program and **identified improvements for NASDAQ and SEC internal procedures.**

NATIONS FINANCIAL SERVICES, INC. — Neptune City, NJ   5.1996 to 6.1998
SALES REPRESENTATIVE

Charged with offering term life insurance and Nations' mutual funds as member of the XX Group. Assisted customers in selection of mutual funds and insurance products consistent with clients' overall investment plan.

Key Achievements

- Developed new clients through referrals and prospecting.
- Researched and evaluated mutual funds and performed comparisons with funds not offered.
- Maintained knowledge of all funds offered and educated clients on tax issues, legalities and IRS policies.

SMITH ROCKS — Red Bank, NJ   2.1994 to 6.1995
CLIENT SUPPORT REPRESENTATIVE

Provided extensive customer support; developed new account leads, administrative tracking and follow-up. Primarily presented fixed-income products to small-business owners and arranged client opportunities for V.P. *First position directly out of college.*

BS, Accounting — Monmouth, University — West Long Branch, NJ

a paragraph under each job position indicates duties and responsibilities. After each paragraph is a Key Achievements side heading and bulleted achievements. This regular pattern makes the section easy to grasp.

DAVID R. JONESON

98 Ben Franklin Drive   Home: (609) 666–1111
Cherry Hill, New Jersey 07896   drjoneson@aol.com   Home Fax: (609) 666–7777

QUALIFICATIONS PROFILE

Top-performing senior executive with 14 years of experience in property operations and management for residential development and investment/development property markets. Delivered $800 million in revenue/profit growth through innovative hands-on operating leadership and high-profile property management. In-depth knowledge and experience in business planning, management, and implementation, contributing significantly to bottom-line efficiency and profitability. Possess broad-based management skills, with strong planning, communication, organizational, team building, and decision-making skills.

- ☑ Due Diligence
- ☑ Asset Management
- ☑ Project Development
- ☑ Profit & Loss Management
- ☑ Purchasing Scope Definition
- ☑ Budget Planning & Forecasting
- ☑ Lease Negotiations
- ☑ Team Building/Leadership
- ☑ Client Relationship Building
- ☑ Judgment/Problem Solving
- ☑ Anticipating Economic Climates
- ☑ Diverse Market/Industry Knowledge

KEY ACHIEVEMENTS

- Established Hunter Street Investments (HSI) direct property development/investment portfolio throughout New York worth more than $600 million.
- Key driver in development of an organization-wide strategic planning and visionary process. Focused investment business on being a capital player and residential developers of apartments and residential land markets.
- Leadership of more than $800 million in property projects, with complete development and management responsibility for more than 40 projects. Currently includes $400 million in investment property and $200 million in development projects.
- Instrumental in instigating strategic directional papers for current and future development/ investment portfolios, enabling HSI to expand internationally into Australia, Germany, and the United Kingdom.
- Spearheaded strategic process improvements to expand portfolio, successfully increasing HSI's revenue/profit to $600 million.
- Outstanding mentor and coach, leading teams to identify new opportunities as well as contracting/developing residential, industrial, and commercial properties across New York worth more than $600 million.
- Established strategic business relationships with brokers and agents for early access to potential investment sites, expanding new and existing business opportunities.

PROFESSIONAL EXPERIENCE

HUNTER STREET INVESTMENTS (HSI) — New York, NY   **1991–Present**
Director (2001–Present)

Provide vision and tactical leadership for New York's largest private-property investor while managing a staff of more than 20. Manage all stages of property development process; P&L management; financial and operational management; direct and oversee property acquisitions; project management; direct half-yearly valuations to track development/capital/income growth; research property trends; develop property investment and development objectives; oversee asset management of investment properties; and business relationship building.

- Exceed company benchmarks for Return on Investment (ROI) through the implementation of market factor influences and strong property management techniques.
- Lead and negotiate all contract negotiations for property development/investment opportunities throughout New York, including securing under due diligence provisions allowing company to purchase development/investment properties.

87

Combination. *Jennifer Rushton, N. Richmond, New South Wales, Australia*

The original resume listed only responsibilities and lacked achievements, keywords, and so on. It didn't tell what the applicant could actually do for a company. He wanted only to "update the

Professional Experience Continued

- Expanded HSI's portfolio nationally and internationally through the design of direct/indirect property portfolios and development investment strategies.
- Increased staff morale and performance through the implementation of an employer bonus incentive scheme delivering profits to employees.
- Provide strong organizational leadership and active participation in business development by offering tactical direction to enhance business plans. Recommend and coordinate the purchase and sale of development/investment properties to optimize profit.
- Led and negotiated strategic business alliances with banks to finance HSI's development/investment portfolio, further expanding market reach.
- Redesigned and streamlined company infrastructure by relocating staff nationally in New Jersey, capitalizing on human resource, operational, and financial competencies in line with company objectives.

Manager of Acquisitions (1995–2001)

- Negotiated the acquisition of $800 million in development and investment properties as part of HSI's objectives.
- Effectively documented business processes and procedures, identifying issues that may represent risk to the business or its clients and providing asset management solutions where necessary.

Property Analyst (1991–1994)

- Identified expansion and market opportunities through successfully researching property trends.

WALTER GIRMOND & ASSOCIATES — New York, NY   1989–1991
Valuer

- Independently performed valuations and market research on vacant land, development sites, and residential properties throughout New York.
- Implemented strong client focus and communication processes, continually building long-term relationships and cementing existing relationships.

EDUCATION & PROFESSIONAL CERTIFICATIONS

University of New York — New York	**Graduate Diploma Property Investment & Finance** (anticipated completion June 2003)
University of New York — New York	**Bachelor of Business — Valuation & Land Economy** (1991)
New York Property Institute — New York	**Land Economist** (1992)
Professional License:	**Real Estate & Business Agent's License**

PUBLIC SPEAKING ENGAGEMENTS & FEATURED NEWSPAPER ARTICLES

Speaking Engagements:	Property Council of New York, "Owner-Manager Relation: Best Practice," 2004
	Property Council of New York, "Property Investment Trends for 2004," 2004
Newspaper Articles:	Property Council of New York, "Personal Style — David Joneson," 2002
	The *New York Times*, "Softer Trend Seen for City Properties," 2004

PROFESSIONAL AFFILIATIONS

New York Property Institute
Property Council of New York
Securities Institute of New York
Urban Development Institute of New York
Real Estate Institute of New York (REINY)

REFERENCES AVAILABLE UPON REQUEST

format," but the writer overhauled the resume completely. Here's the final product. The Qualifications Profile makes skills prominent, and the Key Achievements within a pair of horizontal lines stand out. Bullets point to these and additional achievements throughout the resume.

FRANK JAKOVAC

609 Candlewood Lane
Pittsburgh, PA 15212
412.302.1218
fjakovac@msn.com

* SENIOR EXECUTIVE PROFILE *
Providing Financial & Operating Leadership to
High-Growth Ventures, Start-Ups & Turnarounds

Top-performing, **solutions-driven** executive with 25+ years of experience leading organizations through start-up, change, revitalization, turnaround, and accelerated growth. Personally credited with driving significant gains in revenues and bottom-line profits through strategic financial leadership. **Decisive** and **results-oriented** with **outstanding negotiation** and **crisis management** skills. An engaging, **professional communicator** with the ability to put others at ease, quickly building relationships based on mutual trust and benefit. Combine cross-functional expertise and experience in different arenas.

Business Development, Leadership, and Management

- Built entrepreneurial venture from start-up to $300M in four years; built another privately held venture from start-up to $100M in assets in five years.
- Develop and nurture proactive working relationships with chief executive officers, Fortune 500 corporations, bankers, investors, business partners, and other personnel critical to corporate growth, expansion, and profitability.
- Design and implement organizational infrastructures and business plans that maximize performance, quality, efficiency, and bottom-line profits.
- Key executive in successful turnaround and merger of a public company into restructured business opportunity.

Network Technology

- Astute strategic understanding of leading-edge technologies to leverage resources and to optimize productivity.
- Designed, implemented, and maintained large Local Area Networks (LANs) for major corporations—equipment included that of IBM, Amdahl, Hitachi, Memorex, and Compaq.

PROFESSIONAL EXPERIENCE

* President/CEO/Director *

A-FIRST SPORTSWEAR & GOLF CORPORATION   2001–PRESENT
A wholly owned subsidiary that designed, manufactured, and marketed distinctive premium and moderately priced sportswear. A-First sold its products primarily through golf pro shops and resorts, corporate sales accounts, and better specialty stores.

Challenge: To lead a financially unstable organization through aggressive dissolution, turnaround, and business process reengineering initiatives for corporate restructuring.

Key Accomplishments:

- Executive management responsibility for total restructuring and realignment of strategic planning, operations, marketing, finance, regulatory affairs, administration, technology, and P&L.
- Realigned budget process and developed/implemented strategic plans to achieve organizational goals through 2003 in the Homeland Security arena.
- Completed successful merger with United Companies Corporation. Credited with leading AFSG through the revitalization process into business decisions that left the corporation able to pursue business opportunities.

88

Combination. *Sharon Pierce-Williams, Findlay, Ohio*

An attractive font (Imprint MT Shadow) for the name is the first sign that this is a distinctive resume. Next, the horizontal lines are in two colors if you use a color printer to print the

FRANK JAKOVAC

609 Candlewood Lane
Pittsburgh, PA 15212
412.302.1218
fjakovac@msn.com
Page 2

PROFESSIONAL EXPERIENCE (continued)

* President & Co-Founder *

AVID VENTURES, INC., Pittsburgh, PA   1998–2001
- Worked with other venture capitalists to develop and manage projects ranging from information technology to land development.

* Chairman, CEO, & Founder *

Challenge: To launch entrepreneurial ventures from start-up in an intensely competitive market while creating strong infrastructures supporting continued growth.

GATEWAY MANAGEMENT SERVICES & GATEWAY ARCHIVES, INC.   1992–1998
  Largest independent disaster recovery provider in the country. Also provided information management and IT consulting services. Merged with Business Records Management to form BRM/Gateway.

GATEWAY CAPITAL FUNDING, INC.   1990–1997
  Specialized in large-scale, mixed-use land development projects in the Southeast with major focus in North and South Carolina.

GATEWAY GROUP, INC., *parent corporation of*   1987–1995
  Gateway Financial Corp., Inc.
  Gateway Network Services, Inc.
  GFC specialized in the leasing arena concentrating on the large-scale mainframe market. The equipment included that of IBM, Amdahl, Hitachi, Memorex, and Compaq. GNS provided on-site maintenance and data processing services to corporations with a minimum of 200 computer terminals and PCs. The major focus was on utility markets.

Key Accomplishments:

- **Entrepreneur of the Year Nominations** by *The Pittsburgh Business Times/INC. Magazine*—1989, 1990, and 1992.
- Built new privately held Gateway Archives from concept to $3M in annual revenues—an off-site business information retrieval and retention service that provided 21st-century solutions to old storage requirements.
- Gateway Capital funded $100M in assets from leasing operations. Launched 1,000-acre development of "King's Grant," the largest retail land development project in the history of the Carolinas. In 1999, the Concord Mills regional mall opened on King's Grant.
- *Who's Who in America, Who's Who in Business and Industry, Who's Who of Emerging Leaders in America.*

* President *

MEMOREX FINANCE CO., *A wholly owned "captive finance" organization of Memorex Corp.*   1975–1986
MEMOREX CORP., *Started as sales trainee within Memorex Corp. and became President of Memorex Finance Co.*

Key Accomplishments:

- **Leasing Manager of the Year**—1981, 1982, 1983, and 1984
- Key player in building Memorex Finance Co. from start-up to $300M in annual revenues in four years.
- Selected as one of three to start the first captive financial organization for a peripheral manufacturer—a prototype that IBM Credit Corp. currently uses.
- Branch Manager of the Year, 1979
- Senior Salesman of the Year, 1977

EDUCATION & AFFILIATIONS

Bachelor of Science, Edinboro University of Pennsylvania
Executive Extended Master Program in Business Administration, University of Pittsburgh
Board of Trustees, Alumni Board of Directors, Edinboro University of Pennsylvania

resume. The colors are one of MS Word's "picture clip" options for horizontal lines—a capability many Word users don't know about. A pair of opening and closing asterisks (not a common feature in resumes) flags several centered headings of particular importance. Explanations in italic promote understanding.

WALTER D. SAKS

98 Ben Franklin Drive
P.O. Box 219
Cherry Hill, New Jersey 07896   wdsaks@aol.com

Home: (609) 666-1111
Cell: (609) 666-5555
Home Fax: (609) 666-7777

REAL ESTATE DEVELOPMENT MANAGER / ENTERPRISE MANAGER

Results-driven management executive with an in-depth understanding of real estate development and construction. Exceptional ability to comprehend multifaceted problems and frame effective solutions, achieving multiple goals. Proficient in financial analysis, strategic development and implementation, staff management, and preparation of financial reports and statements. Outstanding communication and interpersonal skills, with expertise in developing and maintaining strong and productive working relationships with clients and staff at all levels.

- Land Purchase Contracts
- Strong Real Estate Knowledge
- Requisite Feasibility (Due Diligence)
- Construction Contracting & Negotiation

- Leasing Criteria
- Lease Negotiations
- Purchasing Scope Definition
- End-User Space Use Requirements

Career Chronology

Treasurer—New Jersey County Airport Association	1998–Present
General Partner—Daikcons, Inc.	1981–1998
President/CEO—Saks Construction, Inc.	1965–1981
Manager/Partner—Marble Products, Inc.	1961–1965
U.S. Navy	1955–1961

REAL ESTATE EXPERIENCE

DAIKCONS, INC.—New Jersey, NJ

General Partner

President/CEO of partnership developing commercial real estate projects in metro New Jersey area. Managed and directed construction of partnership ventures; negotiated sales and leases; performed evaluations and due diligence studies; negotiated loan draw schedules and terms; prepared loan packages and projections; developed marketing/sales material; directed architects, engineers, and staff.

- Recognized within the local real estate community as a credible professional with a track record of closing early sales/leases and meeting client delivery requirements. Interest saved due to early sales resulted in increased profits for venture partners and permitted acceleration of project phasing.
- Established strategic business relationships with brokers and agents for early access to potential development sites, expanding new and existing business opportunities.
- Championed project management of Corrs Professional Village ($12.2 million), Kinney Office Park ($19.5 million), Syman Office Park ($24 million), and Bowen Office Park ($18 million).
- Successfully prepared loan packages and projections for efficient line of credit construction loans, maximizing use of relatively small loan values.
- Led and negotiated strategic business alliances with commercial real estate developers to further expand market reach.
- Astutely controlled and established budgets for hard and soft costs, cash-flow projections, project phasing, and sales projections.
- Successfully performed evaluations and due diligence studies on sites, including evaluations for office parks, commercial warehousing projects, shopping centers, and commercial condominium projects.

89

Combination. *Jennifer Rushton, N. Richmond, New South Wales, Australia*

This individual wanted to return to the real estate/construction industry after having worked a little while for a nonprofit organization. The writer listed a Career Chronology first to let potential

WALTER D. SAKS

Experience Continued

CONSTRUCTION EXPERIENCE

SAKS CONSTRUCTION, INC. — New Jersey, NJ
President/CEO
President/CEO for general contracting company managing construction projects for federal government agencies and departments, state governments, large corporations, and individuals.

- Successfully created financially viable company within 6 months by securing industry relationships, enhancing profile and market awareness.
- Led project management of 15–20 construction projects each year, with scope of projects ranging from commercial renovations to major new construction projects.
- Successfully bid for and performed contract construction work for local government agencies and the federal government through its various contracting arms, including General Services Administration, U.S. Navy, Army Corps of Engineers, Air Force, and NASA.
- Encouraged team communication by holding regular staff meetings, maintaining and facilitating communication about projects, avoiding potential problems, and contributing to a successful, results-driven organization.
- Pioneered innovative technological improvements through the design and installation of a detailed cost accounting system. Cost reports, which were taking several weeks to produce by hand, were available for weekly labor production analysis.

MARBLE PRODUCTS, INC. — Cherry Hill, NJ
Manager/Partner

- Full autonomy for profitability of operations, including margins, mark-ups, contracting, billing, collections, and negotiation of all disputes.
- Evaluated competitive market trends and implemented product positioning strategies to ensure long-term, sustainable growth. Re-engineered light structural steel designs of architects and structural engineers, conforming to applicable codes, to gain price edge over competing iron/steel companies.

ADDITIONAL EXPERIENCE

NEW JERSEY COUNTY AIRPORT ASSOCIATION (NJCAA) — New Jersey, NJ
Treasurer
Currently serving as Treasurer for NJCAA, a volunteer non-profit organization. Former roles included President and Vice President.

- Instrumental in doubling active membership during tenure as President, through increased association activity and relationships with FAA and county government.
- Initiated and developed programs and safety presentations for local airport pilot community; liaised with county government and officials on behalf of local airport and general aviation community.

EDUCATION
UNIVERSITY OF NEW JERSEY — New Jersey, NJ
Bachelor of Civil Engineering

PROFESSIONAL TRAINING
Management & Managerial Development • Construction Scheduling & CPM Implementation
Managerial Accounting • Purchasing Agent Practices & Principles
Contract Negotiations & Principles

REFERENCES AVAILABLE UPON REQUEST

employers know that the applicant was currently working, and then followed it with his real estate and construction experience. The contact information, presented in a balanced format, includes an e-mail address. Bullets in the Experience sections point to achievements. See Cover Letter 4 (page 380).

Roger H. Jones

111 Somewhere Ave. NE ▪ Seattle, WA 98115   (206) 222-2222   email: finance@attbi.com

CAREER TARGET: FINANCIAL ANALYST in a banking, corporate or M&A consulting environment.
Proficiencies include Financial Analysis & Reporting ▪ **Modeling** ▪ **O&M** ▪ **Capital Planning** ▪
Business Planning ▪ **Client Relations** ▪ **Process Improvement** ▪ **Databases** ▪ **Reseller Tracking**

- Strong analytical and problem-solving skills.
- Expert technical abilities in Excel. Adept with technology.
- Proven communicator and team player. Strong work ethic.
- Thorough understanding of operations and business risk.
- Excel at analyzing a proposal's strengths and weaknesses.

> *Roger carefully listens, asks questions.... No detail is too small or unimportant. A detail-oriented self starter, he coordinates all elements to "get the job done, done right and on time." —Jason Rodes, Rainier Property Management*

EDUCATION

Post-Graduate Studies: BUSINESS VALUATION, INVESTMENT AND FINANCING, U.W., Spring 2003. Pursuing class work to further M&A capabilities. Studies include evaluating shareholder value and equity value of a corporation, economic interdependencies among investments, inflation, capital rationing, transfer pricing, lease & capital strategies, employee stock options and taxes. Other topics: total cash flow, ratio analysis, takeover target evaluations, basic tax issues, leveraged buyouts, spin-offs, carve-outs and split-ups.

B.A., Business Administration. Focus: Finance/Operations Management (O&M). Major GPA 3.2.
University of Washington (U.W.), Seattle, WA. Graduated June 2003.
U.W. Business School rated 13th during 1999 (year of acceptance).
Studies included Accounting, Corporate Finance, Economics (micro & macro), Strategic Planning & Forecasting, Ratio Analysis, Business Measurements, M&A Case Studies, Portfolios & Investments.

FINANCIAL ANALYSIS PROJECTS
➢ **NPV Loan Analysis**—Evaluated financial statements and tracked the risk-free rate and S&P 500 average annual growth rate. Calculated the spread of a bank from raw numbers, using this information to prepare NPV Analysis on a loan from the bank's view.
➢ **Security/S&P 500 Benchmark Project**—Calculated average daily returns for Caterpillar Equipment and S&P 500. Determined average returns, variances and standard deviations on both to perform extensive regression analysis and statistical analysis. Made recommendations based on alpha and beta scores.

HONORS: **Skills 2000 Business Assessment Test**—Scored in the 97th percentile.

EXPERIENCE
Customer Service/Retail Sales, Home Depot, Seattle, WA 03/02–present
➢ Trusted to train peers, act as ad-hoc floor manager and set promotional pricing for volume clients.
➢ Commended for ability to plan and proactively identify potential weaknesses in customers' projects.

General Manager/Partner, Jones & Jones/Ross Jones Family Farms, Ritzville, WA 01/94–03/02
Managed operations for the family's $.5M wheat farm overseeing seasonal hiring, workflow tasking & resource management, facilities planning & construction, purchasing & vendor oversight and budgeting & financial planning. Raised to value hard work, risk taking and prudent business practices.
➢ Valuated capital projects and purchases of highly customized equipment and facilities.
➢ Designed Access database, programming equipment list queries for accounting purposes.
➢ Performed critical analysis of separate operating units.
➢ Compared leasing, buying and selloff scenarios, strategizing economic plans for growth.

COMPUTERS
Expert: Excel, Word, PowerPoint. Intermediate: Access. Beginner: SQL, AS400, Visual Basic.
Capabilities: Internet Research, macros, VBA, pivot tables, spreadsheet modeling, database building.

AFFILIATIONS/COMMUNITY INVOLVEMENT
Habitat for Humanity ▪ U.W. Alumni Association, 2001–present ▪ Psi Upsilon Fraternity, 1997–2001

90

Combination. *Alice Hanson, Seattle, Washington*

This recent graduate had searched for a job for a year without success because of stiff competition. With this resume he received multiple interviews within six weeks and landed a great job.

Healthcare

Resumes at a Glance

RESUME NO.	OCCUPATION	GOAL	PAGE
91.	Occupational Therapist	Occupational Therapist	185
92.	Asst. Director, Hospital Food Services	Not specified	186
93.	Medical/Billing Assistant	Pharmaceutical Sales Rep.	188
94.	High School Special Ed. Teacher	Medical Transcriptionist	190
95.	Laboratory Technician	Laboratory Technician	192
96.	Interim Office Manager	Nurse	193
97.	Mental Health Worker	Not specified	194
98.	Staff Nurse	Registered Nurse	196
99.	Nurse-Midwife	Nurse-Midwife	198
100.	Family Nurse Practitioner	Not specified	200
101.	Forensic Investigator	Television/Film Consultant	202
102.	Clinical Nursing Supervisor	Not specified	204
103.	Nurse Manager	Nurse Manager/Case Manager	206
104.	Field Case Manager	Case Mgr./Critical Care Nurse	208
105.	RPN IV	Pharmaceutical Salesperson	210
106.	Director, Quality Management	Nurse Administrator	212
107.	President, Dental Services	Not specified	214
108.	Attending Physician/Staff	Physician	216
109.	Reg. Director, MRI & CT Facilities	Administration Management	218
110.	Public Health Technician	Not specified	220
111.	President, Health Software Co.	Not specified	222
112.	Admissions Coordinator	Healthcare Marketing Director	224
113.	Home Economics Student	Not specified	226
114.	Clinical Coordinator	Clinical Research Operations	228
115.	Medical Director	Senior Healthcare Executive	230
116.	Business/Technology Consultant	Senior Healthcare Executive	232

Cheryl Ruiz
Two Hundred Maine Road
Huntington, NY 11743
(631) 382-2425

OCCUPATIONAL THERAPIST

Innovative healthcare provider with 14 years of experience with the following populations:

- Cerebral Palsy
- Head Trauma
- Sensory Integration

- ADD
- HIV
- Neurological Disorders

- Metabolic Disorders
- Juvenile Arthritis
- Orthopedic Conditions

- Developmental Delays
- Chromosomal Disorders
- Burn Victims

Demonstrate strong performance in the areas of communications, problem solving and organization. Licensed to practice in New York State. Certified by the American Occupational Therapy Association.

PROFESSIONAL EXPERIENCE

Evaluate children's abilities; recommend and provide therapeutic services. Incorporate imagination in adapting activities to stimulate client needs. Perform evaluations of home safety in preparation for discharge. Create a healing, safe, and nurturing environment.

> **Occupational Therapist,** JumpStart Park Therapy, New York, NY, 1995–Present
> **Occupational Therapist,** New Beginnings, Hauppauge, NY, 1992–1995
> **Occupational Therapist,** Smithtown, NY, 1987–1992

- Plan and direct administrative and operational activities of the O.T. Department. Supervise a cohesive team that includes 3 occupational therapy aides and 2 certified occupational therapy assistants.

- Function as a member of an interdisciplinary team, encouraging parental involvement by providing training and education.

- Working knowledge of the latest equipment and modalities, including e-stim, ultrasound and short-wave diathermy equipment.

- Work cooperatively with social workers, psychologists, doctors and other healthcare members to maintain a progressive healing environment.

- Implement and modify treatment programs based on patients' needs; maintain accurate documentation on patient progress.

- Provide specialized post-surgical wound care, burn therapy and scar management as well as splinting.

EDUCATION

B.S., Occupational Therapy, New York University, New York, New York, 1987
> **Licensed and Certified,** New York State, 1987

Associate's, Liberal Arts, Nassau Community College, Garden City, New York, 1981

LANGUAGES
Fluent in Spanish and Italian. Knowledge of Portuguese.

AFFILIATIONS

American Occupational Therapy Association
New York State Occupational Therapy Association

91

Combination. *Linda Matias, Smithtown, New York*

The applicant had the same job at three different sites for many years. To avoid repetition in the description of duties, the writer grouped the jobs and then indicated what was common to all three.

TONI M. DEMARCO

452 Burns Court • Port Washington, New York 11554 • (516) 535-6221
tmdemarco@optonline.net

PROFILE

Proactive MBA Management professional with expertise in process and performance improvement, administration, human resources, training and development, and creative business channeling. Excellent team building and interpersonal relations skills. Ability to provide a team-oriented management style focused on motivation and success. Precise, resourceful problem-solver. Effective leader and mentor.

PROFESSIONAL EXPERIENCE

SLOAN KETTERING HOSPITAL • New York, NY   **11/68 to Present**
Assistant Director / Food Nutritional Services • 2000 to Present
Production Manager • 1984 to 2000

Co-direct, coordinate, and supervise the general production of the Food & Nutritional Services Department. Service approximately 1,200 to 1,600 meals per day for patients, staff, employees, and off-site meal-service hospitalization program. Provide sit-down service for up to 100 people daily. Train, schedule, mentor, and supervise staff of 30–32 per shift, including cooks, cooks' helpers, nutritional service aides, and cafeteria staff. Recruit, train, and schedule new employees.

- Provide catering for in-service medical programs, partial-hospitalization meal programs, snack programs, fund-raising events, and community affairs.
- Organize projects and service with all departments.
- Participate in $3,000,000 capital budget and special functions planning.
- Purchase food/supplies/equipment and maintain inventory control; review cost-control records.
- Oversee safety and sanitation procedures; enforce New York State Department of Health and Joint Commission Association (JCAHO) mandates, and interpret guidelines for staff.
- Facilitate "Meals-On-Wheels" service as part of community outreach, continuum-of-care program sponsored by hospital. Plan menus; supervise staff production and related areas of communication.
- Conduct weekly patient rounds.
- Confer with Infection Control Director for patient-related safe food-handling protocol.
- Serve on Environment of Care Committee, Wellness Committee, and Performance Improvement Committee.

  ~ *Play key role in Performance Improvement Program for Food & Nutritional Services Department.*
  ~ *Pioneered and streamlined Dysphasia Food Program with Clinical Nutrition Manager and Speech Pathologist.*
  ~ *Spearheaded Mentor Program for administrative rotation of Suffolk County Community College Diet Technician Program, and the New York Tech's Dietetic Masters Program.*
  ~ *Developed Emergency Preparation Plan for Food & Nutritional Services Department.*
  ~ *Create and implement departmental job descriptions, evaluation forms, and competency testing. Formulate safety program and departmental recording procedures.*
  ~ *Continually develop new menu selections; research recipes, survey patients for input, and coordinate menu planning. Developed Heart Healthy Menu Program for employee dining.*
  ~ *Developed and executed 15 standardized forms to maintain HACCP compliance.*
  ~ *Participated in capital campaign for the ambulatory surgical pavilion as team captain, committee member for hospital fund-raising event, and family walk committee team captain.*

92

Combination. *Donna M. Farrise, Hauppauge, New York*

Distinctive page borders mark the resume as unique at first glance. In the Professional Experience section, bulleted items tell of more duties beyond those indicated in the paragraphs

TONI M. DEMARCO
- Page Two -

Diet Technician • 1980 to 1984
Supervisor • 1971 to 1980
Nutrition Service Aide • 1968 to 1971

RESIDENTIAL CARE FACILITY • Bay Shore, NY   **11/97 to 1/02**
Consultant Nutritionist
 Consulted in preparation of meal service to clients in residential treatment center. Coordinated nutritional care of residents.

- Formulated menu and production sheets for School Lunch Program and residential living for residents; mindful of cultural diversity and age-specific needs of population.
- Performed nutritional screening and recorded nutritional care intervention in medical records.
- Maintained list of residents with special nutritional needs.
- Visited with clients to obtain food preferences and tolerances, and provided nutritional counseling for staff, clients, and family.
- Planned in advance for both general and therapeutic diets.
- Coordinated the nutritional care and recording of information related to nutritional needs with nursing staff.
- Posted current menus in food-preparation area for staff review and information.

EDUCATION

Dowling College, Oakdale, NY
Master of Business Administration, 1999
Bachelor of Business Administration, 1996

Suffolk County Community College, Riverhead, NY
Associate of Applied Science, 1980

CERTIFICATIONS

New York State Certified Dietitian Nutritionist, 1996

MEMBERSHIPS / ASSOCIATIONS

American Dietetic Association
Long Island Dietetic Association, Registered Dietetic Technician
Hospital Federal Credit Union, Board Member

COMPUTER SKILLS

MS Word/Excel/PowerPoint • TimeCare for Windows • Windows
WordPerfect • Internet

after the job positions. Tilde (~) bullets point to achievements in italic. Boldfacing makes the individual's name, centered headings, job positions, dates, and degrees stand out. The headings and some center-aligned text pull the reader's eyes down the pages.

CHRISTY N. SMITH

Home: (555) 555-5555
Cell: (555) 555-5551

5555 Lake Street, #K-55, San Diego, California

Smith34@smithmail.com

Seeking Position As…

PHARMACEUTICAL SALES REPRESENTATIVE

Profile: Recent graduate with a B.S.B.A. degree—completed concurrently with full-time and additional part-time employment. Four years of experience in medical environment, including work as Medical Assistant in orthopedic rehab clinic and Administrative Assistant in physical therapy clinic. Willing and able to work independently or in collaborative environment. Challenge oriented.

Customer Service • Relationship Building • Medical Terminology • Physician Relations
Sales • Record Keeping • Teamwork Facilitation • Problem Resolution

Valued as an articulate, professional communicator.

EDUCATION

BACHELOR OF SCIENCE IN BUSINESS ADMINISTRATION, Corporate Communication
Southern California University—San Diego, California, Dec. 2003

Relevant Coursework: Public Relations, Public Speaking, Marketing, International Marketing, Advertising, Promotion Management, Mass Media, Business Policy, Accounting.

Classroom Accomplishment: Collaborated to win district for National Advertising Association's National Student Advertising Competition. Planned real-world advertising campaign for National Bank.

EMPLOYMENT HISTORY

MEDICAL ASSISTANT/BILLING ASSISTANT   **Jan. 2002–Present**
Oceanview Orthopedic Rehabilitation—San Diego, California
Staff consists of 3 MDs, 1 chiropractor, 1 acupuncturist, 2 massage therapists, 4 physical therapists, 10 support staff.

Accountabilities include coordinating care, scheduling appointments, handling insurance authorizations, processing claim forms, entering charges, preparing deposits, and discharging patients. Assist doctors and chiropractor in patient care.

- **Given Additional Responsibility:** Cross-trained to cover any position or department in clinic.
- **Increased Timely Insurance Authorizations:** Created new, more effective charting method to track patients' physical therapy sessions.
- **Clear Communications:** Trained new chiropractic assistant. Patiently and articulately explain procedures/tests in simple terms to reduce patient anxiety.

93

Combination. *Peter Hill, Honolulu, Hawaii*

This recent graduate was looking for a position in pharmaceutical sales. The writer capitalized on skills gained from administrative experience in physicians' offices and from retail sales

CHRISTY N. SMITH

ACCOUNTING ASSISTANT   **Jan. 2003–Present**
John Doe, CPA, MBA—Del Mar, California
1 CPA, 3-5 assistants.

> Accountabilities include journalizing information, reconciling bank statements, processing tax returns, bookkeeping, performing data entry.
>
> • **Charged with Additional Responsibility:** Hired part-time based on performance accounting course that the owner taught. Offered more bookkeeping responsibilities with selected clients. Received a raise after only 2 weeks on the job.

BRAND REPRESENTATIVE   **Oct. 2001–Present**
College Gap —San Diego, California
High-profile, nationwide clothing retailer marketing fashions for teens and college students.

> Accountabilities include brand representation (required to wear current styles at all times), customer service and sales, cashiering, visual placement, stocking, store maintenance. Train new brand reps.
>
> • **Achieve Aggressive Marketing Objectives:** Collaborate with store management and colleagues to secure #1 company-wide ranking for sales and customer service.
> • **Surpass "Last Year" Benchmarks:** As part of a motivated team, contribute to store consistently outperforming previous year's sales numbers.

ADMINISTRATIVE ASSISTANT   **Jan. 2000–May 2002**
SD Rehab—San Diego, California
Physical therapy clinic. 2 therapists, 1 PTA.

> Performed routine medical office duties such as scheduling appointments, checking in/out patients, setting up patient accounts, monitoring and obtaining insurance approvals, assisting with billing.

COMPUTER SKILLS

Competent in MS Word, PowerPoint, Excel, Publisher, Access; Lotus 1-2-3; e-mail and Internet.

Familiar with QuarkXPress, Adobe Photoshop, QuickBooks.

~ Professional References Gladly Furnished on Request ~

experience. The shaded box and the statement in it are seen almost immediately. Lines extending from the side section headings to the right margin have a different look about them and help the reader spot the sections quickly. In the Employment History section, bullets and boldfacing call attention to achievements.

JUDITH C. FRENCH

9 Fox Hill Drive ~ Howell, New Jersey 07731
Phone: 732.761.9106 ~ E-mail: judyfrench@aol.com

MEDICAL TRANSCRIPTION ~ WORD PROCESSING ~ DATA MANAGEMENT

Professionally trained and skilled *Medical Transcriptionist*. Well organized and versed in medical terminology. Keen understanding of cardiac, pulmonary, and radiology transcription terms. Member of *American Association of Medical Transcriptionists*. Fluent in English and French. Computer literate with experience with Microsoft Office (Word, Excel, Access), Windows 95/98, e-mail, and Internet. *Certified Medical Transcriptionist* from Professional Career Development Institute, Ocean County Community College.

- Self-disciplined
- Problem Solver
- Excels under Pressure
- Professionalism
- Motivated
- Research Techniques
- Superb Memory
- Quick Learner

HIGHLIGHTS

- Detail-oriented educator with exceptional grammar, editing, proofreading, and spelling skills.
- Taught Biology and Anatomy for 15 years.
- Senior editor with five years of experience editing, proofreading, and writing testing procedures for government agencies.
- Experience in accounting, creating databases, data entry, and bookkeeping with various companies.
- Twelve years of experience writing curricula for high-school-level students; subjects include Life Skills, English, Math, and Life Sciences.
- Nineteen years of experience teaching Special Education.

PROFESSIONAL EXPERIENCE

HIGH SCHOOL SPECIAL EDUCATION TEACHER   1995–Present
Milltown Board of Education, Milltown, NJ

BOOKKEEPER ~ DATA ENTRY   2000–2001
Home Depot, Old Bridge, NJ

HIGH SCHOOL TEACHER ~ ALL SUBJECTS   1994–1995
Middlesex County Educational Services Commission, Piscataway, NJ

Continued...

94

Combination. *Beverley and Mitchell I. Baskin, Marlboro, New Jersey*

The page borders are thin but still tie the two pages together. The horizontal bars make the main sections evident at a glance. Italic is useful in the Profile to make key positions and the

PROFESSIONAL EXPERIENCE (continued)

SPECIAL EDUCATION TEACHER   1991–1994
Moorestown Board of Education, Moorestown, NJ

JUNIOR HIGH SCHOOL SPECIAL EDUCATION TEACHER   1988–1991
Moorestown Board of Education, Moorestown, NJ

SENIOR EDITOR ~ COMBAT SYSTEMS ENGINEERING   1984–1989
Development Group, General Electric, Moorestown, NJ

TRAINING AND EDUCATION

Certified Medical Transcriptionist ~ OCEAN COUNTY COLLEGE, Toms River, NJ

M.Ed. ~ PENNSYLVANIA STATE UNIVERSITY, State College, PA   Graduated with Distinction

BA ~ LAFAYETTE COLLEGE, Easton, PA
        Major: Psychology/French, Minor: Biology
        Dean's List

MEDICAL SPECIALTY WORK

Enjoy medical specialty work including *cardiac, pulmonary, and radiology transcription projects.*

Excel quickly—comfortable with new terms and procedures.

Work well under pressure and stringent deadlines.

Possess a track record of project accuracy and attention to details.

Considered an efficient, organized project manager with an excellent memory.

Completed Pre-Med courses in college—instructor in Biology and Anatomy.

Avid health/science reader.

Working knowledge of foreign languages, including French and Latin.

~ Excellent References upon Request ~

related membership stand out. Adequate white space throughout avoids a cramped look and encourages reading. The "Continued..." flag at the foot of the first page is thus a welcome sign. The reader would dread it, however, in an overpacked resume without breathing space.

LORI GREEN

55 Southern Bend Way
Brentwood, New York 22222
(555) 555-0000 • labtech@health.com

LABORATORY TECHNICIAN

PROFESSIONAL EXPERIENCE	**Laboratory Technician** **Briarcliff Medical Center, The Islips, New York**	**1986–present** **Evening Shift**

▶ *Profile*

♦ 17+ years of comprehensive in-service training and experience managing multifaceted laboratory functions; A.A.S., Medical Laboratory Technology.

♦ Broadly cross-trained in areas that include, but are not limited to, hematology, phlebotomy and blood-bank procedures interfacing directly with professional staff and patients in ER, ICU, OR and Recovery.

♦ Perform and interpret laboratory tests, demonstrating a keen ability to identify and correct discrepancies; record and communicate test results.

♦ Recognized for ability to organize, prioritize, coordinate and perform tasks concurrently during periods of limited staffing and supervision.

♦ Ensure quality control of laboratory procedures, staff communication, equipment functionality, and OSHA/FDA compliance.

♦ Render in-house and off-site phlebotomy services utilizing exceptional organizational, time-management and interpersonal skills.

♦ Effectively train personnel in all areas of laboratory procedures; coordinate staff schedules; maintain timely and accurate computerized data entry.

▶ *Diagnostic Testing*

– Hematology
– Phlebotomy
– Blood Bank
– Bone Marrow Slides
– Urinalysis
– Coagulation
– Chemistry
– Serology

▶ *In-service Training*
15 years, ongoing

– CPR
– Vital Signs
– Venipuncture
– Specimen Handling
– Infection Control
– Fire and Safety
– Information Systems
– OSHA/FDA

▶ *Equipment*

– Beckman CX3, CX7
– TDX
– IMX
– Hemo-Cell-Dyne 1600
– Coulter S+4
– Coulter T-660

Secretary, Computer Department, Storage Warehouse **1978–1986**
Space Savers, The Islips, New York

♦ Provided secretarial support in areas of typing and customer service.

♦ Operated and maintained functionality of IBM and Hitachi mainframes to ensure accurate and timely processing of sensitive government information.

♦ Organized, labeled and supervised the release of tape inventory.

EDUCATION   **Bachelor of Science, Medical Laboratory Technology, 1987**
Stony Brook University, Stony Brook, New York

95

Chronological. *Ann Baehr, Brentwood, New York*

A Profile and three groups of skill areas *embedded in* the information about the current position in the Professional Experience section give this resume in effect a chronological format.

CHRISTINA WOODS, RN

333 Sherman Street • Brentwood, New York 55555 • (555) 222-4444 • newnurse@health.com

EDUCATION

Bachelor of Science in Nursing, 2004; GPA 3.9
STONY BROOK UNIVERSITY, Stony Brook, New York

Certificate of Completion, Diabetic Nurse Education, 2003
LONG ISLAND UNIVERSITY *at* C.W. POST, Brentwood, New York

LICENSES & CERTIFICATIONS

New York State Registered Nurse License, 2004, # 555555
CPR; BLS Certification

CLINICAL TRAINING

Upheld high standards of nursing care for a diverse population of patients ranging from newborn to geriatric in a variety of settings including Medical Surgical, Pediatrics, ER, OR, PICU, and Ambulatory Surgery.

Assessment
- Performed total patient assessments including neurologic, cardiovascular, respiratory, gastrointestinal, genitourinary, IV site/line, PICC lines, CVP lines, surgical/trauma wound, nephrostomy tubes, trachiostomy, urinary catheters, NG tubes, G tubes, chest tubes, and ostomies.

Planning
- Educated patients and their families on disease processes, medical-surgical procedures, and broad aspects of therapeutic regimens, including medication and pain-management techniques.
- Attended in-service training on IV and PICC line management.
- As an observer, learned the legal role that chart-based medical records hold during court proceedings.

Implementation
- Followed aseptic procedures and provided care in accordance with universal precautions with an emphasis on surgical/traumatic wound care and debriding, intake and output, and ostomies.
- Administered oral and intramuscular and subcutaneous medications.
- Cared for perinatal and postpartum patients and their newborns, and evaluated fetal monitoring strips.

Evaluation
- Worked effectively with an interdisciplinary team and performed accurate charting procedures.
- Successfully recommended and implemented changes to the medical unit regarding assignment delegation and prioritization, resulting in a higher standard of patient care, and reassessed/revised plan of care as needed.

WORK HISTORY

Interim Office Manager, LONG ISLAND CARES, New Hyde Park, New York	10/99–present
Senior Fundraiser, UNICEF, Great Neck, New York	5/97–10/99

96

Chronological. *Ann Baehr, Brentwood, New York*

This newly licensed RN had clinical training but no clinical experience. The writer placed office management experience at the end and made clinical training resemble clinical experience.

PAMELA E. SWENSEN

333 Hibiscus Lane   swensenp@aol.com
Jackson, MO 00000   (901) 852-7744

EDUCATION

Jackson College, Jackson, MO
Bachelor of Arts Degree in **Psychology,** May 2004
o   Dean's List, three semesters
o   GPA: 3.65/4.0

Community College of Lafayette, Lafayette, MO
Associate Degree in **Nursing,** May 2000

CLINICAL EXPERIENCE

Spring 2004   **Bensen Heights Hospital,** Jackson, MO
                 Psychiatric Unit.
                 • Interacted with broad range of inpatient psychiatric clients to complete
                   assessments and care plans.

Fall 2003   **Jackson City Hospital,** Jackson, MO
                 Med-surg Post-surgical Unit.
                 • Changed dressings, administered meds and IVs, removed catheters.
                 • Assisted with insertion of various drains used post-surgically.
                 • Assessed inputs and outputs.
                 • Performed EKGs.

Spring 2003   **Phillip Rheims General Hospital,** Belton, MO
                 Maternity.
                 • Trained new parents with proper care of newborns.
                 • Performed postpartum assessments.
                 • Assisted nurses during newborn assessments and birthing procedures.
                 • Evaluated and observed diagnosed procedures during labor and delivery.

Fall 2002   **Saint Theresa Hospital,** Fallon, MO
                 Pediatric Unit.
                 • Administered medications as prescribed.
                 • Interacted with children during diversionary activities.

Spring 2002   **Saint Theresa Hospital,** Fallon, MO
                 Medications and IV Therapy.
                 • Prepared care plans and medications prior to administration.
                 • Completed physical assessments on all patients.

Fall 2001   **James L. Betts Retirement Home,** Jackson, MO
                 PTs with ADLs.
                 • Interacted with PTs during group meals.
                 • Administered medications to PTs as required.

97

Combination. *Edward Turilli, Newport, Rhode Island*

Without the brief Certification/Skills section on page two, the resume's format would be
chronological. Enclosing the name in a shaded box makes the reader see the name first, even

Pamela E. Swensen **Page Two**

RELATED EMPLOYMENT

January 2002– **Jackson City Hospital,** Jackson, MO
Present Mental Health Worker, Part-time.
- Assess and complete BIWA withdrawal assessment sheets.
- Interview PTs to complete daily process notes.
- Complete observation sheets with levels of observation for each patient.
- Maintain safe milieu appropriate for patient safety.
- Provide crisis intervention as needed.
- Interact with peers and colleagues in a positive and therapeutic environment.

August 2000– **Child and Family Services of Lafayette County,** Lafayette, MO
January 2002 Residential Counselor, Part-time.
- Supervised residents' activities, recording daily personnel accountability.
- Administered prescription medication as needed.
- Interacted with peers to ensure safe and enjoyable environment.

OTHER EMPLOYMENT

Summers **Lafayette County Summer Recreation Center,** Lafayette, MO
1998–2000 Lifeguard, Swim Instructor.

CERTIFICATIONS / SKILLS

- Registered Nurse
- CPR, First Aid
- Lifeguard (three seasons)
- Health Care Provider
- American Red Cross
- Crisis Intervention

VOLUNTEER

- First Aid and Safety Member, U.S. Lifeguard Association
- Sylvan Children's Care Center: Outpatient Services
- Jackson Youth Intervention Association

EXCELLENT REFERENCES / LETTERS OF RECOMMENDATION FURNISHED UPON REQUEST

though the contrast between the letters of the name and the shaded background is less than that between black letters and a white background. With experience limited to part-time work and work during academic semesters, bullets point to duties and responsibilities at the various workplaces.

Gerard P. Carlisle, MPA, RN, CNOR

167 Florida Street • South Brunswick, NJ 07080 • 908.555.5555 • jerrypcar@comcast.net

HEALTHCARE PROFESSIONAL

Operations Management ~ Healthcare Review ~ Clinical Consultant

Extremely competent, well-organized, and professional **REGISTERED NURSE** with a consistent track record of surpassing standards and goals at New Jersey's premier hospital...motivator and detailed problem-solver who takes pride in meticulous work. Continually strives to expand professional knowledge and responsibilities.

Excellent leadership, scheduling, interpersonal, and safety skills. Establish rapport and confidence while building strong and lasting relationships with a diverse group of individuals...possess exceptional planning, prioritizing, and goal-setting skills to achieve optimal patient outcome...ability to create, implement, and document efficient methods of operations.

Competencies Include

- Patient Relations
- Clinical Review
- Project Management
- Patient Case Management
- Clinical Practice Management

- Staff Training/Motivation/Development
- HIPAA Compliance
- Clinical Case Analysis
- Surgical Nursing
- Pain Management Nursing

Professional Accomplishments

- Contributor to the success of the Pain Institute of Beth Israel. The Institute was named one of the top 35 facilities in the United States by *Good Housekeeping* magazine for 2003.

- Member of the Pain Management Committee, a multidisciplinary team that develops policies and procedures for treating pain.

- As Head Nurse of the Same Day Surgery Unit, hired, trained, and monitored the level of performance of a staff of 30 healthcare professionals.

- As Head Nurse, 6 Tower Surgery Unit, supervised, developed, and evaluated a staff of 60 healthcare professionals.

- Provide leadership to monitor cases for appropriate utilization of services, completeness of documentation, and proper compliance with HIPPA, state, and hospital policies and procedures.

- Selected by the Vice President of Nursing to be an internal consultant in the emergency room for the purpose of upgrading the level of nursing.

- Chosen as a recipient of a full scholarship to Nursing School by the State of New Jersey, Trenton Development Center.

- As Head Nurse, ensure that problems are addressed with appropriate auditing and resolution.

Education and Certifications

MPA ~ Master of Public Administration ~ *Fairleigh Dickinson University*, Madison, NJ
AAS ~ Nursing ~ *Elizabeth General Medical Center School of Nursing*, Elizabeth, NJ
BS ~ Sociology ~ *University of Scranton*, Scranton, PA
ANCC ~ Certified in Medical/Surgical Nursing
AORN ~ Certified in Perioperative Nursing

Additional certification in Telemetry and Intravenous Lines.

Continued

98

Combination. *Beverley and Mitchell I. Baskin, Marlboro, New Jersey*

Everything except experience is put on the first page so that the Professional Experience section can appear in full on the second page. Boldfacing aids comprehension on both pages. On the

Page Two GERARD P. CARLISLE

Professional Experience

Newark Beth Israel Hospital, *Newark, NJ (1995–Present)*
New Jersey Pain Institute
Staff Nurse (2001–Present)
- **Chosen for this elite position in a very high-profile unit.** Extensive familiarity with patient assessment, intervention, and compliance with medical policies and procedures.
- Provided health services to ambulatory patients within the Department of Anesthesia in a prestigious division of a hospital that serves as a teaching affiliate of the University of Medicine and Dentistry of New Jersey.
- Ability to create and implement efficient methods for operations.
- Interact with patients of all ages, levels of development, and ethnic backgrounds.
- Maintained calm, caring environment throughout shifts.

Same Day Surgery
Head Nurse (1999–2001)
- Managed the admission, surgery, and recovery of an ambulatory surgical center that treated 45 patients per day.
- Streamlined the admission and discharge process through performance improvement and program development initiatives.
- Oversaw, monitored, and performed budget analysis for the unit to ensure objectives were achieved.

Perioperative Services
Staff Nurse (1998–1999)
- Utilized assessment skills to identify and monitor patients' needs and consulted with physicians to provide timely and efficient treatments to patients recovering from surgery.
- Administered medications, reviewed patient charts, and implemented interventions as necessary.
- Surgical rotations included oncology, thoracic, and vascular procedures.

6 Tower Surgical Unit
Head Nurse (1996–1998)
- Supervised, trained, and provided administrative direction to a 60-staff team in this 34-bed surgical unit.
- Planned and managed the care of post-operative patients from admission to the unit until their discharge.
- Collaborated with a multidisciplinary team to provide excellent patient care that exceeded federal, state, and hospital regulations.
- Responsible for ensuring that the unit's budget objectives were met.

New Jersey Department of Human Services, Division of Developmental Disabilities, Trenton Developmental Center, *Trenton, NJ (1986–1995)*
Staff Nurse (1994–1995)
- Provided skilled nursing care for developmentally and physically challenged children and adults in a long-term-care facility. Supervised and monitored 4 Licensed Practical Nurses.

Acting Principal Community Program Specialist (1990–1993)
- Supervised 5 caseworkers serving 360 developmentally and physically challenged individuals.
- Trained and mentored staff on policies and procedures.
- Negotiated residential service contracts with sponsors and group home providers.

Habilitation Plan Coordinator (1986–1990)
- Caseworker for 75 developmentally and physically challenged adults and children.
- Conducted field visits to families, managing their benefits and verifying client's eligibility.

first page, boldfacing calls attention to the person's name, degrees, certifications, competencies, and professional achievements. On the second page, boldfacing makes evident the two workplaces and the different positions held at these sites. Page borders unite the two pages, and lines delineate sections.

PAMELA MURPHY

238 Waterton Avenue • Troy, NY 12180
Home: 518-274-4565 • Mobile: 518-274-0022 • pmrmurphy2@aol.com

Seeking Position as...

NURSE-MIDWIFE

"20 Years of Experience Dedicated to the Care of Women and Newborns"

Experienced Nurse-Midwife with licensure in NY, CT, and the U.S. Virgin Islands.
15 years as Clinical Nurse in Labor and Delivery at Yale–New Haven Hospital.
5 years as Gynecological Teaching Associate at Yale School of Medicine.
Massage Therapist with training in pregnancy and infant massage.
Qualified to first-assist physicians with cesarean births.

Skilled in providing culturally competent care for ethnically diverse populations.
Maintain calm, reassuring demeanor in high-risk and trauma situations.
Proficient with, and appreciative of, varied styles of practice.
Value safe, positive, and respectful care for all women.
Conversant in Spanish.

PROFESSIONAL EXPERIENCE

Nurse-Midwife   2002–Present
Oncelet Healthcare Center, Troy, NY

- Deliver full scope of midwifery care in private office setting and in association with Samaritan Hospital.
- Provide in-hospital night-shift coverage: Offer triage and backup evaluation for community physicians, serve as technical resource for nursing staff, and provide breastfeeding assistance to new mothers.
- First-assist physicians with cesarean births.

Staff Midwife   2001–2002
Governor Juan Francisco Luis Hospital and Medical Center, Christiansted, St. Croix; U.S.V.I.

- Provided midwifery and nursing care of high-risk antepartum, intrapartum, and postpartum women from ethnically diverse populations, including women from surrounding islands.
- Documented and communicated to appropriate team members patient condition, treatment, progress, and other pertinent information relative to maternal/fetal/newborn status.
- Performed triage of pregnant women presenting through the emergency room.

Clinical Nurse, Labor and Birth   1986–2001
Childbirth Educator   1986–1996
Yale–New Haven Hospital, New Haven, CT

- Delivered expert nursing care to childbearing women from local communities referred for high-risk care at this university teaching hospital emphasizing evidence-based practice and customer satisfaction.
- Served as preceptor and mentor to nursing, midwifery, medical, and other allied-health students.
- Provided skilled nursing assistance in operating room and recovery room care of obstetric patients.
- Designed and implemented educational programs for pregnant women and their families.
- Guest lecturer for other educators on the benefits of massage for pregnancy, labor, and birth.

99

Combination. *Jeanne Knight, Melrose, Massachusetts*

Resume writer's comments: "The strong and creatively formatted summary section quickly and clearly highlights this person's expertise as a Nurse-Midwife." The effect was accomplished

PAMELA MURPHY–Resume   Page 2

PROFESSIONAL EXPERIENCE (cont'd)

Lecturer/Gynecological Teaching Associates   1995–2001
Yale School of Medicine, New Haven, CT

Certified Licensed Massage Therapist (private practice)   1995–2001
Guilford Center for Alternative Healing, Guilford, CT

Labor and Delivery Nurse   1985–1986
St. Margaret's Hospital for Women, Dorchester, MA

Neonatal Intensive Care Nurse   1981–1983
Hartford Hospital, Hartford, CT

EDUCATION

Master of Science in Nursing, Midwifery Program   2001
State University of New York at Stony Brook

Bachelor of Science in Nursing   1981
University of Connecticut at Storrs

CLINICAL ROTATIONS

Danbury Hospital Women's Center, Danbury CT (3/1999–9/1999)
Delivered well woman, antepartum, and postpartum care.

Loyola-Yale Schools of Nursing National Health Care Project, Corozol District, Belize (3/2000)
Provided preventative health care to high-risk women and children. Designed and delivered workshops to
traditional birth attendants on pregnancy complications.

Northern Navajo Medical Center, Shiprock, NM (10/2000–12/2000)
Provided culturally competent nurse-midwifery care of Navajo women and their families during labor and birth.
Performed triage, antenatal testing, induction of labor, and treatment of women with pregnancy complications.

Yale–New Haven Hospital Women's Center, New Haven, CT (1999–2001)
Led group Prenatal Care sessions and provided guidance on comfort measures in pregnancy and labor.

CERTIFICATES, LICENSURE, AND TRAINING

Certified by the American College of Nurse-Midwives since 2001

RN and Midwifery licensure held in New York, Connecticut, and the U.S. Virgin Islands
Licensed Massage Therapist in New York and Connecticut

Certificate, New York Massage Therapist Program, Connecticut Center for Massage Therapy; Newington, CT
Certificate, Sexual Assault Nurse Examiner (SANE) course, Quinnipiac University; Hamden, CT
Certificate (in progress), First Assist for Nurse-Midwives

Current in newborn resuscitation and CPR

through inverted-pyramid formatting of two groups of lines, center-aligning each line (with a hard return at
the end of each line) and making each new line shorter than the preceding line. The appearance of the section is distinctive and captures the reader's attention.

Elizabeth Gallagher, RN, FNP

669 Kinsey Road
Akron, OH 44313
(222) 222-2222
lizgal@worldnet.att.net

KEY QUALIFICATIONS

Family Nurse Practitioner with 20 years of nursing experience • Variety of clinical experiences: hospital, office, clinic, and home care • Strong problem-solving and diagnostic skills • ACLS certified • Effective communicator who enjoys teaching staff and patients • Proven ability to build rapport with patients and earn their trust

PROFESSIONAL EXPERIENCE

Family Nurse Practitioner   1998 to 2004
Mahoning County Family Clinic, Warren, OH
 • Obtained patient histories and performed physical examinations.
 • Diagnosed and treated patients of all ages.
 • Conducted wellness care, health maintenance, and patient education.
 • Recommended and developed a patient satisfaction survey.

Family Nurse Practitioner   1996 to 1998
Joel Blumberg, M.D., Warren, OH
 • Treated acute illnesses and minor injuries in adults and children.
 • Operated a low-cost general medicine clinic for uninsured individuals.
 • Developed experience with indigence, physical abuse, substance abuse, and psychological disorders.

Clinical Nurse Specialist   1991 to 1996
Baxley Home Health Care, Lancaster, PA
 • Developed curriculum and taught classes to 150+ staff members. Presented material in a relevant and engaging manner that encouraged interest.
 • Reviewed patient charts and identified potential adverse medication interactions, then recommended modifications to physicians.
 • Updated facility's in-home fall-prevention policies.
 • Trained, scheduled, and supervised nursing staff.

Staff Nurse—Intensive Care   1987 to 1991
Lancaster Regional Hospital, Lancaster, PA
 • Provided patient care, including insertion of invasive lines, intubations, continuous venous hemodialysis, and assistance with bedside surgeries.
 • Selected as Intensive Care Nurse of the Year in 1990.

100

Combination. *Rima Bogardus, Garner, North Carolina*

Resumes can sometimes be simple and easy to read when an individual has a solid record of work, belongs to the "right" organizations, acquired the appropriate degrees, and participated

- Served on the Clinical Practice Committee (1989–1991), which researched practices and implemented various changes. Results included improved patient satisfaction, reduced length of stay, decreased nosocomial infections, and increased staff efficiency.

Previous employment was as a Registered Nurse in a hospital and a physician's office.

PROFESSIONAL MEMBERSHIPS

American Academy of Nurse Practitioners
Advanced Practice Nurses of Ohio
Sigma Theta Tau (Nursing Honor Society)

EDUCATION

Master of Science in Nursing—Family Nurse Practitioner Concentration   1995
Franklin and Marshall College, Lancaster, PA   GPA: 3.8

Bachelor of Science in Nursing
University of Maryland, Baltimore, MD

CONTINUING EDUCATION

Management of Chest Pain	2003
Meeting the Health Care Needs of the Uninsured and Underinsured	2002
New Developments in Treating Diabetes	2002
Comprehensive Case Management Intensive	2001
Dermatology Seminar	2000
Leadership Skills for Health Care Professionals	1999
Pediatrics Seminar	1999

in expected continuing education. There are no holes to patch, gaps to fill, or weaknesses to cover. This resume is one of them and mentions both employment duties and contributions. In the Professional Experience section, boldfacing for job positions makes them seem more important than workplaces.

JOHN R. DELROSARIO, RPA-C

701 Park Avenue • Setauket, New York 11771 • (631) 563-7209
johnrdelrosario@yahoo.com

PROFILE

Professional Forensic Investigator/Physician Assistant seeking to transition background and experience into a new consulting venue for television/film. Successfully combine literary consultant experience and published crime-scene authoring. Natural ability to communicate professionally with individuals of all levels. Organized, detail-oriented, and efficient administrative abilities.

TRANSITIONAL SKILLS

➤ Investigated approximately 500 deaths a year, over a 23-year career, in role as Forensic Investigator, including homicides, suicides, accidental deaths, undetermined deaths, and deaths from natural causes.

➤ Supervised crime scene for Medical Examiner's Office; pronounced death, conducted physical examination of the deceased, investigated scenes, reconstructed accidents, identified and preserved evidence.

➤ Advised detectives, crime-scene technicians, and morgue drivers.

➤ Obtained biological exemplars for evidentiary purpose at direction of police agencies, courts, or their authorized agents.

➤ Identified and established evidentiary value of items, i.e., samples for toxicological analysis, documented evidence, and directed removal while safeguarding quality and chain of evidence.

➤ Testified in court. Assisted in prosecutions in more than 1,000 DWI cases.

➤ Conducted formal lectures, educational programs, and conferences in forensic medicine for physicians, NYSSPA, and staffs.

➤ Provided regulatory reporting to OSHA, Long Island Police Departments, FBI, New York State Health Department, Centers for Disease Control, and Consumer Product Safety Commission.

➤ Participated in research of Huntington's Disease.

PROFESSIONAL EXPERIENCE

MEDICAL EXAMINER'S OFFICE • Riverhead, NY   10/78 to 10/01
Forensic Investigator

   Conducted independent and confidential investigations of deaths. Interviewed witnesses, recorded detailed observations of scenes, took photographs, collected evidence, and reviewed physician and hospital records. Obtained factual history and recorded events with emphasis on manner and circumstances of death. Prepared and submitted detailed reports.

➤ *Senior Forensic Investigator for Suffolk County Medical Examiner's Office investigating 1997 TWA Flight 800 disaster.*

➤ *Assisted in implementing new Medical Examiner's facility, 1988.*

➤ *Co-founder and creator of the "Forensic Investigator" role in 1978—replacing 20 P/T police surgeons and deputy medical examiner positions.*

STONY BROOK HOSPITAL • Stony Brook, NY   10/91 to 7/93
Hospice Nurse On-Call—P/T

   Provide comfort and patient care, and administer medications to 40–50 ill and dying patients. Interact with family members and loved ones to educate them on patient status and care.

Prior to 1978, served as a Physician Assistant and EMT/ORT at several surgical and medical practice centers: Huntington Surgical Group, New York Group, Good Samaritan Memorial Hospital, and Massachusetts Memorial Hospital.

101

Combination. *Donna M. Farrise, Hauppauge, New York*

Strong page borders unite visually the two pages of this resume for a Vietnam War veteran who was seeking to leave a long-term career as a forensic investigator in order to become a

JOHN R. DELROSARIO, RPA-C
— Page Two —

EDUCATION

Regents College, NY
Associate of Applied Science in Nursing, 1990

New York University, New York, NY
Bachelor of Science in Health Science Technology, 1974

State University of New York at Stony Brook School of Allied Health, Stony Brook, NY
Physician Associate, 1973

LITERARY CONSULTANT

Technical Adviser to Tom Philbin on Precinct Siberia Crime Novels for Fawcett Publishing: Precinct Siberia / Undercover / A Matter of Degree / Cop Killer / Jamaica Kill / Death Sentence / Street Killer
Antiquarian Book Dealer—Flitcraft Books

PUBLICATIONS

American Journal of Forensic Pathology:
"Open Revolver Cylinder at the Suicide Death Scene" (Pending)
Wrote Stories for Physician Assistant Update Magazine

CERTIFICATIONS / LICENSES

**Certification by The National Commission on Certification of Physician Assistants (NCCPA)—
#981744
New York State Licensed Registered Nurse—#426200
Registered Physician Associate—# 000149**

MEMBERSHIPS / ASSOCIATIONS

Founding Member of New York State Society of Physician Assistants
Original Member of the American Academy of Physician Assistants
Pioneering Member of Physician Assistant Profession
Attended First Physician Assistant Program at the State University of New York at Stony Brook
Life Member of the First Marine Division Association

TASK FORCE SERVICE

Emergency Medical Service (EMS) Council of Suffolk County

MILITARY SERVICE

U.S. Navy, 1965–1971
2nd Battalion—1st Marines
1st Marine Division—Vietnam

consultant for television/film. Bold, centered, and underlined headings guide the reader's eyes downward through the two pages. Attractive 3-D, arrow-tip bullets point to the individual's transitioning skills and to his significant attainments as a forensic investigator.

Nancy Viggner, RN, BSN

555 Parston Road, Apt. 1, Wellington, WA 98888
(777) 777-1777

Healthcare professional with more than 20 years of nursing experience demonstrates strengths in the following key areas:

- Multi-Specialty Group Practice Management
- Medical and Clinical Services
- Clinical Process Improvement
- Total Quality Management
- Policy Development and Implementation
- Health Education and Training
- Provider, Staff, and Interdepartmental Facilitation
- Public Speaking / Event Management

CAREER SUMMARY

CEDAR WOODS MEDICAL GROUP, Wellington, WA, 1998–present
Clinical Nursing Supervisor, 1999–present
Medical Records Supervisor, 1999
Referral Coordinator, 1998

- Supervise 100 clinical personnel and coordinate 20 specialty departments in compliance with group and regulatory standards.

- Recommend and implement departmental policies and procedures.

- Collaborate with colleges to set up extern programs, placements, evaluations.

- Set up training classes and coordinate in-service education.

- Ensure accreditation processing / CPR recertification.

- Assess, adjust, and forecast staffing needs.

- Select, train, and evaluate all departmental personnel.

- Implement and develop OSHA and WISHA biohazard safety clinical training programs and specialized training.

- Set up, staff, and oversee MMG vaccine coordinators for public health department—vaccine implementation, benchmarking, etc.

- Collaborate with local hospitals, public agencies, insurance companies, and nursing homes to improve patient care delivery.

COMMUNITY COLLEGE, Wellington, WA, 1997
Adjunct Faculty Position

KAISER PERMANENTE MEDICAL CENTER
Rancho Cordova, CA, 1995–1996
Float RN—Internal Medicine, Pediatrics, and OB / GYN

CORVEL CORPORATION, Rancho Cordova, CA, 1994–1995
Supervisor / Medical Case Manager

KAISER PERMANENTE MEDICAL CENTER
Sacramento, CA, 1979–1990
Pediatric Advice Nurse, Relief Charge Nurse, Triage Nurse

UC DAVIS MEDICAL CENTER, Sacramento, CA, 1978–1979
Pediatric ICU Nurse, Relief Charge Nurse, ICU Float Nurse

" … great patient advocate … hardworking with a positive attitude… very supportive ."

"…exceptional motivator." "…excellent leader."

" … straightforward and easy to work with… can analyze problems well and offer good solutions… willing to be flexible and try new ideas… learns very quickly."

"… flexible … personable, responsible… fellow employees respect her and find her fair."

"…exceeded our expectations in her teaching and management abilities…intelligent… self-reliant."

excerpts from performance evaluations

LICENSES / CERTIFICATIONS

Washington RN License, current

California RN License, current

HIV / AIDS Education Certificate, current

BCLS, current

Case Management Certificate, current

TQM Certificate, current

California Public Health Nurse, prior

Arterial Blood Puncture Certified, prior

ACLS / PALS, prior

NY Licensed Vocational Nurse, prior

PROFESSIONAL DEVELOPMENT

Member, Community College
Advisory Board
Corvel Total Quality Management
Health Care Delivery Improvement
Workers' Compensation
Claims Insurance
OSHA / WISHA Biomedical / Biohazard
Waste
Clinical Safety Orientation
Patient Confidentiality
LastWord / Phamis

EDUCATION

Continuing Education Classes
30+ hours annually
BS, Nursing, Adelphi University,
Garden City, NY
Graduated with Honors cum Laude
Dean's List, 3 years

102

Combination. *Janice M. Shepherd, Bellingham, Washington*

This resume is distinctive because of (1) the shape of the shaded area on page one and (2) the dedication of page two to Continuing Education Classes. Bullets in the left column of page one

Nancy Viggner, RN, BSN

555 Parston Road, Apt. 1, Wellington, WA 98888
(777) 777-1777

CONTINUING EDUCATION CLASSES

2004

May	Diabetes Update
April	Safety in the Workplace
	Referral Training
	Ambulatory Care Nursing Conference
March	Trainer, Biomedical / Biohazard Waste
February	Basic CPR—Recertification
January	Legal Documentation
	Minimizing Liability through the Medical Record

2003

December	Office Evaluation / Triage Nursing Review
November	Healthcare Delivery Improvement
October	Dealing Effectively with Unacceptable Employee Behavior
August	Surgical Emergencies
July	Stress Management / Biofeedback
	Conscious Sedation
May	Common Joint Pain / Problems
	Ambulatory Care Nursing Conference
April	Skin Cancer
March	Depression
February	Diabetes
	Basic CPR
January	Chest Pain

2002

November	Healthy Practices—Risk Reduction
	Strategies for Medical Office Staff
October	Hypertension
	Emotions
September	Rashes
	Immunization—Update 2002
July	Dizziness / Fainting
June	Headaches
April	Urinary Tract Infections
	Pediatric Palliative Case Project
	Telephone Triage
March	Cough
	Understanding Anger
February	Limb Pain
	Basic CPR
January	Upper Respiratory Infections

CONTINUING EDUCATION CLASSES EVERY YEAR PREVIOUS

point to key strengths and to significant responsibilities in the candidate's role as Clinical Nursing Supervisor. In the right column, the excerpts from performance evaluations help to overcome any doubts a reader may have about the candidate. Page two is a handy list of knowledge areas.

KELVIN M. PARKER
555 River Lane • Sunset Beach, Hawaii 00000
(808) 555-5555 • kmparker@islandmail.net

NURSE MANAGER • CASE MANAGER • DIRECTOR OF NURSING
Offering 20+ Years of Experience in Both Inpatient and Outpatient Settings

Background includes managing nurse staffs in medical facilities of 36 to 530 beds, including personnel selection, training and development, and dismissal. Maximize quality of care through needs identification and resource optimization. Work well as team member, and with people from other cultures and ethnic backgrounds. Working knowledge of nurse association and Teamster contracts.

> *Expertise in Patient, Nurse, and Physician Relations; Project Management; Team Development; and Conflict Resolution.*

- **Computer skills** include WordPerfect, E-mail, Internet, and various hospital documentation and order-entry systems.
- BLS Certified (expires 10/05); RN Licensure Hawaii #5555; ACLS Certification pending.

EMPLOYMENT HISTORY

PAN PACIFIC REHABILITATION HOSPITAL—Honolulu, Hawaii   2002–Present

Nurse Manager
95-bed acute care rehabilitation services facility. Serve as call-in administrative officer. Accountable for house-wide supervisory coverage, including nurse staffing.

ISLAND MEDICAL CENTER—Honolulu, Hawaii   1988–2002

Nurse Manager
530-bed medical center. Charged with hospital-wide managerial coverage. Handled staff hiring, dismissal, counseling; continuing education and development; $1.5 million multi-unit budget creation and administration; capital improvements; contract negotiations; and grievance reconciliation. Served as Nursing Administrative Coordinator.

- Directed 24-hour coverage for 32-bed neurology, 24-bed orthopedic, and 21-bed pediatric medical/surgical units.
- Identified need and developed 4-bed step-down telemetry neurovascular unit for stroke patients.
- Implemented cost-effective chronic ventilator program, opening up beds in critical care unit.
- Administered sick-child daycare program. Handled marketing and community outreach.
- Member of Information Services Committee. Took active role in evaluation, selection, and realization of progressive hospital-wide technology.
- Selected by physicians to receive **Nursing Leadership Award** for 1999.

103

Combination. *Peter Hill, Honolulu, Hawaii*

This individual wanted to move from Hawaii to the United States mainland. The writer's task was to position the applicant for this transition. With this resume he received interview offers

KELVIN M. PARKER

Page 2 of 2

JONES HOSPITAL—Seattle, Washington   1980–1988

Nurse Manager
36-bed surgical unit. Accountable for 24-hour coverage. Established 4 post-ICU beds.

HOSPITAL OF THE NORTHWEST—Vancouver, Washington   1978–1980

Charge Nurse
42-bed hospital. Provided shift coverage for OB, ER, CCU, and medical/surgical units as night charge nurse.

THE MONUMENT HOSPITAL—Portland, Oregon   1977–1978

Staff Nurse
27-bed hospital. Performed routine nurse duties. Assisted Nurse Practitioner in outpatient clinic.

PROFESSIONAL ACTIVITIES/COMMUNITY INVOLVEMENT

Co-chair, American Association of Neuroscience Nurses (AANN)—Local Chapter
Active Member, American Organization of Nurse Executives (AONE)

Co-chair, "Think First" Spinal Cord and Head Injury Prevention Program
Yearly Supervisor of Health Care, Hawaii Special Olympics
Yearly Participant, Honolulu Health Fair

EDUCATION

B.S., Nursing, Walla Walla College—Walla Walla, Washington

•   •   •

from many of the best hospitals in the country. The pair of horizontal lines encloses a profile and a shaded box that indicates areas of expertise. This strong beginning sets the tone for the rest of the resume. Boldfacing makes managerial positions, the leadership award, and other leadership roles stand out.

GLORIA SIMMONS, RN, CCRN, CMC

445 Parker Street
(555) 555-5555   Ridgewood, NJ 00000   simms@aol.com

PROFESSIONAL SUMMARY

Certified Case Manager and Certified Critical Care Nurse with demonstrated accomplishments in medical case management, critical care and utilization management in managed and acute care environments. Proven clinical proficiency in performing thorough patient assessments and caring for a broad range of acute and chronically ill adults. Proven leadership and administrative qualifications include program development, staff supervision and management. Well versed in Medicare regulations and managed care.

- Extensive background in patient/family education, discharge planning and community resources.
- Sensitive and responsive to patients' needs with a strong commitment to ensuring cost-effective care while optimizing quality.
- Strong interpersonal and organizational skills; effective communicator with patients, families, physicians, agency and other healthcare professionals.
- Recognized as an excellent trainer/preceptor with the ability to lead and motivate others to higher levels of performance.

CAREER HISTORY

BLUE CROSS BLUE SHIELD OF NEW JERSEY, Ridgewood, NJ (1996–present)
Field Case Manager

Manage large caseload with up to 90 clients for a leading HMO with 35,000 Medicare and 100,000 commercial members, representing 25% of the New Jersey market. Coordinate all care/services and discharge planning for acute and chronically ill patients and average 30 visits each day in skilled nursing, rehab and home health environments. Accountable for cost-effective utilization and management of resources while maximizing quality care, provider/vendor negotiations and precepting field case managers. Present bimonthly utilization management reports to Network Advisory Board and represent healthcare management department at multidisciplinary task force as well as corporate/regional planning meetings.

Accomplishments

- Recognized for leadership of the Utilization Management Department, saving $125 million in medical care costs in 1998.
- Selected by management to serve on Standard Operation Procedures Committee (SOP) to develop and implement procedures on quality management.
- Named Most Valuable Team Player in 1996 for contributions to SOP Committee, including procedural documentation, streamlining grievance process and internal communications.
- Initiated and designed skilled nursing facility tracking mechanism for field case managers that facilitated time management and efficiency.
- Managed multiple special projects involving reconciliation of claims and other documents, ensuring regulatory compliance in a timely manner.

WILDER HOSPITAL, Ridgewood, NJ (1993–1996)
Case Manager (1994–1996), *ICU Nurse* (1993–1994)

Managed and provided skilled nursing care to a caseload of 18 patients daily and 50–75 patients on weekends as the only case manager in 100-bed facility. Coordinated patient education, quality management and cost-effective utilization of community services. Served as preceptor and trainer to nursing staff. Developed and implemented patient discharge plans.

104

Combination. *Louise Garver, Enfield, Connecticut*

The applicant, a nurse/case manager, was competing for a position in another state. The writer presented the individual's experience in a chronological format and highlighted her quantifiable

GLORIA SIMMONS, RN, CCRN, CMC

(555) 555-5555 • Page 2

WILDER HOSPITAL continued...

- Designated by management as 1 of only 3 nursing professionals to plan and launch new inpatient care-management program, which included development of policies, procedures, social services resource manual and staff training.
- Won support from all departments for new critical-care program, which was created in just 6 months and received an "outstanding" review from JCAHO.
- Commended by senior management for role in saving $200,000 by reducing average patient stay from 9 to 5.5 days and contributing to 98% patient satisfaction rating.

SIMMONS HOSPITAL, New York, NY (1990–1997)
Coronary Care Charge Nurse

Provided skilled nursing care to critical cardiac patients and supervised/mentored nursing staff as well as patient care technicians at 400-bed medical center. Chosen to participate on Acuities Committee to determine appropriate staffing levels.

MEMORIAL HOSPITAL, Springfield, MA (1988–1990)
ICU Nurse

Coordinated and delivered nursing care to critically ill patients in ICU, collaborated with medical staff and precepted new nursing professionals at 400-bed medical facilities.

EDUCATIONAL CREDENTIALS

M.S., Health Care Administration, New Jersey University, New Jersey, NY
B.S., Nursing, Columbia University, New York, NY

CONTINUING EDUCATION

Completed seminars in Critical Care, Case Management and Cardiology
Domestic Violence ... HIV ... IV Therapy ... Flight Nursing Training

CERTIFICATIONS & LICENSES

Critical Care Nursing (CCRN)
Medical Case Management (CMC)
Advanced Cardiac Life Support (ACLS)
IABP and IV Therapy

Registered Nurse, State of New Jersey

ASSOCIATIONS

American Association of Critical Care Nurses
Case Management Association

accomplishments. The result landed her an interview and a job offer over numerous other candidates (she was told) because her document displayed her leadership strengths and showed how she had saved the organization money without sacrificing patient care.

MARGARET ADAMS

5555 Main Street ◆ Los Angeles, California 00000
Home & Fax: (808) 555-5555 ◆ Cellular: (808) 555-5556 ◆ E-mail: email@email.com

PROFILE

Seasoned healthcare professional executing transition into **PHARMACEUTICAL SALES.**
Background includes ten years of experience as Registered Nurse (includes six years in emergency
room; one year in OR). Energetic, competitive, and health-conscious. Strong time-management
and organizational skills.

Sold pharmaceutical products and health services as business owner. Experienced seminar speaker,
workshop presenter, and instructor. Extensive community involvement. Willing to travel.

Core Competencies

Relationship Development	Persuasive Communications	New Client Generation
Sales Presentations	Medical Terminology	Physician Relations
Research	Marketing Initiatives	Customer Service

PROFESSIONAL EXPERIENCE

1999–PRESENT STATE CORRECTIONAL CLINIC—IRVINE, CALIFORNIA

RPN IV—Performed intake screenings for contagious diseases, pregnancy, and cervical
and breast cancer. Run clinics for Nurse Practitioner, Medical Director, Psychiatrist, Dentist,
Gynecologist, and Midwife. Accountable for 300 female inmates. Supervise staff of up to five
(RNs, LPNs, CNAs).

➤ **Developed relationships and recruited professionals** such as dietitian to provide
  nutritional counseling, aerobics instructor to augment anger-management program, and
  yoga teacher.
➤ **Saved money and increased efficiency** by designing new formulary spreadsheet
  to provide reliable information on drug availability and pricing. Average monthly
  pharmaceutical bill dropped from $35,000 to $27,500. Also resulted in better continuity
  of care and more accurate prescriptions.
➤ **Created and taught inmate health-education program.** Included stress and anger
  management, personal hygiene, and hepatitis B and C. Led to fewer STDs and contagious
  diseases, and more responsibility and self-empowerment for inmates.
➤ **Boosted peak-hour nursing coverage and clinic efficiency** by reworking schedules
  from eight-hour shifts to ten-hour shifts. Provided two-hour overlap.
➤ **Ensured adequate coverage** by designing new assignment sheets.

1991–1995 PRIVATE PRACTICE—FRANCE

Licensed Naturopath—Cultivated strong provider/client relationships. Taught health
fundamentals: exercise, diet, mental attitude, acupuncture, ozone therapy, classic homeopathy,
and detoxification. Researched and sold European pharmaceutical products (plant-based/over-
the-counter) in city of roughly one million citizens.

105

Combination. *Peter Hill, Honolulu, Hawaii*

The writer's task was to position this seasoned, well-traveled healthcare professional for a transition into pharmaceutical sales. The Profile section states the career objective and indicates that

MARGARET ADAMS
Page 2 of 2

- ➢ **Built client base from scratch to 1,750** within four years.
- ➢ **Implemented marketing initiatives.** Led workshops and seminars in health clubs and medical centers. Wrote articles on relevant topics for local newspapers. Published monthly newsletter.
- ➢ **Made presentations** on holistic medicine and chronic diseases at convention center in Paris, France.

1995   EUROPEAN COMMITTEE FOR EMERGENCY DOCTORS—FRANCE

RN Volunteer for Ethiopia—Collaborated to provide basic medical services to approximately 10,000 refugees following devastating famine. Distributed food and clothing, primarily to women and children.

- ➢ **Facilitated international relationships** by having French students develop "bridge program" with Ethiopian school to exchange thoughts, photographs, and customs.
- ➢ **Started vaccination program** for weak and undernourished refugees.
- ➢ **Received specialized training** prior to departure at prestigious European Institute for Tropical Medicine in Paris.

** Previous positions include **Night Nurse** (Orthopedic Rehabilitation Hospital, 1990–1991), and **Intensive Care Nurse** (Anesthesiology Unit, 1987–1988 and Surgical Unit, 1981–1987).*

EDUCATION & LICENSURE

RN Degree (Psychiatric Nursing), 1997
University of California
Los Angeles, California
GPA 3.5/4.0

RN Degree (Maternity Nursing), 1999
Texas State University
Dallas, Texas
GPA 4.0/4.0

Licensed RN in California and France; Licensed Naturopath in France; Licensed as RN for Tropical Medicine

LANGUAGES

French: verbal and written fluency

German: verbal competence

COMMUNITY INVOLVEMENT

California Adventurer's Club
Southern California Kayaking Club
California European Association

the individual has already sold pharmaceutical products. The Core Competencies shown in three columns are those most relevant to the objective. Attractive bullets point to Professional Experience achievements that also are relevant to a future career in pharmaceutical sales.

MARYANN FRENCH, R.N., B.S., C.A.C.

44 Carol Drive, Brentwood, NY 22222 • (555) 222-5555 • nurseadmin@health.com

<u>NURSE ADMINISTRATOR</u>

Accomplished Career Path

THE ISLAND SHORE HEALTH SYSTEM, Great Neck, NY   1990–present

The Island Shore Medical Center at Bethpage   5/97–present
  DIRECTOR, QUALITY MANAGEMENT   (On-call)

The Island Shore Health System   2/96–5/97
  ASSISTANT DIRECTOR, QUALITY MANAGEMENT

The Island Shore Medical Center at Syosset   10/90–2/96
  DIRECTOR, REGULATORY AFFAIRS   (On-call)
  DIRECTOR, RISK MANAGEMENT
  DIRECTOR, MEDICAL STAFF CREDENTIALING

<u>Quality Management / Performance Improvement</u>
- Directly responsible for hospital-wide quality management and performance improvement encompassing
  - Utilization Review   – Social Services and Physical Therapy Departments
  - Risk / Quality Management   – Regulatory Agencies
  - Performance Improvement   – Medical Staff Credentialing
- Ensure staff focus on individual, departmental, and hospital-wide initiatives, as well as team concepts.
- Guide the process of root cause analysis to identify, track, and resolve adverse events encompassing the development, implementation, and monitoring of corrective action plans.
- Prepare and process monthly statistical reports and analysis of hospital-wide operations.

<u>Program Development and Implementation</u>
- Direct the planning, development, implementation, and monitoring of case management (Care Guide®).
- Guide the development, implementation, and monitoring of healthcare practices to assess, identify, maintain, and improve the community standard of care.
- Initiate the development and analysis of hospital-wide studies to track and monitor specific patterns and trends.

<u>Regulatory Affairs</u>
- Coordinate and direct the multidisciplinary education and compliance of the New York State Department of Health Codes and the Joint Commission standards, maintaining staff development, program objectives, and risk-management oversight.
- Develop programs designed to reduce liability and increase staff awareness, education, and reporting activities.

<u>Medical Staff Credentialing</u>
- Develop and initiate the implementation of system-wide medical staff credentialing, allowing for a concise and expeditious application process.
- Ensure full compliance with New York State and Joint Commission regulatory requirements.

<u>Presentations</u>
- The Island Shore Health System, Medical Staff Credentialing Presentation, 2004
- The Island Shore Health System, Quality Management Presentation, 2003
- The Island Shore Health System, Medical Staff Credentialing Presentation, 2002
- The Island Shore Health System, Department of Quality Management Presentation, 2002

— Continued —

106

Combination. *Ann Baehr, Brentwood, New York*

This resume uses a combination format to showcase specific experience: the most recent experience on page one, and the Earlier Chronology on page two. Boldfacing directs attention down

MARYANN FRENCH, R.N., B.S., C.A.C.
Page 2

Earlier Chronology

Alcoholism Recovery Center, Brentwood, NY   1985–1990
  NURSE II

The Pharmaceutical Company, Hauppauge, NY   1982–1985
  INVENTORY MANAGER

Sachem Hospital, Sachem, NY   1980–1982
  STAFF REGISTERED NURSE

St. Jude Medical Center, Roosevelt, NY   1974–1980
  STAFF REGISTERED NURSE

Education & Training

Certificate of Completion, JCAHO, 2004
CONSULTANT'S CLINICAL CENTER, Brentwood, NY

Bachelor of Science in Health Administration, 1997
SAINT JOHN'S COLLEGE, Patchogue, NY

Alcoholism Counseling, 1989
INSTITUTE of ALCOHOLISM STUDIES, SOUTH OAKS HOSPITAL, Amityville, NY

Associate of Applied Science in Nursing, 1974
NASSAU COMMUNITY COLLEGE, Garden City, NY

Licenses & Certifications

New York State Certified Alcoholism Counselor #5555, 1989

New York State Licensed Registered Nurse #555555-1, 1974

Professional References and Portfolio of More Than 75 Letters of Recognition Available upon Request

the left margin of the first page so that the reader can see easily the applicant's career path, leadership roles, and areas of responsibility and expertise. Boldfacing on page two directs the reader once again to the left margin and then down the center of the page to view the applicant's credentials.

ROBERT MARTIN, D.D.S.
477 Covington Avenue
Bloomfield, CT 00000

(555) 555-5555   rmartin@yahoo.com

PROFESSIONAL SUMMARY

Expertise in all areas of dentistry combines with equally strong qualifications in business planning, development and management to enhance productivity and profitability.

Recognized internationally as a pioneer in the implementation of leading-edge techniques with a specialization in restorative and periodontal dentistry.

Distinguished career encompasses consulting, teaching and leadership roles with a major medical center as well as national and state professional associations in the dental field.

SPECIAL AWARDS & LICENSURE

Fellow of the Academy of General Dentistry
Master-candidate of the Academy of General Dentistry
State of Connecticut License in Dentistry

SELECTED ACHIEVEMENTS

- **Grew dental practice to a profitable business through effective business planning, cost controls, consistent service excellence and referral-based marketing.**
- **Achieved reputation for innovation and expertise in the dental profession as one of the first to implement state-of-the-art nonsurgical periodontal techniques.**
- **Elected President of the Connecticut Academy of General Dentistry and spearheaded the development and implementation of innovative programs that improved profitability.**
- **Honored as "Dentist of the Year" by the American Dental Association for contributions and dedication to the field of dentistry.**
- **Invited to join Connecticut State Board of Dentistry as consultant and provide expertise on program development and consumer relations.**
- **Fostered a motivating work environment and promoted open communications, resulting in high performance and staff retention.**

MANAGEMENT EXPERIENCE

HARTFORD DENTAL GROUP • Hartford, CT • 1970–present
President

Established and built highly successful business providing comprehensive dental services to several thousand patients. Acquired 3 private practices and led office through steady growth. Recruited and managed team of professional and support personnel. Provided ongoing staff training and development, leading to peak productivity, exceptional patient relations and continual referrals.

CONSULTING & TEACHING EXPERIENCE

CONNECTICUT BOARD OF DENTISTRY • Hartford, CT
Consultant (1984–present)

Selected as consultant to the statewide organization in the design and implementation of educational, consumer relations and other programs.

107

Combination. *Louise Garver, Enfield, Connecticut*

This dentist wanted to close his private practice in dentistry and become a manager in a corporate environment related to his specialty. The writer focused the applicant's resume on his

ROBERT MARTIN, D.D.S. – Page 2

UNIVERSITY OF CONNECTICUT SCHOOL OF DENTISTRY • Hartford, CT
Instructor (1990–present)

Revamped and expanded the curriculum. Teach operative dentistry and other courses in the School of Dentistry.

NEW YORK MEDICAL CENTER • New York, NY
Consultant (1999–present)

Consultant to medical center's pain-management program for patients suffering from TMJ disorder.

EDUCATIONAL CREDENTIALS

Doctor of Dental Science
University of Connecticut School of Dentistry, Hartford, CT
Graduated with high honors

Continuing Education

Successfully completed more than 1,000 hours of continuing education, earning graduate credits in all areas of general dentistry and practice management, including

TM Disorders	Tooth-Colored Restorations	Soft Tissue Surgery
Implants	Overlay Dentures	Endodontics Esthetics
Ceramic Restorations	Oral Pathology	Orthodontics
Auxiliary Utilization	Pharmacotherapeutics	Fixed Prosthodontics
Dental Materials	Dental Jurisprudence	Operative Dentistry
Table Clinics	Partial Dentures	Radiology
Treatment Planning	Clinical Diagnosis	Surgical Endodontics
Oral & Maxillofacial Surgery	Removable Prosthetics	Financial Management
Practice Management	Periodontics	Patient Education
	Patient Insurance Programs	

AFFILIATIONS

American Dental Association
Connecticut Dental Association
Academy of General Dentistry
Connecticut Dental Research Group

management qualifications and accomplishments in order to show that he was more than just a private practitioner. The applicant was successful in finding an R & D management position at a company that provides products to the dentistry field.

MICHELLE JONES, M.D.

98 Ben Franklin Drive
P.O. Box 219
Cherry Hill, New Jersey 07896   mjones@aol.com

Home: (609) 654–1040
Cell: (609) 654–5809
Home Fax: (609) 654–1755

HEALTHCARE PHYSICIAN

Senior Medical Resident in Internal Medicine with extensive knowledge of community medical diagnostic and patient care services in various settings, including inpatient and outpatient clinics, and government/private hospitals and clinics. Strong understanding of current principles, methods, and procedures for the delivery of medical evaluation, diagnosis, and treatment in women's healthcare, including rotation in OB/GYN. Outstanding interpersonal and cross-cultural communication skills: Fluent in English, Romanian, and French, combined with a basic command of Hungarian.

☑ Obstetrics/gynecology
☑ General surgery
☑ Internal medicine
☑ Infectious diseases
☑ Hospital medical service
☑ Private practice experience

☑ Pediatrics
☑ Outpatient clinic/office
☑ Emergency room experience
☑ Rheumatology
☑ Urology
☑ Nursing home/rehab/long-term care

☑ Cardiology
☑ Orthodontic
☑ Neurology
☑ Pulmonary
☑ Vascular
☑ Psychiatry/behavioral/substance abuse

EDUCATION

Institute of Medicine & Pharmacy—New York

Doctor of Medicine (*1998*)
Class Rank: Top 8%

Institute of Medicine—Hungary

Doctor of Medicine (*1991*)
Class Rank: Top 10%

Certifications:

Advanced Cardiac Life Support (ACLS)
Basic Life Support (BLS)
Advanced Trauma Life Support (ATLS)
American Board of Internal Medicine (ABIM)

Professional Licenses:

Doctor of Medicine (MD)—New Jersey
Doctor of Medicine (MD)—California

PROFESSIONAL EXPERIENCE

CLIFTON MEDICAL CENTER—Clifton, New Jersey   Oct 1998–Present
Attending Physician/Staff
Reporting directly to Chief of Medical Service and Chief of Staff M.D for 140-bed medical center providing hospital, outpatient clinic, rehabilitation unit, and nursing home services. Scope of responsibilities includes health care; supervising/teaching rounds; teaching clinic; supervising on-call residents; and working with residents on Internal Medicine Residency Program.

- Provide and manage direct patient care, including physical examinations, evaluations, assessments, diagnoses, and treatment.

108

Combination. *Jennifer Rushton, N. Richmond, New South Wales, Australia*

The individual was looking at senior practitioner roles in a small practice. The writer helped the applicant show potential employers that she had worked in leading roles and could manage

MICHELLE JONES, M.D.

Professional Experience, Continued

- Train and supervise residents and on-call residents engaged in specialty activities and procedures, including emergency room on-call duties, inpatient area, outpatient clinic, nursing home/rehabilitation and long-term care/hospice unit, and off-site outpatient clinics.
- Effectively manage ER, medical floor inpatients, emergencies in ICU/CCU, and all in-house medical residents while on call as attending Medical Officer of the day.
- Frequently function as acting Chief Resident, directing and coordinating the patient care activities of nursing and support staff.
- Collaborate with residents on Internal Medicine Residency Program.

MEDICINE ASSOCIATES OF BLOOMFIELD—Bloomfield, New Jersey   Jan 1999–Jan 2001
Associate Physician
Reported directly to partner physicians while supervising a staff of 4 for small private practice. Scope of responsibilities included providing internal medicine; daily office functions; managing in-hospital patients; and managing patients at several local nursing homes and personal care homes.

- Developed and implemented patient management plans, recorded progress notes, and assisted in provision of continuity of care.
- Managed in-hospital patients at 3 local hospitals; provided appropriate patient education explaining the necessity, preparation, nature, and anticipated effects of scheduled procedures to the patient.
- Managed patients at several local nursing homes and personal care homes; examined patients, performed comprehensive physical examinations, and compiled patient medical data, including health history and results of physical examination; and prescribed pharmaceuticals, other medications, and treatment regimens as appropriate to assessed medical conditions.

PROFESSIONAL AFFILIATIONS

Member, American Medical Association (AMA)
Member, American Society of Internal Medicine (now called the American College
of Physicians—American Society of Internal Medicine, ACP—ASIM)

PUBLICATIONS

*The Use of a Correction Factor for the Calculation of Suprarenal Outputs as a Function of
Arterial Pressure*, diploma thesis, 1982.

Baucht, J., and <u>Jones, M.,</u> "The Use of a Correction Factor for the Calculation of
Suprarenal Outputs as a Function of Arterial Pressure," presented at and published in
the proceedings of The National Symposium of Physiology, New York, August 16–18,
Vol. 1, 2:20–24, 1981.

RESEARCH

Determination by E-testing of sensitivity of gram-negative microorganisms to
Levoflaxacin, sponsored by Baxter Pharmaceuticals (submitted for publication).

Measurement of adrenal blood flow in an experiment model.
Advisor: Dr. James Baucht

REFERENCES AVAILABLE UPON REQUEST

staff. The writer also displayed the applicant's patient care and knowledge. The opening profile lists in three columns her areas of expertise. Bulleted items in the Professional Experience section point to activities and responsibilities related to her care of patients.

Theodore R. Fitzgerald

123 S.E. Top O' Scott Circle • Seattle, Washington 44444

555-555-5555 *home*   12345678@msn.com   *cell* 555-555-5555

Administration Management

Professional Profile

Cross-functional *Management* professional with more than ten years of experience and a Bachelor of Science degree in the field of *Medical Imaging Technology.* Expertise in strategic planning, development and operations of multiple facilities. Skilled in combining leadership success in staffing, training and development; budgeting and cost controls; contract negotiations and mediation; and securing technical equipment, skilled physicians and technologists. Excellent organizational, communication and analytical skills.

Outstanding Accomplishments

- Increased facilities from two to eight locations performing 1,700 CT, MRI and X-ray procedures per month
- Manage facility and marketing budgets
- Assisted in selecting new center locations and full facility development
- Extensive personnel development and management
- Manage technical protocols on machines for overall consistency
- Recruitment and contract negotiations with staff radiologists
- Established private network among eight facilities
- Certified MRI scanners with American College of Radiology
- Implemented Teleradiology
- Development of customized patient and referring physician database
- Guest lecturer at alma mater with emphasis on CT and MRI

Professional Experience

Regional Director • Washington Advanced MRI & CT • Seattle, Washington • *1999–present*
Execute daily operations including management of eight facilities located in Oregon and Washington, ensuring delivery of highest service and quality to patients and referring physicians. Provide personnel management and development; contract negotiations with insurance carriers and provider radiologists; and develop regional marketing plan, budgets and growth opportunities.

Lead CT Technologist/Co-Manager of MRI and CT Department
Providence Seattle Medical Center • Seattle, Washington • *1997–1999*
463-bed research and teaching facility in the Seattle metropolitan area with a five-scanner (MRI and CT) department
Developed performance evaluations; processed payroll; managed protocol; monitored quality assurance; and maintained supplies. Trained technologists, developed feasibility studies and provided employee counseling and radiologist/technologist mediation.

continued . . .

109

Combination. *Rosie Bixel, Portland, Oregon*

This former radiologic technologist was, as a regional director of a multisite, two-state MRI and CT firm, working on an MBA to enhance his management skills and credentials. The writer

Theodore R. Fitzgerald   **Page Two**

Radiologic Technologist (CT/MRI) • *1992–1999*
Providence Seattle Medical Center • Seattle, Washington
Provided quality and compassionate care to all patients. Produced high-quality imaging services for radiologists and referring physicians. Represented PPMC for Helical CT including one week of training in Milwaukee, Wisconsin. Provided quality-assurance monitoring of Contrast Media. Experienced on the following: GE Signa 5X MRI, GE Hilite Advantage CT, GE Helical Cti and Windows Workstation.

Certifications
American Registry of Radiologic Technologists • #25333
Advanced Certification, Computed Tomography
Advanced Certification, Magnetic Resonance Imaging
Washington Board of Radiologic Technology • #103444

Awards, Honors & Achievements
Leadership 2000 Course • PPMC
Most Dedicated Student Award • OIT
Medical Imaging Program, Most Outstanding Student Award • OIT
Guest Lecturer • Washington Institute of Technology in CT and MRI

Professional and Community Affiliations
Member • American Society of Radiologic Technologists
Member • Washington Society of Radiologic Technologists
Member • Metropolitan Association for Common Good (MACG) • *2001–2004*
Member • Washington Health Forum • *2000–2004*
Chairman • Pastoral Council • St. Therese Parish and School • *2001–2002*
Member • Pastoral Council • St. Therese Parish and School • *1999–2001*
President • Society of Medical Imaging Students • OIT • *1990–1991*

Education
Master of Business Administration • Colorado State University • *Degree expected 2005*
Bachelor of Science • Medical Imaging Technology • *1992*
Washington Institute of Technology • Klamath Falls, Washington

makes prominent the person's management abilities and experience. Lines enclosing "Administration Management" seem like a banner just below the contact information. The word Management is boldfaced in the Professional Profile, and managing is a recurrent theme in the Outstanding Accomplishments.

Melissa Tarkington

9803 Clinton Avenue ▪ Houston, TX 77000 ▪ (281) 000-0000 ▪ name@cox.net

HEALTH & HUMAN SERVICES PROFESSIONAL

Dedicated health and human services professional with 15 years of experience in customer service delivery, management of administrative processes, and quality control. Qualifications include excellent services-management abilities, strong communication skills, administrative experience, comprehensive knowledge of federal/state healthcare and social-service regulations, and ability to team with diverse work groups in achieving organizational objectives. Deliver effective presentations in both large and small group settings. Computer proficient; highly adaptable to new systems and processes. Work well under pressure in multi-task management environments. Able to work well in self-managed and team-based environments. *Additional strengths include*

- Public Speaking & Presentations
- Work Planning & Prioritization
- Needs Assessment Interviewing
- Eligibility Determination

- Confidential Files/Correspondence
- Caseload Management/Administration
- Quality Assurance Standards
- Medicaid Regulations

- Customer Service Delivery
- Regulatory Compliance
- Medical Terminology
- HR Generalist Affairs

"Thanks for all you do; you add to morale around here and I appreciate it. And I appreciate your efficiency and unflappable calm, too." —Name Withheld, Dean, School of Allied Health

PROFESSIONAL EXPERIENCE

TEXAS DEPARTMENT OF HEALTH—HOUSTON, TX   1997–Present
Public Health Technician, Medical Transportation

Hold full responsibility for diverse range of administrative and caseload-management activities involving Medical Transportation Program (based on Medicaid policies), including intake interviews, eligibility determinations, transportation authorizations/arrangements, file and records management, contract agreements, service delivery reviews and resolutions, and recovery of Medicaid funds. Assist in training of new MTP intake staff and provide insight into Medicaid policies and procedures for clients, staff, and partner healthcare professionals. Challenged to fulfill various program/caseload goals in deadline-driven environment.

SELECTED ACCOMPLISHMENTS:
- Successfully manage average of 90–100 calls per day and maintain excellent track record of customer service delivery and records documentation. Developed strong knowledge base in Medicaid policies/procedures.
- Awarded eight hours of administrative leave by Commissioner of Health for recommending strategy to improve operational processes and reduce costs.
- Achieved highest success rate in division for recouping Medicaid funds related to medical transportation.
- Delivered series of well-received presentations to professional groups, service providers, and community groups/members regarding general and specific aspects of MTP program.

HEALTH SCIENCES CENTER—HOUSTON, TX   1995–1997
Administrative Assistant, School of Allied Health (1996–1997)

Served in highly visible position as primary assistant to dean of School of Allied Health; scope of accountability included maintaining schedule for appointments/meetings and events, preparing and distributing information for various programs throughout the school, handling finances and confidential documents/correspondence, planning travel itinerary, and verifying multimillion-dollar inventory list.

- Commended by dean for overall exemplary performance and maintaining consistent on-time, on-target scheduling, task management, and special-event coordination.
- Maintained excellent relationships with all staff and faculty personnel, including president and other top administration heads.
- Completed annual inventory report for all schools within School of Allied Health with 100% accuracy.

…Continued…

110

Combination. *Daniel J. Dorotik, Jr., Lubbock, Texas*

The bold horizontal lines direct the reader's eyes to the profile paragraph and three-column list of strengths, which indicate areas of expertise. The quotation just after the list is effective

Melissa Tarkington - Page Two
(Professional Experience Continued)

Medical Transcriptionist, Radiology (1995–1996)

Transcribed routine and specialty pathology reports, including autopsies, bone marrow evaluations, and cytology reports, to document patient care and ensure proper delivery of healthcare services. Planned and conducted quality assurance evaluations on work; researched and retrieved prior history data for patient cases.

- Noted for transcribing large volume of routine/specialty reports with highest possible accuracy rating.

TEXAS DEPARTMENT OF HEALTH—HOUSTON, TX   1994–1995
Eligibility Specialist, CIDC (1995)
Social Service Technician, CIDC (1994–1995)

Promoted to perform wide range of administrative and supervisory duties for eligibility program, including supervision of entire eligibility process, volunteer activities, and maintenance of client and general office files. Planned and directed in-services for medical service providers, community service agencies, and other public health agencies; helped assistant program director with training and orientation of new employees. As Social Service Technician, maintained case records and assisted in office and caseload-management functions.

- Conceptualized and developed database program that generated monthly report, resulting in elimination of manual counting and quicker retrieval of client data.
- Created format that led to automation of CIDC monthly statistical report and subsequent expedient distribution; coded CIDC program files to clearly distinguish differentiation among various programs.
- Increased awareness of program policies and procedures through in-service presentations and comprehensive training/mentoring of new employees.

TEXAS DEPARTMENT OF HUMAN SERVICES—HOUSTON, TX   1993–1994
Administrative Assistant, Long-Term Care Unit

Recruited to oversee and meet objectives for all aspects of administrative work, including filing, processing, correspondence, editing/reviewing, scheduling, and other office-management duties.

- Developed training manual for new administrative staff that shortened learning curve and eased transition.

SCHOLASTIC BOOK FAIRS—HOUSTON, TX   1992–1993
Administrative Assistant

Fulfilled all administrative responsibilities as assistant to branch manager. Entrusted to serve as acting office manager in supervisor's absence. Facilitated payroll, inventory, mail/messenger, and database tasks.

"I am truly saddened to hear of your leaving your post…your upbeat personality, warm smile, and efficient work always made me look forward to coming over there." —Name Withheld, Ph.D., Assistant Dean, SAH

EDUCATION & TRAINING

BS in Human Services, 2002
UNIVERSITY—HOUSTON, TX

Selected Professional Development Coursework:
Employee Interview & Selection Training, 2002 ▪ Creating a Harassment-Free Environment, 2001 Emotional Intelligence on the Job, 2001 ▪ Computer File Management, 2001 ▪ Developing Leadership Ability, 2001 ▪ Reducing Conflict at Work, 1999 ▪ Communicating with Clients from Poverty, 1998 ▪ 7 Habits of Highly Effective People, 1997

Computer Skills:
Microsoft Word, Excel, PowerPoint, Access; Adobe Photoshop, Acrobat; WordPerfect; Harvard Graphics; Internet

because its thanks "for all you do" acts like an endorsement of all the activities stated or implied in the list. At the end of the Professional Experience section, another quotation, lamenting the departure of the individual, suggests to the reader that hiring this individual would be a great gain.

DEBORAH PRESCOTT, B.SC.P.T., MBA

6666 Victoria Street • Augusta, Nova Scotia B2B 2B2
Phone: 555.555.5555 • Alt: 222.222.2222 • deb.prescott@ns.email.ca

STRATEGIC PLANNING & BUSINESS DEVELOPMENT PROFESSIONAL
Start-up, Turnaround, and High-Growth Ventures

Winner—National ABC / IVY MBA Business Plan Competition 2003
Winner—Meta Corp Venture Capital Fast Pitch Competition 2002 (Austin, Texas)
Represented Canada at World Venture Capital Competition 2002 (Austin, Texas)

Innovative and results-driven professional combining award-winning business development and consulting expertise with career experience in healthcare, life sciences, and biotech industries. Full range of hands-on managerial and business experience, including strategy, financing, operations, sales, and marketing. Expert at problem solving and decision making—able to compress large issues into manageable solutions. Outstanding communication, negotiation, and public-speaking skills. Expert in all MS Office applications and corporate pro forma models.

Management Consulting Expertise	*BioTech / Life Sciences Expertise*
Business Plan Development	Start-up Management Consulting
Strategic Planning & Development	Technology Transfer Skills
Venture Capital / Debt & Equity Financing	Medical Industry Experience
Project Management	Registered Physiotherapist

PROFESSIONAL EXPERIENCE

AlzheimerGuide Inc., Augusta, Nova Scotia   2001–Present

President
Co-founded Internet-based company providing interactive health-management software for patients and caregivers dealing with Alzheimer's disease worldwide (www.alzheimerguide.com). Responsible for all business planning, financing negotiations, strategic partnerships, internal accounting, and overall software production management.
- Negotiated all strategic relationships with pharmaceutical companies throughout North America—closed critical licensing deal for educational materials with major Canadian pharmaceutical company.
- Leveraged comprehensive medical knowledge to effectively translate and communicate business vision to medical community.
- Successfully led business to best-to-date revenue gains following complete redesign of business model and strategy.

MegaTel Consulting, Pinehurst, Nova Scotia   2001–Present

Sole Proprietor
Provided consulting services for start-up and early-stage companies operating in the healthcare/life science and biotech fields.
Major projects:
- Developed business plan, R&D schedules, financing, negotiations, and cooperative research agreements between pharmaceutical companies and a new biotech spinoff company from Houseman University. Acquired financing from Atlantic Opportunities Agency and House-Tek (Technology Transfer Arm of Houseman University), and mentored principal scientists and managers in development of achievable operational goals.
- Created vision and developed business plan proposal for e-health incubator (E-Home Initiative) at Houseman University—joint project among the Deans of Medicine, Architecture, and Computer Science.
- Provided management consulting expertise with House-Tek. Facilitated initial stages of licensing agreement between researchers and international pharmaceutical companies interested in the field of dementia pharmaceutical compounds.

111

Combination. *Ross Macpherson, Pickering, Ontario, Canada*

This candidate was only a few years out of school with an MBA but had tremendous achievements in two key areas of expertise. The writer highlighted these up front in the Profile. In the

DEBORAH PRESCOTT 555.555.5555 Page 2

_____

MegaTel Consulting _(continued)_:

- Completed comprehensive assessment and feasibility study for new service delivery (The Centre for Health Care for the Elderly, QEII Health Science Centre).
- Redesigned business plan in anticipation of North American product relaunch for firm specializing in health education (Auguste Productions).
- Provided business planning and consultative expertise for commercialization of innovative wireless technology applied to e-health and home / institutional-based healthcare (Atlantic Canada Opportunities Agency).
- Prepared funding plan, operating costs, and budgets for Geriatric Medicine Research Unit in preparation for submission to the Canadian Foundation for Innovation.

SciTel Wireless Inc., Augusta, Nova Scotia 2000–2001
Management Consultant
Hired as business consultant and promoted to lead start-up company providing wireless applications for health-related products and services (e.g., data management and gathering for clinical trials in pharmaceuticals).
- Developed entire corporate structure and coordinated all initial business-development activities, including business planning, financing, and development of R&D plans.

**Previous experience includes**
Registered Physiotherapist, PhysioWorld, Augusta, Nova Scotia 1996–1999
Cardio-Respiratory Physiotherapist, Health Science Institute, Augusta, Nova Scotia 1996

EDUCATION & AWARDS

M.B.A.—Finance, Strategy, Entrepreneurship, Houseman University, Augusta, Nova Scotia May 2000
B.Sc.—Physical Therapy, King's University, Queenston, Ontario 1996

Awards:
- MBA Entrance Scholarship, Houseman University 1998
- King's University Appeal Bursary (outstanding academic achievement) 1994–95
- King's Anniversary Scholarship 1992

VOLUNTEER ACTIVITIES

Volunteer—Foundation for Children 1999–Present
Volunteer Physiotherapist—International, National, and Provincial sporting events 1995–Present
Coordinator—Houseman University Varsity Therapy Program 1997–1998

ADDITIONAL ACHIEVEMENTS & ACTIVITIES

Judge—Houseman University MBA Case Competition April 2001
Keynote Speaker—Atlantic Conference on Entrepreneurship, Houseman University 2000
Speaker—Technology Round Table, Augusta Club 2000
Board Member—Alzheimer's Society Board for Continuing Medical Education 2000–Present
Board Member / Advisor—E-Home Committee at Houseman University 2000–Present
One of five MBA graduates profiled in **_Canadian Business Review._**
Additionally featured in the following publications: _Silicon Valley North, Chronicle Herald, Daily News._

Professional Experience section, italic calls attention to the activities related to each position held. Bullets point to main achievements. The "Major projects" subheading is effective because it implies that the ones listed are only a selection of many project achievements. Not long ago she was "just" a college graduate!

Jennifer Williamson

9803 Clinton Avenue
Houston, TX 79424

(281) 000-0000
name@aol.com

MARKETING DIRECTOR/HEALTHCARE

Delivering Breakthrough Marketing Initiatives That Drive Revenue Growth and Build Strategic Partnerships

Customer-driven Marketing Specialist with over nine years of experience in the healthcare industry demonstrating strong marketing leadership and uncompromising focus on client needs fulfillment. Consistently successful in increasing revenues, improving profitability, accelerating business growth, and enhancing the quality of service offerings. Combine expert communication, negotiation, team-building, and presentation skills.

Consistently successful in building win-win relationships with staffs, physicians, government agencies, and business partners. Strong business-development and public relations skills, with demonstrated strength in implementing strategies and tactics necessary for successful financial and organizational growth. Solid network of professional contacts in healthcare industry.

AREAS OF EXPERTISE

- Client Relationship Development
- Organizational Leadership
- Marketing Communications
- Solutions-Selling Initiatives
- Special Events Management

- Public Speaking & Presentations
- Strategic Partnerships & Alliances
- Marketing Campaign Management
- Competitive Positioning & Branding
- Staff Training & Development

- Community Outreach
- Media & Press Relations
- Regulatory Compliance
- Insurance Affairs
- Crisis Management

PROFESSIONAL EXPERIENCE

REHABILITATION AND CARE CENTER—Houston, TX   2000–Present

ADMISSIONS COORDINATOR

Hold full responsibility and accountability for wide range of activities driving patient admission/retention, business development, and market share growth in highly competitive market. Coordinate all issues surrounding resident admission to the facility for long-term or rehabilitation care. Advise families regarding long-term-care insurance, Medicare, Medicaid, and private payment options. Establish and maintain win-win marketing contacts with area medical professionals. Responsible for screening physical and fiscal appropriateness of all potential residents. Challenged to jump-start occupancy rate growth by developing marketing strategies to outdistance competition and position facility as #1 service provider in area.

SELECTED ACCOMPLISHMENTS:

- **Grew occupancy rate to 98%, representing highest rate among major facilities in surrounding area** (up from previous average of 87–92%) through strategic marketing contacts and relationship-building strategies.
- **Boosted Medicare patient average from 6–7 to 18–19** by addressing needs of skilled patients and using educational forums to sell potential clients on facility program.
- **Negotiated favorable service rates with insurance companies** for physical and occupational therapy programs, resulting in enrollment increase and bottom-line growth for facility.
- **Introduced marketing communications initiatives** that educated patients and families about complicated financial, legal, and medical options and facilitated decision-making, leading to steady stream of repeat and referral business.
- **Played key role in facility receiving "zero nursing violations"** during 2002 state survey of facility conducted by state surveyors and HCFA representative.

FAMILY HOSPICE—Houston, TX   1999–2000

PROFESSIONAL RELATIONS COORDINATOR

Apprised patients and families of healthcare options regarding hospice and the terminally ill. Conducted presentations to healthcare professionals, physicians, and the general public. Negotiated contracts with administrative bodies of long-term healthcare facilities and area hospitals. Developed and implemented short-term and long-range marketing plans/goals.

...Continued...

112

Combination. *Daniel J. Dorotik, Jr., Lubbock, Texas*

This resume displays the effective use of italic and boldfacing. Italic focuses attention in the summary profile. On page two, italic is used for the explanation of a gap in the individual's

Jennifer Williamson—Page 2

(Professional Experience Continued)

SELECTED ACCOMPLISHMENTS:

- **Increased business and referral growth by 30+% with physicians/discharge planners,** targeting Lubbock and the surrounding areas.
- **Facilitated transfer of hospice patients to long-term healthcare facilities,** working jointly with hospice/primary care physicians, patient care managers, CNAs, and other industry professionals to expedite process.
- **Maintained excellent record of compliance with JCAHO, state laws, and federal regulations.**

NETWORK SERVICES—Houston, TX   1998–1999

PHYSICIAN SERVICE REPRESENTATIVE

Hired as radiologic technologist and promoted to representative position based on educational background and organizational need for new strategic marketing program. Oversaw budget and designed marketing activities to increase new patient visits for PPO and multiple PNS clinics. Reported directly to Marketing Coordinator; coordinated all activities surrounding implemenation of new physician practice within network. Held responsibility for preparation and administration of company-wide special events.

SELECTED ACCOMPLISHMENTS:

- **Coordinated and executed successful events and programs,** including KidFest and similar outreach programs, that promoted positive image for organization and resulted in increased referrals and subsequent revenue growth.
- **Created successful newspaper ads in the *Houston Chronicle* for several clinics** that effectively pre-sold clients on services through inclusion of special marketing initiatives for each individual clinic.

* Fulfilled full-time child care responsibilities through 1997 and subsequently transferred to Houston region in beginning of 1998. Attended workshops and completed independent study to maintain professional development during this period.

MEDICAL CENTER—Santa Fe, NM   1994–1996

SPECIAL PROCEDURES TECHNOLOGIST/RADIOLOGIC TECHNOLOGIST

Assisted and performed peripheral, pulmonary, and cerebral angiography, as well as other interventional exams. Assisted in mammiographic biopsies; monitored and performed QA equipment testing.

CHIROPRACTIC HEALTH CENTER—Santa Fe, NM   1992–1994

ASSISTANT OFFICE MANAGER

Oversaw pre-certification of all patient insurance claims. Transcribed all physician notes regarding patient information and managed all receivables for office.

EDUCATION

BA, Speech Communications, STATE UNIVERSITY—Houston, TX

AA, Radiologic Science, MEDICAL INSTITUTE—Santa Fe, NM

- **Attendee,** wide range of workshops and professional development courses throughout career.
- **Trainer and Program Coordinator,** Continuing Education Unit courses (hospice) for discharge planners.

COMMUNITY AND EVENT INVOLVEMENT

- **Presentation,** Rotary Club: Delivered informative speech covering various hospice functions and benefits.
- **Co-Host,** Charity Event, Junior High School: Benefited local organization in fund-raising efforts.
- **Co-Coordinator,** Annual Luncheon: Honoring social workers, discharge planners, and other professionals.

work experience. The chief use of boldfacing is to highlight key points in bulleted achievements in the Selected Accomplishments sections. If, as a reader of the resume, you want a quick assessment of "what the person did," search for bullets and boldfacing, and you will have a fast, useful impression.

Tori Grace Ulrich

3 Woodland Court
Knoxville, TN 00000

(000) 000-0000
tori416@yahoo.com

OBJECTIVE
To contribute acquired administrative skills and recent educational preparation to a position in the health/nutrition industry.

EDUCATION
B.S., Home Economics, concentration in Nutrition—May 2004
Texas Christian University, Ft. Worth, TX
Maintained overall GPA of 3.45 while working part-time.

CAREER STRENGTHS

➢ Resourceful self-starter, effective in researching and analyzing data.
➢ Knowledge of marketing concepts and scientific principles related to food-product labeling and dietary information.
➢ Effective written and oral communications skills utilized in reporting evaluations on comparative products and educating adults on healthier lifestyle issues.
➢ Equally comfortable working independently as well as collaboratively in group efforts.

FIELD EXPERIENCE

➢ Observed and interviewed dietitians in the community to learn and evaluate their teaching techniques.
➢ Counseled two individual clients in weekly sessions on meal planning and exercise to achieve their weight-loss goals.
➢ Planned, organized, developed, and conducted lecture on nutrition to a group of recovering substance abusers.
➢ Teamed with another student to design a cycle menu for a nursing home, taking into account factors such as food specifications, portion costs, production schedules, and nutrient content.
➢ Practiced time-management, organizational, and assessment skills while involved in multiple ongoing projects that focused on planning, preparation, and attractive presentation of meals for specific dietary needs (i.e., diabetic or sodium-restricted populations).

EMPLOYMENT/COMMUNITY SERVICE

ELITE TEMPORARY AGENCY, Ft. Worth, TX   2002–2004

Various administrative assignments, including telemarketing. Gained experience in promoting an idea, basic computer proficiency (MS Word, Excel, and Access), paperwork organization, and dealing with customer problem-solving situations.

CHILI PEPPER'S GRILL, Ft. Worth, TX   2000–2002

Hired as hostess and later promoted to wait staff. Demonstrated superior abilities and was appointed as trainer for new employees.

PLEASANTVILLE NURSING HOME, Ft. Worth, TX   2000–2004

Volunteer, providing companionship to the elderly and assisting with meal service.

113

Combination. *Melanie Noonan, West Paterson, New Jersey*

This graduating student wanted to portray education fieldwork as experience in her search for a position in the health/nutrition industry. The heading "Field Experience" accomplishes her aim.

Word Version
ASCII Version

ANN MARTIN, R.N., B.S.N.
568 East Windsor Drive, Collegeville, PA 99999
(555) 555-5555 • amartin@dotresume.com

CAREER FOCUS: CLINICAL RESEARCH OPERATIONS

SUMMARY OF QUALIFICATIONS

More than 15 years' nursing experience plus training in clinical research. Highlights:

- **Clinical Research**—Screened patients for in-hospital research studies and acted as liaison to research nurse. Administered stage III/IV trial medications. Assisted with development of New Drug Application. Completed 50% of **graduate-level training in clinical research operations with 4.0 average;** anticipate 2004 graduation.

- **Patient Assessment and Evaluation**—Analyzed diagnostic studies, observed and monitored patients, assessed conditions, and evaluated effects of multiple-drug treatment plans. Performed triage for interhospital transfers and nuclear disaster trial runs.

- **Patient, Family, and Staff Education**—Taught patients and families about conditions, procedures, and medications to improve compliance with protocols. Trained staff in medications and conditions.

- **Communication and Administration**—Served as mediator in staff conflicts and facilitated communication among medical professionals, patients, and families. Coordinated interhospital and intrahospital patient transfers. Maintained written and computerized logs.

- **Computer Skills**—Proficient in Microsoft Windows and Word. Familiar with Excel, Access, and PowerPoint. Internet savvy.

EDUCATION

Graduate Program in Clinical Research Operations, Western University, Norristown, PA, 4.0 GPA (expected completion, December 2004)

B.S.N., Wayne State University, Bradford Falls, PA, 3.65 GPA (1982)

PROFESSIONAL EXPERIENCE

REDMOND UNIVERSITY HOSPITAL, Philadelphia, PA

Clinical Coordinator, Triage Transfer Center (1997–2001)

Highlights: Telephonically coordinated interhospital transfers working with staff of 3 or independently. Managed entire process including triage, arrangement of transport and life support, insurance precertification/LOS, and extensive assessment for caretakers at destination. **Screened transfer patients for research studies, acting as liaison to research nurse** and counseling patients and families regarding medications and preoperative procedures. Maintained detailed written and electronic logs: patient-study screening and protocol matches, medications, demographics, and transportation. Worked closely with cardiac catheterization lab.

Selected Accomplishments

- **Successfully applied nursing experience in cardiac care to clinical research.**
- Maintained efficient, timely, and safe interhospital patient transfers despite 80% increase to 250–300 transfers per month.
- Helped ensure smooth operation of cardiac cath lab through effective coordination and scheduling.

CENTRAL HOSPITAL, Abington, PA

Nurse Manager, Cardiac Progressive Care Unit (1989–1993)
Charge Nurse, Telemetry Step-Down Unit (1984–1989)
Team Leader, Medical-Surgical Floor (1982–1984)

Highlights: Implemented transition of 45-bed medical-surgical floor into 30-bed telemetry unit. Supervised and coordinated staff of 6–11 RNs, LPNs, and monitor technicians. Analyzed diagnostic studies, observed and monitored patients, and assessed response to treatment. Offered treatment recommendations and worked with team to develop health care plans. Educated patients and conducted staff training in dysrhythmia and cardiac drugs. Provided IV therapy and **administered medications, including drugs in stage III/IV trials.** Participated in triage for nuclear emergency trials.

Selected Accomplishments

- Developed extensive knowledge of pharmaceuticals: indications, actions, and side effects.
- Increased outpatient compliance and decreased returns-to-hospital by providing discharge and healthful living instruction.
- Improved patient care through staff mediation and facilitation of interdepartmental communication.

VOLUNTEERISM

Assisted in development of NDA for niphedipine (Procardia) by providing technical writer with foundation in cardiology and drug action on circulatory system. Also reviewed and interpreted prior research for writer—case studies and statistics from Great Britain, and trials conducted in the United States.

Served as volunteer parish nurse; former Red Cross volunteer.

114

Web version. *Jan Holliday, Harleysville, Pennsylvania*

In this Web version of a regular resume, the horizontal bar serves two purposes: to highlight the career focus and to hold navigation buttons. The two-column resume layout works well.

TERRENCE WONSEN, M.D., M.B.A., F.A.C.O.E.M.

1057 Forest Park Boulevard
St. Louis, MO 55555

E-mail: wonsenMD@earthlink.net

(555) 555-5555 (home)
(555) 555-5556 (pager/cell phone)

CAREER PROFILE

SENIOR EXECUTIVE—OCCUPATIONAL AND ENVIRONMENTAL MEDICINE
Corporate Medical Director/Corporate Health Services Director/Vice President of Medical Affairs

Distinguished 22-year career as manager and practicing physician in corporate and hospital settings. Combine business acumen with medical/clinical expertise. Excel at aligning medical goals with business objectives. Record of implementing cost-effective programs and processes that improve employee health and safety, reduce expenses from absenteeism, and cut healthcare costs. Strong operational, project-management, team-building, and leadership skills. Experienced in managing international, multi-site, employee-health-delivery systems. Skills and areas of expertise include

- Policy & program development
- Strategic planning
- Project management
- Process improvement
- Workers' Compensation
- Disability management
- Health & disability benefits

- Medical surveillance testing
- Wellness & health promotion
- Travel medicine
- Immunization programs
- Ergonomic issues
- HMO, indemnity, & commercial insurance

- Bioterrorism readiness
- Regulations—OSHA, EPA
- Industrial hygiene & safety
- Toxicology
- Sick-building syndrome
- FAA & FHWA drug/alcohol testing programs

PROFESSIONAL CREDENTIALS

Education

M.B.A.	School of Business Administration, Washington University, St. Louis, MO 1989
M.D.	School of Medicine, Washington University, St. Louis, MO 1985
B.A.	Yale University, New Haven, CT 1978

Medical Licensure MO, IL, FL

Certifications American Board of Preventive Medicine/Occupational Health 1999
American Board of Emergency Medicine 1996
American Board of Medical Management 1992
Fellow, American College of Occupational and Environmental Medicine 2002

Affiliations President, Midwest College of Occupational and Environmental Medicine 1998–Present
Fellow, American College of Occupational and Environmental Medicine
Member, American College of Physician Executives

PROFESSIONAL EXPERIENCE

CONSOLIDATED INDUSTRIES, INC., St. Louis, MO   1997–Present
Multibillion-dollar global engineering-and-construction company.

Medical Director—Midwest Region (7 sites, 15 staff)

Manage occupational and environmental medicine (OEM) operations and drive strategic initiatives at multiple sites in the U.S. and internationally. As lead physician, supervise and mentor healthcare professionals. Treat patients. Serve as an expert clinical resource for multi-site, health-services personnel and as internal consultant on high-level corporate projects. Oversee health and safety issues related to overseas travel. Provide consulting services to the Environmental Health and Safety Department on environmental health issues and to the corporate legal department on ADA, FMLA, workplace violence, and environmental exposure litigation. Member of the Medical Standards Committee.

115

Combination. *Jean Cummings, Concord, Massachusetts*

This physician-executive wanted to move up to the next level, from regional manager to corporate medical director. The writer combined the elements of a medical curriculum vitae with a

TERRENCE WONSEN, M.D., M.B.A., F.A.C.O.E.M.   PAGE 2

PROFESSIONAL EXPERIENCE (CONTINUED)

Selected Achievements—Consolidated Industries, Inc.

Strategic Planning and Internal Consulting
- Identified the strategic OEM requirements of a complex global organization. Defined short- and long-term organizational and business goals.
- Reviewed and updated corporate medical policies and procedures. Ensured OSHA compliance.
- Collaborated with environmental health-and-safety executives to establish criteria for medical surveillance.
- Provided expertise on the potential impact of bioterrorism. Contributed to development of a corporate response.
- Key player in developing and piloting a corporate wellness program.

Program Reengineering and Process Redesign
- Reengineered clinic operations—identified and captured opportunities for efficiency and quality improvements.
- Created a high degree of uniformity throughout the 26-clinic program, reducing risk of error, improving quality of patient care, and decreasing costs of medical-director-level oversight.
- Achieved impressively high "retention of care" metrics. Enabled the manufacturing-facility clinic with the heaviest caseload to handle 95% of injuries onsite in 2002 (industry standard for excellence is considered to be 80%+). Results: reduced absenteeism and slashed costs previously incurred by relying on offsite treatment.
- Redesigned staffing model. Instituted nurse-based patient-care guidelines with oversight by a consulting physician. Defined and developed a position for a disability-nurse case manager.

Program Initiatives
- Created a detailed disability-training manual. Standardized processes and procedures for performing disability evaluations and handling insurance issues. Trained physicians. Results: streamlined operations, returned employees to work earlier, and increased number of modified-duty solutions.
- Rolled out the AED (automatic external defibrillator) program in the Midwest in 2001.
- Collaborated on a corporate-wide, 26-site initiative to vaccinate employees against influenza. Achieved an aggressive 30% target for employee participation, significantly exceeding corporate benchmarks.
- Developed an overseas-assignment and travel-immunization program. Served as physician-consultant to troubleshoot and solve expatriate medical emergencies and problems.
- Launched company's first integrated disability program. Results: saved on direct costs of disability and medical payments by enabling employees to return to work with modified duties; saved on indirect costs related to lost productivity, replacement hiring, and overtime; and reduced costs of Workers' Compensation payments.

ILLINOIS GENERAL MEDICAL CENTER, Chicago, IL   1994–1997
Associate Medical Director for the Corporate Health Program

Accountable for both management and clinical roles. Developed policies and procedures, visited client company sites, conducted evaluations, and treated patients. Worked closely with the PT and OT teams to coordinate efforts.

- Increased the number of workers who returned to full- or modified-work duties.
- Decreased the number of days workers missed work due to disability.
- Achieved high levels of customer satisfaction.
- Made key contributions to growing the client base and increasing program revenues.

ST. JOSEPH HOSPITAL, Chicago, IL   1989–1994
Chairman, Department of Emergency Medicine
Director, Occupational Health Program

- Conceived, developed, and implemented the hospital's first occupational health program.

CHICAGO GENERAL HOSPITAL, Chicago, IL   1985–1989
Director, Emergency Department

- Reengineered the E.D. delivery system. Results: increased patient volume and revenues by 15%, raised customer satisfaction levels, enhanced the E.D.'s reputation, and improved Quality Control.

HARVARD MEDICAL SCHOOL, BETH ISRAEL HOSPITAL, Boston, MA   1983–1985
Intern and Resident in Surgery

resume marketing quantifiable achievements of a management executive. The resume is thus unique, with a mix of medical and management areas of expertise in the profile, a separate Professional Credentials (medical) section, and a Professional Experience (management) section.

PAUL JEPSON

14 Westlake Drive
Framingham, MA 01702

Email: paul@jepson.com

Cell: 508 875 1699
Residence: 508 789 0098

Senior Executive	Healthcare / Medical

Profile

Results-focused senior executive offering 20 years of experience positioning hospitals and healthcare facilities for growth, increased shareholder value, and refined business infrastructure. Acknowledged for capacity to build consensus and drive solutions that meet short-, medium-, and long-term goals. Communicative, energetic style coupled with strategic vision has transformed multimillion-dollar losses to strong profit performances in months, while projects under personal direction have won national awards for innovation. Expert in restoring profitability, assessing potential acquisitions, devising case-management programs, and managing sensitive cultural change integrations that challenge the status quo, yet win the unqualified support of key stakeholders and staff.

Areas of Expertise

- Organizational/Cultural Change
- Business Analysis/Management
- Executive Presentations & Negotiations
- Mergers & Acquisitions
- Healthcare Management/Operations
- Strategic Planning & Market Expansion
- Communications/Success Recognition
- Due Diligence Research & Recommendations

- Process Reengineering
- Business Development
- Not-for-Profit Organizations
- Clinical Process Revitalization
- Quality Healthcare Delivery
- Case Management Solutions
- Tendering Processes
- Hospital Business Administration
- Healthcare Industry Best Practice

Executive Performance

Change Management

Executed comprehensive change-management program for **Christian Church Community Care**—a not-for-profit organization that had experienced significant growth, yet remained stagnant in terms of processes and service delivery protocols. Incrementally introduced new philosophies and methods that automated routine tasks, cut inefficiencies, and slashed costs—winning the support of key stakeholders via step-by-step communication programs encouraging problem "ownership."

Cut administration errors by up to 15% and elevated direct nursing care by 200% through reduced reliance on administrative follow-up.

Program delivered return on $255K investment within 15 months, outstripping all board expectations.

• • •

Case Management

Spearheaded revitalized **case management practices** across New Zealand for the **Workplace Compensation Enterprise** as part of a $100M collaborative initiative to arrest escalating claims costs and introduce holistic infrastructure change. **Project managed $880K bid** against aggressive competition and presided over a team of 8 to design, develop, and commission an organizational-change project contributing **$37.5M per annum in savings**.

Against a backdrop of intense media and public scrutiny, **created transparent and accountable work practices** and regularly briefed the CEO to convey expected healthcare service improvements across New Zealand. Curtailed lead times, elevated customer service delivery, cut paperwork, employed dedicated caseworkers for each case, introduced recuperation plan negotiations, and reduced rehabilitation, compensation, and tail costs.

• • •

Due Diligence

Enhanced salability of business unit, conducting all due diligence work on behalf of **WorkComp.** Examined products, internal processes, liquidity, debt position, markets, demand and supply capabilities, competitors, management, and skill retention post-sale. Board fully embraced all product and service recommendations.

116

Combination. *Gayle Howard, Chirnside Park, Melbourne, Australia*

The applicant was "a consultant with vast experience in technology and project management to a number of diverse sectors, including healthcare." He believed that over many years as a

Paul Jepson

Executive Performance

Efficiency Improvements

Inadequate systems, procedures, and controls were the key challenges faced by **Hatchett Mitch Pathology.** Produced a complete suite of recommendations to refine workflows and internal controls, and revamp business methods. Pruned costs and delivered 10% improvement in operational and customer service efficiencies.

• • •

Cost Savings & Revenue Growth

Revealed numerous cost-saving and revenue growth opportunities to principals of **The Princeton Hospital.** Worked in partnership to deliver a long-term business/growth strategy, formalize information and clinical management, and optimize financial operations. Recommended methods to enforce compliance to debt collections, assume a stronger commercial stance, restructure divisions to prune budget expenditures, introduce technology enhancements, and review clinical management processes.

Recommendations accepted and implemented across the board, resulting in **reduction in days' accounts outstanding from 90+ days to 9.** "Payment on Discharge" recommendation **tripled cash flows** and **slashed cost of debt by $200K per annum.**

• • •

Tender Evaluation

Countered public concerns over the integrity of **Burswood Health's** tender process in awarding the multimillion-dollar GADHH software project. Under "impossible" deadlines and a zero-tolerance error environment, meticulously re-evaluated assessment processes, tenders, and the veracity of solutions offered for effectively managing medical records/reports, admissions/transfers/discharges, surgery, theatre, and pharmacy management, billing, and more.

Produced comprehensive report of findings to federal legal representatives citing minor "human error" breaches; tender was given "green light" and **system implemented with no political fallout.**

• • •

Hospital Metrics Analysis

Assessed financial health of the **South East Private Hospital** to leverage improved performances across all divisions at the lowest practicable cost. Analyzed all key hospital metrics that reflected desired outcomes and produced reports forecasting trends, winning management support.

Employment Chronology

BUSINESS/TECHNOLOGY CONSULTANT   7/2002–Present

Devised a formal value creation model for management to analyze the validity of proposed infrastructure expenditures over multiple timeframes of up to 10 years.

CAMDEN RAIL

Examined future business and technology infrastructures, and identified a need to realign perceptions and practices to reflect technology as a business "investment."

United existing processes with industry best practice to create a methodology that integrated seamlessly with evolving activity-based costing initiatives and strategic goals. **Model forecasted productivity savings of up to 30%,** together with improved focus on technology investments and business value.

• • •

TRANTON INC.

Advanced business and technology solution provider servicing medical, healthcare, human resources, education, and executive management.

VICE PRESIDENT, BUSINESS DELIVERY   6/2000–6/2002

Reported to Chairman & CEO (Monaco); Managing Director, Asia Pacific
Projects: AUD $600K–$4 million

Instrumental in transforming a fledgling business unit to the most prominent and successful unit in the group—despite the challenges of global downturns in technology.

As the pivotal operations-based driver, steered complete solution development phases—from creation to market launch and project implementation. Sustained momentum, scheduling, and delivery objectives, while simultaneously building client relationships through intense communication and scrutiny of individual business strategies, objectives, and infrastructure.

consultant to healthcare/medical sectors he had gained enough knowledge to run a hospital. This resume targets the skills important for a hospital CEO and plays down the individual's technology background. Most of the resume is therefore a functional resume for a CEO; the Employment Chronology section is about

Paul Jepson

TRANTON INC.,
(CONTINUED)

Turned around employee reluctance for merging intellectual property development and client development areas by exposing key international staff to the advantages of linking these complementary operations; devised well-received training programs conveying future vision. Relocation saved $2 million per annum, and in service delivery areas **delivered 70% productivity improvement.**

Devised and developed corporate- and program-based activities spanning organizational management, corporate profile enhancement/creation, funding, capital raising, budgeting and planning, strategy and financial planning and execution, and business and market development.

• • •

UNISAVILLE
AUSTRALIA LTD.

*Business Solutions,
Consulting,
e-Business
Divisions.*

PROGRAM (EXECUTIVE) DIRECTOR, QUEENSLAND, AUSTRALIA   7/1994–6/2000

Reported to South Pacific Director, Sydney

Consulted to large corporates, healthcare/medical facilities, and government, and led team of 10 in project implementations, bids, and delivery of specialist healthcare engagements. Key catalyst in spearheading the innovative "Organizational Agility" practice that positioned the company for more responsive service delivery and allowed greater flexibility to meet market demand. Initiative prompted significant interest from the U.S.-based head office, inviting input on methods to drive cultural change.

Consultancies/Project Scope: Business strategy formulation, process reengineering, training and education, organizational and cultural change, operational analyses, executive guidance, productivity improvements, and cost-containment programs.

Project Highlights:

Winner, Gold National Government Productivity Award, for contributions in boosting employee productivity as part of a $15 million office management system for the Department of County Industries.

Reduced "tail" costs by $2 billion as part of a collaborative $100 million national business process reengineering initiative to contain spiraling litigation and accident insurance issues for the **Workplace Compensation Enterprise in New Zealand.**

Consolidated myriad disparate technology systems, designing a comprehensive knowledge base for the City of Bundaberg that connected all systems for consolidated access from all areas. **Cut annual running costs by 96%.**

• • •

CRAYDON &
LINDSOM

SENIOR MANAGER   7/1989–7/1994

*Direct Reports: 12 (managers, senior consultants, consultants, support staff)
Operational budget: $12 million*

Profit-and-loss accountability in this senior management role overseeing daily operations while driving tactical market plans to capture new business within premium markets. With high fees and high-quality deliverables, expectations were strong and necessitated continuous monitoring. Steered client relationship-management strategies, delegated priorities, monitored project progress, identified trends, hired consultants, appraised staff performances, and positioned the business for continued prosperity.

Education

Master of Business Administration, University of Illinois, Urbana, Illinois

Bachelor of Science. *Majors: Management, Business Administration, Technology.* Monash University, Melbourne, Australia

Graduate Certificate in Quality, Worldwide Organization of Quality

---

technology. Note the use of boldface in the Executive Performance and Employment Chronology sections to call attention to the names of workplaces and significant achievements. The left column is used effectively to display performance subcategories, workplaces, and explanations in italic.

Hospitality

Resumes at a Glance

RESUME NO.	OCCUPATION	GOAL	PAGE
117.	VP and Pricing Administrator	Not specified	235
118.	Food Service Manager	Food Services Manager	236
119.	President, COO, Manager	Hospitality Industry Specialist	238

MARIANNE L. PERRAULT

900 East Shelter Road
Oldetown, Rhode Island 09999

Fax: (401) 555-6666
E-mail: marip@foxx.net
Phone: (401) 333-8877

QUALIFICATIONS

➤ Proven ability to train, schedule, supervise, and effectively manage 60 employees preparing 1,000 airline passenger meals per day.
➤ Competent leader with extensive experience in prioritizing, delegating, and controlling work flow in municipal government and high-volume private-industry work environments.
➤ Proficient in effectively organizing, handling, and monitoring a wide variety of tasks.
➤ Comfortable with operating Microsoft 2000, ME, Corel, and Internet research on PC and Macintosh platforms.

EXPERIENCE

Food-Air Associates, Inc., Providence, RI
Vice President and Pricing Administrator for family-owned business, 1994–present
o Manage accounts payable / receivable for very profitable, high-volume airline catering kitchen serving American, USAirways, United, Northwest, Southwest, and Delta Air Lines.
o Review and analyze monthly P&L statement generated by accounting firm.
o Establish costs of goods and services; audit and reconcile inventory.
o Negotiate contract terms with major airline clients.
o Hire, train, schedule, and manage up to 60 employees.
o Design and implement quality-assurance measures to maintain high standards and consistent business retention to clients serving a total of 1,000 passenger meals per day.

Oldetown Police, Oldetown, RI
Administrative Assistant to the Chief of Police (part-time), 1992–1994
o Researched, prepared, and wrote grants for municipal benefit.
o Assisted in assembling data for annual police budget submissions to town council.
o Provided accurate, courteous responses to inquiries on police matters of a sensitive nature.

EDUCATION

John Phelps University, Newport, RI
o Master of Science in Business Administration, 1994

Rhode Island University, Providence, RI
o Bachelor of Science in Finance, 1992
o Cecelia H. Belknap Scholar: GPA over 3.85 (four years)

VOLUNTEER

Providence Chamber of Commerce; Oldetown Animal League; Providence GRO-Business Associates; Air-Transportation League; R.I. Fraternal Order of Police.

– EXCELLENT REFERENCES FURNISHED UPON REQUEST –

117

Combination. *Edward Turilli, Newport, Rhode Island*

Two boxes make this resume different from most others. The hollow bullets also are not common. Boldfacing and italic make the name, headings, workplaces, jobs, and universities stand out.

CHERYL R. COOKMAN

1548 Northshore Blvd., #109
Las Vegas, NV 05326

555/555-3697 (home)
555/555-5469 (cell)

FOOD SERVICES MANAGEMENT PROFESSIONAL
...Oklahoma Food Management Certification/Serve Safe Certified Instructor...
...Consistently promoted to higher levels of responsibility through exceptional work performance...

Well-qualified Food Service professional with strong management, decision making, supervision, and leadership skills. Proven ability to delegate, problem solve, prioritize projects, manage personnel, and meet deadlines without compromising quality. Create and implement menu plans, oversee food selection, contain cost, and maintain quality control. Computer literate: Word, Excel, and Internet. Bachelor of Arts. **Key skills:**

Culinary Arts:
- Superior culinary skills in food preparation, recipe experimentation/development, and full-service catering. Proven success in developing food budgets and negotiating contracts. Ensure cleanliness, quality, and food-service standards and procedures. Significantly upgraded quality of food operations, profitability, and standards of service through innovative menu planning.

Staff Training & Motivation:
- Successful career record of motivating personnel to perform at high efficiency levels. Talent for recruiting, hiring, and developing support staff. Team player; always willing to share knowledge to attain corporate goals.

Leadership & Management:
- Exceptionally strong multitasking abilities. Planned and served catered affairs for 250+; developed menus, coordinated deliveries, and supervised personnel. Directed kitchen operations, purchasing budget, inventory planning, menu development and pricing, staff scheduling, vendor contracts, regulatory compliance, and food/labor cost and controls.

PROFESSIONAL BACKGROUND

BETTER LIVING, INC., Norman, OK   1994–Present
Publicly held, global food-service-management company. Divisions include Vending, Fine Dining, Schools, and Catered Dining.

Food Service Manager (1998–Present)
Oversee food-service operations at 4 local high schools; provide lunch for student population of up to 950 at each location. Manage 17 staff, including food prep cooks, cashiers, cooks, and fryers. Recruit, train, schedule, and perform employee evaluations. Responsible for payroll, documenting man-hours, and tracking sick leave and vacation time. Accountable for volume sales on budget of $889K annually. Generate sales of $1,500–$1,900 daily at each location; control $12K–$15K inventory. Perform menu planning, inventory control, and purchasing. Design menus for special school events. Negotiate with outside vendors, conduct monthly staff meetings, perform end-of-day cash balances, handle bank deposits, submit vendor bills electronically, determine food pricing, provide sales/profit analysis, and conduct food reviews.
Performance Highlights:
- Reduced cost 11% through vendor negotiations.
- Increased profits 14% through in-house preparation of pizza.
- Recognized by senior-level management; consistently receive annual bonuses based on corporate budget expectations.
- Qualified to administer state-mandated Serve Safe test.
- Maintain 100% rating on county health inspections and corporate safety and health inspections.
- Boosted profits through maintaining food costs at 38–42%; exceed corporate budget of 47%.
- Facilitated smooth transition process during corporate merger.

Food Service Worker (1998)
Fast-track promotion to management. Hands-on experience in all phases of food-service operations.

118

Combination. *Cathy Fahrman, Tampa, Florida*

When a summary of qualifications indicates many skills, it is helpful to group the skills in some way to aid comprehension. Culinary Arts, Staff Training & Motivation, and Leadership &

CHERYL R. COOKMAN
Page 2

PROFESSIONAL BACKGROUND (continued)

THE AMERICAN DREAM, Norman, OK   1997–2002
Bed-and-breakfast hotel.

Caterer/Server/Bartender (part-time)
Provided catering services, including menu planning and food preparation, for special events; up to 180+ guests. Upscale dining with up to 5 main courses.

END OF THE DAY, Norman, OK   1999–2002
80-seat fine-dining restaurant serving lunch and dinner.

Caterer/Server/Bartender (part-time)
Provided catering services for special events and parties for up to 90+ guests.

WHOLESALE, INC., Norman, OK   1991–1994
Food and merchandise wholesaler.

Cake Decorator (1992–1994)
Decorated cakes for weddings and large parties.

Team Leader/Produce Department (1991–1992)
Oversaw produce staff, including scheduling and performance evaluations. Managed produce rotation, product ordering, and inventory levels.

Stock Person (1991)
Quickly promoted to Team Leader position (within 3 months).

EDUCATION

COLLEGE UNIVERSITY, Norman, OK
Bachelor of Arts, Fine Arts (1992)
Personally paid for all college expenses

CONTINUING EDUCATION

Diversity Training [2001; 2002]
Quality Assurance [2001; 2002]
Power of Many [2002]
Contribution Analysis and Pricing is Very Effective (C.A.P.T.I.V.E.) [2002]
Creating a dynamic, fun, and enjoyable working environment (FISH) [2002]
Profit Improvement Methods:
Interactive program focusing on learning and using the action planning process to improve profitability [2001]
Beginner's Excel [2001]

CERTIFICATIONS

Serve Safe Certified [2001]
Oklahoma Food Manager Certified [1999]

Management are three categories used as bold italic side subheadings for grouping this applicant's skills. In the Professional Background section, italic emphasizes a brief description of each workplace. Bullets draw attention to Performance Highlights for the current position. Many of these are quantified with percentages.

Gerald F. Hewlitt

Hospitality Industry Specialist
Senior-level Operations Manager

Sales + Marketing + Owner Mentality + Technology + Daring Creativity = SUCCESS

Executive Profile

More than 20 years of experience in every facet of the hospitality industry in positions as general manager, consultant, and / or owner with a solid background in successful traditional and entrepreneurial venues. Use a real-world approach to problem solving and a deep well of experience to meet the challenges of this fast-paced, high-turnover industry.

- Have operated multiple restaurants accommodating 900+ patrons and managed events for up to 2,000 attendees while partnering with diverse management, overseeing a multitude of activities, and managing half-million-dollar budgets / P&Ls.

- Proven team-forming and motivational skills have delivered unmatched loyalty and a nearly unheard-of staff turnover rate of less than 25%, far below the 61% industry standard. Consistently develop cost-cutting and profit-building initiatives.

- Honed and demonstrated project-planning and management skills in supremely high-stress scenarios where failure was not an option and the wrong decision could end a career and / or deliver substantial personal loss.

- Skilled at simultaneously supervising several restaurants and projects. Directed management of two separate restaurants, 20 miles apart, for five years. Worked 18+ hours concurrently managing early-morning renovations and late-night operations.

- Use lifelong interest in computers / IT to enhance every business opportunity and activity from marketing, to inventory control, to menu preparation, to catering scheduling, etc. Hold Certificate in Computer Science from Adelphi University (2001).

- Strategic business sense, uncompromising work ethic, and natural sincerity have helped create consistent profits and have won loyal support and motivation of customers, employees, partners, managers, community leaders, suppliers, and local officials.

Summary of Qualifications

- multi-unit operation management
- multimillion-dollar P&L management
- facility management
- event management & promotion
- troubleshooting & change management

- project planning & systems development
- advanced IT knowledge
- risk management & inventory control
- purchasing & negotiating skills
- vendor sourcing & negotiating

- sales / product / market analysis
- food / labor / marketing cost controls
- customer relations and satisfaction
- human resources management
- team-building & staff-retention programs

Career Development

PRESTIGE FOOD AND SPORTS ENTERPRISE, INC. (PFS), OYSTER BAY, NY
1988 to present

President and COO
Partner / Manager

PFS operated two consecutive successful theme restaurants on Long Island. Original concept, Charlie's Big City Grill, opened in 1989 as an 800-patron sports-bar restaurant much like the ESPN Zone restaurants.

- In f / y 1990, Charlie's grossed over $2 million and $2.4 million in f / y 1992 and 1993. Well-trained staff (only 25% turnover rate), value menu, and "almost as good as being at the game" mentality built a loyal customer base of young professionals, over-30 single clientele, families, and out-of-town guests.

- Restaurant was featured in numerous publications as a top sports bar/cafe and was one of the first sites in Metro New York to feature complete sports broadcast from satellite transmission, with Sunday NFL football afternoons attracting more than 1,500 guests.

In proactive response to increased competition from satellite dishes and sports-bar market saturation, renovated site and in 1995 transitioned Charlie's to the New Orleans Roadhouse, a Cajun menu "House of Blues"–style restaurant.

- Took only four months to plan and develop this restaurant / entertainment concept entirely new to Metro New York. Handled politicking / project planning necessary to get permits, plans, contractors, and equipment in place for summer renovation (slow season). Opened on Labor Day weekend 1995, two weeks ahead of schedule and below $750,000 budget.

- Negotiated with property-management company for an additional 10 years on lease and lower rent (both valuable assets for future sale). Fine-tuned, upgraded, and enhanced facility including handicap access, risk management, and venue flexibility. Planned menu, hired kitchen staff, developed company's first employee manual, created marketing plans, and booked live entertainment.

- Now a top rhythm & blues showcase and popular Cajun / Creole dining destination, the Grill was recently sold for a profit.

25 Bay Drive, Amityville, NY 11701
phone: 631-555-5555 ■ fax: 631-000-0000 ■ cell: 516-555-5555 ■ e-mail: GH.PFS@email.com

Combination. *Deborah Dib, Medford, New York*

This resume has all the characteristics of many executive resumes that offer a greater amount of information: relatively smaller type; narrower margins for wider lines; adequate line spacing to

Gerald F. Hewlitt / page two of three

Career Development, continued

Key Leadership Initiatives at Prestige Food & Sports Enterprise

Developed Successful Theme Restaurant in Highly Competitive Area

Developed and operated a major theme restaurant in Nassau County, NY. Created concept from emerging sports-bar trend, incorporated local venue elements into large-scale restaurant. Composed business plan and sought financing from U.S. Small Business Administration. Took possession of 10-year lease, construction, and physical development in less than four months. Driven by desire to succeed, took Charlie's Big City Grill from concept to creation in under a year.

Key Results:

- First year's gross sales exceeded $2 million, with sales growing by more than 20% in next four years.

Reduced Staff Turnover in High-Turnover Industry

Challenged with creating a strong team environment to reduce turnover of staff. Trained managers in "team management" principles, focusing on workplace pride. Compiled PC-based employee guidebook. Shared company's success with employees through annual bonuses, social gatherings, and benefit options.

Key Results:

- Delivered industry-low 25% turnover rate, even keeping 25% rate during renovation closure.
- Retaining competent and recognizable employees increased sales by building repeat customer / staff bond.
- Increased service quality and customer loyalty through better, more knowledgeable employees.

Managed Redevelopment and Construction of Successful Theme Restaurant

Challenged to co-develop and implement a new, next-generation theme-restaurant concept; to outperform, within five years, previous years' flat growth; to implement changes within a 90-day window; and to retain core customer base, as well as staff crucial to immediate success and profitability.

Identified key areas of planning and attention, set calendar, assigned management / partner responsibilities. Researched themes / concepts. Established $750,000 budget, developed project plan, and scheduled major construction for traditionally low-performing period. Renegotiated a lengthened lease, concessions for capital improvements, and lower rent. Established cooperative dialogue with town and county officials to expedite necessary permits and approvals.

Key Results:

- Completed construction of the New Orleans Roadhouse below budget and two weeks ahead of schedule.
- After renovation, year-one gross revenue rose to $2.6 million from $2.3 million.
- Reduced daily maintenance costs by 18% and energy consumption by 8%+ by updating infrastructure, HVAC, and layout.
- Achieved reduced insurance risk through facility changes that allowed full handicap accessibility.
- Retained market share, provided exposure to different market areas, and positioned firm for strong short-term growth.
- Booked live performances by top entertainers and expanded catering capacity.

Rebranded Local Restaurant to Attract New Customers

Challenged with marketing the New Orleans Roadhouse without conveying rural image. Recognized traditional radio spots did not take advantage of new theme, so explored and implemented 30- and 60-second local television spots with a major Metro NY cable television provider.

Key Results:

- Quarterly sales increased 21%. Ads generated qualified first-time customers and helped in rebranding.

Reduced Marketing Costs While Increasing Market Visibility to Targeted Customers

Challenged to develop effective, low-cost method of advertising to main customer base. Researched and implemented customer databases for direct-mail and target-marketing strategies, integrated direct-mail software for in-house mail sorting, and added POSTNET barcoding to meet USPS regulations. Appended 80,000-member database with phone numbers leading to telemarketing efforts. Eliminated manual removal of outdated customer information from database by using USPS National Change of Address files to automate process.

Key Results:

- Slashed direct-mail costs to 33%, from $63,000 to $42,000. Reduced marketing budget to 15%.
- Realized 3% to 7% annual postage and labor cost savings by updating database with USPS.

ensure white space between sections; and bullets, boldfacing, and italic to make important information more easily seen. To make the best use of the top third of the first page, the writer puts contact information at the bottom of each page. In the Career Development section, achievements are cast as five Key

Gerald F. Hewlitt / page three of three

Career Development, continued

THE LINDEN TREE CAFE, BABYLON, NY   **General Manager & Principal**
1999 to 2000 & 1982 to 1995

The Linden Tree Cafe is a well-established neighborhood cafe located in a historical building in one of Long Island's largest downtowns, Babylon, an urban / suburban town attempting revitalization from ongoing effects of "mall creep."

- In 1982 identified closed cafe as a good prospect—surrounding area's demographics were upscale, community revitalization efforts were strong, and circa-1880 building matched current trend for historic charm. Successfully negotiated 10-year lease with option to purchase building within five years at 1982 value, with half of paid rent credited towards purchase price.

- Working with Town of Babylon officials, the Babylon Historical Society, and the Chamber of Commerce, renovated building's façade to circa 1880, funding 70% of work through state and federal historic preservation funds. Purchased fixtures with no money down.

- Opened in November of 1982 and quickly established a local clientele. Then marketed to non-local population using regional magazine advertisements, popular radio stations, and supplier co-op ads.

- Cafe steadily grossed over $700,000 annually in early '80s. Although maintaining a historic building with apartments was an ongoing challenge, in 1986, purchased building at 1982 negotiated price of $110,000 rather than appraised price of $225,000.

- Restaurant's revenues began to falter in the late '80s as national recession reached Long Island, mall creep continued to deflect downtown business, town's road and sidewalk repairs limited access for months, and the large summer beach crowd started to gather at bayfront restaurants close to the ferries rather than in the downtown area.

- In 1990 planned complete building renovation including infrastructure, new kitchen, HVAC, handicap access, 100% fire sprinklers, increased dining area, and all-new outside dining area. To reduce effect on business, completed entire renovation in under four months. Kept core customer base informed of upcoming grand re-opening with a 20,000+ newsletter mailing, and invited best customers and community leaders to menu tastings and mock service dining shortly before reopening.

- Renovation and new menu generated results above initial projection, but with unsteady growth. Decided to sell when a generous offer was received in 1994. Completed sale in 1995. Kept possession of building and separate real estate company; transitioned professional activities into new investment areas.

- New owners' establishment closed after only four years through owners' series of business-devastating decisions. Owners changed name and concept; invested heavily in fad, not trend; maintained business cash flow with questionable business practices; tarnished establishment's reputation; damaged property with brew-pub equipment; and drove away original clients.

- Determined to personally rebuild and reestablish business and then sell to a buyer or team who could maintain and enhance it. Repossessed property in winter of 1998, facing enormous challenges as landlord of a building in need of a tenant and as a member of a community that wanted to see / solicit a fine establishment in the area.

- Achieved this goal in less than 18 months with under $100,000 investment after reestablishing cordial community and business working relationships. Reopened in Spring 1999 with Chamber of Commerce celebrating the event with a party at the establishment in June 1999. In August 2000, business was sold for a profit and continues to develop.

Education and Certification

Bachelor of Science in Management, Adelphi University, Garden City, New York

Adelphi University, Garden City, New York
Certificate, 320 hours, Computer Science, 2001
Earned while running two businesses.

Comp USA
MS Excel (2 days)
Advanced use of CorelDRAW software (2 days)

Hospitality Certifications
Food Service Manager's Certificate, No. 92122, County of Suffolk Department of Health Services
Food Service Manager's Certificate, Nassau County Department of Health

National Restaurant Association
Preventing Sexual Harassment in the Workplace
Restaurant Catering
Trends in Restaurant Design

New York Restaurant Association
Writing an Operation Manual (2 days)

25 Bay Drive, Amityville, NY 11701
phone: 631-555-5555 ■ fax: 631-000-0000 ■ cell: 516-555-5555 ■ e-mail: GH.PFS@email.com

Leadership Initiatives with bulleted Key Results specified for each initiative. Most of the results are quantified in dollar amounts and percentages. For the workplace mentioned on page three, the bulleted items tell in sequence the interesting history of the cafe.

Human Resources

Resumes at a Glance

RESUME NO.	OCCUPATION	GOAL	PAGE
120.	CFA Administrator, Waste Removal	HR/Corporate Trainer	243
121.	HR Manager	Not specified	244
122.	HR Director	Not specified	246
123.	HR Director	HR Executive	248
124.	General Counsel/VP	Senior HR Executive	250
125.	Senior HR Manager	Senior HR Manager	252
126.	HR Manager	HR Executive	254
127.	VP, e-HR	HR Executive	256

Joseph D. Morten

167 Helman Lane • Bridgewater, New Jersey 08807
908.555.5555 (H) • 908.444.4444 (Fax) • jMorten439@aol.com

HUMAN RESOURCES / CORPORATE TRAINING

Supervision ~ Business Management ~ Employee Relations ~ Coaching

Energetic, reliable and adaptable professional with a solid understanding of human resources, business operations and various corporate environments. Proven abilities in creatively identifying methods for improving staff productivity and organizational behavior. Recognized for ability to incorporate innovative management techniques into a multicultural workforce.

Results-oriented professional with excellent communication and interpersonal skills. Accurately perform challenging tasks with precision and attention to detail. Excel at organizing and setting up new procedures, troubleshooting and taking adverse situations and making them positive.

Competencies Include

- Human Resources Management
- Operations Management
- Teambuilding/Leadership
- Organizational & Project Management

- Training & Development
- Staffing Requirements
- Problem Resolution
- Employee Scheduling

Professional Experience

Waste Removal, *Plainfield, NJ (August 1997–September 2002)*
CFA Administrator
Waste Removal is the nation's largest full-service waste removal / disposal company
- Maintained and monitored multiple databases for the more than 120 pieces of equipment in the trucking company inventory.
- Generated accurate reports of budgets, repair costs, and personnel scheduling.
- Dramatically improved maintenance shop productivity through close budget monitoring.
- Served as a key link between management and mechanics, utilizing excellent interpersonal and communications skills. Acknowledged for improving the overall flow of information throughout the organization.
- Initiated, planned and managed the implementation of high-turn inventory-management systems and procedures. The new inventory system was credited with improving the operation of a very high-volume parts operation.
- Assumed a leadership role in the company by completely reorganizing the physical inventory process to ensure greater accuracy and system integrity.
- Managed the successful integration of two new parts operations, turning a possible negative situation into a very positive one.

Easy Video Entertainment, *Colonia, NJ (March 1994–August 1997)*
Store Manager
Retail video rental and sales chain with over 600 outlets and 5,000 employees worldwide
- Managed all daily store operations including a staff of 5 employees. Responsible for recruitment, hiring, firing, training and scheduling of all staff members.
- Ability to train and motivate staff to maximize productivity and control costs with hands-on management and close monitoring of store budgets.
- Attained a 25% increase in sales over a 12-month period, leading all 45 stores in the district. The store ranked 40th in overall sales volume of the 600 stores in the company.
- Maintained a consistent Top 20 ranking for sales of high-profit coupon books.
- Used excellent leadership, team-building and communication skills to develop subordinates and encourage cooperation and responsibility. Ensured compliance with corporate HR programs.
- Developed and implemented creative and aggressive promotional techniques that resulted in the store consistently exceeding its sales goals.

Education

BA ~ Psychology, *FAIRLEIGH DICKINSON UNIVERSITY, Madison, NJ*

120

Combination. *Beverley and Mitchell I. Baskin, Marlboro, New Jersey*

The tilde (~), used to separate fields of activity in the profile, is echoed in the Education section at the bottom of the page. Each workplace in boldface is "explained" by a statement in italic.

JOHN THOMPSON

5001 West Washington Avenue
Milwaukee, Wisconsin 53200

E-mail: johnthompson@mail.com
Residence: (414) 445-5555

HUMAN RESOURCES PROFILE

Results-oriented, hands-on human resources professional with 6+ years of experience and PHR certification. Excellent interpersonal and written communication skills with the ability to relate effectively to individuals at all levels within the organization. Highly organized, analytical, and decisive with strong problem-solving capabilities. Strong customer-service orientation and business sense. Demonstrated HR Generalist competencies include

- Staffing, Recruitment, Interviewing, & New-Hire Orientations
- Policy Development & Implementation
- Organizational Development
- Labor Law & Practices
- EEOC/AA Compliance

- Compensation & Benefits Administration
- Training & Development
- Labor & Contract Negotiations
- Communications & Community Relations
- Grievance & Conflict Resolution

PROFESSIONAL EXPERIENCE

MIDWEST CONSUMER PRODUCTS
Milwaukee, Wisconsin

Jan 1998 to Present

Acquired by Consumer Enterprises in July 2001. Formerly a privately held distributor with 6% of U.S. market share and 5,000 total employees. Midwest operation consists of Milwaukee-based headquarters and 6 state distribution centers.

HUMAN RESOURCES MANAGER—MIDWEST OPERATION (Apr 1999 to Present)
EMPLOYMENT MANAGER (July 1998 to Apr 1999)
EMPLOYMENT COORDINATOR (Jan 1998 to July 1998)

Promoted to Department Manager with accountability for Policy & Procedure Development/Implementation, Staffing, Recruitment & Selection, Labor Relations, Compensation, Training & Development, Organizational Development, and Regulatory Compliance. Directly manage HR staff consisting of Employment Representative and Administrative Assistant. Midwest operation composed of 70% non-exempt and 30% exempt employees, with one-third belonging to labor unions.

<u>Selected Accomplishments</u>
- Successfully implemented employee referral program that emphasized succession planning, rewarded strong performance, and resulted in 20% decrease in print advertising expenses.
- Developed/implemented comprehensive Affirmative Action plans and contemporary recruitment strategies (including community outreach, on-site job fairs, dial-up job line, and Internet job board advertising) to attain workforce diversity and ensure EEO objectives/legal guidelines. Conducted on-site AAP audit with OFCCP; preliminary results appeared positive.
- Successfully handled labor-relations issues, including grievance procedures and arbitration; assisted with labor negotiations.
- Conducted compensation analysis for manufacturing segment, brought starting salaries in line with market, and instituted step program for entry-level employees.
- Increased retention 5% and reduced cost-per-hire 10%.

121

Combination. *Michele J. Haffner, Glendale, Wisconsin*

A distinctive feature of this resume is the use of partially shaded horizontal lines to enclose the centered main headings. These are in small caps and boldfaced. The result is that you can look

PROFESSIONAL EXPERIENCE (continued)

MAJOR CONSUMER PRODUCTS OF WISCONSIN (continued)

- Consulted with managers on employee productivity, efficiency, and product quality issues. Coached and assisted manufacturing management staff in the design and implementation of incentive programs (tied to quality standards) with consistently higher product quality results.
- Co-facilitated diversity initiatives with third-party training organization (Spherion Group) to include Management Leadership/Inclusion Training. Created peer-based advisory council (Midwest Employee Advisory Council) and served as chair member.
- Facilitated employee-relations sessions with management, emphasizing staffing and corrective action procedures.
- Involved with creation, development, and implementation of the Midwest University Management Training Program—a collaborative effort with Brown County Technical College. Program emphasized managerial core competencies.
- Assisted with total organizational planning effort that standardized performance review processes.
- Successfully defended third-party interventions of state and federal compliance offices (WFEA, EEOC, OSHA).

SERVICE GREATER MILWAUKEE—Milwaukee, Wisconsin   May 1996 to Dec 1997
Wisconsin Works contract participant.

EMPLOYMENT RESOURCE SPECIALIST & WORK EXPERIENCE COORDINATOR

Accountable for teaching job-search techniques to low-income participants transitioning from government subsidy within the W-2 program. Marketed program and secured area employers willing to provide on-site work-skills training.

<u>Selected Accomplishments</u>
- Developed and monitored 200+ Work Experience Program sites and program participants.
- Cultivated relationships within local religious and educational communities to assist with life-skills coaching efforts.

PROFESSIONAL AFFILIATIONS & CERTIFICATIONS

Society for Human Resource Management, Employment Management Association, and Human Resources Management Association of SEWI
Certified Professional in Human Resources (PHR)

EDUCATION

Master of Business Administration—Marquette University—Milwaukee, 1996
Bachelor of Arts—University of Illinois—Champaign, 1994

BUSINESS TECHNOLOGY SKILLS

Proficient using Microsoft Word, Excel, PowerPoint; AS400 Software; and electronic resume databases including Monster.com and CareerBuilder.com

at either page and easily spot the resume's main sections. In the Professional Experience section, each workplace is explained by one or more italic statements. Underlined Selected Accomplishments subheadings and bullets draw attention to important achievements.

CAREN ALEXANDER
65 Darvon, Edinburgh EH6, Scotland
Home: +44 666799 8682
Office: +44 999000 2323
E-mail: CAXR@aol.com

■ **SUMMARY**

Management professional with expertise in human resources systems, operations and programs encompassing information technology/Web-based tools, mergers/acquisitions, compensation, benefits, payroll, records, reporting and other related functions. Proven record in creating and managing high-quality, cost-efficient domestic and global HR initiatives responsive to organizational needs and the achievement of business objectives. Strategic/tactical planning and leadership strengths combine with technical and project management skills.

■ **EDUCATION**

M.S., Human Resources Management, Boston University, Boston, Massachusetts, 1994
Research Project: "Breaking Through the Glass Ceiling: Gender Discrimination Initiatives"

B.S., Economics, University of California, Irvine, California, 1991

Diploma, Johnson High School, Irvine, California, 1987
  Awards/Honors:
  ◆ Captain and MVP of State Championship Team—Cross Country and Track
  ◆ Member of Honors Society, French Club and Public Speaking Club; Awarded Franklin Scholarship

■ **PROFESSIONAL EXPERIENCE**

LARSON TECHNOLOGIES, INC., United Kingdom and United States   Jan. 1996–Present
Fast-track advancement through progressively responsible management positions at a global technology leader in communications networking; assumed an integral HR role in 11 corporate mergers/acquisitions during tenure.

Director, HR Systems, Operations & Programs—Edinburgh, Scotland   May 1999–Present

Selected to spearhead integration of worldwide HR systems, operations and initiatives for division in Scotland as well as manage workforce reductions resulting from merger; key executive team member throughout integration efforts. Accountable for division-level HR reporting and records management, domestic and international integration into corporate systems, multimillion-dollar budget and staff of 23.

Oversight of all HR applications includes PeopleSoft Web-based compensation, Restrac Web-Hire, HR Intranet Website and employee self-service (e-serv). Provide consulting expertise to systems-integration activities in company's Ireland division as well as issues-resolution guidance/support for systems and process integration in Europe, Middle East and Africa.

Accomplishments

◆ Directed conversion of legacy systems and operations to corporate environment following merger, including PeopleSoft HR, benefits, payroll, data interfaces, forms, processes and more.
◆ Saved division's HR organization $3 million through design and introduction of HR service charge-back.
◆ Consolidated and trained worldwide HR staff on division-wide HR policies, procedures and processes.
◆ Initiated implementation of Web-based HR tools for compensation, benefits open enrollment and e-serv.
◆ Succeeded in closing all global HR systems, operations and programs in division on time and within budget.
◆ Retained team during critical 18-month shutdown period of HR organization without any resignations.

continued...

122

Combination. *Louise Garver, Enfield, Connecticut*

This individual was transferred to Scotland to close the company's division. Her job was going to be eliminated as well. She decided to remain in that country and seek employment. The writer

CAREN ALEXANDER—Page 2

FARRELL COMMUNICATIONS, INC., Alameda, CA
Senior Manager, HR Systems, Operations & Programs   Oct. 1998–May 1999

Provided strategic planning and leadership in the company-wide restructuring/integration efforts following company's merger with a technology company employing 2,300 people worldwide. Directed staff of 15, workforce reduction initiatives, employee-related reporting and records and immigration program.

Accomplishments

♦   Enhanced system's capability to support multiple benefit programs and address issues resulting from the merger.

♦   Evaluated acquisition's HR systems; within 3 months, migrated legacy data to PeopleSoft, an enhanced system to incorporate benefits and implemented Web-based compensation program.

Manager, HR Systems, Operations & Programs   Jan. 1998–Oct. 1998

Directed all HR systems, operations, program development and support, immigration, EEO/Affirmative Action Program, records administration, mergers and acquisitions and intranet Web development.

Human Resources Generalist   Jan. 1997–Jan. 1998

Managed expatriate and immigration programs, records administration, analysis and reporting activities. Directed data analysis, support and integration for 5 acquisitions. Provided compensation analysis support, participating in compensation surveys for sales employees, executives and management/individual contributors. Led implementation of PeopleSoft 6.0 application for workforce management and base benefits administration. Developed and managed spreadsheet-based annual merit and bonus programs.

Staffing Operations Specialist   Jan. 1996–Jan. 1997

Implemented processes to manage and track headcount and personnel requisitions. Developed tracking and auditing process for managing contingent workforce. Supported 3 acquisitions. Created and implemented company's expatriate, relocation and immigration policies and procedures.

Prior Experience: Human Resources Generalist, CONSTAR, INC., Falls Church, Virginia (Nov. 1994–Jan. 1996).

■ **ADDITIONAL TRAINING**

Completed Management Development, Public Presentation, Personal Effectiveness, EEO/Affirmative Action, PeopleSoft HRM & Benefits I & II, People Tools I, SS7 Technology, Remote Access Networking and other company-sponsored professional training/seminars.

■ **COMPUTER/SPECIAL SKILLS**

Microsoft Word (advanced), Excel (advanced), PowerPoint, Access, Project, and FrontPage; OrgPlus; Lotus Notes; PeopleSoft 5.0–7.5. Fluent in Spanish and French languages.

■ **INTERESTS**

Hill walking, mid-distance running, modern art, reading and travel.

References Available on Request

created this document to emphasize the person's accomplishments and give her an edge in the market-place. Diamond bullets and centered, underlined, and italicized Accomplishments subheadings ensure that the applicant's achievements are seen. The resume achieved results for her.

SUSAN B. ALMANN

589 Brighton View
Croton, NY 55555

(555) 555-5555

Sbalm345@aol.com

CAREER PROFILE

Strategic **Human Resources Executive** and proactive business partner to senior operating management to guide in the development of performance-driven, customer-driven and market-driven organizations. Demonstrated effectiveness in providing vision and counsel in steering organizations through accelerated growth as well as in turning around underperforming businesses. Diverse background includes multinational organizations in the medical equipment and manufacturing industries.

Expertise in all generalist HR initiatives:

Recruitment & Employment Management … Leadership Training & Development … Benefits & Compensation Design … Reorganization & Culture Change … Merger & Acquisition Integration … Union & Non-Union Employee Relations … Succession Planning … Expatriate Programs … Long-Range Business Planning … HR Policies & Procedures.

PROFESSIONAL EXPERIENCE

MARCON MANUFACTURING COMPANY, Peekskill, NY
Director, Human Resources (1996–Present)

Challenge: Recruited to create HR infrastructure to support business growth at a $30 million global manufacturing company with underachieving sales, exceedingly high turnover and lack of cohesive management processes among business entities in U.S. and Asia.

Actions: Partnered with the President and Board of Directors to reorganize company, reduce overhead expenses, rebuild sales and institute solid management infrastructure.

Results:
- Established HR with staff of 5, including development of policies and procedures; renegotiated cost-effective benefit programs that saved company $1.5 million annually.
- Reorganized operations and facilitated seamless integration of 150 employees from 2 new acquisitions within parent company.
- Reduced sales force turnover to nearly nonexistent; upgraded quality of candidates hired by implementing interview skills training and management development programs. Results led to improved sales performance.
- Recruited all management personnel; developed HR policies, procedures and plans and fostered team culture at newly built Malaysian plant with 125 employees.
- Initiated business reorganization plan, resulting in consolidation of New York and Virginia operations and $6.5 million in cost reductions.

BINGHAMTON COMPANY, New York, NY
Manager, Human Resources & Administration (1993–1996)

Challenge: Lead HR and Administration function supporting 1,600 employees at $500 million manufacturer of medical equipment. Support company's turnaround efforts, business unit consolidations and transition to consumer products focus.

Actions: Established cross-functional teams from each site and provided training in team building to coordinate product development efforts, implement new manufacturing processes and speed products to market. Identified cost-reduction opportunities; instrumental in reorganization initiatives that included closing union plant in Texas and building new plant in North Carolina. Managed HR staff of 12.

123

Combination. *Louise Garver, Enfield, Connecticut*

The applicant wanted to move to a VP-level position at another organization. The writer created this resume, which demonstrated—with a Challenge-Actions-Results approach—the depth of

SUSAN B. ALMANN • PAGE 2

Manager, Human Resources & Administration, continued...

Results:
- Instituted worldwide cross-functional team culture that provided the foundation for successful new product launches and recapture of company's leading edge despite intense competition.
- Led flawless integration of 2 operations into single, cohesive European business unit, resulting in profitable business turnaround.
- Restructured and positioned HR organization in the German business unit as customer-focused partner to support European sales and marketing units.
- Initiated major benefit cost reductions of $3 million in year one and $1 million annually while gaining employee acceptance through concerted education and communications efforts.

ARCADIA CORPORATION, New York, NY
Assistant Manager, Human Resources (1989–1993)

Challenge: Provide HR support to corporate office and field units of an $800 million organization with 150 global operations employing 4,500 people.

Actions: Promoted from Assistant Director of HR to lead staff of 10 in all HR and labor-relations functions. Established separate international recruitment function and designed staffing plan to accommodate rapid business growth. Negotiated cost-effective benefits contracts for union and non-union employees.

Results:
- Oversaw successful UAW, Teamsters and labor contract negotiations.
- Established and staffed HR function for major contract award with U.S. government agency.
- Introduced incentive plans for field unit managers and an expatriate program that attracted both internal and external candidates for international assignments in the Middle East.
- Managed HR issues associated with 2 business acquisitions while accomplishing a smooth transition and retention of all key personnel.
- Restructured HR function with no service disruption to the business while saving $500,000 annually.

EDUCATION

M.B.A., Cornell University, New York, NY
B.A., Business Administration, Amherst College, Amherst, MA

AFFILIATIONS

Society for Human Resource Management
Human Resource Council of Albany

the person's expertise and contributions. The resume successfully attracted interviews and offers at the VP level. Note the use of ellipses between areas of expertise in the Career Profile section. This resume was the winner in the 2002 Professional Association of Resume Writers' Best Executive Resume category.

GARRY CROSSLEY

66 Madrona Drive ~ Santa Monica, California, 55555

555.555.5555 (A/H)   g_cross@hotmail.com

SENIOR HR EXECUTIVE

HR Infrastructure & Planning ~ Generalist Functions ~ Employment & Business Law

Multi-faceted, results-oriented Senior HR Executive with comprehensive experience demonstrating quantifiable achievements and expertise encompassing all facets of legal, management and human resource generalist functions. Combines unique blend of visionary leadership and executive business savvy with competencies to spearhead strategic planning and execution of core staffing, operational and administrative initiatives to drive overall HR, organizational and bottom-line financial performance.

♦ Multi-Site Operations Management	♦ Project/Financial Management	♦ Merger/Acquisition Integration
♦ Industrial/Employee Relations	♦ Benefits/Compensation Design	♦ Policy/Process/Systems Design
♦ Staff Performance Optimization	♦ Union/Non-Union Relations	♦ Business/Corporate Litigation

CAREER ACCOMPLISHMENTS

TimeField Corporation

- Revitalized morale of support services staff, improved client satisfaction and optimized overall organizational efficiencies through motivation/mentoring of underperformers and streamlining policies and procedures, including implementation of computerized work-order systems.
- Captured cost savings of $200,000 for contracted services within first year through elimination of previous reliance on expensive outside contractors.
- Transformed support services functions into high-producing team through execution of numerous turnaround strategies including corporate-wide conversion to Kronos computerized payroll system that secured improved attendance, payroll processing and performance-management functions.
- Consistently captured cost savings on premium renewals for employee benefit plans while obtaining improved benefit plans through facilitation of strategic negotiations.

PROFESSIONAL EXPERIENCE

TimeField Corporation, Los Angeles, CA   1987–Present
Human Services and Healthcare Provider to 25,000 clients locally, regionally and internationally with $60 million budget and 1,200 employees spanning 52 sites, across four states.

General Counsel / Vice President of Support Services (1990–Present)

- Diverse role, accountable for $4 million budget and 13 staff, spearheading direction and execution of strategic initiatives to secure optimal performance across 10 functions encompassing legal, human resources, corporate and healthcare services procurement, risk management, training and development, information management, conference management and office services and telecommunications.
- Key member of executive team, providing ongoing tactical support, advice and presentations to President and Board of Directors in goal setting and achievement of corporate growth objectives.
- Distinguished track record for management and delivery of corporate-level functions and activities within HR, compensation/benefit administration, recruitment, training, performance management, diversity, EEO/AAP, HRIS, Safety, corporate-wide MIS, purchasing and risk management.
- Legal counsel handling a broad spectrum of corporate and program matters with sole responsibilities with investigation, negotiation, litigation and settlement across business law, employment law, commercial transactions, housing law, construction, real estate, elder-care law, corporate law, mergers and acquisitions, due diligence, bond financings, risk management and family law matters.

124

Combination. *Annemarie Cross, Hallam, Victoria, Australia*

As an executive, this individual had vast expertise. The writer put experience and achievements related to the applicant's goal toward the beginning of the document. She mentioned

PROFESSIONAL EXPERIENCE
(Continued)

Accomplishments

- Pioneered and directed five functions that improved organizational effectiveness, reduced costs and generated revenue including risk management, corporate purchasing, conference-management services, telecommunications and office services.
- Championed consistently high ratings from local, state and federal inspections, demonstrating leadership and direction expertise.
- Exceptional litigation record, winning 100% of 150 cases handled since 1990 within Administration, State and Federal court matters.
- Collected $700,000 in damages across broad spectrum of cases, and captured over $500,000 cost savings in legal fees by personally performing work previously assigned to external high-profile legal firms.
- Improved collection system and dispute-resolution system for three nursing homes, 550 hospital beds and 2,000 housing units through creation and execution of turnaround solutions.
- Designed, planned, executed and directed successful $400,000 telecommunications project.

Vice President of Support Services (1987–1990)

- Oversaw administration and operation departments with $6 million budget, including employee benefit programs and purchasing volume across 52 sites, with increasingly responsible duties proportionate to 300% budget increase during that time.
- Directed, supported and mentored 12–100 employees located at 50 sites across four states.
- Reviewed all employment disciplinary and employment law-related matters.

Accomplishments

- Re-engineered six core departments that facilitated 300% corporate growth.
- Achieved successful outcomes in all employment law matters, spearheading management of each case independently from beginning through completion.
- Captured significant improvement in staff morale and productivity through participative management style and introduction of innovative performance-optimizing strategies.
- Implemented strategic cost-reduction initiatives that secured consistent budget savings of 5%–10%.

Previous experience demonstrating expertise spearheading development and expedition of grievance-resolution and arbitration programs; litigation of unfair labor practices; and staff training and development across both public and private sectors, including Fortune 500 entity.

EDUCATION

UNIVERSITY OF CALIFORNIA, Los Angeles, CA
Juris Doctor

CAPITOL UNIVERSITY, Washington, DC
Master of Science—**Major: Industrial Relations**

STANFORD UNIVERSITY, Stanford, CA
Bachelor of Arts in Urban Studies

CERTIFICATIONS

Senior Professional in Human Resources—Society for Human Resource Management

less-related experience with a Fortune 500 company in a short italic paragraph at the end of the Professional Experience section. Achievements stand out in the Career Accomplishments section after the profile, and in the Professional Experience section under each Accomplishments side subheading in italic.

Michelle Reinecke

7263 Callaghan Rd., San Antonio, Texas 78217   (H) 210-783-2574   (W) 210-558-6327   (C) 210-852-5237   e-mail: mreinecke@tisd.net

> ***Senior Human Resource Manager***
> *with 13 years of human resource experience including a strong background in regional and corporate-level support in multiple U.S.-based, culturally diverse call center operations with a workforce total of up to 600 local and 2,500 regional associates.*

Core Professional Strengths

Human Resource Management
State / federal employment law / unemployment compensation/ policy interpretation / safety & health / benefits administration / departmental budget / HRIMS / performance management

Recruiting
Exempt & non-exempt level sourcing / selection / on-boarding / orientation / employee relations / community relations / pre- & post-hire assessments / applicant tracking / per-hire costs analysis

Training and Development
Grant attainment / instructional systems design / training facilitation / organizational development / quality improvement

Retention
Retention strategy analysis / workforce surveys / case studies / development & implementation of employee-retention programs

Professional Achievements

* **Educated** the corporate sales team in the components of Outsourcing's staffing package—*Call Source Plus.*
* **Initiated $350K worth of annual bottom-line savings** by implementing employee equipment purchase programs, redesigning differential / vacation pay policies and reducing starting salaries.
* **Maximized the call-based routing** initiative of the call center group by providing human resource expertise in the area of employee profiling, behavior profiling and pre- and post-hire assessment processes.
* **Provided human resource expertise** as part of Spherion's Customer Development Solutions sales presentation design team and facilitate the presentation on an "as-needed" basis to current and potential outsourcing clients as part of the contract retention strategy.
* **Assimilated** the division's human resources data and talent in support of the launch of the corporate HRIMS initiative—**"Project Meteor."**

Professional Experience

Senior Human Resource Manager
DIGICOM TELESERVICES, INC., San Antonio, Texas—1998 to present
24/7 inbound customer service call center servicing DigiCom calling-card and long-distance customers. The center staffs 450–600 local employees. This position is also indirectly responsible for human resources consultation for 1,500–2,500 regional employees and currently reports to corporate human resources.

* Awarded **CEO recognition** for representing the Customer Development Solutions group as the subject-matter expert on the **corporate team** that led the organization through the 2001 / 2002 **corporate payroll system implementation.**
* Received local recognition for *2001 Employer of the Year* by the State of Texas; *2001 Employer of Excellence* and *2001 Transitional Employer of the Year* by Bexar County Employment Services Development Board.

125

Combination. *MeLisa Rogers, Victoria, Texas*

The applicant had a human resource generalist background and extensive achievements. The writer consolidated these into a two-page resume so as to capture the highlights of the

Michelle Reinecke
-2-
Professional Experience—continued

- ❖ **Achieved 100% of hiring goals** while maintaining the lowest recruiting costs of the division at $275.00 per hire.
- ❖ **Implemented an Integrated Voice Response** unit to capture 100% of survey data from a workforce of 2,500 associates for the 2001 Associate Survey project. Achieved an above-average response rate of 42%.
- ❖ **Increased associate retention by 47%** to achieve industry-standard excellence rate of 53% and maintained this rate for three consecutive years.
- ❖ **Led the regional succession planning and performance management** process to ensure talent development and quality bench strength.
- ❖ **Secured $100K+ of community funds** for employee training and development programs.
- ❖ **Repeatedly achieve a win rate of 99%** on unemployment claims for three locations across the U.S., resulting in **savings of $90K** for the division.

Human Resource Supervisor / Management Trainer
GRAYSON FOODS, Rochester, New York—1989 to 1997
Food processing facility—800 local employees.
- ❖ **Managed** hiring / orientation for dayshift.
- ❖ **Facilitated 100% of management training** programs for the operation.
- ❖ **Secured $100K + of state grant** training funds.
- ❖ **Developed and implemented employee mentor program.**
- ❖ **Developed and implemented** the night-shift human resources department.
- ❖ **Managed grievance process** for non-exempt employees under the UFCW union contract.

Agriculture Science Instructor
ROCHESTER INDEPENDENT SCHOOL DISTRICT, Rochester, New York—1988 to 1989

Quality Supervisor
HENSLEY FARMS OF TEXAS, San Angelo, Texas—1985 to 1988

Education and Professional Training

- ❖ **Master of Science—Human Resource Development**—Penn State University, 1997
- ❖ **Bachelor of Science—Agriculture Science**—Texas A&M University, 1985
- ❖ **Professional Training:**
  Vital Learning Management Development—certified facilitator
  Dale Carnegie—certified assistant
  Microsoft Project and Publisher
  Multiple legal and human resource management training seminars

Professional Organizations

- ❖ **American Society for Training and Development (ASTD)**
- ❖ **American Association of Human Resource Management (AAHRM)**
- ❖ **Rochester Economic Development Corporation (REDC)**
- ❖ **Rochester Chamber of Commerce**
- ❖ **Rochester Independent School District (RISD) Volunteer: Innovative Research Team—Curriculum for Real World Application**

individual's background and yet cover the vast amount of experience in her field. A box for the profile and shaded boxes for the centered section headings make the resume sections visible at a glance. Compound diamond bullets help to draw attention to the achievements.

JONATHAN F. MARLEY, MBA

7589 Weathering Avenue
Chicago, IL 44596

(715) 555-7662
jfm255@yahoo.com

HUMAN RESOURCE EXECUTIVE
...Excel in designing & administering HR plans to drive revenue increases...

Highly qualified professional with 15 years of experience in all core corporate HR functions; exceptional strengths in administration and systems development. Strong analysis, organizational, and problem-solving skills. Proven record of establishing successful HR processes and systems for start-up ventures. Extensive experience in creating team-based environments. Solid leadership, talent assessment, and management recruiting abilities. Demonstrated knowledge in

- Compensation & Staff Relations
- Regulatory Compliance
- Recruiting & Staffing
- Assessment & Evaluation

- Training & Development
- HRIS Systems
- Leadership & Motivation
- Benefit Administration

- Goal Setting & Strategic Planning
- Budget Management
- Affirmative Action
- Third-Party Vendor Negotiations

PROFESSIONAL BACKGROUND

ANCO & DOLNER, Chicago, IL   2002–2003
Global employee assessment, testing, and screening company for large corporations.
Human Resources Manager, Sacramento, CA
Directed testing/assessment center to conduct employment screening for airport security personnel. Project encompassed securing management and non-management staff for 7 major airports. Managed 25 staffing specialists at 1 of 150 centers nationwide. Project secured 44,000+ staff nationwide; personally accountable for 600+.
- Recognized as one of the most successful testing sites nationwide; completed project 2 weeks prior to deadline.
- Met all goals and established 800+ reserve pool for future employment.

GLOBAL COMMUNICATIONS, Chicago, IL   2000–2002
Publicly held telecommunications company with $1.1 billion annual revenues.
Senior Director of Human Resources
Executive staff leader; directed team of 11 HR generalists and managers; indirectly managed 4 recruiters. Created and implemented HR initiatives to drive business plan. Provided day-to-day support for 3,500+ employees in sales and operations departments. Performed organizational climate electronic surveys to design initiatives for improving employee relations. Generated detailed monthly analysis and matrix reports.
- Decreased employee turnover by 30% through climate surveys, intensified training, career targets, improved appraisal process, and enhanced work environment.
- Reduced vacancy turnaround time from 45 to 15 days; reduced cost by decreasing external recruiting services.
- Designed 2-day management development training for front-line supervisors; provided ongoing training to consistently improve management staff (2000).
- Spearheaded downsizing from 5,500 to 500 staff during acquisition. Teamed with line managers regarding legal issues; trained managers on downsizing procedures, and developed and administered severance packages.

SONIC INTERNATIONAL, New York, NY   2000
Software development company; primary focus on educational, sports, and financial industries.
Human Resource Consultant (contract)
Recruited to create compensation structures for 2,500+ employees. Established job titles/descriptions, compensation packages, and benefits. Partnered with Towers Perrin to conduct market analysis.
- Successfully streamlined compensation administration.

MEDFORD HEALTH PLANS, New York, NY   1997–1999
Managed care insurance provider.
Regional Human Resources Manager
Recruited to direct day-to-day activities for start-up of HR functions and staffing of Operations Center for expansion into NY market. Set up HR department, including staff recruiting and training. Tasked to recruit 600+ employees; coordinated transfer of 10% of staff from northeast operations.
- Facilitated development of annual HR Business Plan.
- Assumed consultant role for management staff integration of 2 HMOs acquired by Medford.
- Conducted downsizing and designed severance plans; interacted with third-party vendor to staff all key positions.

126

Combination. *Cathy Fahrman, Tampa, Florida*

This resume directs the reader's attention through bullets and other devices. The pair of horizontal lines enclosing the opening profile pulls the reader's eyes to it. Boldfacing makes the

JONATHAN F. MARLEY, MBA   Page 2

PROFESSIONAL BACKGROUND (continued)

BANKAMERICA CREDIT CORP., New York, NY   1985–1997
Diverse financial corporation.
Director of Human Resources/World Wide Securities Services Division (1989–1997)
Recruited to interface with Senior Management Team to design and implement processes and support systems to transition operations to team-based environment. Oversaw 2 management staff and directed the day-to-day activities involved in start-up of the HR department, including relocation of 200 employees/functions and staffing of Financial Service Operations Center. Established entire HR department; teamed with recruiting division of company for advertising and job fair participation. Conducted interviews and designed assessment protocols.

- Accomplished full staffing in 7 months.
- Designed and implemented selection tools, award recognition programs, climate surveys and action plans, organizational development, and talent assessment.
- Achieved Top Performance Rating.
- Facilitated cross-functional teams in designing efficient and cost-effective organizational structures.

Director of Human Resources/Student Loan Division (1985–1989)
Oversaw and forecasted $2M HR department budget. Created benefit plans and job descriptions.

- Designed employee policy/procedure manuals and HRIS systems.
- Initiated and implemented plans for company IPO offering.
- Designed employee training programs.
- Acted as company representative and responded to all third-party complaints; maintained 100% resolution rate.
- Designed compensation program using PC-based model to streamline tracking, forecasting, and reporting processes to benchmark internal and external equity.

EDUCATION

ACADEMY WEST COLLEGE, Santa Fe, NM
Master of Business Administration (1992)

UNIVERSITY OF CHICAGO, Chicago, IL
Bachelor of Business Administration (1983)

BAYSIDE COMMUNITY COLLEGE, Brooklyn, NY
A.A.S., Accounting

PROFESSIONAL DEVELOPMENT & ACTIVITIES/PUBLIC SPEAKING

- *Myers-Briggs, Career Development, Evaluation Interview, ABRA CADABRA systems, HR Partner systems, Commercial Banking & Financial Management*
- Promoting Employee Recognition, Effective Communication Skills (University of Chicago)
- American Institute of Banking (AIB), Board Member
- Society of Human Resource Professionals (SHRP), Executive Board Member
- Public Speaking: Company presentations, up to 600 attendees

MILITARY

UNITED STATES AIR FORCE, *Airman*

COMPUTER PROFICIENCY

Excel, Word, Lotus 1-2-3, custom payroll systems, PeopleSoft, and Internet

applicant's name, the centered section headings, the job positions in the Professional Background section, the academic degrees, and the individual's military role as Airman more visible. Bold italic captures attention in the profile. By itself, italic helps to explain the various workplaces.

BRENDA HAMILTON

222 Lakeridge Place
Augusta, Alberta A1A 1A1
555.222.4444
bhamilton@email.com

HUMAN RESOURCES EXECUTIVE
Specialist in the Creation and Implementation of Leading-Edge Corporate HR Initiatives

DYNAMIC AND HIGHLY SKILLED STRATEGIC HR EXECUTIVE credited with building and leading award-winning and best-in-class Human Resources initiatives in the areas of cultural transformation, organizational change, e-Human Resources, and employee development. Career expertise designing, creating, launching, and leading innovative programs to enhance corporate culture, improve employee performance, and support change across the organization. Highly skilled in communications, mentoring, and integrating diverse teams around a common vision.

Key areas of speciality include

- Values-Based Initiatives
- Organizational Change
- Strategic Planning
- Merger & Acquisition Integration
- HR Policy, Process, & Systems Design

- e-Human Resources
- Learning & Education
- Leadership & Mentoring
- Restructuring & Revitalization
- HRIS Technology Solutions

PROFESSIONAL EXPERIENCE

TELCO COMMUNICATIONS INC., Augusta, Alberta   1997–Present

Vice President—e-Human Resources (2002–Present)

Selected to lead the strategizing and implementation of a best-in-class online HR function integrating Recruitment, Performance, Recognition, and HR Administration for 30,000 employees nationally. Defined and spearheaded all strategic work to meet four key measurables: to build a self-service model, reduce HR costs, build a high-performance corporate culture, and enhance Data / IP skills across the organization. Concurrently responsible for Ombudsman, HR Website Design and Maintenance, Equity & Ethics, and Workplace Accommodation functions.

- Created in-house e-performance management system currently used by all managers across all lines of business enterprise-wide.
- Introduced a highly successful online data / IP learning curriculum and corresponding learning management system; success of program and efficacy of communications evidenced by 11,000 users within first 60 days.
- Sourced, purchased, and implemented RecruitSoft to enable and facilitate e-recruiting function.
- Championed and currently chairing e-Human Resources Steering Committee consisting of key cross-functional stakeholders.

Vice President—Learning Services / Chief Learning Officer (2000–2002)

Built, launched, and guided internal "corporate university" designed to provide training and performance enhancement across the areas of Technology, Management, Sales, and Marketing. Established Learning Services model, assembled the leadership team, and built the curricula to support and develop over 30,000 employees. Managed $22 million budget and 147-person staff.

- Recognized opportunity to sell technology, management, and sales training modules worldwide—concurrently managed this independent business entity that generated an additional $5 million in annual revenue.

127

Combination. *Ross Macpherson, Pickering, Ontario, Canada*

This executive's many quality contributions justify the three-page format. Professional Accreditation & Education and Volunteer Leadership round out her outstanding qualifications.

BRENDA HAMILTON
555.222.4444 • bhamilton@email.com
Page 2

<u>**Vice President—Enterprise-Wide Change for People**</u> (1999–2000)

Seconded on 8-month project to spearhead and launch enterprise-wide cultural transformation to establish pillars of high performance across the organization. As leader of the "Energy Team," surveyed 1,000 employees, communicated and branded 4 core values, and launched supporting performance management system (Team Machine).

- Built communications strategy around hugely successful 4-hour "Igniter Sessions" that delivered new values, culture, and strategy to over 23,000 employees in person across 45 cities in less than 6 months.
- Following rollout, Pulse Check Analysis identified **78% increase** in how engaged employees were in TELCO values.
- Initiative recently won **International Verizon Leadership Award** for excellence in Leadership and Cultural Change (January 2004).
- Feature articles in *Telecom Edge* (May 2003) and *Business in Augusta* (December 2003).

<u>**Vice President—Human Resources**</u> (1997–1999)

Selected to lead all HR functions throughout TELCO Alberta—payroll, labour-relations, policy, compensation, and learning—and spearhead all critical HR process changes. Concurrently represented HR interests through 2 major corporate mergers.

- Led HR due diligence team for ABCTel merger—investigated HR practices, labour relations climate, contracts, and associated costs, and reported into Prime Due Diligence team.
- Created highly successful career transition structure and processes to support corporate restructuring—recognized as one of the top initiatives throughout North America for its creativity, support, efficacy, and feedback.
- Led successful cultural merger following purchase and integration of PEN-Tel.
- Spearheaded extensive values-based work to support ABCTel merger, effectively identifying, branding, and communicating the new organization's core values.

AGM LIMITED, Augusta, Alberta   1986–1997
(Alberta-based telecommunications company—merged into TELCO Alberta 1997)

<u>**Director—Employee Programs & Services**</u> (1994–1997)

Coordinated creation and maintenance of all HR policies and services prior to merger. Established and administered all policies concerning compensation, payroll, pension, administration, benefits, and labour relations.

- Beta-tested first SAP payroll in Canada—oversaw massive conversion process and led organization through smooth implementation.
- Successfully introduced a new flex benefit program accepted by both unionized and non-unionized workforce—effectively negotiated with all bargaining units and communicated program across entire corporation.
- Reduced costs through exhaustive cost analyses and updated policies annually to consistently meet proprietary and growth needs.

<u>**Director—Organization Development**</u> (1993–1994)

Selected to lead change-management priorities throughout AGM, with particular focus on restructuring initiatives in anticipation of PEN-Tel merger.

- Built highly successful career transition model to support restructuring—developed strategy, created and communicated process, and effectively supported restructuring of 2,800 employees representing 25% of the total AGM workforce.

After a centered heading for the profile with centered key specialty areas in two columns, side section headings establish the layout for the rest of the resume. Boldfacing and underlining make evident the positions held at the different workplaces. Bullets point to the applicant's significant achievements. Many of these are

<u>**Director—Management & Quality Education**</u> (1990–1993)

Developed and launched in-house training and development division providing Total Quality training and Management development programs across the organization. Defined the strategy, developed the curricula, and coordinated the launch and management of all learning programs. Managed staff of 22 direct reports.

Previous AGM positions include
Finance Supervisor
Finance Training Supervisor
Total Quality Training

PROFESSIONAL ACCREDITATION & EDUCATION

Executive Management Program in Telecommunications	*University of Southern California*, 2002
Revitalizing the Workforce	*Center for Creative Leadership, Greensbow, NC*, 1997
Human Resource Executive Program	*University of Michigan*, 1996
PSOD (Organizational Development)	*National Training Labs, Alexandria, VA*, 1991
Personnel Administration (with Distinction)	*University of Augusta*, 1988
BA—Psychology / B.Ed.	*Pinehurst University*, 1979

VOLUNTEER LEADERSHIP

Advisory Board—*University of Augusta, Augusta, AB*	2002–Present
Advisory Board—*University of Augusta (TELCO Centre for Management Development)*	1989–2001
Board—*USC Center for Telecommunications Management (Marshall School of Business)*	1998–2000
President / Chair—*Skills Alberta, Augusta, AB*	1990–1998
Advisory Board—*Simon Pritchard University, Centennial, BC*	1998–2000
HR Management Committee—*Saint Royal College, Augusta, AB*	1998–2000
Chair—*Conference Board Education Forum*	1988–1991

quantified with numbers, dollar amounts, and percentages. Boldfacing highlights two exceptional achievements. Extra line spacing above each main section ensures adequate white space and avoids a crowded appearance. The overall impression is that the resume is long for good reasons.

Information Systems/Technology

Resumes at a Glance

RESUME NO.	OCCUPATION	GOAL	PAGE
128.	Software Developer	Software Programmer/Engineer	261
129.	Computer & Information Systems Manager	Computer & Information Systems Manager	262
130.	E-Commerce Manager	E-Commerce Manager	264
131.	Application Development Supervisor	Not specified	266
132.	Information Systems Consultant	Not specified	268
133.	IT Senior Technical/Project Mgr.	Senior Technology Executive	270
134.	Senior Software Engineer	Technical Project Manager	274
135.	Senior Solutions Manager	Corporate Executive	276
136.	Project Manager, IVR Replacement	IT Project Manager	278
137.	Assoc. VP/Onsite Program Director	IT Development Executive	280

RICHARD LEVINSON
0000 Preston Avenue ◆ Houston, TX 77000 ◆ (281) 000-0000 ◆ myname@aol.com

Career Target: Software Programmer / Software Engineer

PROFILE

Talented software programmer with BBA degree, strong educational background in programming, and experience using cutting-edge development tools. Articulate and professional communication skills, including formal presentations and technical documentation. Productive in both team-based and self-managed projects; dedicated to maintaining up-to-date industry knowledge and IT skills.

Knowledge & Skill Areas:

- Software Development Lifecycle
- Object-Oriented Programming
- Problem Analysis & Resolution
- Web Site Design & Development

- Requirements Gathering & Analysis
- Technical & End User Documentation
- Software Testing & Troubleshooting
- Project Teamwork & Communications

TECHNICAL SUMMARY

Languages:	Java, C, C++, JSP, ASP, Rational, HTML, SQL, Unified Process
Operating Systems:	Linux, Windows XP/2000/9x
Object-Oriented Design:	UML, Design Patterns

EDUCATION

TEXAS UNIVERSITY, Houston, TX
Bachelor of Business Administration in Computer Science, 2002

- ◆ Earned place on President's List for 3 semesters (4.0 GPA)
- ◆ Member, Golden Key National Honor Society & Honors Fraternity
- ◆ Selected for listing in *Who's Who Among Students in American Universities and Colleges*

Relevant Coursework:

- Software Engineering
- Project Management
- Database Design

- Systems Engineering
- Differential Equations
- Classical / Modern Physics

- Calculus I, II, III
- Logic Circuits
- Systems Analysis

Project Highlights:

- ◆ **Software Engineering**—Served as Design Team Leader and member of Programming group for semester-long project involving development of software for actual implementation within Texas University Recreation Center. Determined requirements, created "look and feel" for user interface, and maintained explicit written documentation.

- ◆ **Systems Engineering**—Teamed with group of 4 in conceptualizing and designing client-server application to interconnect POS and inventory systems for retail outlet, delivering class presentation that highlighted specifications and projected $2 million in cost savings.

COMMUNITY COLLEGE, Houston, Texas
- ◆ 3.96 GPA / Concentration in Computer Science coursework

EXPERIENCE

DATAFRAME CONCEPTS, L.L.C., Houston, TX   2000–Present
Software Developer

- ◆ Worked with small team of developers to brainstorm and implement ideas for shipping/receiving software representing leading-edge concept within transportation industry.

- ◆ Planned and initiated redesign of existing standalone application, utilizing object-oriented design/programming and Java in creating thin-client GUI for new distributed system.

- ◆ Collaborated with marketing director in strategies to further business growth, including Web site enhancement that drove 65% increase in visitor interest for product offering.

* References and additional information will gladly be provided upon request.

128

Combination. *Daniel J. Dorotik, Jr., Lubbock, Texas*

The applicant had limited work experience, so the writer emphasized skills and education. To de-emphasize experience, the writer put the Experience section at the bottom of the resume.

DAVID KENT

5555 Kalanianaole Hwy. • Honolulu, Hawaii 00000
808-555-5555 • dkent@islandemail.com

COMPUTER AND INFORMATION SYSTEMS MANAGER
Administrative Intranets/Public Web Sites/Software Engineering

7+ years of Web planning, development, and administration experience. Thorough knowledge and effective execution of state-of-the-art Internet and intranet systems technology. Proven communication and presentation skills. Easily introduce technical information to project participants and to the public. Project management expertise spans single and multi-institutional organizations, and academia.

- Information and Reporting Systems
- Real-Time Database Management Systems
- IT/Web-Based Media Support
- Scientific Document/Media Support
- Science Communication
- Web/Database Servers
- Project Quality Control
- Content Development

Specializing in the development and implementation of automated and paperless systems for data collection; procedures reporting; information submission, storage, and retrieval; and formal report and Web content production.

───────────────── **RELEVANT EXPERIENCE** ─────────────────

RESEARCH CORPORATION OF THE UNIVERSITY OF HAWAII, Honolulu, 1998–Present

Computer and Information Systems Manager (1/2000–Present)
Marine Bioproducts Engineering Center (MarBEC)

Supervise Information and Reporting System (IRS) software development team of up to 8 (2 faculty and 6 students). Establish IRS content management and administrative procedures. Provide comprehensive annual report preparation support, including research updates and timely production and delivery. Plan and meet marketing, IT, and AV requirements of MarBEC-sponsored meetings and symposiums.

- Designed and developed proprietary IRS software, securing $500,000 in additional funding. Anticipated time savings of 40%–60% in annual report content preparation, 80%–90% in research-related Web content publishing. Has potential to save NSF $2.2 million of ERC annual expenditures if fully deployed.
- Completed special project: Culture Collection (CC) database management system resulting in real-time online availability of CC content.
- Delivered Beta version of Annual report Volume II reporting system 8 weeks ahead of schedule. Delivered full system version 1.01 on schedule and within budget.
- Presented several successful Web development and software engineering multimedia seminars: PowerPoint site visit presentations; ERC annual meeting IRS demonstrations; IRS demo to University Information and Computing Sciences (ICS) Department.
- Assisted with planning and production of Fourth Asia-Pacific Marine Biotechnology Conference (produced proceedings and coordinated AV requirements) and Microalgae Production for the Aquaculture Industry Workshop (produced workshop video).

Database/Web Development Specialist (7/1999–1/2000)
MarBEC

Coordinated planning, development, and implementation of Relational Database Management System (RDMS), including time frame for deliverables. Maintained and estimated budgets for subcontracted work and personal assistant. Created Internet and intranet content/applications in support of internal and external activities. Trained users at multiple sites. Developed related standards, policies, and procedures.

129

Combination. *Peter Hill, Honolulu, Hawaii*

The applicant wrote his own resume; it was six pages long. The writer consolidated it into this strong two-page resume, positioning this CIS Professional/Webmaster for the next step in his

Computer Specialist III (6/1998–6/1999)
NOAA National Marine Fisheries Service (NMFS) Honolulu Laboratory

Coordinated NMFS Honolulu Laboratory, PIAO, WPCFIN, and Coast Watch Web sites to comply with NOAA standards. Collaborated to develop and implement standards for these and other sub-webs. Established and chaired laboratory's Web committee. Established laboratory's Web presence. Identified, obtained, and published Web site material.

- Designed and developed intranet and Internet Web sites in 6 months, 10 weeks ahead of schedule. Conceptualized and built from scratch NOAA R/V *Townsend Cromwell* student connection outreach Web site.

CHESAPEAKE BAY RESEARCH CONSORTIUM, Annapolis, Maryland, 1995–1998

Environmental Management Fellow
EPA Chesapeake Bay Program (CBP) Office

Worked closely and in coordination with CBP management committee members and other federal, state, and university staff to provide means of publishing and maintaining CBP Web site material.

- Established notable Web presence through coding, designing, and administering intranet and Internet World Wide Web sites. Co-authored CBP *Web Document Guidance.*

TECHNICAL EXPERTISE

HARDWARE: Intel-Based Systems • Macintosh • UNIX • Digital Imaging Devices • Telecommunications • Local Area Networks

SOFTWARE: Operating Systems • HTML • Database/Spreadsheet • Microsoft Project 2000 • Graphics Packages • File Manipulations • E-mail Editors • GIS • FTP • Word Processors • Directory Manipulations • Multimedia Digital Imaging

PROGRAMMING AND CODING PROFICIENCIES/FAMILIARITIES: HTML Editors • XHTML • CSS • JavaScript • Dynamic HTML • SQL • CGI Scripting • Visual Basic • DOM • COM • ColdFusion Markup Language • DTDs • XML • XSL • XSLT

ADDITIONAL TRAINING

Troubleshooting and Maintaining the Macintosh • XML Certification • Web Process and Project Management • Web Site Development and Design • Brochure, Catalog Ad, Newsletter, and Report Design • Graphics and Animation Creation • Data and Information Presentation • Windows-Based Environment Programming

EDUCATION

Bachelor of Science—Oceanography (Mathematics Emphasis), 1992
Humboldt State University, Arcata, California

career. Boldfacing and bullets do their job of calling attention to the most important information. Center-alignment is used for attractive formatting of the contact information, the banner over the profile, concluding profile information, the section headings, the workplaces, and the header on page two.

Stephen Wolf

1632 Red Hills Drive • San Diego, CA 99999
Home: 555.555.5555 • stevew@yahoo.com • Cell: 555.555.5555

E-COMMERCE MANAGER

Project Management • Application Development • EDI Management

Highly qualified IT professional with successful record determining and documenting requirements for IT products, logistics and financial applications. Outstanding problem-solving, analytical and decision-making skills with proven ability to conceptualize solutions to challenging situations and implement practical, cost-effective project plans. Characterized as a talented strategist, communicator, project leader and customer relationship manager. Areas of expertise encompass the following:

- Quality & Productivity Improvement
- Client Relationship Management
- Supply Chain & Product Management
- Product & Design Research
- International Transportation & Logistics

- Budget & Resource Planning
- EDI & Systems Integration
- Troubleshooting & Test Management
- Team Building & Leadership
- Technology Needs Assessment & Solutions

BA — Political Science — University of California, Berkeley
Accounting — Technical College — Schwandorf, Germany

Post-University Training Courses — Project Management; Introduction to SQL;
Leadership, Training & Conflict Resolution

PROFESSIONAL EXPERIENCE

BARKLEY SYSTEMS, San Diego, CA   **Apr 2001–Present**
Develops software solutions that completely manage marine terminal operations and communications.

E-Commerce Manager

Currently manage EDI group; leading the development of EDI applications of several internally developed large-scale software packages. Instrumental in establishing the internal business and resource infrastructure to support development, implementation and operations.

- Improved productivity through development of appropriate procedures, which ensured ISO certification for organization. Decreased customer complaints and dramatically reduced post-implementation support; achieved trading partners' functional expectations by 100%.

- Implemented project tracking tools; successfully communicated status of each project to company executives and key operations personnel, ensuring projects were completed.

- Instrumental in initiating and implementing several technical improvements to existing infrastructure, drastically reducing error rate and network traffic.

- Established formal communication channels with trading partners, resulting in improved communications with external trading partners, improved reputation, fewer complaints and reduced support.

- Wrote requirements for e-commerce module addressing existing EDI requirements and anticipated B2B integration needs.

- Executed EDI processes for large-scale software implementations, including requirements gathering, process design, development of data conversion, communications procedures and user acceptance testing.

130

Combination. *Denette D. Jones, Boise, Idaho*

This resume is nicely laid out with a variety of alignment and indentation patterns. Line spacing and margins are controlled so that information about the current workplace ends at the bottom

CRAFT INCORPORATED, Alameda, CA   Apr 2000–Feb 2001
Internet startup providing B2B payment and invoicing services over Internet.

Product Manager

Managed new B2B product for an e-commerce company producing a coherent product strategy including defining product, documenting requirements, evaluating prospective vendors, researching competitors, producing marketing materials and coordinating sales efforts.

- Identified, contacted and evaluated potential software vendors with the goal of keeping start-up costs minimal. Maintained strategic vendor partnerships and participated in contract negotiations.

- Completed comprehensive requirements document for new, Web-enabled invoicing/purchase order management application; process included interviewing potential customers and investigating legal and industry-specific requirements.

- Wrote and developed marketing materials and prototype HTML interface, resulting in interest among potential clients through quality presentations illustrating product.

- Identified potential integration partner and incorporated integration strategy into marketing material, which became major selling point with prospective clients.

- Strategically planned and coordinated with marketing on possible sales targets. Presented product to potential clients including live demonstrations of product capabilities.

BARTLETT SYSTEMS, San Diego   May 1995–Apr 2000
$1 billion international transportation/logistics company in more than 100 countries with 10,000 employees.

EDI Manager/Lead Business Analyst — (1997–2000)

Managed ten business analysts, technical resources and several ongoing EDI and non-EDI projects, including numerous multimillion-dollar, high-profile accounts. Primary resource for technical, business and procedural questions regarding mapping, U.S. Customs, transportation industry and internal policies.

- Developed and implemented project management procedures for electronic commerce group. Assigned projects based on experience, nature of project and potential development of new skills, resulting in quicker turnover while ensuring successful completion of projects.

- Increased productivity through department reorganization, improving staff effectiveness without increasing workload. Improved relationship between EDI group and other departments by establishing formal communications channels with other departments.

- Prioritized and published list of all projects and assigned resources based on client need, company priority and resources required to complete project.

Business Analyst — (1995–1997)

- Wrote programmer specifications for systems modifications and data conversion programs for Unisys mainframe and UNIX environment. Performed EDI mapping of all EDI standards as well as application-to-application, using Mentor (Sterling Gentran) on UNIX and PC platforms.

- Followed up with programming staff before project deadline; notified clients of potential problems, resulting in better reputation and fewer complaints.

- Designed and implemented report writer procedures to fit the assessed reporting needs of internal and external clients. Report output varied from hard-copy reports to proprietary flat files.

TECHNOLOGY SKILLS & QUALIFICATIONS

Operating Systems:	Windows, Mac, UNIX
Software:	MS Office (Word, Excel, PowerPoint, Access), Front Page, Project; Dreamweaver; Eudora; Internet Explorer; Netscape Navigator, Composer; Visio
Basic Understanding:	SQL, PL/SQL, HTML, XML, JavaScript
EDI Tools:	Sterling Gentran, Harbinger TLE Client Tools, Specbuilder

of page one and information about the preceding workplace begins at the top of page two. Small italic statements about each workplace in the Professional Experience section are useful for those who are not familiar with the companies. The boldfacing of job positions makes them readily apparent.

RONALD E. WHITTINGTON, CNE, MCP

1100 Residence Lane
Westings, IL 55555

Residence: (630) 555-0000
ronwhittington@cne.com

EXPERIENCED INFORMATION TECHNOLOGY PROFESSIONAL

Certified professional with eight-plus years of field experience. Expert in project management, design, development, migration and implementation of enterprise networking technology. Diverse technical expertise derived from rapid learning and effective application of cutting-edge technology. Highly communicative team leader who motivates and mentors people at all levels of technical expertise. Facilitate problem-solving teams that accurately assess technical challenges and successfully transform ideas into appropriate workable solutions.

PROFESSIONAL EXPERIENCE

ZOISE OFFICE SOLUTIONS, CHICAGO, IL
APPLICATION DEVELOPMENT SUPERVISOR

FEBRUARY 2000–PRESENT

In May 2002, received promotion from senior information systems engineer to application development supervisor. My team is responsible for Contracts and Pricing application development and backline support. Accountable for yearly performance evaluations, project management, total quality management and priority resource scheduling. Meet with business analysts, mangers and directors to coordinate resources, forecast budgets and meet deadlines.

Major project contributions include

*   Automated Pricing Review for quarterly contract reviews: multi-CPU Intel platform with SQL database on EMC storage.
*   SOS Catalog, creation of a new pricing logic.
*   Timán-Zoise tier-one joint venture, creation of new DB/2 database and contract reporting structure.
*   Contract Access and Security, security profile and architecture enhancements in CICS environment.
*   Contract Purge Re-Architecture to reduce operating costs and make available valuable resources on AS/400.
*   Mainframe Elimination by providing analysis information for proof of concept to reduce operating costs.

SENIOR INFORMATION SYSTEMS ENGINEER

Top-level technical contributor responsible for highly available e-mail infrastructure and virus countermeasures. Provided technical consulting, evaluation and reviews on complex projects. Qualifications in all facets of project life cycle development. From initial feasibility analysis and conceptual design through documentation, implementation, quality review and enhancement. Provided long-range capacity planning of enterprise applications and operating systems, database management and data networks. Effective communicator with associates and senior management. *Earned the Outstanding Achievement Award October 2000 for demonstrating 110% total quality toward company goals.*

Defined project management methodology to optimize technology resources and applications:

*   Implemented Sendmail MultiSwitch on Sun Solaris utilizing EMC storage and Cisco Local Director.
*   Replaced outbound fax acknowledgments for e-mail acknowledgment of orders placed by customers.
*   Designed a "stopgap" solution for our customers to e-mail orders.
*   Designed maintenance and support programs for the Enterprise Technology Assistance Center.
*   Contributed to enterprise management project to centralize monitoring of e-mail and antivirus software.
*   Upgraded Norton AntiVirus to the corporate edition as project manager.
*   Contributed to design of migration from GroupWise to Microsoft Exchange 2000.

❏ ❏ ❏

131

Combination. *Stephanie Whittington, Bolingbrook, Illinois*

This is a two-color (black and blue) resume if you print it on a color printer. Blue ink appears in the applicant's name and certification designations, the decorative square bullets at the bottom

RONALD E. WHITTINGTON, CNE, MCP

(630) 555-0000   ronwhittington@cne.com

SENIOR TECHNOLOGY SPECIALIST—FRANKLIN HENDERSON L.L.C., GLEN BROOK, IL   APRIL 1998–DECEMBER 1999

In June 1999, received promotion from technology specialist to senior technology specialist. Was in charge of client relations. *Awarded the Client Partnership Award for 3rd and 4th fiscal year 1999.* Standardized on Microsoft Windows NT, Novell, Compaq, Cisco and Computer Associates' ARCserve*IT*, Inoculate*IT* and FAXserve products.

- Evaluated, tested and implemented technologies and communications services.
- Developed database, procedures and systems to support technology deployment.
- Delivered over $95,000 in additional profit through value-added network consulting in less than one year.

INFORMATION TECHNOLOGY MANAGER—SPI MANAGEMENT ASSOCIATES, INC., NAPERBROOK, IL   JULY 1997–APRIL 1998

Planned and implemented the opening of a branch office. Used Nortel routers for WAN connectivity; 3Com work group hubs and Cisco switches for LAN connectivity. Operated on Novell intraNetWare 4.11 network operating system. Multiple Compaq brand file servers, communications and e-mail servers enabled task-specific operations.

- Managed help desk and software development personnel and tasks.
- Deployed, trained and supported Novell GroupWise document management.
- Implemented Novell Application Launcher for central administration of applications.
- Planned Internet connectivity using ISDN dedicated service, IP to IPX gateway and firewall technology.

COMPUTER SYSTEMS MANAGER—ON TOP OF LIFE, INC., DES MOINES, IA   DECEMBER 1995–JUNE 1997

This 24/7 multi-office traumatic brain injury rehabilitation center utilized NetWare 4.1 network operating system. Supported Marktech clinical and billing application, Kronos time tracking and DaVince e-mail system. Established key business relationships with the CEO and various upper-level managers. Revitalized operations and led the corporation's launch into emerging technology designed specifically for healthcare organizations.

- Saved $1 million in travel by implementing video teleconferencing technology over fiber using PictureTel equipment.
- Updated network infrastructure to support switched fast Ethernet using 3Com switches and workgroup hubs.

"Our organization has grown and benefited from [Ronald E. Whittington's] knowledge and expertise . . . his interpersonal skills are excellent . . . he is customer oriented and responds quickly to any and all requests made of him" (President and CEO).

EDUCATION & CERTIFICATIONS

BACHELOR OF SCIENCE IN TECHNICAL MANAGEMENT
DeVry University—anticipated completion summer 2004

ASSOCIATE IN APPLIED SCIENCE
Joliet Junior College—graduated 1994

Microsoft Certified Professional   **Certified Novell Engineer**

Continuing Professional Education sponsored by Zoise, Sendmail, Omicron and Martin Training Associates:

Accelerating Project Team Performance	Project Management Framework
Meeting Facilitation Skills	Your Role in Quality
Manager / Supervisor Training	Sendmail MultiSwitch
Negotiations and Conflict Resolution	Project Planning and Controls

Directory Technology—Active Directory, NDS, Netscape and LDAP

REFERENCES AVAILABLE UPON REQUEST

❏ 2 ❏

of each page (plus the page number on page two), and the header at the top of page two. The color is tasteful and distinguishes this resume from others of similar merit.

NORMAN LATHROP
450 Spencer Road
San Jose, California 00000
(555) 555-5555 • lathropn@aol.com

INFORMATION SYSTEMS CONSULTANT

Experienced **Certified Disaster Recovery Planner (CDRP)** and **Certified Business Continuity Planner (CBCP)** serving a diverse client base in finance and banking, healthcare, telecommunications, insurance, gas, chemicals, publishing and government. Project management qualifications combine with demonstrated ability to develop and implement technical solutions to meet critical business needs. Outstanding leadership and interpersonal skills resulting in effective working relationships and top performance among staff. An excellent communicator between technical and business units who can translate complex data into easily understood terms.

AREAS of EXPERTISE

Information Systems Integrity • Business Impact Analysis • Systems Applications
Disaster Recovery Planning & Auditing • Technical Support & Training • Compliance
Business Continuity Planning • Information Protection Analysis • Technical Documentation

PROFESSIONAL EXPERIENCE

DEP SOLUTIONS • San Jose, California • 1999–present
Information Systems Consultant

Recruited to manage development, implementation and enhancement of business resumption and computer disaster recovery programs for corporate clients in finance/banking, healthcare, publishing, insurance, gas/chemicals, telecommunications and government. Achieved distinction as first recipient of company's recognition award for outstanding performance.

Key Projects

♦ Developed and implemented business recovery program with 5 platforms, data center and complex network at financial services organization with 32 business units at 6 regional sites.
♦ Created business recovery plans with 2-year maintenance program for 2 major customer service centers supporting client company and its operations globally.
♦ Designed voice systems disaster recovery plans and models for corporate headquarters/field locations of major telecommunications corporation.

APEX SYSTEMS • San Jose, California • 1993–1999
Manager of Planning Services (*1995–1999*)

Planned, developed and managed all disaster and business recovery projects for entire company. Functioned as information systems security administrator controlling user identification creation and distribution as well as menu creation and distribution access. Researched, planned and provided technical support for workflow and document management projects.

Key Projects

♦ Performed risk assessment, analyzed business impact and led crisis-management team in the development of data and business recovery plan.
♦ Instrumental in saving $7 million annually through coordination and transition to an in-house claims data processing system.
♦ Collaborated on the design and implementation of mainframe-based system completed in just 15 months.
♦ Analyzed workflow procedures and downtime costs for utilization management and provided recommendations to maximize future growth potential.

132

Combination. *Louise Garver, Enfield, Connecticut*

With his own "shell" resume, this candidate was getting no interviews. The writer transformed it into this strong document that emphasizes the individual's certifications and

NORMAN LATHROP • (555) 555-5555 • Page 2

Manager of Special Projects (1994–1995)

Managed all phases of MIS project planning, development, implementation and management. Represented MIS department to all business units and with subcontractors. Initiated and wrote procedures to automate MIS request system, increasing efficiency, accountability and control.

Key Projects

♦ Strengthened confidence and productivity level of 100+ nontechnical staff through training in microcomputers and software applications.
♦ Created new system to organize and categorize 350 internal/external reports for a state contract.
♦ Provided technical solutions to expedite completion of Medicare contract; company was awarded contract out of 450 bids nationwide.

Manager of Enrollment Services (1993–1994)

Reorganized and supervised staff in the daily operations of department. Reviewed, developed and implemented new policies and procedures. Involved in the development of system enhancements and participated in the design and implementation of a new automated membership system.

Key Projects

♦ Significantly improved productivity through outstanding team-building and leadership skills.
♦ Increased applications processing 25% in just one month by redesigning workflow procedures.
♦ Introduced cross-training program, turning around employee morale and performance.

RYAN-LANCE CORPORATION • San Jose, California • 1992–1993
Systems Analyst

EDUCATIONAL BACKGROUND

B.S. (Computer Science) New York University, New York, New York

Additional Training

Hewlett Packard Product Support • NEC Product Marketing
UNIX & 3b2 • Development of Disaster Recovery Strategies
Novell NetWare Engineer • IBM Business Partner
Voice/Data Telecommunications (ATM, SONET & Frame Relay)
Bell Atlantic Disaster Recovery Institute Training Program

COMPUTER CAPABILITIES

Hardware: IBM 9672 • IBM 9221 • HP 3000-III • AT&T 3b2
Compaq Systempro • HP Vectra • Epson • various PC platforms

Software: Microsoft Windows, Word, Access, Project & Excel • dBASE III

ASSOCIATIONS

Disaster Recovery Institute • Business Continuity Institute
Information Systems Audit & Control Association

---

accomplishments. He began to get interviews. The depth of his expertise as presented on the resume secured him a higher position with 35 percent more income. Notice the location and extent of the bold-facing. It draws attention to the Areas of Expertise and the Key Projects subsections with diamond bullets.

RAMJEET CHAPRA

5898 North Broome Street, Chesterfield, MN 22222
Home: 666-666-6666 • Cell: 888-888-8888 • RChapra@netzero.com

SENIOR TECHNOLOGY EXECUTIVE

Expert in Partnering IT with Enterprise Strategies, Operations & Goals

Ten+ years of IT management experience with world-class manufacturers and service providers. Known for exceptional technical proficiency and astute understanding of business operations / performance drivers across tech and management lines. Manage senior-level responsibilities far exceeding job titles.

Personal and business watchwords are EXCELLENCE—continuously strive for perfection; ECONOMY—seek simplicity and elegance in planning and execution; and ETHICS—demonstrate personal integrity in all endeavors.

Deliver exceptional rather than expected results through strategic thinking, innovative problem-solving, and managing teams / change for performance excellence. Self-directed, disciplined, flexible, confident, and ready for new responsibilities.

MANAGEMENT & TECHNICAL ABILITIES

Business & IT Vision, Strategy & Leadership • Departmental Operations Management • Organizational Restructure & Change
Project, Performance & Budget Analysis • Project Planning & Management • Systems Development & Implementation
Enterprise-Wide & Global Solutions • Applications Analysis & Development • Team Building • Internal & External Customer Service

Operating Systems • UNIX (several flavors), Windows (all versions), Linux, DOS
Languages • C/C++, Perl, TCL, UNIX Shell Scripting, Visual Basic, VBA, Java, Javascript
Databases • Oracle, DB2, Access, MySQL, Real-time databases
Software • Business Objects Crystal Reports, MS Office, multiple other commercial packages
Comprehensive IT skills / project list available upon request.

EDUCATION

MS in Computer Integrated Manufacturing—4.00 GPA. Chatworth Institute of Technology, Chicago, IL, 1992

BE in Electronics & Communications—First Class Honors / 4.00 GPA. University of Bombay, India, 1986

Honors Diploma in Systems Management—Outstanding / Highest Grade. NIIT, Bombay, India, 1987

PERSONAL & BUSINESS DRIVERS

"Visionary, creative, out-of-box thinker; exhibits professionalism in the face of adversity; decisive when faced with chaos and uncertainty; [demonstrates] self-initiative." Director of IT • "Ramjeet has the ability to understand very complex technical issues and communicate them in an appropriate level of detail to whatever audience he is facing." Director IT Planning

Business • Get It Right the First Time

Invest appropriate time to fact-finding and planning. Dare to risk, act decisively with full-throttle effort into execution, and tenaciously move forward and achieve objectives, despite constraints and obstacles. *Example:* Independently authored and delivered technology presentations to staff and management to improve lagging knowledge of IT staff and allow CIO to forge ahead with new technology initiatives.

Technology • Practice Pragmatic Application of Relevant Technology

Look to technology as first-line option / solution for enhancing operational performance, increasing productivity, improving efficiency, eliminating bottlenecks, reducing errors, and solving problems. *Example:* Improved performance of reporting from new GL system by identifying and addressing system bottlenecks.

Project Management • Take a Big-Picture View

Create plan that fits scope; define and clearly articulate project goals and milestones (stretch, yet realistic); assemble, coach, manage, and motivate team; intervene to resolve technical and business issues using problem-solving skills that are second to none. *Example:* Brought stalled project on track within two weeks by setting / communicating clear vision, goals, and milestones.

Leadership • Interact, Motivate, Lead by Example

Combine technical knowledge / proficiency with unique ability to identify / leverage individual strengths of team members, truthfully deliver good / bad news, avoid / mediate conflicts, encourage communication / cooperation, and inspire / lead professionally, functionally, and culturally diverse individuals / groups. *Example:* Negotiated with feuding teams to resolve issue hindering completion of PVCS systems implementation. Agreement enabled department to become more organized around change-management and change-audit efforts.

133

Combination. *Deborah Dib, Medford, New York*

Why would a resume ever be four pages long? This dynamite resume illustrates why. It deserves close study. If you take the time to examine it, your effort will be rewarded with lessons in

PROFESSIONAL EXPERIENCE

UNIVERSAL LIFE INSURANCE COMPANY, Cranford, MN **1999 to Present**

A division of AmerUs, an $18.3 billion holding company, ULICO develops, markets, and services a full line of life insurance and annuity products to consumer and business customers. Employs 1,200 in offices in Illinois, Missouri, Ohio, and New York.

IT SENIOR TECHNICAL / PROJECT MANAGER

Direct accountability for managing IT projects (conversions, installations, integrations, upgrades) and providing systems / technical support to four operating locations and 1,200 users.

Provide technical / managerial oversight (design, development, implementation, evaluation) to multiple intra- and inter-company projects and initiatives of strategic and tactical importance—business and financial reporting solutions; data warehouse and data marts; and Web-based applications for internal and external customers.

Distinctions

- *"Always the right man for the job."* CIO—Universal Life Insurance Company

- *"He would be a candidate to run any business unit or department … [demonstrates] analytical and organizational skills, accountability, intelligence, customer focus, and leadership."* Current supervisor

- *"In the top 5% of the company. One of the most talented individuals I have had the pleasure to work with."* Former supervisor

- Recognized as the go-to for attacking and solving complex technology issues.

- Retained and given additional responsibility / authority in post-merger downsizing staff in IT department from 65 to 30.

Business & Leadership Contributions

- Participate in enterprise-level IT strategy and department-level operations management. As internal IT consultant / advisor, interface routinely with top-tier corporate executives and senior department managers across all functional lines.

- Recommended and / or implemented high-impact initiatives for measuring, tracking, and improving productivity, business matrix, systems performance / data quality indicators, and product management / progress.

- Led training sessions on basics of Web servers and TCP / IP technology to members of IT department, enabling CIO to move forward with new technology initiatives.

- Credited with personal contributions to effecting enterprise-wide culture change, upgrading the technical competency of IT department personnel, opening channels of communication, and fostering cooperation among internal departments.

IT Projects & Results

- *Multiple-Phase Financial Reporting Project*—Succeeded in bringing lagging project back on track within four weeks. Restaffed project; worked with client to redefine requirements; renewed sense of urgency; and provided strong, decisive, technically astute leadership. (Project Manager and Team Lead)

- *Web-based Project Tracking Solution*—Contributed technical expertise, innovation, and conceptualization of key business drivers to design, development, and implementation of IT solution providing instant / near real-time access to project information / status to internal and external customers. (Architect)

- *Enterprise Sales Reporting*—Managed recommendation, development, and implementation of data warehousing technologies for standardized and consolidated sales reporting. Provided one-stop-shop for information from multiple disparate systems as well as easy-to-use management dashboard. (Project Manager and Technical Lead)

- *Enterprise Reporting and Business Intelligence Solution*—Managed and coordinated enterprise-wide deployment of a standard corporate reporting and information-presentation solution. Coordinated activities of multiple team members and external consultants. Provided leadership and expertise for technical issues. (Project Manager and Lead Architect)

resume writing. In the profile, all of the keywords are capitalized for emphasis. If you wonder why the Education section was put so near the beginning, check out the information. Someone whose undergraduate and graduate GPAs are 4.00, with an additional outstanding/highest grade in a related field, is someone

PROFESSIONAL EXPERIENCE, continued

AUTO ELECTRONICS INC., Valley Stream, MO   **1992 to 1999**

Division of $26 billion company, Genius AutoSystems, originally formed by joining former major parts divisions. World's largest manufacturer and global distributor of automotive components, modules, fully integrated systems, and aftermarket replacement parts.

SENIOR PROJECT ENGINEER, Factory Information Systems Group (FIS)—led team of three engineers
LEADER, Manufacturing Technology Team—led team of 12 global representatives

Technical lead for newly formed department providing critical IT solutions / operational support for all manufacturing tracking and monitoring requirements. Reported directly to manager of FIS, indirectly to director of manufacturing engineering. Led teams in design, development, and implementation of IT solutions. Managed related functions / project cycles—staffing and training, resource planning / allocation, cost / progress analysis, on-floor testing and troubleshooting, technical and business problem-solving.

Distinctions
- *"Give the task to accomplish [and] Ramjeet will quickly and efficiently assess the situation; make recommendations; marshal resources; and lead the effort by directing both business and technical resources."* Supervisor
- *"Ramjeet has more breadth of perspective than most engineers or managers."* Senior Engineer
- Earned numerous "Lightning Awards" for vision, innovation, and personal performance excellence.
- Chosen to lead global Manufacturing Technology Team (MTT). Traveled worldwide to conduct training and lead presentations on topics related to technology's role / value in high-performance manufacturing.

Business & Leadership Contributions
- Successfully lobbied for the formation of Factory Information Systems Group to replace outside systems vendor and expensive, ineffective applications. Played principal role in evolving department to become critical manufacturing partner.
- Led MTT meetings—cross-departmental, cross-functional, trans-global team of 12 involved in enterprise-wide IT strategies, projects, and solutions for the production floor.
- Served as internal IT consultant, advisor, and front-line point of contact to stakeholders—senior management, manufacturing managers, key department heads, union representatives—in multiple global operational locations.

IT Projects & Results
- *Factory Information System*—Conceived and built proof of concept / prototype, and won consensus / approval for IT specifications and business matrix. Developed and positioned $200,000 project for 80-site global deployment and provided ongoing system support / improvement through MTT.
- *In-sourcing of FIS*—Facilitated $60 million to $80 million cost saving by recommending bringing project in-house, redefining IT strategy / specifications, and providing strong technical and managerial leadership throughout project cycle.
- *Web-based Equipment & Manufacturing Management Solution*—Improved ability to monitor remote manufacturing equipment. Co-developed and built versatile Web-based front-ends, enabling management of manufacturing lines from any location, without need for specialized access software.

NPG GROUP, Bombay, India   **1991**

$149 million market leader in manufacture of industrial yarn and fabric and refrigerant gases—2,500 employees and operations in 14 locations throughout India, UAE, and US.

ASSISTANT MANAGER—Management Services Department

Assisted in management, systems operation, and supervision of 12 programming / technical support staff. Developed / implemented PERQS monitoring system within six weeks of hire. Designed, developed, and deployed methods-time ordering / product information. Reengineered and streamlined business / reporting processes.

SIDDIQUI MANUFACTURING COMPANY, Bombay, India   **1989 to 1991**

$790 million diversified enterprise—manufacturer, marketer, and distributor of wide range of durable consumer goods and industrial products in global markets.

SENIOR SERVICE OFFICER—CAD / CAM Division

Provided field support for CAD / CAM workstations, pre-sale technical support, post-sale hardware / software installation, and on-site and remote UNIX systems administration. Reduced time to connect machines to computers from 6–10 weeks to less than 2 hours. Assumed role of liaison to technology R&D teams. Provided client training.

to pay attention to. Take time to read the testimonials in the resume. They are more than just glowing; they make the choice between "hiring this guy" or purchasing a supercomputer a tough one. Study the use of full- and center-justification for variety. Note the consistent use of heavier bullets for Distinctions on pages

RAMJEET CHAPRA

5898 North Broome Street, Chesterfield, MN 22222
Home: 666-666-6666 ● Cell: 888-888-8888 ● RChapra@netzero.com

CRITICAL PROJECTS & INITIATIVES

Expert in Partnering IT with Enterprise Strategies, Operations, & Goals

Developed and delivered system that allowed company to manufacture new and profitable high-tech product.

As *Project Engineer, Auto Electronics Systems*, challenged to create new manufacturing data collection system and update / implement more functional companion systems. Researched, designed, and built proof-of-concept system. Worked with management to restore control of this initiative back internally (away from old system's outside vendor). Led team to write SOW and perform evaluation / bidding effort.

Result   State-of-the-art system is now in use in more than 80 global manufacturing sites, providing effective and standardized means to control, gather, and process data from the shop floor (product would have been extremely difficult, if not impossible, to build without functions of this system). System provided company with data gathering / archiving abilities as required by regulatory agencies.

Strength   *"I deliver cost-effective, functional systems and develop the team and business processes to enable the global deployment of these systems."*

Revitalized stalled mission-critical project.

As *Project Manager, Universal Life*, challenged to revitalize stalled project providing standardized way of supplying financial, accounting, and statutory reporting from company's new general ledger system. Reviewed client needs and team skill sets, and made staffing changes. Set up a formal project plan and assigned priorities. Provided technology assistance where required.

Result   The project was back on track and delivering high-quality reports to a happy client. Without this, the GL system would not have gone live, forcing enterprise to rely on previous-generation GL systems at much greater costs.

Strength   *"I understand and comprehend difficult situations, build and rally a team around a problem, and provide superior technical and project management to achieve tangible results."*

Standardized data gathering into a universal, cost-effective, and accurate reporting tool.

As *Project Manager, Universal Life*, challenged to implement new version of reporting tool while previous generation still ran live in production. In addition, solved multiple problems in data integrity. Brought together team of DBAs, data administrators, consultants, and end-users; developed project plan; and managed execution. Installed new version within five weeks with little user disturbance. Implemented Web-based tools to provide less complex user interface. Developed training plans to ensure success.

Result   Project has been adopted as the corporate reporting standard for the enterprise (post-merger). New version allows for easier reporting, simpler maintenance of the infrastructure, and saving licensing / maintenance costs.

Strength   *"I focus on business drivers and strive to provide the most effective and simple solution that can be standardized across the enterprise."*

Developed customer solution on personal initiative, directly leading to new contracts.

As *Senior Service Officer, Siddiqui Manufacturing*, took on personal challenge to resolve longstanding parametric software / training issue causing customer to work harder and longer to send designs out the door. Worked on program from home, on own time, to deliver solution, and implemented at customer's site during a regular service call.

Result   Customer was ecstatic that two-year problem was finally resolved and a parametric design now took 80% less time to execute. As a direct result, he renewed annual contract and within six months bought two more licenses.

Strength   *"I look to customer satisfaction as a business driver and strive to provide outstanding service and support to both internal and external customers."*

Built global consensus for crucial manufacturing enterprise system.

As *Leader, Manufacturing Technology Team, Auto Electronics Systems*, challenged to adopt a badly needed enterprise statement-of-work (SOW) for factory information systems (FIS) across all global sites. Organized virtual and on-site global team meetings (traveled to USA, Europe, Mexico), leading team to consensus on final version.

Result   Standard FIS platform was adopted and evaluation / bid effort using this SOW was conducted. Company realized substantial savings in cost avoidance and implementation delays due to adoption of a common global standard.

Strength   *"Using initiative, team leadership, presentation, and persuasion skills, I build consensus and deliver cost-effective business benefits, keeping IT a value-add rather than a revenue drain."*

two and three. Observe the use of boldfacing and italic to capture attention. Finally, observe the recurrent rhythm of Challenge...Response...Result...Strength on page four.

Jeff Staffly

TECHNICAL PROJECT MANAGER
DEVELOPING PROFITABLE COMMERCIAL SOFTWARE PRODUCTS

LEADERSHIP STRENGTHS

- Envisioning practical implementations of product concepts and technologies.
- Integrating the latest resources and equipment; incorporating new technologies quickly and proficiently.
- Evaluating/managing projects from a technical, operational, logistical, and financial perspective.
- Optimizing processes and operations to realize cost reductions.
- Developing/sharing best practices to increase effectiveness, productivity, and customer satisfaction.
- Managing stress, unpredictable workloads, conflicting deadlines, and interruptions.

TECHNICAL KNOWLEDGE AND EXPERTISE

Platforms	Wintel Platforms, Macintosh, IBM System 390, RS/6000
Operating Systems	Windows, UNIX (IBM AIX, Linux), IBM OS/390, Mac (OS9 and OSX)
Programming Languages	JAVA, C, C++, Visual Basic, Pascal, FORTRAN
Development Tools	Microsoft Visual C++, Borland J Builder, Visual Cafe
Standards/Specifications	DCE, CORBA, JAVA RMI
Performance Analysis	DevPartner
Configuration Management	SafeSource
Project Management	Microsoft Project
Protocols	TCP/IP, HTTP, SNMP, IPP

AWARDS AND RECOGNITION

1998 IBM outstanding Technical Achievement for OS/390 Print Server
1989 International Communications Association Student of the Year
Author—IBM Technical Disclosure (White Paper), "Thin Client Architecture"
Presenter—IBM User Group, "AIX Print System"

PROFESSIONAL EXPERIENCE

Hands-on program manager responsible for leading teams from initial concept through definition, design, development, test/debug, and production. Developed and released educational software and printing protocol systems. Provided software development guidance to design/production teams, influenced product feature set, and facilitated customer-requested enhancements. Led cross-functional teams throughout entire project cycle. Managed relationships with marketing, information developers, product managers, and production.

PROJECT HIGHLIGHTS AND ACHIEVEMENTS

At Education Labs Corporation
- ✓ Improved product usability. Extended functionality to include visual tools, enabling easy reading and understanding of classroom scientific experiments.
- ✓ Delighted science teacher by increasing classroom experiment time after reducing setup steps from 12 to 3 by automating manual configuration and detection processes on the classroom's legacy systems.
- ✓ Built intuitive GUIs that incorporated customer functionality requests with planned features and defect fixes. Accommodated customer requests while adhering to published update schedules, enabling achievement of revenue goals.
- ✓ Extended target market and reduced development costs/time by creating mechanisms to develop on Windows and Mac platforms simultaneously.
- ✓ Strengthened customer relationships and deepened customer use model knowledge by observing customer sites and classrooms. Transformed knowledge gained into product development plans.
- ✓ Developed/delivered customer presentations to introduce new technology and facilitate technology adoption.

555 Rolland Place • Lafayette, CO 00000 • 555.555.5555 • jfstaff@atcom.net

134

Combination. *Roberta F. Gamza, Louisville, Colorado*

The applicant's own original resume was filled with tasks and history. The writer turned the resume into a marketing document that demonstrates the value he brought to his previous

Jeff Staffly

At IBM

- ✓ Collaborated with IEEE committee to develop leading-edge IPP technology standards. Worked with leading manufacturers (HP, Microsoft, Sun Microsystems, and Apple Computer) to ensure interoperability.

- ✓ Led a team of 5 to design and implement a distributed printing system from concept through prototype and production for OS/390 operating system based on the IPP specification. Specified team and resource requirements; developed and managed schedule; collaborated with product managers, marketing, and information developers; and tested to ensure project success. Launched functionality as part of OS/390 scheduled release on time and on budget.

- ✓ One of three chief architects for client component of a new print server for the OS/390 operating system that exceeded all sales goals within the first year. Challenged to build a brand-new printing subsystem that must interface with existing printing subsystems. Conducted extensive customer research and worked closely with marketing and product engineers to specify subsystem. Subsystem was released as part of the operating system, but was offered as a high-profit, add-on component.

- ✓ Developed add-on AIX Print Server client component that leveraged RS/6000 sales. Developed print management system for heavy-use clients (banks, credit card companies, statement producers) that significantly reduced printing costs.

- ✓ Enabled IBM to extend printing architecture throughout the customer enterprise, displacing competitive desktop printers throughout customer sites. Developed a print submission client for Windows operating system, allowing employees in any part of the enterprise to access centralized printing resources and eliminating the need for desktop printers.

PROFESSIONAL HISTORY

Senior Software Engineer, Education Labs Corp., Boulder, CO	January 2000–April 2003
Senior Software Engineer, IBM Printing Systems, IBM Corp., Boulder, CO	June 1996–December 1999
Software Engineer, Productive Data Systems (at IBM), Boulder, CO	November 1992–June 1996
Software Engineer, Internet Communications, Boulder, CO	June 1991–November 1992
Telecommunications Engineer, Data Systems, Boston, MA	December 1984–June 1991

EDUCATION

M.S. Telecommunications, University of Boulder, Boulder, CO, 1989

B.A. Business Administration, Massachusetts State University, Boston, MA, 1980

MEMBERSHIP

Member, Association of Computing Associates (ACA)

COMMUNITY SERVICE

Volunteer Math Tutor for Boulder's Riverview Elementary School

555 Rolland Place • Lafayette, CO 00000 • 555.555.5555 • jfstaff@atcom.net

employers while highlighting his technical skills. The first page is the marketing page, grouping the most important information according to topics most prospective employers would want to cover. Because the positions in the Professional History seem somewhat similar, not telling the duties of each avoids dull repetition.

Vince Conlan

000 Bluff Street ♦ P.O. Box 000 ♦ Des Moines, IA 00000-0000 ♦ 000-000-0000 (H) ♦ 000-000-0000 (C)

CORPORATE-LEVEL EXECUTIVE
VICE PRESIDENT ♦ DIRECTOR
Information Technology ♦ Management Information Systems ♦ Sales and Marketing ♦ Business Development

Positive, results-driven, and innovative individual with proven success in balancing operational efficiencies and business growth with client satisfaction, offering more than 20 years of progressive and stable experience with world-class, Fortune 100 organization. Take pride in ability to effectively combine corporate objectives and values with personal and professional goals and work ethics. Employ proactive management and strong leadership techniques to generate accomplishment-driven workplace environment, resulting in employee loyalty. Build and foster strategic business relationships with C-level executives, maintaining customer satisfaction at all levels. Possess extraordinary capabilities in the areas of

New Business Development	*Account Management*	*Global Sales and Marketing*
Budget Administration	*Total Quality Management*	*Change Implementation*
Strategic Planning	*Human Resources Leadership*	*Product Development*

CAREER ACCOMPLISHMENTS:

➤ Recognized by XYZ Corporation as #1 Sales Professional: Received President's Club Award for achievement of $7.8M in sales on $3.2M budget for FY 2002.
➤ Led start-up activities of Technical Operations division from ground floor, developing and implementing departmental structure and strategies. Generated $226M in revenues on $143M operating budget.
➤ Negotiated acquisition of distribution rights of Barr Systems Software and Data/Ware systems on behalf of XYZ, resulting in exceptional levels of revenue growth and receipt of President's Award, 1996.

PROFESSIONAL EXPERIENCE:

XYZ CORPORATION   **1981–present**
Senior Solutions Manager—Industrial Business Unit (2000–present)
- Direct and monitor all facets of product and service sales and marketing, technical project development and implementation, and contract negotiation.
- Maintain P&L responsibility for unit: Set direction and manage changes, resulting in continuously meeting and achieving organizational goals and project timelines.
- Build, lead, and foster highly qualified multitasking, cross-functional teams capable of meeting timelines and bringing projects to completion while remaining within budget and scope specifications.
- Conceive, develop, execute, and implement state-of-the-art knowledge-sharing solutions for global enterprises, resulting in client savings of up to 20% and increased revenues, enhancing profitability for client and company.
- Achieved 222% of quota for FY 2001, generating $10.8M in revenues.

Project Manager/Technical Liaison (1999–2000)
- Served as key member of team responsible for development and implementation of Technical Operations Services and Support division's Technical Delivery Unit.
- Liaised between NASG Launch Team and technical advisor, ensuring all parties remained knowledgeable of organizational goals.
- Consulted with Analyst, CBU Specialist, and Sales Representatives to develop standard operating processes and procedures.

Manager of Technical Operations—CBU Senior Staff (1999)
- Developed and monitored efficient and productive teams with operations budget in excess of $10M annually.
- Directed activities of 47 personnel in areas of strategic operations, technical sales, and billable services.

135

Combination. *Lea J. Clark, Macon, Georgia*

The thin, empty box near the contact information serves as a graphic that ties together (1) the two pages of the resume and (2) the resume and the cover letter. See Cover Letter 24

Vince Conlan

(EXPERIENCE...CONTINUED)

Technical Program Manager (1997–1999)
- Led teams to generation of $200M in gross revenues over 21 months.
- Managed all aspects of production printing, technical equipment and application viability, product and customer support services, environmental configuration consultation, and training.
- Maintained responsibility for product validation and acquisition, vendor relations, and contract negotiations.

Service Marketing Manager (1996–1997)
Marketing Consultant (1993–1996)
Worldwide Product Manager (1991–1993)
Program Manager (1987–1991)
Senior Applications Consultant (1985–1987)
Product Marketing Consultant (1983–1985)
Senior Systems Analyst (1981–1983)

TECHNICAL SKILLS:

OS/Environments: TOS, DOS, MFT, MVS, TSO, CICS, IMS, OS2, Apple-OS, MAC-OS, VMS, UNIX, AIX, HPUX, MS-DOS, PC DOS, DR-DOS, Windows NT, Networks
Platforms/Protocols: Mainframes (IBM, Cray, Amdahl, Sperry, Univac, Burroughs); Minicomputers (Digital, Data General, HP, Compaq, Tandem, Texas Instruments); personal computers, servers, routers, hubs, switches, bridges; XNS, Ethernet, Token Ring, TCP/IP, Banyan VINES, Frame Relay, ATM, VPN, OSI
Software: Office suites (Lotus, Corel, Microsoft), printer descriptor languages (PostScript, HPCL, TROFF, ASCII, EBCDIC, Interpress), preprocessor applications (e.g., Adobe Acrobat), project management, document management, archiving/retrieving
Languages: FORTRAN, COBOL, PL/1, Assembler, RPG, C, C+, C++, Pascal, Visual Basic, BASIC, SQL, HTML
Hardware: PCs, servers, printers, scanners, and various peripherals
Networking: LAN, MAN, WAM, W-LAN, NAS and SAN, TCP/IP

EDUCATION:

Bachelor of Science in Mathematics—1977
California State University at Los Angeles—Maintained 3.86 GPA

TRAINING:

Managing People and Processes • Quality Improvement • Middle Management School • Inspecting for Quality
Leading Cross-Functionality • Measures of Quality • Advanced Management School • Leading the Enterprise
Leadership Through Quality • New Manager School • Problem-Solving Process • Effective Listening Skills
Business Leadership Series • Implementing Diversity • Exercising Influence • Managing Technical People

MEMBERSHIPS & AFFILIATIONS:

Member, Who's Who in America • Member, New Life Presbyterian Men's Council
Member, Alpha Phi Alpha Fraternity • Member, Des Moines Urban League

(page 400). The writer paid attention to phrase length, which led to a visually satisfying arrangement of capabilities at the end of the profile. Interesting arrow-tip bullets point to three important Career Accomplishments. Technical skills are conveniently grouped according to important categories.

WALTER BLAKE

98 Ben Franklin Drive		Home: (609) 444-1111
Cherry Hill, New Jersey 07896	walterblake@aol.com	Home Fax: (609) 444-2222

PROFILE

IT Project Manager with 24 years of experience directing cross-functional teams of technical experts to analyze systems and processes and implement infrastructure improvements. Recognized for leadership in planning, scheduling, crisis and risk management, and definition of scope for information systems projects. Proven record developing solutions that improve efficiency of IT and business operations. Cross-cultural experience, having worked both in England and Canada.

Expertise includes

- ☑ Project Management
- ☑ Strategic Business Planning
- ☑ Team Building/Leadership
- ☑ Diverse Market/Industry Knowledge

- ☑ Research & Analysis Skills
- ☑ Problem Identification & Resolution
- ☑ Cross-Cultural Communications
- ☑ Business/Project Strategy & Direction

PROFESSIONAL EXPERIENCE

HAWKSBURY SYSTEMS—New Jersey, NJ   Jan 2001–Present
Project Manager—IVR Replacement (Dec 2003–Present)

- Achieved project objectives, ensuring completion in a timely and cost-effective manner.
- Directed and negotiated terms with various vendors to replace existing IVR application, including coordinating with CGI for the development of IVR replacement application.
- Led project planning and management of internal resources for IVR replacement project, formulating strategies to improve business and operational processes; coordinated with IBM for voice support.

Technical Consultant—Infrastructure Outsourcing Project (Jul 2003–Present)

- Key player in the development of strategies for several in-house systems, including assisting with validation and data collection on all USII systems and development of test strategies for transitioned applications.
- Coordinated the planning and scheduling of hardware transitions with IBM, identifying needs and providing solutions where necessary.
- Planned and executed transition of hardware from Hawksbury to IBM premises in order to support USI applications with minimal impact to USI's business.

Project Manager—Pride Payne Proof of Concept (Sept 2002–Jul 2003)

- Instrumental in planning and executing innovative strategies to achieve objectives for infrastructure improvement; redefined scope of project and coordinated resources from Hawksbury and Pride Payne to progress project, resulting in a successful Proof of Concept demonstration to management in less than 3 weeks.
- Built and managed successful client relationships with IBM and Pride Payne, ensuring all business needs were met.
- Achieved all project objectives within a short period of time; defined Statement of Work for project with Pride Payne, identified server and application, created a copy of server and application at Pride Payne's office, and coordinated with Pride Payne to execute Statement of Work.

Service Manager—USII Division (Feb 2002–Sept 2002)

- Spearheaded efforts to develop successful communications between Customer Service area of Production Services and the IS area of USI; coordinated monthly meetings, maintaining and facilitating communication on projects, avoiding potential problems.
- Appointed as Account Manager for U.S. Insurance Division for Production Services, ensuring duties were properly performed and procedures followed.
- Initiated continual efforts to improve operations to achieve business targets by identifying opportunities to employ IT to enhance business opportunities.

136

Combination. *Jennifer Rushton, N. Richmond, New South Wales, Australia*

For a sense of an applicant's career development, read a resume backward. That is, start with the earliest job toward the end of the resume and read *up* the page(s) until you come to the

WALTER BLAKE   Page 2 of 2

Professional Experience Continued

Project Manager—Infrastructure for ASC Project (Jan 2001–Feb 2002)
- Led cross-functional teams in designing and implementing an infrastructure to support new GL; key strength is communicating project goals and maintaining focus on results throughout project life cycle.
- Championed project management of infrastructure changes required to support ASC project, including coordination between ASC project and production services, development of SLA to support ASC application, and coordination of operational readiness requirements.

ZURICH—New York, NY   Dec 1996–Jan 2001
Technology Services Year 2000 Coordinator (Feb 1998–Jan 2001)
- Instrumental in planning and coordinating upgrades and validation testing for all hardware and system software on all platforms for Year 2000 rollover; rollover was successful with no infrastructure problems.

Implementation Coordinator (Nov 1998–Dec 1999)
- Acted as direct liaison between SAP project and Technology Services teams; coordinated development of Interim SLA for SAP application and ensured all infrastructure changes required to support project were scheduled and completed on time.

Year 2000 Validation Team Leader (Dec 1996–Nov 1998)
- Spearheaded project objectives; defined strategy for Enterprise Time Machine Testing for Year 2000 compliance, led team carrying out Year 2000 compliance validation for CAPSIL, and planned and estimated Year 2000 compliance validation for 19 other applications.

INTERNATIONAL RESEARCH BOARD—New Jersey, NJ   Aug 1993–Nov 1996
Manager—Year 2000 Infrastructure Support Team (Apr 1996–Nov 1996)
- Oversaw testing of all tools for Year 2000 Project while defining testing strategy to ensure Year 2000 compliance; monitored and assisted Technology and Support Services with Year 2000 compliance.

Manager—Reset Development Team (Apr 1995–Apr 1996)
- Successfully transitioned support and ongoing development of Reset Development Project from software house to in-house staff.

Testing & Implementation Coordinator (Aug 1993–Apr 1995)
- Engineered testing and implementation for mainframe development project; executed system testing of interfaces between new system and existing system, tested existing downstream systems, carried out Acceptance Testing, and provided on-site support for release of new system.

AP ASSISTANCE CENTRE LTD—Birmingham, England   Apr 1992–Jul 1993
Business Analyst/Team Leader

HELMERK INTERNATIONAL LTD—Birmingham, England   Mar 1983–Feb 1992
Business Analyst

DIXILYN IMPERIAL PLC—Birmingham, England   Oct 1976–Mar 1983
Principal Analyst Programmer/Senior Analyst Programmer

PROFESSIONAL DEVELOPMENT

360 Management • Total Quality Management • Managing for Achievement • Purposeful Management • Getting Started & Applying PMW • SSADM Version 4 • Project Management & Control • Structured Testing • Introduction to Data Manager • Easytrieve Plus • System Analysis • APL & Advanced APL Programming • BASIC Programming • MVS/JCL Utilities • Structured Programming • COBOL Application Programming

current or most recent position. You will then better understand the profile, summary of qualifications, areas of expertise, or whatever else begins the resume. This resume, which documents chronologically the person's work experience and achievements, is perfect for this kind of analysis.

JAMES ROBERT

Results-driven, highly successful Information Technology Executive interested in applying proven project management and system conversion skills along with exceptional global team management ability to progressive IT leadership team.

EXECUTIVE SUMMARY

A flexible and seasoned **Information Technology Development Executive** with a proven background in **global multimillion-dollar project management.** Possess 19 years of successful, progressive experience in fixed-price and fixed-material projects, **legacy system maintenance,** software / system development, **offshore / onsite team management,** consulting, account development, and product development. Recognized as an effective, solution-oriented analyst who effectively **delivers seamless system conversions** for a **geographically diverse** range of clientele and industries across North America, Europe, the Middle East, and Asia. Exceptional ability to mentor emerging Project Managers and perform in challenging environments.

AREAS OF EXPERTISE

- Global Technology Systems Development
- Reverse Engineering & Re-engineering
- Information Technology Operations
- Program Management
- Onsite & Offshore Delivery Models
- Multicultural Team Building
- Legacy System Maintenance

TECHNICAL PROFICIENCIES

Operating Systems: Windows 2000 Professional & NT; MS Access & Project, Lotus Notes, Solaris, Oracle9i, Weblogic, UNIX.

Software Applications: PeopleSoft 7.54.1, EPM 8.02, Peopletools 7.5, Sheridan Active X Suite, Business Objects 5.1.2, Platinum, CICS, COBOL, BD2, DB2 Connect, MS SQL server, VB Visual Studio, J2EE, Rational Rose, RUP, ASP, Dream Weaver, Fireworks 3, RoboHelp, PVCS, Java, and Websphere.

HIGHLIGHTS OF ACCOMPLISHMENTS

ABC CORPORATION, Anytown, U.S.   2002 to Present
Associate Vice President / Onsite Program Director

Spearhead project management of IT process engineering and re-engineering for multimillion-dollar accounts, ensuring on-schedule and on-budget delivery of business process contracts. Hold full responsibility for project functions, including legacy systems maintenance, reverse engineering, re-engineering, project planning / implementation, and resource management. Oversee global onsite and offshore project coordination, monitoring product development and quality, remote connectivity, data security, and system integration. Engage in cross-functional team project coordination and deliver executive briefings.

- **Engineered** IT phase of a **multimillion-dollar** Business Process **Outsourcing Project** of the HR systems for a **Fortune 500** insurance company, executing knowledge and responsibility transfer of payroll for 50,000 employees 1 day **ahead of 45-day timeline** and **within budget.**

Continued...

5555 Apple Court ● Anytown, U.S. 55555 ● 555-555-5555 ● E-mail address

137

Combination. *Rita Fisher, Columbus, Indiana*

With contact information at the bottom of the page, the writer can display the most important information about the applicant at the top of the first page. The reader can see at any time a

➢ **Forged key relationships** with outgoing employees, gaining invaluable organizational insight and **allowing more efficient infrastructure transition** of multiple organizations.
➢ Currently **implementing 20-million euro legacy system conversion** for a leasing company on a 6-year business plan to be #3 in the European market, **preserving optimal features** of previous system **while enhancing system** to support present and future growth.
➢ **Streamlining onsite / offshore project** execution including 10 managers, 160 consultants, **18,000 function points,** and task of re-engineering the Offerings and Contract system in 8 months with **optimal resource utilization.**

XYZ COMPANY, Anytown, U.S.   1997 to 2002
Engagement (Program) Manager

Held full multimillion-dollar program management responsibility for offshore / onsite outsourcing teams and offshore development centers. Led ITO functions of reverse engineering and re-engineering, technology recommendation, and project planning and implementation. Presented effective proposal development and accurate project estimations to prospective clients. Assessed and redirected delinquent projects. Managed project budgets and resources. Oversaw help desk operations and third-party vendors.

➢ **Salvaged** a Y2K 12 million LOC **conversion project,** solving quality issues and **restoring project timeline, maintaining operation** of **35,000 trucks** for transportation company.
➢ **Won** 4 new accounts with **clientele** completely **unfamiliar with** application **outsourcing** and maintenance, delivering system conversions **beyond customer expectations.**
➢ **Pioneered innovative outsourcing** delivery **model** of an 80% offshore / 20% onsite 80-member team distribution for large insurance company, **capturing cost savings of 43%** and seamlessly enhancing applications while maintaining legacy technology.
➢ **Selected** for **superior management ability** to participate in Project Management Program, **earning PMI certification** and subsequently mentoring 30 project managers.

ABC CONTROL CORPORATION, Anytown, Somewhere in Europe   1996 to 1997
Project Manager

Directed preparations of project proposals and built client inroads for client/server development and Y2K conversion projects. Conducted contract negotiations, setting work specifications and financial terms. Supervised onsite and offshore delivery teams and maintained standard operational methodology for legacy system conversions.

➢ **Successfully managed company's first onsite / offshore team** for a 15 million LOC Y2K conversion, monitoring project progress and delivering technology products on schedule.
➢ Collaborated on **Y2K conversion project** to maintain operations for **3 major European banks.**

XYZ CONSULTANTS, Anytown, U.S.   1987 to 1996
Product Manager

Rapidly promoted from Senior Systems Analyst to product management. Developed in-house and third-party products utilizing Ingress, Oracle, and UNIX. Directly involved in product development and launch. Engineered sales and marketing of products, consistently exceeding sales projections. Supervised a consulting branch office and related third-party collaborations. Assisted with ISO certification and business process re-engineering projects.

Continued...

number for calling the applicant. The profile in bold italic is center-aligned for an initial impression of symmetry. The resume ends with center-alignment on page three. A distinctive feature of this resume is the boldfacing of important words and phrases in the Executive Summary and bulleted achievements for each

➢ **Completed fixed-price** integrated software development **assignments under** previously ineffective **constraints** of isolated development or undefined scope of assignment.
➢ **Forged** new **consulting operations** in undeveloped territories, completing strategy studies and migration assignments.

PROFESSIONAL CERTIFICATION & DEVELOPMENT

Project Management Institute, Member
Effective Negotiating—Karrass
Advanced Project Management—Syntel

EDUCATION

Post-Graduate Diploma in Management
NAME OF INSTITUTION, ANYTOWN, U.S.

Master of Arts in Philosophy
NAME OF UNIVERSITY, ANYTOWN, U.S.

Bachelor of Arts in Accounting
NAME OF UNIVERSITY, ANYTOWN, U.S.

of the four jobs held. Having an Executive Summary at the beginning of the document is itself distinctive. It shows that the writer knows what technical and business executives expect to find at the beginning of a document.

Law

Resumes at a Glance

RESUME NO.	OCCUPATION	GOAL	PAGE
138.	Assistant Property Manager	Legal Assistant	285
139.	Associate General Counsel	Corporate Counsel	286
140.	Senior Counsel	Not specified	288
141.	Counsel	Corporate Counsel	290
142.	Legal Assistant	Legal Asst./Paralegal Asst.	292

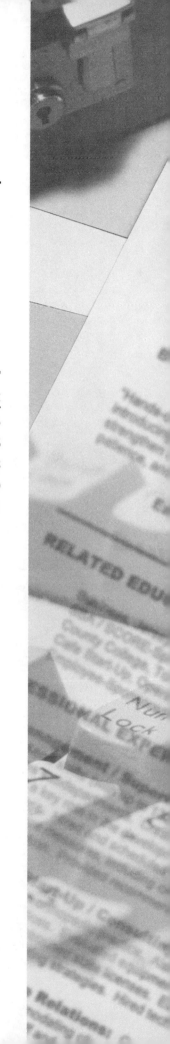

Shawna Peterson

2804 Lawndale Sugarland, TX 77862 H: 713-682-5357 C: 713-679-8953 e-mail: shawna_peterson@yahoo.com

LEGAL ASSISTANT

Energetic new graduate experienced in property management with core strengths in creative problem solving, negotiating conflicts and motivating others toward goals.

ACHIEVEMENTS

- *Implemented professional property management practices:* Generate 5–10 new tenant leases per month; close leases of 2–3 tenants per month.
- *Secured the lease on a client who had been targeted for several years:* Built professional relationships and provided proactive communication of open properties in response to client needs.
- *Saved $600 annually in certified mail:* Transitioned to telecommunication of rent notification.
- *Financed 100% of college education:* Full / part-time employment and scholarships.

EDUCATION

TEXAS A&M, College Station, Texas—***Bachelor of Applied Arts and Sciences***—May 2003.
- Representative Coursework—Legal Assistant, Criminal Justice, Literature Writing, Real Estate Law, Corporate Law, Criminal Law, Law Office Management, Research Methods.
- Recognized "program pioneer" as one of first to graduate with the legal assistant degree.
- Proficient in Microsoft Office suite, WordPerfect and legal office management software.

PROFESSIONAL EXPERIENCE

Assistant Property Manager   September 2000–present
<u>Ronald Craiger Properties</u>—Sugarland, Texas
Ronald Craiger Properties is a property management firm specializing in commercial leasing with approximately 300 current tenants. The position of Assistant Property Manager is primarily responsible for account management—including overdue account collection, building relationships with real estate representatives and reporting account summaries to the owner.

Challenge: **Minimize confrontation in "Lock-Out" process** with tenants of overdue accounts.
Action: Analyzed legal terms of tenants' lease agreements, commercial lease and lease history.
Result: Conduct tenant "Lock-Out" processes with confidence and professionalism while maintaining firm's positive reputation so as to secure new, revenue-generating tenants.
***

Challenge: **Manage account collection with limited records** of accounts paid, overdue or unpaid.
Action: Researched firm's 300 tenant accounts: 10–15% were overdue and 5% of these were not paid for 5 months. Tenants were personally notified and informed of their account status.
Result: Positive tenant rapport was achieved and 100% of accounts were either brought current or closed. Developed a monthly report to keep the owner informed of tenant status.

Legal Assistant—Part-time   March 2000–present
<u>William Mead—Corporate Attorney</u>—Sugarland, Texas
Special project—managed, organized and developed a file system for the firm's real estate files.

Legal Assistant—Internship   Spring 1999
<u>David McDowell—Corporate Attorney at Law</u>—Sugarland, Texas
Organized corporate client books.

138

Combination. *MeLisa Rogers, Victoria, Texas*

The writer turned a resume template that lacked zest into a professional document that showcases the talents and achievements of this new graduate to appeal to law firms in metropolitan areas.

Roberta Jennings

555 E. Alabama Avenue • Aurora, CO 00000 • 555.555.5555 • rjesq@atti.net

Corporate Counsel

Accomplished corporate counsel with more than seven years of experience devising and implementing practical solutions to complex problems. Skilled in dispute resolution and client management. Articulate communicator and clear, concise writer with polished presentation and interpersonal skills. Impeccable ethics and integrity.

Areas of Expertise

Real Estate • Transportation • Commercial Transactions

Professional Credentials

Admitted to Colorado Bar, 1992
Juris Doctor, University of Denver, College of Law (Top 20% of Class)

Legal Expertise

- Property Acquisition/Sales/Transfer
- Property Leases/Deeds
- Trespass Claims/Relocation Issues
- Easements/Right of Way
- Tower Site Agreements
- Evictions
- Default Letters/Releases
- Condemnation Actions

Professional Experience

The Broe Companies, Inc., Denver, CO   **1996–2002**

Associate General Counsel since 1999. In-house counsel for privately held company with holdings and operations in commercial real estate, senior living communities, railroad and related transportation services and healthcare technology. Served as Director of Legal Affairs, 1996–1999. Legal expertise includes

Contracts	Managed contracts process, including negotiations, dispute resolution and collections for equipment sales and leases; commercial property acquisitions and leases; vendor agreements; confidentiality agreements; service agreements for start-up operations.

✓ Processed high volumes of contracts in short timeframes. Meticulously reviewed each contract. Prudently selected points to argue, winning them in negotiations.

✓ Successfully negotiated corporate accounting and telecommunications software usage contracts.

Litigation Management	Directed and determined litigation and resolution strategy for commercial, property and personal injury disputes; prepared reports advising CEO, CFO and Managing Director of status of company legal matters. Served as the liaison between corporate and outside counsel and facilitated exchange of information.

✓ Selected and retained outside counsel as needed. Weighed the merits/costs of the case against the efforts necessary to establish relationship with outside counsel and made go/no-go decisions.

✓ Strived for speedy resolution through mediation and arbitration to reduce costs.

✓ Encouraged clients/departments to budget for litigation to meet budget objectives.

139

Combination. *Roberta F. Gamza, Louisville, Colorado*

The individual wanted to test the waters and see how marketable she was. The writer demonstrated the person's value and growth within her profession. A distinctive feature is the use of

R o b e r t a   J e n n i n g s

Intellectual Property	Managed company's intellectual property portfolio and provided advice on trademark-related issues.
	✓ Creatively resolved several naming disputes, avoiding costly litigation.
Human Resources	Handled resolution of wrongful termination, discrimination, sexual harassment and ADA claims; provided counsel on immigration matters, use of independent contractors, and development of personnel policies and procedures.
	✓ Resolved more than 80% of discrimination and wrongful-termination claims without incurring incremental costs and avoiding lengthy litigation.
Risk Management	Served as primary liaison between subsidiaries and insurance carriers; evaluated, monitored and settled claims; ensured compliance with policy reporting requirements. Provided legal assistance in company's efforts to establish captive insurance company.
	✓ Established timely notifications and accurate record keeping of all incidents and claims.
	✓ Interpreted insurance coverage/policies for all concerned parties.
Corporate Formation Records Maintenance	Supervised formation and records maintenance for company subsidiaries structured as corporations, limited liability companies and partnerships.
	✓ Formed companies in 20 different states, Canada and the Caribbean.
	✓ Developed database and maintained accurate corporate records in compliance with IRS regulations for 200 companies.

Law Office of Bertrand F. Marsh, P.C., Denver, CO   1994–1995
Associate Attorney. Firm's primary undertaking was defense of a Fortune 500 company in multimillion-dollar litigation involving sale of product technology. Supervised paralegal team in responding to discovery requests; responsible for privilege review of documents responsive to discovery requests.

Project Attorney, Denver, CO   1992–1993
Clients included Colorado Attorney General Department of Natural Resources and PRC Environmental Consulting, Inc., a U.S. Environmental Protection Agency contractor. Research and writing regarding federal and state hazardous substances, water and air-quality regulations in support of state's position in clean-up negotiations. Investigation, verification of evidence and compilation of reports for use by EPA in identifying and bringing actions against potentially responsible parties in environmental clean-up actions.

Affiliations
Member, American Corporate Counsel Association
Member, Colorado Bar Association

Education
J.D.   University of Denver, College of Law, Denver, CO, 1991
B.A.   International Studies, Rutgers University, New Brunswick, NJ, 1986

two columns to indicate—by categories in the left column and details in the right column—the person's areas of expertise at the most recent workplace. Check-mark bullets draw attention to achievements listed for each of the categories. The two columns add to the impression of adequate white space.

NICHOLAS T. SPERRY

6880 Whitney Avenue • New York, New York 00000
(555) 555–5555
NTSPERRY788@cox.net

CAREER PROFILE

Experienced attorney with expertise in corporate law, bankruptcy/insolvency, commercial lending and commercial real estate in banking and private-practice environments.

- Effective litigator in both state and federal courts. Successful negotiator of complex transactions and contracts.
- Preparation of opinion letters, loan documents, pleadings, contracts and memoranda.
- Strengths include cultivating and managing client relationships, marketing and business development. Computer proficient in legal research software.

PROFESSIONAL EXPERIENCE

TRANS-AMERICA CORPORATION, Madison, New York   1993–present
Senior Counsel/Department Head—Legal Services Unit

Direct law department and professional staff of multibillion-dollar financial services division. Manage personal portfolio of active litigation and transaction matters while overseeing caseloads of legal staff. Represent organization in bankruptcy and collection proceedings (foreclosures, replevins, liquidations) and in defensive litigation. Provide counsel to internal management and account officers.

- Resolved numerous litigation and workout cases, resulting in $29M in cash recoveries for division within first year after assuming department leadership.
- Expanded client services to include defensive litigation and loan closings for Commercial Lending and Community Banking divisions.
- Effectively negotiated complex Chapter 11 bankruptcies, including cash collateral orders and reorganization plans.
- Negotiated and drafted documents for real estate and asset-based loan workouts and restructures.
- Drafted master environmental engineering contract used in all site assessments organization-wide.
- Educated officers, division senior staff and law department personnel on various legal issues including bankruptcy, eviction process and limited liability companies.

MANAGEMENT CORPORATION LAW DEPARTMENT, Hartford, Connecticut   1991–1993
Senior Counsel/Litigation Team Leader   1992–1993
Counsel   1991–1992

Promoted to manage litigation team specializing in legal issues and remedies of FDIC, including application of FIRREA and FDIC authority in liquidation of failed banking institutions. Managed personal portfolio averaging 60 high-profile corporate cases. Counsel to approval committees, providing written legal opinions to support proposed settlements/restructures. Researched FDIC, fraud and bankruptcy issues.

- Represented organization in bankruptcies, foreclosures, liquidations, collections and deeds-in-lieu of foreclosures, resulting in multimillion-dollar cash recoveries each quarter.
- Negotiated and drafted documents for commercial real estate and asset-based workouts.
- Trained loan assistants on Article 9 filings, and all officers and legal staff on bankruptcy issues.

140

Combination. *Louise Garver, Enfield, Connecticut*

Rather than provide a traditional curriculum vitae, the writer created this resume, which focuses on the applicant's professional achievements to set him apart from the competition. The resume

NICHOLAS T. SPERRY • Page 2

PETERSON, SCHMIDT AND TOWNSEND, P.C., New York, New York   1985–1991
Associate

Managed diverse caseload in commercial lending, commercial real estate and corporate law for large private legal practice. Incorporated businesses and formed limited partnerships, including preparation of incorporation documents, shareholder and partnership agreements and certificates of limited partnerships. Negotiated and drafted employment contracts and licensing agreements.

- ◆ Negotiated and drafted loan documents, and closed commercial real estate and asset-based loans of up to $10M.
- ◆ Restructured $55 million line of credit for a major retail chain and represented buyers in a stock purchase for an automotive parts business.
- ◆ Researched Regulation D and Regulation A private offerings and assisted senior counsel in preparing Form D documents and prospectus.
- ◆ Developed and marketed expertise in bankruptcy, foreclosures and loan workouts through informational seminars for officers of financial institutions.
- ◆ Generated $300,000-plus annually for the firm and maintained a full-time caseload from new business developed.

COLE, DAVIS AND ROBINSON, P.C., New York, New York   Summers 1984–1985
Law Clerk
OFFICE OF THE U.S. ATTORNEY, New York, New York   Summers 1983–1984
Law Clerk

EDUCATION

J.D., NEW YORK UNIVERSITY SCHOOL OF LAW, New York, New York, 1985
B.A. (Political Science), HARVARD UNIVERSITY, Cambridge, Massachusetts, 1982

Additional
Advance Trial Practice Training, National Institute of Trial Advocacy, 1994

ADMISSIONS and MEMBERSHIPS

New York Bar, 1985
District of New York Federal Court, 1986
New York Bar Association, Commercial Law & Bankruptcy Section

"drew a 100% response rate for positions in corporate and private practice environments in his specialty areas." For the past three workplaces, the writer uses diamond bullets and boldfacing to direct attention to achievements. A pair of lines encloses each main heading.

DENNIS E. RIGGS

1234 Carrolton Drive • Bloomington, IL 61704 • 309.555.5555 • deRiggs@aol.com

CORPORATE COUNSEL
Litigation Management ~ Attorney Management

Dynamic, proactive Corporate Counsel with **multiple responsibilities and the ability to direct a large staff. Outstanding leadership and teambuilding strengths** that generate optimum productivity and performance from legal staff. Excellent communication and presentation skills. Proven capabilities in litigation, mediation, and arbitration. Supervise the selection process for retaining outside attorneys.

Possess the vision necessary to develop and implement successful action plans. Demonstrated proficiency directing multiple ongoing cases in a productive and cost-effective manner.

Areas of Expertise

◆ Litigation Management	◆ Institutional Litigation
◆ Attorney Management	◆ Organizational Compliance
◆ Arbitration/Mediation	◆ Mentoring/Teambuilding
◆ Legal Review	◆ Claim Audits
◆ Risk Management/Remedial Measures	◆ Project Management

Professional Experience

LIBERTY MUTUAL INSURANCE, *Bloomington, IL*
Counsel	2002–Present
Assistant Counsel	1998–2002
Attorney	1997–1998

Promoted twice over a five-year period after demonstrating exceptional legal and managerial expertise. Acknowledged for superior interpersonal skills and the ability to interface with individuals of all levels.

Leadership:
Senior Management Bonus Committee member; Legal Resource Management Committee member; Section Interview Team; Corporate Summer Intern Mentor; About Our Business Table Leader—Selected to conduct multiple six-hour corporate business presentations to all staff, from administrative to executive level personnel.

Litigation:
Manage complex institutional bad-faith litigation for the state of West Virginia (trial and appellate).

- Select and hire attorneys, assign cases, and oversee all aspects of the litigation (state and federal).
- Review suits, evaluate corporate institutional exposure, and formulate strategies. Conduct interviews of company employees to determine exposure of cases.
- Determine whether to proceed to trial or negotiate settlements.
- Provide updates to executive management concerning multimillion-dollar exposure cases. Advise on strategy, progress, and resolution.
- Direct trial/deposition preparation of all levels of institutional personnel (administrative to executive).
- Additional duties include the management, review, and assignment of cases in other states on an as-needed basis.
- Assist in drafting public relations message points concerning high-profile cases.
- Television interview preparation of retained counsel concerning insurance industry issues.

Managerial Responsibilities:
Managed all phases of the litigation budget and supervision of 10 to 15 outside attorneys and staff.

- Interview, select, and negotiate the contracts of outside attorneys.
- Assist in the formulation of corporate legislative strategies for West Virginia.
- Create remedial measures/risk-management strategies concerning institutional litigation.
- Interview prospective in-house attorneys for the corporate law department and provide hiring recommendations.
- Conduct corporate executive and regional management presentations as needed concerning status of institutional litigation. Report on compliance issues.
- Interview corporate summer interns and provide hiring recommendations.
- Conduct statewide claim file audits.
- Accountable for the approval of all litigation fees and expenses with check-signing duties.
- Assist in the administration of support-staff evaluation.

141

Combination. *Beverley and Mitchell I. Baskin, Marlboro, New Jersey*

Boldfacing makes key information stand out in the profile. Large diamond bullets direct attention to each area of expertise. Four categories—Leadership, Litigation, Managerial

Page Two   **DENNIS E. RIGGS**

Professional Experience *(Continued)*

Corporate Achievements:
- Supervised more bad-faith jury trials than any other member of the department.
- Authored corporate law department's *Guidelines for Employee Deposition Preparation.*
- Managerial responsibility for two of Liberty Mutual's top five institutional bad-faith states (volume and financial exposure): Pennsylvania, '97 to '98 and West Virginia, '98 to present.

LIBERTY MUTUAL INSURANCE, *Baltimore, MD*
Claim Litigation Counsel   1992–1997

Trial counsel for lawsuits ranging from auto bodily-injury claims to premises liability injuries. Composed opinion letters related to potential exposures. Prepared all motions and other materials needed for trial. Conducted EUO (fraud investigations) proceedings of insureds and provided advice on the merits of claims (accept or deny). Assisted in the interviewing and hiring recommendations of prospective in-house trial attorneys.
- Tried more jury trials than any other member of the 300+-member department.
- Selected to provide presentations to claim management on trial strategy.
- First-chaired approximately 100 jury trials, which required excellent time-management and organizational skills.
- First-chaired approximately 40 bench trials; conducted approximately 200 to 250 depositions.
- First-chaired approximately 30 arbitration/mediations.
- Demonstrated ability to communicate thoughts and ideas to advance the causes of individual insureds, as well as the corporation.
- Supervised and trained younger attorneys and summer interns.

KESSLER, HARDY AND FARRELL, *Landover, MD*
Associate   1991–1992
Law Clerk   1989–1991

Practices included insurance and medical malpractice defense. Drafted motions, legal memoranda, opinion letters, and briefs concerning a variety of insurance and medical issues. Drafted all forms of discovery and conducted depositions. Second-chaired medical malpractice trial.

LIBERTY MUTUAL INSURANCE, *Fairmont, WV, and Frederick, MD*
Claims Representative   1986–1988

Responsible for all phases of the investigation, evaluation, and negotiation of automobile claims presented by insureds and claimants for bodily injuries and property damage.

Personal Lines Underwriter (Intern)   1985

Assisted in the evaluation and determination of the acceptance of insurance risks involving personal property.

Education

UNIVERSITY OF MARYLAND SCHOOL OF LAW, Baltimore, MD ~ Juris Doctor   1990
FAIRMONT STATE COLLEGE, Fairmont, WV ~ BS (Cum Laude), Business Management 1985
All-American—Football

Bar Admissions and Affiliations

Maryland   1990
District of Columbia   1992
U.S. Court of Appeals, District of Columbia   1992
U.S. District Court, Maryland   1992
U.S. Court of Appeals, Fourth Circuit   1992
U.S. District Court, District of Columbia   1992

CPCU—Insurance Institute of America, ongoing
Multiple national institutional litigation seminars
Powell/Tate Media Communications Training (print & television)
National Institute of Trial Advocacy School—Diploma   1994
Licensed Maryland Real Estate Agent
Automobile Insurance Claim School
Basic Insurance Claim Course
Basic Insurance Course
Personal Lines Underwriting Course
Toastmasters International

Responsibilities, and Corporate Achievements—are used to indicate aspects of the applicant's professional experience at the Bloomington, Illinois, site of his employer. Smaller type enables the reporting of more information in the allotted space. Dates of promotions are easily seen.

PATRICIA JUHASZ

555 Riddle Avenue • Smithtown, NY 55555 • (888) 999-0000 • Pjuhasz@telcomm.net

Legal Assistant/Paralegal Assistant

Experienced Legal Assistant with excellent office management and client-attorney relation skills seeking an entry-level Paralegal Assistant position where a working knowledge of legal terminology, general law, and legal proceedings, and continuing education in Paralegal Studies will be utilized and expanded. Bring experience working within a Legal Department/Collection Agency environment in the following select areas:

*Civil Litigation…Collections…Settlements…Affidavits…Skip Tracing…Attorney Sourcing & Selection
Bankruptcies…Judgments…Liens…Summons & Complaint…Estate Searches…Statute of Limitations*

PROFESSIONAL EXPERIENCE

Legal Assistant, Legal Recoveries, Inc., Lake Grove, NY   1998–present

Joined this Collection Agency's legal department at a time of unit-wide staffing changes. Responsible for managing a high volume of civil litigation case files for major accounts that partially included Century Detection, Credit Union of New York, AB Bank National Association, and St. Mary's Hospital.

- Collaborate extensively with internal departments including collections, medical billing, finance, production, special projects, and clerical to obtain, verify, and process documentation pertaining to the status of more than 50 weekly referred collections cases forwarded to the legal department.
- Carefully source and select nationally based bonded attorneys utilizing the *American Lawyers Quarterly, Commercial Bar Directory, National Directory List,* and *Columbia Directory List;* determine the appropriate choice upon obtainment and review of résumés, copies of insurance policies, and court filing fees.
- Perform estate searches and integrate traditional investigative methods and the DAKCS database system to gather account histories and case-sensitive documentation for attorneys including
    debtors and guarantors, credit bureau reports, court affidavits, judgments, skip-tracing records, bankruptcy notices, banking statements, proof of statute of limitations, proof of assets, and trial letters
- Maintain communications with attorneys and clients from point of referral/discovery to trial phase to facilitate and expedite case settlements that historically award clients a minimum of 80% in recovered funds.

EDUCATION

Bachelor of Science in Paralegal Studies, 1998
ST. JOSEPH'S COLLEGE, Brentwood, NY

COMPUTER SKILLS

DOS/Windows 2000; WordPerfect and Microsoft Word; DAKCS

EARLIER WORK HISTORY

Administrative Assistant, State Insurance, Patchogue, NY	1997–1998
Office Support Assistant, Financial Association of America, Inc., Islip, NY	1995–1997
Appointment Coordinator, Phlebotomy Services, Huntington, NY	1991–1996
Senior Office Support Assistant, AB National Bank, Hicksville, NY	1986–1991

Professional References Provided upon Request

142

Combination. *Ann Baehr, Brentwood, New York*

The focus is on the most relevant experience. Earlier experience is put near the bottom. Keywords are used to indicate areas of expertise at the end of the profile. The page border is shadowed.

Law Enforcement

Resumes at a Glance

RESUME NO.	OCCUPATION	GOAL	PAGE
143.	Receptionist	Law Enforcement	295
144.	Patrol Supervisor, U.S. Air Force	Not specified	296
145.	Lieutenant, Detective Division	Not specified	298
146.	Assistant Chief of Police	Law Enforcement Official	300
147.	Senior Parole Officer	Not specified	302

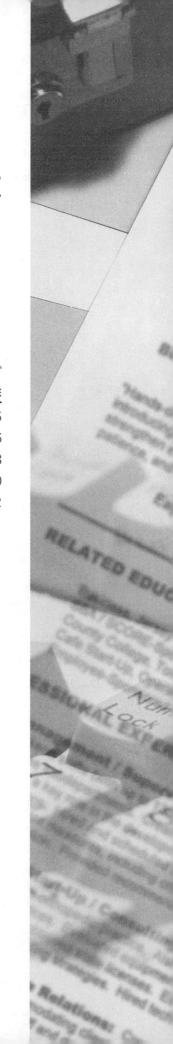

JENNIFER GONZALES

334–30 Kissena Blvd., Flushing, NY 55555 ● (555) 222-7777 ● JGonzales@lawandorder.net

Seeking a position in the field of

Law Enforcement

CITY——STATE——FEDERAL——PRIVATE

➢ Highly motivated, energetic law enforcement student with strong work ethic and professional goals.
➢ Bring five years of experience in office support and retail sales positions while attending college full time.
➢ Bilingual with an articulate fluency in English and Spanish; personable, easygoing communication style.
➢ Meet challenges head on; work well in stressful situations and in a fast-paced setting.
➢ Analytical with a lot of common sense, intuitive instincts, and ability to think outside of the box.
➢ Maintain excellent research, organization, time-management, and problem-assessment/resolution skills.

Education

Bachelor of Arts, Forensic Psychology—expected August 2004
John Jay College of Criminal Justice, New York, NY
Honors Candidate: Psi Chi Chapter National Honor Society in Psychology

Academically trained in criminalistics and psychology:

Select Courses: Analysis of Criminal Behavior, Concepts of Forensic Science, Abnormal Psychology,
Physical Fitness in Law Enforcement, Criminal Law, Group Dynamics
Select Projects: Crime Scene Observation, Forensic Study of Microscopic Fibers, Fingerprint Analysis

Work Experience

Receptionist, Volvoville, Massapequa, NY	4/98–Present
Payroll Clerk, People's Alliance Federal Credit Union, Hauppauge, NY	4/00–7/00
Sales Associate, Annie Sez, East Northport, NY	2/98–6/98
Senior Sales Associate, Rainbow Shops, Commack/Bay Shore, NY	9/97–2/98

● Provide front-desk representation, clerical support, and customer service for Volvo and subsidiary, Land Rover, directing customer traffic with a proven ability to maintain open lines of communication.

● Managed more than 50 business payroll accounts utilizing cross-trained experience in teller and payroll services.

● Prepared and uploaded weekly exempt/non-exempt payroll data into network system for clients to download.

● Completed mandatory training that included a film study on a mock robbery to learn observation techniques.

● Held increasingly responsible sales positions, achieving recognition for over-quota floor sales and cashier management skills, and manager-requests to return during school breaks based on performance and reliability.

● Provided excellence in customer service while assisting in all areas of inventory and display merchandising.

Computer Skills

Windows XP/Me; Microsoft Word, LexisNexis, PsychInfo, Criminal Justice Abstracts,
InfoTrak Health, Sociological Abstracts, Internet research

143

Combination. *Ann Baehr, Brentwood, New York*

Making explicit four areas of interest—city, state, federal, and private—directly below the Law Enforcement heading reduced the risk that this new graduate would be limited to just one area of interest in her job search.

BRUCE S. ALEXANDER

1010-L Park South Drive ▪ Charlotte, NC 28888
Home: (704) 555-5555   Cell: (704) 666-1111
shadowman@mindspring.com

CAREER PROFILE

Results-oriented professional with more than 15 years of security management and law enforcement experience in both the military and private sector, including drug surveillance, anti-terrorism activities, nuclear security and operations leadership. Highly developed situational problem-solving and analytical skills. Advanced knowledge of military (grounds) weapons, special experience identification (SEI) training and drug-testing procedures. Expert Marksman and Security Craftsman (7-Skill Level). Consistently commended for professionalism and outstanding performance—played key role in several major operations and investigations. Qualified by:

▪ Investigative Techniques	▪ Emergency Response	▪ Cross-Cultural Relations
▪ Conflict Resolution	▪ Search & Seizure	▪ Physical Security & Theft Prevention
▪ Supervision & Training	▪ Technical Surveillance	▪ Community Partnerships

---

AWARDS & RECOGNITION

- Air Force Achievement Medal (First Oak Leaf Cluster) for Outstanding Achievement, 1992
- Air Force Achievement Medal for Outstanding Achievement, 1987
- Air Force Commendation Medal, 1987
- Armed Forces Expeditionary Medal, 2001
- National Defense Service Medal, 1990–1991

PROFESSIONAL EXPERIENCE

U.S. AIR FORCE—Charleston, SC   2001–2004
Patrol Supervisor
Second-in-command of day-to-day operations. Led and trained staff of 15–20 personnel, including supervisory staff of 5. Conducted general law enforcement protection activities. Apprehended, controlled and detained suspects. Conducted interviews with witnesses and suspects. Provided first-responder action. Developed, planned and implemented security force programs.

- Participated in supervisory capacity in "Operation Enduring Freedom/Noble Eagle" in response to the World Trade Center and Pentagon attacks. As member of 13-person team, provided surveillance and security for sites in Spain, Italy, Saudi Arabia, Afghanistan, Pakistan, Turkmenistan and Uzbekistan. Conducted interrogations of two Saudi intelligence officers.

- Received Armed Forces Expeditionary Medal for contributions in training of U.S. Armed Forces personnel in intelligence gathering and security operations.

- Participated in apprehension of 44 illegal aliens, serving as preliminary investigator. Performed discovery and analysis; interviewed suspects, gathered evidence and filed report.

- Played key role in defusing many internal incidents involving military personnel (e.g., smuggling and illegal possession of firearms, criminal domestic violence and violent assault altercations).

144

Combination. *Doug Morrison, Charlotte, North Carolina*

The individual was seeking a new position in law enforcement with either a federal or state agency. He possessed a strong security, surveillance, and covert operations background in the

-2-

MONTGOMERY COUNTY SPECIAL POLICE & SAFETY SERVICE, INC.—Raleigh, NC   1996–2001
Special Police Officer (1999–2001)
Security Officer (1996–1999)
Provided security service to 12 Bank of America facilities. Investigated suspicious activities, complaints and reports of violence. Worked with other law enforcement officers throughout the Raleigh area.

- Improved charge/arrest rate through better surveillance while providing onsite security.

- Arrested 15 suspects for acts of domestic violence, B&E, traffic felonies and possession of illegal drugs.

U.S. AIR FORCE—Southeast Region, U.S.   March–July 1992
Shift Leader, Night Crew
Supervised 13-member team as leader during a major drug operation in southwestern U.S. Collaborated directly with U.S. Border Patrol, U.S. Customs Service and local police officials.

- Directed designated activities during 3½-month covert investigation of a major drug enterprise leading to the seizure of 250 lbs. of marijuana, 6 kilos of uncut cocaine, 1 lb. of crystal methamphetamine ("ice") and 1 lb. of heroin, and the indictment of numerous individuals.

- Awarded the Air Force Achievement Medal for outstanding service achievement, March 1993:

> Recognized by senior officials for "outstanding achievement while performing as team member of Joint Task Force Six Mission . . ." Cited by commander for "playing vital role in this unique narcotics smuggling activity," including surveillance, analysis of intelligence reports, mapping of reconnaissance areas and instruction and supervision of personnel.

U.S. AIR FORCE—Charleston, SC   1990–1991
Fire Team Leader/Squad Leader (Staff Sergeant, E-5)
Assigned to 315th Security Force Squadron (SFS)/437th SFS, Charleston A.F.B.
Participated in air base security activities to protect federal government resources and property in Cairo, Egypt vicinity, as well as Joint Task Force in Southwest Asia. Worked closely with Egyptian military police and Special Forces, among others.

Security Specialist (Sergeant, E-4)—Kirtland AFB, Albuquerque, NM (1985–1989)
Led 2-person team. Planned, coordinated and supervised field threat protection (Level 1) operations.

- Distinguished with the Air Force Achievement Medal (contributions during July 28–September 2, 1987 mission) and the Air Force Commendation Medal (identification of sniper location, use of cross-cultural diplomacy, among other mission activities in Europe).

EDUCATION

B.S., Human Sciences, Gardner-Webb University, Boiling Springs, NC, 1996
A.A.S., Law Enforcement Technology, Central Piedmont Community College, Charlotte, NC, 1994
U.S. Air Force: N.C.O. Preparatory Course, *Distinguished Graduate,* (2nd among 52), 1988; N.C.O. Academy, 1996; Security Forces Training (7-Skill Level), 1999. **Civilian:** Introduction to Community Policing, January 2000; BLET, State of NC, 2000

military—in both domestic and international operations. The writer created a three-column box in the Career Profile section to draw attention to important qualifications. Another box on the second page makes conspicuous the person's Air Force Achievement Medal for outstanding service.

CHARLES WILSON

2158 Hampton Lane, Cincinnati, OH 45219
513.426.9568
cwilson@ci.cincinnati.oh.us

CAREER PROFILE

A results-oriented, high-energy LAW ENFORCEMENT LIEUTENANT with 20+ years of progressively responsible experience in the Public Service area. Highly developed administrative and analytical skills as evidenced by the ability to continuously improve division operations. Qualified by:

Investigative Techniques	DEA Certification	Evidence Collection
Police Media Relations	Supervision & Training	Emergency Response
Conflict Resolution	Search & Seizure	Technical Surveillance
Protection Programs	Defense Management	Professional Development

PROFESSIONAL EXPERIENCE

CINCINNATI POLICE DEPARTMENT, Cincinnati, OH   1984–Present

Lieutenant of Detective Division, 1997–Present
Lieutenant of Patrol Division, 1996–1997
Sergeant of Patrol Division, 1994–1996
Detective Division—Forensics, 1992–1994
Field Training Officer, 1989–1992
Patrol Officer, 1984–1989
Prior police experience in various security positions, 1981–1984

KEY ACCOMPLISHMENTS

- Supervise seven investigators assigned 330+ cases per year who gather and analyze sufficient evidence in major crime cases, resulting in an average solvability rate of 40%.

- Supervised three-year investigation of a major drug enterprise leading to the seizure of 200 kilos of cocaine and the indictment of 40+ individuals on state and federal charges.

- Increased charge rate 10% due to advanced investigative techniques and technology training.

- Redesigned police department schedules to allow for 100 hours per year of in-service training for all officers in the department.

- Modernized Detective Division's infrastructure by purchasing new computers and reconfiguring office space to allow for increased communications.

- Equipped cruisers with laptop computers and CAD-RMS (Computer-Aided Dispatch—Records Management System) software, increasing report-writing efficiency and reducing paperwork 80% for Patrol Division officers.

- Led Patrol Division with 50 drunk-driving arrests, accounting for 10% of total arrests.

- Updated forensic lab equipment and coordinated training for all officers, leading to increased evidence-collection capabilities for the police department.

- "Police Officer of the Month" presented by the Cincinnati Police Department—October 1993.

145

Combination. *Sharon Pierce-Williams, Findlay, Ohio*

During 20 years of working for the police department, this detective never needed a resume. He was completing a BA degree; thinking of retiring from the force; considering future career

CHARLES WILSON

2158 Hampton Lane, Cincinnati, OH 45219
513.426.9568
cwilson@ci.cincinnati.oh.us

Page 2

EDUCATION

UNIVERSITY of CINCINNATI, Cincinnati, OH
Bachelor of Arts Degree
Major: Criminal Justice
GPA: 4.0 Anticipated Graduation: 2004

TERRA COMMUNITY COLLEGE, Fremont, OH
Associate in Law Enforcement Degree
GPA: 3.84 *Magna Cum Laude*
Distinguished Alumni Award, 2001

NORTHWESTERN UNIVERSITY TRAFFIC INSTITUTE, Evanston, IL
School of Police Staff and Command (19 semester hours)

FEDERAL BUREAU of INVESTIGATION NATIONAL ACADEMY, Quantico, VA
Criminal Justice Education (17 semester hours)

OHIO PEACE OFFICER TRAINING COUNCIL (386 hours), Fremont, OH—**Top Honors**

PROFESSIONAL DEVELOPMENT

FBI U.S. Department of Justice, Media Relations for the Law Enforcement Executive,
    Quantico, VA—2001
Crime Stoppers Annual Training Conference, Pueblo, CO—2001
Combating Violent Crimes in the 21st Century Information Sharing Conference, MAGLOCLEN,
    Cleveland, OH—2000
FBI Hostile School Environment: Causes and Solutions Conference, Cleveland, OH—1999
Exploring Economic, Electronic and Financial Crimes in Our Society Information Sharing
        Conference, MAGLOCLEN, Atlantic City, NY—1999
Crime Stoppers International Conference, Gillette, WY—1998
Crime Trends in America, MAGLOCLEN, Pittsburgh, PA—1998

AFFILIATIONS & LEADERSHIP

Board of Crime Stoppers of Cincinnati, **Law Enforcement Coordinator/Liaison,** 1997–Present
Benevolent Protective Order of the Elks #75, **Chairman of Youth Activities,** 2001–Present
Free and Accepted Masons of Ohio—32nd Degree, 2002
Fraternal Order of Police Lodge #20 Member, **President,** 1989–1990

CONTINUING EDUCATION

Ohio Department of Health, Alcohol Testing, Approval & Permit Program, Senior Operator Permit
Search and Seizure Update, Cincinnati Academy (16 hours)
The Dispatch Institute: Liability and Public Image Concerns in Public Safety Telecommunications
Laws of Arrest, Search & Seizure, Firearms Training (50 hours)
Ohio Peace Officer Training Council, Evidence Technician (40 hours)
Lucas County Coroner Forensic Medical Sciences, Evidence Related to Blood (8 hours)
Front-Line Effective Police Supervision Skills (14 hours)
Defensive Tactics Training (16 hours)
Public Safety Training, Saving Our Own Lives (16 hours)
FBI U.S. Department of Justice DEA, Basic Narcotics and Dangerous Drug Law Enforcement (80 hours)

options; and realizing that it was time to put his credentials, experience, and accomplishments on paper. This resume won "Best Law Enforcement/Security Industry Resume" at the Professional Association of Resume Writers' 2002 national convention in Dallas, Texas.

Tom Collier

000 15th Street ▪ Oakland, CA 00000 ▪ name@aol.com
Home: (000) 000-0000 ▪ Work: (000) 000-0000 ▪ Cell: (000) 000-0000

LAW ENFORCEMENT OFFICIAL

With Track Record of Strengthening Safety/Security Programs and Success in Providing Community of Oakland, CA with 20+ Years of Excellent Public Service

Dedicated law enforcement officer with more than 20 years of experience in planning and managing investigations, security, public service, and police force activities. Strong qualifications in budgeting, personnel affairs, training, resource management, public safety, and emergency response. Excellent research and problem-solving skills; maintain strict confidentiality on sensitive information. Confident public speaker with experience in media and civic leadership relations. Reputation for strong work ethic and uncompromising devotion to service.

SPECIFIC SKILL AREAS

- Public Safety Programs
- Emergency Response
- Internal Investigations
- Crisis Communications
- Team Building & Leadership

- Community Event Coordination
- Policy & Procedure Development
- Budget Planning & Management
- Staffing, Training, & Retention
- Time & Resource Allocation

- City Council Presentations
- Community Outreach
- External Communications
- Regulatory Compliance
- Media & Public Relations

AWARDS & RECOGNITIONS

Service Above Self Award, "Outstanding Community Service" — by Oakland Rotary Club (1996)
Two-Time Recipient, County Outstanding Peace Officer Award — by Oakland College (1982 & 1983)
Representative, Advisory Committee in Washington, D.C. — selected by CA Police Chiefs Association (1999)

PROFESSIONAL EXPERIENCE

CITY OF OAKLAND POLICE DEPARTMENT — Oakland, CA   1979–Present
Assistant Chief of Police (1985–Present)
Shift Supervisor (1980–1985)
Police Officer (1979–1980)

Distinguished 20-plus-year career ensuring public safety for city of Oakland with culturally diverse population. Progressed rapidly through strict promotion requirements to handle increasingly responsible positions, culminating in supervisory duty for staff of 25 employees. Hold key accountability and co-responsibility for budget management, staff training, lead work on investigations, program/policy development, and public safety programs, along with regulatory documentation and filing requirements. Maintained consistent performance in core law enforcement disciplines. **Selected Accomplishments:**

TEAM BUILDING & LEADERSHIP

- Use tact and professionalism in responding to citizen complaints against officers and allegations of misconduct, applying corrective strategies on minor infractions and stricter measures on serious offenses.
- Co-developed Employee Evaluation program that enhanced targeting of strengths/weaknesses and resulted in measurable, sustainable performance improvements.
- Earned high level of loyalty from staff and maintained excellent retention rate through fair, consistent evaluations and modeling effective on-the-job performance in both criminal and administrative matters.

PROGRAM & DEPARTMENT DEVELOPMENT

- Recognized for contributions to organizational development through supervision of following departments:
  - *Patrol Division*
  - *K-9/Animal Control*
  - *Investigation Division*
  - *School Resource Office*
  - *Communications Division*
  - *Community Policing Division*

…Continued…

146

Combination. *Daniel J. Dorotik, Jr., Lubbock, Texas*

Usually, personal information is not included in a resume—often to avoid breaking sensitive regulations about hiring. The personal information at the bottom of page two was judged

Tom Collier

Professional Experience, Continued

(PROGRAM/DEPARTMENT DEVELOPMENT)

- Modified key departmental policies to reflect changes in the law following high-profile court cases that involved such issues as high-speed pursuit, search and seizure, and domestic violence.
- Implemented new technologies and applications that resulted in increased efficiency and accuracy for file and records management functions.

CRISIS MANAGEMENT & RESPONSE

- Repeatedly recognized by citizens, community groups, and supervisors for quick-thinking, calm, and correct response to multitude of crisis and emergency situations, both in the field and as shift supervisor.
- Developed strong relationships with members of Fire Department and local/regional emergency medical services that led to improved, expedited emergency responses.

COMMUNITY & CITY COUNCIL RELATIONS

- Built good will between citizens and police department over 20-year period, with emphasis on youth crime prevention and community service initiatives.
- Deliver well-received, comprehensive presentations to City Council of Levelland detailing department's year-to-date statistics and activities from written report.

EDUCATION & TRAINING

Associates Degree in Law Enforcement
COLLEGE, Oakland, CA (1979)

Selected Professional Development Coursework:
Asset Forfeiture & Racial Profiling ▪ Leadership Principles ▪ Supervising Problem Solving ▪ Cultural Diversity
Leadership Survival Skills ▪ Manpower Allocation & Deployment ▪ Chief's Administrative Conference
Law Enforcement Liability ▪ Command Staff Leadership Series ▪ Principles of Management

* 576 hours total in professional development. A comprehensive course list will gladly be provided upon request.

Certifications & Licenses:

- Master Peace Officer, 2000
- Intermediate Peace Officer, 1988
- Peace Officer License, 1981
- Advanced Peace Officer, 1988
- Instructor Proficiency, 1984
- Basic Peace Officer, 1980

AFFILIATIONS & CIVIC INVOLVEMENT

Member — City of Oakland Police Association (1988–Present)

Advisory Board Member — County Family Center (1992–1996)
Advisory Board Member — County Children's Welfare Board (1995–2001)

President — Girls Softball (1993–Present)
President — Youth Soccer League (1993–1995)
President — Girls Little Dribblers Association (1996–1997)

PERSONAL

Married, 23 years, to Sandra Collier, Nursing Supervisor at Oakland Clinic
Three children: Amy (22), Josh (19), and Alyssa (16)

appropriate for this candidate because background checks on personal information are standard in the field of law enforcement, and he was being hired to represent the community. Information about his affiliations and civic involvement paints him as a model citizen.

FRANKLIN HARRIS

84 Park Boulevard • East Syracuse, NY 13900
315/999-5555 • fharris@myemail.com

SUMMARY

- Diverse professional experience gained in human services, local and state government, academic settings and not-for-profits in addition to extensive community involvement as a volunteer
- Skilled in Project/Program Development and Implementation, Strategic Planning and the management of human, financial and other resources, with a solid record of accomplishments and contributions
- Extensive hands-on involvement in the creation, update and execution of procedures and policies
- Well-developed interpersonal, communication and problem-solving capabilities
- Successfully achieve individual goals and serve as an effective team member

HIGHLIGHTS OF ACCOMPLISHMENTS

Program and Operations Management
- ▶ Eighteen-year career with the NYS Division of Parole, beginning as a Parole Officer based at a state prison facility and promoted several times, most recently serving as Senior Parole Officer.
  - ✧ Managed personal caseloads as well as multiple parole offices and teams of parole officers. In last position, directed six officers overseeing approximately 450 parolees in an urban area.
  - ✧ Represented Syracuse field operations on citywide task force to target homicide reduction.
  - ✧ Selected for committee involvement, assigned projects and sought out for advice relative to criminal justice and parole operations knowledge.
- ▶ Transitioned Cayuga County's Child Protection Services when state law refocused the agency's purpose.
- ▶ Doubled Junior Achievement involvement during tenure as Director of Cayuga County operations.
- ▶ Held several newly created positions.

Project/Program Development and Implementation
- ▶ Designed and implemented the Cease Fire Program in conjunction with the City of Syracuse's task force on homicide reduction. The program was deterrent-focused and targeted at parolees.
- ▶ Developed a home/school liaison program for an area public school and served as the first Home/School Coordinator for that district.
- ▶ Created and launched an innovative program for at-risk children in the Foster Care Program. Authored new operating procedures and manuals for staff as well as foster-home parents.

Financial Management
- ▶ As director of two agencies, guided fiscal decision-making and planning.
- ▶ As a school board President, serve as Financial Officer for that school. Involved in bargaining contracts for superintendent and principals.
- ▶ Reorganized a non-profit agency's accounting system to achieve better financial control.

Teaching/Training
- ▶ Developed and delivered course curriculum at the university/college level for a variety of learners.
- ▶ Assessed training needs for organizations.
- ▶ Drove the creation of the Institute for Child Abuse Training.

147

Combination. *Salome A. Farraro, Mount Morris, New York*

This individual had retired from the state and wanted a resume that captured the diversity of his background, including extensive civic involvement, and highlighted his accomplishments. He

GOVERNMENT & HUMAN SERVICES EXPERIENCE

NEW YORK STATE, DIVISION OF PAROLE   *1985–2004*
Senior Parole Officer, Field Operations (Syracuse, NY & Onondaga County)
  Managed six parole officers, five overseeing 400+ parolees in the Main Street section of the City of
  Syracuse and the sixth supervising 30 individuals in the electronic monitoring/home confinement program
  throughout Syracuse. Reviewed and made determinations on requests for parolee arrest warrants.

Facility Parole Officer 2, Cayuga Correctional Facility
Facility Parole Officer 2, Auburn Incarceration Facility
  Managed the activities of these Parole Offices, facilitating the prisoner release process from case assessment
  to inmates' interviews, release orientation and presentation to Parole Board, as well as post-release support
  coordination. Supervised seven staff members in total. Cayuga's medium-security prison houses 850 inmates
  and the Auburn behavior-modification program services 300 inmates.

Field Parole Officer, Syracuse, NY & Parole Officer, Cayuga Correctional Facility

CAYUGA COUNTY DEPARTMENT OF SOCIAL SERVICES—Auburn, NY   *1983–1985*
Cluster Home Coordinator
  Successfully created and implemented a program for at-risk children, which maintained children's ties with
  their families/communities while providing services at a reduced cost compared to institutional care.

CAYUGA COUNTY DEPARTMENT OF SOCIAL SERVICES—Auburn, NY   *1970–1980*
Supervisor of Child Protection Services/Case Worker
  As first Supervisor of Child Protection Services in this county, oversaw the transition from a broad focus on
  child welfare to child protection services as regulated by a 1973 New York State law. Directed five case
  workers and three home aides in the management of an average of 100 cases.

EDUCATION & NON-PROFIT EXPERIENCE

AUBURN COMMUNITY COLLEGE—Auburn, NY   *1991*
Instructor, Sociology Department (at Cayuga Correctional Facility)

SYRACUSE UNIVERSITY—Syracuse, NY   *1985; 1980–1982*
Adjunct Professor
  Provided Human Services Development training to social workers throughout New York State. Performed
  an assessment of New York City's Bureau of Children's Services to identify staff development needs.
  Collaborated in the creation of a video illustrating family communication, which was marketed and sold.

Instructor/Program Development
  Working via the New York State Research Foundation in conjunction with Cornell University and Syracuse
  University, contributed to curriculum development of social worker training. Delivered training across the
  state. Instrumental in the creation of the Institute for Child Abuse Training now based at Cornell.

NORTH SYRACUSE CENTRAL SCHOOL DISTRICT—North Syracuse, NY   *1984*
Home/School Coordinator
  Developed, implemented and managed a home/school liaison program to improve communication between
  school and home for the benefit of students with educational and/or behavioral issues.

**ONONDAGA COMMUNITY COUNSELING SERVICES & SPECIAL FRIENDS
PROGRAM**—DeWitt, NY   *1984*
Executive Director

JUNIOR ACHIEVEMENT OF CAYUGA COUNTY—Auburn, NY   *1974–1977*
Director

intended to use the resume for flexible, part-time, nonprofit operations and management positions. The
writer wrote also a cover letter (see Cover Letter 30, page 406) to an area coalition of churches about a
Projects Coordinator position. The applicant gained an interview for the position because of the resume and

EDUCATION & PROFESSIONAL DEVELOPMENT

Graduate Studies: *Psychology:*   State University of New York at Buffalo—Buffalo, NY
                          Social Work: Syracuse University—Syracuse, NY
                          Social Work: State University of New York at Buffalo—Buffalo, NY

Bachelor of Science, Criminal Justice: State University College at Buffalo—Buffalo, NY

Associate in Applied Science, Police Science: Auburn Community College—Auburn, NY

Certified Peace Officer: State of New York

Maxwell Human Services Management School at Syracuse University
- *23-hour program devoted to social services training and development*

RECENT ACTIVITIES & AFFILIATIONS

Board of Education, East Syracuse—Minoa Central School District
- President, *2001–present;* Vice President, *1998–2001*

U.S. Sea Cadets, Syracuse, *2001–present*
- Uniform Instructor; previously volunteer
- Trained at Fort Drum and coordinate programming with three other instructors for approximately 40 cadets ranging in age from 11 to 20

Town of East Syracuse, *2000–present*
- Councilman
- Current liaison to ambulance corps, cemeteries and parks and recreation
- Past liaison in planning, zoning and health matters

East Syracuse–Minoa PTA, *1994–present*

Troop 99, Boy Scouts of America, *current*
- Committee Member; past volunteer troop leader and soccer coach

Masons, East Syracuse Lodge and formerly Auburn Lodge, *1994–present*

United Church, East Syracuse, NY, *1994–present*

New York State Parole Officer Association, *1985–present*
- Past Representative for Syracuse Field Office
- Former Vice President of Central New York

cover letter. Shaded section headings are readily spotted at a glance and therefore make it easy to size up the design of the resume. A variety of bold bullets direct attention to key information. The first page especially is an appealing door to the rest of the resume.

Management

Resumes at a Glance

RESUME NO.	OCCUPATION	GOAL	PAGE
148.	Office Manager	Office Manager	307
149.	Manager, Retail	Manager, Retail	308
150.	Clubhouse Manager	Country Club Manager	309
151.	County Executive Director	Not specified	310
152.	Independent Contractor/ Consultant	Not specified	312
153.	Director of Community Development	Not specified	314
154.	Director of Training and Management Development	Organization Development/ Training Manager	316
155.	Div. Director of Operations	Not specified	318
156.	General Manager	General Manager	320
157.	Chemical Operator	Maintenance Reliability Engineer	322
158.	Senior VP	Senior-Level Executive	324
159.	Domain Expert	Director of SOCC	326
160.	Career and Life Coach	Non-Profit Organization Mgr.	328
161.	General Manager	Not specified	330

Collins Mackey

5th Street • Centereach, NY 55555 • (555) 444-2222

OFFICE MANAGER

Bringing 25+ Years of Office Administration and Full-charge Bookkeeping Experience as Follows:

- ◆ Accounts Payable / Receivable
- ◆ Weekly Payroll
- ◆ Credit and Collections
- ◆ Statement Billings

- ◆ Expense Control
- ◆ Account Management
- ◆ Account Reconciliation
- ◆ Month-end Closings

- ◆ Human Resources Management
- ◆ Staff Training and Supervision
- ◆ Customer Service / Client Relations
- ◆ Computerized Processes

PROFESSIONAL EXPERIENCE—*Overview*

Recognized throughout longstanding career for ability to develop, implement, and manage full-charge, computerized bookkeeping functions while overseeing multifaceted office administration procedures

- As Office Manager for August Publications, fully manage company-wide accounting and reporting functions for five subsidiaries, as well as weekly payroll processes for 45 salaried employees.
- Liaison between senior management, employees, and clients to ensure proper lines of communication critical in addressing myriad problems and issues requiring immediate attention and resolve.
- Manage Accounts Payable/Receivable and expense-control procedures, including bank and account reconciliation, cash receipts, disbursements, finance charges, billings, invoicing, purchase order and inventory verification, chargebacks, rebates, and preparation of daily bank deposits.
- Negotiate and enforce collections to recover funds and expedite the clearance on delinquent accounts.
- Collaborate extensively with external auditors, providing in-depth assistance with periodic corporate audits.
- Perform thorough credit analyses, research financial histories, and review account status as a prerequisite to qualifying new accounts, authorizing purchases, and extending/increasing lines of credit of up to $200,000.
- Establish and maintain Human Resources–related employee files reflecting salary increases, deductions, garnishments, benefits, payroll exceptions, and W-2 withholdings, exercising a high level of confidentiality.
- Skilled at interviewing, hiring, training, and evaluating employees in areas of accounting procedures.
- Research account transactions, demonstrating a keen ability to recognize and resolve discrepancies.
- Follow through on timely and accurate month-end closings and financial reporting activities.

WORK CHRONOLOGY

Office Manager,	August Publications, Hauppauge, NY	1996–present
Office Manager,	Quality Insurance, Huntington, NY	1986–1996
Office Manager,	DSG Management Corp., Melville, NY	1983–1985
Controller's Assistant,	Georgia Interiors, Farmingdale, NY	1979–1983
Credit/Collections Supervisor,	EastTel Sales Corp., New York, NY	1978–1979
Accounts Payable/Receivable Clerk,	Syobel Corp., New York, NY	1973–1978

COMPUTER PROFICIENCIES

Windows 2000; MS Word and Excel; WordPerfect; Lotus; Peachtree Accounting

EDUCATION

Bachelor of Arts, Business Management/Accounting, Banes College, 1982

148

Combination. *Ann Baehr, Brentwood, New York*

The writer condenses extensive experience onto one page, using keywords, an Overview section representing many similar positions to avoid repetition, and a compact Work Chronology section.

LAURA D. WENN

899 Lancona Road
Dallas, TX 00000

(555) 555-5555
ldw56@yahoo.com

RETAIL MANAGEMENT PROFESSIONAL

Nine years of retail management experience demonstrating a consistent track record of outstanding sales, merchandising and customer service results. Equally strong qualifications in all areas of fine jewelry department operations: P&L, budgeting, inventory control, training, security and other functions. Effective communicator, leader and problem solver who builds teamwork and possesses the initiative to exceed goals.

EXPERIENCE

LAWRENCE FINE JEWELRY CORPORATION, Seattle, WA (1993–present)
Progressed rapidly from part-time position to manager at several stores, including the following:

Manager—G. Fox, Randolph Mall, Dallas, TX (1999–present)
Manager—G. Fox, Valley Mall, Phoenix, AZ (1995–1999)
Manager—G. Fox, Turner Mall, Tucson, AZ (1994–1995)
Assistant Manager—G. Fox, Forest Mall, San Antonio, TX (1993–1994)

Summary of Responsibilities

Operations Management—Hold profit and loss accountability; manage all aspects of day-to-day department performance of stores ranging from $500,000 to $2M in annual sales. Direct sales, inventory control, visual merchandising, housekeeping, security, administration and compliance to company policies/procedures. Managed 2 stores concurrently over 4-month period with highly successful sales results during busy Christmas season.

Staff Supervision & Training—Supervise teams of up to 13 fine-jewelry specialists. Experienced in personnel recruiting, selection, training, developing, scheduling and supervising associates. Motivate staff to achieve performance goals and ensure productive department operations.

Customer Relations & Service—Develop and manage customer relations to maximize service satisfaction, promote goodwill and generate repeat/referral business that contributes to sales growth. Monitor and resolve any service issues.

Selected Achievements

- Increased Randolph store sales from $1.1M to $1.4M (27%) in 2000 and maintained .02% shrink—well below company average of 2.1%.
- Increased percent-to-store sales at Valley Mall from 2.8% to 5.2%, surpassing company average of 2.5%. Grew annual sales at Valley Mall from $.8M in 1995 to $1.1M (37%) in 1996, $1.4M (27%) in 1997, $1.7M (21%) in 1998 and $2M (18%) in 1999.
- Selected by Regional Manager to serve as Training Store Manager for the region; recognized for the ability to recruit quality candidates who have successfully advanced with the company.

Awards

- Earned **Branch Manager of the Year** and **Branch of the Year** awards in 2000 in the Southwest Region.
- Twice named **Manager of the Year** out of 50 stores in 1998 and 1996 in the Southwest Region.
- Winner of 3 sales performance awards in 2000: **Goal Achievers**, **Best Increase in % to Store** and **Best Event Business. Christmas Contest** winner in 1999, exceeding sales goal by 15%.
- Selected runner up for 3 awards in 2000: **Best in Operations**, **Best Visual Department** and **Best Buyer Communication.** Ranked #3 in **Christmas Contest** in 2000, exceeding sales goal by 21%.

EDUCATION / PROFESSIONAL DEVELOPMENT

B.A., Retail Management, Valhalla College, Dallas, TX

Completed various company-sponsored training courses in management, personnel recruiting, staff training and development, sales, customer service and related topics.

149

Combination. *Louise Garver, Enfield, Connecticut*

The applicant was applying for a position with a competitor in Arizona. She had held positions with the same responsibilities at several stores. To eliminate repetition, the writer summarized key duties.

EDWARD J. BROWER

999 Wilson Drive ▪ Dallas, TX 75200 ▪ (972) 555-7777 ▪ ejbrower@email.com

Country Club Management Professional
Proven track record of driving revenues to unprecedented levels

Challenge-driven visionary with comprehensive knowledge of all aspects of country club management, seven years of experience in hospitality industry, and core competencies in

Club Management	*Strategic Marketing*
Member Service & Satisfaction	*Crucial Planning & Execution*
Interdepartmental Communications	*Revenue & Profitability Acceleration*

EDUCATION & PROFESSIONAL DEVELOPMENT

UNIVERSITY OF HOUSTON—Houston, TX
Conrad N. Hilton College of Hotel & Restaurant Management
Bachelor of Science, Hotel and Restaurant Management (1996)

WHARTON COUNTY JUNIOR COLLEGE—Wharton, Texas
Associate of Applied Sciences, Supervisory Management (1993)

CLUB MANAGERS ASSOCIATION OF AMERICA
Pursuing **Certification in Club Management**

RELEVANT EMPLOYMENT CHRONICLE

LOVELY COUNTRY CLUB—Dallas, TX (1996–Present)
Clubhouse Manager / Assistant Manager

Progressed from assistant manager to clubhouse manager and assumed challenge of reconstructing food, beverage, service, housekeeping, maintenance/repair, and security processes for 5,800-sq.-ft. clubhouse, ballroom with 250 capacity, large bar/ lounge, and kitchen. Oversee staff of 25–30 (five directs), all club marketing, budget of $1.3 million, and inventory of $672,000; and placate and ensure satisfaction of 833 membership. **Direct all operations in absence of general manager.**

Selected Accomplishments

- **Successfully revamped and revitalized club;** developed innovative strategies and processes, which **boosted morale and productivity,** slashed labor and food costs, and escalated annual **revenues** from approximately **$900,000 to $1.3 million.**
- **Devised and launched exciting youth, social, and dining activities,** which **dramatically enhanced member interest and participation.**
- **Honored with challenge** of organization, planning, and execution of **Annual Eisenhower International Golf Classic,** which resulted in being named **Host Club** for its annual events.
- **Recognized as club's "computer system guru";** troubleshoot and diagnose system malfunctions throughout club.

Positions held while pursuing degree:

Server / Busboy, WILDWOOD HOTEL—Houston, TX (1995–1996)

- **Promoted to server within five months** because of demonstrated commitment to personalized, superior customer service.

Guest Service Agent, GARDEN SUITES HOTEL—Houston, TX (1993–1995)

- **Awarded highest customer service/excellence award** possible by guest nominations while attending front desk.

PROFESSIONAL AFFILIATIONS & HONORS

CLUB MANAGERS ASSOCIATION OF AMERICA (Since 1996)

Chronicled in "Who's Who Among Students in American Junior Colleges"
Recipient of Phi Beta Lambda's "Outstanding Student Award"
Volunteer Director, House Services—*Gourmet Night* (1995)
Historian / Parliamentarian, Phi Beta Lambda (1991, 1992)

150

Combination. *Ann Klint, Tyler, Texas*

Much center-justified information in this resume creates adequate white space even inside a page border. Boldfacing ampersands and the first letter of certain words in headings is distinctive. See Cover Letter 26 (page 402).

Victoria Chamberlain

5441 Sycamore Lane
St. Louis, MO 00000

(000) 000-0000
name@aol.com

CAREER PROFILE

15+ Years of Diversified Experience and Documented Contributions in Office Management, Human Resources, and Insurance Disciplines

Dedicated, quality-focused professional offering strong qualifications in office administration, service delivery, personnel affairs, and insurance-related activities, including claims adjustment and customer service. Precise, detail-oriented worker with proven skill in managing large volumes of information and facilitating multiple tasks in deadline-driven environment. Sound judgment and decision-making skills. Recognized at every step of career path for positive attitude and work effort; maintain highest professional ethics and standards.

Core Competencies:

Workflow Planning & Prioritization

• • •

Time & Resource Optimization

• • •

Regulatory Compliance Filing and Recordkeeping

• • •

Team Member Training and Mentoring

• • •

Service Quality Improvement

• • •

Multi-Task Management

• • •

Customer Needs Assessment

• • •

Quality Control Standards

• • •

Loan Administration

• • •

Budget Management

• • •

Creative Problem Solving

• • •

Interviewing, Hiring, Retention

• • •

Public Presentations

RELEVANT EXPERIENCE

COUNTY EXECUTIVE DIRECTOR, 1988–2000
X County FSA Office ▪ Y County FSA Office
Z County FSA Office ▪ A County FSA Office (trainee)

Amassed track record of results spanning more than 10 years of management in a government-funded agency supporting local farmers and producers. Scope of responsibility included program management, staffing and training, community and Board of Director meetings, loan administration, quality assurance, and regulatory compliance in deadline-driven environment.

Continually monitored member and staff activities, identifying and analyzing key financial data and performance indicators, applying cost-benefit analysis to decisions, and demonstrating strong understanding of organizational missions and capabilities.

Drove achievement of organizational goals
- Projected confidence and took decisive steps to achieve objectives.
- Kept efficiency levels high and produced consistently top results, earning recognitions for exemplary performance:
  - **Finished regularly in top 10 among 100+ counties statewide in timely, on-target payment submissions.**
  - **Earned consistent recognition from State of Missouri for efforts in establishing and maintaining excellent operations.**

Provided excellent service to program recipients
- Wrote newsletters, press releases, and other informational materials to keep farmers/producers abreast of new developments.
- Implemented emergency procedures to aid program members during disaster/crisis events. Authorized loan extensions in special situations.

Motivated and contributed to enhanced team performance
- Trained and mentored staff through series of changes from manual to automated systems, engaging in one-on-one training to ease transition.
- Selected to train State of Missouri employees based on crop insurance and appraisal knowledge.

151

Combination. *Daniel J. Dorotik, Jr., Lubbock, Texas*

The shaded box displaying core competencies is eye-catching and draws attention away from the individual's lack of formal education. The Career Profile and Relevant Experience sections

Victoria Chamberlain **Page Two**

OTHER EXPERIENCE

Federal Crop Insurance Corporation ▪ *St. Louis, MO*
CONTRACT CLAIMS ADJUSTER/FIELD SUPERVISOR

Hired as field representative in charge of appraising crops and determining cause of loss on per-situation basis, earning promotion within two years to oversee all job assignments, recruit and train new employees, review insurance claims, and make final determinations on courses of action. Managed adjusting activities over multi-county territory and assigned losses to field staff. Addressed and resolved customer issues, including management of complex claims resolutions. Worked in tandem with Underwriting Department.

Accomplishments:

- Earned appointment as District Reviewer covering entire district area, with responsibility for employee reviews, random loss claims, and assistance with unusual/controversial claims.
- Built strong, sustainable relationships with farmers and producers by providing excellent service while protecting company interests and bottom line.
- Developed advanced abilities in analyzing and tracking claims results, pinpointing and correcting deficiencies, and delivering presentations to management regarding evaluations.
- Built loyal, top-performing staff through prudent hiring decisions and ongoing training initiatives.

Name of Company ▪ *St. Louis, MO*
PROGRAM ASSISTANT

- Assessed program compliance and worked directly with customers to answer questions and solve small- and large-scale problems.
- Fulfilled various objectives in filing, mail/courier services, and general office duties.

PROFESSIONAL DEVELOPMENT

Professional Development Coursework:

- ❑ Executive Director Management Training, Parts I and II
- ❑ Time Management/Stress Management
- ❑ EEO/Civil Rights Training
- ❑ Farm Loan Training
- ❑ Federal Crop Insurance
- ❑ Certified Appraiser—All Crops
- ❑ Instructor & Sales Training

Computer Skills:

MS Word and Windows, WordPerfect, proprietary applications, PC and mainframe computer systems

References:

Will be gladly provided upon request

---

offset the Other Experience section, which is silent about the dates of the person's earlier jobs. Bulleted accomplishments for these experiences, however, are signs of management potential. Note in the Relevant Experience section the underlined statements about achievement, service, and teamwork.

MELINDA FORMAN
7765 Hazel Lane
Portland, OR 00000

(555) 555–5555   mforman@hotmail.com

NONPROFIT MANAGEMENT PROFESSIONAL

Operations/Project Management: Proven record in conceiving and transmitting vision into reality, mission into action and philosophy into practice. Strategic planning expertise combines with dynamic leadership, resulting in the efficient operation of organizational programs. Focused problem solver who identifies organizational needs and delivers effective solutions on time and under budget in both nonprofit and business environments.

Human Resources/Training: Recruiting, mentoring and supervising staff in the delivery of quality programs. Development and facilitation of staff development, leadership training and other workshops. Adept at fostering cooperation and building successful cross-functional team relationships at all levels in multicultural environments.

Fiscal & Grant Management: Planning and administration of all financial and budgeting activities related to program operations, including preparation of audits and financial reports as well as securing grant funding.

Program Development/Community Relations: Experienced in designing and managing innovative programs that achieve organizational goals. Effective in developing community partnerships and building awareness for organizational activities/events through public relations, fundraising and outreach efforts.

CONSULTING EXPERIENCE

FORMAN GROUP, Portland, OR
Independent Contractor/Consultant (1997–present)

Consult with companies to provide expertise in the areas of strategic planning, training and development, operations, information technology, sales and customer service. **Major Engagements:**

- **Lane-Brown Consulting Group:** Designed content and facilitated various sales training programs for management-level personnel of client companies in diverse industries. Created templates and developed processes for core consulting projects; designed and implemented e-business website to market organizational development products. Contributed to development and design of human resources policy and procedural manuals.

- **McKenzie Worldwide:** As consultant/liaison with 500+ staff members of the Business Consulting Practice, provided strategic planning for technology projects, including ongoing technical support coordination, research, resolution of high-end customer issues and continuous improvement. Contributed to development of an effective implementation process to assess resource requirements, communications and accountability procedures.

- **First Bank:** Provided leadership support for an online banking project and trained 12 project managers on desktop tools; maintained and authored key project database; maintained and audited $250,000 in asset inventory. Assisted in defining project scope, scheduling of resources and cost controlling.

- **Morris Corporation:** Contributed technical support and project management capabilities to ITS Group Field Engineering, Professional Services and Sales. Effectively defined project scope, scheduled resources and controlled costs. Produced key documents: critical path analysis, project implementation plans and fault escalation procedures.

NONPROFIT MANAGEMENT EXPERIENCE

TJ CHILDREN'S ASSOCIATION, Portland, OR
Program Director (1996–1997)

Provided strategic planning and leadership in the administration of youth programs for boys and girls ages 5–18 of diverse multicultural backgrounds. Scope of responsibilities included operations, human resources, financial/grant management, program development, fundraising, facilities, marketing, public relations and community outreach. Recruited, trained and supervised staff of 10. Managed $300,000 annual budget. **Key accomplishments:**

- Initiated and implemented innovative programs such as anger management, diversity awareness, book club, boys' programs, coed programs and girls' program incorporating health/fitness, self-esteem and related themes.
- Led successful efforts in preparation for American Camping Association Accreditation; managed programs that surpassed all governmental standards.
- Redesigned, revitalized and expanded a floundering day-camp program, increasing attendance to 400 participants.
- Built a cohesive team environment through training, staff/leadership development and diversity initiatives.
- Wrote grants and secured funding from a variety of private and governmental resources for new programming.

152

Combination. *Louise Garver, Enfield, Connecticut*

The applicant had started a consulting business so that she could control her hours while raising children. Now that they were in school, she wanted to return to nonprofit management. Her

MELINDA FORMAN • Page 2

CAMP ROSEN, Portland, OR
Program Director (1994–1996)

Initially managed the 8-week residential camp program and subsequently selected for the Program Director position to increase minority participation and staffing as well as design and manage day-camp program. Directed all aspects of approximately 50 youth programs annually serving 1,100 girls of all economic and social backgrounds. Accountable for program design, development and delivery, staff recruitment and training, and day-to-day management of facilities and operations. Program specialty areas included HIV/AIDS training for adults and youths and life skills planning. Community outreach efforts included public relations and presentations to various groups. Managed $250,000 annual budget. Ensured continuing accreditation with local, state and camping associations. **Key accomplishments:**

♦ Designed and implemented leadership training program for teenage girls; program included mentoring and job skills training.
♦ Expanded the introduction of innovative programs in health and safety, HIV/AIDS awareness, environmental education, conflict resolution, recreational and others.
♦ Succeeded in building minority staffing by 50% and minority campers by 75% through active recruitment efforts. Designed and delivered training to national and international teams. Infused troops with new program options.
♦ Produced public relations and recruiting materials; researched and authored articles on current issues affecting girls, which were published in area newspapers.
♦ Member of fund-raising council, planning and coordinating annual event generating $200,000.

PORTLAND YOUTH CENTER, Portland, OR
Program Director (1992–1994)
Assistant Program Director (1991–1992)
Village Director (1987–1989)

Joined organization while attending college and promoted through series of progressively responsible management positions to direct summer camp for 200 urban youth. Recruited, mentored and trained team of 60 multicultural staff members in all aspects of program operations. Responsible for fiscal management, marketing, community outreach, program development and other functions. Supervised, tracked and monitored program activities. Developed and coordinated administrative policies, procedures and controls. Administered $500,000 annual budget.
Key accomplishments:

♦ Initiated and facilitated organization's first leadership training and several other programs for boys and girls, including opening programs for physically challenged individuals.
♦ Increased year-round programming and boosted participation in leadership training and camping programs.
♦ Worked closely with the Board of Directors on strategic planning, program direction and funding. Partnered with community groups and social service agencies in services administration throughout the year.
♦ Recruited numerous volunteers as member of Board of Directors to serve on special committees of the American Camping Association.

EDUCATION

B.S. in Sociology, University of Oregon, Portland, OR, 1989
Participated in study-abroad programs in South America, France and Italy.

Additional:

Completed Camp Training courses
Previously certified to teach CPR/First Aid courses

COMPUTER & OTHER SKILLS

Microsoft Office suite (Word, Excel, PowerPoint), Microsoft Project
Lotus SmartSuite (WordPro, Lotus 1-2-3, Freelance Graphics)
Foreign-language skills: Conversational Spanish and French

original four-page resume listed every short-term consulting assignment and buried nonprofit experience at the end. She looked like a job hopper and was getting no interviews. The writer created a two-page resume that put nonprofit experience first. The client received multiple job offers within two months.

9727 Sunrise Avenue, Philadelphia, PA 00000

Home: (000) 000-0000
Fax: (000) 000-0000
Cell: (000) 000-0000
E-mail: lindseyb@taskforce21.org

Barbara Lindsey

Executive Profile

Offering more than 20 years of broad-based management advisory experience, combining administrative, sales, and marketing skills in challenging multitasking environments. Successful in utilizing a consultative approach to access key decision makers or benefactors, network effectively, and create synergistic relationships. Excel in focusing the efforts of diverse groups to work toward common goals. Strong ability to plan and organize high-level business affairs while maintaining efficient control of financial and human resources. Areas of expertise include

- Program design, development, and implementation
- Project management
- Staff training and team leadership
- Special event planning and management
- Scheduling, logistics, and detail coordination
- Negotiations and contracting
- Public relations

- Budget development, allocation, and monitoring
- Community outreach
- Proposal and grant writing
- Fundraising and promotional campaigns
- Policy and procedure implementation
- Public speaking and presentation delivery
- Computer literacy

Professional Experience

PHILADELPHIA IN THE 21ST CENTURY TASK FORCE at Rutgers Camden Law School   2000–Present

A public and privately funded task force of civic leaders drawn from the professional, philanthropic, cultural, and social sectors of the metropolitan region, established to evaluate Philadelphia's strengths, assess its role in the regional economy, and articulate a vision of the city in the decades ahead.

Director of Community Development
- Joined the Task Force in its early stages as an Assistant to the Executive Director. Assigned to special project to coordinate a dinner meeting for 26 prominent attendees from the fields of healthcare, education, foundations, and community development, which culminated in the establishment of a Board of Directors.
- Successfully accomplished this initial effort and demonstrated further abilities to manage the day-to-day affairs of the Task Force, freeing executive's time to focus on organization development strategies. After 3 months, was promoted to Administrative Director.
- Took charge of all planning and details for subsequent monthly Task Force meetings as well as workshops, seminars, dinners, and related activities, all within very tight lead times.
- Carried out primary mission of the Task Force in directing compilation of an inventory of City of Philadelphia assets, designed to attract future investors in the city's economic development. Managed student interns who assisted in completing this large-scale project within a $250,000 budget and 18-month timeline.
- Produced the *Directory of City Assets* book, which the Task Force made available and distributed as a public service to libraries, educational institutions, businesses, and cultural organizations throughout the City of Philadelphia.
- As representative of the Task Force, conveyed a professional image and played a critical role in fulfillment of its goals by chairing or participating in several advisory committees within the community. These included the Regional Plan Association, Philadelphia Arts Council, United Way of Greater Philadelphia, and Rutgers Camden Law School.
- Sat on the Advisory Board of the Northeast Regional Economic Development Conference to plan for its being hosted in Philadelphia in 2004.

(Continued)

153

Combination. *Melanie Noonan, West Paterson, New Jersey*

A "different" font (Lucida Handwriting) for the individual's name and for centered headings sets the tone for this resume. Comments about the current workplace are in italic and draw special

Barbara Lindsey

WEBBER AGENCY, Camden, NJ
1996–2000

Employee Benefits Consultant
- Consulted and acted on behalf of the client companies to analyze health benefits, perform cost comparisons, and recommend solutions to lower employer costs. Maintained a book of business that included non-profit agencies, state-funded Community Action programs/day care centers, and municipalities.
- Represented University Health Plans, the HMO of the University of Medicine and Dentistry of New Jersey (UMDNJ) in its initiative to expand from Medicare only to a commercial managed-care company. Implemented strategy that facilitated introduction of the plan to a large corporation, a large financial institution, and county government.
- Served as codirector for the State Health Benefits open enrollment, coordinated special events, and developed marketing strategies for on-site campaigns and health fairs in conjunction with local hospitals.

COMED HMO, Philadelphia, PA
1990–1996

Marketing Manager/Senior Account Executive, New Jersey and Eastern Pennsylvania
- Increased new business and expanded existing customer base throughout the state of New Jersey and was promoted to Philadelphia corporate office after 3 months. Managed a staff of 22 in the sale of group health insurance to commercial accounts as well as the sales efforts of account executives, service representatives, and telemarketing staff to increase market share and obtain sales goals.
- Increased existing business by 150% through restructuring former market strategies and improving customer service.
- Successfully led the marketing department to attain sales quota and meet budget for the first time in 6 years.
- In conjunction with the Director of Marketing: Developed and implemented marketing policies and procedures; designed and delivered sales training modules that became procedure for all new hires; conducted presentation skills training for all field sales representatives.

CUSTOM INFORMATION SOFTWARE, Haverford, PA
1988–1990

Sales Supervisor/Field Sales Training Coordinator
- Hired as sales representative and promoted within 9 months after increasing territory 50% through new business with accounts such as QVM, Parsons Corp., and Columbia National.
- Supervised a staff of 5 in marketing IBM mainframe software education seminars to data processing personnel. Trained and acted as consultant to 20 sales representatives on sales techniques.
- Conducted internal sales training, which consisted of formal instruction sessions and interactive workshops, including team building, assertiveness training, and listening skills.

GLK CONSULTANTS, Princeton, NJ
1985–1988

Account Representative
- As consultant to the data processing industry, marketed systems/applications to programmers and support personnel.

Education

UNIVERSITY OF ROCHESTER, Rochester, NY
B.A. Psychology, 1985

attention. Bullets point to important information: first, the areas of expertise in the Executive Profile; then, the achievements in the Professional Experience section. Achievements are presented for each of the workplaces. Small caps highlight workplace names and the university's name.

RONALD T. BROWNING

221 Forest Lane
Chicago, IL 00000
(555) 555-5555
RTB678@aol.com

ORGANIZATIONAL DEVELOPMENT / TRAINING MANAGER

Dynamic management career designing and directing innovative organization development, management development, and training programs for a global Fortune 500 corporation. Expertise:

Management/Employee Development • Performance Management Systems • Succession Planning • Change Management • Continuous Improvement Process • Team Building

Achieved recognition for successful collaboration with senior management to plan and implement strategies for improving customer focus, productivity, profitability, and employee satisfaction.

Honored with numerous corporate Quality Awards for excellent performance in change management, business negotiations, and team-building initiatives.

CAREER EXPERIENCE

RAND CORPORATION, Chicago, IL   1984–2004
Director of Training & Management Development   *1987–2004*
Assistant Director of Management Education   *1984–1987*

Senior training and organizational development executive for diversified multibillion-dollar corporation with 30,000 employees worldwide. Designed and introduced management development and employee training programs at all corporate/field business units. Directed team of senior training consultants and an annual $1.7 million budget. **Key Achievements:**

Organization Development
- ♦ Transitioned corporation into learning and development environment, fostering teamwork and high employee involvement resulting in significant improvements in performance and morale.
- ♦ Created a nationally acclaimed performance management and succession planning system implemented company-wide; featured in Tom Peters' newsletter *On Achieving Excellence.*
- ♦ Designed and implemented culture-change training division-wide to support more than 20% growth in product lines.
- ♦ Recommended external consultants to facilitate improvement in product line performance, resulting in increased automation systems, streamlined workflow, and decreased expenses by $14 million.

Management Development
- ♦ Innovated internal enterprise marketing Management/Leadership Training and Consulting Services for external customers, saving $300,000 in year one of implementation.
- ♦ Developed and facilitated Leadership and Teamwork seminars/retreats for CEO and senior management teams. Results strengthened coordination between market segments, reduced product development cycle time, improved profitability, and increased customer satisfaction.
- ♦ Created company's first core Management/Leadership Development curriculum organized into 3 skill levels (foundation, operational, and strategic); expanded program to include all employees.

Employee Development
- ♦ Planned and created highly effective employee development planning process (SOLID) introduced company-wide.
- ♦ Consulted with incoming senior management and facilitated effective transition of new staff within unit in record time.

154

Combination. *Louise Garver, Enfield, Connecticut*

This applicant had spent most of his career with one employer and progressed through the ranks. His position was eliminated in a massive downsizing. To illustrate the depth of his

Manager, Training and Organizational Development   *1983–1984*

Promoted to create all training and organizational development programs for division with 500 employees. Assessed organizational needs and developed programs for all employees. Managed $650,000 annual budget.

◆ Conducted customized training in effective negotiation skills, resulting in renewal of a major 10-year contract surpassing company's established return-on-equity objectives.

LENNOX CORPORATION, Chicago, IL   1981–1983
Senior Training Coordinator

Designed and implemented training programs for managers and professionals on performance management and coaching, leadership, conflict management, communications, and negotiations. Conducted train-the-trainer programs for line managers. Led 15 trainers in several plant locations. Reduced external training costs by $175,000. Served on Policy Development Committee.

EDUCATION & AFFILIATIONS

Ed.D. in Organizational Development
YALE UNIVERSITY, New Haven, CT

M.Ed. in Counseling and B.A. in Psychology
COLUMBIA UNIVERSITY, New York, NY

Certified Trainer: Zenger Miller Supervision Training

American Association for Training and Development

PROFESSIONAL ACTIVITIES & HONORS

- Advisory Board for U.S. Training Industry Survey "Report to the President of the United States of America."

- Recipient of Training Director Forum's Award for "Managing Change" and for "Selling Training to Senior Management."

- Named "Rising Star" by *Human Resources Executive* journal in September 2003.

- Invited as panelist to address "Large-scale Change" at the Association for Training and Development International Conference.

experience and to position him for a VP-level assignment, the writer presented the individual's experience and key achievements in three development areas (organization, management, and employee). The resume helped him land three interviews, and he received two offers for a VP-level position in his field.

JACKSON BRAUN

3000 Peak Vista Drive • Dallas, TX 55555 • Home: (000) 000-0000 • Cell: (000) 000-0000

EXECUTIVE PROFILE

Successful executive with 27 years of proven success in revitalizing failing business units. Proven career record of producing multimillion-dollar profits through pinpointing operational inefficiencies and encouraging the revitalization of employee morale and corporate culture change. Possess solid understanding of food distribution industry in diverse markets and cultures, including profit and loss, market analysis, operations analysis, and logistics. Demonstrated ability to communicate business principles to distribution center personnel on all levels in order to facilitate change and initiate turnaround. Expertise in

◈ Cost Reductions	◈ Profit Generation	◈ Strategic Planning
◈ Distribution Management	◈ Process Redesign	◈ Multi-Site Operations
◈ Operations Start-Up	◈ Multi-Level Communications	◈ Sales/Market Growth

CAREER EXPERIENCE

CST CORPORATION   2002–PRESENT
DIVISIONAL DIRECTOR OF OPERATIONS, Savannah, SC
Recruited for abilities to successfully revitalize failing business units. Currently responsible for more than $1 billion in annual sales from Fort Worth, Oklahoma City, and Denver facilities. Accountable for all P&L, equipment, utilities, personnel, and operating procedures. Directed overhaul from the ground up of San Diego distribution center, including bringing warehouse, offices, refrigeration, and transportation facilities up to code and fully staffing the center. Mobilized correction of gross inefficiencies in Oklahoma City and Fort Worth facilities, resulting in quick turnarounds. Facilities currently maintain monthly profits.

- ◈ Launched San Diego distribution center and built into a profit-producing facility within 3 months.
- ◈ Reduced substantial losses at Oklahoma City distribution center of $6 million per year to generating a profit within 3 months. Cost per case drastically fell 85–90 cents per case—excluding marketing monies—resulting in $8+ million turnaround (running rate).
- ◈ Directed operational changes in Fort Worth center, resulting in cost per case drastically falling from $2.35 per case to $1.80 per case, with $5+ million gain in profits realized in 4 months (running rate).

GALLEY'S FOOD SERVICE, INC.   1998–2002
GENERAL MANAGER, Lincoln, NE
Recruited to modernize operations in return for potential significant equity position. Restructured business financially and reorganized personnel. Monitored P&L and administered daily supervision of staff. Developed strong relationships with key accounts. Boosted bottom-line profitability in order to strengthen personal purchasing position.

- ◈ Achieved notable increase in profits, including a 60% increase in 1996, a 26% increase in 1997, and an 11% increase in 1998. (All profits are EBIT.)

155

Combination. *Michele Angello, Aurora, Colorado*

Unique dot-in-a-diamond bullets point to areas of expertise in the Executive Profile and to accomplishments in the Career Experience section. Horizontal lines enclosing section headings

JACKSON BRAUN (Page 2)

CAREER EXPERIENCE (continued)

NAUTILUS FOOD SERVICE, INC.   1994–1998
DIVISION PRESIDENT, Sioux City, IA

- ◈ Initiated operational changes within one year that revitalized Sioux City center from 7-year record of losses to $350,000 EBIT in fiscal 1996.

BEST FOODSERVICE, INC.   1991–1994
DIVISION PRESIDENT, Boca Raton, FL.
EXECUTIVE VICE PRESIDENT, Baltimore, MD
Accountable for all P&L and administration of all personnel, including sales, procurement, marketing, operations, customer service, finance, transportation, and warehouse staff. Directed $450 million distribution center with 1,350 employees, overseeing sales, procurement, and marketing.

- ◈ In 1994/95, transformed Schmidt acquisition with 9 straight years of losses to a turnaround of $250,000 EBIT, an overall gain of $1 million.
- ◈ Negotiated additional $1.2 million in additional EBIT through fourth-quarter vendor buy-in conference.

EDUCATION

University of Notre Dame, Notre Dame, IN
Executive M.B.A. Program. Accepted into exclusive program; completed 8-week course prior to acceptance of Best promotion and transfer.

University of Houston, Houston, TX
Best Management School, 1991

Ivy League University, East Coast, PA
Bachelor of Arts Degree, Business Administration
> **Honors**—Received full scholarship for music and sports. Varsity baseball, Captain; Theta Delta Chi, President and Treasurer; All-Conference Outfielder, State of Pennsylvania; Recruiter and Mixed Quartet member.

HONORS & AWARDS

CST Corporation, Distribution Company of the Year—2000
Best Foodservice, Branch of the Year—1993
Nautilus Food Service, Highest Margin and Highest Sales Gross—Attained awards 11 out of 12 months
Galley's Food Service, National Sales Award
Numerous Sales Awards

make the overall layout easy to see. The writer likes to use a larger font size (12 points) for the text in the Executive Profile to make that information stand out from the resume's other information (at 11 points). Note that all of the achievements are quantified in some way.

EDWARD P. TOMPKINS

266 Haggerty Road   (555) 555-5555
Audubon, PA 00000   etompkins@dotresume.com

PROFESSIONAL PROFILE

General Manager with extensive experience leading multiple departments in multimillion-dollar corporations. Consistent track record of improving bottom line by growing revenue, improving efficiency, reducing expenses, and maximizing employee productivity. Strong leader, excellent communicator, progressive change agent, and creative problem solver.

- *Management & Leadership*—Accomplished in leading personnel at all levels, including managers, supervisors, department heads, and staff. Proven ability to collaborate with executives. Exceptional team-building skills. Long-term vision coupled with detail orientation.

- *Communication & Professionalism*—Customer- and employee-oriented. Effective and articulate. Savvy in interacting with management, staff, clients, vendors, consultants, and subcontractors. Accessible, flexible, and energetic. Consistent demeanor in all situations.

- *Business Improvement & Problem Resolution*—Resourceful in implementation of operational improvements and management of challenging projects. Excellent analytical and problem-solving skills. Proven ability to identify needs, enhance efficiencies, and cut costs. Lean Enterprise certified.

AREAS OF EXPERIENCE

General/Operations Management	Vendor Relations	Finance/P & L
Purchasing/Materials Management	Customer Management	Production
Marketing & Sales	Human Resources	Credit & Collections

CAREER HIGHLIGHTS

E. J. FORESTER, INC., Valley Forge, PA (2000–2004)
A multimillion-dollar industry leader employing 150 and specializing in structural steel, modular mezzanines, material-handling products, and miscellaneous metal fabrication.

General Manager
Reported to president with 10 direct reports and 36 indirect reports. Managed all aspects of operations, production, engineering, purchasing, process maximization, and manpower utilization. Spearheaded development of standard operating procedures. Initiated and led implementation of programs for organizational clarity, quality improvement, employee initiative, and preventive maintenance.

Key Accomplishments
- Increased employee productivity 20 percent through application of Lean Enterprise concepts and organizational restructuring.
- Boosted production 25 percent while reducing work hours 20 percent—a result of maximizing efficiency of labor and equipment.
- Reduced operating costs approximately 15 percent through increases in efficiency.
- Improved employee job satisfaction and morale through introduction of employee initiative program and projects to clarify organization structure and standard operating procedures.
- Laid groundwork for better product quality and plant safety with creation of Quality and Compliance Department.

156

Combination. *Jan Holliday, Harleysville, Pennsylvania*

The Professional Profile includes three bulleted skill areas in bold italic. Information grouped according to the three categories is easier to understand than if the same information had been

EDWARD P. TOMPKINS

page 2

CAREER HIGHLIGHTS, continued

VALLEY PRIDE, INC., King of Prussia, PA (1990–2000)
A multimillion-dollar corporation with 100 employees and end markets in transportation, construction, environment, and industry.

General Manager
Promoted to general manager (1995–2000) after serving as acting general manager (1994–1995) and purchasing/office manager (1990–1993).

As general manager and acting general manager, directed all departments, supervising 45 management, administrative, and floor personnel. Collaborated with top management and consultants on business and strategic planning, and established business goals, production quotas, and manpower requirements. Managed employee-management relations, maintaining teamwork environment and generating positive morale through creation of steering committee and employee initiative program. Implemented improvements in production processes and office technology. Created Internet presence and strategy.

In all positions, oversaw purchasing, sales, marketing, vendor and customer relations, accounting, and credit and collections.

Key Accomplishments
- Increased sales/revenues on a 20-percent annual basis.
- Boosted distributor sales 500 percent by expanding network from 2 to 14.
- Improved customer retention through implementation of comprehensive customer service program.
- Decreased employee training time 40 percent with introduction of streamlined processes and written standard operating procedures.
- Cut operating costs 15 percent by reducing non-value-added operations, improving employee efficiency, and obtaining process-improvement input from vendors.
- Reduced uncollectible accounts to less than 1 percent of sales.
- Pared inventory 25 percent through product re-engineering.
- Achieved 25-percent reduction in product material expense through collaboration with customers and vendors.

EDUCATION, SEMINARS

Lean Enterprise Certificate, National Manufacturing Certification Agency, Allentown, PA (2004)

Leadership Seminar, Duff Management Institute, Philadelphia, PA (2003)

B.A., Finance, Eastern State University, Philadelphia, PA (1989)

COMPUTER SKILLS

Internet savvy. Working knowledge of Microsoft Word, Access, and Outlook. Familiar with Microsoft Excel.

presented in one long paragraph. Italic comments about the workplaces in the Career Highlights section enhance understanding of the applicant's experience. Bulleted Key Accomplishments for each workplace make a strong case for his worth as an employee.

John Savage
maintenance reliability engineer

1000 State Drive
Memphis, Tennessee 38100
℗ 901.555.5555 – js1@tide.net

"Your contribution over the past 10 years has been a key factor to our success."
— Site General Manager

"Finding a better way to do something is what helps us become the best in the business."
— Production Manager and Maintenance Manager

WHAT I CAN OFFER TOPLINE

❏ Moving maintenance from a cost center to a **productivity center** as well ❏ Getting the right information to the right people in time to **save money and boost production** ❏ **Building and motivating teams** who think of my suggestions as their own good ideas ❏ Solving the right problems — the first time ❏ **Forging "success partnerships" with vendors**

RECENT WORK HISTORY WITH EXAMPLES OF PROBLEMS SOLVED

❏ **Chemical Operator** *promoted over 250 tough competitors to be* **Industrial Maintenance Mechanic;** *promoted over 70 others (some more senior) to be* **Industrial Maintenance Leader;** *promoted before 75 others to be* **Maintenance Coordination Leader,** GE, Centerville, Tennessee   86–Present

Our plant operates 24/7 from its 300 acres of production space. Our 425 employees produce polycarbonate resins and engineered plastics as raw materials for products that range from automotive instrument panels to CDs and DVDs.

Serve as direct reporting official for 12 maintenance mechanics.

Gave management the production maintenance reports they needed to run the business after others tried — and failed — using our mainframe. Led 20 team members from across three states to build our new reporting system. *Payoffs:* **Saved $240K in direct labor.** Now every team member has immediate, on-site ability to track more than 48K stock items and assets. Project **on time and on budget. Our system now the GE standard.**

Got control of our high non-fill rate by overhauling our MRO. Did my homework to marry best practices to just the right metrics applied to just the right data points. Replaced our expensive, twice-yearly inventory with a rolling system. *Payoffs:* The new approach easily handles 10,900 stock issue requests. **Non-fill rate dropped to zero and stayed there for 16 months.**

Helped management rethink how we could comply with tough EPA standards for our transformers. Proposed, and got complete support for, an approach that let us get maximum ROI from existing equipment. *Payoffs:* My fix complete in just a few days for only $30K — **$720K less than the cost of the original plan.**

Worked closely with the production team to solve a chronic problem that caused too many costly production-line shutdowns. When I reevaluated vendor's equipment against EPA standards, I saw a new engineering solution that promised a long-term solution. *Payoffs:* We **met Federal regulations better than ever** and we **saved $140K** in raw materials.

Championed the idea of predictive maintenance as a complement to preventative maintenance. Sold senior management on the idea and my approach to implementing it. *Payoffs:* **Reduced production budget by $900K** *and* **increased** production **12.5 percent.**

More indicators of performance **TopLine** *can use …*

157

Combination. *Don Orlando, Montgomery, Alabama*

The way to examine this resume (and others by this writer) is to search for the many ways it does not look like resumes by others. Note the creative use of font enhancements (boldfacing,

Built a mutually beneficial relationship with vendors that served us, them, and our customers better. Tapped into their expertise to redesign a critical component that didn't fail gracefully. *Payoffs:* **Lowered replacement part cost by 35 percent**. **Saved $110K more** by tripling the MTBF.

❏ **Industrial Maintenance Mechanic,** Delta Chemical Company, Longview, Louisiana

           75–85

EDUCATION AND PROFESSIONAL DEVELOPMENT

❏ Pursing BS, Education, with special emphasis on Adult Education in Industrial Operations
Center State University, Center, Tennessee   Degree expected in 04
Earning this degree at night and on the weekends while working 50 hours a week.

❏ Associate Degree (Applied Technology)
Union State Technical College, Memphis, Tennessee   95
Completed this degree while holding down a 50-hour-a-week job.

❏ Reliability-Centered Maintenance Training, Manufacturing Technologies, Inc.   03
Volunteered for this 88-hour course. One of 20 selected from a field of 200 eligibles.

❏ Electrical and Instrumentation Craft Training, National Center for Construction Education and Research   Jul 99

❏ Planning and Scheduling Maintenance Management Resources, Hartford Steam Boiler Company   98
Selected and funded by my employer for this week-long workshop.

❏ Millwright Craft Training, National Center for Construction Education and Research   Dec 94

COMPUTER SKILLS

❏ Expert in EMPAC, a purchasing, asset, work-management, and maintenance software suite.

❏ Proficient in Primavera, a project planning and management software package; MS Word, Excel, PowerPoint, Outlook, and Money; and Internet search protocols.

PROFESSIONAL ACCREDITATIONS

❏ **Certified Systems Administrator for Enterprise Maintenance Planning and Control** by Corker International   01

❏ Certified Instructor in millwright craft training from the National Center for Construction Education and Research   99

PROFESSIONAL AFFILIATIONS

❏ Member, Program Advisory Committee for Electrical and Instrumentation Programs, Union State Technical College, Memphis, Tennessee   Since Mar 99
Selected by the president to help guide how the college matches its curriculum with industry best practices.

italic, bold italic, and small caps) and font styles (sans serif and serif). Look for the word "Payoffs" to see a novel way to present quantified information about achievements. Notice the use of headers (at the top of pages) and footers (at the bottom of pages) to impress on the reader the need for confidentiality.

CHARLES STRAIGHT

SENIOR-LEVEL EXECUTIVE

Operations ● General Management ● Business Development

Improve financial and operational performance of dynamic multimillion-dollar service and supply-based enterprises in domestic and international markets.

- Delivered $200 million in total career business development revenue.
- Contributed millions of dollars in efficiency / cost savings by developing and championing innovative systems.
- Drive ROI-based operational direction in growth, M&A, restructure, turnaround, and change.
- Overcome complex business challenges and serious financial constraints in volatile markets.
- Achieve operational and financial discipline across all functional lines. Experience spans two full market cycles.

Areas of Excellence

- Strategic & Tactical Planning...Market Development...Multimillion-Dollar P&L Management / Improvement...M&A
- Innovative Solutions & Efficiency Creation...Crisis Management...Contract Negotiations...ISO Certifications
- Purchasing, Distribution & Warehousing...Quality Control...Customer & Vendor Management...Labor Relations
- Systems & Process Reengineering...Logistics...Global Supply Solutions...Statistical Process Control

CAREER DEVELOPMENT

THE LATHAM CO., Garfield, CA	Senior Vice President	1993 to Present
1988 to Present	Vice President of Operations	1990 to 1993
	Operations Manager	1988 to 1990

Nation's largest purchasing, logistics, and global supply solutions company, serving marine / offshore industries. Hold full P&L / operations accountability for four-division Vessel Supply and Purchasing Management Groups, with operations in Milton, Oklahoma, and California. Oversee M&A functions, planning, purchasing, warehousing, distribution, quality control, human resource management, and union negotiations. Manage ISO 9002 quality system. Oversee seven direct reports.

Budget: $3.5 Million / Sales: $40 Million / Reporting Staff: 76

Operational Management

- *Reduced labor costs 25%* through manpower efficiencies generated by consolidating company-wide order entry, warehousing, and purchasing functions.
- *Contained costs and increased employee satisfaction* by negotiating consistent win-win labor union contracts.
- *Directed creation / implementation of enterprise-wide customized application* (warehouse, logistics, purchasing, and customer service). Conceptualized / introduced technology infrastructure for integration of virtually all business functions.
- *Orchestrated company's NY-to-NJ relocation.* Spearheaded renovation, including planning, design, and construction.
- *Managed relocation hiring strategies / up-staffing.* Developed formal job descriptions and performance appraisal system.
- *Provided complete outsourced purchasing / logistics* to largest U.S. publicly owned bulk shipping company.
- *Delivered continuous process improvement* with ISO 9002 Quality Management System and Statistical Process Control.

Business Development

- *Increased U.S. Gulf sales by 63%* and opened new sales markets by initiating / negotiating joint venture and later acquisition of Tipton USA, a $15 million annual revenue competitor in Milton market.
- *Expanded company's revenue base by $3 million* and enhanced service by establishing Technical Supply Division to improve sales, procurement, and distribution of essential spare parts, components, and capital equipment.
- *Oversee two accounts representing 33% of current sales.* Cultivate / maintain profitable business relationships (including contract negotiation) with key clients.
- *Developed $8 million revenue stream* (from an initial $400,000) by establishing new markets throughout Scandinavia, the United Kingdom, and Greece.

348 Mill Road, Chatham, CA 11111 ● 777.777.7777 (h) ● 666.666.6666 (f) ● cstraight@att.net

158

Combination. *Deborah Dib, Medford, New York*

Areas of Excellence amount to key phrases. Capsule descriptions of each company are useful for assessing the individual's stature. A distinctive feature is the Budget/Sales/Reporting Staff line

CHARLES STRAIGHT

Career Development / Latham Co., continued

Acquisitions Management

- *Researched and evaluated all new business ventures.* Assessed 15 possible acquisition candidates across the U.S.
- *Led acquisition contributing $100,000 in annual profit* and broadened strategic sales / distribution to U.S. Gulf. (Gulf Maritime Services Corporation, Houston, TX). Negotiated terms / agreements and managed venture's first year.

ISO Certification Initiative

- *Championed achievement of ISO 9002 Certification within only 13 months.*
- *Preemptively envisioned benefits of certification* prior to widespread embrace by the industry, sold idea up- and down-stream within company.
- *Directed entire initiative:* processes, procedure development, documentation, employee training, and auditing. Created definitive methodology to measure results and produce consistent and ongoing improvement.
- *Delineated five performance metrics:* customer satisfaction, vendor performance, returned products, customer issues, and product fulfillment rates.
- *Provided semi-annual management review reports* to executive management documenting results and recommending process improvements.

ISO-Related Distinctions

- *Commended by outside auditors* for establishment of excellent documentation and metrics measurement procedures.
- *Credited with a true turn-around of the company's operational procedures.* Achieved or exceeded established benchmarks and produced operational cost efficiencies while improving all levels of customer satisfaction.

ANDERSON & ROWE, INC., New City, MD   Vice President & General Manager
1978 to 1988

Full-service marine supplier and outfitter, among foremost U.S. companies in the marine industry. Held strategic and tactical responsibility for management of daily ship supply operations, including sales / business development, financial management, union negotiations, purchasing, distribution, staffing, and legal issues. Oversaw four direct reports.

Budget: $1 Million / Revenue: $6 Million / Reporting Staff: 20

Operational Management

- *Reduced operating expenses by 20%* through staff redeployment and several contract renegotiations.
- *Increased revenues 18%* by securing commission-based consignment commodity handling agreements.
- *Planned and managed company's successful relocation* to a new state-of-the-art facility. Funded the move with a grant from the New City Business Relocation Corporation (BRAC).
- *Negotiated facility purchase and arranged financing* through New City Industrial Agency Bonds, achieving favorable interest rates and 33% tax abatement.

Business Leadership

- *Managed acquisition of key competitor,* increasing market share and reducing overhead through economies of scale.
- *Pioneered creation of an industry-based collective-bargaining group,* ultimately saving each member company substantial dollars in labor costs. Served as group's lead negotiator in interactions with union representatives.

EDUCATION & AFFILIATIONS

Bachelor of Arts, English
Burnham University, Western Campus
Burnham, OH

International Supply Association (ISSA)
National Association of Marine Suppliers (NAMS)
Society of Marine Port Engineers

348 Mill Road, Chatham, CA 11111 ● **777.777.7777 (h)** ● **666.666.6666 (f)** ● **cstraight@att.net**

under each workplace description to quantify company size. Note how italic is used in the bulleted achievements in the Career Development section, and how they are grouped according to side headings. A big surprise at the end is that this individual was an English major in his college days.

JEFFREY A. DAVENPORT

227 Meadowvale Drive
Centreville, VA 20121

703.222.7777
email: jeffreydaven222@com.com

VICE PRESIDENT, FLIGHT OPERATIONS / DIRECTOR OF SOCC

Bottom-line-driven manager supported by progressively responsible experience throughout a 15-year aviation-industry career. Proven accomplishments in the productive leadership over system operations control center (SOCC) encompassing dispatch, crew scheduling, customer service and maintenance control. Combine strong industry knowledge and business leadership skills to consistently manage complex scheduling; lead high-performance, motivated teams; and implement efficient processes that ensure smooth operations and quality customer service. Strong communicator, effective negotiator and motivational team builder; able to effectively communicate needs and merge disparate teams in the support of market/industry objectives. Respected for wide range of industry knowledge, solid sense of integrity and demonstrated passion for industry as a whole. **Executive MBA in Airline Management in progress.**

Industry Expertise: Extensive knowledge of FAR 121 Scheduling (Federal Aviation Regulation Part 121); Licensed 121 Aircraft Dispatcher; Technical and Logistical Support for Active Fleet Maintenance Discrepancies; Aircraft Mechanical Systems and Flight Controls; Real-time Flight Following; Post-Situational Replay; Route Planning; Flight & Ground Crew Operations; System Customer Service; Policies & Procedures Development; Labor Agreements; Emergency Management; Budgeting & Personnel Administration.

EXECUTIVE CAREER HIGHLIGHTS

DOMAIN EXPERT / CUSTOMER SUPPORT & TRAINING MANAGER
CONSTANABLE AVIATION GROUP—Washington, DC (March 2000 to Present)
(A subsidiary of the Airline Company and SOC Domain Expert with more than 500 employees)

Charged with providing key input into development of SOC planning and decision optimization support tool. Created user definition, quality assurance and business development functions for the product entitled ATLAS v1.0, Advanced Tracking and Look Ahead Solution, an intelligent situation display system capable of reading live air-traffic data such as ASDI, radar, satellite, ground tracking position updates, and flight plans of all aircraft on any given day.

- **Credited with contributing to successful SOC redesign** based on expertise of SOC environment and management of irregular operations; played pivotal role in innovation and creation of functionality and "look and feel" of software.
- **Customized product ability to project current situation** ahead in "fast time": the decision-support capability to improve activity / response time of airlines' operational control centers, airport and station managers.
- **Ensured optimum usage and workability of product** to increase reliability of current aircraft activity monitoring while allowing for current aircraft activity to be projected into the future.
- **Delivered gate-to-gate flight tracking and position updates** within one second and currently integrating results with flight planning, crew scheduling and maintenance planning activities.
- **Key input in development of connectivity** between carriers' other decision-support systems and SOC database and potential connectivity with Constanable.
- **Eased usability for dispatchers and ATC coordinators** by leading creation of advanced rerouting function with "spotlight" point-and-click user interface.
- **Identified and secured numerous business development** opportunities without incurring additional costs by actively promoting product and remaining visible within the industry.

SOC MANAGER (OPERATIONS CONTROL)
AMERICA'S BEST AIRLINE COMPANY—New York, NY (April 1998 to March 2000)

Held full accountability for directing daily operations of 500+ flight schedule, including all customer service, aircraft routing, crew scheduling and dispatch functions. Coordinated operational control activities in conjunction with worldwide operations (including timing and variety of airline activities) and based on support of meteorologists, engineering and route planning staff tasked with providing critical information and plans in support of daily operations.

159

Combination. *Kim Little, Victor, New York*

One way to compress much information onto two pages is to resort to paragraphs. Without enhancements, paragraphs are difficult to read, and a reader's tempo in reading them can be

Continued...

- **Fostered optimum staff performance** despite challenging work environment/deadline commitments by cultivating well-motivated, focused staff committed to overall team success.
- **Smoothed communication flow between disparate divisions** of SOC staff by focusing on team efforts related to bottom-line objectives and increasing employee value through incentives.
- **Sustained cost-effective operations and positive revenue** results by constantly employing cost vs. profit analysis in all decisions.
- **United employee commitment** and realized quantifiable employee confidence/decision-making by facilitating comprehensive training programs on all aspects of SOC environment/activities.

SOC DUTY MANAGER / CREW RESOURCES MANAGER
FLYING WORLD AIRLINES—Farmington, NM (June 1995 to April 1998)

Promoted from initial position as Licensed 121 Dispatcher to SOC Management position responsible for all activities related to the delivery of smooth and timely flight operations. Charged with providing consistent monitoring of all weather, scheduling, crew and mechanical issues and coordinating an aircraft's flying time with required maintenance and repair schedules.

- **Instrumental role in securing conversion of a 135 carrier rating to a 121 carrier rating** by proving RUNS to the FAA.
- **Gained high approval ranking** from pilot group by achieving exceptional reliability rating and by employing calm, focused and decisive leadership despite challenging, time-sensitive environment.
- **Marshaled resources and planning strengths** to ensure efficiency and compliance with FAA regulations and contractual guidelines through appropriate assignments of open flights to crew members.

MANAGER OF AIRCRAFT PLANNING
CARRIER POSSIBILITIES—McLean, VA (1993 to 1995)

Scope of responsibility was diverse and included development, maintenance and fine tuning of all flight schedules. Coordinated wide variety of activities, including crew scheduling, fueling, catering, maintenance, sales/marketing and tour operator sources to develop integrated and viable system-wide departure/arrival schedule.

PRINCIPAL PARTNER
DAVENPORT HOSPITALITY SERVICES—Miami, FL (1991 to 1993)

Launched this travel/tourist organization to complement local hoteliers' host of offerings and services. Directed all public relations, advertising, marketing tools, travel development and entertainment promotions. Coordinated activities of guest services desk and reception hotline. Produced narrated overview tour that combined local history, geographics and entertaining points of interest.

Early career includes positions as Fuel Supervisor-EWR (Jennings Airlines); Operations Supervisor, Duty Manager EWB/HYA/EWR (Worldwide Union); PBA Station Manager, Operations Supervisor and Ramp Agent (Pan Trans Express) between 1985 and 1993.

EDUCATIONAL ACHIEVEMENTS & PROFESSIONAL DEVELOPMENT

E.M.B.A., Airline Management—The George Washington University's Aviation Institute, January 2005
(Accepted into program concurrent with B.A. studies)
B.A., Aeronautical Science, Embry Riddle Aeronautical University, June 2004

Member, Airline Dispatchers Federation (ADF)

slow. In this resume, see how paragraphs are formatted differently so that it does not look like a book. Many blank lines ensure adequate white space in spite of the number of paragraphs. Horizontal lines enclosing section headings help to ensure that the document looks like a resume.

LISA DAVIDSON

5555 West King Street, Honolulu, Hawaii 00000 • (808) 555-5555 • iluvyoga@coconut.org

*Seeking **Management** position in a*
NON-PROFIT ORGANIZATION

QUALIFIED TO PERFORM

- *Mission Planning and Implementation*
- *Organizational Development*
- *Leadership Training*
- *Marketing Communications*
- *Media Relations*
- *Public Relations*
- *Corporate Relations*
- *Fund-raising*
- *Grassroots Campaigns*
- *Community Outreach*
- *Educational Programming*
- *Member Development and Retention*
- *Member Communications*
- *Volunteer Recruitment*
- *Volunteer Training*
- *Special Events Management*

EDUCATION

Columbia College, Columbia University—
New York, NY
B.S., English Literature
(Journalism/Ancient Religions concentration)
- Editor of campus weekly magazine
- Awarded Cornell Woolrich Fellowship

PROFILE

18+ years of experience in dynamic organizational settings, including past 8 years in positions of bottom-line accountability. Background includes history of creating and building various small businesses. Effective communicator highly skilled in multiple environments—public speaking, groups, and one-on-one. ***Core skills include***

Organizational Leadership	Project Management
Persuasive Communications	Problem Resolution
Staff Management	Training and Development
Presentations	Workshops
Customer Service	Cross-Cultural Awareness
Research	Written Communications

PROFESSIONAL HISTORY

Career and Life Coach   **1995–Present**
Honolulu, HI; Seattle, WA; Florence, Italy; London, England

Consult with and advise—in person and by telephone—clients of a variety of personal backgrounds and professional levels. Select clients include lawyers, child services professionals, non-profit board members, non-profit fund-raisers, artists, and cultural diversity trainers. Work closely with one assistant on scheduling matters.
- Successfully partner with clients, assisting them through major life transitions.
- Conceptualize, plan, and write all marketing materials for life- and career-development workshops.
- Communicate with media regarding workshop promotional plans. Consistently attract 5 to 20 participants.
- Mentor other professional teachers and workshop presenters on planning, implementation, and problem resolution.
- Publish quarterly client newsletter with circulation of 150.
- Have designed and led weekly workshops on subjects ranging from stress management to decision making.

Certified Yoga Instructor   **1999–Present**
Honolulu, HI; London, England

Currently perform private therapeutic sessions. Have taught daily classes of up to 40 students, including new student orientations. Handle all administrative functions.
- Employ various levels of persuasive communication according to individual student's level, expectations, and goals.
- Have assisted hundreds of people in recovering from injuries, addiction, and stress, helping them develop positive mind and body attitudes.

PROFESSIONAL HISTORY Continued on Page 2 →

160

Combination. *Peter Hill, Honolulu, Hawaii*

The applicant had a successful business/entrepreneurial background and wanted a nonprofit management position. The writer plays up the variety of the applicant's core skills, job positions

Founder/Manager/Sales Representative   1997–1999
Handworks, Inc.—Seattle, WA

Accountable for bottom-line success of this on-site chair-massage service at natural food supermarket franchises. Contracted out and supervised 11 massage therapists. Acted as liaison between customers, employees, and corporate management.
- Spearheaded comprehensive public relations campaign to educate public about services.
- Successfully planned and built business from scratch. Sold it after only two years.

Jin Shin Jyutsu Practitioner   1994–1999
Private Practice—Seattle, WA

Built thriving private practice providing Japanese *Jin Shin Jyutsu* style of bodywork.

Founder/Manager/Sales Representative   1994–1995
Davidson Delicacies—Seattle, WA

Managed all aspects—production, sales, distribution—of this wholesale natural food venture, including materials procurement, kitchen operations, order fulfillment, and account maintenance. Negotiated terms for 20+ accounts throughout Seattle area.
- Launched and grew profitable business, starting with no knowledge of business world or industry.
- Positioned company for success by implementing unique marketing message. Attracted attention of national buyers (including a national food distributor).
- Created *Climbing Cookie* and other unique concept products. Customers still ask for them at area stores.

Administrative Assistant   1992–1993
The Family Schools—Seattle, WA

Oversaw all front- and back-office operations for experimental alternative school program of the Boulder public school system. Program focused on community development of elementary school programs.

Program Assistant   1990–1992
Neighborhood Initiative Programs—Seattle, WA

Accountable for program and event planning for this government-funded leadership training and education for low-income and minority communities. Wrote grant proposals, press releases, business communications, and marketing materials. Assisted in design of Community Leadership Training Program.

Communications Assistant   1989–1990
Williams & Stevenson—Baltimore, MD

Collaborated to compose marketing proposals and newsletter pieces. Managed administrative functions in communications department of this international law firm.

Communications Assistant   1984–1988
Pratt, Gregg, & Nakamoto—Baltimore, MD

Charged with authority to assess prospective client case potential. Generated press releases and marketing materials for this entertainment law firm. Researched and wrote one partner's weekly column for New York newspaper.

~ References Furnished on Request ~

held, qualifications, and work experiences to make her appealing to a wide range of organizations. The two-column look of the first page helps to convey a sense of diversity at a glance. A reader can see something of the individual's qualifications, education, and experience in one sweep of the eyes.

Candace L. Kugle

520 E. Ogden Avenue
Naperville, Illinois 06060

000-983-8882
ckugle@internetservice.com

PROFESSIONAL QUALIFICATIONS AND KEY STRENGTHS

Professional manager with a broad-based background in business development, human resources, personnel management and store operations. Strong leadership and motivational skills; proven ability to quickly build rapport, establish trust, and train and motivate people of all levels. Recognized for professionalism, positive mental attitude, commitment to excellence and demonstrated ability to communicate and interact effectively with senior management, associates and customers. Big-picture focus on company goals has produced increased efficiencies in production and sales.

*Human Resource Management • Interviewing/Training/Developing Personnel • Benefits-Wage Administration
Project Management • Expense and Inventory Control • Policies, Programs and Procedures*

CAREER HIGHLIGHTS

Human Resources

- Established training priorities for 110 stores throughout Illinois, Wisconsin, Minnesota, Iowa and Michigan.
- Recruited personnel at college campuses.
- Evaluated human resources programs and directives.
- Ensured proper execution of federal and state laws and customer service initiatives.
- Evaluated hiring decisions and identified high potential field management personnel.
- Presented benefits and corporate policies overview to new hires.

Management

- Improved expense control; identified efficiencies for controllables and salary expenditures.
- Enhanced management/staff team productivity through motivational training and mentoring.
- Responsible for overall store operations.
- Developed and sustained new and existing business.
- Contributed to store-management team effort to maintain efficient operating conditions and ensure in-stock position.

EMPLOYMENT HISTORY

General Manager, WESTRIDGE APPAREL, Schaumburg, Illinois, 08/99 to Present
- Supervised all aspects of the opening of the Weekend Only Warehouse concept store.
- Recruit, hire and train sales staff.
- Schedule sales and support staff.

General Manager, VENTURE CORPORATION, Chicago, Illinois, 09/98 to 08/99
- Executed merchandising and operations for hardlines /softlines.
- Controlled office/freight receiving procedures; salary budgets.
- Supervised management staff, emphasizing sales performance and high standards of store operations.
- Directed complete remodeling of assigned fashion areas.
- Trained management personnel in operations and supervision.
- Managed job assistance efforts for multiple stores during business close-down.

Previous roles:

Regional HR Trainer, Ft. Wayne, IN—09/95 to 09/98	**Fashion Manager,** Quincy, IL—04/84 to 11/90
District Manager, Ft. Wayne, IN—11/91 to 09/95	**Apparel Manager,** Green Bay, WI—04/81 to 04/84
Softline Manager, Garden City, MI—11/90 to 11/91	**Assistant Manager/Trainee,** Kenosha, WI—07/80 to 04/81

EDUCATION

University of Michigan, Ann Arbor, Michigan
Bachelor of Science in Clothing, Textiles and Design (cum Laude), 1980

161

Combination. *Pat Chapman, Naperville, Illinois*

This individual had retail management experience and wanted to move into human resource management. The writer plays up human resources both in the profile and in the Career Highlights.

Manufacturing

Resumes at a Glance

RESUME NO.	OCCUPATION	GOAL	PAGE
162.	Creative Director	Toy Manufacturing	333
163.	Military Program Manager, Overhaul & Repair	Not specified	334
164.	VP of Manufacturing	Plant/Operations Executive	336
165.	Local Systems Administrator/ Corrugator Scheduler	Not specified	338

BAXTER A. LEEDS

45 Kaiwan Street   Taipei, Taiwan   555-05050505   bestoys@xix5.net

PROFESSIONAL GOAL

Opportunity in the toy manufacturing industry where experience in creative product development, team leadership, and mass production will contribute to business growth and success in the USA and Asia.

PROFESSIONAL PROFILE

- Successful background in the toy industry with a leading manufacturer in both the USA and Asia.
- Highly creative in design, construction, and production of seasonal, novelty, and licensed products.
- Broad understanding of living and working in Asia; knowledge of customs, beliefs, and culture.
- Dedicated commitment to quality products, expense control, and customer satisfaction.
- Valued by colleagues for work ethic, team leadership, creativity, and open-mindedness.

EXPERIENCE

BESTOYS, INC.—Taipei, Taiwan   **1992–Present**
Creative Director
USA-based toy company with manufacturing operations in Taiwan.

Creative Product Development
- Manage product aesthetic and function during product engineering and development process.
- Conceptualize in 3D with mechanical ability to develop pattern, starting with minimal item definition.
- Strong knowledge of model-building techniques and experience with all relevant materials.
- Collaborate with company's CEO and Asian Division President on product development initiatives.

Management/Team Leadership
- Direct 100-member Taiwan prototype staff in all phases of the prototyping/manufacturing process.
- Independently supervise work, coping with fluctuating work loads while maintaining accuracy to product design without missing deadlines.
- Effective interpersonal skills and a respect for people of all backgrounds and nationalities.
- Communicate via e-mail with USA product management on daily item needs and changes.

Manufacturing for Mass Production/Licensed Products
- Skilled in meeting mass production costs, scheduling, and engineering specifications.
- Work directly with BesToys' Asian engineering staff and production vendor engineering on item construction to meet aesthetic, function, schedule, and item cost.
- Manufacture a vast number of products including boys', girls', spring, seasonal, novelty, and licensed products for vastly successful brand names.
- Effectively complete a large volume of licensed goods for sale/distribution in various world markets.

Key Contributions:

- Opened a new prototype facility in Taiwan to meet increased corporate demands, maximize output of sales samples, and reduce prototyping costs.
- Utilize a management style of empowerment, support, and assertiveness in meeting deadlines.
- Monitor and control USA designs built in Taiwan to ensure highest quality standards.

EDUCATION

BFA with Honors
Marketing and Advertising Design—Santa Rosa Fine Arts Academy, Santa Rosa, California, 1992

162

Combination. *Billie Ruth Sucher, Urbandale, Iowa*

The applicant brought the writer "vast pages of information about his background." The writer organized and categorized this information into keyword/skills areas to showcase his experience.

> *"Susan is by far the most promising young professional to come along in many years. Her intelligence, skills, and interpersonal relationships mix together to make her a star."*
> John Smith, Military Program Vice President

SUSAN K. STEELE
200 Steele Street, Chicago, IL 00000
555.555.5555
steelesus@xxxxx.xxx

PROFILE

- Achievement-oriented and accomplished operations professional with aerospace manufacturing, management, merger, and union experience.
- Excellent written and oral communication, presentation, and computer skills.
- Exceptional leadership, organizational, interpersonal, process-improvement, and problem-solving ability.

AWARDS

- **Apex President's Award, 2003**
- **Senior Management Awards, 2002, 2001, 2000**

EXPERIENCE

APEX COMPANY, Chicago, IL   1996–Present
Major Aerospace and Defense Contractor

Military Program Manager Overhaul & Repair, 2001–Present
- Managed $2 million overhaul/repair of military aircraft components, reducing turn time from one year to 30 days.
- Coordinated with all business/operational disciplines to manage competing resources and demands to maximize customer satisfaction and production efficiencies.
- Worked with sales and marketing to develop strategies for new business, along with regular interface with customers, project team members.
- Negotiated and managed large, complex, multimillion-dollar contracts.
- Monitored financial performance to ensure earnings before interest and tax (EBIT) targets were met.

Operations Management Development Program, Management Investment Candidate, 1999–2001
One of four high-potential operations management candidates selected for two years of management training in various operations areas. Three of these assignments occurred during the merger with another company of equal size and ran an average of six months. Assignments included

    Program Manager—Overhaul & Repair Facility Transition
- Transitioned $8 million commercial, military business to The Netherlands and West Coast.
- Managed $1 million budget for construction of new materials crib and mezzanine to hold 9,000 parts, valued at $12 million; net result was on-time completion, 25% under budget, and no loss of business-to-business units.
- Union, non-union personnel utilized to move material without any issues.
- Used Microsoft Project to develop timeline to manage business transition, construction, suppliers, and material move.

163

Combination. *Ellen Mulqueen, Hartford, Connecticut*

This high achiever wanted the quotation to be the first item any reader saw. The box in the upper-left corner of the first page accomplishes that goal. Airplane bullets are distinctive and

Operations Management Development Program, Management Investment Candidate (cont'd)

Program Manager—Manufacturing Operations Systems
- ✈ Planned and implemented Manufacturing Execution System (MES), a time and attendance, labor, and work-in-process (WIP) tracking system with minimal disruption to manufacturing operations.
- ✈ Led manufacturing operations through process of information technology improvements, with objective of one-process, one-system solutions to simplify and solve complex business issues.

Manufacturing Engineer—Assembly and Test Precision Controls & Accessories
- ✈ Implemented statistics process control (SPC) tracking analysis and process specification capabilities for PC&A assembly and test.
- ✈ Worked with cross-functional teams to identify root cause analysis.
- ✈ Developed, implemented corrective action plan that increased test yields on Jet Fuel Control from 25% to 100%.

Business Unit Manager—Propulsion Business Unit
- ✈ Managed Regional, Military Aircraft Blade and Composite lines of 100 hourly union associates, 3 production supervisors.
- ✈ Assumed day-to-day management functions covering production of 300 military, 500 regional blades; all associated composites; and plastic tooling department.
- ✈ Oversaw linear flow of production, overdue reduction, process improvements, continuous improvement, cost management/reductions, and management liaison to union safety team.

Buyer, 1996–1998
- ✈ Managed connector commodity in coordination with suppliers, using JDE and MRP systems, resulting in **95% success rate**; this involved getting right parts at right time by using negotiating, buying, expediting, and problem-solving skills. Supervised and managed daily activities of contractors.

EDUCATION

New York University Graduate College of Business, New York, NY
- ✈ MBA, with 3.85 GPA

University of Chicago, Chicago, IL
- ✈ BBA, Management, Summa cum Laude

Chicago Community College, Chicago, IL
- ✈ Computer Programming Certificate

topically relevant. Boldfacing effectively directs attention to the person's name, the section headings, the positions held, the major assignments, and a notable achievement. Indentation patterns help to keep levels of information straight and to ensure adequate white space.

WILLIAM T. PARKERSON

35 Sunderland Drive
Cedar Grove, NJ 55555

E-mail: parkersonw@compuserv.com

Home: (555) 555-5555
Fax: (555) 555-5555

PLANT / OPERATIONS / GENERAL MANAGEMENT EXECUTIVE

Multi-site manufacturing plant/general management career building and leading high-growth, transition and start-up operations in domestic and international environments with annual revenues of up to $680 million.

Expertise: Organizational Development • Productivity & Cost Reduction Improvements • Supply-Chain Management • Acquisitions & Divestitures • IPOs • Plant Rationalizations • Safety Performance • Customer Relations • Change Agent

CORE COMPETENCIES

Manufacturing Leadership—Strong P&L track record with functional management experience in all disciplines of manufacturing operations • Developing and managing operating budgets • Spearheading restructuring and rationalization of plants and contracted distribution facilities • Initiating lean manufacturing processes, utilizing SMED principles • Establishing performance metrics and supply-chain management teams.

Continuous Improvement & Training—Designing and instituting leadership-enhancement training program for all key plant management • Instituting Total Quality System (TQS) process in domestic plants to promote the business culture of continuous improvement and leading ISO 9001 certification process.

New Product Development—Initiating plant-based "New Product Development Think Tank" that developed 130 new products for marketing review, resulting in the successful launch of 5 new products in 2000.

Engineering Management—Overseeing corporate machine design and development teams • Developing 3-year operating plan • Directing the design, fabrication and installation of several proprietary machines • Creating project cost tracking systems and introducing ROI accountability.

PROFESSIONAL EXPERIENCE

BEACON INDUSTRIES, INC., Maspeth, NY (1997–Present)
Record of continuous promotions to executive-level position in manufacturing and operations management despite periods of transition/acquisition at a $680 million Fortune 500 international manufacturing company. Career highlights include:

Vice President of Manufacturing (1997–Present)

Senior Operating Executive responsible for the performance of 7 manufacturing/distribution facilities for company that experienced rapid growth from 4 plants generating $350 million in annual revenues to 14 manufacturing facilities with revenues of $680 million. Charged with driving the organization to become a low-cost producer. Established performance indicators, operating goals, realignment initiatives, productivity improvements and cost-reduction programs that consistently improved product output, product quality and customer satisfaction.

Achievements:

- Selected to lead corporate team in developing and driving forward cost-reduction initiatives that will result in $21 million saved over the next 3 years through capital infusion, process automation and additional rationalizations.

- Saved $13 million annually by reducing fixed spending 11% and variable overhead spending 18% through effective utilization of operating resources and cost-improvement initiatives.

- Cut Workers' Compensation costs 40% ($750,000 annually) by implementing effective health and safety plans, employee training, management accountability and equipment safeguarding. Led company to achieve recognition as "Best in Industry" regarding OSHA frequency and Loss Workday Incident rates.

- Reduced waste generation 31%, saving $1 million in material usage by optimizing manufacturing processes as well as instituting controls and accountability.

- Enhanced customer service satisfaction 3% annually during past year (measured by order fill and on-time delivery percentage) through supply-chain management initiatives, inventory control and flexible manufacturing practices.

- Trimmed manufacturing and shipping–related credits to customers from 1.04% to .5% of total sales in 1999, representing annual $1.8 million reduction.

- Decreased total inventories 43% from 1997 base through combination of supply-chain management, purchasing, master scheduling and global utilization initiatives.

- Rationalized 3 manufacturing plants and 6 distribution facilities, saving $6 million over 3 years.

164

Combination. *Louise Garver, Enfield, Connecticut*

The applicant's experience was concentrated in one industry throughout his career. He wanted to relocate and find a VP of Operations or Division Management position in another industry.

WILLIAM T. PARKERSON • (555) 555-5555 • Page 2

General Manager, Northeast (1994–1997)

Assumed full P&L responsibility of 2 manufacturing facilities and a $20 million annual operating budget. Directly supervised facility managers and indirectly 250 employees in a multi-line, multicultural manufacturing environment. Planned and realigned organizational structure and operations to position company for high growth as a result of acquiring a major account, 2 new product lines and 800 additional SKUs.

Achievements:

- Reduced operating costs by $4.5 million through consolidation of 2 distribution locations without adverse impact on customer service.

- Accomplished the start-up of 2 new manufacturing operations, which encompassed a plant closing and the integration of acquired equipment into existing production lines for 2 new product lines without interruption to customer service; achieved 2 months ahead of target and $400,000 below budget.

- Increased operating performance by 15% while reducing labor costs by $540,000.

- Reduced frequency and severity of accidents by 50% in 3 years, contributing to a Workers' Compensation and cost-avoidance reduction of $1 million.

- Decreased operating waste by 2% for an annual cost savings of $800,000 in 2 manufacturing facilities.

- Negotiated turnkey contracts for 2 distribution warehouses to meet expanded volume requirements.

- Maintained general management and administrative cost (GMA) at a flat rate as sales grew by 25% annually over 3 years.

ROMELARD CORPORATION, Detroit, MI (1980–1994)
Division Manufacturing Director (1989–1994)

Fast-track advancement in engineering, manufacturing and operations management to division-level position. Retained by new corporate owners and promoted in 1994 based upon consistent contributions to revenue growth, profit improvements and cost reductions. Scope of responsibility encompassed P&L for 3 manufacturing facilities and a distribution center with 500 employees in production, quality, distribution, inventory control and maintenance.

Achievements:

- Delivered strong and sustainable operating gains: Increased customer fill rate by 18%; improved operating performance by 20%; reduced operating waste by 15% and reduced inventory by $6 million.

- Justified, sourced and directed the installation of $10 million of automated plant equipment.

- Implemented and managed a centralized master scheduling for all manufacturing facilities.

- Reduced annual Workers' Compensation costs by $600,000.

- Created Customer Satisfaction Initiative program to identify areas of concern and implemented recommendations, significantly improving customer satisfaction.

Prior Positions: Manufacturing Manager (1987–1989); Plant Manager (1986–1987); Engineering Manager (1984–1986); Plant Industrial Engineer (1980–1984).

EDUCATION & PROFESSIONAL DEVELOPMENT

Bachelor of Science in Manufacturing Engineering
Syracuse University, Syracuse, NY

Continuing professional development programs in
Executive Management, Leadership and Finance

The writer created a strong introduction and Core Competencies section that positioned him effectively. He was soon offered a VP-level position in a totally different industry. Substantial bulleted lists of quantified achievements for each position held since 1989 are impressive.

Bernard T. Bailey

123 Main Street
Park Point, IL 00000

555-555-5555
xxxx@aol.com

HIGHLIGHTS OF VALUE TO A POTENTIAL EMPLOYER

- In-depth knowledge of **manufacturing and distribution operations and logistics**, with a particular strength in improving efficiency with effective **supply-chain analysis, production planning and scheduling.**
- Hands-on experience in **materials forecasting, purchasing and inventory management.**
- Versatile problem-solver, especially in the application of technology to the planning process, as well as day-to-day operations.
- Computer and related equipment skills: Microsoft Office suite, Crystal Reports, AS400, Novell NetWare, IBM PCs, HP printers.

PROFESSIONAL EXPERIENCE

Northern Industries, Inc., Portland, OR, 1992 to Present
Local Systems Administrator / Corrugator Scheduler for the Pleasant Park, IL, plant of this major manufacturer of corrugated containers and point-of-purchase products. Firm recently merged into the XYZ Company.
- Maintain plant LAN systems; provide training and first-line user support for systems issues.
- Install and repair computer equipment.
- Plan and direct production schedules for two-shift machine operation.
- Forecast, purchase and manage raw materials inventory within sales budget.
- Manage finished-for-release inventories for key accounts.
- Provide expertise for sales and production departments to establish new product requirements.

Tech Systems, Park Point, IL, 1990–1992
- Established and operated a company selling and servicing computer products for small businesses.

ABC Housewares Manufacturing, Inc., Western Park, IL, 1985–1990
Assistant Warehouse Manager
- Developed significant improvements in layout and operational procedures to increase productivity.
- Installed warehouse management computer system; provided liaison to data processing staff and system vendor.
- Trained operations staff and led the transition to new procedures.

Additional experience gained with the following:
- **Distribution Systems Analyst** with **DDD Corporation,** Chicago, IL, 1978–1985. Completed projects to develop and maintain layouts of multi-warehouse distribution center, analyze material-handling requirements and branch store inventory sharing, and research computer support requirements.
- Intelligence Analyst with the U.S. Army, 1967–1974, and the Central Intelligence Agency, 1974–1975.

EDUCATION

Big State University, Big State, IL
Bachelor of Science in Administrative Science, 1978

165

Combination. *Christine L. Dennison, Lincolnshire, Illinois*

Companies assume that mature applicants want a high position or high salary, but this applicant wanted only a "decent" amount of responsibility. The writer presents him as low key and reliable.

Media

Resumes at a Glance

RESUME NO.	OCCUPATION	GOAL	PAGE
166.	Host, Writer, & Executive Producer	Author/Producer/Speaker	341
167.	Account Executive, Radio & TV	Not specified	342
168.	Business Development Manager	Media Manager	343
169.	Television Director	Television Production	344
170.	Production Assistant	Video Editing/Production	346

Gregg S. Lane

Ph.: (555) 555-5555
Fax: (800) 000-0000

129 Avenida del Sol, Apt. 136
Northview, CA 99999
www.spirit.com
soul2@gsl.com

Author ▪ *Producer* ▪ *Inspirational Speaker*

FCC Certified Cable Access Producer:

➢ *Well-versed in FCC rules and regulations.*

➢ *Proficient in problem solving, with ability to quickly adapt to the unexpected.*

➢ *Experienced in: Preparing Run Sheets ▪ Editing ▪ Writing ▪ Program Planning and Coordinating ▪ Managing Logistics and Personnel ▪ Virtually all aspects of production.*

➢ *Effective communicator who interacts well with people from a wide range of social and cultural backgrounds.*

➢ *Able to tackle issues by producing programs that are relevant, informative, and stimulating.*

CAREER HIGHLIGHTS	▪ **Host, Writer, and Executive Producer—*The Spirited Soul*** Cable Television Broadcast—Weekly 30-minute teaching program applying philosophy and phenomenology to inspire awareness and appreciation for the spiritual presence in our daily lives. *Originally aired 1992–1996; updated and revived Feb 2004.* Multicultural demographic for both programs: Casitas Heights, Westview, Norwood, Thousand Hills, San Lopez, West/South Marina.	2004
	▪ **Host, Writer, and Executive Producer—*The Spirited Soul*** Radio Broadcast Station KTYM—30-minute teaching program with presentations derived from philosophical and spiritual works. Audience demographic: Culturally diverse, encompassing Casitas Heights, Westview, Norwood, Thousand Hills, West Marina.	1992 to 1996
	▪ **Founded Spiritual Essence—A nonprofit outreach program.**	1992
	▪ **Host and Producer—*Computer Awareness*** Cable Television Broadcast—Weekly 30-minute show that focused on desktop publishing and related technology. Featured guests who were experts in the field.	1992

EDUCATION	▪ State University—Loma Pointe, CA
	  – *Bachelor of Arts in Communications Studies—2001*
	     Emphasis on Speech and Broadcast Communications, Rhetoric, Advanced Phenomenology
	  – Enrolled in Master's Program—Communications Studies major
	
	▪ Central College—Central City, CA
	  – *Broadcasting—1990*	

PROFESSIONAL AFFILIATIONS	Member—Elite Communications Association Member—Nationwide Communication Association	
PUBLICATIONS	Lane, Gregg S.: *Heritage Unveiled,* Second Edition. Lane Pub. Co. 210 p. Copyright 1993. Lane, Gregg S.: *Modern Predictions.* Jolie Enterprises. 54 p. Copyright 1990. Lane, Gregg S.: *Heritage Unveiled.* Lane Pub. Co. 144 p. Copyright 1972.	

166

Combination. *Gail Taylor, Torrance, California*

The bold script type for the applicant's name and roles captures attention first. The gray box and gray horizontal line are almost as eye-catching. Next, special tip bullets direct eyes down the page.

Marilyn Forester

900 Limrock Avenue
Windsor, CT 00000
(555) 555-5555
mforester@yahoo.com

Career Profile

Results-oriented Sales, Marketing and Account Management Professional with a solid history of verifiable accomplishments in the competitive broadcast arena. *Key Strengths:*

- Proven ability to identify and acquire new accounts, retain existing clients, design creative promotions and generate revenues and profitability.
- Effective negotiator with expertise in the sales process; adept at selling conceptually by using qualitative information.
- Committed to building long-term relationships and finding solutions to address customer needs, resulting in mutual growth.
- Sales leadership skills are evident in the ability to train and mentor new recruits to achieve results.
- Computer proficient in Tapscan, Qualitap, Media Master, Target One and other software programs.
- Bilingual in English and Spanish.

Professional Experience

WPTX-AM & WPTX-FM, Hartford, CT   1994–present
Part of Channel Communications One, a global organization that owns and operates numerous radio stations, television stations and billboard companies, as well as holds equity interests in other media companies.

Account Executive (1996–present)

Promoted to build new and expand existing account base in the greater Springfield metropolitan and northern Connecticut territory. Experienced and successful in selling advertising on both stations (adult contemporary and news/talk formats). Build strong partnerships with local direct clients and advertising agencies in the local, regional and national marketplace. Accountable for sales and marketing strategies, copywriting, proposal writing and promotional planning.

- *Grew annual revenues from zero base to more than $380,000, developing and managing 75 accounts.*
- *Won 2003, 2002, 2001 President's Club Award; consistently recognized as one of the top performers.*
- *Chosen out of 15 account executives from 3 different radio stations to win 2003 Team Spirit Award for leadership and outstanding sales performance.*
- *Designed several creative promotional tie-ins that generated profits for both the radio station and clients.*
- *Cultivate and maintain strong, ongoing relationships with clients while working collaboratively to meet their advertising needs. Commended for excellent service and follow-up.*
- *Selected by management to train and mentor new account executives, providing effective coaching in sales techniques, marketing strategies, proposal writing and related topics.*

Business Manager (1994–1996)
Coordinated accounts payable, accounts receivable and payroll for 70 employees at both stations. Posted entries to the general ledger, invoiced customers and performed credit checks as well as collections. Prepared month-end and year-end closings and financial reports for corporate management.

- *Implemented system that cut days outstanding by 50% (down to 30–60 days), significantly reducing backlog of past-due accounts and bringing accounts receivable under control.*
- *Instituted credit approval system where none previously existed, which included performing extensive account research and reconciliation.*
- *Initiated recordkeeping system for accounts payable that improved accuracy and ensured on-time payments.*

Education

Bachelor of Arts in Communications, UNIVERSITY OF CALIFORNIA, Riverside, CA, 1993

167

Combination. *Louise Garver, Enfield, Connecticut*

The individual was planning to relocate and was seeking a similar position. The writer emphasized the depth of the applicant's skills, experience, and achievements. The person got a new job quickly.

JASON PETERS

928 Arthur Road • Port Reading, New Jersey 22222 • (333) 333-3333 • jpeters@aol.com

Media manager whose accomplishments reflect effective leadership, an innovative mindset, strong sales and client management skills, and expertise in identifying effective means of corporate communications

SUMMARY OF QUALIFICATIONS

Forward-thinking professional with 15 years of experience in the audio-visual services field. Demonstrated expertise in both the development of promotional materials and the production and orchestration of media events. Innovative and resourceful with strong grasp of how to best reach target audiences. Proven record in delivering communications solutions that hit the mark. Respected business partner with extensive array of industry contacts. Able to successfully identify client needs and create cost-effective programs that are consistent with company image and style. Valued for vision in finding new and better ways to do business. Effective leader who embraces the ideals of customer satisfaction and encourages creativity and risk-taking to make it happen. Top-notch communications skills. Effective in adapting messages to regional, national, and international audiences. Progressive in outlook and quick to adopt new technologies.

PROFESSIONAL EXPERIENCE

MEDIAMASTERS, Franklin Park, New Jersey   Apr 1988 to present
Business Development Manager – New Jersey (Mar 1993 to present)

Manage department of six, overseeing all aspects of client engagement and client projects. Develop promotional materials to generate new business. Communicate with prospects to identify needs, developing and presenting client proposals and implementing project plans. Hired as technician, earned promotion to assistant manager after only one year. Earned second promotion to current position in 1993.

- Successfully manage company advertising to bring in new prospects. Designed brochure sent out in mass mailing and developed multimedia advertising plan that integrated print ads, radio spots, and website to promote services.

- Designing creative and cost-effective proposals, successfully built client base and customer confidence while ensuring frequent repeat business. Grew client base by 60% since becoming manager, successfully bringing on several major well-known international companies.

- Developed innovative presentation proposal for major client that saved thousands of dollars by converting a company warehouse into a temporary theatre, eliminating the need for offsite facilities. Plan was later adapted and successfully used to orchestrate cost-effective presentations for many other clients.

- Positioned company to compete more effectively for staging contracts by successfully streamlining labor and eliminating waste to significantly reduce program costs.

- Developed webcast for well-known car manufacturer that allowed CEO to address employees from overseas location, saving both time and money.

EDUCATION & CONTINUING DEVELOPMENT

WESTERN UNIVERSITY, Sunnyvale, California
Bachelor of Science degree in Radio, Television and Film (Emphasis: Media Management)
➤ Worked at Panavision, scheduling, operating and maintaining film and video equipment.

Seminars and Workshops:
Writing, Producing and Directing Workshop, American Film Institute
Media Management Program, ICIA
Extensive product training on Sony and Panasonic products

TECHNOLOGY SKILLS

PowerPoint ◆ Word ◆ Excel ◆ Internet ◆ Script Writing ◆ Video Editing ◆ Video Shooting ◆ Video Teleconferencing

168

Combination. *Carol A. Altomare, Three Bridges, New Jersey*

This media manager wanted to show that he could "do it all" in developing and coordinating media events and in communicating effectively. The writer uncovered and displayed his innovativeness.

George Johnson

3346 Main Street ▪ New Haven, CT 00000 ▪ (555) 555-5555 ▪ gjohnson@attbi.com

Television Production Professional

Offering broad knowledge and 5 years of progressive experience in all facets of television production, including directing live daily TV newscasts, promotions and local programming. Solid academic foundation; bachelor's degree in broadcast journalism.

Value Offered ...

✓ Adept at enhancing graphic elements and content quality in newscasts and utilizing technology and other broadcasting tools.
✓ Keen eye for camera composition and a solid understanding of the flow and tone of news stories.
✓ Resourceful problem solver who can lead, delegate and troubleshoot effectively, lending balance, focus, structure and creativity to the newsroom.
✓ Efficiently prioritize a broad range of responsibilities to consistently meet tight deadlines, budget and expectations. Work well under pressure in time-driven, demanding environments.
✓ Foster collaborative working relationships and positive communications with all departments for successful program broadcasts.
✓ Effective in training, coaching and leading staff in a team-oriented environment.
✓ Versatile, organized, take-charge professional with exceptional follow-through abilities and detail orientation.
✓ Proven ability to showcase journalistic content in a compelling manner. Ability to sustain an on-air look that is clear, consistent, contemporary and focused on viewer needs.

Production & Related Skills ...

Live Television ▪ Technical Directing ▪ Studio Cameras & Techniques ▪ Master Control ▪ Video Production ▪ DAT Recording ▪ Audiovisual Production ▪ Control Room ▪ Load In/Load Out ▪ Promotions/Commercial Production

Proficiency in Technical Equipment & Applications ...

Phillips Diamond Digital 30 Switcher ▪ Dveous DVE ▪ Pinnacle Still Store ▪ Odetics TCS2000 ▪ DVC Pro ▪ Adobe Photoshop ▪ Deko FX (Computer Graphics)

Professional Experience & Accomplishments

WCTX-TV 30   New Haven, CT
Advanced through series of progressively responsible production positions based on performance results and skills:
Director (2001–present)
Master Control Director (1999–2001)
Production Assistant (1998–1999)

▪ **News/Technical Directing**—Direct live TV newscasts, commercial production and taped local programming; hands-on experience using Phillips Diamond Digital 30 Switcher, Dveous DVE, Deko FX and Pinnacle Still Store. Accountable for myriad activities, including reviewing production schedule for morning programming; entering graphics sequence; preparing log of stories and related graphics; marking scripts and camera shots; operating Deko FX machine, directing shows and taping news cut-ins, along with other production activities such as promotions for various shows on WCTX and two other area stations; handling pre-production setup and direction for Showcase 50.

▪ **Supervision/Team Leadership**—Manage, train, evaluate and develop team of 6: audio technician, production assistants, assistant director and broadcast journalism interns. Supervise lighting of news and production studios.

▪ **Master Control**—Aptitude for quickly learning technical equipment and directing on-air switching between commercials and programming, excluding newscasts and live programming. Responsible for satellite dishes, tuning in microwave live shots, rolling tapes for newscasts, dubbing commercial spots into Odetics TCS2000 playback system and aiding in commercial production. Editing experience includes 1/2", 3/4", 1" and DVC Pro formats.

▪ **Production Operations**—Operated camera for news, locally produced programming, commercial, promotional and public service production. Maintained established studio lighting, checked and maintained all sets, performed setup, struck staging, and operated equipment at remote broadcast locations.

169

Combination. *Louise Garver, Enfield, Connecticut*

The applicant was interested in relocating to the Southwest to a large station in a similar capacity with growth potential. The writer created a document that demonstrated the individual's

George Johnson - Page 2

(555) 555-5555 ▪ gjohnson@attbi.com

WCTX-TV 30 continued…

Accomplishments

✓ Awarded as Employee of the Month in September 2002: "George directed the September 11th broadcast flawlessly. He always keeps his cool and rarely makes mistakes. He cares about the on-air product, and he always gives 150% to the station."

✓ Contributed to significant increase in ratings after taking over direction of the 6 a.m. news show by opening up the show's structure through improvisation and improving quality with fresher news content.

✓ Recognized by supervisor for skill in handling any area of production and getting the job done right, along with technical equipment expertise, troubleshooting and problem-solving capabilities.

FORMAN MEDIA   New Haven, CT
Intern   **1997–1998**

▪ Acquired invaluable knowledge base in television production; developed skills in camera operation at hockey and basketball games on both college and professional levels.

▪ Performed audio, camera and director duties for city council and school board meetings.

▪ Provided assistance with master control procedures, prepared air tapes and completed air tape changes.

Prior Management Experience

SOUNDTRACK INC.   Stamford, CT
Manager   **1995–1997**

▪ **Operations Management**—Profit and loss management responsibility for retail business in the music industry. Diverse functions encompassed oversight of daily operations to ensure efficiency, quality and productivity.

▪ **Human Resources**—Hired, trained, scheduled, evaluated and supervised team of associates; monitored overall job performance to maintain accuracy and adherence to company policies and procedures. Encouraged individual employee contributions and fostered an atmosphere of teamwork.

▪ **Sales & Marketing**—Implemented company's marketing strategies, including creating product displays to enhance merchandise and increase sales. Worked closely with music company representatives; maintained thorough knowledge of market trends.

▪ **Customer Service/Relations**—Provided excellent service to customers by assisting them with merchandise selection, providing information on musical releases/products, responding to requests and addressing any concerns.

WBGY-AM 1460   Stamford, CT
Production Assistant/Board Operator   **1994–1995**

▪ Wrote and recorded commercial advertising and promotional material; taped network satellite feed. Broad experience base included monitoring and switching of satellite sports events and local programming.

Education

Bachelor of Arts in Broadcast Journalism, New York University, New York, NY, 1994

Other Media Experience

WQPM-FM 98.8—Production Director (1 year) and DJ (3 years)
The Pinnacle campus newspaper—Arts & Entertainment Writer (3 years)

versatility and range of skills, including his prior management experience in a retail business. The combination helped him get a new position at a larger TV station. Note the effective use of boldfacing throughout the resume. Italic has special roles to play in the Professional Experience & Accomplishments section.

CHAD CARPENTER

504 Bickford Drive
Hermitage, Tennessee 00000

Home (555) 000-0000
ccarpenter@comcast.net

CAREER FOCUS

VIDEO EDITING—POST PRODUCTION—VIDEO PRODUCTION

Broad understanding of video-editing, post-production, and video-production techniques. Uniquely creative in applying technical abilities to production operations to complement and enhance the storytelling process. Completed five-month internship with MegaStar, a post-production facility in Nashville.

EDUCATION

Degree:

BACHELOR OF SCIENCE—MASS COMMUNICATION—2003
Concentration in **Electronic Media Production**
Austin Peay State University—Clarksville, Tennessee

Relevant
Courses:

Television Production—Single Camera Directing and Producing—Multi-Camera Directing and Producing—Television Series Production—Nonlinear Editing—Remote Truck Production

TECHNICAL SKILLS

Proficient with both Macintosh (Mac OS 9) and PC (Windows 95/98, DOS) platforms. Confident in learning and using new technology.

Video Editing
Software:

FAST 601 Silver—Final Cut Pro 2.0—Avid Media Composer 1000 v. 7.0—Adobe Premiere 5.0

Additional
Software:

Adobe After Effects 5.0—Adobe Photoshop 5.5—WordPerfect—Microsoft Excel—Internet navigation and research—e-mail

PROFESSIONAL EXPERIENCE

PRODUCTION ASSISTANT (Internship)—Aug. to Dec. 2003
MegaStar, a division of Jake Young Productions—Nashville, Tennessee

MegaStar is a post-production facility offering editing, graphics, and soundstage services. Creative projects include network specials, episodic TV, music and concert videos, documentaries, promotional campaigns, and electronic press kits (EPKs).

▸ Observed firsthand numerous editing sessions between clients and producers, acquiring an understanding of the logic and reasoning behind shot selection and video- and audio-track sequencing.
▸ Participated in the taping of a live concert production, "Ripples in the Pond—The Best of Matthew Cage Live," for contemporary Christian singer and musician Matthew Cage. Assisted with equipment setup, set construction, running errands, purchasing supplies, striking the set, and general cleanup.
▸ Edited a behind-the-scenes video entitled "Beyond the Music" using Avid Media Composer 1000.
▸ Gained a practical understanding of real-world production projects, as well as the business side of the industry.

170

Combination. *Carolyn S. Braden, Hendersonville, Tennessee*

This recent college graduate was looking for his first real position in his chosen field of Video Editing and Production. Emphasis is on education, technical skills, and an internship. See Cover Letter 2 (page 378).

Sales and Marketing

Resumes at a Glance

RESUME NO.	OCCUPATION	GOAL	PAGE
171.	Inside Sales Account Manager	Inside Sales/Office Manager	349
172.	Wireless Consultant	Marketing & Sales Management	350
173.	Sales Dev. Mgr./Sales Director	Not specified	352
174.	Gas Scheduler/Trader Associate	Energy Trader/Scheduler	354
175.	Corporate Account Manager	Sales/Account Mgmt. Executive	356
176.	Mgr., Networking-Hardware Sales	Networking-Hardware Sales	358
177.	Business Development Director	Sales & Marketing Manager	360
178.	Enterprise Server Manager	Not specified	362

Catherine M. Sipowicz

36 Algonquin Drive • East Brunswick, New Jersey 08816 • 732.555.5555 • jcsipowicz2003@yahoo.com

INSIDE SALES MANAGER ~ OFFICE MANAGER

Professional Inside Sales Manager and Office Manager with more than 10 years of experience in all phases of the business cycle. Consistently exceed objectives and increase bottom-line profits for employers. A quick learner and an excellent communicator with an ability to perform well in a multitasking environment.

Extensive experience in the sales process from order entry through customer service. Thrive in manufacturing and production arenas; a detail-oriented individual, friendly and personable, and a self-starter with a willingness to work well as a member of a team.

Creative and skilled analyst with strong problem-solving skills offering outstanding systems expertise (conversions, upgrades, and training), and excellent computer and Internet skills.

Areas of Expertise:

- Office Management
- Project Management
- Customer Service
- Customer Sales Profiles
- Inventory Control

- Credit and Collections
- Problem Identification/Solutions
- Sales Management Support
- Commission Reporting
- Inside Sales

Professional Experience

AMERICAN BOUQUET COMPANY, INC.—*Edison, New Jersey (1990 to Present)*
Inside Sales Account Manager   *(1998 to Present)*
Responsible for maintaining $7 million of current business and coordinating all functions between the outside sales staff and the internal departments of the company.

- Directed and coordinated activities concerned with the sales organization, including screening and evaluating new customers, performing credit authorizations, verifying clients' sales histories, and compiling monthly sales comparisons.
- Appointed as inside Sales Account Manager to handle a major supermarket chain buying $3 million of floral products, resulting in a 23% sales increase in the first year.
- Provided sales forecasts for holidays and special events, which greatly increased the efficiency and accuracy of production schedules and purchasing requirements.
- Designed an innovative program to evaluate effectiveness of new marketing campaigns. Hired and supervised a merchandiser to track the program on a weekly basis.
- Assisted the marketing department in designing individual color layouts for major customers, as well as writing advertising copy and product-pricing bulletins.
- Developed an automated monthly sales comparison analysis with the IT department, reducing the report-generation time from 8 hours to 1 hour.

Office Manager   *(1993 to 1998)*
Manage a multitude of tasks contributing to the daily operations of American Bouquet Company. Responsible for hiring, training, motivation, and supervision of the telemarketing staff.

- Developed and implemented various systems for optimizing production resources and increasing efficiency. Designed Excel spreadsheets and standardized forms for use by all departments.
- Enhanced interdepartmental communications, resulting in reduced production and billing errors.

Administrative Assistant   *(1990 to 1993)*
Coordinated communications between sales and production. Performed credit checks, made collections, and resolved price discrepancies. Responsible for inventory, price lists, and customer lists.

- Project Manager for developing, implementing, and maintaining an inventory-control system that utilized coding to correlate new orders with production scheduling.

Education

BA in Political Science, ***RUTGERS UNIVERSITY***, New Brunswick, New Jersey—1990

171

Combination. *Beverley and Mitchell I. Baskin, Marlboro, New Jersey*

A page border, horizontal lines, larger type, boldfacing, italic, and two sizes of bullets all contribute to the solid design and layout of this resume. Areas of Expertise in two columns provide white space.

1783 Florence Avenue
Uniontown, OH 44685
Phone: 330.414.1258
Email: willi30@uakron.edu

Seeking position in ...
* Marketing & Sales Management *
Product Development / Brand Management /
Product Analysis

VALUE TO YOUR ORGANIZATION

A well-rounded, results-oriented individual looking to apply *energetic sales capabilities* in the *Marketing, Sales, and Business Management* arena where a proven ability to communicate effectively and a determined focus on success and achievement can play a vital role in increasing revenue and market share. *Highly motivated . . . team player . . . personable . . . professional.* Core competencies include the following:

Market Research & Analysis	Project Planning & Management
Promotional Marketing	Customer Relationship Management
Sales & Marketing Leadership	Financial Analysis & Report Documentation
Customer to Business & B2B Liaison	Proactive Work Ethic/Good Attitude

EDUCATION

UNIVERSITY OF AKRON, **Bachelor of Science,** Akron, OH
Double Major: Marketing & Sales Management
Minor Studies in Professional Sales, **Fisher Institute for Professional Selling**
Anticipated Graduation: 2003   Marketing & Sales GPA: 3.1

PROFESSIONAL SALES EXPERIENCE

Wireless Consultant, UNITED WIRELESS, Montrose, OH   11/02–Present
- After one month, tied for 1) **Top Salesman** in Montrose store among three-year employees and 2) **Top Salesman** in company out of 150+ employees.

Account Executive
VERIZON, SPRINT, AT&T, MCI, T-MOBILE DBA WIRELESS DEPOT, Akron, OH   2/01–11/02
- Recognized as **Top Salesman** by multiple cellular companies.
- Demonstrated skill in **building relationships and customer loyalty** in a highly competitive market to sell cellular service to business owners, mall customers, and retailers.
- Developed outside sales curriculum and employee handbook. Wrote marketing/business plan for new stores.

Associate Manager, MC SPORTING GOODS, Medina, OH   5/00–2/01
- Coached 10 employees on sales techniques and customer service; budgeted employee payroll and schedules.
- Managed $500K inventory through cycle accounts; reduced loss by 80%.

Senior Salesman, BEST BUY, INC., Cuyahoga Falls, OH   9/99–4/00
- **Promoted to Senior Salesman in 6 months. Recognized nationally** for cellular and satellite sales. Achieved **Salesman of the Month** two consecutive months.
- Trained and advised sales representatives on effective sales presentations, success strategies, and closing methods, concentrating on customer needs.

ACTIVITIES & AWARDS

PI SIGMA EPSILON, National Professional Fraternity in Marketing, Sales Management, & Selling
   Vice President of Finance   2002–2003

   SPECIAL ACHIEVEMENTS:
   - **President's Award** for leadership skills, 2002; **Work Award** for hard work and dedication, 2002
   - **Exceptional Sales & Marketing Collegiate Award Nominee,** 2003

UNIVERSITY OF AKRON INTRAMURAL SPORTS, **Team Captain**

172

Combination. *Sharon Pierce-Williams, Findlay, Ohio*

Many hiring managers believe that resumes for recent college graduates should be only one page. That makes sense when graduates have few noteworthy accomplishments and little work

1783 Florence Avenue
Uniontown, OH 44685
Phone: 330.414.1258
Email: willi30@uakron.edu
Page 2

* Key Project & Leadership Experience *

PI SIGMA EPSILON—Gamma Kappa Chapter
NATIONAL PROFESSIONAL FRATERNITY IN MARKETING, SALES MANAGEMENT, & SELLING

Pro-Am Regional Sell-A-Thon, **Top 5 Finish** (out of 55 individuals), National Cincinnati Conference, 2003
Special Events Competition—**3rd Place,** National Cincinnati Conference, 2003
Top Marketing and Sales Fraternity—**3rd Place,** Atlanta Conference, 2002; Cincinnati Conference, 2003
Top Marketing and Sales Fraternity—**2nd Place,** National Dallas Conference, 2001

Vice President of Finance   2002–2003
Lead general board meetings and set agendas, collect and deposit chapter money, log receivables and payables in general ledger, devise operating statements for nationals, budget/allocate chapter money for various projects, and place funds in money market account to draw interest on savings.

University of Akron

PROJECT: **Marketing Research Plan for Online Graduate Program**

Challenge: Chosen through competitive interview process by Assistant Dean of Business School to analyze low enrollment of the online graduate program.

Action: Collaborated with other students to survey and evaluate data. Presented findings to Assistant Dean.

Result: Developed campus marketing promotions, increasing program awareness and enrollment by 25%.

Green Township YMCA

"Bill's work in designing the survey, conducting hundreds of interviews with our members and potential members, and compiling the results for our review will be invaluable to us as we consider our options with respect to expanding the Green YMCA."
—John Paul Davis, Green YMCA

"Bill and his team gave the best presentation of research findings that I have seen in my professional career at First Energy."
—Ralph Dinicola, First Energy Executive

PROJECT: **YMCA Expansion—As Project Chair**, collaborated with top executive board members, convincing them to hire PSE for the analytical research involved in this strategic decision, as opposed to a marketing company.

Challenge: To determine if a multimillion-dollar expansion is necessary.

Action: Coordinated weekly meetings with PSE committee/YMCA staff to update project status and findings.

Result: Competed at PSE National Convention for "Top Marketing Research Award" using this project.

"The Cup" Sales Project
3rd-Place Finish at Cincinnati PSE National Convention, 2003

PROJECT: Conceptualized "The Cup" theme Sales Project for 2002.

Challenge: To promote 16-oz.-cup sales to students and the community to make a profit for PSE and for donations to the Akron Children's Home.

Action: Sold and marketed "The Cup" project to downtown Akron bars. Hired graphics design service to apply bars' logos on cups. Consulted with attorney to meet Akron liquor regulations.

Result: Generated revenues of $10,000+ in two weeks and profits of $8,000; $1,500 to charity.

experience. This resume writer writes for graduates who belong to Pi Epsilon, a national marketing group, and who are offered jobs in the $50K–$60K range. Page two of this resume shows a depth to this outstanding graduate that would have been lost in a one-page format.

       *READY TO RELOCATE TO THE **SEATTLE** AREA*

Charles W. Broadway

4200 Centre Street   Montgomery, Alabama 36100   cbroad555@aol.com   ☎ 334.555.5555

WHAT I CAN OFFER TOPLINE AS YOUR NEWEST SALES PROFESSIONAL

○ Penetrating and holding **new markets,**

○ Gathering and leveraging **sales intelligence** faster than our competition,

○ Mastering our customers' business so well we **anticipate** their **needs,**

○ Putting together "win-win" sales deals that yield **enduring profits,**

○ Communicating so powerfully that **sales** are **closed** — at every level from shop floor to boardroom, and

○ **Managing risk** prudently.

RECENT WORK HISTORY WITH EXAMPLES OF PROBLEMS SOLVED

○ *Hired away by the CEO to be* **Sales Development Manager** *and then promoted over four more experienced eligibles to be* **Sales Director,** Arista Corporation, Montgomery, Alabama   Oct 04 to Present
Arista is the world's largest auto transmission manufacturer.

Supervise three regional sales managers directly. Lead a territory that covers all of America east of the Mississippi River and portions of Canada. Build and defend a travel budget of $400K. My district generates $45M in annual sales.

Chosen by the President to **guide us into a new market** dominated by four tough competitors. Found, and really listened to, all potential customers. Identified our market niche. Then made the calls that led to **20 presentations nationwide,** many at presidential levels. *Payoffs:* **From $0 sales to $3.5M** in sales in just 16 months.

Moved faster than our competition to discover an RFP before it hit the street. When none of our products met this customer's needs, **put together a win-win deal** that shared both risks and profits. *Payoffs:* When I showed our customer's CEO how I could **save him $2M** over the life of the contract, I **won a $4M contract for us.**

Used polite persistence to **"steal" a customer from a competitor** who had served them for a decade. Soon uncovered our competitor's weakness. **Carefully timed and executed "cold calls"** on the right people. *Payoffs:* By appealing right to their specific needs, brought in **$8M** in the last two years alone.

Saw opportunity a potential customer missed — even after he awarded his contract to another company. Tracked our competitor's performance right up until contract renewal. *Payoffs:* My presentation, made on the same day as other firms, carried the **sale: $4M** over several years — even though we weren't the lowest bidder.

       *More indicators of performance **TopLine** can use ☞*

173

Combination. *Don Orlando, Montgomery, Alabama*

A resume that's different from other resumes gets attention. Hiring officials want to know what a new employee can do for the company. This resume is distinctive in indicating immediately

Charles Broadway	**Sales Professional**	334.555.5555

Uncovered an unmet need in a major market. Worked with the customer and a manufacturer to design a new product. Persuaded our leadership to invest $200K in the prototype I knew we would need for the competition. *Payoffs:* **Won a $14M sale** and **took away our competitor's dominance** in this market.

Picked up the signs that a competitor's customer wasn't happy, and then found out why. Got a 100-percent response to our needs-analysis survey to define the best new product for the market. *Payoffs:* **Profit margin up** four percent—**double the industry average.** My methods became the **corporate standard** for customer analysis.

○ Plant Manager, Plantar Corporation, Montgomery, Alabama   May 98 to Sep 04

○ **Sales Manager for Business Products,** Mylar Corporation, Montgomery, Alabama
Mar 96 to May 98

EDUCATION & PROFESSIONAL DEVELOPMENT

○ MPA, Auburn University—Montgomery, Montgomery, Alabama   00

○ BS, Troy State University, Troy, Alabama   96
Earned this degree working 10 hours a week.

○ Instructed classes in Value Analysis for Product Improvement and Cost of Sales
96 to 98

Selected from five more experienced professionals to teach these six-week courses, preparing 100 sales professionals to represent up to ten different products.

IT SKILLS

○ Expert in proprietary **sales, billing, and customer contact software** suite; proficient in Outlook, Word, Excel, PowerPoint, and Internet search methods

what the sales applicant can bring to "TopLine." Uncommon bullets point to six boldfaced sales results of top importance to executives responsible for sales: getting and keeping new markets, beating competitors, anticipating customer needs, staying profitable, closing sales, and controlling risk.

JAMES R. BELLMAN

8888 Garden Valley Lane <> Houston, TX 77777
Residence: (832) 999-2222 <> Cellular: (832) 777-8888

ENERGY TRADER / SCHEDULER with proven track record in **generating highest-ever revenues, producing optimal volume,** and **acquiring new accounts** with key energy corporations. Competencies:

Revenue & Market Share Acceleration	*Gas / Power Marketing & Commodity Trading*
Client Relationship Management	*Oil & Gas Infrastructure Restructuring*
Electronic & Technical Analysis	*Risk & Project Management*
Strategic Scheduling & Nominating	*Financial / Physical Positioning*
Natural Gas / Energy Flow Optimization	*Critical Portfolio & Volume Management*

PROFESSIONAL EXPERIENCE

AUSTIN MERCHANT ENERGY — Houston, TX   2001–Present

Principal Gas Scheduler / Trader Associate

Nominate, schedule, and optimize natural gas flow in large West Region (Texas to California) on interstate pipelines (EPNG, PG&E, California, Transwestern), implementing Internet, electronic bulletin boards, and facsimile methodologies. Utilize electronic trading systems, technical analysis systems, and published financial data to acquire pricing, trends, and forecasting to attain forecasting acumen.

Selected Achievements
> * **Promoted** from scheduler to trader associate; retained as principal gas scheduler after drastic company downsizing.
> * **Nominated** *"Most Volume Transporter"* (1.4 Bcf) from Texas to California in company's history.
> * **Commended for being one of the most efficient and concise schedulers** on the team.
> * **Consistently received excellent annual / biannual performance reviews.**

CONNOLEY ENERGY SERVICES, INC. — Dallas, TX   1999–2001

Account Executive

Recruited to develop / integrate physical trading and financial positions throughout the U.S. Consulted with clients to evaluate / determine energy needs. Established strategic alliances with clients to gain trust / confidence. Recommended methodologies / strategies to maximize clients' profitability and facilitated clients' OTC energy trades.

Selected Achievements
> * **Generated company's highest-ever revenue months** ($40,000–$70,000 / month in brokerage fees) from approximately 50 key accounts.
> * Successfully **acquired new business with major corporations** such as BP Energy, Southern Company / Mirant, Duke Energy, Virginia Power, TXU Energy, and Florida Gas Utilities.

EXXON NATURAL GAS COMPANY — Dallas, TX   1998–1999

Senior Trader — Gulf Coast

Recruited because of astute trading reputation; challenged to increase trading volume and market share for major industry leader. Actively traded 200,000–250,000 mm BTUs of natural gas daily on all Texas intrastate and many interstate pipelines (Transco, Texas Eastern, Tennessee, Texas Gas, Columbia Gulf, Florida Gas) throughout eastern half of U.S. Managed portfolio in Gulf and Northeast, implementing EFPs, Triggers, Indexes, Swaps, and other pricing methodologies to gain volume and maximize profits. Evaluated physical and financial positions and calculated / projected monetary results.

Selected Achievements
> * **Escalated trading volume from 300 Mcf to 1.5 Bcf, gaining significant market share.**
> * **Created system to track gas location, trading volume, and amount / rate of transport,** which **improved tractability** and **accelerated profitability.** Optimized transport through strategic trend analysis.

174

Combination. *Ann Klint, Tyler, Texas*

The applicant's competencies stand out because they are within a pair of horizontal lines and center-justified in each of the two columns. Achievements are certain to be seen in a repeated

JAMES R. BELLMAN
Page Two

P&G ENERGY MARKETING, INC. — Dallas, TX   1995–1998

Trader — East Region (1997–1998)

Promoted to Trader; traded physical natural gas in Gulf and East Coast Regions, implementing strategies and various pricing tools (Indexes, Swaps, EFPs, Triggers, Options) to increase revenues and volume. Actively contributed in research, development, and execution of term deals. Cultivated business alliances with producers, end-users, and marketers.

Volume Management Representative (1995–1997)

Recruited because of acquired nominating expertise. Approached and fostered business relationships with producers, marketers, pipeline representatives, and end-users (retailers / wholesalers) to determine flow preferences and critical gas routing strategies. Nominated / scheduled natural gas on various intrastate and interstate pipelines (FGT, TETCO, TGP), utilizing electronic bulletin boards and facsimile machines. Allocated, tracked, and recorded all transactions and flow data into spreadsheets, gas control modules, and customized systems.

Selected Achievements
- ➤ **Selected to participate in software pilot program** initiated to evaluate and refine AltraEnergy Dealmaker program; **drastically improved efficiency of program through critical refinement.**
- ➤ **Spearheaded research, development, and execution of key long-term trading transactions.**
- ➤ Recognized as **"best gas nominator," "highest number generator,"** and **"most efficient scheduler"** in company.

RELIABLE RESOURCES MARKETING COMPANY — Houston, TX   1995

Support Associate

Acquired in-depth knowledge of natural gas trading transactions; coordinated reporting efforts between traders, suppliers, marketers, gas schedulers, and accounting personnel. Created spreadsheets to facilitate data entry of all natural gas transactions; imported data; monitored daily exposure; and analyzed baseload (month / year) to swing (daily) basis. Prepared margin summary analysis monthly.

EDUCATION

TEXAS A&M UNIVERSITY — College Station, TX
Bachelor of Business Administration in Marketing (1994)

➤<>➤<>➤<

pattern that "works": first, the company's name in all caps with place names and dates; second, the applicant's job position(s) in boldface; third, a paragraph indicating responsibilities; and fourth, Selected Achievements, indented, bulleted with special arrow tips, and enhanced with boldfacing.

DAVID R. PERLMAN

405 Weatherspoon Drive
Ehldridge, NC 56974

(555) 555-1834
daveperl@yahoo.com

SALES / ACCOUNT MANAGEMENT EXECUTIVE
...Consistently exceed corporate goals & increase key account base...

Well-qualified executive with proven expertise in global/national sales, strategic marketing, team building, and contract negotiations. Re-acquired major corporate account and increased sales 220%; committed to a high level of customer service to build trust and enhance sales. Highly motivated to outperform the competition; consistently set and achieve personal goals above corporate expectations. Exceptional "deal closing" expertise; keen understanding of corporate dynamics. PC literate; B.S., Business Administration.

CORE STRENGTHS

...National Accounts / Building & Maintaining Long-term, Loyal Business Relationships...
...Consultative Selling / International Expertise / Team Building / New Business Development...
...Creative & Strategic Planning / New Product Introduction / Sales Process Planning & Implementation...

CAREER BACKGROUND

THE WIRELESS NETWORK, Walson, NC   1990–Present
2nd largest global provider of cellular, voice, and data applications.

International Corporate Account Manager (2002–Present)
Fast-track promotion to oversee corporate, city, county, and federal clients. Manage 10 national contracts and 20+ remote accounts in the NC market. Market voice and data to multimillion-dollar accounts. Negotiate contracts; team with business care personnel and account managers to increase data sales. Train clients on benefits-features of Extranet (Web-based site for customer service and new products). Function as remote account manager for national accounts not based locally.

Executive Account Sales Manager (2002)
Tasked to drive government account sponsorships in 8 counties serving 13 retail locations. Focused on city, county, and federal clients. Managed advertising and marketing initiatives for national accounts.
Highlights:
- Increased sales by 31% (1st year).
- Acquired major government account (Marion County elections), resulting in $3M annual revenues.

Senior International Account Manager (1997–2001)
Accountable for attaining corporate sales quotas, increasing revenues, acquiring 80+ new high-profile national accounts per month ($7M+ in annual revenues), and maintaining existing accounts. Managed 1 sales associate and 75 accounts. Teamed with other professionals to create high-impact PowerPoint presentations for new clients. Extensive interaction with clients and business sales departments to facilitate resolution of customer service and billing issues.
Highlights:
- Decreased client churn 7.5% below industry standards.
- Successfully initiated and closed federal government contracts through attention to detail and response time, resulting in 12% increase in annual revenues.
- Re-acquired and grew Buy It Here Online Network account 220% through aggressive leadership and advertising strategies.
- Consistently exceeded sales goals; maintained 122% average status of corporate expectations.
- Coordinated quarterly on-site benefit expos for large nationally contracted companies, which increased gross activations by 7%.
- Recruited new accounts, including United Shipping, Pepsi, and Warethon.
- Achieved 197% sales quota (2002); ranked 3rd in the state and 36th nationwide.
- Elite *10 Top Producers* (2001); 151% quota (4th Quarter); 116% quota (2nd Quarter); 104% quota (1st Quarter).
- *Presidents Club Winner* (1997, 1998, 2001, 2002).
- Awarded *Top Federal Account Executive* (2nd Quarter 2000).
- *Gold Club Winner* (1999).
- Ranked among the *Top Producers* in NC (1997–2001).

175

Combination. *Carol Heider, Tampa, Florida*

Center-justification is evident in part of the profile, in the Core Strengths section, and in the small sections on the second page. An advantage of center-justification in sections with short

DAVID R. PERLMAN
Page 2

CAREER BACKGROUND (continued)

THE WIRELESS NETWORK, Walson, NC (continued)

Corporate Account Executive (1992–1997)
Promoted to senior-level management following merger acquisition of One Cellular. Managed major account acquisition and maintenance for large corporate clients ($500K+ annual revenues) through target research and cold-call sales. Territory included central North Carolina and 9 surrounding counties. Served as mentor for sales associates. Managed 2 sales executives and 120+ accounts. Conducted weekly sales meetings.
Performance Results:
- Increased account base by 25 accounts.
- Personally recruited University of New Bedford and ABC accounts.
- *100% Club Achiever* (1990–1992; 1994–1996).
- *Top Producer of Voice Mail Sales* (1995).
- One of the *Top 10% in Company* for digital sales introduction (1992–1993).
- *North Carolina Rookie of the Year Award*—Corporate Accounts Division (1992).
- *Circle of Excellence Award* (1991); determined through employee balloting for integrity, team player, displaying good judgment, pursuit of excellence, and customer satisfaction skills.

EDUCATION

UNIVERSITY OF NORTHERN CALIFORNIA, Bakersfield, CA
Bachelor of Science, Business Administration (1984)
Activities: Dean's List

CONTINUING EDUCATION / TRAINING

The Best Sales Training
Getting There Sales Training
Magic Sales Training
Know Your Client Sales Training
SPIN Training
Microsoft Word & Outlook training classes

ACTIVITIES

Board of Directors, Wireless International
Board of Directors, Lend a Hand
Captain, Neighborhood Watch
Volunteer, "Adopt A Family"

CERTIFICATIONS

Account Management & Maintenance (AMM) certified

COMPUTER EXPERTISE

Microsoft Excel, PowerPoint, Word, and Outlook; Internet

phrases is that eyes can travel quickly down the center of the page. Bold italic draws attention to positions held, to Highlights and Performance Results sections, and to the candidate's academic degree. The Highlights and Performance Results sections present quantified achievements and notable awards.

JOSEPH A. SUTTON

128 Driscoll Avenue
Atlanta, GA 55555

(555) 555-5555
Sutton128@aol.com

SENIOR SALES PROFESSIONAL

High-Tech Industry—Networking-Hardware Sales

—Pioneered wholesale networking-hardware sales & propelled company to a dominant market position—
—Grew annual revenues from $50 million to $150 million within five years—

➢ Top global-sales performer with the big-picture vision, leadership, and tenacity to successfully penetrate new markets, capture market share, and accelerate corporate-revenue growth.

➢ 15 years of progressively responsible experience; consistently exceeded sales goals and forecasts.

➢ Extensive network of contacts with major players in the global networking-equipment market—OEMs, VARs, retail distributors, Fortune 100 / 1000 companies, and strategic partners.

➢ Dynamic sales manager skilled at developing sales teams to peak performance; training expertise in

needs assessment / solution selling / consultative selling
market research / niche marketing / prospecting / channel & account development / pricing / forecasting
presentations / overcoming objections / closing / negotiating contracts / customer support

PROFESSIONAL EXPERIENCE

NETCONNECT, INC., Atlanta, GA
1996 to Present
Semiconductor & networking equipment reseller with annual revenues of $250 million.

Manager of Worldwide Networking Hardware Sales (1999 to Present)

Launched the new networking-hardware division. P&L responsibility. Established product-line sales strategy. Built global relationships and made high-level presentations to customers and vendors. Hired staff. Trained, developed, and managed 100+ representatives.

▪ As team leader and individual contributor, tripled global networking sales during tenure.

▪ Transformed networking equipment from a small percentage of the corporate product mix to its dominant product line, accounting for 60% of the company's 2001 sales.

▪ Drove the product line to its current ranking as the most profitable within the company.

▪ Made strategic decisions about product diversification that enabled the company to dominate the market, owning 52% of the market space.

▪ Ramped up new product-line sales quickly, attaining $12 million in revenues in the first eight months.

Senior Sales Representative (1996 to 1999)

Developed and managed accounts. Negotiated contracts. Trained sales personnel in U.S., Asia, and Europe.

▪ Expanded into new markets. Built a broad and loyal customer base with leading networking VARs, resellers, retail distributors, and Fortune 100 companies.

▪ Presidents Club Winner three times.

▪ Personally accountable for 8% of company revenues in 1998 with $22 million in sales.

▪ Developed the company's first formal sales agreement incorporating volume incentives; document was later adopted company-wide.

176

Combination. *Jean Cummings, Concord, Massachusetts*

Relatively thick page borders and horizontal lines make the resume look strong. The two lines on the first page enclose the profile and capture the reader's attention. Special arrow-tip bullets

JOSEPH A. SUTTON

Page 2

PROFESSIONAL EXPERIENCE (CONTINUED)

SPAULDING, INC., Atlanta, GA   1995 to 1996
A $50 million sheet-metal manufacturer.

Senior Sales Representative

- Turned around an underperforming territory, accelerating sales to 130% of the prior year's revenues.
- Grew business to top accounts by 10%.
- Closed the most profitable order in the U.S. to date with a 45% profit margin.
- Doubled the number of accounts in the territory.

STANDARD SUPPLY COMPANY, St. Louis, MO   1988 to 1995
Construction equipment manufacturer with $2 billion in annual revenues.

Sales Planning Manager (1993 to 1995)
Developed and implemented strategic business planning for the mechanical / electrical small business unit (SBU). Managed operating budgets, developed sales forecasts, established pricing guidelines, and set sales targets for all 260 divisional sales representatives and managers. Reported to the VP of Sales. Contributed to high-level decision-making.

- Developed and managed a $30 million budget.
- Successfully implemented market segmentation.

Sales Specialist, Wilmington, DE (1991 to 1993)

- Turned around downward-trending sales and increased product-line penetration by 27%.
- Established 38 new accounts, a 30+% increase over the previous year.
- Introduced a team-selling approach that was adopted by the company nationwide.
- Awarded divisional "Sales Specialist of the Month" 15 times. Achieved 200% of sales quota in 1992.

Sales Representative (1988 to 1991)

- Opened up new territory, selling to hospitals, municipalities, schools, and industry.
- Built a base of 250 accounts.

EDUCATION AND SKILLS

THE UNIVERSITY OF NORTH CAROLINA, Chapel Hill, NC
   Bachelor of Arts degree in Economics   1988
   Extensive coursework in Spanish

Languages: Working knowledge of spoken and written Spanish

Computer Software: Microsoft Word and Excel; proprietary contact-manager software

point to stellar information in the profile. Bullets elsewhere signal achievements—most of them quantified. Duties and responsibilities, if indicated, appear in a short paragraph after some of the job positions. Notice the consistent and effective use of boldfacing and italic.

Timothy Kaplington

9803 Clinton Avenue ▪ Lubbock, TX 79424
(000) 000-0000 ▪ name@yahoo.com

SALES & MARKETING MANAGER

*With Deep Experience in Sales and Sales Management of Commercial Roofing
Products/Services and Documented Success in Start-Up and Turnaround Environments*

Results-focused sales/marketing manager with distinguished career leading national and global business development initiatives and generating more than $35 million in sales of roofing and waterproofing products/services throughout career. Repeated success guiding sizeable, cross-functional teams in the design and launch of business solutions driving record-setting revenues. Polished presenter and astute negotiator able to forge solid relationships with strategic partners, Fortune 500 customers, and institutional clients. Entrepreneurial thinker and deal-maker.

AREAS OF EXPERTISE

- Account Retention Strategies
- Sales Development Lifecycle
- Business-to-Business Sales
- Channel/Pipeline Growth
- Strategic Partnerships

- Team Building & Leadership
- Staff Training & Mentoring
- Key Account Management
- Trade Show Presentations
- Relationship-Building Initiatives

- Low-Slope Roofing Products
- Steep Roofing Products
- Roofing Design Services
- Waterproofing Design Services
- Roofing Construction Services

PROFESSIONAL EXPERIENCE

COMPANY NAME, Lubbock, TX   2000–Present
Business Development Director

Led efforts to identify prospects and secure commitments for start-up local fiber-optic provisioner. Developed strategic plans and conferred with members to provide expertise on business development.

- Paved the way for potentially lucrative contracts through customer relationship–building initiatives and leveraged extensive industry contacts and prior sales experience to implement win-win strategies.
- Negotiated **5** long-term deals with **multimillion-dollar clients** and enhanced profit margin **89%** through cost-containment strategies.

WOOD ROOFING COMPANY, San Antonio, TX   1989–2000
Sales & Marketing Director

Launched start-up firm and held full responsibility, accountability, and decision-making authority for core business development functions, including sales, marketing, finance, HR, and customer service. Recruited, staffed, trained, and mentored team of 10+ sales representatives in the fulfillment of revenue and service objectives. Created strategic/tactical sales plans that targeted key accounts for roofing maintenance services and territory expansion. Challenged to grow business through highly volatile and competitive market conditions.

- Spearheaded breakthrough **300%** sales growth (from zero to **$3 million** in annual sales) within first year of operations while maintaining bottom-line strength by overseeing entire sales cycle function.
- Drove print/radio advertising initiatives to achieve **12%** of budget allotment; expanded sales program through print advertising and cold-calling efforts into new key market, generating **25%** sales increase.
- Initiated in-house telemarketing campaign that expanded customer base and jumped sales **12%**.

…Continued…

177

Combination. *Daniel J. Dorotik, Jr., Lubbock, Texas*

A pair of horizontal lines—the first is thick and the second is thin—enclose the main section headings and help to make them conspicuous. Small caps make these and the centered title of

Timothy Kaplington – Page 2

Professional Experience, Continued

MICHELIN, Brussels, Belgium   1985–1989

Director of Sales

Managed sales and marketing of Belgium division of European manufacturer selling to Northern Europe distributor partnerships. Directed advertising/PR functions; served as Product Manager for EPDM roof systems line; and forged relationships with country-specific independent marketing firms, distributors, and major account end users. Created sales program, initiated specific sales strategies, and directed performance of independent sales representatives specifically designed for each country.

- Optimized national accounts by providing total service solutions to maintain relationships, maximize profits, and minimize problems with industry-leading clients, including **British Telecom, Total France, Laidlaw Waste, The Rank Organization, U.S. Corporation of Engineers, and Trammel Crow Real Estate**.
- Contacted senior decision makers at major European firms to obtain approvals for product use on behalf of distributor partners; solicited potential partners/distributors and increased alliances **150%**.
- Spearheaded trade show participation via exhibits at various European and national trade shows, providing impetus and forum for expanded client base and tripled business growth.
- Implemented innovative, cost-effective consultative selling program using outsourced, in-country professionals. Built long-term partnerships with distributors and their applicators/fabricators.

DEA GROUP, Boston, MA   1983–1985

VP of Marketing

Directed marketing programs and activities for architectural and engineering services that targeted private and institutional clients (e.g., hospitals and schools) throughout Midwest region. Personally initiated efforts in soliciting new business and forging strong, sustainable partnerships to outdistance competition and increase market position. Grew and managed key end-user accounts, including institutional and government entities. Supported NY office in sales program functions and activities.

- Delivered winning sales and marketing strategies to capture institutional clients for A&E consulting services, resulting in volume increase of **50%** representing more than **$1.5 million** in annual revenues.
- Streamlined business development efforts and increased revenue potential by developing program for divisions that facilitated exchange of customer information and consolidated marketing initiatives.
- Directed and trained engineering/technical team in growing sales successfully by expanding sales functionality across diversified products and services.

JONES-SMITH, Baton Rouge, LA   1982–1983

Sales Representative

Directed sales development efforts toward distributors and contractors for industry leader in commercial insulation and roofing industry.

- Exceeded management expectations by reaching sales of **more than $1 million** each year of tenure.

EDUCATION

Dual BA Degree in Economics and Government, 1980
Texas University, San Antonio, TX

the profile look compatible. The difference is that the title is spread apart slightly with extra space between adjacent characters. More than the usual information is provided on two pages by allowing almost all bulleted items in the Professional Experience section to be at least two lines long. Note the boldfacing in these items.

GEORGE B. WILLIAMS

11 Elm Court ▫ Anywhere, NY 00000 ▫ 555.555.5555 ▫ gw345@xxxxx.xxx

PROFILE

- Highly successful **Sales / Support Professional**, dealing with IBM servers, storage devices, associated software, and services.
- Achieved **nine IBM Sales Leadership Awards** in last ten years.
- Consistently exceed sales quotas.
- Strong customer relation and negotiation skills in Insurance, Health, Retail, Consumer Products, and Manufacturing industries.
- Excellent oral and written communication skills at all levels of enterprise.

□ □ □ □ □

EXPERIENCE

IBM Corporation, New York, NY
Enterprise Server Manager   2001–Present
- **Grew sales revenue 175% in 2003, 150% in 2002, and 125% in 2001.**
- Lead team of 20+ Server Sales Specialists, Storage Sales Specialists, and IBM Business Partners selling to Fortune 500 and above accounts.
- Provide customer guidance on IBM product selection, product roadmaps, and competitive offerings; and lease, purchase, and finance alternatives.
- Negotiate complex acquisition agreements with and on behalf of customers.
- Assemble and manage RFP response teams.
- Formulate sales strategies, generate proposals, and manage team quota.

Server and Storage Sales Specialist   1995–2000
- Sold high-end IBM servers and storage to small, medium, and large accounts.
- Conducted product presentations, planned and coordinated customer briefings, and arranged travel logistics for hosted customer at key IBM customer events.
- Negotiated pricing and contracts with customers.
- Configured, ordered, scheduled, and facilitated timely customer equipment delivery and installation.

Server and Storage System Engineer   1987–1995
- Developed new program that identified and resolved customer concerns, resulting in significant increase in customer satisfaction with products and services.
- Provided technical pre- and post-sales support to sales team.
- Worked one-on-one with customers to determine technical requirements and develop implementation project plan.
- Conducted pre- and post-implementation System Assurances to ensure customer success.

□ □ □ □ □

EDUCATION/ TRAINING

BBA, Pace University, New York, NY. Double Major: Management, Marketing
IBM-Certified Sales Specialist

178

Combination. *Ellen Mulqueen, Hartford, Connecticut*

A single gray vertical line crosses two black horizontal lines to make this resume look unique. Boldfacing directs attention especially to the applicant's excellent sales record.

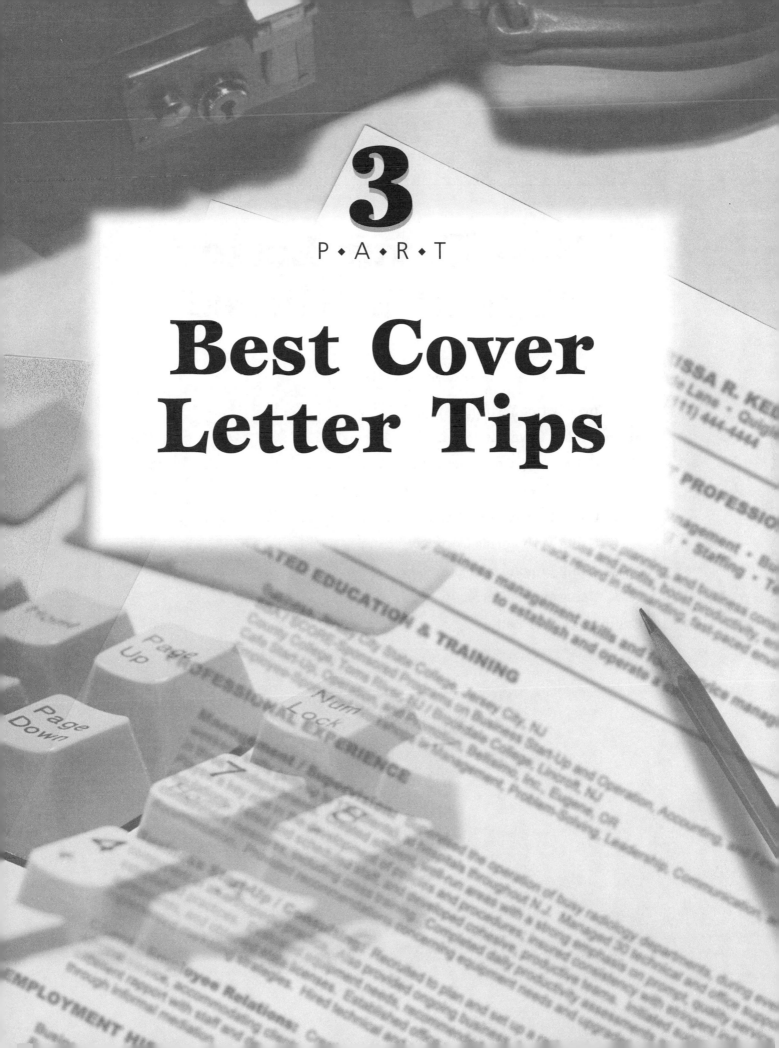

3
P·A·R·T

Best Cover Letter Tips

Best Cover Letter
Tips at a Glance

Best Cover Letter Writing Tips 365

Myths About Cover Letters 365

Tips for Polishing Cover Letters 366

   ■ Using Good Strategies for Letters 366

   ■ Using Pronouns Correctly 367

   ■ Using Verb Forms Correctly 368

   ■ Using Punctuation Correctly 369

   ■ Using Words Correctly 373

Exhibit of Cover Letters 375

Best Cover Letter Writing Tips

In an active job search, your cover letter and resume should complement one another. Both are tailored to a particular reader you have contacted or to a specific job target. To help you create the "best" cover letters for your resumes, this part of the book mentions and debunks some common myths about cover letters and presents tips for polishing the letters you write.

Myths About Cover Letters

1. **Resumes and cover letters are two separate documents that have little relation to each other.** The resume and cover letter work together in presenting you effectively to a prospective employer. The cover letter should mention the resume and call attention to some important aspect of it.

2. **The main purpose of the cover letter is to establish a friendly rapport with the reader.** Resumes show that you *can* do the work required. The main purpose of cover letters is to express that you *want* to do the work required. But it doesn't hurt to display enthusiasm in your resumes and refer to your abilities in your cover letters.

3. **You can use the same cover letter for each reader of your resume.** Modify your cover letter for each reader so that it sounds fresh rather than canned. Chances are that in an active job search, you have already talked with the person who will interview you. Your cover letter should reflect that conversation and build on it.

4. **In a cover letter, you should mention any negative things about your education, work experience, life experience, or health to prepare the reader in advance of an interview.** This is not the purpose of the cover letter. You might bring up these topics in the first or second interview, but only after the interviewer has shown interest in you or offered you a job. Even then, if you feel that you must mention something negative about your past, present it in a positive way, perhaps by saying how that experience has strengthened your will to work hard at any new job.

5. **It is more important to remove errors from a resume than from a cover letter because the resume is more important than the cover letter.** Both your resume and your cover letter should be free of errors. The cover letter is usually the first document a prospective employer sees. The first impression is often the most important one. If your cover letter has an embarrassing error in it, the chances are good that the reader may not bother to read your resume or may read it with less interest.

6. **To make certain that your cover letter has no errors, all you need to do is proofread it or ask a friend to "proof" it.** Trying to proofread your own cover letter is risky, even if you are good at grammar and writing. Once a document is typewritten or printed, it has an aura about it that may make it

seem better written than it is. For this reason, you are likely to miss typos or other kinds of errors.

Relying on someone else is risky, too. If your friend is not good at grammar and writing, that person may not see any mistakes either. Try to find a proof-reader, a professional editor, an English teacher, a professional writer, or an experienced secretary who can point out any errors you may have missed.

7.   **After someone has proofread your letter, you can make a few changes to it and not have it looked at again.** More errors creep into a document this way than you would think possible. The reason is that such changes are often done hastily, and haste can waste an error-free document. If you make *any* change to a document, ask someone to proofread it a final time just to make sure that you haven't introduced an error during the last stage of compo-sition. If you can't find someone to help you, the next section gives you advice on how to eliminate common mistakes in cover letters.

Tips for Polishing Cover Letters

You might spend several days working on your resume, getting it "just right" and free of errors. But if you send it with a cover letter that is written quickly and contains even one conspicuous error, all of your good effort may be wasted. That error could be just the kind of mistake the reader is looking for to screen you out.

You can prevent this kind of tragedy by polishing your cover letter so that it is free of all errors. The following tips can help you avoid or eliminate common errors in cover letters. If you become aware of these kinds of errors and know how to fix them, you can be more confident about the cover letters you send with your resumes.

Using Good Strategies for Letters

1.   **Use the postal abbreviation for the state in your mailing address.** See resume writing strategy 1 in Part 1.

2.   **Make certain that the letter is addressed to a specific person and that you use this person's name in the salutation.** Avoid using such general salutations as *Dear Sir or Madam, To Whom It May Concern, Dear Administrator, Dear Prospective Employer,* or *Dear Committee.* In an active job search, you should do everything possible to send your cover letter and resume to a particular individual, preferably someone you've already talked with in person or by phone, and with whom you have arranged an interview. If you have not been able to make a personal contact, at least do everything possible to find out the name of the person who will read your letter and resume. Then address the letter to that person.

3.   **Adjust the margins for a short letter.** If your cover letter is 300 words or longer, use left, right, top, and bottom margins of one inch. If the letter is short-er, you should increase the width of the margins. How much to increase them is a matter of personal taste. One way to take care of the width of the top and bot-tom margins is to center a shorter letter vertically on the page. A maximum width for a short cover letter of 100 words or fewer might be two-inch left and right margins. As the number of words increases by 50 words, you might decrease the width of the left and right margins by two-tenths of an inch.

4. **If you write your letter with word-processing or desktop-publishing software, use left-justification to ensure that the lines of text are readable and have fixed spacing between words.** The letter will have a "ragged" look along the right margin, but the words will be evenly spaced horizontally. Don't use justification in an attempt to give a letter a printed look. Unless you do other typesetting procedures, such as "kerning" and hyphenating words at the end of some lines, full justification can make your letter look worse by giving it some extra-wide and extra-narrow spaces between words.

Using Pronouns Correctly

5. **Use *I* and *My* sparingly.** When most of the sentences in a cover letter begin with *I* or *My,* the writer may appear self-absorbed, self-centered, or egotistical. If the reader is turned off by this kind of impression (even if it is a false one), you could be screened out without ever having an interview. Of course, you will need to use these first-person pronouns because most of the information you put in your cover letter will be personal. But try to avoid using *I* and *My* at the beginnings of sentences and paragraphs.

6. **Refer to a business, company, corporation, or organization as "it" rather than "they."** Members of the Board may be referred to as "they," but a company is a singular subject that requires a singular verb. Note this example:

   > New Products, Inc., was established in 1980. It grossed more than a million dollars in sales during its first year.

7. **If you start a sentence with *This,* be sure that what *This* refers to is clear.** If the reference is not clear, insert some word or phrase to clarify what *This* means. Compare the following lines:

   > My revised application for the new position will be faxed to you by noon on Friday. *This* should be acceptable to you.

   > My revised application for the new position will be faxed to you by noon on Friday. This *method of sending the application* should be acceptable to you.

   A reader of the first sentence wouldn't know what *This* refers to. Friday? By noon on Friday? The revised application for the new position? The insertion after *This* in the second sentence, however, tells the reader that *This* refers to the use of faxing.

8. **Use *as follows* after a singular subject.** Literally, *as follows* means *as it follows,* so the phrase is illogical after a plural subject. Compare the following lines:

Incorrect:	My plans for the day of the interview are as follows:
Fixed:	My plans for the day of the interview are these:
Correct:	My plan for the day of the interview is as follows:
Better:	Here is my plan for the day of the interview:

   In the second set, the improved version avoids a hidden reference problem—the possible association of the silent "it" with *interview.* Whenever you want to use *as follows,* check to see whether the subject that precedes *as follows* is plural. If it is, don't use this phrase.

Using Verb Forms Correctly

9. **Make certain that subjects and verbs agree in number.** Plural subjects require plural forms of verbs. Singular subjects require singular verb forms. Most writers know these things, but problems arise when subject and verb agreement gets tricky. Compare the following lines:

Incorrect:	My education and experience has prepared me...
Correct:	My education and experience have prepared me...
Incorrect:	Making plans plus scheduling conferences were...
Correct:	Making plans plus scheduling conferences was...

   In the first set, *education* and *experience* are two things (you can have one without the other) and require a plural verb. A hasty writer might lump them together and use a singular verb. When you reread what you have written, look out for this kind of improper agreement between a plural subject and a singular verb.

   In the second set, *making plans* is the subject. It is singular, so the verb must be singular. The misleading part of this sentence is the phrase *plus scheduling conferences.* It may seem to make the subject plural, but it doesn't. In English, phrases that begin with such words as *plus, together with, in addition to, along with,* and *as well as* usually don't make a singular subject plural.

10. **Whenever possible, use active forms of verbs rather than passive forms.** Compare these lines:

Passive:	My report will be sent by my assistant tomorrow.
Active:	My assistant will send my report tomorrow.
Passive:	Your interest is appreciated.
Active:	I appreciate your interest.
Passive:	Your letter was received yesterday.
Active:	I received your letter yesterday.

   Sentences with passive verbs are usually longer and clumsier than sentences with active verbs. Passive sentences often leave out the crucial information of who is performing the action of the verb. Spot passive verbs by looking for some form of the verb *to be* (such as *be, will be, have been, is, was,* and *were*) used with another verb.

   In solving the passive language problem, you might create another, such as using the pronouns *I* and *My* too frequently (see Tip 5 in this list). The task then becomes one of finding some other way to start a sentence while keeping your language active.

11. **Be sure that present and past participles are grammatically parallel in a list.** See Tip 48 in Part 1. What is true about parallel forms in resumes is true also in cover letters. Present participles are action words that end in *-ing,* such as *creating, testing,* and *implementing.* Past participles are action words that usually end in *-ed,* such as *created, tested,* and *implemented.* These types of words are called *verbals* because they are derived from verbs but are not strong enough to function as verbs in a sentence. When you use a string of verbals, control them by keeping them parallel.

12. **Use split infinitives only when *not* splitting them is misleading or awkward.** An *infinitive* is a verb preceded by the preposition *to,* as in *to create, to test,* and *to implement.* You split an infinitive when you insert an adverb between the preposition and the verb, as in *to quickly create, to repeatedly test,* and *to slowly implement.* About 50 years ago, split infinitives were considered grammatical errors; these days, however, opinion about them has changed. Many grammar handbooks now recommend that you split your infinitives to avoid awkward or misleading sentences. Compare the following lines:

Split infinitive:	I plan to periodically send updated reports on my progress in school.
Misleading:	I plan periodically to send updated reports on my progress in school.
Misleading:	I plan to send periodically updated reports on my progress in school.

The first example is clear enough, but the second and third examples may be misleading. If you are uncomfortable with split infinitives, one solution is to move *periodically* further into the sentence: "I plan to send updated reports periodically on my progress in school."

Most handbooks that allow split infinitives also recommend that they not be split by more than one word, as in *to quickly and easily write.* A gold medal for splitting an infinitive should go to Lowell Schmalz, an Archie Bunker prototype in "The Man Who Knew Coolidge" by Sinclair Lewis. Schmalz, who thought that Coolidge was one of America's greatest presidents, split an infinitive this way: *"to instantly and without the least loss of time or effort find..."*[1]

Using Punctuation Correctly

13. **Punctuate a compound sentence with a comma.** A compound sentence is one that contains two main clauses joined by one of seven conjunctions (*and, but, or, nor, for, yet,* and *so*). In English, a comma is customarily put before the conjunction if the sentence isn't unusually short. Here is an example of a compound sentence punctuated correctly:

> I plan to arrive at O'Hare at 9:35 a.m. on Thursday, and my trip by cab to your office should take no longer than 40 minutes.

The comma is important because it signals that a new grammatical subject (*trip,* the subject of the second main clause) is about to be expressed. If you use this kind of comma consistently, the reader will rely on your punctuation and be on the lookout for the next subject in a compound sentence.

14. **Be certain not to put a comma between compound verbs.** When a sentence has two verbs joined by the conjunction *and,* these verbs are called *compound verbs.* Usually, they should not be separated by a comma before the conjunction. Note the following examples:

---

[1] Sinclair Lewis, "The Man Who Knew Coolidge," *The Man Who Knew Coolidge* (New York: Books for Libraries Press, 1956), p. 29.

I *started* the letter last night *and finished* it this morning.

I *am sending* my resume separately *and would like* you to keep the information confidential.

Both examples are simple sentences containing compound verbs. Therefore, no comma appears before *and.* In either case, a comma would send a wrong signal that a new subject in another main clause is coming, but no such subject exists.

Note: In a sentence with a series of three or more verbs, use commas between the verbs. The comma before the last verb is called the *serial comma.* For more information on using the serial comma, see resume writing style Tip 63 in Part 1.

---

15. **Avoid using *as well as* for *and* in a series.** Compare the following lines:

Incorrect:	Your company is impressive because it has offices in Canada, Mexico, as well as the United States.
Correct:	Your company is impressive because it has offices in Canada and Mexico, as well as in the United States.

    Usually, what is considered exceptional precedes *as well as,* and what is considered customary follows it. Note this example:

    Your company is impressive because its managerial openings are filled by women as well as men.

16. **Put a comma after the year when it appears after the month and day.** Similarly, put a comma after the state when it appears after the city. Compare the following pairs of lines:

Incorrect:	On January 4, 1994 I was promoted to senior analyst.
Correct:	On January 4, 1994, I was promoted to senior analyst.

Incorrect:	I worked in Chicago, Illinois before moving to Dallas.
Correct:	I worked in Chicago, Illinois, before moving to Dallas.

17. **Put a comma after an opening dependent clause.** Compare the following lines:

Incorrect:	If you have any questions you may contact me by phone or fax.
Correct:	If you have any questions, you may contact me by phone or fax.

    Actually, many writers of fiction and nonfiction don't use this kind of comma. The comma is useful, though, because it signals where the main clause begins. If you glance at the example with the comma, you can tell where the main clause is without even reading the opening clause. For a step up in clarity and readability, use this comma. It can give the reader a "feel" for a sentence even before he or she begins to read the words.

18. **Use semicolons when they are needed.** See resume writing style Tip 64 in Part 1 for the use of semicolons between items in a series. Semicolons are used also to separate main clauses when the second clause starts with a *conjunctive adverb* such as *however, moreover,* and *therefore.* Compare the following lines:

Incorrect:	Your position in sales looks interesting, however, I would like more information about it.
Correct:	Your position in sales looks interesting; however, I would like more information about it.

The first example is incorrect because the comma before *however* is a *comma splice,* which is a comma that joins two sentences. It's like putting a comma instead of a period at the end of the first sentence and then starting the second sentence. A comma may be a small punctuation mark, but a comma splice is a huge grammatical mistake. What are your chances for getting hired if your cover letter tells your reader that you don't recognize where a sentence ends, especially if a requirement for the job is good communication skills? Yes, you could be screened out because of one little comma!

19. **Avoid putting a colon after a verb or a preposition to introduce information.** The reason is that the colon interrupts a continuing clause. Compare the following lines:

Incorrect:	My interests in your company *are:* its reputation, the review of salary after six months, and your personal desire to hire handicapped persons.
Correct:	My interests in your company *are these:* its reputation, the review of salary after six months, and your personal desire to hire handicapped persons.
Incorrect:	In my interview with you, I would like *to:* learn how your company was started, get your reaction to my updated portfolio, and discuss your department's plans to move to a new building.
Correct:	In my interview with you, I would like to discuss *these issues:* how your company was started, what you think of my updated portfolio, and when your department may move to a new building.

Although some people may say that it is okay to put a colon after a verb such as *include* if the list of information is long, it is better to be consistent and avoid colons after verbs altogether.

20. **Understand colons clearly.** People often associate colons with semicolons because their names sound alike, but colons and semicolons have nothing to do with each other. Colons are the opposite of dashes. Dashes look backward, whereas colons usually look forward to information about to be delivered. One common use of the colon does look backward, however. Here are two examples:

My experience with computers is limited: I have had only one course on programming, and I don't own a computer.

I must make a decision by Monday: That is the deadline for renewing the lease for my apartment.

In each example, what follows the colon explains what was said before the colon. Using a colon this way in a cover letter can impress a knowledgeable reader who is looking for evidence of writing skills.

21. **Use slashes correctly.** Information about slashes is sometimes hard to find because *slash* often is listed in grammar reference books under a different

name, such as *virgule* or *solidus*. If you are not familiar with these terms, your hunt for advice on slashes may lead to nothing.

At least know that one important meaning of a slash is *or*. For this reason, you often see a slash in an expression such as *ON/OFF*. This usage means that a condition or state, like that of electricity activated by a switch, is either ON or OFF but never ON and OFF at the same time. This condition may be one in which a change means going from the current state to the opposite (or alternate) state. If the current state is ON and there is a change, the next state will be OFF, and vice versa. With this understanding, you can recognize the logic behind the following examples:

Incorrect:	ON-OFF switch (on and off at the same time!)
Correct:	ON/OFF switch (on or off at any time)
Correct:	his-her clothes (unisex clothes, worn by both sexes)
Correct:	his/her clothes (each sex had different clothes)

Note: Both his-her and his/her are clumsy. Try to find a way to avoid them. One route is to rephrase the sentence so that you use the plural possessive pronoun *their* or the second-person possessive pronoun *your*. [Campers should make their beds before breakfast. Please make your beds before breakfast.] Another way is to rephrase the sentence without possessive pronouns. [Everyone should put on clothes before going to breakfast.]

22. **Think twice about using *and/or*.** This stilted expression is commonly misunderstood to mean *two* alternatives, but it literally means *three*. Look at the following example:

> If you don't hear from me by Friday, please phone and/or fax me the information on Monday.

What is the person at the other end to do? The sentence really states three alternatives: just phone, just fax, or phone *and* fax the information by Monday. For better clarity, use the connectives *and* or *or* whenever possible.

23. **Use punctuation correctly with quotation marks.** A common misconception is that commas and periods should be placed outside closing quotation marks, but the opposite is true. Compare the following lines:

Incorrect:	Your company certainly has the "leading edge", which means that its razor blades are the best on the market.
Correct:	Your company certainly has the "leading edge," which means that its razor blades are the best on the market.
Incorrect:	In the engineering department, my classmates referred to me as "the guru in pigtails". I was the youngest expert in programming languages on campus.
Correct:	In the engineering department, my classmates referred to me as "the guru in pigtails." I was the youngest expert in programming languages on campus.

Note this exception: Unlike commas and periods, colons and semicolons go *outside* double quotation marks.

Using Words Correctly

24. **Avoid using lofty language in your cover letter.** A real turn-off in a cover letter is the use of elevated diction (high-sounding words and phrases) as an attempt to seem important. Note the following examples, along with their straight-talk translations:

    Elevated: My background has afforded me experience in...

    Better: In my previous jobs, I...

    Elevated: Prior to that term of employment...

    Better: Before I worked at...

    Elevated: I am someone with a results-driven profit orientation.

    Better: I want to make your company more profitable.

    Elevated: I hope to utilize my qualifications...

    Better: I want to use my skills...

    In letter writing, the shortest distance between the writer and the reader is the most direct idea.

25. **Check your sentences for an excessive use of compounds joined by *and*.** A cheap way to make your letters longer is to join words with *and* and do this repeatedly. Note the following wordy sentence:

    Because of my background and preparation for work and advancement with your company and new enterprise, I have a concern and commitment to implement and put into effect my skills and abilities for new solutions and achievements above and beyond your dreams and expectations. [44 words]

    Just one inflated sentence like that would drive a reader to say, "No way!" The writer of the inflated sentence has said only this:

    Because of my background and skills, I want to contribute to your new venture. [14 words]

    If, during rereading, you eliminate the wordiness caused by this common writing weakness, an employer is more likely to read your letter completely.

26. **Avoid using abstract nouns excessively.** Look again at the inflated sentence in the preceding tip, but this time with the abstract nouns in italic:

    Because of my *background* and *preparation* for *work* and *advancement* with your *company* and new *enterprise,* I have a *concern* and *commitment* to implement and put into *effect* my skills and *abilities* for new *solutions* and *achievements* above and beyond your *dreams* and *expectations.*

    Try picturing in your mind any of the words in italic. You can't because they are *abstract nouns,* which means that they are ideas and not images of things you can see, taste, hear, smell, or touch. One certain way to turn off the reader is to load your cover letter with abstract nouns. The following sentence, containing some images, has a better chance of capturing the reader's attention:

    Having created seven multimedia tutorials with my videocamera and Gateway Pentium computer, I now want to create some breakthrough adult-learning packages so that your company, New Century Instructional Technologies, Inc., will exceed $50,000,000 in contracts by 2005.

Compare this sentence with the one loaded with abstract nouns. The one with images is obviously the better attention grabber.

27.   **Avoid wordy expressions in your cover letters.** Note the following examples and the shorter alternatives that follow them in parentheses:

> at the location of (at)
>
> for the reason that (because)
>
> in a short time (soon)
>
> in a timely manner (on time)
>
> in spite of everything to the contrary (nevertheless)
>
> in the event of (if)
>
> in proximity to (near)
>
> now and then (occasionally)
>
> on a daily basis (daily)
>
> on a regular basis (regularly)
>
> on account of (because)
>
> one day from now (tomorrow)
>
> would you be so kind as to (please)

Trim the fat wherever you can, and your reader will appreciate the leanness of your cover letter.

28.   **At the end of your cover letter, don't make a statement that the reader can use to reject you.** For example, suppose that you close your letter with this statement:

> If you wish to discuss this matter further, please call me
> at (555) 555-5555.

This statement gives the reader a chance to think, "I don't wish it, so I don't have to call." Here is another example:

> If you know of the right opportunity for me, please call me
> at (555) 555-5555.

The reader may think, "I don't know of any such opportunity. How would I know what is right for you?" Avoid questions that prompt yes-or-no answers, such as "Do you want to discuss this matter further?" If you ask this kind of question, you give the reader a chance to say no. Instead, make a closing statement that indicates your optimism about a positive response from the reader. Such a statement might begin with one of the following clauses:

> I am confident that…
>
> I look forward to…

In this way, you invite the reader to say yes to further considering your candidacy for the job.

Exhibit of Cover Letters

The following Exhibit contains sample cover letters that were prepared by professional resume writers. In most cases, the names, addresses, and facts have been changed to ensure the confidentiality of the original sender and receiver of the letter. For each letter, however, the essential substance of the original remains intact.

Use the Exhibit of cover letters as a reference whenever you need to write a cover letter for your resume. If you have trouble starting and ending letters, look at the beginnings and ends of these letters. If you need help with writing about your work experience, describing your abilities and skills, or mentioning some of your best achievements, look at the middle paragraph(s). Search for features that will give you ideas for making your own cover letters more effective.

As you examine the Exhibit, consider the following questions:

1. **Does the writer show a genuine interest in the reader?** One way to tell is to count the number of times the pronouns *you* or *your* appear in the letter. Then count the number of times the pronouns *I, me,* and *my* occur in the letter. Although this method is simplistic, it nevertheless helps you see where the writer's interests lie. When you write a cover letter, make your first paragraph *you*-centered rather than *I*-centered. See also Tip 5 under "Using Pronouns Correctly," earlier in Part 3.

2. **Where does the cover letter mention the resume specifically?** The purpose of a cover letter is to call attention to the resume. If the letter fails to mention the resume, the letter has not fulfilled its purpose. In addition to mentioning the resume, the cover letter might direct the reader's attention to one or more parts of the resume, increasing the chances that the reader will see the most important part(s). It is not a good idea, however, to put a lot of resume facts in the cover letter. Let each document do its own job. The job of the cover letter is to point to the resume, not repeat it verbatim.

3. **Where and how does the letter express interest in an interview?** The immediate purpose of a cover letter is to call attention to the resume, but the *ultimate* purpose of both the cover letter and the resume is to help you get an interview with the person who can hire you. If the letter doesn't display your interest in getting an interview, the letter has not fulfilled its ultimate purpose.

4. **How decisive is the writer's language?** This question is closely related to the preceding question. Does the writer express interest in an interview directly or indirectly? Does the person specifically request an interview on a date when the writer will be in the reader's vicinity, or does the person only hint at a desire to "meet" the reader someday? When you write your own cover letters, be sure to be direct and convincing in expressing your interest in an interview. Avoid being timid or wishy-washy.

5. **How does the person display self-confidence?** As you look through the Exhibit, notice the cover letters in which the phrase "I am confident that..." (or a similar expression) appears. Self-confidence is a sign of management ability but also of essential job-worthiness. Many of the letters display self-confidence or self-assertiveness in various ways.

6. **How does the letter indicate that the person is a team player?** From an employer's point of view, an employee who is self-assertive but not a team

player can spell T-R-O-U-B-L-E. As you look at the cover letters in the Exhibit, notice the many letters in which the word *team* appears.

7. **How does the letter make the person stand out?** As you read the letters in the Exhibit, do some letters present the person more vividly than other letters? If so, what does the trick—the middle paragraphs or the opening and closing paragraphs? Use what you learn here to help you write distinctive cover letters.

8. **How familiar is the person with the reader?** In a passive job search, the reader will most likely be a total stranger. In an active job search, the chances are good that the writer will have had at least one conversation with the reader by phone or in person. As you look through the cover letters in the Exhibit, see whether you can spot any letter which indicates that the writer has already talked with the reader.

After you have examined the cover letters in the Exhibit, you will be better able to write an attention-getting letter—one that leads the reader to your resume and to scheduling an interview with you.

THOMAS DORAN   555 555-5555
■■

April 29, 2004

Mr. Alex J. Madrid
Advertising Director
Creative Spanish Advertising, Inc.
5555 Ignacio Road
Concordo, Mexico YZ555-55

Dear Mr. Madrid:

A **bachelor of arts in advertising, a minor in marketing** from Academia University, and experience building several competitive advertising campaigns add credibility to my candidacy for an advertising position with Creative Spanish Advertising, Inc. Your *Today's Journal* classified ad for an advertising assistant sparked my interest. The enclosed resume reflects an **energetic, highly competitive, and committed** individual with **relevant experience.** The following **achievements and personal characteristics** are additional reasons to take a closer look at my qualifications.

CONTRIBUTING IDEAS THAT WORK...

- Provided advertising skills as **integral team player** on several campaigns. Fully involved in creating a plan book and **creative brief** to promote awareness of how the state lottery uses funds to better the state public school system. Contributed to **all aspects of project.**
- Earned a place on the Advertising Coalition Student Competition Team of 2003 due to **abstract concepts** and **creative impact.** Incorporated **appeal techniques** in the creation of a four-year integrated marketing communications plan book for auto dealership. Chosen for **creative team.**

EXPERIENCE THAT BRINGS INSIGHT...

- Used initiative to gain opportunity and funding for **foreign study programs** in Mexico and Holland. Studies covered **Spanish, international marketing, management, and law.** Submersion into these cultures and observation of foreign **advertising techniques, nontraditional media,** and **economic structures** greatly enhanced **insight** into international business.
- Gained a stronger **acceptance of differences,** expanded **cultural awareness,** and became more **self-reliant and confident** through **travel experiences** and **interaction with people of diversity.**

PROFICIENCIES THAT REFLECT DISTINCTION ...

- Creative idea generation and problem solving for unique presentations.
- Brainstorming and openness to new ideas for increasing productivity.
- Group facilitation and organization for effective teamwork.
- Effective decisions based on overall picture for positive outcomes.
- Interpersonal skills such as mediation and negotiation for maintaining strong business relationships.
- Effective writing talent for creative copy.
- Mac and IBM computer literacy with experience in QuarkXPress, Adobe Illustrator and Photoshop, and Microsoft Works and Word for optimum layouts.
- Conversational Spanish for interfacing with peers and clients.

I will contact you within the week to confirm receipt of my resume and set up a **personal interview** at your convenience. In the meantime, thank you for your time and consideration.

Sincerely,

Thomas Doran

Enclosure: Resume

■ ■ ■ ■ ■

5555 55ᵗʰ Street ▪ Camary, Texas 55555 ▪ tdoran@yahoo.com

Edith A. Rische, Lubbock, Texas

The letter has only two paragraphs. Sandwiched between them are three sections with bulleted achievements, areas of development, and personal qualifications. See Resume 21 (page 53).

CHAD CARPENTER

504 Bickford Drive
Hermitage, Tennessee 00000

Home (555) 000-0000
ccarpenter@comcast.net

May 1, 2004

WTEN Channel 7
Human Resource Department
924 Streamline Drive
Nashville, TN 00000

Re: PRODUCTION ASSISTANT

No doubt there is keen competition for jobs as a Production Assistant at Channel 7, and I'm sure you are interested in finding creative, imaginative, and technically qualified individuals to fill these positions. As a recent graduate from APSU, I believe I have the qualifications and enthusiasm you are looking for.

As you will see in the attached resume, I have completed an internship with MegaStar, a post-production facility in Nashville. Under their mentoring, I gained a practical understanding of the critical interaction among various members of the production team—producers, directors, talent, editors, and crew members. I am accustomed to the hectic pace of a production environment and have hands-on experience with a variety of technical applications. My academic training and internship experience have worked together to enhance my knowledge and increase my confidence in my abilities. I realize, however, that beginning positions often involve routine tasks, which I will be happy to perform.

I am confident that within a very short time I can prove my value as a contributor to the Channel 7 production team. I would appreciate the opportunity to meet with you and discuss my qualifications in further detail. Thank you for your time, and I look forward to speaking with you.

Sincerely,

Chad Carpenter

Enclosure

2

Carolyn S. Braden, Hendersonville, Tennessee

The first two paragraphs show that this recent graduate believes he can do well the work of a production assistant. The third paragraph indicates that he wants to. See Resume 170 (page 346).

Dorothy Bond
555 Winding Lane
Pleasant Park, IL 00000
555-555-5555
xxxxxxx@aol.com

October 15, 2004

Job Code M5555
Chicago Tribune
P.O. Box 806883
Chicago, IL 00000

Dear Sir/Madam:

In response to the advertisement you placed in the *Chicago Tribune* for an Administrative Supervisor, Hospital Fundraising Development Department, I have enclosed my resume for your review. My successful experience in administrative management, new business development, marketing, and promotion, combined with my strong work ethic and MPA/Healthcare degree, would be a good match for this position.

In my career, I have enjoyed creating strategies that expand and improve the client relationship base and marketing efforts. I have also developed a variety of effective administrative procedures and programs. From the beginning I have maintained an interest in public administration, and I completed a Masters in Public Administration–Healthcare through City University in 2000. I am now targeting positions in the field of public administration that would combine these skills and experiences and would appreciate the opportunity to talk with you about your plans and philosophies. In my search, I am targeting a compensation range in the mid-thirties to mid-fifties.

You can reach me at the phone number or e-mail listed above. Thank you for your time and attention.

Sincerely,

[signature]

Resume enclosed

Christine L. Dennison, Lincolnshire, Illinois

The letter is somewhat generic as a response to a blind box ad, which did not allow research of the company. Instead of a requested salary history, the letter gives a wide salary range that indicates flexibility.

WALTER D. SAAKS

98 Ben Franklin Drive		Home: (609) 666–1111
P.O. Box 219		Cell: (609) 666–5555
Cherry Hill, New Jersey 07896	wdsaaks@aol.com	Home Fax: (609) 666–7777

<Date>

<Title, Name of Hiring Manager>
<Name of Company>
<Address>
<City, State ZIP>

Dear <Courtesy><Last Name>,

Throughout my 40-year career in real estate development and construction, I have built and led numerous successful development, construction, and property management companies. For each organization, I have provided the strategic, marketing, financial, and operating expertise to deliver strong earnings and sustained revenue streams. Please consider the following in addition to my resume:

- 15+ years of management experience in a general contracting company, including construction management, owner/client negotiations, sub-contract scope designs and negotiations, project cost accounting/reporting, design-build, estimating, purchasing, design/expense analysis, and bidding.

- 15 years of experience in real estate development and management, including site selection, building conception designs, establishing and maintaining owner associations, acting as representative on condominium boards, and establishing budgetary goals and life expectancies of building and site features.

- Recognized as a credible professional within the real estate community of New Jersey; proven track record of closing early sales/leases and meeting client delivery requirements.

- Leadership of more than $190 million in construction projects, with complete development and management responsibility for more than 470 projects ranging from commercial renovations to major new construction projects.

- Astute business manager with an outstanding ability to build dynamic teams and generate strong results; successfully assembled teams to solve engineering, architectural, and mechanical problems associated with all phases of construction and development.

As a successful entrepreneur, I possess a wealth of positive, proven methods and solutions to diverse obstacles. Most significant is my ability to drive projects through complex political channels by providing a strong community vision and decisive action plan. In addition, my enthusiasm for the entire process, from product conception and planning to delivery and sales/leasing, is undaunted by any negativity or economic difficulty. There is always a consumer for a product selected and executed with pride and grace.

I would welcome the opportunity to discuss how my credentials and expertise can benefit your organization, and will therefore contact your office next week to arrange a mutually convenient time for us to meet. In the interim, I thank you for reviewing this letter and the accompanying material.

Sincerely,

Walter Saaks
Enclosure

4

Jennifer Rushton, N. Richmond, New South Wales, Australia

The writer expanded this three-paragraph letter after the first paragraph by adding five bulleted items about experience, esteem, scope of accomplishments, and outstanding managerial abilities. See Resume 89 (page 180).

LOUELLA SCIENTIST, PH.D.
9999 Chemistry Street • New Haven, Connecticut 06511
louellascientist@net.net • 999.999.9999 (W) • 999.999.9999 (H)

May XX, 2004

Name, Title
Company
Address
City, ST, 99999

Dear Hiring Executive:

The cures for various types of cancer (including Hodgkin's Lymphoma) may be closer than we think, thanks to my work in discovery of *survivin,* an anti-apoptosis gene. Original thinking and outstanding problem-solving abilities have distinguished my eight years of experience in molecular biology and biochemistry research, fields vital to progress in pharmacology. In addition, I have experience in researching the effects of GH regulation, leptin expression, and other factors in regard to obesity. My record of success makes me an excellent candidate for a challenging position as a **Research Scientist in Molecular/Cell Biology and Oncology.**

As a member of research teams seeking new breakthroughs in cancer treatment, gene therapy, and other exciting areas, I have taken on increasing levels of responsibility in the laboratory. My latest position has been in scientific research for the Department of Molecular Biology at Branford's prestigious Institute of Pharmaceutical Discovery. As a postdoctoral researcher, I worked in the Pathology Department of the Yale University School of Medicine and at the Scripps Research Institute in La Jolla, California. Areas of research have included the following:

- Mechanisms of growth hormone (GH) action through regulated production of GH binding proteins

- Transcriptional regulation of human leptin gene by hypoxia

- Development of DNA constructs for gene therapy

- Use of a novel anti-apoptosis gene, *survivin,* to combat the spread of cancer

Please take a few moments to review my enclosed curriculum vitae. I would welcome the opportunity for an interview, in which we might discuss targets of research in your organization's laboratories. I believe I could make significant contributions that could lead to development of breakthrough drugs by your company. In the interim, I thank you for your interest and look forward to hearing from you.

Sincerely,

Louella Scientist, Ph.D.

Enclosure

5

Cathy Childs, Grand Island, Florida

An impressive first paragraph displays the applicant's experience and originality. The second paragraph and bulleted items show areas of expertise. The third shares a hope for breakthroughs.

KARA MANN
karamann@email.com

5555 Meadow Hill Drive
Los Angeles, CA 55555

Residence (310) 555-5555
Mobile (310) 555-0000

[Date]

[Name]
[Address]
[City, State ZIP]

Dear [Salutation]:

Perhaps your organization is in search of a highly motivated recent college graduate who is passionate about the Entertainment / Music Industry and has the energy and drive to "pay my dues," acquire knowledge and advance professionally. If so, then we should talk!

I offer a combination of creative talents and a strong work ethic, as well as the following qualifications:

- BA in Film Studies from the University of Southern California…

- Hands-on experience directing, acting in and producing short independent and student films…

- Realistic understanding of the demands of the entertainment industry…

- Operating knowledge of a variety of audio and video equipment…

- Experience (two summers) as an intern at a top research marketing firm…

While my enclosed resume provides a brief overview of my background, I look forward to a personal meeting, at which time we can discuss your needs and my qualifications in detail. I will call you next week to schedule a meeting; in the meantime, you can contact me at the above numbers. Thank you in advance for your time and consideration.

Sincerely,

Kara Mann

Enclosure

6

Vivian VanLier, Los Angeles, California

This letter is for an entry-level position in entertainment/music. The entire first paragraph is in bold italic to capture attention. Bulleted items begin with the highly regarded degree from the USC film school.

Matsutoka "Mike" Suehiro

Ph: (555) 555-5555
matsus@home.com

578 Cherrybrook Lane
Mesa City, CA 99999

Media Relations · Marketing · Communications

January 12, 2004

Millennium Media Productions
1212 Dulane Canyon Road
Dulane Canyon, CA 99999

Marketing, advertising and sales. All intrinsically competitive, results-driven enterprises. For me, therein lies the attraction. If you're looking for a Photographer/Art Director who is capable and creative, with great interpersonal skills and a powerful work ethic, please take a closer look at my qualifications.

I am a forward-thinking and effective team player who doesn't hesitate to roll up his sleeves and get the job done—whatever it takes. When I roll my sleeves back down, it could be 8 hours later; could be 16 hours later. But, rest assured that when I do close up shop, it's because the work is done; not because the clock strikes 5:00. This entrepreneurial-type conscientiousness and team member dedication have helped me to

- Successfully create brand images for new product lines.
- Routinely exceed expectations for all positions I've held.
- Lead by example and elicit peak performance from supporting players.
- Devise methods that resulted in significant savings in operational costs.
- Regularly complete high-quality projects on time and, most often, well under budget.
- Formulate photography systems and creative processes for $3 million website redesign.

If, after reviewing my resume, you'd like to discuss how my creativity, experience and business acumen can benefit Millennium Media, I am available to meet at your convenience. I can be reached at (555) 555-5555, or by e-mail—matsus@home.com.

Sincerely,

Mike Suehiro

7

Gail Taylor, Torrance, California

The casual style of this letter reflects the applicant's desire to work in a "fun place." His view is that a person can have fun *and* be productive. "It's easy to envision his enthusiasm at work."

ALBERT W. BAXTER

5555 Sea Breeze Ave. ~~ Glasscot, Iowa 55555 ~~ **(555) 555-5555**
awbaxter@aol.com

August 23, 2004

Mike Preston
Corporate Human Resources Manager
Ranch Style Cookin' Restaurants
5555 Steak Ave.
Marigold, Texas 55555-5555

The best executive is the one who has sense enough to pick good men to do what he wants done, and self-restraint enough to keep from meddling with them while they do it. ~~ Theodore Roosevelt

RE: SOUTHERN DIVISION MANAGER FOR RANCH STYLE COOKIN' RESTAURANTS

Dear Mr. Preston:

As I consider new career options that offer opportunities to "own" my future, experience new challenges, and expand my expertise, I am excited by your job posting for a **division manager.** As a general manager in a competitive customer service market, I offer many transferable skills that would add distinction to this position, such as the ability to **recruit and train leaders; empower entrepreneurs; build long-term peer, team, and client relationships; effect superior customer service; and make sound decisions.** The enclosed resume not only demonstrates these skills, but it reflects several major career achievements.

The following **key strengths** also exemplify highly marketable skills and characteristics that I possess:

- *Functional experience in operations turnaround, marketing and new business development, budgeting and financing, planning and forecasting, and personnel staffing.*

- *Strategic planning that enables restructuring of company personnel, processes, and goals to realize major improvement.*

- *Aptitude for defining problems, pitching and selling ideas, setting timelines, initiating steps, and facilitating positive change.*

- *A talent for selecting, recruiting, training, and retaining top producers.*

- *A management style that promotes integrity, unity, teamwork, shared decision-making, support, recognition, and justice.*

- *Honest, straightforward communication techniques that promote development of strong and lasting rapport and trust.*

- *Dedication and loyalty as demonstrated by longevity with a single employer.*

- *The ability to recognize and reinforce the potential in every person.*

An interview to further investigate your needs and my qualifications would be mutually beneficial. Please anticipate a call within the week to confirm receipt of my resume and to explore convenient appointment times. In the meantime, thank you for your time and consideration.

Sincerely,

Albert W. Baxter

Enclosure: Resume

8

Edith A. Rische, Lubbock, Texas

The candidate recently earned his CPA status and wants a senior accounting position. Key strengths listed after the second paragraph and enhanced with boldfacing capture attention.

555 ● 555 ● 5555

B. Rae French
5555 Toton Avenue ● Skyview, Texas 79000
brfrench@nts-online.net

May 27, 2004

Sally Monarch
Human Resources Director
CORPORATE AMERICA
5555 Broadview Lane
Macro City, Texas 99999

...an ordinary person who is motivated, enthusiastic, who has dreams, and who works hard; who has the ability to laugh, to think, to cry; and who can give the gift of belief to other people can accomplish anything.
Unknown

RE: CORPORATE TRAINER

Dear Ms. Monarch:

After a successful eight-year teaching career in academia, I am seeking change. To be more specific, as a **corporate trainer,** I hope to realize more latitude for **creativity** and **original training techniques** in a company where upward mobility is an option. **Communication, interpersonal relations, coordination, and organization** are among my most highly developed skills—all practical resources for managing a corporate training program. The enclosed resume reflects a **multitalented, energetic achiever** who enjoys making **positive contributions.**

The following **additional skills** further exhibit a **strong candidacy** for a corporate trainer position:

Interpersonal / Communication Skills
- **Personable, cheerful demeanor** and a **relaxed style** cultivate an **effective learning environment.**
- **A sense of humor makes training enjoyable.**
- **Perceptiveness** and **attentiveness** allow appropriate **responses to student needs.**
- Ability to develop **rapport and trust** with a **diverse population** strengthens **trainer / trainee relationships.**
- **Articulation** and **good grammar** ensure **clear, credible delivery** of **instructions** and **training materials.**

Leadership Qualities
- Readiness to **assume responsibility** and **accountability** alleviates stress on upper management.
- **Integrity, diligence,** and **commitment** model **leadership** and **reflect distinction.**
- **A positive attitude** and **willingness to adapt to change** suggest **cooperation** and **easy transitions.**
- **Discernment, prioritization,** and **delegation** encourage **teamwork** and **productivity.**
- **Analytical thinking** and **common sense** foster **effective problem solving.**
- **Proven training techniques** fortify **information retention.**

Administrative Abilities
- **Restructuring curriculum** and **writing directives** supplement **program development.**
- Capacity to **coordinate activities, focus on details,** and **follow up** promotes **smooth-running events.**
- **Organization** and **forward planning** imply **efficiency** and **successful outcomes.**
- **Time management, multitasking,** and **follow through** facilitate **consistently met deadlines.**

I am **confident** that my abilities can benefit your company's training department, and consider a **personal interview to be mutually beneficial.** Relocation is an option for the opportune job offer. I will contact your office within the week to confirm receipt of my resume and set up an appointment at your convenience. Thank you for your consideration.

Sincerely,

B. Rae French

Enclosure: Resume

9

Edith A. Rische, Lubbock, Texas

The novel page border sets this letter apart from most cover letters. The letter appears to set the applicant apart from other applicants through the bulleted lists of skills. See Resume 64 (page 130).

Bill Raymond, CFA

555 Lowell Street
Lawrence, MA 01746

billraymond@alumni.mit.edu
978-555-1210

May 22, 2004

Mr. Tom Marston, Director of Fixed Income
International Financial Investments, Inc.
200 Federal Street, 26th Floor
Boston, MA 02110

Dear Mr. Marston:

In response to your search for the **Money Market Analyst/Portfolio Manager** position your firm placed on Bloomberg, I bring more than 15 years of experience in the market.

My years of experience at Boston Investors, Inc., including more than a dozen years managing money market portfolios, indicate that I could step right into this position and add value immediately. It combines my passion for analysis with my knowledge of money markets.

Your Needs	My Qualifications
CFA, MBA degree or equivalent	◆ CFA since 1996
	◆ B.A. in Economics from M.I.T.
Several years of experience in Money Markets, fund analysis and trading	◆ More than a dozen years of experience managing taxable 2a-7 funds
Creating credit files	◆ Created institutional 2a-7 from scratch, including credit files

My enclosed resume provides further details of my accomplishments. I look forward to discussing a career opportunity with you. I will call you in the next few days to discuss your company's needs in greater detail.

Sincerely,

Bill Raymond
Senior Vice President
Boston Investors, Inc.

Enclosure

10

Gail Frank, Tampa, Florida

The "Your Needs…My Qualifications" two-column table is distinctive. Diamond bullets and the additional line about the M.I.T. degree suggest that his qualifications surpass the reader's needs.

BRENDA B. STEVENS

5555 55th Street ▪ Ft. Cloud, Mississippi 55555 ▪ *(555) 555-5555*

May 12, 2004

TROY PHARMACEUTICALS
5555 Magnum Street
Ft. Cloud, Mississippi 55555

Re: Pharmaceutical Sales Specialist, Code SPMDT

Dear Human Resources Coordinator:

I am committed to improved patient care, a quality that characterizes value to medical professionals. As an *established pharmaceutical sales representative* covering the whole of Mississippi, I offer *beneficial industry knowledge* from *six years of experience.* It would be an honor to represent TROY, a highly regarded pharmaceutical company whose mission to enhance and preserve quality of life coincides so closely with mine.

The enclosed resume reflects a *match between my credentials and your requirements for the pharmaceutical sales specialist position.* A qualification summary follows:

JOB REQUIREMENTS	PERSONAL QUALIFICATIONS
Five years of sales experience, preferably pharmaceutical	▪ *Six years of proven success* in the pharmaceutical / medical sales industry. ▪ *Established rapport with 200+ Mississippi physicians* specializing in a spectrum of healthcare disciplines.
Bachelor's degree	▪ *Bachelor of Science* in political science with minor in public relations.
Project and account management experience	▪ Exclusively *acquired six-figure surgical center account,* orchestrated *total equipment installation,* and *troubleshot logistical problems.* ▪ Employ *continuous customer contact, needs assessment, and strategic planning* to manage and grow 180+ accounts.
Sales / persuasion skills	▪ Consistently rank in *top 10% of regional sales* representatives for exceeding 100% of annual sales goals. ▪ Use *scientific / consultative sales approach* to gain customer acceptance of products and services.
Communication and presentation skills	▪ Relate to physicians through *lighthearted, yet authoritative, communication style* to create enjoyable sales environment. ▪ Incorporate analogies, illustrations, sales / detail aids, and humor into presentations and training seminars to *engage audiences, retain interest, and improve comprehension.*

Given a *pre-established client network, technical knowledge, and personal values,* I am confident I would well serve TROY PHARMACEUTICALS' goals and objectives. I hope to *share business development ideas* during a personal interview, and look forward to scheduling an appointment at your convenience. In the meantime, thank you for your consideration.

Sincerely,

Brenda B. Stevens

Enclosure: Resume

11

Edith A. Rische, Lubbock, Texas

This similar "Job Requirements…Personal Qualifications" two-column table shows that you can easily expand the Qualifications column to suggest that your qualifications outweigh the job's requirements.

Neve Lawrence

Summer 2004

**POSITION REFERRAL CLIENT, ASTD DENVER
POSITION #2569**

Dear Hiring Professional:

In response to your posted search through the Denver chapter of the American Society for Training and Development (ASTD) for a quality **Trainer and/or Instructional Designer,** I bring more than 10 years of experience in the training field as well as familiarity with the business environment.

I am an extremely high-energy and innovative professional. I consistently produce strong feedback and lots of spirited interaction in my workshops. My employers and clients have been very pleased with my level of expertise and my enthusiasm for what I do.

More than 9,400 people have been through one or more sessions with me during the last 9 years. I have taught "soft-skills" and management topics (delivering more than 25 different topics and often juggling 2 or 3 at a time!). Many of these programs were either designed or presented by me, or I radically researched and revised outdated materials and exercises to improve knowledge transfer and participation in the class. I love adding value to my job and to my trainees.

My enclosed resume provides further details of my accomplishments, professional history and topics taught. I look forward to discussing yet another career opportunity with you and your company. I hope we can arrange a meeting so we may discuss your company's needs in greater detail.

Sincerely,

Neve Lawrence

Enclosure

555 Santa Fe Drive, Littleton, Colorado 80161   (303) 555-8238   nlawrence@hotmail.com

12

Gail Frank, Tampa, Florida

The applicant is at a disadvantage in having to write to an unnamed hiring professional. Each of the four succinct paragraphs attempts to motivate the reader to contact the applicant for an interview.

ALVIN ENGINEER

1234 Autocad Street • Phoenix, Arizona 99999
aengineer@net.net • 999.999.9999

May XX, 2004

Name, Title
Company Name
Address
City, State, ZIP

Dear Hiring Executive:

Your company's performance on a current contract will go a long way in determining your eligibility for subsequent work. As a fiscally responsible **Engineering Manager,** I will accept full ownership of every initiative, taking profit-and-loss responsibility for government work the same as for commercial environments. My expertise in strategic planning will ensure that technological capabilities keep pace with your evolving business requirements.

My diversified career includes spearheading multimillion-dollar R&D efforts for NCS Pearson and Raytheon. Prior to my tenure with these industry leaders, I gained experience in full-cycle development of prototype systems for various clients. Among the highlights of my technical leadership have been

- Serving as one of only five technical managers company-wide for a $3M initiative.
- Leading a CMM software accreditation project to achieve certification under budget and three months early.
- Being selected for participation in a corporate stock bonus plan.

I would appreciate the opportunity to discuss how I may be of service to <corporation name>. In the interim, I appreciate the time you have spent reviewing this letter and the accompanying material.

Thank you for your consideration.

Sincerely,

Alvin Engineer

Enclosure

Cathy Childs, Grand Island, Florida

This three-paragraph letter has bulleted highlights introduced after the second paragraph. Note the correct use of parallelism in starting each item with a participle (Serving… Leading…Being …).

BETHANY MITCHELL

619 Winston Terrace   Longwood, CA 99999 Teachkids@cc.com   (888) 000-0000

Elementary School Teacher—Grades K–5

February 5, 2004

Juanda Jefferson
Administrator—Recruitment (Elementary)
South Valley Unified School District
800 South Barkley
Boulder Canyon, CA 99999

Dear Ms. Jefferson:

"Begin with the end in mind." Whoever said that could have easily been referring to the job of an elementary school teacher. Where our children end up depends largely on where—and how—they start out. I am committed to helping them get the substantial foundation they need and deserve.

Teaching is not just my calling; it is my passion. To be entrusted with influencing these young minds is an enormous responsibility, and one I take very seriously. To contribute to the growth of these students, who come with so much potential, curiosity, and energy, is uniquely rewarding. I just can't imagine myself doing anything other than teaching. My philosophies are simple:

- Teach with patience and creativity.
- Be consistent.
- Present challenges.
- Judiciously apply discipline.

Each child comes with his or her own imaginings, fears, dreams, and abilities. With these tools, the student and I can form the basis for a lifelong journey of growth—and we can have fun doing it.

I believe the enclosed resume will portray me as a qualified candidate who is devoted to providing a sound teaching program and establishing within the classroom a healthy learning environment. If you would like to discuss how I might contribute to South Valley's educational system, I'm available to meet at your convenience. Meanwhile, I will call in a few days to confirm you received my resume and to check your availability.

Sincerely,

Bethany Mitchell

P.S. I'm particularly interested in learning more about your recent implementation of a reading intervention program.

14

Gail Taylor, Torrance, California

Parallel lines make the contact information easier to spot. The crayons graphic is a positive touch. What wins over the reader is the applicant's enthusiasm throughout. See Resume 44 (page 94).

Jon Stevens, PE

55 Roman Lane ♦ East Bronx, NY 00000
(H) 000-000-0000 ♦ (C) 000-000-0000 ♦ user@optonline.net

(Date)

(contact name)
(company name)
(street address)
(city, state, ZIP code)

Dear Hiring Professional (or insert contact name):

As an experienced, corporate-level executive with more than 15 years of progressive and stable experience in facilities and operations management, finance management, and budget administration, I believe I would be ideally suited to fill an executive position within your organization.

I have developed a proactive, hands-on style of management that allows me to create and foster an efficient and productive work environment. Possessing excellent human resources administration, engineering, written / oral communication, and computer skills has positioned and qualified me to become an immediate and viable asset to your team. My qualifications include proven strengths in the following areas:

**Client Retention ♦ Recruiting ♦ Team Coordination ♦ Cost Controls ♦ Staff Development
Change Management ♦ Contract Negotiation ♦ Mechanical Engineering ♦ Human Resources
P & L Responsibilities ♦ Budget Development and Administration ♦ Project Management**

The enclosed resume briefly outlines my experience and accomplishments. I would be happy to further discuss my background in a meeting with you. Please feel free to contact me, at your convenience, if you have any questions or would like to schedule an interview.

Thank you for your consideration. I look forward to hearing from you soon.

Sincerely,

Jon Stevens

Lea J. Clark, Macon, Georgia

This four-paragraph letter has areas of strength introduced by the second paragraph. These are placed on three single-spaced lines, center-justified, boldfaced, and separated by diamond bullets.

15

Darrin Wilson

1124 Liberty Street, 3rd Floor • Chester, PA 18940 • 267.757.5462 • dWilson53@excite.com

MARKET RESEARCH ANALYST

Dear Sir/Madam:

As a research professional, I understand that success depends on a strong commitment to **customer satisfaction.** Executing the basics and using logic and reasoning to identify the strengths and weaknesses of alternative solutions, conclusions or approaches to problems are key to increasing performance and market share. I believe that my background and education reflect a commitment and ability to find solutions to these challenges. I developed excellent skills in **project coordination and the design and development of research projects** that increased the effectiveness of my organization.

I am considered an energetic, aggressive and innovative leader who is extremely client-oriented.

My position encompasses multiple tasks and responsibilities that include the following:

♦ Examining and analyzing statistical data to forecast future trends and to identify potential markets.

♦ Designing and implementing new formats for logging and transferring information while working as part of a team researching data and statistics.

Thank you for your consideration. I approach my work with a strong sense of urgency, working well under pressure and change. I look forward to meeting with you personally so that we may discuss how I may make a positive contribution to your organization.

Sincerely yours,

Darrin Wilson

Enclosure

16

Beverley and Mitchell I. Baskin, Marlboro, New Jersey

This four-paragraph letter displays bulleted responsibilities introduced by the third paragraph. Boldfacing of phrases in the first paragraph calls attention to concerns that are of interest to the reader.

Robert V. Carlino

6 Phillips Drive • Princeton Junction, NJ 08550 • (609) 209-8349 • rCarlino17@aol.com

CHIEF FINANCIAL OFFICER

June 12, 2004

Mr. John Promo
President
American Construction
PO Box 1844
Bridgewater, NJ 08807-0884

Dear Mr. Promo:

As a Certified Public Accountant with solid experience as a **Chief Financial Officer** and a **Vice President of Finance,** I understand that success depends on the bottom line, with special attention to financial and managerial teamwork. I believe that my background and accomplishments have proven to be a productive combination.

Throughout my career, I have been assigned increasing responsibilities and significantly contributed to corporate growth. I believe I have mastered the art of contact management, corporate networking, and personal relationship building. In doing so, I developed a working knowledge of several service-oriented industries, including Architectural, Engineering, and Construction.

Following are some accomplishments of which I am proud:

- Increased shareholder distribution from zero in 1998 to $1.3 million and $1.5 million in 2001 and 2002, respectively, in spite of a 20% revenue shrinkage over the same time period.
- Improved cash flow more than $3 million in 6 months.
- Grew profit margin from 3% to 10% for 3 consecutive years, *the best in company history.*
- Reduced overhead from 170% to 120% in direct labor.
- Trimmed DOS 21% from 85 to 67 days.

Thank you for your consideration. I am a forward thinker and a team player who has a strong commitment to my people and the organizations I work for. I look forward to speaking with you to discuss how I may make a positive contribution to your operation.

Sincerely yours,

Robert V. Carlino

Enclosure

17

Beverley and Mitchell I. Baskin, Marlboro, New Jersey

The design is like that of the preceding letter, but the design is flexible. Differences are in the expansion of the second paragraph and the increased number of bullets after the third paragraph.

19500 SW 64 Avenue
Miami, Florida 33157
(305) 555-8688
smr555@aol.com

SHAUN M. REINHARDT

April 17, 2004

Medical Technologies
HR Department
8561 The Reserve Circle
Tamarac, FL 33321

Dear Hiring Professional:

In response to your search for a quality sales professional, I bring more than 13 years of experience in medical product sales; specifically, practice-management software systems and support.

I am an extremely high-energy and innovative salesperson who leads by example. I consistently produce strong results with a high degree of integrity, dedication and organized communication skills.

Many of my achievements are due to my ability to identify prospects, develop relationships and then close deals. This quality, coupled with a drive to think strategically and capitalize on opportunities, has given me a track record of success. Some highlights include the following:

- Consistently exceed sales quotas and bring in new accounts.
- Increased territorial revenue more than 300%.
- Achieved highest overall upgrade system sales performance of more than 26%.
- Closed the largest number of system sales in the Southeast Region in 1997.
- Created numerous profitable programs, such as the System Support Partner program: a way to increase both customer service and profit levels.
- Won numerous awards and recognition: the "Presentation" contest, a telemarketing script contest, member of the "Winner's Circle" and the "Giant Slayer Award."

My resume and a summary page provide further details of my accomplishments. I look forward to discussing a new career opportunity with you. I will contact you next week to arrange a meeting so we may discuss your company's needs in greater detail.

Sincerely,

Shaun M. Reinhardt

Enclosure

18

Gail Frank, Tampa, Florida

This candidate could have been a manager but wanted to stay in the field and sell. The first three paragraphs and almost all of the bulleted items play up the person's sales interest and achievements.

MEG ANISTON

555 Overlake Street, Oakland, CA 94601   maniston@earthlink.com
510-555-4242   Fax 510-555-4243

May 22, 2004

VISIONEER FINANCIAL PRODUCTS
ATTN: Position #5490
56 Hillside Drive, Suite 285
Oakland, CA 94601

Dear Hiring Professional:

In response to your search for a quality sales professional, I bring more than 15 years of experience in financial sales and consultation.

I am an extremely high-energy and innovative salesperson who leads by example. I consistently produce strong results with a high degree of integrity, dedication and organized communication skills.

Many of my achievements are due to my ability to create and maintain rapport with clients. This quality, coupled with a drive to think strategically and capitalize on opportunities, has given me a track record of success. Some highlights include

♦ Consistently exceed sales quotas and bring in new accounts
♦ Closing rate over 80%
♦ Client retention of 92%
♦ Increased revenue by 146% within first 6 months of current position
♦ Annually generated between $14–20 million in revenue
♦ Hired, trained and developed team of 85 people
♦ Created and delivered hundreds of impactful presentations and meetings

My resume and a summary page provide further details of my accomplishments. You will note that I have worked for some major companies and have progressed in responsibility levels. I look forward to discussing yet another career opportunity with you. I shall contact you next week to arrange a meeting so we may discuss your company's needs in greater detail.

Sincerely,

Meg Aniston

Enclosure

19

Gail Frank, Tampa, Florida

This letter is for an individual without a degree but with a strong work ethic and a results-oriented attitude. Diamonds as bullets call early attention to the person's qualifications.

MARIA M. LEAL

(555) 555-5555 (H)   555 Quad Street, Prairie Stream, Texas 55555   **(555) 555-0000 (C)**
mariamleal@mindspring.net

April 29, 2004

Mr. Francis Rolly
Assistant Superintendent for Personnel Services
Prairie Stream Independent School District
5555 Main Street
Prairie Stream, Texas 55555

Re: GENERIC ADMINISTRATOR APPLICATIONS   *All our children deserve teachers who believe their students can
learn and who will not be satisfied until they do. —Joe Nathan*

Dear Mr. Rolly:

Please accept this letter of application and resume as representation of sincere interest in an **administrator position** within the Prairie Stream Independent School District. Not only have I been a PSISD Title I educator for the past 13 years, but I am proud to be a product of PSISD, wherein I was raised. Additionally, a **master of education in educational leadership, with a mid-management/principal certification, and a master of education in elementary education, with a specialty in math,** add to my qualifications for this esteemed position. However, though I offer an impressive educational background, nothing can replace the hands-on teaching and administrative experiences afforded me by tenure at Heartgood Elementary. My record at Heartgood of **strong interpersonal, communication, and problem-solving skills** speaks for itself.

Over the years, I have contributed to the implementation of several money-saving and learning-centered enhancements. I have

- Consistently returned from training seminars to **empower the staff** and teachers with newly gained knowledge, an endeavor for staff development that has saved substantial funding.
- Initiated inventory awareness, **cutting costs** on ordering manipulatives and supplies that could be acquired or shared by teachers from existing inventory.
- Helped **transition** first-graders to second-grade spiral math curricula by restructuring their program to coincide with Sharon Wells' math curriculum.
- **Increased TAAS/TAKS scores** through tutor programs. I am highly involved in implementing other excellence programs and directing academic team competitions.

The following communication and interpersonal practices also reinforce credibility for an administrator position. I

- Regard **personal contact** as the first and optimum vehicle for relating needs and information.
- Use **assertive communication,** calm demeanor, active listening, compromise, and negotiation to create win-win situations.
- **Overcome resistance** by communicating both perspectives of an issue, as well as the cause, need, and expected outcome. Then offer positive choices.
- **Acknowledge everyone**—teachers, staff, students, parents, and visitors—for overall success in education.
- **Know every student by name,** especially the challenging ones, and interact with them at every opportunity. Relate to each of them in the manner that works with that particular child.
- **Support teachers** in every way feasible: with resources, encouragement, help, positive feedback, and coaching/mentoring. Instill pride with positive comments.
- **Make parents partners** in their children's educations. Draw on their strengths and treat them with respect. Invite them to participate wherever possible.
- Set **high expectations** to increase performance.

You will find me an exceptional candidate for an **instructional specialist or principal position.** Outstanding references are at your disposal upon request. Since the opportunity to further discuss your needs and my qualifications will be mutually beneficial, I look forward to an upcoming **personal interview.** In the meantime, thank you for your consideration.

Sincerely,

Maria M. Leal

Enclosure: Resume

20

Edith A. Rische, Lubbock, Texas

This letter has only four paragraphs, but a developed first paragraph and many substantial bulleted items after the second and third paragraphs fill a page—even with small print. See Resume 58 (page 118).

GEORGE POWELL

SENIOR EXECUTIVE ● STRATEGY ● MARKETING ● LEADERSHIP

2859 Albany Avenue, Littletown, PA 22222
Home: 444-444-4444 ● Cell: 555-555-5555
E-mail: GeorgePow@yahoo.com
Website: www.GPowell.info

October 31, 2003

«First_Name» «Last_Name»
«Title»
«Company»
«Postal_Address»

To become healthy, consumer electronics companies will need to find new sources of revenue while developing sustainable areas of differentiation that are in tune with customer needs and wants.

Dear «Courtesy_Title» «Last_Name»:

These are tough times in the consumer electronics industry.

As a seasoned senior-level marketing professional with a Fortune 100 background, start-up experience, and cross-industry expertise, I can help. Coupled with experience in communications and IT, my background provides a thorough foundation to position «Company» for the coming convergence of PCs and consumer electronics.

With a profound understanding of computing and Internet trends as well as the wants, needs, and buying behaviors of potential customers, I can anticipate and evaluate the issues associated with this new market direction. By taking a holistic approach to planning, I can leverage the strengths of your organization through targeted strategic and marketing efforts. I know how to drive vigorous strategy development and implementation, construct solid organizational and product line plans, optimize the use of funds, and, most importantly, get it right the first time!

Critical marketing and revenue-generating strengths and contributions include the following:

Identifying opportunities to reposition uncompetitive / limited market products.
To protect a $42 million revenue stream and slow margin erosion, I repositioned a networking product line to meet an emerging need in enterprise networking (Intel). Faced with a slow developing market, I created a pre-market product concept that produced 50% of the firm's revenue in its first 18 months and opened doors with Apple, IBM, and several telcos (GPC).

Constructing powerful positioning, differentiation, and value propositions.
As a consultant, I developed a market identification methodology that became a key differentiator, driving sales of lucrative planning exercises (PAL Associates and Graves).

Understanding channels of distribution and the use of hybrid channels.
During my career I received hands-on education about resellers and their targets (Intel)...worked with communications resellers and top PC distributors (Teleos and DEBCOM)...established a channels-consulting practice (Graves)...and conducted a global study of networking-product distribution channels (IBM).

Using in-depth experience in the marketing / planning process for successful product launch.
Working as a consultant, I have assisted several Fortune 100 firms—including IBM, Telcordia, Lucent, and HP—with strategic and go-to-market planning. As a senior manager, I have been directly involved in product launches, including servers at Intel, the award-winning LAWN at DEBCOM, and ISDN products.

«First_Name», having enjoyed the experience of operating a successful consulting firm for six years, I find I miss the challenges associated with developing markets. That is why I am contacting you—to discuss bringing my strategic and revenue-generating expertise to «Company». Let's schedule an informal exploratory meeting to review your needs and my ideas. I will call you next week and look forward to speaking with you soon.

Sincerely,

George Powell

Enclosure

21

Deborah Dib, Medford, New York

Another way to develop a letter so that it fills a page is to add a paragraph for each item in a series of items introduced by a colon—in this letter, the colon is after the fourth paragraph.

555 Reynolds Road
Berlin, Maryland 21811

410-555-8080
czenith@hotmail.com

CHARLENE ZENITH
♦ PHARMACEUTICAL SALES REP ♦

To: Schering Plough, Pharmaceutical Division
Re: Online Posting #2651

In response to your search for a **quality pharmaceutical sales professional,** I bring more than 8 years of experience in sales. I am a quick learner with a strong track record of recognizable increases of sales in my product. People describe me as an extremely high-energy and innovative salesperson who leads by example. I consistently produce strong results with a high degree of integrity, dedication and organized communication skills.

Many of my achievements are due to my ability to create and maintain rapport with clients. This quality, coupled with a drive to think strategically and capitalize on opportunities, has given me an extremely high client retention rate. My work managing the egos and needs of corporate clients and celebrities will transfer well to a pharmaceutical sales environment. I thrive on setting aggressive goals and then meeting them.

I meet and exceed all the qualifications detailed in your online job posting:

Your Needs	My Qualifications
B.A. degree or equivalent.	♦ B.A. in Communication Studies with a Concentration in Public Relations from Virginia Polytechnic Institute.
Previous outside business-to-business sales experience.	♦ More than 3 years of experience as Marriott Event & Sales Manager, selling to top corporate clients.
Demonstrated sales and communication abilities.	♦ Results include 90–95% retention of clients, $1.3 million direct contribution to profit, and highest area market share. ♦ Developed all promotional materials, collateral and sales kits for the property.
Excellent interpersonal, organizational and time-management skills.	♦ Outgoing, dynamic personality. ♦ Have run hundreds of events and tournaments that require outstanding time-management and service skills. ♦ History of thriving on networking, prospecting and working odd hours to meet diverse client needs.
Computer office suite literacy at an intermediate level.	♦ Sourced and installed network for entire office, plus developed database systems to facilitate administrative work and increase available selling and service time.
Valid driver's license and safe driving record.	♦ Licensed in the state of Virginia; safe record.

My resume provides further details of my accomplishments. If you will add me to the interview roster for this open position, I'll be ready…anytime or anywhere!

Thank you,

Charlene Zenith

22

Gail Frank, Tampa, Florida

Still another way to expand a letter is to develop further a "Your Needs…My Qualifications" two-column table. This one is keyed to the items in an online job posting.

May 12, 2004

AMY VESTAL

Target:

Events Planning

Ideas are the root of creation.

—Ernest Dimnet

5555 55th Street
Flower, Texas 79400

avestal@aol.com

(555) 555-5555

Rita Coleman
Vice President of Marketing
CAPITAL IDEAS AND EVENTS
5555 Main Street
Crestview, Texas 79000

RE: Events Planner / Marketing Position

Dear Ms. Coleman:

Generating creative ideas spanning from decorating to effective problem solving energizes me! Other talents include **planning and coordinating the logistics of complex projects or exciting events, revitalizing a failing business, and increasing profits through innovative marketing strategies.** Additionally, a **bachelor's degree** adds credibility to my candidacy for the above-named position.

Upon reviewing the enclosed resume, you will discover a background rich in **sound leadership, skillful negotiation, effective networking, and active public relations experience,** all of which have enhanced the promotion of several personal businesses. As an entrepreneur, I have an understanding of the factors needed to run a winning business—insight that can enhance relationships with the business community.

The following character traits would reward any employer:

Personal Trait	Company Benefit
Ownership of responsibility—	Sound leadership.
Perceptiveness and understanding—	Effective interaction with team.
Attentive listening—	Accurate response to customer needs.
Loyalty, honesty, and diligence—	Company distinction.
Competitiveness and optimism—	Increased profits.
Self-motivation and resourcefulness—	Stimulated productivity.
Passion—	Dedicated service.
Energetic action—	Met deadlines.

A personal interview at your convenience would be mutually advantageous. I will contact your office within the week to set up a meeting. In the meantime, **thank you for your valued time and consideration.**

Sincerely,

Amy Vestal

Enclosure: Resume

23

Edith A. Rische, Lubbock, Texas

In this two-column cover letter, the left column is shaded slightly to define the column visually. Content within the column is center-justified and spread down the column for a balanced look. See Resume 24 (page 58).

Vince Conlan

000 Bluff Street ◆ P.O. Box 000 ◆ Des Moines, IA 00000–0000 ◆ 000–000–0000 ◆ 000–000–0000

October 4, 2004

Kevin James
James & Associates
Tampa, FL 00000-0000

Dear Mr. James,

As a National Solutions Manager with XYZ Corporation and a growth-oriented management professional with exceptional skills in information technology—as well as new business development; client services; and personnel leadership, training, and motivation—I believe I am ideally suited to meet the needs of your organization. I am submitting my resume to you for review and consideration for the position of Director of Operation—Product Development as posted with jobsearch.msn.com.

I have developed exceptional and proven skills in new business development, global sales and marketing, budget administration, change development and implementation, strategic planning, human resources management, and product development. My revenues for FY 2003 reached 247% of organizational goal, earning corporate recognition and receipt of the President's Club Award. Throughout my tenure with XYZ, I have held several progressive positions.

My ability to generate revenues, develop business relations, negotiate and solidify contractual agreements, and provide top-notch client services and satisfaction are well recognized. As a result of my cross-functionality, multitasking abilities, and organizational skills, I was selected to serve in my current position. I believe many of these experiences and qualifications would easily transfer to the position you are seeking to fill.

If you have any questions or would like to schedule an interview, please do not hesitate to contact me at the telephone numbers or e-mail address listed above. Thank you for your careful consideration.

I look forward to your reply.

Sincerely,

Vince Conlan

24

Lea J. Clark, Macon, Georgia

Boldfacing and a narrow, empty box for the contact information draw attention to the letter. The first three paragraphs show that the applicant can do the targeted job. See Resume 135 (page 276).

BRIAN LANGE

2400 Daphne Way
Walnut Creek, CA 94000

925-555-0000
BrianLange@pacbell.net

April 12, 2004

Mr. Henry Newton
Vice President, Administration & Operations
Alliance Technical, Inc.
111 Pontiac Drive
Santa Cruz, CA 95060

Reference: Employment Opportunity—Director of Customer Service & Support

Dear Mr. Newton:

Could you use a senior manager with a track record of building and managing teams that ensure strong customer satisfaction by providing high-quality solutions to customer issues? If so, I believe you will find the enclosed resume worth a close look.

Throughout the past several years, I have enjoyed leading my own teams and working with cross-functional groups to analyze and resolve a variety of customer concerns. In addition to establishing and mentoring customer-focused teams, I also gain great satisfaction from improving the way things are done and the results that are achieved, either by streamlining existing methods or by creating and implementing new processes and procedures. Continuous improvement is more than a buzzword to me!

At both Prentiss and Acquire, I spearheaded development of the entire infrastructure, policies and procedures, while simultaneously carrying out all the standard management responsibilities—including staff recruitment, hiring and training. I also participated in major budget development, planning and management activities. At Acquire, the initiatives I led enabled the company to turn around relationships with several key customers, which prevented loss of that business.

My combination of management and technical strengths has repeatedly proven valuable to employers. I utilize it to plan and manage complex technical projects while also accomplishing management objectives related to those projects. For example, I drove the establishment of an international Critical Customer Escalation department that substantially reduced escalation time and, as a result, greatly improved the customer support experience.

In the current challenging business environment, I believe my strong experience can benefit employers who need to produce exceptional results. Specifically, I am confident I can add substantial value to Alliance Technical as the Director of Customer Service and Support, and I would like to arrange a personal interview to discuss your needs. I will call you within the next few days to follow up and, if appropriate, schedule an interview. I look forward to speaking with you.

Sincerely,

Brian Lange

Encl.

25

Georgia Adamson, Campbell, California

This applicant wanted to move up in customer-relations management in either a technical or a nontechnical company. The letter refers to both management and technical strengths.

EDWARD J. BROWER

999 Wilson Drive ▪ Dallas, TX 75200 ▪ (972) 555-7777 ▪ ejbrower@email.com

May 31, 2004

Mr. Lawrence M. Ball
Ball Property Services, Inc.
5566 Second Place
Dallas, TX 75701

Dear Mr. Ball:

Mr. Bill Anderson informed me that you are leading the search committee in replacing him as general manager of Westhaven Country Club. Because I am regarded as a highly dedicated manager with a strong background in management and the vision to perceive—and competency to execute—a master plan to drive the success of Westhaven to unprecedented levels, he is confident that I am the prime candidate to ensure Westhaven's continued success.

Upon attaining my B.S. in Hotel and Restaurant Management in 1996, I joined Westhaven Country Club as the assistant manager and was promoted to clubhouse manager last August. For the past month, I have willingly assumed all responsibilities of both positions. Perfecting the art of club management is an ongoing goal of mine. I am currently pursuing this through mentoring by Mr. Anderson, concentrated studies through the Club Managers Association of America in an effort to earn my certification in club management, and attendance at national conferences.

You will note a few recent accomplishments on my enclosed resume, the most significant of which is escalating revenues from approximately $900,000 to $1.3 million. This success, I believe, is attributed to the following:

- Unique creativity, integrated with the tenacity to attain desired results;
- Broad-based knowledge of food and beverage;
- Success in developing a cohesive team committed to excellence, respect, and cooperation; and
- Treating each member as I would a member of my family, ensuring their enjoyment and satisfaction.

Another accomplishment, not mentioned on my resume, includes winning the "Idea Fair" contest at last year's National Club Managers Association of America Conference. My entry was the children's menu that I designed for Westhaven; it won top honor in its category.

Mr. Ball, I am a goal-setter and a goal-achiever. These qualities have contributed toward goal attainment in all my endeavors. As Dallas continues to grow, the competition in our industry only becomes more demanding. Two requirements are necessary for this to occur: (1) The leader must be able to envision the potential of Westhaven in our emerging marketplace, and (2) he must be able to develop and orchestrate a master plan. As general manager, I will go the extra mile to ensure Westhaven's success, and look forward to the exciting challenges this new opportunity offers. Thank you for your consideration, and I sincerely look forward to visiting with you soon.

Respectfully,

EDWARD J. BROWER

Enclosure

26

Ann Klint, Tyler, Texas

A strong page border, echoed by the line in the contact information, defines this letter visually. The last paragraph "sells" the applicant as one with vision, ability, and enthusiasm. See Resume 150 (page 309).

JOSEPH P. BLODGETT
20040 Beacon Street #601   617-555-6375
Brookline, MA 02446   617-555-4587 Fax
jpblodgett@blodgett.com

March 21, 2004

EXCEL TRIUMPH PRODUCTS
ATTN: John Roberts, CEO
134 Andover Street
Lowell, MA 01851

Dear Mr. Roberts:

As Vice President of Finance for an international manufacturing company that grew from $10 million to more than $300 million, I was challenged to develop and support a complete financial infrastructure as the company grew and changed. Along with other senior management, I eventually led an effort to purchase the company through the creation of a general partnership.

I am now ready to return to corporate America and am seeking a new opportunity to exercise my financial expertise.

I am an extremely creative and innovative executive always looking for new ways to grow a company. Many of my achievements are due to my ability to create and maintain rapport with individuals. These qualities, coupled with a drive to think strategically and capitalize on opportunities, have given me a track record of success.

After reading the recent article about your business in the *Boston Globe,* I conducted some more background research on your company on the Internet. Some areas I can help you with include the following:

- ◆ Management of all financial reporting, strategic planning and operating procedures
- ◆ Long-term relationships with outside bankers, vendors and investment professionals
- ◆ Capital expenditures planning, budgeting and timing
- ◆ Analysis, decision making and negotiations with internal and external parties, including acquisitions
- ◆ Leadership of Purchasing and MIS functions and project execution
- ◆ Focus on risk management and employee benefit areas

My enclosed resume provides further details of my accomplishments. I look forward to discussing another new and challenging career opportunity with you. I shall contact you next week to arrange a meeting so we may discuss your company's needs in greater detail.

Sincerely,

Joe Blodgett

Enclosure

Gail Frank, Tampa, Florida

This applicant retired but learned that he was not ready to retire. After a long term with his company and with expertise in virtually every area of finance, he wants to be a part-time consultant.

BILL STEADMAN, CPP

CORPORATE EXECUTIVE ● CHIEF SECURITY OFFICER

"Security is always too much...until it's not enough."
— Daniel Webster

«Date»

«First_Name» «Last_Name»
«Title»
«Company»
«Postal_Address»

Dear «Courtesy_Title» «Last_Name»:

Within minutes, the disastrous events of September 11, 2001, transformed our conceptualization of corporate security—changed its significance, scope, and strategy—from an optional "diligence" to an absolute requirement. Undoubtedly, the 15,000+ companies that were directly affected that day have since created, expanded, and / or upgraded corporate security.

In these perilous times, today's socially and financially conscientious enterprise is obligated to take a serious, urgent, and comprehensive approach to protecting infrastructure, property, and people from internal and external threats. Globally, companies are reprioritizing corporate security in their plans and actions, despite the soft economy.

Today's conundrum? Do more with less—again! This is where I come in! Through 20+ years of experience in the planning, deployment, and management of full-scale corporate security programs, I can provide <Name of Company> with the capacity to efficiently and cost-effectively avoid / mitigate risk and loss. In addition, I bring the added value of senior-level executive achievement, advanced academics, and an understanding of technology.

The following are highlights of my successes:

- Served as Head of Security for all of Your Cable's corporate entities and assets and managed related strategies, projects, and inventories for corporate headquarters and two operating divisions. Controlled $7 million capital and expense budget.

- Assisted SVP of Security (solid line to CEO) with enterprise-wide budget and team oversight ($24+ million / 800+ employees).

- Contributed to $1+ million in annual cost savings related to corporate security.

- Formed and managed an internal organization—Intelligence Services Group—as a solution to employee and vendor security issues.

- Planned and managed technology-based security—personnel, proprietary, and intellectual property protection—systems projects representing investments, some in excess of $1 million.

- Contributed to post-9/11 strategic plans and actions for high-profile venues and events (e.g., West Side Arena, Lyman Recital House, and Senior GMA Tournament). Consulted on Metropolis Plaza security issues after the '93 bombing.

<Name of Contact>, if you see value in the breadth of my experience, scope of my knowledge, and caliber of my management qualifications, please get in touch so we can set up a meeting. I look forward to discussing your needs and my solutions. I can guarantee you a substantial ROI.

Sincerely,

Bill Steadman

Enclosure

vulnerability assessment ● access security ● event security ● workplace / employee security
executive protection ● electronic surveillance / countermeasures ● competitive intelligence / countermeasures
emergency preparedness ● crisis response ● intellectual / proprietary property protection

25 Bristol Road, Smallville, New Jersey 33333 ● Home: 444-444-4444 ● Cell: 777-777-7777 ● E-mail: bstead@verizon.net

28

Deborah Dib, Medford, New York

The writer put bulleted successes, keywords, and contact information in a footer (a designated area) at the bottom of the page in order to start selling the need for security at the top with the Webster quotation.

Edward Field
16 Land Street
Streator, IL 55104
Cell: 312.555.0514

edfield@hope.com

(Customize/personalize name and address here, or write:)

Dear Hiring Executive:

I believe that you will find my experience as Director of Finance very intriguing. I specialize in financial analysis, budgeting, planning, acquisitions and mergers. In addition, my background includes detailed product pricing analysis to ensure success in highly competitive markets.

Currently, I am Director of Finance and Business Development at Hi-Technologies, a software development company. My duties include establishing pricing strategies and authoring business plans, which have raised $5 million in capital over the last year.

Prior to this position, I was Director of Finance for Automart, Inc., a startup procurement automation firm. I negotiated the sale of the company for $20.5 million and performed all due diligence and contract review.

At my previous position, I was the Financial Manager at a $250 million healthcare services company. I reported directly to the President and directed the corporate strategic planning process, leading the annual budget process for four business units with revenues of $150 million.

With my strong financial expertise and operational experience, including advising the decision makers, I strongly believe that my skills in the following areas can bring you continued success:

→ Financial planning and analysis
→ Budgeting and planning
→ A strong knowledge of acquisitions and mergers

I would like to discuss mutual business interests, and will contact you in a few days to set a convenient time for us to meet. Thank you for your time and consideration.

Sincerely,

Edward Field

Steven Provenzano, Schaumburg, Illinois

Because the six paragraphs are short, the tempo in reading the paragraphs is quick. This means that a reader is more likely to read the entire letter. Bullets point to skill areas.

FRANKLIN HARRIS

84 Park Boulevard • East Syracuse, NY 13900
315/999-5555 • fharris@myemail.com

February 10, 2004

Reverend Henry Richmond
President
Onondaga County Coalition of Churches
PO Box 857
Syracuse, NY 13909

RE: Projects Coordinator

Dear Reverend Richmond:

Your posting referenced above from the *Syracuse Daily News* is of great interest to me. In the next month, I will be retiring from the State of New York and am seeking a challenging, rewarding and flexible opportunity. My resume is enclosed for your review.

Project and program coordination/management have been a staple of my career with the state, beginning in Social Services (Foster Care and Child Protection Services) and concluding in the Division of Parole. Beyond tenure in these departments, I have been an instructor, trainer and curriculum developer… director of two non-profit organizations … and the designer and first coordinator of a public school's home/school program. Contributing to my community has always been important, and notable current involvement includes President of the East Syracuse–Minoa Central School Board, Uniform Instructor for the Sea Cadets, and Councilman for the Town of East Syracuse.

Educational credentials earned include a BS in Criminal Science with graduate studies in Social Work as well as Psychology. I am a Certified Peace Officer in line with my Parole Division experience. I have completed diverse professional development as well as training necessary to serve responsibly in several volunteer capacities.

In addition to my well-honed interpersonal and communication skills, positive attitude, and dedication, my familiarity with your service area and established contacts in it would be beneficial. I am very comfortable having accountability for an organization's effective use of its resources and am confident in my ability to contribute positively as your Projects Coordinator.

It would be a pleasure to discuss this opportunity with you in greater detail, and I invite you to contact me at 999-5555 or via e-mail at fharris@myemail.com. I look forward to talking with you soon.

Thank you for your time and consideration.

Sincerely,

Franklin Harris

30

Salome A. Farraro, Mount Morris, New York

Six paragraphs in turn indicate the applicant's situation, experience, educational credentials, worker traits and skills, interest in an interview, and thanks. See Resume 147 (page 302).

List of Contributors

List of Contributors

The following professional resume writers contributed the resumes and cover letters in this book. To include in this appendix the names of these writers and information about their businesses is to acknowledge with appreciation their voluntary submissions and the insights expressed in the e-mails that accompanied their submissions. Resume and cover letter numbers after a writer's contact information are the *numbers of the writer's resumes and cover letters* included in the Gallery, not page numbers.

Australia
Victoria
Hallum

Annemarie Cross
Advanced Employment Concepts/AEC Office
    Services
P.O. Box 91, Hallam, Victoria, 3803
Phone: 61 3 9796 4464
Fax: 61 3 9796 4479
E-mail: success@aresumewriter.net
Web site: www.aresumewriter.net/
Member: CMI, PARW/CC, PRWRA
Certification: CEIP, CPRW, CRW, CCM, CECC
Resume: 124

Melbourne

Gayle Howard
Top Margin Résumés Online
P.O. Box 74
Chirnside Park, Melbourne, Victoria 3116
Phone: 61 3 9726 6694
Fax: 61 3 9726 5316
E-mail: getinterviews@topmargin.com
Web site: www.topmargin.com
Member: CMI, PARW/CC, PRWRA, ASA
Certification: CPRW, CRW, CCM, CERW
Resume: 116

New South Wales
North Richmond

Jennifer Rushton
Keraijen
20 Enfield Ave.
N. Richmond, NSW, 2754
Phone: 61 2 4571 1123
Fax: 61 2 4571 1971
E-mail: vbss@keraijen.com.au
Web site: www.keraijen.com.au
Member: CMI, PRWRA
Certification: CRW
Resumes: 87, 89, 108, 136
Cover letter: 4

Canada
Ontario
Pickering

Ross Macpherson
Career Quest
1586 Major Oaks Rd.
Pickering, Ontario L1X 2J6
Phone: (905) 426-8548
Toll-free: (877) 426-8548
Fax: (905) 426-4274
E-mail: ross@yourcareerquest.com
Web site: www.yourcareerquest.com
Member: CMI, PARW/CC
Certification: MA, CPRW, CJST, CEIP, JCTC
Resumes: 56, 111, 127

United States
Alabama
Montgomery
Don Orlando
The McLean Group
640 S. McDonough St.
Montgomery, AL 36104
Phone: (334) 264-2020
Fax: (334) 264-9227
E-mail: yourcareercoach@aol.com
Member: CMI, PARW/CC, Phoenix
   Career Group
Certification: MBA, CPRW, JCTC,
   CCM, CCMC
Resumes: 52, 157, 173

California
Campbell
Georgia Adamson
A Successful Career/Adept Business
   Services
180 W. Rincon Ave.
Campbell, CA 95008-2824
Phone: (408) 866-6859
Fax: (408) 866-8915
E-mail: success@
   ablueribbonresume.com
Web site:
   www.AblueRibbonResume.com
Member: CMI, NRWA, PARW
Certification: CCMC, CCM, CEIP,
   CPRW, JCTC
Resume: 79
Cover letter: 25

Los Angeles
Vivian VanLier
Advantage Resume & Career
   Services
6701 Murietta Ave.
Valley Glen, CA 91405
Phone: (818) 994-6655
Fax: (818) 994-6620
E-mail: vvanlier@aol.com
Web site:
   www.CuttingEdgeResumes.com
Member: CMI, NRWA, PARW/CC
Certification: CPRW, JCTC, CEIP,
   CCMC
Resumes: 16, 25
Cover letter: 6

Torrance
Gail Taylor
A Hire Power Résumé
21213-B Hawthorne Blvd. #5224
Torrance, CA 90503
Phone: (310) 793-4122
Fax: (310) 793-7481
E-mail: hirepwr@yahoo.com
Web site: www.call4hirepower.com
Member: CMI, NRWA, PARW/CC
Certification: CEIP, CPRW
Resumes: 12, 44, 166
Cover letters: 7, 14, 19

Valencia
Myriam-Rose Kohn
JEDA Enterprises
27201 Tourney Rd., Ste. 201
Valencia, CA 91355-1857
Phone: (661) 253-0801
Toll-free: (800) 600-JEDA
Fax: (661) 253-0744
E-mail: myriam-rose@
   jedaenterprises.com
Web site: www.jedaenterprises.com
Member: CMI, NRWA, PARW/CC
Certification: CPRW, CEIP, IJCTC,
   CCM, CCMC
Resume: 35

Colorado
Arvada
Tracy Laswell Williams
CAREER-Magic.com
5738 Olde Wadsworth Blvd.
Arvada, CO 80002
Phone: (303) 424-5451
Toll-free: (888) 384-1744
Fax: (303) 424-1700
E-mail: tracy@career-magic.com
Web site: www.career-magic.com
Member: NRWA, PARW/CC
Certification: JCTC, CPRW
Resume: 1

Aurora
Michele Angello
Corbel Communications
19866 E. Dickenson Pl.
Aurora, CO 80013
Phone: (303) 537-3592
Fax: (303) 537-3542
E-mail: corbelcomm1@aol.com
Web site: www.corbelonline.com
Member: PARW/CC
Certification: CPRW
Resume: 155

Louisville
Roberta F. Gamza
Career Ink
Louisville, CO 80027
Phone: (303) 955-3065
Fax: (303) 955-3065
E-mail: roberta@careerink.com
Web site: www.careerink.com
Member: CMI, NRWA, PARW/CC,
   PRWRA
Certification: CEIP, JCTC, CJST
Resumes: 78, 134, 139

Connecticut
Enfield
Louise Garver
CAREER DIRECTIONS, LLC
115 Elm St., Ste. 203
Enfield, CT 06082
Phone: (860) 623-9476
Toll-free: (888) 222-3731
Fax: (860) 623-9473
E-mail: careerpro@cox.net
Web site: www.resumeimpact.com
Member: CMI, NRWA, PARW/CC,
   ACA, NCDA, ACPI, CPADN
Certification: MA, JCTC, CMP,
   CPRW, MCDP, CEIP
Resumes: 7, 81, 83, 104, 107, 122,
   123, 132, 140, 149, 152, 154,
   164, 167, 169

Hartford
Ellen Mulqueen
Vocational Counselor, The Institute
   of Living
Department of Rehabilitation
   Services
200 Retreat Ave.
Hartford, CT 06106
Phone: (860) 545-7000, ext. 77678
Fax: (860) 545-7140
E-mail: emulque@harthosp.org
Web site:
   www.instituteofliving.org/
   Programs/rehab.htm
Member: CMI, NRWA, PARW/CC,
   PRWRA
Certification: MA, CRW
Resumes: 15, 31, 163, 178

Florida
Grand Island

Cathy Childs
1510 Lake Dr.
Grand Island, FL 32735
Phone: (352) 669-6419
E-mail: hitchy-koo@juno.com
Member: PARW/CC
Certification: CPRW
Cover letters: 5, 13

Tampa

Cathy Fahrman
The Resume Place
10014 N. Dale Mabry Hwy.,
Ste. 101
Tampa, FL 33618
Phone: (813) 282-0105
Fax: (813) 926-0170
E-mail: hssheider@aol.com
Web site: www.theresumeplace.com
Member: CMI
Certification: CPRW
Resumes: 118, 126

Gail Frank
Frankly Speaking: Resumes That Work!
10409 Greendale Dr.
Tampa, FL 33626
Phone: (813) 926-1353
Fax: (813) 926-1092
E-mail: gailfrank@post.harvard.edu
Web site:
www.callfranklyspeaking.com
Member: PARW/CC, NRWA,
PRWRA, CMI, SHRM, ASTD
Certification: NCRW, CPRW, JCTC,
CEIP, MA
Resumes: 27, 43, 49, 63, 67
Cover letters: 10, 12, 18, 22, 27

M. Carol Heider
The Resume Place
10014 N. Dale Mabry Hwy.,
Ste. 101
Tampa, FL 33618
Phone: (813) 282-0011
Fax: (813) 926-0170
E-mail: hssheider@aol.com
Web site: www.theresumeplace.com
Member: PARW/CC, NRWA, CMI
Certification: CPRW
Resume: 175

Valrico

Cindy Kraft
Executive Essentials
P.O. Box 336
Valrico, FL 33595
Phone: (813) 655-0658
Fax: (813) 354-3483
E-mail: careermaster@
exec-essentials.com
Web site: www.exec-essentials.com
Member: CMI, Coachville, IACC,
AACC
Certification: CCMC, CCM, JCTC
Resumes: 65, 80

Georgia
Macon

Lea J. Clark
Lea Clark & Associates
4521 Dorset Dr.
Macon, GA 31206
Phone: (478) 781-4107
Fax: (478) 781-6960
E-mail: lclark352001@cox.net
Member: PRWRA, Who's Who in
Executives and Professionals
Certification: CRW, BIT
Resumes: 5, 135
Cover letters: 15, 24

Hawaii
Honolulu

Peter Hill
Distinctive Resumes
Honolulu, HI
Phone: (808) 306-3920
E-mail:
distinctiveresumes@yahoo.com
Web site: www.peterhill.biz
Member: CMI, NRWA, PARW/CC
Certification: CPRW
Resumes: 9, 54, 55, 62, 93, 103,
105, 129, 160

Idaho
Boise

Denette D. Jones
Jones Career Specialties
4702 Gage St.
Boise, ID 83706
Phone: (208) 331-0561
Fax: (208) 361-0122
E-mail: ddjones@gowebway.com
Web site:
www.jonescareerspecialties.com
Member: CMI, NRWA, PRWRA
Resume: 130

Illinois
Bolingbrook

Stephanie Whittington
Prairie Professional
Bolingbrook, IL 60440
Phone: (630) 378-1167
E-mail:
swhittington@prairieprof.com
Web site: www.prairieprof.com
Member: NRWA
Resume: 131

Elk Grove Village

Joellyn Wittenstein-Schwerdlin
A-1 Quality Résumés & Career Services
1819 Oriole Dr.
Elk Grove Village, IL 60007
Phone: (847) 285-1145
Fax: (847) 285-1838
E-mail: Joellyn@interaccess.com
Web site: www.prwra.com/
a-1resumes
Member: CMI, PRWRA
Certification: JCTC, CPRW
Resume: 72

Lincolnshire

Christine L. Dennison
Dennison Career Services
Lincolnshire, IL 60069
Phone: (847) 405-9775
E-mail:
chris@thejobsearchcoach.com
Web site:
www.thejobsearchcoach.com
Member: PARW/CC, Greater
Lincolnshire Chamber of
Commerce
Certification: CPC
Resume: 165
Cover letter: 3

Naperville

Patricia Chapman
CareerPro-Naperville, Inc.
520 E. Ogden Ave., Ste. 3
Naperville, IL 60563
Phone: (630) 983-8882
Fax: (630) 983-9021
E-mail: pat@career2day.com
Web site: www.career2day.com
Member: CMI, PRWRA, NAFE
Certification: CRW
Resume: 161

Schaumburg

Steven Provenzano
A-Advanced Résumé Service, Inc.
850 E. Higgins Rd., #125-Y
Schaumburg, IL 60173-4788
Phone: (630) 289-1999
E-mail: advresumes@aol.com
Web site: TopSecretResumes.com
Member: PARW/CC
Certification: CPRW
Cover letter: 29

Indiana

Columbus

Rita Fisher
Career Change Résumés
2826 Hawcreek Blvd.
Columbus, IN 47203
Phone: (812) 375-6190
Toll-free: (866) 645-6350
Fax: (928) 569-5114
E-mail: resumes@reliable-net.net
Web site:
    www.careerchangeresumes.com
Member: PARW/CC
Certification: CPRW
Resume: 137

Iowa

Urbandale

Billie Ruth Sucher
Billie Ruth Sucher & Associates
7177 Hickman Rd., Ste. 10
Urbandale, IA 50322
Phone: (515) 276-0061
Fax: (515) 334-8076
E-mail: betwnjobs@aol.com
Member: CMI, SHRM
Certification: M.S., CTMS, CTSB
Resume: 162

Massachusetts

Concord

Jean Cummings
A Resume For Today
123 Minot Rd.
Concord, MA 01742
Phone: (978) 371-9266
Toll-free: (800) 324-1699
Fax: (978) 964-0529
E-mail: jc@aresumefortoday.com
Web site:
    www.AresumeForToday.com
Member: CMI, PARW/CC
Certification: M.A.T., CPRW, CEIP
Resumes: 115, 176

Framingham

Rosemarie Ginsberg
Creative Staffing Associates, Inc.
15 Michael Rd.
Framingham, MA 01701
Phone: (508) 877-5100
Fax: (508) 877-3511
E-mail: csadirecthire@aol.com
Web sites:
    www.creativeresumesnjobs.com
    and www.ecreativestaffing.com
Member: CMI, NRWA, PARW/CC,
    PRWRA
Certification: CPRW, CEIP, CECC
Resume: 37

Melrose

Jeanne Knight
Career and Job Search Coach
P.O. Box 828
Melrose, MA 02176
Phone: (617) 968-7747
E-mail: jeanne@careerdesigns.biz
Web site: www.careerdesigns.biz
Member: CMI, NRWA
Certification: JCTC
Resumes: 76, 99

Westborough

Jessica Robinson
RA Résumé
P.O. Box 513
Westborough, MA 01581
Phone: (508) 284-9950
Fax: (508) 870-0911
E-mail: Jessica@raresume.com
Web site: www.raresume.com
Member: PARW/CC
Certification: CPRW
Resume: 14

Michigan

Flint

Janet L. Beckstrom
Word Crafter
1717 Montclair Ave.
Flint, MI 48503-2074
Phone: (810) 232-9257
Toll-free: (800) 351-9818
Fax: (810) 232-9257
E-mail: wordcrafter@voyager.net
Member: CMI, PARW/CC
Certification: CPRW
Resume: 82

Missouri

St. Louis

Sally McIntosh
Advantage Résumés
11611 Misty Moss Ct.
St. Louis, MO 63146
Phone: (314) 434-7599
Fax: (866) 728-9323
E-mail: sally@reswriter.com
Web site: www.reswriter.com
Member: NRWA, CMI
Certification: NCRW, JCTC
Resume: 84

New Jersey

Flemington

Carol A. Altomare
World Class Résumés
P.O. Box 483
Three Bridges, NJ 08887-0483
Phone: (908) 237-1883
Fax: (908) 237-2069
E-mail:
    caa@worldclassresumes.com
Web site:
    www.worldclassresumes.com
Member: PARW/CC
Certification: CPRW
Resumes: 19, 27, 29, 46, 168

Iselin

See Marlboro.

Mahwah

Igor Shpudejko
Career Focus
23 Parsons Ct.
Mahwah, NJ 07430
Phone: (201) 825-2865
Fax: (201) 825-7711
E-mail: Ishpudejko@aol.com
Web site: www.CareerInFocus.com
Member: CMI, PARW/CC
Certification: CPRW, JCTC, MBA,
   BSIE
Resume: 34

Marlboro

Beverley Baskin and Mitchell I.
   Baskin
BBCS Counseling Services
6 Alberta Dr.
Marlboro, NJ 07746
Also at Iselin, NJ,
   and Princeton, NJ
Toll-free: (800) 300-4079
Fax: (732) 972-8846
E-mail: bbcs@att.net and
   info@bbcscounseling.com
Web sites: www.baskincareer.com
   and www.job-research.com
Member: NRWA, NCDA, NECA,
   MACCA, AMHCA
Certification: Ed.S, MA, LPC,
   NCCC
Resumes: 22, 73, 74, 75, 94, 98,
   120, 141, 171
Cover letters: 16, 17

Princeton

See Marlboro.

West Paterson

Melanie Noonan
Peripheral Pro, LLC
560 Lackawanna Ave.
West Paterson, NJ 07424
Phone: (973) 785-3011
Fax: (973) 256-6285
E-mail: PeriPro1@aol.com
Member: NRWA, PARW/CC
Certification: CPS
Resumes: 13, 113, 153

New York

Brentwood

Ann Baehr
Best Resumes
122 Sheridan St.
Brentwood, NY 11717
Phone: (631) 435-1879
Fax: (631) 435-3655
E-mail: resumesbest@earthlink.net
Web site: www.ebestresumes.com
Member: CMI, NRWA, PARW/CC
Certification: CPRW
Resumes: 8, 17, 23, 36, 59, 61, 95,
   96, 106, 142, 143, 148

Hauppauge

Donna M. Farrise
Dynamic Resumes of Long Island, Inc.
300 Motor Pkwy., Ste. 200
Hauppauge, NY 11788
Phone: (631) 951-4120
Toll-free: (800) 528-6796 and (800)
   951-5191
Fax: (631) 952-1817
E-mail:
   donna@dynamicresumes.com
Web site:
   www.dynamicresumes.com
Member: CMI, NRWA, PARW/CC
Certification: JCTC
Resumes: 92, 101

Hicksville

Deanna Verbouwens
Ace in the Hole Resume Writing &
   Career Services
14 Mitchell Ct.
Hicksville, NY 11801
Phone: (516) 942-5986
E-mail: verbouwens@yahoo.com
   and info@aceinthehole.net
Web site: www.aceinthehole.net
Member: PARW/CC
Resumes: 33, 41

Huntington

MJ Feld
Careers by Choice, Inc.
205 E. Main St., Ste. 2–4
Huntington, NY 11743
Phone: (631) 673-5432
Fax: (631) 673-5824
E-mail: mj@careersbychoice.com
Web site:
   www.careersbychoice.com
Member: PARW/CC
Certification: MS, CPRW
Resume: 6

Medford

Deborah Dib
Advantage Resumes of NY
77 Buffalo Ave.
Medford, NY 11763
Phone: (631) 475-8513
Fax: (501) 421-7790
E-mail: deborah.dib@
   advantageresumes.com
Web sites:
   www.advantageresumes.com
   and www.
   executivepowercoach.com
Member: CMI, NRWA, PARW/CC
Certification: CCM, NCRW, CPRW,
   CEIP, JCTC, CCMC
Resumes: 119, 133, 158
Cover letters: 21, 28

Mount Morris

Salome A. Farraro
Careers TOO
3123 Moyer Rd.
Mount Morris, NY 14510
Phone: (585) 658-2480
Toll-free: (877) 436-9378
Fax: (585) 658-2480
E-mail: sfarraro@careers-too.com
   and srttoo@frontiernet.net
Web site: www.careers-too.com
Member: PARW/CC
Certification: CPRW
Resume: 147
Cover letter: 30

Poughkeepsie

Kristin M. Coleman
Custom Career Services
44 Hillcrest Dr.
Poughkeepsie, NY 12603
Phone: (845) 452-8274
Fax: (845) 452-7789
E-mail:
   kristincoleman44@yahoo.com
Member: CMI
Resumes: 4, 10, 50, 60

Smithtown

Linda Matias
CareerStrides
34 E. Main St., #276
Smithtown, NY 11787
Phone: (631) 382-2425
Fax: (631) 382-2425
E-mail: careerstrides@bigfoot.com
Web site: www.careerstrides.com
Member: CMI, NRWA
Certification: CEIP, JCTC
Resumes: 48, 77, 91

Staten Island

La-Dana R. Jenkins
LRJ Consulting Services
200 Pierce St.
Staten Island, NY 10304
Phone and fax: (718) 448-5825
E-mail: lrjconsulting@hotmail.com
Web site: www.lrjconsulting.net
Member: NRWA, NCDA
Resume: 85

Victor

Kim Little
Fast Track Resumes
1281 Courtney Dr.
Victor, NY 14564
Phone: (585) 742-2467
Toll-free: (877) 263-7581
Fax: (585) 742-1907
E-mail: ServPCR@aol.com
Web site:
    www.fast-trackresumes.com
Member: CMI, PARW/CC
Certification: JCTC
Resumes: 86, 159

North Carolina

Asheville

Dayna Feist
Gatehouse Business Services
265 Charlotte St.
Asheville, NC 28801
Phone: (828) 254-7893
Fax: (828) 254-7894
E-mail: Gatehous@aol.com
Web site: www.BestJobEver.com
Member: CMI, PARW/CC, NRWA
Certification: CPRW, JCTC, CEIP
Resume: 53

Charlotte

Doug Morrison
Career Power
2915 Providence Rd., Ste. 250-B
Charlotte, NC 28211
Phone: (704) 365-0773
E-mail: dmpwresume@aol.com
Web site:
    www.careerpowerresume.com
Member: CMI, PARW/CC, PRWRA
Certification: CPRW
Resumes: 71, 144

Garner

Rima Bogardus
Career Support Services
P.O. Box 2026
Garner, NC 27529
Phone: (919) 779-9772
Toll-free: (877) 939-1099
E-mail: rima@
    careersupportservices.com
Web site:
    www.careersupportservices.com
Member: PARW/CC
Certification: CPRW, CEIP
Resume: 100

Ohio

Athens

Melissa L. Kasler
Resume Impressions
One North Lancaster
Athens, OH 45701
Phone: (740) 592-3993
Toll-free: (800) 516-0334
Fax: (740) 592-1352
E-mail: resume@frognet.net
Web site:
    www.resumeimpressions.com
Member: CMI, PARW/CC
Certification: CPRW
Resumes: 47, 57

Findlay

Sharon Pierce-Williams, M.Ed.
The Résumé.Doc
609 Lincolnshire Ln.
Findlay, OH 45840
Phone: (419) 422-0228
Fax: (419) 425-1185
E-mail:
    Sharon@TheResumeDoc.com
Web site:
    www.TheResumeDoc.com
Member: CMI, PARW/CC,
    Findlay–Hancock County
    Chamber of Commerce
Certification: CPRW
Resumes: 88, 145, 172

Oregon

Portland

Rosie Bixel
A Personal Scribe
4800 SW Macadam Ave., Ste. 105
Portland, OR 97239
Phone: (503) 254-8262
Fax: (503) 255-3012
E-mail: aps@bhhgroup.com
Web site:
    www.bhhgroup.com/resume.asp
Member: NRWA
Resumes: 42, 109

Jennifer Rydell
Simplify Your Life Career Services
6327-C SW Capitol Hwy. PMB 243
Portland, OR 97239-1937
Phone: (503) 977-1955
Fax: (503) 245-4212
E-mail: Jennifer@
    simplifyyourliferesumes.com
Web site: www.
    simplifyyourliferesumes.com
Member: CMI, NRWA, PARW/CC
Certification: CPRW, NCRW, CCM
Resume: 26

Pennsylvania

Harleysville

Darlene Dassy
Dynamic Résumé Solutions
602 Monroe Dr.
Harleysville, PA 19438
Phone and fax: (215) 368-2316
E-mail: darlene@
    attractiveresumes.com
Web site:
    www.attractiveresumes.com
Member: CMI, NRWA, PRWRA
Certification: BBA, CRW
Resume: 45

Jan Holliday
Arbridge Communications
Harleysville, PA 19438
Phone: (215) 513-7420
Toll-free: (866) 513-7420 (in the
    U.S.)
E-mail: info@arbridge.com
Web site: www.arbridge.com
Member: NRWA, CMI, IWA
Certification: MA, NCRW, Certified
    Webmaster
Resumes: 3, 11, 69, 114, 156

Sharon

Jane Roqueplot
JaneCo's Sensible Solutions
194 N. Oakland Ave.
Sharon, PA 16146
Phone: (724) 342-0100
Toll-free: (888) 526-3267
Fax: (724) 346-5263
E-mail: info@janecos.com
Web site: www.janecos.com
Member: CMI, NRWA, PRWRA,
    PARW/CC, AJST, NCDA
Certification: CBC, CECC
Resume: 2

Rhode Island
North Kingstown

Edward Turilli
Director, Career Development Center
Salve Regina University
Newport, RI 02842
ARC—Anthem Résumé and Career
    Services
918 Lafayette Rd.
North Kingstown, RI 02852
Phone: (401) 268-3020
Fax: (401) 341-2994
E-mail: turillie@salve.edu
Web site:
    www.salve.edu/office_careerdev
Member: CMI, PARW/CC, NCDA,
    NACE, EACE
Certification: MA
Resumes: 66, 97, 117

Tennessee
Hendersonville

Carolyn S. Braden
Braden Resume Solutions
108 La Plaza Dr.
Hendersonville, TN 37075
Phone: (615) 822-3317
Fax: (615) 826-9611
E-mail:
    bradenresume@comcast.net
Member: CMI, PARW/CC
Certification: CPRW
Resume: 170
Cover letter: 2

Texas
Bishop

Nick V. Marino
Outcome Resumes and Career
710 Aurora Dr.
Bishop, TX 78343
Toll-free phone: (866) 899-6509
Fax: (512) 857-0782
E-mail: outcomerez@earthlink.net
Web site:
    www.outcomeresumes.com
Member: CMI, PARW, PRWRA,
    AJST, CPADN
Certification: CPRW, CRW, CEIP,
    CFCM, CFRW/C, CFJST
Resume: 28

Lubbock

Daniel J. Dorotik, Jr.
100PercentResumes
9803 Clinton Ave.
Lubbock, TX 79424
Phone: (806) 783-9900
Fax: (214) 722-1510
E-mail:
    dan@100percentresumes.com
Web site:
    www.100percentresumes.com
Member: NRWA, PARW/CC
Certification: NCRW
Resumes: 20, 51, 70, 110, 112, 128,
    146, 151, 177

Edith A. Rische
Write Away Resume
5908 73rd St.
Lubbock, TX 79424-1920
Phone: (806) 798-0881
Fax: (806) 798-3213
E-mail: erische@door.net
Web site:
    www.writeawayresume.com
Member: NRWA
Certification: NCRW, JCTC
Resumes: 21, 24, 58, 64
Cover letters: 1, 8, 9, 11, 20, 23

Tyler

Ann Klint
Ann's Professional Résumé Service
2130 Kennebunk Ln.
Tyler, TX 75703-0301
Phone: (903) 509-8333
Fax: (734) 448-1962
E-mail: Resumes-Ann@tyler.net
    and ann_klint@hotmail.com
Resumes: 68, 150, 174
Certification: NCRW, CPRW
Cover letter: 26

Victoria

MeLisa Rogers
Ultimate Career
270 Liveoak Ln.
Victoria, TX 77905
Phone: (361) 574-8830
Toll-free: (866) 573-7863
Fax: (361) 574-8830
E-mail: success@ultimatecareer.biz
Web site: www.ultimatecareer.biz
Member: PARW/CC, SHRM,
    ASTD
Certification: M.S. HRD, CPRW
Resumes: 18, 30, 32, 38, 125, 138

Washington
Bellingham

Janice M. Shepherd
Write On Career Keys
Bellingham, WA 98226-4260
Phone: (360) 738-7958
Fax: (360) 738-1189
E-mail: janice@
    writeoncareerkeys.com
Web site:
    www.writeoncareerkeys.com
Member: CMI, PARW/CC
Certification: CPRW, JCTC, CEIP
Resume: 102

Seattle

Alice Hanson
Aim Resumes
P.O. Box 75054
Seattle, WA 98175-0054
Phone: (206) 527-3100
Fax: (206) 527-3101
E-mail: alice@aimresumes.com
Web site: www.aimresumes.com
Member: CMI, NRWA, PARW/CC,
    PSCDA, NRWA
Certification: CPRW
Resume: 90

Matt Thompson
Northwest Resumes
Seattle, WA
Toll-free phone: (888) 821-9979
Fax: (425) 955-0327
E-mail: matt@nwresumes.com
Web site: www.nwresumes.com
Member: NRWA
Certification: NCRW
Resume: 39

Wisconsin

Glendale

Michele J. Haffner
Advanced Résumé Services
1314 W. Paradise Ct.
Glendale, WI 53209
Phone: (414) 247-1677
Fax: (414) 247-1808
E-mail:
    michelle@resumeservices.com
Web site: www.resumeservices.com
Member: PARW, Coachville
Certification: CPRW, JCTC
Resumes: 40, 121

Professional Organizations

If you would like more recommendations of resume writers and career coaches in your area, see the following information.

Career Masters Institute
119 Old Stable Rd.
Lynchburg, VA 24503
Phone: (434) 386-3100
Fax: (434) 386-3200
E-mail: wendyenelow@
    cminstitute.com
Web site: www.cminstitute.com

**www.CertifiedResumeWriters.
com**

**www.CertifiedCareerCoaches.
com**

National Association of Résumé Writers
P.O. Box 184
Nesconset, NY 11767
Toll-free phone: (888) NRWA-444
E-mail:
    AdminManager@nrwaweb.com
Web site: www.nrwaweb.com

Professional Association of Résumé Writers & Career Coaches
1388 Brightwaters Blvd., NE
St. Petersburg, FL 33704
Toll-free phone: (800) 822-7279
Fax: (727) 894-1277
E-mail: PARWCCHQ@aol.com
Web site: www.parw.com

Professional Résumé Writing and Research Association
1106 Coolidge Blvd.
Lafayette, LA 70503
Toll-free phone: (800) 225-8688
E-mail: laurie@prwra.com
Web site: www.prwra.com

Occupation Index

Resumes are indexed according to the current or last positions listed on them. Job goals do not appear in this index. Numbers are resume numbers in the Gallery, not page numbers.

A

Account Executive
  Financial Services, 86
  Radio and TV, 167
Account Manager
  Cardiology, 8
  Corporate, 175
  Sales, Inside, 171
  Software, 16
Account Supervisor,
    Advertising, 22
Accountant, 20
Accounting Clerk, 17
Accounting Instructor, Adjunct,
    18
Accounting Student, 17
Adjunct Instructor
  Accounting, 18
  History, 67
  Psychology, 60
Administrative Assistant,
    Executive, 12
Administrative Specialist, 12
Administrator
  CFA, Waste Removal, 120
  Local Systems,
      Manufacturing, 165
  Pricing, 117
Admissions Coordinator,
    Rehabilitation Center, 112
Advertising, Account
    Supervisor, 22
Advertising Manager, Senior, 23
Airline Pilot, Commercial, 9
Application Development
    Supervisor, 131
Architect, 35
Assistant
  Administrative, Executive, 12

Legal, 142
Marketing, 25
Production, Intern, 170
Assistant Chief of Police, 146
Assistant Controller, 19
Assistant Director, Hospital
    Food Services, 92
Assistant English Language
    Teacher, 55
Assistant Mgr./Floor
    Supervisor, Retail, 4
Assistant Property Manager,
    138
Assistant Site Manager, Call
    Center, 30
Assistant VP/Trust Officer,
    Banking, 82
Assistive Technology (AT)
    Program Manager, 68
Associate General Counsel, 139
Associate VP/Onsite Program
    Director, 137
Attending Physician/Staff, 108

B

Banking
  Business Development
      Officer, 81
  Customer Associate, 78
  Vice President, 81
Billing Assistant, 93
Business Development
  Director, 177
  Manager, 168
  Officer, Banking, 81
Business/Technology
    Consultant, 116

C

Call Center
  Assistant Site Manager, 30
  Operations Manager, 32
Cardiology Account Manager, 8
Care Center, Admissions
    Coordinator, 112
Career and Life Coach, 260
Case Manager, Field, 104
CFA Administrator, Waste
    Removal, 120
Cheerleading Sponsor, 64
Chemical Operator, 157
Chief Executive Officer,
    Sportswear Corp., 88
Chief Financial Officer,
    Software/Internet Co., 84
Chief of Police, Assistant, 146
Chief Operating Officer, Theme
    Restaurants, 119
Claims Dept. Mgr./Supervisor,
    Insurance, 77
Clerk, Accounting, 17
Client Services Representative,
    31
Clinical Coordinator, 114
Clinical Nursing Supervisor,
    102
Clubhouse Manager, 150
Coach
  Career and Life, 160
  Tennis, 6
Co-Director of Education, 66
Commercial Airline Pilot, 9
Community Development,
    Director, 153
Computer and Information
    Systems Mgr., 129

Construction Consultant, 73
Consultant
  Business/Technology, 116
  Construction, 73
  Information Systems, 132
  Management, 152
  Wireless, 172
Contractor, Independent, 152
Controller
  Assistant, 19
  Senior, 83
Coordinator
  Admissions, Rehabilitation
    Center, 112
  Clinical, 114
  Educational Software, 34
  Event/Program, 7
  Project, 12
Corporate Account Manager,
  175
Corporate Facilities Manager, 1
Corrugator Scheduler, 165
Cosmetic Technician, 24
Counsel, 141
  General, 124
    Associate, 139
  Senior, 140
County Executive Director, 151
Creative Director, 162
Customer Associate, Banking,
  78
Customer Service
  Asst. Site Manager, Call
    Center, 30
  Associate, 51
  Retail, 90
  Specialist, 14
Customer Support & Training
  Mgr., 159

D

Dental Services, President, 107
Dept. Chairperson/Teacher,
  Elementary, 11, 69
Dept. Head, Legal Services, 140
Designer, Senior, 33
Detective, 145
Developer, Software, 128
Director
  Assistant, Hospital Food
    Services, 92
  Business Development, 177
  Community Development,
    153
  Creative, 162
  Executive, County, 151

Expense Mgmt. &
    Procurement, 80
Human Resources, 122, 123
Investments, 87
Management Development,
  154
Medical, 115
Online Development &
    Corporate Planning, 79
Operations, Divisional, 155
Operations & Training, 75
Program, Onsite, 137
Public Relations, 28
Quality Management, 106
Regional, MRI & CT
    Facilities, 109
Sales, 173
Security, 5
Sportswear Corp., 88
Television, 169
Training & Mgmt.
    Development, 154
Div. Director of Operations,
  155
Domain Expert, Aviation, 159

E

E-Commerce Manager, 130
Education, Co-Director, 66
Educational Coordinator,
  Software, 34
E-Human Resources, Vice
  President, 127
Elementary Teacher, 11, 44, 45,
  46, 69
Engineer
  Industrial, 76
  Recording, 13
  Software, Senior, 134
Engineering and Land
  Surveying, VP, 74
English Language Teacher,
  Assistant, 55
Enterprise Server Manager, 178
Esthetician, 10
Event/Program Coordinator, 7
Executive Administrative
  Assistant, 12
Executive Director, County, 151
Executive Producer, Radio and
  TV, 166
Executive VP,
  Software/Internet Co., 84
Expense Mgmt. & Procurement,
  Director, 80

F

Facilities Manager, Corporate, 1
Family Nurse Practitioner, 100
Field Case Manager, 104
Financial Services
  Account Executive, 86
  Representative, 85
Floor Supervisor, Retail, 4
Food Catering Company, VP,
  117
Food Service Manager, 118
Forensic Investigator, 101

G

Gas Scheduler/Trader
  Associate, 174
General Counsel, Associate, 139
General Counsel/VP of Support
  Services (HR), 124
General Manager, 156, 161
General Partner, Real Estate, 89
Grant Writer, 27

H

Health Software Co., President,
  111
High School Special Ed.
  Teacher, 94
History Instructor, Adjunct, 67
Home Economics Student, 113
Hospital Food Services, Asst.
  Director, 92
Host/Writer/Exec. Producer,
  Radio and TV, 166
Human Resources
  Director, 122, 123
  General Counsel/VP, 124
  Manager, 121, 126
    Senior, 125
  Vice President, 127

I

Independent
  Contractor/Consultant, 152
Industrial Engineer, 76
Information Systems
  Consultant, 132
  Manager, 129
Inside Sales Account Manager,
  171
Instructor
  Adjunct
    Accounting, 18
    History, 67
    Psychology, 60
  Kindergarten, 43

Insurance, Claims Dept.
  Mgr./Supervisor, 77
Interim Office Manager, 96
Intern
    Principal, 58
    Production Assistant, 170
Investigator, Forensic, 101
Investments Director, 87
IT Senior Technical/Project
    Manager, 133
IVR Replacement, Project
    Manager, 136

J–K

Japanese Teacher, 54

Kindergarten Instructor, 43
Kindergarten Teacher, 42

L

Laboratory Technician, 95
Language Teacher, English,
    Asst., 55
Law Enforcement, Detective,
    145
Legal Assistant, 142
Legal Services, Dept. Head, 140
Lieutenant of Detective Div.,
    145
Life Coach, 160
Local Systems
    Administrator/Corrugator
    Scheduler, 165

M

Management Consultant, 152
Manager
    Account
        Cardiology, 8
        Corporate, 175
        Sales, Inside, 171
        Software, 16
    Advertising, Senior, 23
    Assistant, Retail, 4
    Business Development, 168
    Case, Field, 104
    Claims Dept., Insurance, 77
    Clubhouse, 150
    Computer and Information
        Systems, 129
    Corporate Account, 175
    Customer Support &
        Training, 159
    E-Commerce, 130
    Enterprise Server, 178
    Facilities, Corporate, 1

Food Service, 118
General, 156, 161
Human Resources, 121, 126
    Senior, 125
Insurance Claims, 77
IT Technical/Project, Senior,
    133
Manufacturing/Engineering,
    72
Marketing, Medical, 3
Networking Hardware Sales,
    176
Nurse, 103
Office, 148
    Interim, 96
Operations, 2, 5
    Call Center, 32
Product, 3
Program
    Assistive Technology (AT),
    68
    Military, Overhaul &
    Repair, 163
Project
    Corporate, 1
    IVR Replacement, 136
    Wastewater Treatment, 71
    Website, 14
Property, Assistant, 138
Retail, 149
    Assistant, 4
Sales Development, 173
Site, Assistant, 30
Software Account, 16
Solutions, Senior, 135
Theme Restaurants, 119
Mgr./Supervisor, Claims Dept.,
    Insurance, 77
Manufacturing, Vice President,
    164
Manufacturing/Engineering
    Manager, 72
Marine Supply Co., Senior VP,
    158
Marketing
    Assistant, 25
    Manager, Medical, 3
    Vice President, 26
Mass Communication Student,
    170
Math Specialist, Elementary, 58
Math Teacher, 64
Medical/Billing Assistant, 93
Medical Director, 115
Medical Marketing Manager, 3
Meeting Planner, 8

Mental Health Worker, 97
Middle School Teacher, 52
Midwife, 99
Military Program Mgr.,
    Overhaul & Repair, 163
MRI & CT Facilities, Regional
    Director, 109

N

Networking Hardware Sales,
    Manager, 176
Nurse
    Registered Practical, 105
    Staff, 98
Nurse Manager, 103
Nurse-Midwife, 99
Nurse Practitioner, Family, 100
Nursing Supervisor, Clinical,
    102

O

Occupational Therapist, 91
Office Manager, 148
    Interim, 96
Officer
    Business Dev., Banking, 81
    Parole, Senior, 147
Online Development &
    Corporate Planning,
    Director, 79
Onsite Program Director, 137
Operations & Training,
    Director, 75
Operations Director, Div., 155
Operations Manager, 2, 5
    Call Center, 32
Operator, Chemical, 157
Overhaul & Repair, Military
    Program Mgr., 163
Owner, Resume Service, 29

P

Parole Officer, Senior, 147
Partner, General, Real Estate,
    89
Patrol Supervisor, U.S. Air
    Force, 144
Peer Education Teacher, 62
Physician/Staff, 108
Pilot, Commercial Airline, 9
Planner
    Meeting, 8
    Strategic, 1
Police Chief, Assistant, 146
Pre-Kindergarten Teacher, 36

President
  Dental Services, 107
  Health Software Co., 111
  Sportswear Corp., 88
  Theme Restaurants, 119
Pricing Administrator, 117
Principal Intern, 58
Producer, Executive, Radio and
  TV, 166
Product Manager, 3
Production Assistant, Intern,
  170
Program Director, Onsite, 137
Program Manager
  Assistive Technology (AT),
    68
  Military, Overhaul & Repair,
    163
Project Coordinator, 12
Project Manager
  Corporate, 1
  IVR Replacement, 136
  Wastewater Treatment, 71
  Website, 14
Property Manager, Assistant,
  138
Psychologist, School, 61
Psychology Instructor, Adjunct,
  60
Public Health Technician, 110
Public Relations Director, 28

Q–R

Quality Management, Director,
  106

Radio and Television
  Account Executive, 167
  Host/Writer/Executive
    Producer, 166
Real Estate, General Partner, 89
Receptionist, 143
Recording Engineer, 13
Regional Director, MRI & CT
  Facilities, 109
Registered Practical Nurse
  (RPN), 105
Representative
  Client Services, 31
  Financial Services, 85
Research Associate, 70
Restaurants,
  President/COO/Manager,
  119

Resume Service, Owner, 29
Retail
  Asst. Manager/Floor
    Supervisor, 4
  Customer Service, 90
  Manager, 149
RPN IV, 105

S

Sales Account Manager, Inside,
  171
Sales Development Mgr./Sales
  Director, 173
Sales Specialist, Territory, 15
School Psychologist, 61
Security Director, 5
Senior Advertising Manager, 23
Senior Controller, 83
Senior Counsel, 140
Senior Designer, 33
Senior HR Manager, 125
Senior Parole Officer, 147
Senior Software Engineer, 134
Senior Solutions Manager, 135
Senior VP, Marine Supply Co.,
  158
Site Manager, Asst., Call
  Center, 30
Software Account Manager, 16
Software Developer, 128
Software Engineer, Senior, 134
Solutions Manager, Senior, 135
Special Education Teacher, 48,
  49
  High School, 94
Specialist
  Administrative, 12
  Customer Service, 14
  Math, Elementary, 58
  Sales, Territory, 15
  Training and Documentation,
    63
Sportswear Corp., President, 88
Staff Nurse, 98
Strategic Planner, 1
Student
  Accounting, 17
  Home Economics, 113
  Mass Communication, 170
Student Teacher, 37, 47, 50, 53,
  57
Substitute Teacher, 38, 39, 40,
  41
Supervisor
  Account, Advertising, 22

Application Development,
  131
Claims Dept., Insurance, 77
Floor, Retail, 4
Nursing, Clinical, 102
Patrol, U.S. Air Force, 144
Trader, Financial Services, 86
Support Services (HR), VP, 124

T

Teacher, 65
  Elementary, 11, 44, 45, 46, 69
    Math Specialist, 58
    Turnkey Trainer, 59
  English Language, Asst., 55
  Japanese, 54
  Kindergarten, 42, 43
  Math, 64
  Middle School, 52
  Peer Education, 62
  Pre-Kindergarten, 36
  Special Education, 48, 49
    High School, 94
  Student, 37, 47, 50, 53, 57
  Substitute, 38, 39, 40, 41
  Visual Arts, 56
Technician
  Cosmetic, 24
  Laboratory, 95
  Public Health, 110
Technology Consultant, 116
Television Director, 169
Tennis Professional, 6
Territory Sales Specialist, 15
Therapist, Occupational, 91
Trader Associate, 174
Training and Doc. Specialist, 63
Training & Mgmt.
  Development, Director, 154
Treasurer/Senior Controller, 83
Treasurer, Software/Internet
  Co., 84
Trust Officer, Banking, 82
Turnkey Trainer, Elementary,
  59

U–V

U.S. Air Force, Patrol
  Supervisor, 144

Vice President
  Assistant, Banking, 82
  Associate, IT, 137
  Banking, 81
  E-Human Resources, 127

Engineering and Land
   Surveying, 74
Executive, Software/Internet
   Co., 84
Food Catering Company, 117
Manufacturing, 164
Marketing, 26
Senior, Marine Supply Co.,
   158
Support Services (HR), 124
Visual Arts Teacher, 56

W–Z

Wait Staff, 21
Waste Removal, CFA
   Administrator, 120
Wastewater Treatment, Project
   Mgr., 71
Website Project Manager, 14
Wireless Consultant, 172
Writer
   Grant, 27
   Radio and Television, 166

Features Index

The following commonly appearing sections are not included in this index of resume features: Work Experience, Work History, Professional Experience, Related Experience, Other Experience, Employment, Education (by itself), Student Teaching, and References. Variations of these sections, however, *are* included if they are distinctive in some way or have combined headings.

As you look for features that interest you, be sure to browse through *all* of the resumes. Some important information, such as Accomplishments, may not be listed if it is presented as a subsection of an Experience section.

Note: Numbers are resume numbers in the Gallery, not page numbers.

A

Academic Projects, 76
Accomplishments, 31
Achievements, 30, 38, 44, 138
Activities, 21, 43, 70, 175
Activities & Awards, 172
Additional Achievements & Activities, 111
Additional Areas of Experience, 50
Additional Information, 10, 60
Additional Skills, 24, 54
Additional Training, 122, 129
Admissions and Memberships, 140
Affiliates and Memberships, 18
Affiliation(s), 48, 62, 91, 107, 123, 139
Affiliations & Civic Involvement, 146
Affiliations & Leadership, 145
Affiliations/Community Involvement, 90
Areas of Experience, 156
Areas of Experience and Strength, 60
Areas of Expertise, 22, 33, 62, 68, 84, 112, 116, 132, 137, 139, 141, 171, 177
Areas of Proficiency, 35
Areas of Strength, 5
Arts Advocacy, 56

Associations, 132
Attributes, 10
Awards, 28, 149, 163
Awards and Activities, 64
Awards and Honors, 78
Awards and Recognition(s), 134, 144, 146
Awards, Honors & Achievements, 109

B

Book Reviews, 67
Business Development and Revenue Growth, 24
Business Development, Leadership, and Management, 88
Business Organizations, 3
Business Skills, 10
Business Technology Skills, 121

C–D

Career Accomplishments, 124, 135
Career Achievements, 78
Career Development, 119
Career Focus, 4, 170
Career Highlights, 12, 35, 156, 161, 166
Career Interests, 12
Career Profile, 70, 115, 123, 140, 144, 145, 151, 167

Career Strengths, 113
Career Target, 90
Certification(s), 29, 36, 40, 46, 58, 62, 65, 66, 71, 75, 80, 92, 109, 118, 124, 175
Certifications & Licenses, 101, 104
Certifications & Professional Affiliations, 19
Certifications, Licensure, and Training, 99
Certifications/Skills, 97
Charitable/Volunteer Contributions (Academic), 56
Charitable/Volunteer Contributions (Non-Academic), 56
Clinical Training, 96
Community Activities, 19, 55
Community and Event Involvement, 112
Community Involvement, 47, 59, 82, 105
Community Involvement & Affiliations, 17
Community Reinvestment, 53
Community Service, 134
Community Work/Professional Affiliations, 60
Competencies Include, 73, 74, 98, 120

Computer & Other Skills, 152
Computer Capabilities, 132
Computer Experience, 33
Computer Expertise, 175
Computer Literacy, 52
Computer Proficiencies, 148
Computer Proficiency, 127
Computer Skills, 16, 17, 26, 31,
    46, 62, 75, 92, 93, 142, 143,
    156, 157
Computer/Special Skills, 122
Computers, 90
Conference Presentations, 67
Continuing
    Education/Training, 175
Core Competencies, 28, 151,
    164
Core Professional Strengths,
    125
Core Strengths, 175
Critical Projects & Initiatives,
    133
Curriculum Development, 56

E

Education/Activities, 4
Education & Affiliations, 88,
    154, 158
Education & Awards, 111
Education and Certification(s),
    45, 74, 98, 119, 131
Education & Continuing
    Development, 168
Education & Credentials, 10,
    60, 68
Education and Honors, 47, 57
Education & Licensure, 105
Education and Professional
    Activities, 1
Education and Professional
    Affiliations, 84
Education & Professional
    Certifications, 87
Education and Professional
    Development, 56, 147, 150,
    157, 164, 173
Education and Professional
    Training, 125
Education and Relevant
    Inservice Development, 52
Education and Skills, 176
Education and Training, 18, 72,
    106, 146
Education, Certification, 3, 37
Education, Certifications, &
    Training, 43

Education/Professional, 73
Education, Professional
    Development, &
    Affiliations, 79
Education, Seminars, 156
Education/Training, 178
Educational Achievements &
    Professional Development,
    159
Employment/Community
    Service, 113
Esthetic Skills, 10
Executive Career Highlights,
    159
Executive Experience, 28
Executive Performance, 116
Executive Profile, 119, 153, 155
Executive Summary, 137
Expertise, 78
Extracurricular Involvement,
    56

F–G

Flight Hours, 9
Focus & Overview, 51
Foreign Exchange Programs, 21

Grant Writing, 59
graphic(s), 6, 36, 44, 53, 56, 57,
    63, 145, 166, 172

H

Highlights, 6, 94
Highlights of Accomplishments,
    82, 137, 147
Highlights of Experience, 11, 69
Highlights of Qualifications, 4,
    39, 58
Highlights of Value to a
    Potential Employer, 165
Honorary Distinction, 68
Honors and Activities, 22
Honors & Awards, 155
Human Resources Profile, 121

I–J

Interests, 10, 40, 41, 122
Internship Experience and
    College Work Project
    Highlights, 4
IT Skills, 173

K

Key Accomplishments, 145
Key Achievements, 87

Key Qualifications, 14, 34, 100
Key Strengths, 26, 63
Key Strengths & Expertise, 79
Keywords, 19, 27

L

Languages, 91, 105
Leadership Strengths, 134
Legal Expertise, 139
Licenses and Certifications, 59,
    96, 102, 106
Licensure, 52
Literary Consultant, 101

M

Management & Technical
    Abilities, 133
Management Profile, 79
Membership, 134
Memberships & Affiliations,
    135
Memberships/Associations,
    101, 92
Military, 126
Military Service, 101

N–O

Network Technology, 88
Notable Highlights, 65

Objective, 47, 50, 64, 85, 113
Overseas Travel & Experience,
    59
Overview, 48

P

Participatory Memberships, 23
Patents and Publications, 35
Personal, 146
Personal Activities, 56
Pertinent Skills and
    Accomplishments, 27
Player Profile, 6
Professional Accomplishments,
    98
Professional Accreditation &
    Education, 127
Professional Accreditations, 157
Professional Achievements, 18,
    32, 73, 125
Professional Activities &
    Honors, 154
Professional
    Activities/Community
    Involvement, 103

Professional Affiliations, 44, 61, 66, 71, 87, 108, 157, 166

Professional Affiliations & Certifications, 121

Professional Affiliations & Honors, 150

Professional and Community Affiliations, 109

Professional Associations, 63

Professional Certification & Development, 137

Professional Credentials, 115, 139

Professional Development, 23, 58, 62, 82, 102, 136, 145, 151

Professional Development Courses, 45

Professional Development/Training, 81

Professional Experience and Accomplishments, 81, 169

Professional Goal, 162

Professional Highlights, 29

Professional Licenses, 85

Professional Memberships, 37, 100

Professional Organizations, 43, 58, 125

Professional Organizations and Training, 38

Professional Profile, 26, 32, 42, 60, 109, 156, 162

Professional Registrations, 71

Professional Summary, 18, 104, 107

Professional Training, 6, 89

Profile, 4, 7, 12, 13, 19, 24, 33, 40, 44, 45, 53, 57, 61, 74, 92, 101, 105, 116, 121, 128, 136, 160, 163, 178

Project Highlights and Achievements, 134

Promotions and Value-added Projects, 24

Public Speaking Engagements & Featured Newspaper Articles, 87

Publications, 67, 101, 108, 166

Published Articles, 56

Q

Qualification Highlights, 86

Qualifications, 37, 41, 66, 77, 117

Qualifications Profile, 87

Qualifications Summary, 3, 12

Qualified to Perform, 160

Qualities, 10

R

Ratings & Certificates, 9

Recent Achievements, 26

Recent Activities & Affiliations, 147

Recent Work History with Examples of Problems Solved, 157, 173

Relevant Projects, 21

Research, 108

Research Awards, 67

Rewards, 44

S

Sales Awards, 23

School Board & Committee Involvement, 56

Selected Accomplishments, 7

Selected Achievements, 107, 149

Selected Career Highlights, 45

Selected Civic Activities, 58

Selected Extended Professional Activities, 58

Seminars/Workshops Attended, 44

Skills, 41, 52

Special Awards & Licensure, 107

Special Skills, 64

Specific Areas of Knowledge, Insight & Experience, 4

Specific Skill Areas, 146

Strengths, 71, 78

Summary, 122, 147

Summary of Qualifications, 11, 27, 29, 46, 63, 64, 69, 85, 114, 119, 168

Summary of Research Experience, 67

Summary of Responsibilities, 149

T–U

Task Force Service, 101

Teaching Testimonials, 45

Technical Expertise, 129

Technical Knowledge and Expertise, 134

Technical Proficiencies, 137

Technical Skills, 135, 170

Technical Summary, 128

Technology, 14

Technology Skills, 85, 168

Technology Skills & Qualifications, 130

testimonial(s), 2, 12, 45, 49, 56, 57, 65, 78, 80, 102, 110, 133, 157

Training, 75, 135

Training & Development, 65

Training and Education, 95

Transitional Skills, 101

V–Z

Value to Your Organization, 172

Volunteer, 39, 66, 97, 117

Volunteer Activities, 42, 111

Volunteer Experience, 50

Volunteer Leadership, 127

Volunteerism, 114

Work History & Summary of Key Skills, 77